Minnesota State Residential Code, Chapter 1309

Made possible by the Association of Minnesota Building Officials

2007

Minnesota State Residential Code®

First Printing

ISBN-13: 978-1-58001-646-9

Publication Date: November 2007

PRINTED IN THE U.S.A.

TABLE OF CONTENTS

Symbols and Notations in the Code

The symbols in the margins shall indicate the status of the code changes.

M
N
M
N   This symbol indicates that a Minnesota amendment has been added to the 2003 *International Residential Code for One- and Two-Family Dwellings*.

>   This symbol indicates deletion of IRC language by Minnesota.

| Solid vertical lines in the margins within the body of the code indicate a technical change between the requirements of the 2003 and 2006 *International Residential Code*.

➡   Deletion indications in the form of an arrow are provided in the margin where an entire section, paragraph, exception, or table has been deleted or an item in a list of items or a table has been deleted since the publication of the 2003 *International Residential Code*.

Part I — Administration

CHAPTER 1
ADMINISTRATION

This code shall be administered according to Minnesota rules, Chapter 1300.

Subp. 2. **Existing buildings and structures.** Additions, alterations, or repairs to existing buildings and structures meeting the scope of the International Residential Code shall be exempt from Minnesota Rules, chapter 1311, Minnesota Conservation Code for Existing Buildings.

Additions, alterations, or repairs to existing one- and two-family dwellings including townhouses may be made without requiring the existing building or structure to comply with all the requirements of this code provided that any addition or alteration conforms to this code. Repairs to existing buildings or structures may be made that are nonstructural and do not adversely affect any structural member or required fire-resistive element with the same methods and materials of which the building or structure is constructed.

Exception: The installation or replacement of glass shall be as required for new installations in accordance with IRC Section R308.

MINNESOTA RULES, CHAPTER 1300

1300.0010
ADMINISTRATION

This chapter provides administrative provisions for all Minnesota State Building Code rule chapters identified in part 1300.0050. If specific administrative provisions are provided in a statute or rule chapter, the specific administrative provisions apply.

Chapter 1315 shall be administered according to chapter 3800, and the Minnesota Electrical Act, Minnesota Statutes, sections 326.01, and 326.241 to 326.248. Provisions of this chapter that do not conflict with the Minnesota Electrical Act also apply.

1300.0020
TITLE

The chapters listed in part 1300.0050, including the standards they adopt by reference, are the Minnesota State Building Code and may be cited as or referred to as the "code."

1300.0030
PURPOSE AND APPLICATION

Subpart 1. **Purpose.** The purpose of this code is to establish minimum requirements to safeguard the public health, safety, and general welfare through structural strength, means of egress facilities, stability, sanitation, adequate light and ventilation, energy conservation, and safety to life and property from fire and other hazards attributed to the built environment and to provide safety to firefighters and emergency responders during emergency operations.

The purpose of the code is not to create, establish, or designate a particular class or group of persons who will or should be especially protected or benefited by the terms of the code.

Subp. 2. **Application.**

A. The code applies statewide except as provided in Minnesota Statutes, sections 16B.72 and 16B.73, and supersedes the building code of any municipality. The code does not apply to agricultural buildings except with respect to state inspections required or rulemaking authorized by Minnesota Statutes, sections 103F.141, subdivision 8, and 326.244.

B. The codes and standards referenced in a rule chapter are considered part of the requirements of the code to the prescribed extent of each reference. If differences occur between provisions of the code and referenced codes and standards, the provisions of the code apply.

C. In the event that a new edition of the code is adopted after a permit has been issued, the edition of the code current at the time of permit application shall remain in effect throughout the work authorized by the permit.

1300.0040
SCOPE

The code applies to the construction, alteration, moving, demolition, repair, and use of any building, structure, or building service equipment in a municipality, except work located primarily in a public way, public utility towers and poles, mechanical equipment not specifically regulated in the code, and hydraulic flood control structures. Structures classified under part 1300.0070, subpart 12a, as IRC-1, IRC-2, IRC-3, and IRC-4 occupancies not more than three stories above grade plane in height with separate means of egress shall comply with chapter 1309 and other applicable rules. Other buildings and structures and appurtenances connected or attached to them shall comply with chapter 1305 and other applicable rules.

Exception: The following structures that meet the scope of chapter 1305 shall be designed to comply with Minnesota Rules, chapter 1311:

(1) existing buildings undergoing repair, alteration, or change of occupancy; and

(2) historic buildings.

If different provisions of the code specify different materials, methods of construction, or other requirements, the most restrictive provision governs. If there is a conflict between a general requirement and a specific requirement, the specific requirement applies.

If reference is made in the code to an appendix, the provisions in the appendix do not apply unless specifically adopted by the code. Optional appendix chapters of the code identified in part 1300.0060 do not apply unless a municipality has specifically adopted them.

1300.0050
CHAPTERS OF MINNESOTA STATE
BUILDING CODE

The Minnesota State Building Code adopted under Minnesota Statutes, section 16B.61, subdivision 1, includes the following chapters:

A. 1300, Minnesota Building Code Administration;

B. 1301, Building Official Certification;

C. 1302, State Building Code Construction Approvals;

D. 1303, Special Provisions;

E. 1305, Adoption of the International Building Code;

F. 1306, Special Fire Protection Systems;

G. 1307, Elevators and Related Devices;

H. 1309, Adoption of the International Residential Code;

I. 1311, Minnesota Conservation Code for Existing Buildings;

J. 1315, Adoption of the National Electrical Code;

K. 1325, Solar Energy Systems;

L. 1330, Fallout Shelters;

M. 1335, Floodproofing Regulations;

N. 1341, Minnesota Accessibility Code;

O. 1346, Minnesota Mechanical Code;

P. 1350, Manufactured Homes;

Q. 1360, Prefabricated Structures;

R. 1361, Industrialized/Modular Buildings;

S. 1370, Storm Shelters (Manufactured Home Parks);

T. 4715, Minnesota Plumbing Code; and

U. 7670, 7672, 7674, 7676, and 7678, Minnesota Energy Code.

1300.0060
OPTIONAL ADMINISTRATION

The following chapters of the code are not mandatory but may be adopted without change by a municipality which has adopted the code:

A. Chapter 1306, Special Fire Protection Systems;

B. Grading, IBC appendix chapter J; and

C. Chapter 1335, Floodproofing Regulations, parts 1335.0600 to 1335.1200.

1300.0070
DEFINITIONS

Subpart 1. Scope; incorporation by reference. The definitions in this part apply to parts 1300.0010 to 1300.0250. For terms that are not defined through the methods authorized by this chapter, the Merriam-Webster Collegiate Dictionary, available at www.m-w.com, shall be considered as providing ordinarily accepted meanings. The dictionary is incorporated by reference, is subject to frequent change, and is available through the Minitex interlibrary loan system.

Subp. 2. Administrative authority. "Administrative authority" means a municipality's governing body or its assigned administrative authority.

Subp. 3. Adult day care center. "Adult day care center" means a facility that provides adult day care to functionally impaired adults on a regular basis for periods of less than 24 hours a day in a setting other than a participant's home or the residence of the facility operator.

A. "Class E" means any building or portion of a building used for adult day care purposes, by more than five occupants, for those participants who are capable of taking appropriate action for self-preservation under emergency conditions as determined according to part 9555.9730, and must meet Group E occupancy requirements.

B. "Class I" means any building or portion of a building used for adult day care purposes, by more than five occupants, for those participants who are not capable of taking appropriate action for self-preservation under emergency conditions as determined according to part 9555.9730, and must meet Group I, Division 4 occupancy requirements.

Subp. 4. Agricultural building. "Agricultural building" means a building that meets the requirements of Minnesota Statutes, section 16B.60, subdivision 5.

Subp. 5. Building official. "Building official" means the municipal building code official certified under Minnesota Statutes, section 16B.65, subdivisions 2 and 3.

Subp. 6. Building service equipment. "Building service equipment" refers to the plumbing, mechanical, electrical, and elevator equipment, including piping, wiring, fixtures, and other accessories, that provides sanitation, lighting, heating, ventilation, cooling, refrigeration, firefighting, and transportation facilities essential to the occupancy of the building or structure for its designated use and occupancy.

Subp. 7. City. "City" means a home rule charter or statutory city.

Subp. 8. Code. "Code" means the Minnesota State Building Code adopted under Minnesota Statutes, section 16B.61, subdivision 1, and includes the chapters identified in part 1300.0020.

Subp. 9. Commissioner. "Commissioner" means the commissioner of labor and industry.

Subp. 10. Designate. "Designate" means the formal designation by a municipality's administrative authority of a certified building official accepting responsibility for code administration.

Subp. 10a. Family adult day services. "Family adult day services" means a program providing services for up to eight functionally impaired adults for less than 24 hours per day in the license holder's primary residence according to Minnesota Statutes, section 245A.143. This includes programs located in residences licensed by the Department of Human Services for adult foster care, provided that not more than eight adults, excluding staff, are present in the residence at any time.

Subp. 11. Family day care home. "Family day care home" means a residence or portion of a residence licensed by the Department of Human Services under chapter 9502 for no more than ten children at one time of which no more than six are under school age, and must meet Group R, Division 3 occupancy requirements.

Subp. 12. Group day care home. "Group day care home" means any residence or portion of a residence licensed by the Department of Human Services under chapter 9502 for no more than 14 children at any one time, and must meet Group R, Division 3 occupancy requirements.

Subp. 12a. International Residential Code (IRC) occupancy classifications. International Residential Code (IRC) occupancy classifications are as follows:

IRC-1 Single-family dwellings;

IRC-2 Two-family dwellings;

IRC-3 Townhouses; and

IRC-4 Accessory structures:

A. Garages;

B. Storage sheds; and

C. Similar structures.

Subp. 13. Mandatory terms. "Mandatory terms" include "must" and "shall," which have the same meaning.

Subp. 14. Manufactured home. "Manufactured home" has the meaning given in Minnesota Statutes, section 327.31, subdivision 3, and for the purpose of determining occupancy separations, is considered a Group IRC-1 occupancy.

Subp. 15. Master plan. "Master plan" is a plan that has been reviewed for code compliance by the building official and stamped "Reviewed for Code Compliance."

Subp. 16. Mayor and city council. "Mayor" and "city council" mean governing body whenever they appear in the code.

Subp. 17. Municipality. "Municipality" means a city, county, or town; the University of Minnesota; or the state of Minnesota for public buildings and state licensed facilities.

Subp. 18. Outpatient clinic. "Outpatient clinic" means a building or part of a building used to provide, on an outpatient basis, surgical treatment requiring general anesthesia, kidney dialysis, or other treatment that would render patients incapable of unassisted self-preservation under emergency conditions. "Outpatient clinic" includes outpatient surgical centers, but does not include doctors' and dentists' offices or clinics for the practice of medicine or the delivery of primary care. Outpatient clinics must meet Group B occupancy requirements.

Subp. 19. Performance-based design. An engineering approach to design elements of a building based on agreed upon performance goals and objectives, engineering analysis, and quantitative assessment of alternatives against the design goals and objectives, using accepted engineering tools, methodologies, and performance criteria.

Subp. 20. Recyclable materials. "Recyclable materials" means materials that are separated from mixed municipal solid waste for the purpose of recycling, including paper, glass, plastic, metals, automobile oil, and batteries. Refuse-derived fuel or other material that is destroyed by incineration is not a recyclable material.

Subp. 21. Recycling. "Recycling" means the process of collecting and preparing recyclable materials and reusing the materials in their original form or using them in manufacturing processes that do not cause the destruction of recyclable materials in a manner that precludes further use.

Subp. 22. Residential hospice facility. "Residential hospice facility" means a facility located in a residential area that directly provides 24-hour residential and support services in a home-like setting for one to 12 persons who have been diagnosed as terminally ill with a probable life expectancy of under one year. A residential hospice facility must meet IBC Group R-4 occupancy requirements.

Subp. 23. Supervised living facility. "Supervised living facility" means a facility in which there is provided supervision, lodging, meals, and according to the rules of the Minnesota Department of Human Services and the Minnesota Department of Health, counseling and developmental habilitative or rehabilitative services to persons who are mentally retarded, chemically dependent, adult mentally ill, or physically disabled.

A. "Class A-1 supervised living facility" means a supervised living facility for ambulatory and mobile persons who are capable of taking appropriate action for self-preservation under emergency conditions as determined by program licensure provisions for six or fewer persons, and must meet Group R, Division 3 occupancy requirements.

B. "Class A-2 supervised living facility" means a supervised living facility for ambulatory and mobile persons who are capable of taking appropriate action for self-preservation under emergency conditions as determined by program licensure provisions for seven to 16 persons, and must meet Group R, Division 4 occupancy requirements. Facilities with more than 16 persons must meet Group I-1 occupancy requirements.

C. "Class B-1 supervised living facility" means a supervised living facility for ambulatory, nonambulatory, mobile, or nonmobile persons who are not mentally or physically capable of taking appropriate action for self-preservation under emergency conditions as determined by program licensure provisions for six or fewer persons, and must meet Group R, Division 3 occupancy requirements.

D. "Class B-2 supervised living facility" means a supervised living facility for ambulatory, nonambulatory, mobile, or nonmobile persons who are not mentally or physically capable of taking appropriate action for self-preservation under emergency conditions as determined by program licensure provisions for seven to 16 persons, and must meet Group R, Division 4 occupancy requirements.

E. "Class B-3 supervised living facility" means a supervised living facility for ambulatory, nonambulatory, mobile, or nonmobile persons who are not mentally or physically capable of taking appropriate action for self-preservation under emergency conditions as determined by program licensure provisions for over 16 persons, and must meet Group I, Division 2 occupancy requirements.

Subp. 24. State building official. "State building official" means the person who, under the direction and supervision of the commissioner, administers the code.

Subp. 25. State licensed facilities. "State licensed facilities" means a building and its grounds that are licensed by the state as a hospital, nursing home, supervised living facility, free-standing outpatient surgical center, or correctional facility.

Subp. 26. State-owned buildings. "State-owned buildings" means buildings and structures financed in whole or in part by state funds that are under the exclusive jurisdiction and custodial control of one or more state department or agency.

1300.0080
CODE ADOPTION AND AMENDMENTS

Under Minnesota Statutes, section 16B.61, the code is adopted and periodically updated to include current editions of national model codes in general use and existing statewide specialty codes and their amendments.

Under Minnesota Statutes, section 16B.64, subdivisions 5 and 6, amendments to the code may be proposed and initiated by any interested person. Proposed amendments must be submitted in writing on a form provided by the commissioner.

1300.0090
DEPARTMENT OF BUILDING SAFETY

Subpart 1. **Creation of enforcement agency.** There is hereby established in the municipality a code enforcement agency and the official in charge is the designated building official. The agency is referred to in the code as the "Department of Building Safety."

Subp. 2. **Appointment.** The building official shall be designated by the municipality according to Minnesota Statutes, section 16B.65.

1300.0110
DUTIES AND POWERS OF BUILDING OFFICIAL

Subpart 1. **General.** The building official shall enforce the code. The building official may render interpretations of the code and adopt policies and procedures in order to clarify its application. The interpretations, policies, and procedures shall be in conformance with the intent and purpose of the code. The policies and procedures shall not have the effect of waiving requirements specifically provided for in the code.

Subp. 2. **Deputies.** According to the prescribed procedures of the municipality and with the concurrence of the appointing authority, the building official may designate a deputy building official and related technical officers, inspectors, plan examiners, and other employees. The employees have the powers delegated by the building official.

Subp. 3. **Applications and permits.** The building official shall receive applications, review construction documents, and issue permits for the erection, alteration, demolition, moving, and repair of buildings and structures, including all other equipment and systems regulated by the code. The building official shall inspect the premises for which the permits have been issued and enforce compliance with the code.

Subp. 4. **Notices and orders.** The building official shall issue all necessary notices and orders to ensure compliance with the code. Notices and orders shall be in writing unless waived by the permit applicant, contractor, owner, or owner's agent. Notices and orders shall be based on the edition of the code under which the permit has been issued.

Subp. 5. **Inspections.** The building official shall make all of the required inspections or accept reports of inspection by approved agencies or individuals. Results of inspections shall be documented on the job site inspection card and in the official records of the municipality, including type of inspection, date of inspection, identification of the responsible individual making the inspection, and comments regarding approval or disapproval of the inspection. The building official may engage expert opinion necessary to report upon unusual technical issues that arise.

Subp. 6. **Identification.** The building official and deputies shall carry proper identification when inspecting structures or premises in the performance of duties under the code.

Subp. 7. **Right of entry.** If it is necessary to make an inspection to enforce the code or if the building official has reasonable cause to believe that there exists in a structure or upon a premises a condition contrary to or in violation of the code that makes the structure or premises unsafe, dangerous, or hazardous, the building official or designee may enter the structure or premises at reasonable times to inspect or to perform the duties imposed by the code, provided that if the structure or premises is occupied, credentials must be presented to the occupant and entry requested. If the structure or premises is unoccupied, the building official shall first make a reasonable effort to locate the owner or other person having charge or control of the structure or premises and request entry. If entry is refused, the building official shall have recourse to the remedies provided by law to secure entry.

Subp. 8. **Department records.** The building official shall be responsible for official records of applications received, plans, specifications, surveys, plot plans, plan reviews, permits and certificates issued, reports of inspections, and notices and orders issued. The records shall be retained for the period required for the retention of public records under Minnesota Statutes, section 138.17. Department records shall be maintained by the municipality and readily available for review according to Minnesota Statutes, section 13.37.

Subp. 9. **Liability.** The building official, member of the Board of Appeals, or employee charged with the enforcement of the code, while acting for the jurisdiction in good faith and without malice in the discharge of the duties required by the code or other pertinent laws or ordinances, is not rendered personally liable and is relieved from personal liability for any damage accruing to persons or property as a result of any act or by reason of an act or omission in the discharge of official duties. Any suit instituted against an officer or employee because of an act performed by that officer or employee in the lawful discharge of duties and under the code shall be defended by the legal representative of the jurisdiction until the final termination of the proceedings. The building official or any subordinate is not liable for cost in any action, suit, or proceeding that is instituted in pursuance of the code.

Subp. 10. **Approved materials and equipment.** Materials, equipment, and devices approved by the building official shall be constructed and installed in the approved manner.

Subp. 11. **Used material and equipment.** The use of used materials that meet the requirements of the code for new materials is permitted. Used equipment and devices shall not be reused unless approved by the building official.

Subp. 12. **Modifications.** If there are practical difficulties involved in carrying out the provisions of the code, the building official may grant modifications for individual cases, upon application by the owner or owner's representative, provided the building official finds that special individual reason makes the strict letter of the code impractical, the modification is in compliance with the intent and purpose of the code, and the modification does not lessen health, life, and fire safety or structural requirements. The details of action granting modifications shall be recorded and entered in the files of the Department of Building Safety.

Subp. 13. **Alternative materials, design, and methods of construction and equipment.** The code is not intended to prevent the installation of any material or to prohibit any design or method of construction not specifically prescribed by the code, provided that any alternative has been approved. An alternative material, design, or method of construction shall be approved where the building official finds that the proposed design is satisfactory and complies with the intent of the code, and that the material, method, or work offered is, for the purpose intended, at least the equivalent of that prescribed in the code in quality, strength, effectiveness, fire resistance, durability, and safety. The details of any action granting approval of an alternate shall be recorded and entered in the files of the Department of Building Safety.

Subp. 14. **Performance-based fire and life safety design.** The code official may approve performance-based fire and life safety designs if the code official finds that the proposed design has been conducted by an approved method. Approved performance-based designs are evidence of compliance with the intent of the code. Approvals under this subpart are subject to the approval of the building code official whenever the design involves matters regulated by the building code.

   A. Design goals, objectives, and performance criteria shall be approved by the code official before submission of a performance-based design report, calculations, or analysis results. As a minimum, an approved performance-based design shall address the following objectives:

      (1) Life safety of occupants;

      (2) Firefighter safety;

      (3) Property protection;

      (4) Continuity of operations; and

      (5) Safeguarding of the environment.

   B. To determine the acceptability of a performance-based design, the code official may require the owner or agent to provide, without charge to the jurisdiction, a technical opinion and report. The code official may require the technical opinion and report to be prepared by, and bear the stamp of, a licensed design professional.

   C. Performance-based designs shall be prepared by, and bear the stamp of, a licensed design professional competent in the area of work. The design professional shall provide written confirmation to the code official before a certificate of occupancy is issued that the performance-based design has been properly implemented, the operation or use of the building is within the limitations of the design, and adequate controls are in place to maintain compliance with the conditions of the design throughout the life of the building.

Subp. 15. **Tests.** If there is insufficient evidence of compliance with the code, or evidence that a material or method does not conform to the requirements of the code, or in order to substantiate claims for alternative materials or methods, the building official shall have the authority to require tests as evidence of compliance to be made at no expense to the municipality. Test methods shall be as specified in the code or by other recognized test standards. In the absence of recognized and accepted test methods, the building official shall approve the testing procedures. Tests shall be performed by an approved agency. Reports of the tests shall be retained by the building official.

1300.0120
PERMITS

Subpart 1. **Required.** An owner or authorized agent who intends to construct, enlarge, alter, repair, move, demolish, or change the occupancy of a building or structure, or to erect, install, enlarge, alter, repair, remove, convert, or replace any gas, mechanical, electrical, plumbing system, or other equipment, the installation of which is regulated by the code; or cause any such work to be done, shall first make application to the building official and obtain the required permit.

Subp. 2. **Annual permit.** In lieu of an individual permit for each alteration to an already approved electrical, gas, mechanical, or plumbing installation, the building official may issue an annual permit upon application for the permit to any person, firm, or corporation regularly employing one or more qualified trade persons in the building, structure, or on the premises owned or operated by the applicant for the permit.

Subp. 3. **Annual permit records.** The person to whom an annual permit is issued shall keep a detailed record of alterations made under the annual permit. The building official shall have access to the records at all times or the records shall be filed with the building official as designated.

Subp. 4. **Work exempt from permit.** Exemptions from permit requirements of the code do not authorize work to be done in any manner in violation of the code or any other laws or ordinances of this jurisdiction. Permits shall not be required for the following:

   A. Building:

      (1) One-story detached accessory structures, used as tool and storage sheds, playhouses, and similar uses, provided the floor area does not exceed 120 square feet (11.15 m²);

      (2) Fences not over six feet (1,829 mm) high;

      (3) Oil derricks;

      (4) Retaining walls that are not over four feet (1,219 mm) in height measured from the bottom of the footing to the top of the wall, unless supporting a surcharge or impounding Class I, II, or III-A liquids;

      (5) Water tanks supported directly upon grade if the capacity does not exceed 5,000 gallons

(18,927 L) and the ratio of height to diameter or width does not exceed 2 to 1;

(6) Sidewalks and driveways that are not part of an accessible route;

(7) Decks and platforms not more than 30 inches (762 mm) above adjacent grade and not attached to a structure with frost footings and which is not part of an accessible route;

(8) Painting, papering, tiling, carpeting, cabinets, countertops, and similar finish work;

(9) Temporary motion picture, television, and theater stage sets and scenery;

(10) Prefabricated swimming pools installed entirely above ground accessory to dwelling units constructed to the provisions of the International Residential Code or R-3 occupancies constructed to the provisions of the International Building Code, which do not exceed both 5,000 gallons in capacity (18,925 L) and a 24-inch (610 mm) depth;

(11) Window awnings supported by an exterior wall that do not project more than 54 inches (1,372 mm) from the exterior wall and do not require additional support, when constructed under the International Residential Code or Group R-3 and Group U occupancies constructed to the provisions of the International Building Code;

(12) Movable cases, counters, and partitions not over five feet, nine inches (1,753 mm) in height;

(13) Agricultural buildings as defined in Minnesota Statutes, section 16B.60, subdivision 5; and

(14) Swings and other playground equipment.

Unless otherwise exempted, plumbing, electrical, and mechanical permits are required for subitems (1) to (14).

B. Gas:

(1) Portable heating, cooking, or clothes drying appliances;

(2) Replacement of any minor part that does not alter approval of equipment or make the equipment unsafe; and

(3) Portable fuel cell appliances that are not connected to a fixed piping system and are interconnected to a power grid.

C. Mechanical:

(1) Portable heating appliances;

(2) Portable ventilation appliances and equipment;

(3) Portable cooling units;

(4) Steam, hot, or chilled water piping within any heating or cooling equipment regulated by this code;

(5) Replacement of any part that does not alter approval of equipment or make the equipment unsafe;

(6) Portable evaporative coolers;

(7) Self-contained refrigeration systems containing ten pounds (4.5 kg) or less of refrigerant or that are actuated by motors of one horsepower (0.75 kW) or less; and

(8) Portable fuel cell appliances that are not connected to a fixed piping system and are not interconnected to a power grid.

D. Plumbing: See chapter 4715 for plumbing work that is exempt from a permit.

E. Electrical: an electrical permit is not required if work is inspected by the State Board of Electricity or is exempt from inspection under Minnesota Statutes, section 326.244. Obtaining a permit from the Board of Electricity does not exempt the work from other Minnesota State Building Code requirements relating to electrical equipment, its location, or its performance.

Subp. 5. Emergency repairs. If equipment replacements and repairs must be performed in an emergency situation, the permit application shall be submitted to the building official within the next working business day.

Subp. 6. Repairs. Application or notice to the building official is not required for ordinary repairs to structures. The repairs shall not include the cutting away of any wall, partition, or portion of a wall or partition, the removal or cutting of any structural beam or load bearing support, or the removal or change of any required means of egress, or rearrangement of parts of a structure affecting the egress requirements; nor shall ordinary repairs include addition to, alteration of, replacement, or relocation of any standpipe, water supply, sewer, drainage, drain leader, gas, soil, waste, vent or similar piping, electric wiring, or mechanical or other work affecting public health or general safety.

Subp. 7. Application for permit. To obtain a permit, the applicant shall file an application in writing on a form furnished by the Department of Building Safety for that purpose. The application shall:

A. Identify and describe the work to be covered by the permit for which application is made;

B. Describe the land on which the proposed work is to be done by legal description, street address, or similar description that will readily identify and definitely locate the proposed building or work;

C. Indicate the use and occupancy for which the proposed work is intended;

D. Indicate the type of construction;

E. Be accompanied by construction documents and other information as required by the code;

F. State the valuation of the proposed work;

G. Be signed by the applicant, or the applicant's authorized agent; and

H. Give other data and information required by the building official.

Subp. 8. Action on application. The building official shall examine or cause to be examined applications for permits and amendments within a reasonable time after filing. If the application or the construction documents do not conform to the requirements of pertinent laws, the building official shall reject the application and notify the applicant of the reasons. The building official shall document the reasons for rejecting the application. The applicant may request written documentation of the rejection and the reasons for the rejection. When the building official is satisfied that the proposed work conforms to the requirements of the code and applicable laws and ordinances, the building official shall issue a permit.

Subp. 9. Time limitation of application. An application for a permit for any proposed work shall be considered abandoned 180 days after the date of filing, unless the application has been pursued in good faith or a permit has been issued; except that the building official is authorized to grant one or more extensions of time for additional periods not exceeding 180 days each. The extension shall be requested in writing and justifiable cause demonstrated.

Subp. 10. Validity of permit. The issuance or granting of a permit or approval of plans, specifications, and computations, shall not be construed to be a permit for any violation of the code or of any other ordinance of the jurisdiction. Permits presuming to give authority to violate or cancel the provisions of the code or other ordinances of the jurisdiction are not valid. The issuance of a permit based on construction documents and other data shall not prevent the building official from requiring the correction of errors in the construction documents and other data. The building official may also prevent occupancy or use of a structure that violates the code or any other ordinance of this jurisdiction.

Subp. 11. Expiration. Every permit issued shall become invalid unless the work authorized by the permit is commenced within 180 days after its issuance, or if the work authorized by the permit is suspended or abandoned for a period of 180 days after the time the work is commenced. The building official may grant, in writing, one or more extensions of time, for periods not more than 180 days each. The extension shall be requested in writing and justifiable cause demonstrated.

Subp. 12. Suspension or revocation. The building official may suspend or revoke a permit issued under the code if the permit is issued in error; on the basis of incorrect, inaccurate, or incomplete information; or in violation of any ordinance or regulation or the code.

Subp. 13. Placement of permit. The building permit or a copy shall be kept on the site of the work until the completion of the project.

Subp. 14. Responsibility. Every person who performs work for the installation or repair of building, structure, electrical, gas, mechanical, or plumbing systems, for which the code is applicable, shall comply with the code.

1300.0130
CONSTRUCTION DOCUMENTS

Subpart 1. Submittal documents. Construction documents, special inspection and structural observation programs, and other data shall be submitted in one or more sets with each application for a permit.

Exception: The building official may waive the submission of construction documents and other data if the nature of the work applied for is such that reviewing of construction documents is not necessary to obtain compliance with the code.

The building officer may require plans or other data be prepared according to the rules of the Board of Architecture, Engineering, Land Surveying, Landscape Architecture, Geoscience and Interior Design, chapter 1800, and Minnesota Statutes, sections 326.02 to 326.15, and other state laws relating to plan and specification preparation by occupational licenses. If special conditions exist, the building official may require additional construction documents to be prepared by a licensed design professional.

Subp. 2. Information on construction documents. Construction documents shall be dimensioned and drawn upon suitable material. Electronic media documents are permitted to be submitted when approved by the building official. Construction documents shall be of sufficient clarity to indicate the location, nature, and extent of the work proposed and show in detail that it will conform to the code and relevant laws, ordinances, rules, and regulations, as determined by the building official.

Subp. 3. Manufacturer's installation instructions. When required by the building official, manufacturer's installation instructions for construction equipment and components regulated by the code, shall be available on the job site at the time of inspection.

Subp. 4. Site plan. The construction documents submitted with the application for permit shall be accompanied by a site plan drawn to scale, showing the size and location of new construction and existing structures on the site, distances from lot lines, the established street grades, and the proposed finished grades, and it shall be drawn according to an accurate boundary line survey. In the case of demolition, the site plan shall show construction to be demolished and the location and size of existing structures and construction that are to remain on the site or plot. The building official may waive or modify the requirement for a site plan if the application for permit is for alteration or repair or when otherwise warranted.

Subp. 5. Examination of documents. The building official shall examine or cause to be examined the accompanying construction documents to ascertain whether the construction indicated and described complies with the requirements of the code and other pertinent laws and ordinances.

Subp. 6. Approval of construction documents. If the building official issues a permit, the construction documents shall be approved in writing or by a stamp, stating "Reviewed for Code Compliance," dated, and signed by the building official or an authorized representative. One set of the construction documents that were reviewed shall be retained by the building official. The other set shall be returned to the applicant, kept at the site of the work, and open to inspection by the building official or an authorized representative.

Subp. 7. **Previous approvals.** The code in effect at the time of application shall be applicable.

Subp. 8. **Phased approval.** The building official may issue a permit for the construction of foundations or any other part of a building or structure before the construction documents for the whole building or structure have been submitted, provided that adequate information and detailed statements have been filed complying with pertinent requirements of the code. The holder of the permit for the foundation or other parts of a building or structure shall proceed at the holder's own risk with the building operation and without assurance that a permit for the entire structure will be granted.

Subp. 9. **Design professional in responsible charge.**

A. The building official may require the owner to engage and designate on the building permit application a licensed design professional who shall act as the licensed design professional in responsible charge. If the circumstances require, the owner shall designate a substitute licensed design professional in responsible charge who shall perform the duties required of the original licensed design professional in responsible charge. The building official shall be notified in writing by the owner if the licensed design professional in responsible charge is changed or is unable to continue to perform the duties.

The licensed design professional in responsible charge shall be responsible for reviewing and coordinating submittal documents prepared by others, including phased and deferred submittal items, for compatibility with the design of the building.

When structural observation is required by the code, the inspection program shall name the individual or firms who are to perform structural observation and describe the stages of construction at which structural observation is to occur.

B. For the purposes of this part, deferred submittals are defined as those portions of the design that are not submitted at the time of the application and that are to be submitted to the building official within a specified period.

Deferral of any submittal items shall have the prior approval of the building official. The licensed design professional in responsible charge shall list the deferred submittals on the construction documents for review by the building official.

Submittal documents for deferred submittal items shall be submitted to the licensed design professional in responsible charge who shall review them and forward them to the building official with a notation indicating that the deferred submittal documents have been reviewed and that they have been found to be in general conformance with the design of the building. The deferred submittal items shall not be installed until their design and submittal documents have been approved by the building official.

C. Work regulated by the code shall be installed according to the reviewed construction documents, and any changes made during construction that are not in compliance with the approved construction documents shall be resubmitted for approval as an amended set of construction documents.

1300.0140
VIOLATIONS

It is unlawful for any person, firm, or corporation to erect, construct, alter, extend, repair, move, remove, demolish, or occupy any building, structure, or equipment regulated by the code, or cause any of those actions, in conflict with or in violation of the code. The building official may serve a notice of violation or order on the person responsible for the erection, construction, alteration, extension, repair, moving, removal, demolition, or occupancy of a building or structure in violation of the code, or in violation of a permit or certificate issued under the code. The order shall direct the discontinuance of the illegal action or condition and the abatement of the violation.

1300.0150
VIOLATIONS, PENALTY

A violation of the code is a misdemeanor under Minnesota Statutes, section 16B.69.

1300.0160
FEES

Subpart 1. **Schedule of permit fees.** The applicant for a permit for a building; structure; or electrical, gas, mechanical, or plumbing system or alterations requiring a permit shall pay the fee set forth by a fee schedule adopted by the municipality.

When submittal documents are required to be submitted by this chapter, a plan review fee shall be required. The plan review fee shall be established by the fee schedule adopted by the municipality.

Exception: The fee schedule adopted by the municipality may exempt minor work from plan review fees.

Subp. 2. **Fees commensurate with service.** Fees established by the municipality must be by legal means and must be fair, reasonable, and proportionate to the actual cost of the service for which the fee is imposed.

Subp. 3. **Building permit valuations.** The applicant for a permit shall provide an estimated permit value at time of application. Permit valuations shall include total value of all construction work, including materials and labor, for which the permit is being issued, such as electrical, gas, mechanical, plumbing equipment, and permanent systems. Building permit valuation shall be set by the building official.

Exceptions: Building permit valuations for the following structures shall be based on the valuation of on-site work only:

A. Manufactured homes containing a Housing and Urban Development (HUD) certification label;

B. Prefabricated buildings with a Department of Labor and Industry prefabrication label; and

C. Industrialized/modular buildings with an Industrialized Building Commission (IBC) label.

Subp. 4. **Building permit fees.** Building permit fees shall be based on valuation.

Exceptions:

A. One- and two-family dwelling maintenance permits for roofing, siding, windows, doors, or other minor projects may be charged a fixed fee;

B. Permits for plumbing, mechanical, electrical, or other building service equipment systems may be based on valuation or charged a fixed fee; and

C. Replacement of a residential fixture or appliance cannot exceed the permit fee limitation established by Minnesota Statutes, section 16B.665.

Subp. 5. **Plan review fees for similar plans.** When submittal documents for similar plans are approved under subpart 6, plan review fees shall not exceed 25 percent of the normal building permit fee established and charged by the jurisdiction for the same structure.

Subp. 6. **Plan review of similar plans.**

A. Any number of similar buildings may be built from a master plan if:

(1) Plan review fees have been paid for the master plan;

(2) A code change has not occurred that impacts the design of a master plan;

(3) The similar building has the same physical dimensions and structural design as the master plan;

Exception: The following modifications to the master plan are not considered to be significant modifications, according to Minnesota Statutes, section 16B.61, subdivision 1, and are permitted for dwelling units and their accessory structures built to the International Residential Code, and residential occupancies built to the International Building Code that are three stories or less in height and their accessory structures:

(a) Foundation types to include walkout, lookout, and full basement;

(b) Foundation materials to include poured concrete, masonry units, and wood;

(c) Garage dimensions;

(d) Roof design changed by a revised truss plan approved by the building official;

(e) Bays or cantilevered floor areas;

(f) Decks and porches; and

(g) Other modifications approved by the building official;

(4) Occupancy groups other than those identified in the exceptions listed in part 1300.0160, subpart 6, item A, subitem (3), must be the same type of construction and occupancy classification and must have the same exit system;

Exception: Minor changes to the exit access; and

(5) The similar plan is based on a master plan for which the municipality has issued a permit within the last 12 months.

B. Plan review fees for similar building plans must be based on the costs commensurate with the direct and indirect cost of the service, but must not exceed 25 percent of the normal building permit fee established and charged by the municipality for the same structure.

C. The plan review fee charged for similar building plans applies to all buildings regulated by the code regardless of occupancy classification including industrialized/modular buildings constructed under a program specified in Minnesota Statutes, section 16B.75.

D. The applicant must submit a new plan set and other information as required by the building official for each building reviewed as a similar building.

Subp. 7. **Payment of fees.** A permit shall not be issued until the fees prescribed by the municipality have been paid.

Subp. 8. **Work commencing before permit issuance.** If work for which a permit is required by the code has been commenced without first obtaining a permit, a special investigation shall be made before a permit may be issued for the work. An investigation fee established by the municipality shall be collected and is in addition to the required permit fees, but it may not exceed the permit fee.

Subp. 9. **Fee refunds.** The municipality shall establish a permit and plan review fee refund policy.

Subp. 10. **State surcharge fees.** All municipal permits issued for work under the code are subject to a surcharge fee. The fees are established by Minnesota Statutes, section 16B.70. Reports and remittances by municipalities must be filed with the commissioner, directed to the attention of the state building official.

Surcharge fees imposed by the state are in addition to municipal permit fees. Surcharge report forms and information may be obtained by writing the commissioner, to the attention of the state building official.

1300.0170
STOP WORK ORDER

If the building official finds any work regulated by the code being performed in a manner contrary to the provisions of the code or in a dangerous or unsafe manner, the building official may issue a stop work order.

The stop work order shall be in writing and issued to the owner of the property involved, to the owner's agent, or to the person doing the work. Upon issuance of a stop work order, the cited work shall immediately cease. The stop work order shall state the reason for the order and the conditions under which the cited work will be permitted to resume.

1300.0180
UNSAFE BUILDINGS OR STRUCTURES

A building or structure regulated by the code is unsafe, for purposes of this part, if it is structurally unsafe, not provided with adequate egress, a fire hazard, or otherwise dangerous to human life.

Building service equipment that is regulated by the code is unsafe, for purposes of this part, if it is a fire, electrical, or health hazard; an unsanitary condition; or otherwise dangerous to human life. Use of a building, structure, or building service equipment constituting a hazard to safety, health, or public welfare by reason of inadequate maintenance, dilapidation, obsolescence, fire hazard, disaster, damage, or abandonment is, for the purposes of this part, an unsafe use. Parapet walls, cornices, spires, towers, tanks, statuary, and other appendages or structural members that are supported by, attached to, or a part of a building and that are in deteriorated condition or otherwise unable to sustain the design loads that are specified in the code are unsafe building appendages.

The building official may order any building or portion of a building to be vacated if continued use is dangerous to life, health, or safety of the occupants. The order shall be in writing and state the reasons for the action.

All unsafe buildings, structures, or appendages are public nuisances and must be abated by repair, rehabilitation, demolition, or removal according to Minnesota Statutes, sections 463.15 to 463.26.

1300.0190
TEMPORARY STRUCTURES AND USES

Subpart 1. **General.** The building official may issue a permit for temporary structures and temporary uses. The permit shall be limited as to time of service, but shall not be permitted for more than 180 days. The building official may grant extensions for demonstrated cause.

Subp. 2. **Conformance.** Temporary structures and uses shall conform to the structural strength, fire safety, means of egress, accessibility, light, ventilation, and sanitary requirements of the code as necessary to ensure the public health, safety, and general welfare.

Subp. 3. **Termination of approval.** The building official may terminate the permit for a temporary structure or use and order the temporary structure or use to be discontinued if the conditions required in this part have not been complied with.

1300.0210
INSPECTIONS

Subpart 1. **General.** Construction or work for which a permit is required is subject to inspection by the building official and the construction or work shall remain accessible and exposed for inspection purposes until approved. Approval as a result of an inspection is not approval of a violation of the code or of other ordinances of the jurisdiction. Inspections presuming to give authority to violate or cancel the provisions of the code or of other ordinances of the jurisdiction are not valid. It shall be the duty of the permit applicant to cause the work to remain accessible and exposed for inspection purposes. Neither the building official nor the jurisdiction is liable for expense entailed in the removal or replacement of any material required to allow inspection.

Subp. 2. **Preliminary inspection.** Before issuing a permit, the building official may examine, or cause to be examined, buildings, structures, and sites for which an application has been filed.

Subp. 3. **Inspection record card.** The building official shall identify which inspections are required for the work requiring a permit. Work requiring a permit shall not be commenced until the permit holder or an agent of the permit holder has posted or otherwise made available an inspection record card that allows the building official to conveniently make all required entries regarding inspection of the work. This card shall be maintained and made available by the permit holder until final approval has been granted by the building official.

Subp. 4. **Inspection requests.** The building official shall provide the applicant with policies, procedures, and a timeline for requesting inspections. The person doing the work authorized by a permit shall notify the building official that the work is ready for inspection. The person requesting an inspection required by the code shall provide access to and means for inspection of the work.

Subp. 5. **Approval required.** Work shall not be done beyond the point indicated in each successive inspection without first obtaining the approval of the building official. The building official, upon notification, shall make the requested inspections and shall either indicate the portion of the construction that is satisfactory as completed or notify the permit holder or an agent of the permit holder of any failures to comply with the code. Any portion that does not comply shall be corrected and the portion shall not be covered or concealed until authorized by the building official.

Subp. 6. **Required inspections.** The building official, upon notification, shall make the inspections in this part. In addition to the inspections identified in this subpart, see applicable rule chapters in part 1300.0050 for specific inspection and testing requirements.

   A. Footing inspections shall be made after excavations for footings are complete and any required reinforcing steel is in place. Materials for the foundation shall be on the job, except that concrete need not be on the job if the concrete is ready mixed according to approved nationally recognized standards.

   B. Foundations:

      (1) Foundation inspections for poured walls shall be made after all forms are in place with any required reinforcing steel and bracing in place, and prior to pouring concrete.

      (2) All foundation walls shall be inspected prior to backfill for specific code requirements.

(3) The foundation inspection shall include excavations for thickened slabs intended for the support of bearing walls, partitions, structural supports, or equipment.

C. Concrete slab and under-floor inspections shall be made after in-slab or under-floor reinforcing steel and building service equipment, conduit, piping accessories, and other ancillary equipment items are in place, but before any concrete is placed or floor sheathing installed, including the subfloor.

D. Rough-in inspection of plumbing, mechanical, gas, and electrical systems shall be made before covering or concealment, before fixtures or appliances are set or installed, and before framing inspection.

E. Inspection of framing and masonry construction shall be made after the roof, masonry, framing, firestopping, draftstopping, and bracing are in place and after the plumbing, mechanical, and electrical rough inspections are approved.

F. Energy efficiency inspections shall be made to determine compliance with Minnesota Energy Code requirements.

G. Lath and gypsum board inspections shall be made after lathing and gypsum board, interior and exterior, are in place, but before any plastering is applied or before gypsum board joints and fasteners are taped and finished.

   Exception: Gypsum board that is not part of a fire-resistive assembly or a shear assembly.

H. Protection of joints and penetrations in fire-resistance-rated assemblies shall not be concealed from view until inspected and approved.

I. Installation of manufactured homes (mobile homes) shall be made after the installation of the support systems and all utility service connections are in place, but before any covering material or skirting is in place. Evaluation of an approved anchoring system is part of the installation inspection.

J. Fireplaces must be inspected for compliance with applicable requirements of the code and the manufacturer's installation instructions.

K. A final inspection shall be made for all work for which a permit is issued.

L. Special inspections shall be as required by the code.

M. In addition to the inspections in items A to K, the building official is authorized to make or require other inspections of any construction work to ascertain compliance with the code and other laws that are enforced by the Department of Building Safety.

Subp. 7. **Inspection agencies.** The building official is authorized to accept inspection reports by approved agencies.

1300.0220
CERTIFICATE OF OCCUPANCY

Subpart 1. **Use and occupancy.** No building or structure shall be used or occupied, and no change in the existing occupancy classification of a building, structure, or portion of a building or structure shall be made until the building official has issued a certificate of occupancy for the building or structure under this part. Issuance of a certificate of occupancy is not approval of a violation of the code or other ordinances of the municipality. Certificates presuming to give authority to violate or cancel the code or other ordinances of the municipality are not valid.

   Exception: A municipality has the option of requiring certificates of occupancy for:

   A. "U" occupancies constructed under the International Building Code;

   B. Accessory structures constructed under the International Residential Code; or

   C. Used manufactured homes moved into or within a jurisdiction.

Subp. 2. **Existing structures.** The legal occupancy of any structure existing on the date of adoption of the code shall be permitted to continue without change except as specifically required in chapter 1311.

Subp. 3. **Change in use.** Changes in the character or use of an existing structure shall not be made except as specified in chapter 1311.

Subp. 4. **Moved buildings.** Buildings or structures moved into or within a jurisdiction shall comply with the provisions of the code for new buildings or structures.

   Exception: A residential building relocated within or into a municipality need not comply with the Minnesota Energy Code or Minnesota Statutes, section 326.371.

Subp. 5. **Certificate issued.** After the building official inspects a building or structure and finds no violations of the code or other laws that are enforced by the Department of Building Safety, the building official shall issue a certificate of occupancy containing the following:

   A. The building permit number;

   B. The address of the structure;

   C. The name and address of the owner;

   D. A statement that the described portion of the structure has been inspected for compliance with the requirements of the code for the occupancy and division of occupancy and the use for which the proposed occupancy is classified;

   E. The name of the building official;

   F. The edition of the code under which the permit was issued;

   G. The use and occupancy classification;

   H. The type of construction;

   I. If an automatic sprinkler system is provided; and

   J. Any special stipulations and conditions of the building permit.

Subp. 6. **Temporary occupancy.** The building official is authorized to issue a temporary certificate of occupancy before the completion of the entire work covered by the permit, provided that the portion or portions shall be occupied safely. The building official shall set a time period during which the temporary certificate of occupancy is valid.

Subp. 7. **Revocation.** The building official may issue a written suspension or revocation of a certificate of occupancy issued under the code if the certificate is issued in error or on the basis of incorrect information supplied, or if the building or use of the building, structure, or portion of the building or structure is in violation of any ordinance or regulation or a provision of the code.

1300.0230
BOARD OF APPEALS

Subpart 1. **Local board of appeals.** In order to hear and decide appeals of orders, decisions, or determinations made by the building official relative to the application and interpretation of this code, there shall be and is hereby created a board of appeals. The building official shall be an ex officio member of said board but shall have no vote on any matter before the board. The board of appeals shall be designated by the governing body. Appeals hearings must occur within ten working days from the date the municipality receives a properly completed application for appeal. If an appeals hearing is not held within this time, the applicant may appeal directly to the State Building Code Appeals Board.

The board shall adopt rules of procedures for conducting its business and shall render all decisions and findings in writing to the appellant with a duplicate copy to the building official and to the state building official within five working days of the decision. For jurisdictions without a board of appeals, the appellant may appeal to an appeals board assembled by the state of Minnesota, Department of Labor and Industry's Construction Codes and Licensing Division.

Subp. 2. **Qualifications.** The board of appeals shall consist of members who are qualified by experience and training to pass on matters pertaining to building construction and are not employees of the affected jurisdiction.

Subp. 3. **Limitations on authority.** An application for appeal shall be based on a claim that the true intent of this code or the rules legally adopted thereunder have been incorrectly interpreted, the provisions of this code do not fully apply, or an equally good or better form of construction is proposed. The board shall have no authority to waive requirements of this code.

Subp. 4. **Final interpretive authority.** The state building official has final interpretive authority for all codes adopted as part of the code except for the plumbing code when enforced by the Commissioner of Health and the electrical code when enforced by the State Board of Electricity. A request for final interpretation must come from a local or state level building code board of appeals. The procedures for final interpretations by the state building official are as established in Minnesota Statutes, section 16B.63.

1300.0240
DISCLAIMER CLAUSE

The inclusion of specific requirements relative to the manner of installation of any building or portion of any building or building equipment in one or more parts of the code does not limit this procedure to any particular type of installer or provide a basis upon which determination of the right to perform a procedure shall be made. The authority for this determination is in the various licensing statutes or ordinances for each type of installer who performs the work.

1300.0250
SEVERABILITY

The invalidity of any provision of the Minnesota State Building Code does not affect any other provisions of the code that can be given effect without the invalid provision and, to this end, the provisions of the code are declared to be severable.

MINNESOTA RULES, CHAPTER 1303

1303.1000
TITLE

This chapter shall be known as "Minnesota provisions."

1303.1100
PURPOSE

This chapter contains requirements of the code that are mandated by Minnesota Statutes, are needed to address Minnesota's climatic conditions, or are otherwise determined necessary to provide a safe minimum level of construction in an area not appropriately regulated in the International Building Code or International Residential Code.

1303.1200
RESTROOM FACILITIES IN PUBLIC ACCOMMODATIONS

Subpart 1. **Ratio.** In a place of public accommodation subject to this part, the ratio of water closets for women to the total of water closets and urinals provided for men must be at least three to two, unless there are two or fewer fixtures for men.

Subp. 2. **Application.** This part applies only to the construction of buildings or structures of public accommodation or where the cost of alterations to an existing place of public accommodation exceeds 50 percent of the estimated replacement value of the existing facility.

Subp. 3. **Definition.** For purposes of this part, "place of public accommodation" means a publicly or privately owned sports or entertainment arena, stadium, theater, community or convention hall, special event center, amusement facility, or special event center in a public park, that is designed for occupancy by 200 or more people.

1303.1300
SPACE FOR COMMUTER VANS

Every parking ramp or other parking facility must include spaces for the parking of motor vehicles having a capacity of seven to 16 persons. The number of required spaces must be determined by two percent of the gross designed parking area with a minimum of two spaces. The minimum vertical clearance to and within required spaces is 98 inches.

1303.1400
AUTOMATIC GARAGE DOOR OPENING SYSTEMS

All automatic garage door opening systems that are installed, serviced, or repaired for garages serving residential buildings, must comply with the provisions of Minnesota Statutes, sections 325F.82 and 325F.83.

1303.1500
RECYCLING SPACE

Subpart 1. **Requirement.** Space must be provided for the collection, separation, and temporary storage of recyclable materials within or adjacent to all new or significantly remodeled buildings or structures that contain 1,000 square feet or more.

Exception: Residential structures with fewer than four dwelling units.

Subp. 2. **Location.** Space designated for recycling shall be located so it is at least as convenient as the location where other solid waste is collected. If feasible, recycling space should be adjacent to other solid waste collection space. Recycling space must be located and designed in accordance with the provisions of this code and ordinances of the jurisdiction.

Subp. 3. **Identification on plans.** Space designated for recycling must be identified on plans submitted for a building permit.

Subp. 4. **Minimum space.** Space designated for recycling must be sufficient to contain all the recyclable materials generated from the building. The minimum amount of recycling space required must be the number of square feet determined by multiplying the gross square feet of floor areas assigned to each use within a building as set forth in subpart 5, Table 1-A, times the corresponding factor.

Subp. 5. **TABLE 1-A MINIMUM RECYCLING SPACE REQUIREMENTS.**

USE[1]	FACTOR
1. Aircraft hangers (no repair)	.001
2. Auction rooms	.0025
3[2]. Auditoriums, reviewing stands, stadiums, gymnasiums, public swimming pools, skating rinks	.001
4. Lodge rooms, conference rooms, lounges, stages, exhibit rooms	.0025
5. Dance floors, churches[3] and chapels, lobby	.001
6. Dining rooms	.003
7[3]. Drinking establishments	.004
8[3]. Bowling alleys (excluding lanes)	.0025
9[3]. Children's homes and homes for the aged	.0025
10. Classrooms	.002
11. Courtrooms	.001
12. Dormitories	.0025
13. Exercise rooms	.001
14. Garages, parking	.001
15[3]. Hospitals and sanitariums, nursing homes	.0025
16[3]. Hotels	.002
17. Apartments	.0025

18. Kitchens - commercial .003

19[3]. Libraries .002

20. Locker rooms .001

21. Malls .0025

22. Manufacturing areas .0025

23. Mechanical equipment rooms .001

24[3]. Nurseries for children (day care) .002

25. Offices .0025

26. School shops and vocational rooms .0025

27. Storage and stock rooms .0025

28. Warehouses .001

29. All others .0025

Footnotes:

[1] The area of a use must include all areas serving or accessory to a use (corridors, accessory use areas, etc.).

[2] Exclude playing areas, courts, fields, and like areas.

[3] The factors for these uses are intended to include all incidental uses typical of these types of facilities.

If the provisions of Table 1-A are excessive due to a specific use, space for recycling may be considered individually by the administrative authority.

1303.1600
FOOTING DEPTH FOR FROST PROTECTION

Subpart 1. **Minimum footing depth.** In the absence of a determination by an engineer competent in soil mechanics, the minimum allowable footing depth in feet due to freezing is five feet in Zone I and $3^1/_2$ feet in Zone II.

Zone I includes the counties of: Aitkin, Becker, Beltrami, Carlton, Cass, Clay, Clearwater, Cook, Crow Wing, Douglas, Grant, Hubbard, Itasca, Kanabec, Kittson, Koochiching, Lake, Lake of the Woods, Mahnomen, Marshall, Mille Lacs, Morrison, Norman, Otter Tail, Pennington, Pine, Polk, Red Lake, Roseau, St. Louis, Todd, Traverse, Wadena, and Wilkin.

Zone II shall include the counties of: Anoka, Benton, Big Stone, Blue Earth, Brown, Carver, Chippewa, Chisago, Cottonwood, Dakota, Dodge, Faribault, Fillmore, Freeborn, Goodhue, Hennepin, Houston, Isanti, Jackson, Kandiyohi, Lac qui Parle, Le Sueur, Lincoln, Lyon, McLeod, Martin, Meeker, Mower, Murray, Nicollet, Nobles, Olmsted, Pipestone, Pope, Ramsey, Redwood, Renville, Rice, Rock, Scott, Sibley, Sherburne, Stearns, Steele, Stevens, Swift, Wabasha, Waseca, Washington, Watonwan, Winona, Wright, and Yellow Medicine.

Less depths may be permitted when supporting evidence is presented by an engineer competent in soil mechanics.

Subp. 2. **Soil under slab on grade construction for buildings.** When soil, natural or fill, is sand or pit run sand and gravel, and of depth in accordance with minimum footing depth requirements for each zone, slab on grade construction which is structurally designed to support all applied loads is permitted. Sand must contain less than 70 percent material that will pass through a U.S. Standard No. 40 sieve and less than five percent material that will pass through a No. 200 sieve (five percent fines), or be approved by an engineer competent in soil mechanics.

Exception: Slab on grade construction may be placed on any soil except peat or muck for detached one-story private garage, carport, and shed buildings not larger than 3,000 square feet.

Footings for interior bearing walls or columns may be constructed to be integral with the slab on grade for any height building. Footings for exterior bearing walls or columns may be similarly constructed for any height building when supporting soil is as described in this subpart. Footing design must reflect eccentric loading conditions at slab edges, soil bearing capacity, and the requirements of International Building Code, chapter 19.

1303.1700
GROUND SNOW LOAD

The ground snow load, Pg, to be used in determining the design snow loads for buildings and other structures shall be 60 pounds per square foot in the following counties: Aitkin, Becker, Beltrami, Carlton, Cass, Clearwater, Cook, Crow Wing, Hubbard, Itasca, Kanabec, Kittson, Koochiching, Lake, Lake of the Woods, Mahnomen, Marshall, Mille Lacs, Morrison, Norman, Otter Tail, Pennington, Pine, Polk, Red Lake, Roseau, St. Louis, Todd, and Wadena. The ground snow load, Pg, to be used in determining the design snow loads for buildings and other structures shall be 50 pounds per square foot in all other counties.

1303.1800
RADIAL ICE ON TOWERS

The effect of one-half inch of radial ice must be included in the design of towers including all supporting guys. This effect must include the weight of the ice and the increased profile of each such tower component so coated.

1303.2000
EXTERIOR WOOD DECKS, PATIOS, AND BALCONIES

The decking surface and upper portions of exterior wood decks, patios, and balconies may be constructed of any of the following materials:

A. The heartwood from species of wood having natural resistance to decay or termites, including redwood and cedars;

B. Grades of lumber which contain sapwood from species of wood having natural resistance to decay or termites, including redwood and cedars; or

C. Treated wood.

The species and grades of wood products used to construct the decking surface and upper portions of exterior decks, patios, and balconies must be made available to the building official on request before final construction approval.

1303.2100
BLEACHER SAFETY

All new bleachers, manufactured, installed, sold, or distributed where the bleachers or bleacher open spaces will be over 55 inches above grade or the floor below, and all bleacher guardrails if any part of the guardrail will be over 30 inches above grade or the floor below must comply with the State Building Code in effect and the provisions of Minnesota Statutes, section 16B.616.

1303.2200
SIMPLIFIED WIND LOADS

Subpart 1. **Section 2200.**

    A. This section applies to the wind loads for the main wind force-resisting systems only.

    B. In order to utilize wind loads from this part, the building shall meet the following requirements:

        (1) 60 feet or less in height;

        (2) Height not to exceed least horizontal dimension;

        (3) Enclosed building;

        (4) Roof shape - flat, gabled, or hip;

        (5) Roof slope of 45 degrees maximum;

        (6) Simple diaphragm building;

        (7) Not a flexible building;

        (8) Regular shape and approximately symmetrical;

        (9) No expansion joints or separations; and

      (10) No unusual response characteristics (for example: vortex shedding, galloping, or buffeting).

Subp. 2. **Simplified design wind pressures.** P_s represents the net pressures (sum of internal and external) to be applied to the horizontal and vertical projections of building surfaces. For the horizontal pressures, P_s is the combination of the windward and leeward net pressures. P_s may be determined from Equation P_{alt}.

$$P_s = K_{zt}I_wP_{alt} \qquad \text{(Equation } P_{alt}\text{)}$$

where:

K_{zt} = Topographic factor as defined in Chapter 6 of ASCE 7.

I_w = Importance factor as defined in Chapter 6 of ASCE 7.

P_{alt} = Alternative simplified design wind pressure from Table P_{alt}.

TABLE P_{alt}

Horizontal and Vertical Pressure*

Exp B	15 psf
Exp C	19 psf
Exp D	22 psf

*For vertical pressure, the above values are negative (upward).

Overhang Vertical Pressure*

Exp B	-25 psf
Exp C	-30 psf
Exp D	-35 psf

*Negative values are upward.

MINNESOTA RULES, CHAPTER 1309

1309.0010
ADOPTION OF INTERNATIONAL RESIDENTIAL CODE (IRC) BY REFERENCE

Subpart 1. Generally. The 2006 edition of the International Residential Code (IRC) as promulgated by the International Code Council (ICC), Washington, DC, is incorporated by reference and made part of the Minnesota State Building Code except as qualified by the applicable provisions in Minnesota Rules, chapter 1300, and as amended in this chapter. The IRC is not subject to frequent change and a copy of the IRC, with amendments for use in Minnesota, is available in the office of the commissioner of labor and industry. Portions of this chapter reproduce text and tables from the IRC. The IRC is copyright 2006 by the ICC. All rights reserved.

Subp. 2. Mandatory chapters. The 2006 IRC Chapters 2 through 10 and 43 must be administered by any municipality that has adopted the code, except as qualified by the applicable provisions in Minnesota Rules, chapter 1300, and as amended by this chapter.

Subp. 3. Replacement chapters. The following 2006 IRC chapters are being deleted and replaced with the provisions listed below:

A. Chapter 1 of the 2006 IRC and any references to code administration in this code are deleted and replaced with Minnesota Rules, chapter 1300, Minnesota Administration Code.

B. Chapter 11 of the 2006 IRC and any references to energy in this code are deleted and replaced with Minnesota Statutes, section 16B.617.

C. Chapters 12 through 24 of the 2006 IRC and any references to mechanical matters in this code are deleted and replaced with Minnesota Rules, chapter 1346, Minnesota Mechanical Code.

D. Chapters 25 through 32 of the 2006 IRC and any references to plumbing in this code are deleted and replaced with Minnesota Rules, chapter 4715, Minnesota Plumbing Code.

E. Chapters 33 through 42 of the 2006 IRC and references to electrical matters in this code, other than Section R313 Smoke Alarms, are deleted and replaced with Minnesota Rules, chapter 1315, Minnesota Electrical Code.

Subp. 4. Seismic or earthquake provisions. Any seismic or earthquake provisions and any references to them are deleted and are not included in this code.

Subp. 5. Flood hazard or floodproofing provisions. Any flood hazard or floodproofing provisions in the IRC, and any reference to those provisions, are deleted in their entirety. Requirements for floodproofing are located in chapter 1335, floodproofing regulations.

Subp. 6. Elevator and platform lift provisions. Any elevator and platform lift provisions in the IRC and any reference to those provisions are deleted in their entirety. Requirements for elevators or platform lifts are located in chapter 1307, elevators and related devices.

1309.0020
REFERENCES TO OTHER ICC CODES

Subpart 1. Generally. References to other codes and standards promulgated by the ICC in the 2006 IRC are modified in subparts 2 to 11.

Subp. 2. Building code. References to the International Building Code in this code mean the Minnesota Building Code, adopted pursuant to Minnesota Rules, chapter 1305, and Minnesota Statutes, section 16B.61, subdivision 1.

Subp. 3. Residential code. References to the IRC in this code mean the Minnesota Residential Code, adopted under Minnesota Rules, chapter 1309, and Minnesota Statutes, section 16B.61, subdivision 1.

Subp. 4. Electrical code. References to the ICC Electrical Code in this code mean the Minnesota Electrical Code, Minnesota Rules, chapter 1315, adopted under Minnesota Statutes, section 326.243.

Subp. 5. Fuel gas code. References to the International Fuel Gas Code in this code mean the Minnesota Mechanical Code, Minnesota Rules, chapter 1346, adopted under Minnesota Statutes, section 16B.61, subdivision 1.

Subp. 6. Mechanical code. References to the International Mechanical Code in this code mean the Minnesota Mechanical Code, Minnesota Rules, chapter 1346, adopted under Minnesota Statutes, section 16B.61, subdivision 1.

Subp. 7. Plumbing code. References to the International Plumbing code in this code mean the Minnesota Plumbing Code, Minnesota Rules, chapter 4715, adopted under Minnesota Statutes, section 16B.61, subdivisions 1 and 2.

Subp. 8. Private sewage disposal code. References to the International Private Sewage Disposal Code in this code mean the Minnesota Pollution Control Agency's minimum standards and criteria for individual sewage treatment systems in Minnesota Rules, chapter 7080, adopted under Minnesota Statutes, chapters 103F, 103G, 115, and 116.

Subp. 9. Energy conservation code. References to the International Energy Conservation Code in this code mean the Minnesota Energy Code, adopted under Minnesota Statutes, section 16B.617.

Subp. 10. Property maintenance code. References to the International Property Maintenance Code in this code do not apply.

Subp. 11. Accessibility code. References to accessibility in this code mean the Minnesota Accessibility Code, Minnesota Rules, chapter 1341.

1309.0030
ADMINISTRATIVE PROCEDURE CRITERIA

Procedures relating to the administration and enforcement of this code under Minnesota Statutes, section 16B.57, are contained in Minnesota Rules, chapter 1300, Minnesota Administration Code. Minnesota Rules, chapter 1300, governs the application of this code.

1309.0040
VIOLATION

A violation of this code is a misdemeanor under Minnesota Statutes, section 16B.69.

Part II — Definitions

CHAPTER 2

DEFINITIONS

SECTION R201
GENERAL

R201.1 Scope. Unless otherwise expressly stated, the following words and terms shall, for the purposes of this code, have the meanings indicated in this chapter.

R201.2 Interchangeability. Words used in the present tense include the future; words in the masculine gender include the feminine and neuter; the singular number includes the plural and the plural, the singular.

R201.3 Terms defined in other codes. Where terms are not defined in this code such terms shall have meanings ascribed to them as in other code publications of the International Code Council.

R201.4 Terms not defined. Where terms are not defined through the methods authorized by this chapter, the *Merriam-Webster Collegiate Dictionary*, available at www.m-w.com, shall be considered as providing ordinarily accepted meanings. The dictionary is incorporated by reference, is subject to frequent change, and is available through the Minitex interlibrary loan system.

SECTION R202
DEFINITIONS

ACCESSIBLE. Signifies access that requires the removal of an access panel or similar removable obstruction.

ACCESSIBLE, READILY. Signifies access without the necessity for removing a panel or similar obstruction.

ACCESSORY STRUCTURE. A structure not greater than 3,000 square feet (279 m²) in floor area, and not over two stories in height, the use of which is customarily accessory to and incidental to that of the dwelling(s) and which is located on the same lot.

ADDITION. An extension or increase in floor area or height of a building or structure.

AIR ADMITTANCE VALVE. A one-way valve designed to allow air into the plumbing drainage system when a negative pressure develops in the piping. This device shall close by gravity and seal the terminal under conditions of zero differential pressure (no flow conditions) and under positive internal pressure.

AIR BREAK (DRAINAGE SYSTEM). An arrangement in which a discharge pipe from a fixture, appliance or device drains indirectly into a receptor below the flood-level rim of the receptor, and above the trap seal.

AIR CIRCULATION, FORCED. A means of providing space conditioning utilizing movement of air through ducts or plenums by mechanical means.

AIR-CONDITIONING SYSTEM. A system that consists of heat exchangers, blowers, filters, supply, exhaust and return-air systems, and shall include any apparatus installed in connection therewith.

AIR GAP, DRAINAGE SYSTEM. The unobstructed vertical distance through free atmosphere between the outlet of a waste pipe and the flood-level rim of the fixture or receptor into which it is discharging.

AIR GAP, WATER-DISTRIBUTION SYSTEM. The unobstructed vertical distance through free atmosphere between the lowest opening from a water supply discharge to the flood-level rim of a plumbing fixture.

ALTERATION. Any construction or renovation to an existing structure other than repair or addition that requires a permit. Also, a change in a mechanical system that involves an extension, addition or change to the arrangement, type or purpose of the original installation that requires a permit.

ANCHORS. See "Supports."

ANTISIPHON. A term applied to valves or mechanical devices that eliminate siphonage.

APPLIANCE. A device or apparatus that is manufactured and designed to utilize energy and for which this code provides specific requirements.

APPROVED. Acceptable to the building official.

APPROVED AGENCY. An established and recognized agency regularly engaged in conducting tests or furnishing inspection services, when such agency has been approved by the building official.

ASPECT RATIO. The ratio of the height to width (h/w) of a shear wall. The shear wall height is the maximum clear height from top of foundation or diaphragm to bottom of diaphragm framing above and the shear wall width is the sheathed dimension in the direction of applied force on the shear wall.

ATTIC. The unfinished space between the ceiling joists of the top story and the roof rafters.

BACKFLOW, DRAINAGE. A reversal of flow in the drainage system.

BACKFLOW PREVENTER. A device or means to prevent backflow.

BACKFLOW PREVENTER, REDUCED–PRESSURE-ZONE TYPE. A backflow-prevention device consisting of two independently acting check valves, internally force loaded to a normally closed position and separated by an intermediate chamber (or zone) in which there is an automatic relief means of venting to atmosphere internally loaded to a normally open position between two tightly closing shutoff valves and with means for testing for tightness of the checks and opening of relief means.

BACKFLOW, WATER DISTRIBUTION. The flow of water or other liquids into the potable water-supply piping from any sources other than its intended source. Backsiphonage is one type of backflow.

BACKPRESSURE. Pressure created by any means in the water distribution system, which by being in excess of the pressure in the water supply mains causes a potential backflow condition.

BACKPRESSURE, LOW HEAD. A pressure less than or equal to 4.33 psi (29.88 kPa) or the pressure exerted by a 10-foot (3048 mm) column of water.

BACKSIPHONAGE. The flowing back of used or contaminated water from piping into a potable water-supply pipe due to a negative pressure in such pipe.

BACKWATER VALVE. A device installed in a drain or pipe to prevent backflow of sewage.

BALCONY, EXTERIOR. An exterior floor projecting from and supported by a structure without additional independent supports.

BALL COCK. A valve that is used inside a gravity-type water closet flush tank to control the supply of water into the tank. It may also be called a flush-tank fill valve or water control.

BASEMENT. That portion of a building that is partly or completely below grade (see "Story above grade").

BASEMENT WALL. The opaque portion of a wall that encloses one side of a basement and has an average below grade wall area that is 50 percent or more of the total opaque and non-opaque area of that enclosing side.

BASIC WIND SPEED. Three-second gust speed at 33 feet (10 058 mm) above the ground in Exposure C (see Section R301.2.1) as given in Figure R301.2(4).

BATHROOM GROUP. A group of fixtures, including or excluding a bidet, consisting of a water closet, lavatory, and bathtub or shower. Such fixtures are located together on the same floor level.

BEND. A drainage fitting, designed to provide a change in direction of a drain pipe of less than the angle specified by the amount necessary to establish the desired slope of the line (see "Elbow" and "Sweep").

BOILER. A self-contained appliance from which hot water is circulated for heating purposes and then returned to the boiler, and which operates at water pressures not exceeding 160 pounds per square inch gage (psig) (1102 kPa gauge) and at water temperatures not exceeding 250°F (121°C).

BOND BEAM. A horizontal grouted element within masonry in which reinforcement is embedded.

BRACED WALL LINE. A series of braced wall panels in a single story constructed in accordance with Section R602.10 for wood framing or Section R603.7 or R301.1.1 for cold-formed steel framing to resist racking from seismic and wind forces.

BRACED WALL PANEL. A section of a braced wall line constructed in accordance with Section R602.10 for wood framing or Section R603.7 or R301.1.1 for cold-formed steel framing, which extend the full height of the wall.

BRANCH. Any part of the piping system other than a riser, main or stack.

BRANCH, FIXTURE. See "Fixture branch, drainage."

BRANCH, HORIZONTAL. See "Horizontal branch, drainage."

BRANCH INTERVAL. A vertical measurement of distance, 8 feet (2438 mm) or more in developed length, between the connections of horizontal branches to a drainage stack. Measurements are taken down the stack from the highest horizontal branch connection.

BRANCH, MAIN. A water-distribution pipe that extends horizontally off a main or riser to convey water to branches or fixture groups.

BRANCH, VENT. A vent connecting two or more individual vents with a vent stack or stack vent.

BTU/H. The listed maximum capacity of an appliance, absorption unit or burner expressed in British thermal units input per hour.

BUILDING. Building shall mean any one- and two-family dwelling or portion thereof, including townhouses, that is used, or designed or intended to be used for human habitation, for living, sleeping, cooking or eating purposes, or any combination thereof, and shall include accessory structures thereto.

BUILDING DRAIN. The lowest piping that collects the discharge from all other drainage piping inside the house and extends 30 inches (762 mm) in developed length of pipe, beyond the exterior walls and conveys the drainage to the building sewer.

BUILDING, EXISTING. Existing building is a building erected prior to the adoption of this code, or one for which a legal building permit has been issued.

BUILDING LINE. The line established by law, beyond which a building shall not extend, except as specifically provided by law.

BUILDING OFFICIAL. The officer or other designated authority charged with the administration and enforcement of this code.

BUILDING SEWER. That part of the drainage system that extends from the end of the building drain and conveys its discharge to a public sewer, private sewer, individual sewage-disposal system or other point of disposal.

BUILDING THERMAL ENVELOPE. The basement walls, exterior walls, floor, roof and any other building element that enclose conditioned spaces.

BUILT-UP ROOF COVERING. Two or more layers of felt cemented together and surfaced with a cap sheet, mineral aggregate, smooth coating or similar surfacing material.

CEILING HEIGHT. The clear vertical distance from the finished floor to the finished ceiling.

CHIMNEY. A primary vertical structure containing one or more flues, for the purpose of carrying gaseous products of combustion and air from a fuel-burning appliance to the outside atmosphere.

CHIMNEY CONNECTOR. A pipe that connects a fuel-burning appliance to a chimney.

CHIMNEY TYPES

> **Residential-type appliance.** An approved chimney for removing the products of combustion from fuel-burning, residential-type appliances producing combustion gases not in excess of 1,000°F (538°C) under normal operating conditions, but capable of producing combustion gases of 1,400°F (760°C) during intermittent forces firing for periods up to 1 hour. All temperatures shall be measured at the appliance flue outlet. Residential-type appliance chimneys include masonry and factory-built types.

CIRCUIT VENT. A vent that connects to a horizontal drainage branch and vents two traps to a maximum of eight traps or trapped fixtures connected into a battery.

CLADDING. The exterior materials that cover the surface of the building envelope that is directly loaded by the wind.

CLEANOUT. An accessible opening in the drainage system used for the removal of possible obstruction.

CLOSET. A small room or chamber used for storage.

COMBINATION WASTE AND VENT SYSTEM. A specially designed system of waste piping embodying the horizontal wet venting of one or more sinks or floor drains by means of a common waste and vent pipe adequately sized to provide free movement of air above the flow line of the drain.

COMBUSTIBLE MATERIAL. Any material not defined as noncombustible.

COMBUSTION AIR. The air provided to fuel-burning equipment including air for fuel combustion, draft hood dilution and ventilation of the equipment enclosure.

COMMON VENT. A single pipe venting two trap arms within the same branch interval, either back-to-back or one above the other.

CONDENSATE. The liquid that separates from a gas due to a reduction in temperature, e.g., water that condenses from flue gases and water that condenses from air circulating through the cooling coil in air conditioning equipment.

CONDENSING APPLIANCE. An appliance that condenses water generated by the burning of fuels.

CONDITIONED AIR. Air treated to control its temperature, relative humidity or quality.

CONDITIONED AREA. That area within a building provided with heating and/or cooling systems or appliances capable of maintaining, through design or heat loss/gain, 68°F (20°C) during the heating season and/or 80°F (27°C) during the cooling season, or has a fixed opening directly adjacent to a conditioned area.

CONDITIONED FLOOR AREA. The horizontal projection of the floors associated with the conditioned space.

CONDITIONED SPACE. For energy purposes, space within a building that is provided with heating and/or cooling equipment or systems capable of maintaining, through design or heat loss/gain, 50°F (10°C) during the heating season and 85°F (29°C) during the cooling season, or communicates directly with a conditioned space. For mechanical purposes, an area, room or space being heated or cooled by any equipment or appliance.

CONFINED SPACE. A room or space having a volume less than 50 cubic feet per 1,000 Btu/h (4.83 L/W) of the aggregate input rating of all fuel-burning appliances installed in that space.

CONNECTOR. A device for fastening together two or more pieces, members, or parts, including anchors, fasteners, and wall ties.

CONSTRUCTION DOCUMENTS. Written, graphic and pictorial documents prepared or assembled for describing the design, location and physical characteristics of the elements of a project necessary for obtaining a building permit. Construction drawings shall be drawn to an appropriate scale.

CONTAMINATION. An impairment of the quality of the potable water that creates an actual hazard to the public health through poisoning or through the spread of disease by sewage, industrial fluids or waste.

CONTINUOUS WASTE. A drain from two or more similar adjacent fixtures connected to a single trap.

CONTROL, LIMIT. An automatic control responsive to changes in liquid flow or level, pressure, or temperature for limiting the operation of an appliance.

CONTROL, PRIMARY SAFETY. A safety control responsive directly to flame properties that senses the presence or absence of flame and, in event of ignition failure or unintentional flame extinguishment, automatically causes shutdown of mechanical equipment.

CONVECTOR. A system-incorporating heating element in an enclosure in which air enters an opening below the heating element, is heated and leaves the enclosure through an opening located above the heating element.

CORROSION RESISTANCE. The ability of a material to withstand deterioration of its surface or its properties when exposed to its environment.

COURT. A space, open and unobstructed to the sky, located at or above grade level on a lot and bounded on three or more sides by walls or a building.

CRAWL SPACE. Areas or rooms with less than 7 feet (2134 mm) ceiling height measured to the finished floor or grade below.

CRIPPLE WALL. A framed wall extending from the top of the foundation to the underside of the floor framing of the first story above grade plane.

CROSS CONNECTION. Any connection between two otherwise separate piping systems whereby there may be a flow from one system to the other.

DALLE GLASS. A decorative composite glazing material made of individual pieces of glass that are embedded in a cast matrix of concrete or epoxy.

DAMPER, VOLUME. A device that will restrict, retard or direct the flow of air in any duct, or the products of combustion of heat-producing equipment, vent connector, vent or chimney.

DAMPPROOFING. Treatment of a surface or structure located below grade to resist the passage of water in liquid form, in the absence of hydrostatic pressure.

DEAD END. A branch leading from a DWV system terminating at a developed length of 2 feet (610 mm) or more. Dead ends shall be prohibited except as an approved part of a rough-in for future connection.

DEAD LOADS. The weight of all materials of construction incorporated into the building, including but not limited to walls, floors, roofs, ceilings, stairways, built-in partitions, finishes, cladding, and other similarly incorporated architectural and structural items, and fixed service equipment.

DECK. An exterior floor system supported on at least two opposing sides by an adjoining structure and/or posts, piers, or other independent supports.

DECORATIVE GLASS. A carved, leaded or Dalle glass or glazing material whose purpose is decorative or artistic, not functional; whose coloring, texture or other design qualities or components cannot be removed without destroying the glazing material; and whose surface, or assembly into which it is incor-porated, is divided into segments.

DESIGN PROFESSIONAL. See definition of "Registered design professional."

DEVELOPED LENGTH. The length of a pipeline measured along the center line of the pipe and fittings.

DIAMETER. Unless specifically stated, the term "diameter" is the nominal diameter as designated by the approved material standard.

DIAPHRAGM. A horizontal or nearly horizontal system acting to transmit lateral forces to the vertical resisting elements. When the term "diaphragm" is used, it includes horizontal bracing systems.

DILUTION AIR. Air that enters a draft hood or draft regulator and mixes with flue gases.

DIRECT-VENT APPLIANCE. A fuel-burning appliance with a sealed combustion system that draws all air for combustion from the outside atmosphere and discharges all flue gases to the outside atmosphere.

DRAFT. The pressure difference existing between the appliance or any component part and the atmosphere, that causes a continuous flow of air and products of combustion through the gas passages of the appliance to the atmosphere.

Induced draft. The pressure difference created by the action of a fan, blower or ejector, that is located between the appliance and the chimney or vent termination.

Natural draft. The pressure difference created by a vent or chimney because of its height, and the temperature difference between the flue gases and the atmosphere.

DRAFT HOOD. A device built into an appliance, or a part of the vent connector from an appliance, which is designed to provide for the ready escape of the flue gases from the appliance in the event of no draft, backdraft or stoppage beyond the draft hood; prevent a backdraft from entering the appliance; and neutralize the effect of stack action of the chimney or gas vent on the operation of the appliance.

DRAFT REGULATOR. A device that functions to maintain a desired draft in the appliance by automatically reducing the draft to the desired value.

DRAFT STOP. A material, device or construction installed to restrict the movement of air within open spaces of concealed areas of building components such as crawl spaces, floor-ceiling assemblies, roof-ceiling assemblies and attics.

DRAIN. Any pipe that carries soil and water-borne wastes in a building drainage system.

DRAINAGE FITTING. A pipe fitting designed to provide connections in the drainage system that have provisions for establishing the desired slope in the system. These fittings are made from a variety of both metals and plastics. The methods of coupling provide for required slope in the system (see "Durham fitting").

DUCT SYSTEM. A continuous passageway for the transmission of air which, in addition to ducts, includes duct fittings, dampers, plenums, fans and accessory air-handling equipment and appliances.

DURHAM FITTING. A special type of drainage fitting for use in the durham systems installations in which the joints are made with recessed and tapered threaded fittings, as opposed to bell and spigot lead/oakum or solvent/cemented or soldered joints. The tapping is at an angle (not 90 degrees) to provide for proper slope in otherwise rigid connections.

DURHAM SYSTEM. A term used to describe soil or waste systems where all piping is of threaded pipe, tube or other such rigid construction using recessed drainage fittings to correspond to the types of piping.

DWELLING.

Single-family. Any building that contains one dwelling unit used, intended, or designed to be built, used, rented, leased, let or hired out to be occupied, or occupied for living purposes.

Two-family. Any building that contains two separate dwelling units with separation either horizontal or vertical on one lot that is used, intended, or designed to be built, used, rented, leased, let or hired out to be occupied, or occupied for living purposes.

Townhouse. A single-family dwelling unit constructed in a group of two or more attached units in which each unit extends from the foundation to the roof and having open space on at least two sides of each unit. Each single-family dwelling unit shall be considered to be a separate building. Separate building service utilities shall be provided to each single-family dwelling unit when required by other chapters of the State Building Code.

DWELLING UNIT. A single unit providing complete independent living facilities for one or more persons, including permanent provisions for living, sleeping, eating, cooking and sanitation.

DWV. Abbreviated term for drain, waste and vent piping as used in common plumbing practice.

EFFECTIVE OPENING. The minimum cross-sectional area at the point of water-supply discharge, measured or expressed in terms of diameter of a circle and if the opening is not circular, the diameter of a circle of equivalent cross-sectional area. (This is applicable to air gap.)

ELBOW. A pressure pipe fitting designed to provide an exact change in direction of a pipe run. An elbow provides a sharp turn in the flow path (see "Bend" and "Sweep").

EMERGENCY ESCAPE AND RESCUE OPENING. An operable exterior window, door or similar device that provides for a means of escape and access for rescue in the event of an emergency.

EQUIPMENT. All piping, ducts, vents, control devices and other components of systems other than appliances that are permanently installed and integrated to provide control of environmental conditions for buildings. This definition shall also include other systems specifically regulated in this code.

EQUIVALENT LENGTH. For determining friction losses in a piping system, the effect of a particular fitting equal to the friction loss through a straight piping length of the same nominal diameter.

ESSENTIALLY NONTOXIC TRANSFER FLUIDS. Fluids having a Gosselin rating of 1, including propylene glycol; mineral oil; polydimethyoil oxane; hydrochlorofluorocarbon, chlorofluorocarbon and hydrofluorocarbon refrigerants; and FDA-approved boiler water additives for steam boilers.

ESSENTIALLY TOXIC TRANSFER FLUIDS. Soil, water or gray water and fluids having a Gosselin rating of 2 or more including ethylene glycol, hydrocarbon oils, ammonia refrigerants and hydrazine.

EVAPORATIVE COOLER. A device used for reducing air temperature by the process of evaporating water into an airstream.

EXCESS AIR. Air that passes through the combustion chamber and the appliance flue in excess of that which is theoretically required for complete combustion.

EXHAUST HOOD, FULL OPENING. An exhaust hood with an opening at least equal to the diameter of the connecting vent.

EXISTING INSTALLATIONS. Any plumbing system regulated by this code that was legally installed prior to the effective date of this code, or for which a permit to install has been issued.

EXTERIOR INSULATION FINISH SYSTEMS (EIFS). Synthetic stucco cladding systems typically consisting of five layers: adhesive, insulation board, base coat into which fiberglass reinforcing mesh is embedded, and a finish coat in the desired color.

EXTERIOR WALL. An above-grade wall that defines the exterior boundaries of a building. Includes between-floor spandrels, peripheral edges of floors, roof and basement knee walls, dormer walls, gable end walls, walls enclosing a mansard roof and basement walls with an average below-grade wall area that is less than 50 percent of the total opaque and nonopaque area of that enclosing side.

FACTORY-BUILT CHIMNEY. A listed and labeled chimney composed of factory-made components assembled in the field in accordance with the manufacturer's instructions and the conditions of the listing.

FASTENER. A device for holding together two or more pieces, parts, or members.

FENESTRATION. Skylights, roof windows, vertical windows (whether fixed or moveable); opaque doors; glazed doors; glass block; and combination opaque/glazed doors.

FIBER CEMENT SIDING. A manufactured, fiber-reinforcing product made with an inorganic hydraulic or calcium silicate binder formed by chemical reaction and reinforced with organic or inorganic non-asbestos fibers, or both. Additives which enhance manufacturing or product performance are permitted. Fiber cement siding products have either smooth or textured faces and are intended for exterior wall and related applications.

FIREBLOCKING. Building materials installed to resist the free passage of flame to other areas of the building through concealed spaces.

FIREPLACE. An assembly consisting of a hearth and fire chamber of noncombustible material and provided with a chimney, for use with solid fuels.

> **Factory-built fireplace.** A listed and labeled fireplace and chimney system composed of factory-made components, and assembled in the field in accordance with manufacturer's instructions and the conditions of the listing.
>
> **Masonry chimney.** A field-constructed chimney composed of solid masonry units, bricks, stones or concrete.
>
> **Masonry fireplace.** A field-constructed fireplace composed of solid masonry units, bricks, stones or concrete.

FIREPLACE STOVE. A free-standing, chimney-connected solid-fuel-burning heater designed to be operated with the fire chamber doors in either the open or closed position.

FIREPLACE THROAT. The opening between the top of the firebox and the smoke chamber.

FIRE SEPARATION DISTANCE. The distance measured from the building face to one of the following:

1. To the closest interior lot line; or

2. To the centerline of a street, an alley or public way; or

3. To an imaginary line between two buildings on the lot.

The distance shall be measured at a right angle from the face of the wall.

FIXTURE. See "Plumbing fixture."

FIXTURE BRANCH, DRAINAGE. A drain serving two or more fixtures that discharges into another portion of the drainage system.

FIXTURE BRANCH, WATER-SUPPLY. A water-supply pipe between the fixture supply and a main water-distribution pipe or fixture group main.

FIXTURE DRAIN. The drain from the trap of a fixture to the junction of that drain with any other drain pipe.

FIXTURE FITTING

> **Supply fitting.** A fitting that controls the volume and/or directional flow of water and is either attached to or accessible from a fixture or is used with an open or atmospheric discharge.

> **Waste fitting.** A combination of components that conveys the sanitary waste from the outlet of a fixture to the connection of the sanitary drainage system.

FIXTURE GROUP, MAIN. The main water-distribution pipe (or secondary branch) serving a plumbing fixture grouping such as a bath, kitchen or laundry area to which two or more individual fixture branch pipes are connected.

FIXTURE SUPPLY. The water-supply pipe connecting a fixture or fixture fitting to a fixture branch.

FIXTURE UNIT, DRAINAGE (d.f.u.). A measure of probable discharge into the drainage system by various types of plumbing fixtures, used to size DWV piping systems. The drainage fixture-unit value for a particular fixture depends on its volume rate of drainage discharge, on the time duration of a single drainage operation and on the average time between successive operations.

FIXTURE UNIT, WATER-SUPPLY (w.s.f.u.). A measure of the probable hydraulic demand on the water supply by various types of plumbing fixtures used to size water-piping systems. The water-supply fixture-unit value for a particular fixture depends on its volume rate of supply, on the time duration of a single supply operation and on the average time between successive operations.

FLAME SPREAD. The propagation of flame over a surface.

FLAME SPREAD INDEX. The numeric value assigned to a material tested in accordance with ASTM E 84.

FLASHING. Approved corrosion-resistive material provided in such a manner as to deflect and resist entry of water into the construction assembly.

FLOOD-LEVEL RIM. The edge of the receptor or fixture from which water overflows.

FLOOR DRAIN. A plumbing fixture for recess in the floor having a floor-level strainer intended for the purpose of the collection and disposal of waste water used in cleaning the floor and for the collection and disposal of accidental spillage to the floor.

FLOOR FURNACE. A self-contained furnace suspended from the floor of the space being heated, taking air for combustion from outside such space, and with means for lighting the appliance from such space.

FLOW PRESSURE. The static pressure reading in the water-supply pipe near the faucet or water outlet while the faucet or water outlet is open and flowing at capacity.

FLUE. See "Vent."

FLUE, APPLIANCE. The passages within an appliance through which combustion products pass from the combustion chamber to the flue collar.

FLUE COLLAR. The portion of a fuel-burning appliance designed for the attachment of a draft hood, vent connector or venting system.

FLUE GASES. Products of combustion plus excess air in appliance flues or heat exchangers.

FLUSH VALVE. A device located at the bottom of a flush tank that is operated to flush water closets.

FLUSHOMETER TANK. A device integrated within an air accumulator vessel that is designed to discharge a predetermined quantity of water to fixtures for flushing purposes.

FLUSHOMETER VALVE. A flushometer valve is a device that discharges a predetermined quantity of water to fixtures for flushing purposes and is actuated by direct water pressure.

FOAM BACKER BOARD. Foam plastic used in siding applications where the foam plastic is a component of the siding.

FOAM PLASTIC INSULATION. A plastic that is intentionally expanded by the use of a foaming agent to produce a reduced-density plastic containing voids consisting of open or closed cells distributed throughout the plastic for thermal insulating or acoustic purposes and that has a density less than 20 pounds per cubic foot (320 kg/m³) unless it is used as interior trim.

FOAM PLASTIC INTERIOR TRIM. Exposed foam plastic used as picture molds, chair rails, crown moldings, baseboards, handrails, ceiling beams, door trim and window trim and similar decorative or protective materials used in fixed applications.

FUEL-PIPING SYSTEM. All piping, tubing, valves and fittings used to connect fuel utilization equipment to the point of fuel delivery.

FULLWAY VALVE. A valve that in the full open position has an opening cross-sectional area equal to a minimum of 85 percent of the cross-sectional area of the connecting pipe.

FURNACE. A vented heating appliance designed or arranged to discharge heated air into a conditioned space or through a duct or ducts.

GLAZING AREA. The interior surface area of all glazed fenestration, including the area of sash, curbing or other framing elements, that enclose conditioned space. Includes the area of glazed fenestration assemblies in walls bounding conditioned basements.

GRADE. The finished ground level adjoining the building at all exterior walls.

GRADE FLOOR OPENING. A window or other opening located such that the sill height of the opening is not more than 44 inches (1118 mm) above or below the finished ground level adjacent to the opening.

GRADE, PIPING. See "Slope."

GRADE PLANE. A reference plane representing the average of the finished ground level adjoining the building at all exterior walls. Where the finished ground level slopes away from the exterior walls, the reference plane shall be established by the lowest points within the area between the building and the lot line or, where the lot line is more than 6 ft (1829 mm) from the building between the structure and a point 6 ft (1829 mm) from the building.

GRIDDED WATER DISTRIBUTION SYSTEM. A water distribution system where every water distribution pipe is interconnected so as to provide two or more paths to each fixture supply pipe.

GROSS AREA OF EXTERIOR WALLS. The normal projection of all exterior walls, including the area of all windows and doors installed therein.

GROUND-SOURCE HEAT PUMP LOOP SYSTEM. Piping buried in horizontal or vertical excavations or placed in a body of water for the purpose of transporting heat transfer liquid to and from a heat pump. Included in this definition are closed loop systems in which the liquid is recirculated and open loop systems in which the liquid is drawn from a well or other source.

GUARD. A building component or a system of building components located near the open sides of elevated walking surfaces that minimizes the possibility of a fall from the walking surface to the lower level.

HABITABLE SPACE. A space in a building for living, sleeping, eating or cooking. Bathrooms, toilet rooms, closets, halls, storage or utility spaces and similar areas are not considered habitable spaces.

HANDRAIL. A horizontal or sloping rail intended for grasping by the hand for guidance or support.

HANGERS. See "Supports."

HAZARDOUS LOCATION. Any location considered to be a fire hazard for flammable vapors, dust, combustible fibers or other highly combustible substances.

HEATING DEGREE DAYS (HDD). The sum, on an annual basis, of the difference between 65°F (18°C) and the mean temperature for each day as determined from "NOAA Annual Degree Days to Selected Bases Derived from the 1960-1990 Normals" or other weather data sources acceptable to the code official.

HEAT PUMP. An appliance having heating or heating/cooling capability and that uses refrigerants to extract heat from air, liquid or other sources.

HEIGHT, BUILDING. The vertical distance from grade plane to the average height of the highest roof surface.

HEIGHT, STORY. The vertical distance from top to top of two successive tiers of beams or finished floor surfaces; and, for the topmost story, from the top of the floor finish to the top of the ceiling joists or, where there is not a ceiling, to the top of the roof rafters.

HIGH-TEMPERATURE (H.T.) CHIMNEY. A high temperature chimney complying with the requirements of UL 103.

A Type H.T. chimney is identifiable by the markings "Type H.T." on each chimney pipe section.

HORIZONTAL BRANCH, DRAINAGE. A drain pipe extending laterally from a soil or waste stack or building drain, that receives the discharge from one or more fixture drains.

HORIZONTAL PIPE. Any pipe or fitting that makes an angle of less than 45 degrees (0.79 rad) with the horizontal.

HOT WATER. Water at a temperature greater than or equal to 110°F (43°C).

HURRICANE-PRONE REGIONS. Areas vulnerable to hurricanes, defined as the U.S. Atlantic Ocean and Gulf of Mexico coasts where the basic wind speed is greater than 90 miles per hour (40 m/s), and Hawaii, Puerto Rico, Guam, Virgin Islands, and America Samoa.

HYDROGEN GENERATING APPLIANCE. A self-contained package or factory-matched packages of integrated systems for generating gaseous hydrogen. Hydrogen generating appliances utilize electrolysis, reformation, chemical, or other processes to generate hydrogen.

IGNITION SOURCE. A flame, spark or hot surface capable of igniting flammable vapors or fumes. Such sources include appliance burners, burner ignitions and electrical switching devices.

INDIRECT WASTE PIPE. A waste pipe that discharges into the drainage system through an air gap into a trap, fixture or receptor.

INDIVIDUAL SEWAGE DISPOSAL SYSTEM. A system for disposal of sewage by means of a septic tank or mechanical treatment, designed for use apart from a public sewer to serve a single establishment or building.

INDIVIDUAL VENT. A pipe installed to vent a single-fixture drain that connects with the vent system above or terminates independently outside the building.

INDIVIDUAL WATER SUPPLY. A supply other than an approved public water supply that serves one or more families.

INSULATING CONCRETE FORM (ICF). A concrete forming system using stay-in-place forms of rigid foam plastic insulation, a hybrid of cement and foam insulation, a hybrid of cement and wood chips, or other insulating material for constructing cast-in-place concrete walls.

INSULATING SHEATHING. An insulating board having a minimum thermal resistance of R-2 of the core material.

JURISDICTION. The governmental unit that has adopted this code under due legislative authority.

KICK-OUT FLASHING. Flashing used to divert water where the lower portion of a sloped roof stops within the plane of an intersecting wall cladding. ^{MN MN}

KITCHEN. Kitchen shall mean an area used, or designated to be used, for the preparation of food.

LABEL. An identification applied on a product by the manufacturer which contains the name of the manufacturer, the function and performance characteristics of the product or material, and the name and identification of an approved agency and that indicates that the representative sample of the product or material has been tested and evaluated by an approved agency. (See also "Manufacturer's designation" and "Mark.")

LABELED. Devices, equipment or materials to which have been affixed a label, seal, symbol or other identifying mark of a testing laboratory, inspection agency or other organization concerned with product evaluation that maintains periodic inspection of the production of the above labeled items that attests to compliance with a specific standard.

LIGHT-FRAMED CONSTRUCTION. A type of construction whose vertical and horizontal structural elements are primarily formed by a system of repetitive wood or light gage steel framing members.

LISTED AND LISTING. Terms referring to equipment that is shown in a list published by an approved testing agency qualified and equipped for experimental testing and maintaining an adequate periodic inspection of current productions and whose listing states that the equipment complies with nationally recognized standards when installed in accordance with the manufacturer's installation instructions.

LIVE LOADS. Those loads produced by the use and occupancy of the building or other structure and do not include construction or environmental loads such as wind load, snow load, rain load, earthquake load, flood load or dead load.

LIVING SPACE. Space within a dwelling unit utilized for living, sleeping, eating, cooking, bathing, washing and sanitation purposes.

LOT. A portion or parcel of land considered as a unit.

LOT LINE. A line dividing one lot from another, or from a street or any public place.

MACERATING TOILET SYSTEMS. A system comprised of a sump with macerating pump and with connections for a water closet and other plumbing fixtures, that is designed to accept, grind and pump wastes to an approved point of discharge.

MAIN. The principal pipe artery to which branches may be connected.

MAIN SEWER. See "Public sewer."

MANIFOLD WATER DISTRIBUTION SYSTEMS. A fabricated piping arrangement in which a large supply main is fitted with multiple branches in close proximity in which water is distributed separately to fixtures from each branch.

MANUFACTURED HOME. Manufactured home means a structure, transportable in one or more sections, which in the traveling mode is 8 body feet (2438 body mm) or more in width or 40 body feet (12 192 body mm) or more in length, or, when erected on site, is 320 square feet (30 m²) or more, and which is built on a permanent chassis and designed to be used as a dwelling with or without a permanent foundation when connected to the required utilities, and includes the plumbing, heating, air-conditioning and electrical systems contained therein; except that such term shall include any structure that meets all the requirements of this paragraph except the size requirements and with respect to which the manufacturer voluntarily files a certification required by the secretary (HUD) and complies with the standards established under this title. For mobile

homes built prior to June 15, 1976, a label certifying compliance to the Standard for Mobile Homes, NFPA 501, in effect at the time of manufacture is required. For the purpose of these provisions, a mobile home shall be considered a manufactured home.

MANUFACTURER'S DESIGNATION. An identification applied on a product by the manufacturer indicating that a product or material complies with a specified standard or set of rules. (See also "Mark" and "Label.")

MANUFACTURER'S INSTALLATION INSTRUCTIONS. Printed instructions included with equipment as part of the conditions of listing and labeling.

MARK. An identification applied on a product by the manufacturer indicating the name of the manufacturer and the function of a product or material. (See also "Manufacturer's designation" and "Label.")

MASONRY CHIMNEY. A field-constructed chimney composed of solid masonry units, bricks, stones or concrete.

MASONRY HEATER. A masonry heater is a solid fuel burning heating appliance constructed predominantly of concrete or solid masonry having a mass of at least 1,100 pounds (500 kg), excluding the chimney and foundation. It is designed to absorb and store a substantial portion of heat from a fire built in the firebox by routing exhaust gases through internal heat exchange channels in which the flow path downstream of the firebox includes at least one 180-degree (3.14-rad) change in flow direction before entering the chimney and which deliver heat by radiation through the masonry surface of the heater.

MASONRY, SOLID. Masonry consisting of solid masonry units laid contiguously with the joints between the units filled with mortar.

MASONRY UNIT. Brick, tile, stone, glass block or concrete block conforming to the requirements specified in Section 2103 of the *International Building Code*.

>   **Clay.** A building unit larger in size than a brick, composed of burned clay, shale, fire clay or mixtures thereof.
>
>   **Concrete.** A building unit or block larger in size than 12 inches by 4 inches by 4 inches (305 mm by 102 mm by 102 mm) made of cement and suitable aggregates.
>
>   **Glass.** Nonload-bearing masonry composed of glass units bonded by mortar.
>
>   **Hollow.** A masonry unit whose net cross-sectional area in any plane parallel to the loadbearing surface is less than 75 percent of its gross cross-sectional area measured in the same plane.
>
>   **Solid.** A masonry unit whose net cross-sectional area in every plane parallel to the loadbearing surface is 75 percent or more of its cross-sectional area measured in the same plane.

MASS WALL. Masonry or concrete walls having a mass greater than or equal to 30 pounds per square foot (146 kg/m²), solid wood walls having a mass greater than or equal to 20 pounds per square foot (98 kg/m²), and any other walls having a heat capacity greater than or equal to 6 Btu/ft² · °F [266 J/(m² · K)].

MEAN ROOF HEIGHT. The average of the roof eave height and the height to the highest point on the roof surface, except that eave height shall be used for roof angle of less than or equal to 10 degrees (0.18 rad).

MECHANICAL DRAFT SYSTEM. A venting system designed to remove flue or vent gases by mechanical means, that consists of an induced draft portion under nonpositive static pressure or a forced draft portion under positive static pressure.

Forced-draft venting system. A portion of a venting system using a fan or other mechanical means to cause the removal of flue or vent gases under positive static pressure.

Induced draft venting system. A portion of a venting system using a fan or other mechanical means to cause the removal of flue or vent gases under nonpositive static vent pressure.

Power venting system. A portion of a venting system using a fan or other mechanical means to cause the removal of flue or vent gases under positive static vent pressure.

MECHANICAL EXHAUST SYSTEM. A system for removing air from a room or space by mechanical means.

MECHANICAL SYSTEM. A system specifically addressed and regulated in this code and composed of components, devices, appliances and equipment.

METAL ROOF PANEL. An interlocking metal sheet having a minimum installed weather exposure of at least 3 square feet (0.28 m²) per sheet.

METAL ROOF SHINGLE. An interlocking metal sheet having an installed weather exposure less than 3 square feet (0.28 m²) per sheet.

MEZZANINE, LOFT. An intermediate level or levels between the floor and ceiling of any story with an aggregate floor area of not more than one-third of the area of the room or space in which the level or levels are located.

MODIFIED BITUMEN ROOF COVERING. One or more layers of polymer modified asphalt sheets. The sheet materials shall be fully adhered or mechanically attached to the substrate or held in place with an approved ballast layer.

MULTIPLE STATION SMOKE ALARM. Two or more single station alarm devices that are capable of interconnection such that actuation of one causes all integral or separate audible alarms to operate.

NATURAL DRAFT SYSTEM. A venting system designed to remove flue or vent gases under nonpositive static vent pressure entirely by natural draft.

NATURALLY DURABLE WOOD. The heartwood of the following species: Decay-resistant redwood, cedars, black locust and black walnut.

Note: Corner sapwood is permitted if 90 percent or more of the width of each side on which it occurs is heartwood.

NONCOMBUSTIBLE MATERIAL. Materials that pass the test procedure for defining noncombustibility of elementary materials set forth in ASTM E 136.

NONCONDITIONED SPACE. A space that is not a conditioned space by insulated walls, floors or ceilings.

OCCUPANCY CLASSIFICATIONS

IRC-1 - Single-family dwelling

IRC-2 - Two-family dwellings

IRC-3 - Townhouses

IRC-4 - Accessory structures:

a. Garages;

b. Storage sheds; and

c. Similar structures.

OCCUPIED SPACE. The total area of all buildings or structures on any lot or parcel of ground projected on a horizontal plane, excluding permitted projections as allowed by this code.

OFFSET. A combination of fittings that makes two changes in direction bringing one section of the pipe out of line but into a line parallel with the other section.

OWNER. Any person, agent, firm or corporation having a legal or equitable interest in the property.

PAN FLASHING. A type of corrosion-resistive flashing that is integrated into the building envelope at the base of a window or door rough opening that diverts incidental water to the exterior surface of a weather-resistive barrier.

PELLET FUEL-BURNING APPLIANCE. A closed combustion, vented appliance equipped with a fuel feed mechanism for burning processed pellets of solid fuel of a specified size and composition.

PELLET VENT. A vent listed and labeled for use with a listed pellet fuel-burning appliance.

PERMIT. An official document or certificate issued by the authority having jurisdiction that authorizes performance of a specified activity.

PERSON. An individual, heirs, executors, administrators or assigns, and also includes a firm, partnership or corporation, its or their successors or assigns, or the agent of any of the aforesaid.

PITCH. See "Slope."

PLATFORM CONSTRUCTION. A method of construction by which floor framing bears on load bearing walls that are not continuous through the story levels or floor framing.

PLENUM. A chamber that forms part of an air-circulation system other than the occupied space being conditioned.

PLUMBING. For the purpose of this code, plumbing refers to those installations, repairs, maintenance and alterations regulated by Chapters 25 through 32.

PLUMBING APPLIANCE. An energized household appliance with plumbing connections, such as a dishwasher, food-waste grinder, clothes washer or water heater.

PLUMBING APPURTENANCE. A device or assembly that is an adjunct to the basic plumbing system and demands no additional water supply nor adds any discharge load to the system. It is presumed that it performs some useful function in the operation, maintenance, servicing, economy or safety of the plumbing system. Examples include filters, relief valves and aerators.

PLUMBING FIXTURE. A receptor or device that requires both a water-supply connection and a discharge to the drainage system, such as water closets, lavatories, bathtubs and sinks. Plumbing appliances as a special class of fixture are further defined.

PLUMBING SYSTEM. Includes the water supply and distribution pipes, plumbing fixtures, supports and appurtenances; soil, waste and vent pipes; sanitary drains and building sewers to an approved point of disposal.

POLLUTION. An impairment of the quality of the potable water to a degree that does not create a hazard to the public health but that does adversely and unreasonably affect the aesthetic qualities of such potable water for domestic use.

PORTABLE FUEL CELL APPLIANCE. A fuel cell generator of electricity, which is not fixed in place. A portable fuel cell appliance utilizes a cord and plug connection to a grid-isolated load and has an integral fuel supply.

POSITIVE ROOF DRAINAGE. The drainage condition in which consideration has been made for all loading deflections of the roof deck, and additional slope has been provided to ensure drainage of the roof within 48 hours of precipitation.

POTABLE WATER. Water free from impurities present in amounts sufficient to cause disease or harmful physiological effects and conforming in bacteriological and chemical quality to the requirements of the public health authority having jurisdiction.

PRECAST CONCRETE. A structural concrete element cast elsewhere than its final position in the structure.

PRESSURE-RELIEF VALVE. A pressure-actuated valve held closed by a spring or other means and designed to automatically relieve pressure at the pressure at which it is set.

PUBLIC SEWER. A common sewer directly controlled by public authority.

PUBLIC WATER MAIN. A water-supply pipe for public use controlled by public authority.

PUBLIC WAY. Any street, alley or other parcel of land open to the outside air leading to a public street, which has been deeded, dedicated or otherwise permanently appropriated to the public for public use and that has a clear width and height of not less than 10 feet (3048 mm).

PURGE. To clear of air, gas or other foreign substances.

QUICK-CLOSING VALVE. A valve or faucet that closes automatically when released manually or controlled by mechanical means for fast-action closing.

R-VALUE, THERMAL RESISTANCE. The inverse of the time rate of heat flow through a building thermal envelope element from one of its bounding surfaces to the other for a unit temperature difference between the two surfaces, under steady state conditions, per unit area (h · ft^2 · °F/Btu).

RAMP. A walking surface that has a running slope steeper than 1 unit vertical in 20 units horizontal (5-percent slope).

RECEPTOR. A fixture or device that receives the discharge from indirect waste pipes.

REFRIGERANT. A substance used to produce refrigeration by its expansion or evaporation.

REFRIGERANT COMPRESSOR. A specific machine, with or without accessories, for compressing a given refrigerant vapor.

REFRIGERATING SYSTEM. A combination of interconnected parts forming a closed circuit in which refrigerant is circulated for the purpose of extracting, then rejecting, heat. A direct refrigerating system is one in which the evaporator or condenser of the refrigerating system is in direct contact with the air or other substances to be cooled or heated. An indirect refrigerating system is one in which a secondary coolant cooled or heated by the refrigerating system is circulated to the air or other substance to be cooled or heated.

REGISTERED DESIGN PROFESSIONAL. An individual who is registered or licensed to practice their respective design profession as defined by the statutory requirements of the professional registration laws of the state or jurisdiction in which the project is to be constructed.

RELIEF VALVE, VACUUM. A device to prevent excessive buildup of vacuum in a pressure vessel.

REPAIR. The reconstruction or renewal of any part of an existing building for the purpose of its maintenance.

REROOFING. The process of recovering or replacing an existing roof covering. See "Roof recover."

RETURN AIR. Air removed from an approved conditioned space or location and recirculated or exhausted.

RISER. A water pipe that extends vertically one full story or more to convey water to branches or to a group of fixtures.

ROOF ASSEMBLY. A system designed to provide weather protection and resistance to design loads. The system consists of a roof covering and roof deck or a single component serving as both the roof covering and the roof deck. A roof assembly includes the roof deck, vapor retarder, substrate or thermal barrier, insulation, vapor retarder, and roof covering.

ROOF COVERING. The covering applied to the roof deck for weather resistance, fire classification or appearance.

ROOF COVERING SYSTEM. See "Roof assembly."

ROOF DECK. The flat or sloped surface not including its supporting members or vertical supports.

ROOF RECOVER. The process of installing an additional roof covering over a prepared existing roof covering without removing the existing roof covering.

ROOF REPAIR. Reconstruction or renewal of any part of an existing roof for the purposes of its maintenance.

ROOFTOP STRUCTURE. An enclosed structure on or above the roof of any part of a building.

ROOM HEATER. A freestanding heating appliance installed in the space being heated and not connected to ducts.

ROUGH-IN. The installation of all parts of the plumbing system that must be completed prior to the installation of fixtures. This includes DWV, water supply and built-in fixture supports.

RUNNING BOND. The placement of masonry units such that head joints in successive courses are horizontally offset at least one-quarter the unit length.

SANITARY SEWER. A sewer that carries sewage and excludes storm, surface and groundwater.

SCUPPER. An opening in a wall or parapet that allows water to drain from a roof.

SEISMIC DESIGN CATEGORY. A classification assigned to a structure based on its Seismic Group and the severity of the design earthquake ground motion at the site.

SEPTIC TANK. A water-tight receptor that receives the discharge of a building sanitary drainage system and is constructed so as to separate solids from the liquid, digest organic matter through a period of detention, and allow the liquids to discharge into the soil outside of the tank through a system of open joint or perforated piping or a seepage pit.

SEWAGE. Any liquid waste containing animal matter, vegetable matter or other impurity in suspension or solution.

SEWAGE PUMP. A permanently installed mechanical device for removing sewage or liquid waste from a sump.

SHALL. The term, when used in the code, is construed as mandatory.

SHEAR WALL. A general term for walls that are designed and constructed to resist racking from seismic and wind by use of masonry, concrete, cold-formed steel or wood framing in accordance with Chapter 6 of this code and the associated limitations in Section R301.2 of this code.

SIDE VENT. A vent connecting to the drain pipe through a fitting at an angle less than 45 degrees (0.79 rad) to the horizontal.

SINGLE PLY MEMBRANE. A roofing membrane that is field applied using one layer of membrane material (either homogeneous or composite) rather than multiple layers.

SINGLE STATION SMOKE ALARM. An assembly incorporating the detector, control equipment and alarm sounding device in one unit that is operated from a power supply either in the unit or obtained at the point of installation.

SKYLIGHT AND SLOPED GLAZING. See Section R308.6.1.

SKYLIGHT, UNIT. See Section R308.6.1.

SLIP JOINT. A mechanical-type joint used primarily on fixture traps. The joint tightness is obtained by compressing a friction-type washer such as rubber, nylon, neoprene, lead or special packing material against the pipe by the tightening of a (slip) nut.

SLOPE. The fall (pitch) of a line of pipe in reference to a horizonal plane. In drainage, the slope is expressed as the fall in units vertical per units horizontal (percent) for a length of pipe.

SMOKE-DEVELOPED RATING. A numerical index indicating the relative density of smoke produced by burning assigned to a material tested in accordance with ASTM E 84.

SOIL STACK OR PIPE. A pipe that conveys sewage containing fecal material.

SOLAR HEAT GAIN COEFFICIENT (SHGC). The solar heat gain through a fenestration or glazing assembly relative to the incident solar radiation (Btu/h · ft^2 · °F).

SOLID MASONRY. Load-bearing or nonload-bearing construction using masonry units where the net cross-sectional area of each unit in any plane parallel to the bearing surface is not less than 75 percent of its gross cross-sectional area. Solid masonry units shall conform to ASTM C 55, C 62, C 73, C 145 or C 216.

STACK. Any main vertical DWV line, including offsets, that extends one or more stories as directly as possible to its vent terminal.

STACK BOND. The placement of masonry units in a bond pattern is such that head joints in successive courses are vertically aligned. For the purpose of this code, requirements for stack bond shall apply to all masonry laid in other than running bond.

STACK VENT. The extension of soil or waste stack above the highest horizontal drain connected.

STACK VENTING. A method of venting a fixture or fixtures through the soil or waste stack without individual fixture vents.

STAIR. A change in elevation, consisting of one or more risers.

STANDARD TRUSS. Any construction that does not permit the roof/ceiling insulation to achieve the required *R*-value over the exterior walls.

STATIONARY FUEL CELL POWER PLANT. A self-contained package or factory-matched packages which constitute an automatically-operated assembly of integrated systems for generating useful electrical energy and recoverable thermal energy that is permanently connected and fixed in place.

STORM SEWER, DRAIN. A pipe used for conveying rainwater, surface water, subsurface water and similar liquid waste.

STORY. That portion of a building included between the upper surface of a floor and the upper surface of the floor or roof next above.

STORY ABOVE GRADE PLANE. Any story having its finished floor surface entirely above grade plane, except a basement, shall be considered as a story above grade where the finished surface of the floor above the basement is:

1. More than 6 feet (1829 mm) above grade plane.

2. More than 6 feet (1829 mm) above the finished ground level for more than 50 percent of the total building perimeter.

3. More than 12 feet (3658 mm) above the finished ground level at any point.

STRUCTURAL INSULATED PANELS (SIPS). Factory fabricated panels of solid core insulation with structural skins of oriented strand board (OSB) or plywood.

STRUCTURE. That which is built or constructed.

SUMP. A tank or pit that receives sewage or waste, located below the normal grade of the gravity system and that must be emptied by mechanical means.

SUMP PUMP. A pump installed to empty a sump. These pumps are used for removing storm water only. The pump is selected for the specific head and volume of the load and is usually operated by level controllers.

SUNROOM. A one-story structure attached to a dwelling with a glazing area in excess of 40 percent of the gross area of the structure's exterior walls and roof.

SUPPLY AIR. Air delivered to a conditioned space through ducts or plenums from the heat exchanger of a heating, cooling or ventilating system.

SUPPORTS. Devices for supporting, hanging and securing pipes, fixtures and equipment.

SWEEP. A drainage fitting designed to provide a change in direction of a drain pipe of less than the angle specified by the amount necessary to establish the desired slope of the line. Sweeps provide a longer turning radius than bends and a less turbulent flow pattern (see "Bend" and "Elbow").

TEMPERATURE- AND PRESSURE-RELIEF (T AND P) VALVE. A combination relief valve designed to function as both a temperature-relief and pressure-relief valve.

TEMPERATURE-RELIEF VALVE. A temperature-actuated valve designed to discharge automatically at the temperature at which it is set.

THERMAL ISOLATION. Physical and space conditioning separation from conditioned space(s). The conditioned space(s) shall be controlled as separate zones for heating and cooling or conditioned by separate equipment.

THERMAL RESISTANCE, *R*-VALUE. The inverse of the time rate of heat flow through a body from one of its bounding surfaces to the other for a unit temperature difference between the two surfaces, under steady state conditions, per unit area (h · ft^2 · °F/Btu).

THERMAL TRANSMITTANCE, *U*-FACTOR. The coefficient of heat transmission (air to air) through a building envelope component or assembly, equal to the time rate of heat flow per unit area and unit temperature difference between the warm side and cold side air films (Btu/h · ft^2 · °F).

TOWNHOUSE. A single-family dwelling unit constructed in a group of three or more attached units in which each unit extends from foundation to roof and with open space on at least two sides.

TRAP. A fitting, either separate or built into a fixture, that provides a liquid seal to prevent the emission of sewer gases without materially affecting the flow of sewage or waste water through it.

TRAP ARM. That portion of a fixture drain between a trap weir and the vent fitting.

TRAP PRIMER. A device or system of piping to maintain a water seal in a trap, typically installed where infrequent use of the trap would result in evaporation of the trap seal, such as floor drains.

TRAP SEAL. The trap seal is the maximum vertical depth of liquid that a trap will retain, measured between the crown weir and the top of the dip of the trap.

TRIM. Picture molds, chair rails, baseboards, handrails, door and window frames, and similar decorative or protective materials used in fixed applications.

TRUSS DESIGN DRAWING. The graphic depiction of an individual truss, which describes the design and physical characteristics of the truss.

TYPE L VENT. A listed and labeled vent conforming to UL 641 for venting oil-burning appliances listed for use with Type L vents or with gas appliances listed for use with Type B vents.

***U*-FACTOR, THERMAL TRANSMITTANCE.** The coefficient of heat transmission (air to air) through a building envelope component or assembly, equal to the time rate of heat flow per unit area and unit temperature difference between the warm side and cold side air films (Btu/h · ft^2 · °F).

UNCONFINED SPACE. A space having a volume not less than 50 cubic feet per 1,000 Btu/h (4.8 m^3/kW) of the aggregate input rating of all appliances installed in that space. Rooms communicating directly with the space in which the appliances are installed, through openings not furnished with doors, are considered a part of the unconfined space.

UNDERLAYMENT. One or more layers of felt, sheathing paper, nonbituminous saturated felt, or other approved material over which a roof covering, with a slope of 2 to 12 (17-percent slope) or greater, is applied.

UNUSUALLY TIGHT CONSTRUCTION. Construction in which:

1. Walls and ceilings comprising the building thermal envelope have a continuous water vapor retarder with a rating of 1 perm (5.7 · 10^{-11} kg/Pa · s · m^2) or less with openings therein gasketed or sealed.

2. Storm windows or weatherstripping is applied around the threshold and jambs of opaque doors and openable windows.

3. Caulking or sealants are applied to areas such as joints around window and door frames between sole plates and floors, between wall-ceiling joints, between wall panels, at penetrations for plumbing, electrical and gas lines, and at other openings.

VACUUM BREAKERS. A device which prevents backsiphonage of water by admitting atmospheric pressure through ports to the discharge side of the device.

VAPOR PERMEABLE MEMBRANE. A material or covering having a permeance rating of 5 perms (2.9 · 10^{-10} kg/Pa · s · m^2) or greater, when tested in accordance with the desiccant method using Procedure A of ASTM E 96. A vapor permeable material permits the passage of moisture vapor.

VAPOR RETARDER. A vapor resistant material, membrane or covering such as foil, plastic sheeting, or insulation facing having a permeance rating of 1 perm (5.7 · 10^{-11} kg/Pa · s · m^2) or less, when tested in accordance with the dessicant method using Procedure A of ASTM E 96. Vapor retarders limit the amount of moisture vapor that passes through a material or wall assembly.

VEHICULAR ACCESS DOOR. A door that is used primarily for vehicular traffic at entrances of buildings such as garages and parking lots, and that is not generally used for pedestrian traffic.

VENT. A passageway for conveying flue gases from fuel-fired appliances, or their vent connectors, to the outside atmosphere.

VENT COLLAR. See "Flue collar."

VENT CONNECTOR. That portion of a venting system which connects the flue collar or draft hood of an appliance to a vent.

VENT DAMPER DEVICE, AUTOMATIC. A device intended for installation in the venting system, in the outlet of an individual, automatically operated fuel burning appliance and that is designed to open the venting system automatically when the appliance is in operation and to close off the venting system automatically when the appliance is in a standby or shutdown condition.

VENT GASES. Products of combustion from fuel-burning appliances, plus excess air and dilution air, in the venting system above the draft hood or draft regulator.

VENT STACK. A vertical vent pipe installed to provide circulation of air to and from the drainage system and which extends through one or more stories.

VENT SYSTEM. Piping installed to equalize pneumatic pressure in a drainage system to prevent trap seal loss or blow-back due to siphonage or back pressure.

VENTILATION. The natural or mechanical process of supplying conditioned or unconditioned air to, or removing such air from, any space.

VENTING. Removal of combustion products to the outdoors.

VENTING SYSTEM. A continuous open passageway from the flue collar of an appliance to the outside atmosphere for the purpose of removing flue or vent gases. A venting system is usually composed of a vent or a chimney and vent connector, if used, assembled to form the open passageway.

VERTICAL PIPE. Any pipe or fitting that makes an angle of 45 degrees (0.79 rad) or more with the horizontal.

VINYL SIDING. A shaped material, made principally from rigid polyvinyl chloride (PVC), that is used to cover exterior walls of buildings.

WALL, RETAINING. A wall not laterally supported at the top, that resists lateral soil load and other imposed loads.

WALLS. Walls shall be defined as follows:

Load-bearing wall is a wall supporting any vertical load in addition to its own weight.

Nonbearing wall is a wall which does not support vertical loads other than its own weight.

WASTE. Liquid-borne waste that is free of fecal matter.

WASTE PIPE OR STACK. Piping that conveys only liquid sewage not containing fecal material.

WATER-DISTRIBUTION SYSTEM. Piping which conveys water from the service to the plumbing fixtures, appliances, appurtenances, equipment, devices or other systems served, including fittings and control valves.

WATER HEATER. Any heating appliance or equipment that heats potable water and supplies such water to the potable hot water distribution system.

WATER MAIN. A water-supply pipe for public use.

WATER OUTLET. A valved discharge opening, including a hose bibb, through which water is removed from the potable water system supplying water to a plumbing fixture or plumbing appliance that requires either an air gap or backflow pre-vention device for protection of the supply system.

WATERPROOFING. Treatment of a surface or structure located below grade to resist the passage of water in liquid form, under hydrostatic pressure and bridges nonstructural cracks.

WATER-RESISTIVE BARRIER. A material behind an exterior wall covering that is intended to resist liquid water that has penetrated behind the exterior covering from further intruding into the exterior wall assembly.

WATER-SERVICE PIPE. The outside pipe from the water main or other source of potable water supply to the water-distribution system inside the building, terminating at the service valve.

WATER-SUPPLY SYSTEM. The water-service pipe, the water-distributing pipes and the necessary connecting pipes, fittings, control valves and all appurtenances in or adjacent to the building or premises.

WET VENT. A vent that also receives the discharge of wastes from other fixtures.

WIND BORNE DEBRIS REGION. Areas within hurricane-prone regions within one mile of the coastal mean high water line where the basic wind speed is 110 miles per hour (49 m/s) or greater; or where the basic wind speed is equal to or greater than 120 miles per hour (54 m/s); or Hawaii.

WINDER. A tread with non-parallel edges.

WOOD STRUCTURAL PANEL. A panel manufactured from veneers; or wood strands or wafers; bonded together with waterproof synthetic resins or other suitable bonding systems. Examples of wood structural panels are plywood, OSB or composite panels.

YARD. An open space, other than a court, unobstructed from the ground to the sky, except where specifically provided by this code, on the lot on which a building is situated.

Part III — Building Planning and Construction

CHAPTER 3

BUILDING PLANNING

SECTION R300
CLASSIFICATION

R300.1 Occupancy classification. Structures or portions of structures shall be classified with respect to occupancy in one or more of the groups in accordance with Table R300.1.

TABLE R300.1
OCCUPANCY CLASSIFICATION

IRC-1	Dwelling, single-family
IRC-2	Dwelling, two-family
IRC-3	Townhouse
IRC-4	Accessory structures

SECTION R301
DESIGN CRITERIA

R301.1 Application. Buildings and structures, and all parts thereof, shall be constructed to safely support all loads, including dead loads, live loads, roof loads, flood loads, snow loads, wind loads and seismic loads as prescribed by this code. The construction of buildings and structures in accordance with the provisions of this code shall result in a system that provides a complete load path that meets all requirements for the transfer of all loads from their point of origin through the load-resisting elements to the foundation. Buildings and structures constructed as prescribed by this code are deemed to comply with the requirements of this section.

R301.1.1 Alternative provisions. As an alternative to the requirements in Section R301.1 the following standards are permitted subject to the limitations of this code and the limitations therein. Where engineered design is used in conjunction with these standards the design shall comply with the *International Building Code.*

1. American Forest and Paper Association (AF&PA) *Wood Frame Construction Manual* (WFCM).

2. American Iron and Steel Institute (AISI) *Standard for Cold-Formed Steel Framing—Prescriptive Method for One- and Two-Family Dwellings* (COFS/PM) *with Supplement to Standard for Cold-Formed Steel Framing-Prescriptive Method for One- and Two-Family Dwellings.*

R301.1.2 Construction systems. The requirements of this code are based on platform and balloon-frame construction for light-frame buildings. The requirements for concrete and masonry buildings are based on a balloon framing system. Other framing systems must have equivalent detailing to ensure force transfer, continuity and compatible deformations.

R301.1.3 Engineered design. When a building of otherwise conventional construction contains structural elements exceeding the limits of Section R301 or otherwise not conforming to this code, these elements shall be designed in accordance with accepted engineering practice. The extent of such design need only demonstrate compliance of nonconventional elements with other applicable provisions and shall be compatible with the performance of the conventional framed system. Engineered design in accordance with the *International Building Code* is permitted for all buildings and structures, and parts thereof, included in the scope of this code.

R301.1.4 Automatic sprinkler systems (general). All IRC-2 and IRC-3 buildings shall be provided with an automatic sprinkler system.

> **Exception:** IRC-2 and IRC-3 buildings less than or equal to 9,250 square feet of floor area. Floor area shall include all floors, basements, and garages.

R301.1.4.1 State licensed facilities. IRC-1, IRC-2, and IRC-3 buildings containing facilities licensed by the state of Minnesota shall be provided with a fire suppression system as required by the applicable licensing provisions or this section, whichever is more restrictive.

R301.1.4.2 Installation requirements. Where an automatic sprinkler system is required in an IRC-2 and IRC-3 building, it shall be installed in accordance with NFPA 13D-2002 edition and the following:

1. Attached garages are required to have automatic sprinklers with a minimum of one dry head, located within five lineal feet of each door installed in the common wall separating the dwelling unit and the attached garage.

2. Attached covered patios, covered decks, covered porches, and similar structures are required to have automatic sprinklers with a minimum of one dry head for every 20 lineal feet of common wall between the dwelling unit and the covered patios, covered decks, covered porches, and similar structures.

   > **Exception:** Attached roofs of covered patios, covered decks, covered porches, and similar structures that do not exceed 40 square feet of floor area.

For the purposes of this section, fire-resistance-rated floor, wall, or ceiling assemblies separating dwelling units of IRC-2 and IRC-3 buildings shall not constitute separate buildings.

R301.2 Climatic and geographic design criteria. Buildings shall be constructed in accordance with the provisions of this code as limited by the provisions of this section. Additional criteria shall be established by the local jurisdiction and set forth in Table R301.2(1).

R301.2.1 Wind limitations. Buildings and portions thereof shall be limited by wind speed, as defined in Table R301.2(1) and construction methods in accordance with this code. Basic wind speeds shall be determined from Figure R301.2(4). Where different construction methods and structural materials are used for various portions of a building, the applicable requirements of this section for each portion shall apply. Where loads for wall coverings, curtain walls, roof coverings, exterior windows, skylights, garage doors and exterior doors are not otherwise specified, the loads listed in Table R301.2(2) adjusted for height and exposure using Table R301.2(3) shall be used to determine design load performance requirements for wall coverings, curtain walls, roof coverings, exterior windows, skylights, garage doors and exterior doors. Asphalt shingles shall be designed for wind speeds in accordance with Section R905.2.6.

R301.2.1.1 Design criteria. Construction in regions where the basic wind speeds from Figure R301.2(4) equal or exceed 100 miles per hour (45 m/s) in hurricane-prone regions, or 110 miles per hour (49 m/s) elsewhere, shall be designed in accordance with one of the following:

1. American Forest and Paper Association (AF&PA) *Wood Frame Construction Manual for One- and Two-Family Dwellings* (WFCM); or

2. *Southern Building Code Congress International Standard for Hurricane Resistant Residential Construction* (SSTD 10); or

3. *Minimum Design Loads for Buildings and Other Structures* (ASCE-7); or

4. American Iron and Steel Institute (AISI), *Standard for Cold-Formed Steel Framing—Prescriptive Method For One- and Two-Family Dwellings (COFS/PM) with Supplement to Standard for Cold-Formed Steel Framing—Prescriptive Method For One- and Two-Family Dwellings*.

5. Concrete construction shall be designed in accordance with the provisions of this code.

R301.2.1.2 Protection of openings. Windows in buildings located in windborne debris regions shall have glazed openings protected from windborne debris. Glazed opening protection for windborne debris shall meet the requirements of the Large Missile Test of an approved impact resisting standard or ASTM E 1996 and ASTM E 1886 referenced therein.

Exception: Wood structural panels with a minimum of $^7/_{16}$ inch (11 mm) and a maximum span of 8 feet (2438 mm) shall be permitted for opening protection in one- and two-story buildings. Panels shall be precut so that they shall be attached to the framing surrounding the opening containing the product with the glazed opening. Panels shall be secured with the attachment hardware provided. Attachments shall be designed to resist the component and cladding loads determined in accordance with either Table R301.2(2) or Section 1609.6.5 of the *International Building Code*. Attachment in accordance with Table R301.2.1.2 is permitted for buildings with a mean roof height of 33 feet (10 058 mm) or less where wind speeds do not exceed 130 miles per hour (58 m/s).

TABLE R301.2.1.2
WINDBORNE DEBRIS PROTECTION FASTENING SCHEDULE FOR WOOD STRUCTURAL PANELS[a, b, c, d]

FASTENER TYPE	FASTENER SPACING (inches)		
	Panel span ≤ 4 feet	4 feet < panel span ≤ 6 feet	6 feet < panel span ≤ 8 feet
No. 6 Screws	16″	12″	9″
No. 8 Screws	16″	16″	12″

For SI: 1 inch = 25.4 mm, 1 foot = 304.8 mm, 1 pound = 4.448N, 1 mile per hour = 0.447 m/s.

a. This table is based on 130 mph wind speeds and a 33-foot mean roof height.

b. Fasteners shall be installed at opposing ends of the wood structural panel. Fasteners shall be located a minimum of 1 inch from the edge of the panel.

c. Fasteners shall be long enough to penetrate through the exterior wall covering and a minimum of $1^1/_4$ inches into wood wall framing and a minimum of $1^1/_4$ inches into concrete block or concrete, and into steel framing a minimum of 3 exposed threads. Fasteners shall be located a minimum of $2^1/_2$ inches from the edge of concrete block or concrete.

d. Where screws are attached to masonry or masonry/stucco, they shall be attached using vibration-resistant anchors having a minimum ultimate withdrawal capacity of 490 pounds.

TABLE R301.2(1)
CLIMATIC AND GEOGRAPHIC DESIGN CRITERIA

ROOF SNOW LOAD[d]	WIND SPEED[c] (mph)	SUBJECT TO DAMAGE FROM		FLOOD HAZARDS
		Weathering[a]	Frost line depth[b]	
$\rho_f = 0.7 \times \rho_g$	90	Severe	See M.R. part 1303.1600	See M.R. Chapter 1335

For SI: 1 pound per square foot = 0.0479 kPa, 1 mile per hour = 1.609 km/h.

a. Weathering may require a higher strength concrete or grade of masonry than necessary to satisfy the structural requirement of this code. The grade of masonry units shall be determined from ASTM C 34, C 55, C 62, C 73, C 90, C 129, C 145, C 216, or C 652.

b. The frost line depth may require deeper footings than indicated in Figure R403.1(1).

c. Wind exposure category shall be determined on a site-specific basis in accordance with Section R301.2.1.4.

d. The ground snow loads to be used in determining the design snow loads for buildings and other structures are given in Minnesota Rules, Chapter 1303.

TABLE R301.2(2)
COMPONENT AND CLADDING LOADS FOR A BUILDING WITH A MEAN ROOF HEIGHT OF 30 FEET LOCATED IN EXPOSURE B (psf)

Each cell shows the two pressures (positive and negative, psf) for the given basic wind speed.

	ZONE	EFFECTIVE WIND AREA (feet²)	85	90	100	105	110	120	125	130	140	145	150	170
Roof > 0 to 10 degrees	1	10	10.0 -13.0	10.0 -14.6	10.0 -18.0	10.0 -19.8	10.0 -21.8	10.5 -25.9	11.4 -28.1	12.4 -30.4	14.3 -35.3	15.4 -37.8	16.5 -40.5	21.1 -52.0
	1	20	10.0 -12.7	10.0 -14.2	10.0 -17.5	10.0 -19.3	10.0 -21.2	10.0 -25.2	10.7 -27.4	11.6 -29.6	13.4 -34.4	14.4 -36.9	15.4 -39.4	19.8 -50.7
	1	50	10.0 -12.2	10.0 -13.7	10.0 -16.9	10.0 -18.7	10.0 -20.5	10.0 -24.4	10.0 -26.4	10.6 -28.6	12.3 -33.2	13.1 -35.6	14.1 -38.1	18.1 -48.9
	1	100	10.0 -11.9	10.0 -13.3	10.0 -16.5	10.0 -18.2	10.0 -19.9	10.0 -23.7	10.0 -25.7	10.0 -27.8	11.4 -32.3	12.2 -34.6	13.0 -37.0	16.7 -47.6
	2	10	10.0 -21.8	10.0 -24.4	10.0 -30.2	10.0 -33.3	10.0 -36.5	10.5 -43.5	11.4 -47.2	12.4 -51.0	14.3 -59.2	15.4 -63.5	16.5 -67.9	21.1 -87.2
	2	20	10.0 -19.5	10.0 -21.8	10.0 -27.0	10.0 -29.7	10.0 -32.6	10.0 -38.8	10.7 -42.1	11.6 -45.6	13.4 -52.9	14.4 -56.7	15.4 -60.7	19.8 -78.0
	2	50	10.0 -16.4	10.0 -18.4	10.0 -22.7	10.0 -25.1	10.0 -27.5	10.0 -32.7	10.0 -35.5	10.6 -38.4	12.3 -44.5	13.1 -47.8	14.1 -51.1	18.1 -65.7
	2	100	10.0 -14.1	10.0 -15.8	10.0 -19.5	10.0 -21.5	10.0 -23.6	10.0 -28.1	10.0 -30.5	10.0 -33.0	11.4 -38.2	12.2 -41.0	13.0 -43.9	16.7 -56.4
	3	10	10.0 -32.8	10.0 -36.8	10.0 -45.4	10.0 -50.1	10.0 -55.0	10.5 -65.4	11.4 -71.0	12.4 -76.8	14.3 -89.0	15.4 -95.5	16.5 -102.2	21.1 -131.3
	3	20	10.0 -27.2	10.0 -30.5	10.0 -37.6	10.0 -41.5	10.0 -45.5	10.0 -54.2	10.7 -58.8	11.6 -63.6	13.4 -73.8	14.4 -79.1	15.4 -84.7	19.8 -108.7
	3	50	10.0 -19.7	10.0 -22.1	10.0 -27.3	10.0 -30.1	10.0 -33.1	10.0 -39.3	10.0 -42.7	10.6 -46.2	12.3 -53.5	13.1 -57.4	14.1 -61.5	18.1 -78.9
	3	100	10.0 -14.1	10.0 -15.8	10.0 -19.5	10.0 -21.5	10.0 -23.6	10.0 -28.1	10.0 -30.5	10.0 -33.0	11.4 -38.2	12.2 -41.0	13.0 -43.9	16.7 -56.4
Roof > 10 to 30 degrees	1	10	10.0 -11.9	10.0 -13.3	10.4 -16.5	11.4 -18.2	12.5 -19.9	14.9 -23.7	16.2 -25.7	17.5 -27.8	20.3 -32.3	21.8 -34.6	23.3 -37.0	30.0 -47.6
	1	20	10.0 -11.6	10.0 -13.0	10.0 -16.0	10.4 -17.6	11.4 -19.4	13.6 -23.0	14.8 -25.0	16.0 -27.0	18.5 -31.4	19.9 -33.7	21.3 -36.0	27.3 -46.3
	1	50	10.0 -11.1	10.0 -12.5	10.0 -15.4	10.0 -17.0	10.0 -18.6	11.9 -22.2	12.9 -24.1	13.9 -26.0	16.1 -30.2	17.3 -32.4	18.5 -34.6	23.8 -44.5
	1	100	10.0 -10.8	10.0 -12.1	10.0 -14.9	10.0 -16.5	10.0 -18.1	10.5 -21.5	11.4 -23.3	12.4 -25.2	14.3 -29.3	15.4 -31.4	16.5 -33.6	21.1 -43.2
	2	10	10.0 -25.1	10.0 -28.2	10.4 -34.8	11.4 -38.3	12.5 -42.1	14.9 -50.1	16.2 -54.3	17.5 -58.7	20.3 -68.1	21.8 -73.1	23.3 -78.2	30.0 -100.5
	2	20	10.0 -22.8	10.0 -25.6	10.0 -31.5	10.4 -34.8	11.4 -38.2	13.6 -45.4	14.8 -49.3	16.0 -53.3	18.5 -61.8	19.9 -66.3	21.3 -71.0	27.3 -91.2
	2	50	10.0 -19.7	10.0 -22.1	10.0 -27.3	10.0 -30.1	10.0 -33.0	11.9 -39.3	12.9 -42.7	13.9 -46.1	16.1 -53.5	17.3 -57.4	18.5 -61.4	23.8 -78.9
	2	100	10.0 -17.4	10.0 -19.5	10.0 -24.1	10.0 -26.6	10.0 -29.1	10.5 -34.7	11.4 -37.6	12.4 -40.7	14.3 -47.2	15.4 -50.6	16.5 -54.2	21.1 -69.6
	3	10	10.0 -25.1	10.0 -28.2	10.4 -34.8	11.4 -38.3	12.5 -42.1	14.9 -50.1	16.2 -54.3	17.5 -58.7	20.3 -68.1	21.8 -73.1	23.3 -78.2	30.0 -100.5
	3	20	10.0 -22.8	10.0 -25.6	10.0 -31.5	10.4 -34.8	11.4 -38.2	13.6 -45.4	14.8 -49.3	16.0 -53.3	18.5 -61.8	19.9 -66.3	21.3 -71.0	27.3 -91.2
	3	50	10.0 -19.7	10.0 -22.1	10.0 -27.3	10.0 -30.1	10.0 -33.0	11.9 -39.3	12.9 -42.7	13.9 -46.1	16.1 -53.5	17.3 -57.4	18.5 -61.4	23.8 -78.9
	3	100	10.0 -17.4	10.0 -19.5	10.0 -24.1	10.0 -26.6	10.0 -29.1	10.5 -34.7	11.4 -37.6	12.4 -40.7	14.3 -47.2	15.4 -50.6	16.5 -54.2	21.1 -69.6
Roof > 30 to 45 degrees	1	10	11.9 -13.0	13.3 -14.6	16.5 -18.0	18.2 -19.8	19.9 -21.8	23.7 -25.9	25.7 -28.1	27.8 -30.4	32.3 -35.3	34.6 -37.8	37.0 -40.5	47.6 -52.0
	1	20	11.6 -12.3	13.0 -13.8	16.0 -17.1	17.6 -18.8	19.4 -20.7	23.0 -24.6	25.0 -26.7	27.0 -28.9	31.4 -33.5	33.7 -35.9	36.0 -38.4	46.3 -49.3
	1	50	11.1 -11.5	12.5 -12.8	15.4 -15.9	17.0 -17.5	18.6 -19.2	22.2 -22.8	24.1 -24.8	26.0 -25.8	30.2 -31.1	32.4 -33.3	34.6 -35.7	44.5 -45.8
	1	100	10.8 -10.8	12.1 -12.1	14.9 -14.9	16.5 -16.5	18.1 -18.1	21.5 -21.5	23.3 -23.3	25.2 -25.2	29.3 -29.3	31.4 -31.4	33.6 -33.6	43.2 -43.2
	2	10	11.9 -15.2	13.3 -17.0	16.5 -21.0	18.2 -23.2	19.9 -25.5	23.7 -30.3	25.7 -32.9	27.8 -35.6	32.3 -41.2	34.6 -44.2	37.0 -47.3	47.6 -60.8
	2	20	11.6 -14.5	13.0 -16.3	16.0 -20.1	17.6 -22.2	19.4 -24.3	23.0 -29.0	25.0 -31.4	27.0 -34.0	31.4 -39.4	33.7 -42.3	36.0 -45.3	46.3 -58.1
	2	50	11.1 -13.7	12.5 -15.3	15.4 -18.9	17.0 -20.8	18.6 -22.9	22.2 -27.2	24.1 -29.5	26.0 -32.0	30.2 -37.1	32.4 -39.8	34.6 -42.5	44.5 -54.6
	2	100	10.8 -13.0	12.1 -14.6	14.9 -18.0	16.5 -19.8	18.1 -21.8	21.5 -25.9	23.3 -28.1	25.2 -30.4	29.3 -35.3	31.4 -37.8	33.6 -40.5	43.2 -52.0
	3	10	11.9 -15.2	13.3 -17.0	16.5 -21.0	18.2 -23.2	19.9 -25.5	23.7 -30.3	25.7 -32.9	27.8 -35.6	32.3 -41.2	34.6 -44.2	37.0 -47.3	47.6 -60.8
	3	20	11.6 -14.5	13.0 -16.3	16.0 -20.1	17.6 -22.2	19.4 -24.3	23.0 -29.0	25.0 -31.4	27.0 -34.0	31.4 -39.4	33.7 -42.3	36.0 -45.3	46.3 -58.1
	3	50	11.1 -13.7	12.5 -15.3	15.4 -18.9	17.0 -20.8	18.6 -22.9	22.2 -27.2	24.1 -29.5	26.0 -32.0	30.2 -37.1	32.4 -39.8	34.6 -42.5	44.5 -54.5
	3	100	10.8 -13.0	12.1 -14.6	14.9 -18.0	16.5 -19.8	18.1 -21.8	21.5 -25.9	23.3 -28.1	25.2 -30.4	29.3 -35.3	31.4 -37.8	33.6 -40.5	43.2 -52.0
Wall	4	10	13.0 -14.1	14.6 -15.8	18.0 -19.5	19.8 -21.5	21.8 -23.6	25.9 -28.1	28.1 -30.5	30.4 -33.0	35.3 -38.2	37.8 -41.0	40.5 -43.9	52.0 -56.4
	4	20	12.4 -13.5	13.9 -15.1	17.2 -18.7	18.9 -20.6	20.8 -22.6	24.7 -26.9	26.8 -29.2	29.0 -31.6	33.7 -36.7	36.1 -39.3	38.7 -42.1	49.6 -54.1
	4	50	11.6 -12.7	13.0 -14.3	16.1 -17.6	17.8 -19.4	19.5 -21.3	23.2 -25.4	25.2 -27.5	27.2 -29.8	31.6 -34.6	33.9 -37.1	36.2 -39.7	46.6 -51.0
	4	100	11.1 -12.2	12.4 -13.6	15.3 -16.8	16.9 -18.5	18.5 -20.4	22.0 -24.2	23.9 -26.3	25.9 -28.4	30.0 -33.0	32.2 -35.4	34.4 -37.8	44.2 -48.6
	5	10	13.0 -17.4	14.6 -19.5	18.0 -24.1	19.8 -26.6	21.8 -29.1	25.9 -34.7	28.1 -37.6	30.4 -40.7	35.3 -47.2	37.8 -50.6	40.5 -54.2	52.0 -69.6
	5	20	12.4 -16.2	13.9 -18.2	17.2 -22.5	18.9 -24.8	20.8 -27.2	24.7 -32.4	26.8 -35.1	29.0 -38.0	33.7 -44.0	36.1 -47.2	38.7 -50.5	49.6 -64.9
	5	50	11.6 -14.7	13.0 -16.5	16.1 -20.3	17.8 -22.4	19.5 -24.6	23.2 -29.3	25.2 -31.8	27.2 -34.3	31.6 -39.8	33.9 -42.7	36.2 -45.7	46.6 -58.7
	5	100	11.1 -13.5	12.4 -15.1	15.3 -18.7	16.9 -20.6	18.5 -22.6	22.0 -26.9	23.9 -29.2	25.9 -31.6	30.0 -36.7	32.2 -39.3	34.4 -42.1	44.2 -54.1

For SI: 1 foot = 304.8 mm, 1 square foot = 0.0929 m², 1 mile per hour = 0.447 m/s.

NOTES: For effective areas between those given above the load may be interpolated, otherwise use the load associated with the lower effective area.

Table values shall be adjusted for height and exposure by multiplying by the adjustment coefficient in Table R301.2(3).

See Figure R301.2(7) for location of zones.

Plus and minus signs signify pressures acting toward and away from the building surfaces.

TABLE R301.2(3)
HEIGHT AND EXPOSURE ADJUSTMENT COEFFICIENTS FOR TABLE R301.2(2)

MEAN ROOF HEIGHT	EXPOSURE		
	B	C	D
15	1.00	1.21	1.47
20	1.00	1.29	1.55
25	1.00	1.35	1.61
30	1.00	1.40	1.66
35	1.05	1.45	1.70
40	1.09	1.49	1.74
45	1.12	1.53	1.78
50	1.16	1.56	1.81
55	1.19	1.59	1.84
60	1.22	1.62	1.87

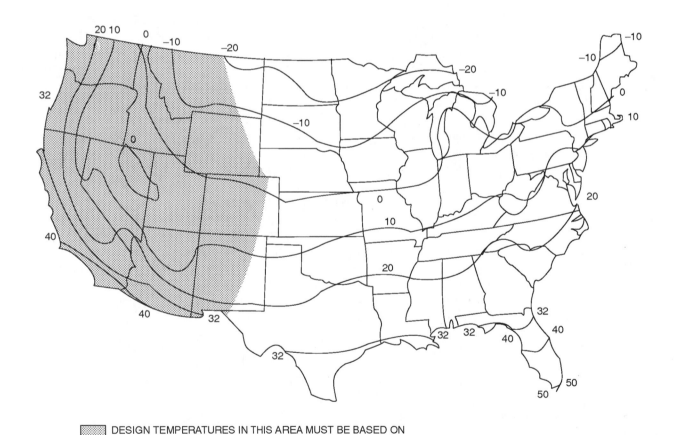

DESIGN TEMPERATURES IN THIS AREA MUST BE BASED ON ANALYSIS OF LOCAL CLIMATE AND TOPOGRAPHY

For SI: °C = [(°F)-32] /1.8.

FIGURE R301.2(1)
ISOLINES OF THE 97$^{1}/_{2}$ PERCENT WINTER (DECEMBER, JANUARY AND FEBRUARY) DESIGN TEMPERATURES (°F)

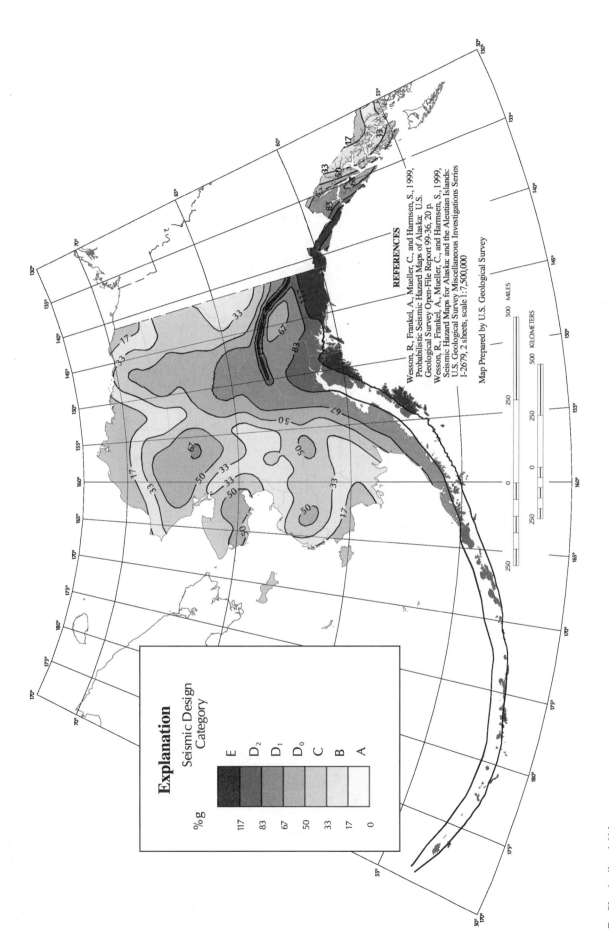

FIGURE R301.2(2)
SEISMIC DESIGN CATEGORIES—SITE CLASS D
(continued)

For SI: 1 mile = 1.61 km.

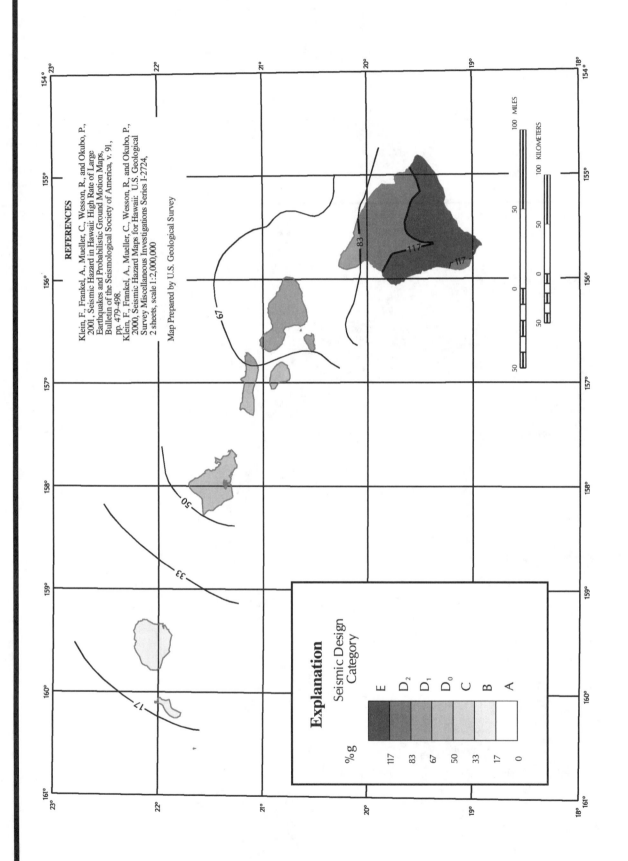

Explanation

Seismic Design
Category

%g	
117	E
83	D₂
67	D₁
50	D₀
33	C
17	B
0	A

REFERENCES

Klein, F., Frankel, A., Mueller, C., Wesson, R., and Okubo, P., 2001, Seismic Hazard in Hawaii: High Rate of Large Earthquakes and Probabilistic Ground Motion Maps, Bulletin of the Seismological Society of America, v. 91, pp. 479-498.
Klein, F., Frankel, A., Mueller, C., Wesson, R., and Okubo, P., 2000, Seismic Hazard Maps for Hawaii: U.S. Geological Survey Miscellaneous Investigations Series I-2724, 2 sheets, scale 1:2,000,000

Map Prepared by U.S. Geological Survey

FIGURE R301.2(2)—continued
SEISMIC DESIGN CATEGORIES—SITE CLASS D

(continued)

For SI: 1 mile = 1.61 km.

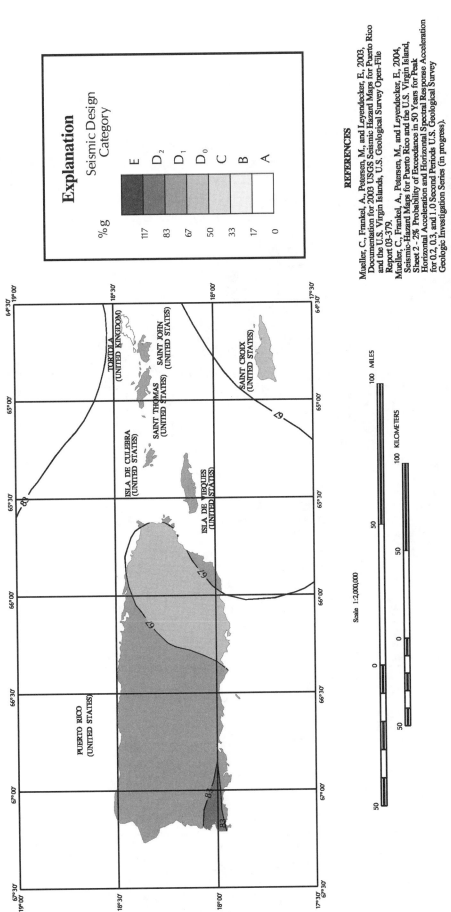

Explanation

Seismic Design Category

%g	
117	E
83	D₂
67	D₁
50	D₀
33	C
17	B
0	A

REFERENCES

Mueller, C, Frankel, A., Petersen, M., and Leyendecker, E., 2003, Documentation for 2003 USGS Seismic Hazard Maps for Puerto Rico and the U.S. Virgin Islands, U.S. Geological Survey Open-File Report 03-379.

Mueller, C, Frankel, A., Petersen, M., and Leyendecker, E, 2004, Seismic-Hazard Maps for Puerto Rico and the U.S. Virgin Island, Sheet 2 - 2% Probability of Exceedance in 50 Years for Peak Horizontal Acceleration and Horizontal Spectral Response Acceleration for 0.2, 0.3, and 1.0 Second Periods U.S. Geological Survey Geologic Investigation Series (in progress).

Map Prepared by U.S. Geological Survey

Scale 1:2,000,000

FIGURE R301.2(2)—continued
SEISMIC DESIGN CATEGORIES—SITE CLASS D

(continued)

For SI: 1 mile = 1.61 km.

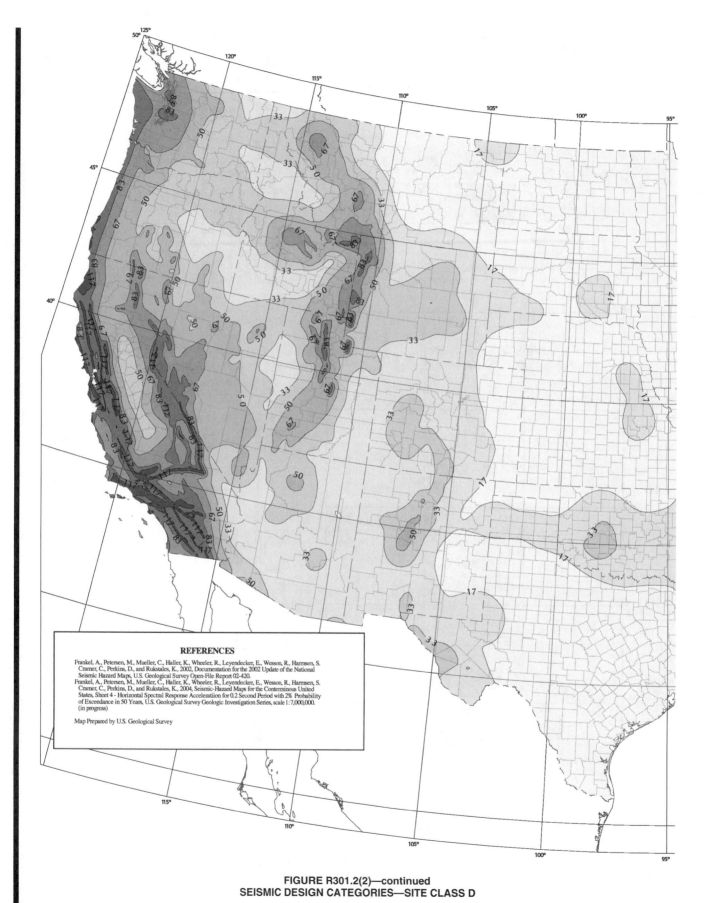

REFERENCES

Frankel, A., Petersen, M., Mueller, C., Haller, K., Wheeler, R., Leyendecker, E., Wesson, R., Harmsen, S.
Cramer, C., Perkins, D., and Rukstales, K., 2002, Documentation for the 2002 Update of the National
Seismic Hazard Maps, U.S. Geological Survey Open-File Report 02-420.

Frankel, A., Petersen, M., Mueller, C., Haller, K., Wheeler, R., Leyendecker, E., Wesson, R., Harmsen, S.
Cramer, C., Perkins, D., and Rukstales, K., 2004, Seismic-Hazard Maps for the Conterminous United
States, Sheet 4 - Horizontal Spectral Response Acceleration for 0.2 Second Period with 2% Probability
of Exceedance in 50 Years, U.S. Geological Survey Geologic Investigation Series, scale 1:7,000,000.
(in progress)

Map Prepared by U.S. Geological Survey

FIGURE R301.2(2)—continued
SEISMIC DESIGN CATEGORIES—SITE CLASS D

(continued)

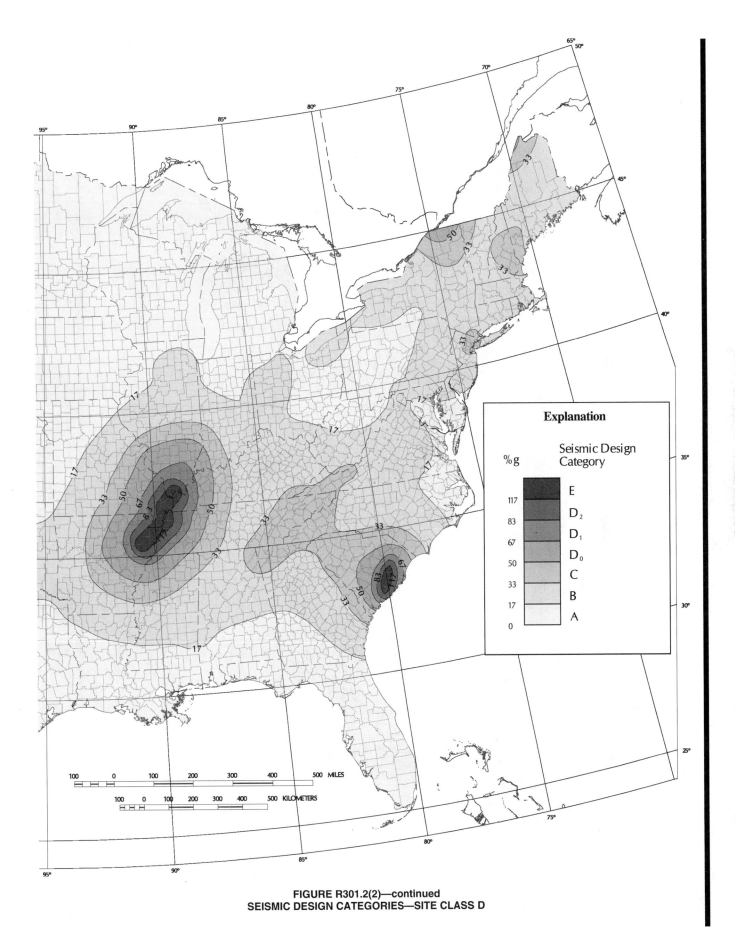

**FIGURE R301.2(2)—continued
SEISMIC DESIGN CATEGORIES—SITE CLASS D**

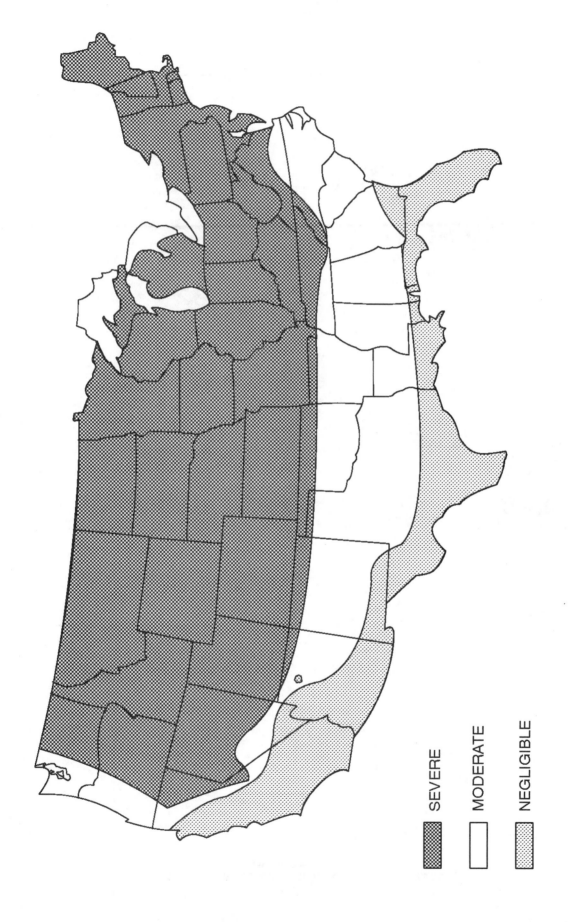

SEVERE

MODERATE

NEGLIGIBLE

FIGURE R301.2(3)
WEATHERING PROBABILITY MAP FOR CONCRETE

a. Alaska and Hawaii are classified as severe and negligible, respectively.

b. Lines defining areas are approximate only. Local conditions may be more or less severe than indicated by region classification. A severe classification is where weather conditions result in significant snowfall combined with extended periods during which there is little or no natural thawing causing deicing salts to be used extensively.

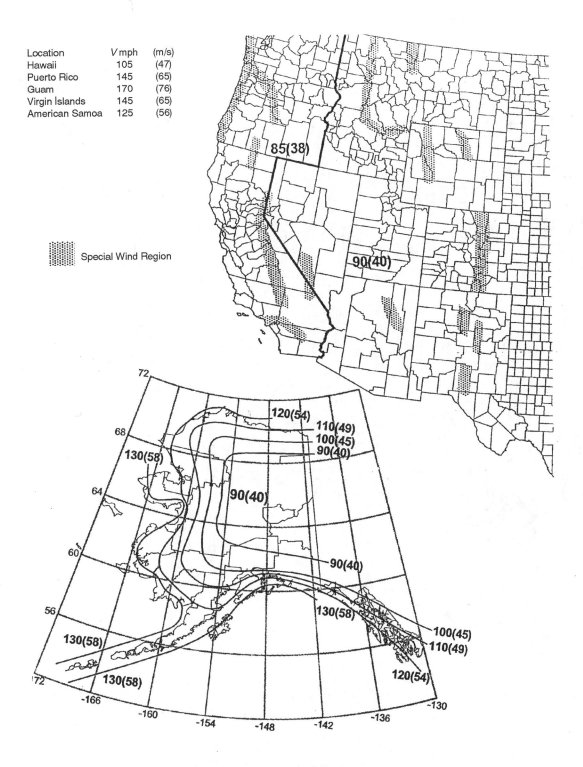

Location	V mph	(m/s)
Hawaii	105	(47)
Puerto Rico	145	(65)
Guam	170	(76)
Virgin Islands	145	(65)
American Samoa	125	(56)

Special Wind Region

FIGURE R301.2(4)
BASIC WIND SPEEDS FOR 50-YEAR MEAN RECURRENCE INTERVAL

(continued)

For SI: 1 foot = 304.8 mm, 1 mile per hour = 0.447 m/s.

a. Values are nominal design 3-second gust wind speeds in miles per hour at 33 feet above ground for Exposure C category.

b. Linear interpolation between wind contours is permitted.

c. Islands and coastal areas outside the last contour shall use the last wind speed contour of the coastal area.

d. Mountainous terrain, gorges, ocean promontories and special wind regions shall be examined for unusual wind conditions.

e. Enlarged view of Eastern and Southern seaboards are on the following pages.

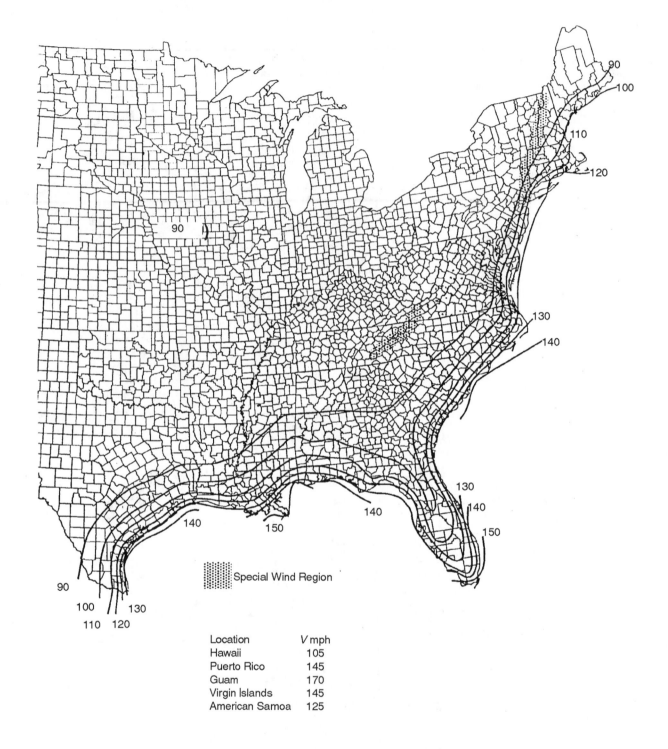

Location	V mph
Hawaii	105
Puerto Rico	145
Guam	170
Virgin Islands	145
American Samoa	125

FIGURE R301.2(4)—continued
BASIC WIND SPEEDS FOR 50-YEAR MEAN RECURRENCE INTERVAL

(continued)

For SI: 1 foot = 304.8 mm, 1 mile per hour = 0.447 m/s.

a. Values are nominal design 3-second gust wind speeds in miles per hour at 33 feet above ground for Exposure C category.

b. Linear interpolation between wind contours is permitted.

c. Islands and coastal areas outside the last contour shall use the last wind speed contour of the coastal area.

d. Mountainous terrain, gorges, ocean promontories and special wind regions shall be examined for unusual wind conditions.

e. Enlarged view of Eastern and Southern seaboards are on the following pages.

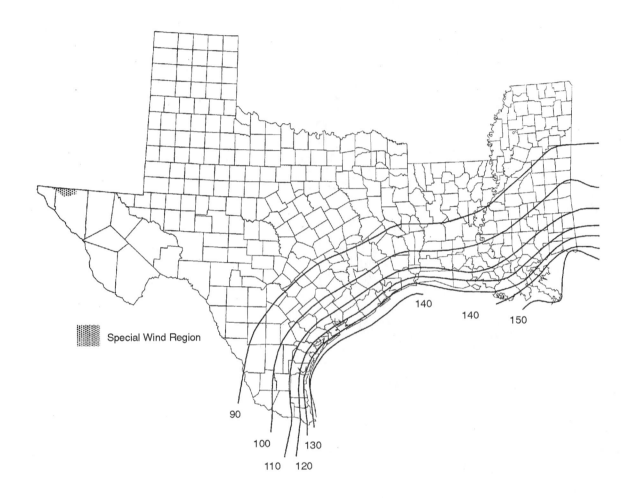

Special Wind Region

140

140   150

90

100   130

110   120

FIGURE R301.2(4)—continued
BASIC WIND SPEEDS FOR 50-YEAR MEAN RECURRENCE INTERVAL

(continued)

For SI: 1 foot = 304.8 mm, 1 mile per hour = 0.447 m/s.

a. Values are nominal design 3-second gust wind speeds in miles per hour at 33 feet above ground for Exposure C category.

b. Linear interpolation between wind contours is permitted.

c. Islands and coastal areas outside the last contour shall use the last wind speed contour of the coastal area.

d. Mountainous terrain, gorges, ocean promontories and special wind regions shall be examined for unusual wind conditions.

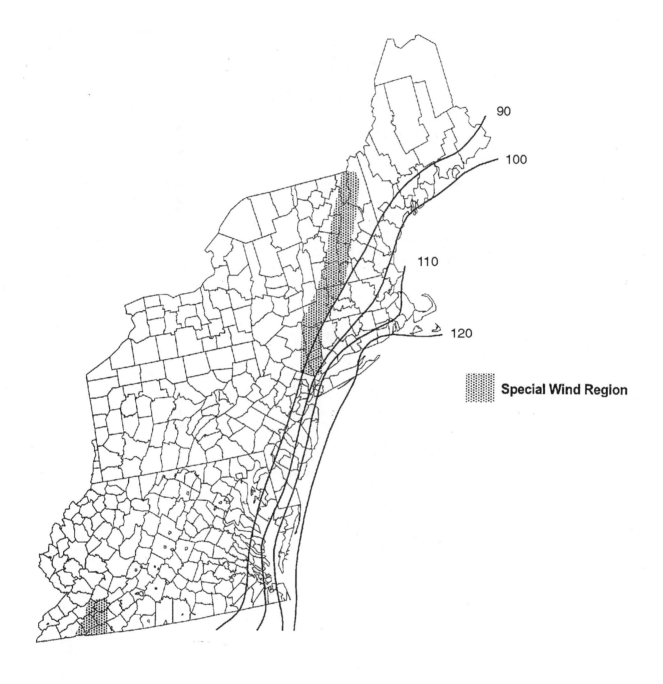

FIGURE R301.2(4)—continued
BASIC WIND SPEEDS FOR 50-YEAR MEAN RECURRENCE INTERVAL

(continued)

For SI: 1 foot = 304.8 mm, 1 mile per hour = 0.447 m/s.

a. Values are nominal design 3-second gust wind speeds in miles per hour at 33 feet above ground for Exposure C category.

b. Linear interpolation between wind contours is permitted.

c. Islands and coastal areas outside the last contour shall use the last wind speed contour of the coastal area.

d. Mountainous terrain, gorges, ocean promontories and special wind regions shall be examined for unusual wind conditions.

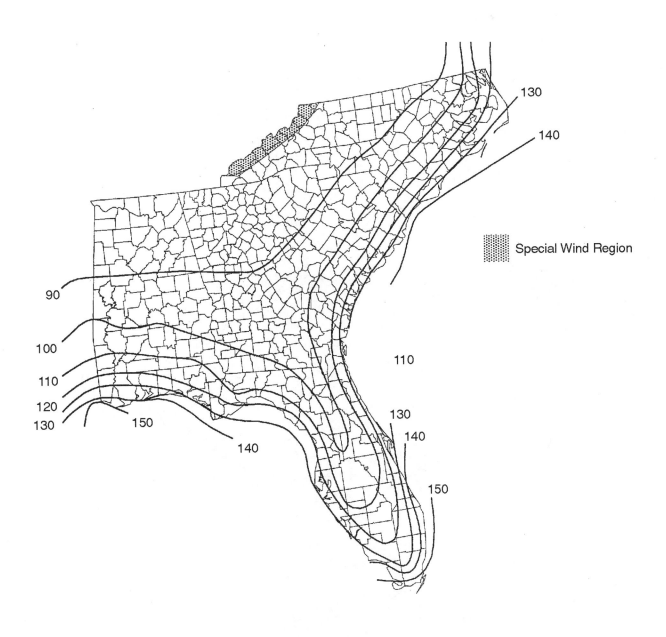

130

140

Special Wind Region

90

100

110

110

120

130

150

140

110

130

140

150

FIGURE R301.2(4)—continued
BASIC WIND SPEEDS FOR 50-YEAR MEAN RECURRENCE INTERVAL

For SI: 1 foot = 304.8 mm, 1 mile per hour = 0.447 m/s.

a. Values are nominal design 3-second gust wind speeds in miles per hour at 33 feet above ground for Exposure C category.

b. Linear interpolation between wind contours is permitted.

c. Islands and coastal areas outside the last contour shall use the last wind speed contour of the coastal area.

d. Mountainous terrain, gorges, ocean promontories and special wind regions shall be examined for unusual wind conditions.

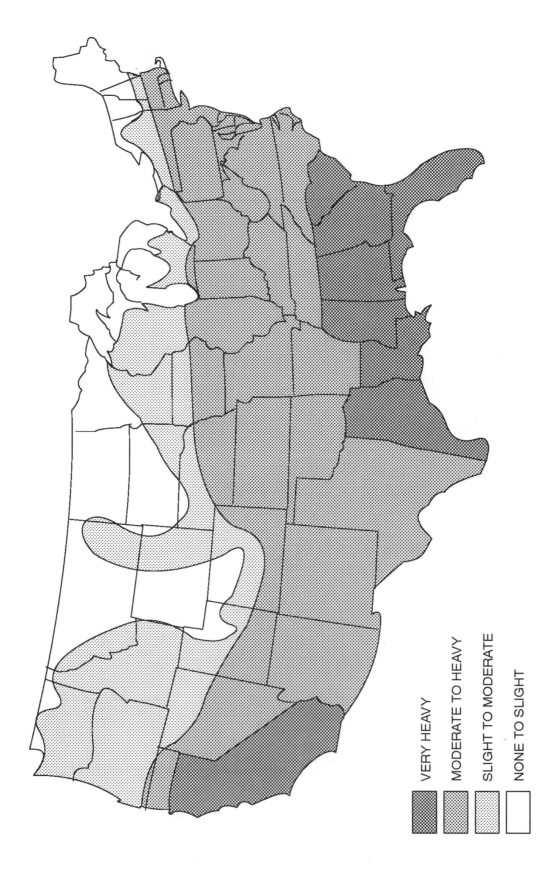

VERY HEAVY

MODERATE TO HEAVY

SLIGHT TO MODERATE

NONE TO SLIGHT

NOTE: Lines defining areas are approximate only. Local conditions may be more or less severe than indicated by the region classification.

FIGURE R301.2(6)
TERMITE INFESTATION PROBABILITY MAP

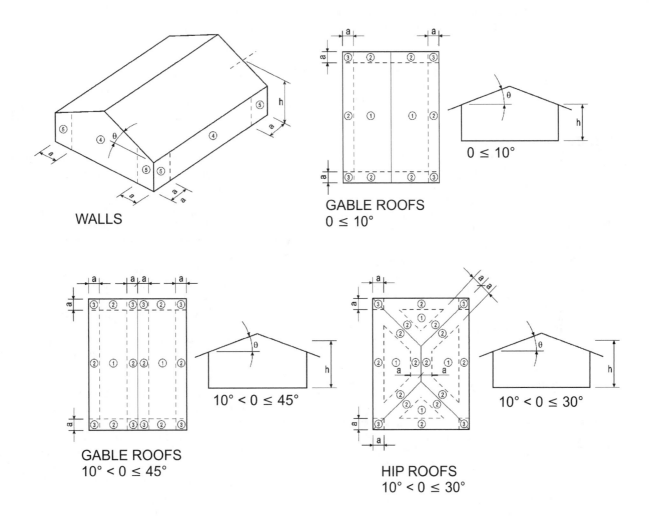

WALLS

GABLE ROOFS
$0 \leq 10°$

$0 \leq 10°$

GABLE ROOFS
$10° < 0 \leq 45°$

$10° < 0 \leq 45°$

HIP ROOFS
$10° < 0 \leq 30°$

$10° < 0 \leq 30°$

For SI: 1 foot = 304.8 mm, 1 degree = 0.0175 rad.
NOTE: a = 4 feet in all cases.

FIGURE R301.2(7)
COMPONENT AND CLADDING PRESSURE ZONES

R301.2.1.3 Wind speed conversion. When referenced documents are based on fastest mile wind speeds, the three-second gust basic wind speeds, V_{3s}, of Figure R301.2(4) shall be converted to fastest mile wind speeds, V_{fm}, using Table R301.2.1.3.

R301.2.1.4 Exposure category. For each wind direction considered, an exposure category that adequately reflects the characteristics of ground surface irregularities shall be determined for the site at which the building or structure is to be constructed. For a site located in the transition zone between categories, the category resulting in the largest wind forces shall apply. Account shall be taken of variations in ground surface roughness that arise from natural topography and vegetation as well as from constructed features. For any given wind direction, the exposure in which a specific building or other structure is sited shall be assessed as being one of the following categories:

1. Exposure A. Large city centers with at least 50 percent of the buildings having a height in excess of 70 feet (21 336 mm). Use of this exposure category shall be limited to those areas for which terrain representative of Exposure A prevails in the upwind direction for a distance of at least 0.5 mile (0.8 km) or 10 times the height of the building or other structure, whichever is greater. Possible channeling effects or increased velocity pressures due to the building or structure being located in the wake of adjacent buildings shall be taken into account.

2. Exposure B. Urban and suburban areas, wooded areas, or other terrain with numerous closely spaced obstructions having the size of single-family dwellings or larger. Exposure B shall be assumed unless the site meets the definition of another type exposure.

3. Exposure C. Open terrain with scattered obstructions, including surface undulations or other irregularities, having heights generally less than 30 feet (9144 mm) extending more than 1,500 feet (457 m) from the building site in any quadrant. This exposure shall also apply to any building located within Exposure B type terrain where the building is directly adjacent to open areas of Exposure C type terrain in any quadrant for a distance of more than 600 feet (183 m). This category includes flat open country, grasslands and shorelines in hurricane prone regions.

4. Exposure D. Flat, unobstructed areas exposed to wind flowing over open water (excluding shorelines in hurricane prone regions) for a distance of at least 1 mile (1.61 km). Shorelines in Exposure D include inland waterways, the Great Lakes and coastal areas of California, Oregon, Washington and Alaska. This exposure shall apply only to those buildings and other structures exposed to the wind coming from over the water. Exposure D extends inland from the shoreline a distance of 1,500 feet (457 m) or 10 times the height of the building or structure, whichever is greater.

R301.2.2 Seismic provisions. The seismic provisions of this code shall apply to buildings constructed in Seismic Design Categories C, D_0, D_1 and D_2, as determined in accordance with this section. Buildings in Seismic Design Category E shall be designed in accordance with the *International Building Code*, except when the seismic design category is reclassified to a lower seismic design category in accordance with Section R301.2.2.1.

> **Exception:** Detached one- and two-family dwellings located in Seismic Design Category C are exempt from the seismic requirements of this code.

The weight and irregularity limitations of Section R301.2.2.2 shall apply to buildings in all seismic design categories regulated by the seismic provisions of this code. Buildings in Seismic Design Category C shall be constructed in accordance with the additional requirements of Section R301.2.2.3. Buildings in Seismic Design Categories D_0, D_1 and D_2 shall be constructed in accordance with the additional requirements of Section R301.2.2.4

R301.2.2.1 Determination of seismic design category. Buildings shall be assigned a seismic design category in accordance with Figure 301.2(2).

R301.2.2.1.1 Alternate determination of seismic design category. The Seismic Design Categories and corresponding Short Period Design Spectral Response Accelerations, S_{DS} shown in Figure R301.2(2) are based on soil Site Class D, as defined in Section 1615.1.1 of the *International Building Code*. If soil conditions are other than Site Class D, the Short Period Design Spectral Response Acceleration, S_{DS}, for a site can be determined according to Section 1615.1 of the *International Building Code*. The value of S_{DS} determined according to Section 1615.1 of the *International Building Code* is permitted to be used to set the seismic design category according to Table R301.2.2.1.1, and to interpolate between values in

TABLE R301.2.1.3
EQUIVALENT BASIC WIND SPEEDS[a]

3-second gust, V_{3s}	85	90	100	105	110	120	125	130	140	145	150	160	170
Fastest mile, V_{fm}	71	76	85	90	95	104	109	114	123	128	133	142	152

For SI: 1 mile per hour = 0.447 m/s.
a. Linear interpolation is permitted.

Tables R602.10.1, R603.7, and other seismic design requirements of this code.

TABLE R301.2.2.1.1
SEISMIC DESIGN CATEGORY DETERMINATION

CALCULATED S_{DS}	SEISMIC DESIGN CATEGORY
$S_{DS} \leq 0.17g$	A
$0.17g < S_{DS} \leq 0.33g$	B
$0.33g < S_{DS} \leq 0.50g$	C
$0.50g < S_{DS} \leq 0.67g$	D_0
$0.67g < S_{DS} \leq 0.83g$	D_1
$0.83g < S_{DS} \leq 1.17g$	D_2
$1.17g < S_{Ds}$	E

R301.2.2.1.2 Alternative determination of Seismic Design Category E. Buildings located in Seismic Design Category E in accordance with Figure R301.2(2) are permitted to be reclassified as being in Seismic Design Category D_2 provided one of the following is done:

1. A more detailed evaluation of the seismic design category is made in accordance with the provisions and maps of the *International Building Code*. Buildings located in Seismic Design Category E per Table R301.2.2.1.1, but located in Seismic Design Category D per the *International Building Code,* may be designed using the Seismic Design Category D_2 requirements of this code.

2. Buildings located in Seismic Design Category E that conform to the following additional restrictions are permitted to be constructed in accordance with the provisions for Seismic Design Category D_2 of this code:

    2.1. All exterior shear wall lines or braced wall panels are in one plane vertically from the foundation to the uppermost story.

    2.2. Floors shall not cantilever past the exterior walls.

    2.3. The building is within all of the requirements of Section R301.2.2.2.2 for being considered as regular.

R301.2.2.2 Seismic limitations. The following limitations apply to buildings in all Seismic Design Categories regulated by the seismic provisions of this code.

R301.2.2.2.1 Weights of materials. Average dead loads shall not exceed 15 pounds per square foot (720 Pa) for the combined roof and ceiling assemblies (on a horizontal projection) or 10 pounds per square foot (480 Pa) for floor assemblies, except as further limited by Section R301.2.2. Dead loads for walls above grade shall not exceed:

1. Fifteen pounds per square foot (720 Pa) for exterior light-frame wood walls.

2. Fourteen pounds per square foot (670 Pa) for exterior light-frame cold-formed steel walls.

3. Ten pounds per square foot (480 Pa) for interior light-frame wood walls.

4. Five pounds per square foot (240 Pa) for interior light-frame cold-formed steel walls.

5. Eighty pounds per square foot (3830 Pa) for 8-inch-thick (203 mm) masonry walls.

6. Eighty-five pounds per square foot (4070 Pa) for 6-inch-thick (152 mm) concrete walls.

Exceptions:

1. Roof and ceiling dead loads not exceeding 25 pounds per square foot (1190 Pa) shall be permitted provided the wall bracing amounts in Chapter 6 are increased in accordance with Table R301.2.2.2.1.

2. Light-frame walls with stone or masonry veneer shall be permitted in accordance with the provisions of Sections R702.1 and R703.

3. Fireplaces and chimneys shall be permitted in accordance with Chapter 10.

TABLE R301.2.2.2.1
WALL BRACING ADJUSTMENT FACTORS BY
ROOF COVERING DEAD LOAD[a]

WALL SUPPORTING	ROOF/CEILING DEAD LOAD 15 psf or less	ROOF/CEILING DEAD LOAD 25 psf
Roof only	1.0	1.2
Roof plus one story	1.0	1.1

For SI: 1 pound per square foot = 0.049 kPa.
a. Linear interpolation shall be permitted.

R301.2.2.2.2 Irregular buildings. Prescriptive construction as regulated by this code shall not be used for irregular structures located in Seismic Design Categories C, D_0, D_1 and D_2. Irregular portions of structures shall be designed in accordance with accepted engineering practice to the extent the irregular features affect the performance of the remaining structural system. When the forces associated with the irregularity are resisted by a structural system designed in accordance with accepted engineering practice, design of the remainder of the building shall be permitted using the provisions of this code. A building or portion of a building shall be considered to be irregular when one or more of the following conditions occur:

1. When exterior shear wall lines or braced wall panels are not in one plane vertically from the foundation to the uppermost story in which they are required.

    Exception: For wood light-frame construction, floors with cantilevers or setbacks not exceeding four times the nominal depth of the wood floor joists are permitted to support braced wall panels that are out of plane with braced wall panels below provided that:

    1. Floor joists are nominal 2 inches by 10 inches (51 mm by 254 mm) or larger and spaced not more than 16 inches (406 mm) on center.

    2. The ratio of the back span to the cantilever is at least 2 to 1.

    3. Floor joists at ends of braced wall panels are doubled.

    4. For wood-frame construction, a continuous rim joist is connected to ends of all cantilever joists. When spliced, the rim joists shall be spliced using a galvanized metal tie not less than 0.058 inch (1.5 mm) (16 gage) and $1^1/_2$ inches (38 mm) wide fastened with six 16d nails on each side of the splice or a block of the same size as the rim joist of sufficient length to fit securely between the joist space at which the splice occurs fastened with eight 16d nails on each side of the splice; and

    5. Gravity loads carried at the end of cantilevered joists are limited to uniform wall and roof loads and the reactions from headers having a span of 8 feet (2438 mm) or less.

2. When a section of floor or roof is not laterally supported by shear walls or braced wall lines on all edges.

    Exception: Portions of floors that do not support shear walls or braced wall panels above, or roofs, shall be permitted to extend no more than 6 feet (1829 mm) beyond a shear wall or braced wall line.

3. When the end of a braced wall panel occurs over an opening in the wall below and ends at a horizontal distance greater than 1 foot (305 mm) from the edge of the opening. This provision is applicable to shear walls and braced wall panels offset in plane and to braced wall panels

offset out of plane as permitted by the exception to Item 1 above.

Exception: For wood light-frame wall construction, one end of a braced wall panel shall be permitted to extend more than 1 foot (305 mm) over an opening not more than 8 feet (2438 mm) wide in the wall below provided that the opening includes a header in accordance with the following:

1. The building width, loading condition and framing member species limitations of Table R502.5(1) shall apply and

2. Not less than one 2×12 or two 2×10 for an opening not more than 4 feet (1219 mm) wide or

3. Not less than two 2×12 or three 2×10 for an opening not more than 6 feet (1829 mm) wide or

4. Not less than three 2×12 or four 2×10 for an opening not more than 8 feet (2438 mm) wide and

5. The entire length of the braced wall panel does not occur over an opening in the wall below.

4. When an opening in a floor or roof exceeds the lesser of 12 feet (3657 mm) or 50 percent of the least floor or roof dimension.

5. When portions of a floor level are vertically offset.

    Exceptions:

    1. Framing supported directly by continuous foundations at the perimeter of the building.

    2. For wood light-frame construction, floors shall be permitted to be vertically offset when the floor framing is lapped or tied together as required by Section R502.6.1.

6. When shear walls and braced wall lines do not occur in two perpendicular directions.

7. When stories above-grade partially or completely braced by wood wall framing in accordance with Section R602 or steel wall framing in accordance with Section R603 include masonry or concrete construction.

    Exception: Fireplaces, chimneys and masonry veneer as permitted by this code.

    When this irregularity applies, the entire story shall be designed in accordance with accepted engineering practice.

R301.2.2.3 Seismic Design Category C. Structures assigned to Seismic Design Category C shall conform to the requirements of this section.

R301.2.2.3.1 Stone and masonry veneer. Stone and masonry veneer shall comply with the requirements of Sections R702.1 and R703.

R301.2.2.3.2 Masonry construction. Masonry construction shall comply with the requirements of Section R606.11.2.

R301.2.2.3.3 Concrete construction. Concrete construction shall comply with the requirements of Section R611 or R612.

R301.2.2.4 Seismic Design Categories D_0, D_1 and D_2. Structures assigned to Seismic Design Categories D_0, D_1 and D_2 shall conform to the requirements for Seismic Design Category C and the additional requirements of this section.

R301.2.2.4.1 Height limitations. Wood framed buildings shall be limited to three stories above grade or the limits given in Table R602.10.1. Cold-formed steel framed buildings shall be limited to two stories above grade in accordance with COFS/PM. Mezzanines as defined in Section 202 shall not be considered as stories.

R301.2.2.4.2 Stone and masonry veneer. Stone and masonry veneer shall comply with the requirements of Sections R702.1 and R703.

R301.2.2.4.3 Masonry construction. Masonry construction in Seismic Design Categories D_0 and D_1 shall comply with the requirements of Section R606.11.3. Masonry construction in Seismic Design Category D_2 shall comply with the requirements of Section R606.11.4.

R301.2.2.4.4 Concrete construction. Buildings with above-grade concrete walls shall be in accordance with Section R611, R612, or designed in accordance with accepted engineering practice.

R301.2.2.4.5 Cold-formed steel framing in Seismic Design Categories D_0, D_1 and D_2. In Seismic Design Categories D_0, D_1 and D_2 in addition to the requirements of this code, cold-formed steel framing shall comply with the requirements of COFS/PM.

R301.2.3 Snow loads. Wood framed construction, cold-formed steel framed construction and masonry and concrete construction in regions with ground snow loads 70 pounds per square foot (3.35 kPa) or less, shall be in accordance with Chapters 5, 6 and 8. Buildings in regions with ground snow loads greater than 70 pounds per square foot (3.35 kPa) shall be designed in accordance with accepted engineering practice.

R301.2.4 Floodplain construction. Buildings and structures constructed in whole or in part in flood hazard areas (including A or V Zones) as established in Table R301.2(1) shall be designed and constructed in accordance with Section R324.

Exception: Buildings and structures located in whole or in part in identified floodways as established in Table R301.2(1) shall be designed and constructed as stipulated in the *International Building Code*.

R301.3 Story height. Buildings constructed in accordance with these provisions shall be limited to story heights of not more than the following:

1. For wood wall framing, the laterally unsupported bearing wall stud height permitted by Table R602.3(5) plus a height of floor framing not to exceed 16 inches.

   Exception: For wood framed wall buildings with bracing in accordance with Table R602.10.1, the wall stud clear height used to determine the maximum permitted story height may be increased to 12 feet without requiring an engineered design for the building wind and seismic force resisting systems provided that the length of bracing required by Table R602.10.1 is increased by multiplying by a factor of 1.20. Wall studs are still subject to the requirements of this section.

2. For steel wall framing, a stud height of 10 feet, plus a height of floor framing not to exceed 16 inches.

3. For masonry walls, a maximum bearing wall clear height of 12 feet plus a height of floor framing not to exceed 16 inches.

   Exception: An additional 8 feet is permitted for gable end walls.

4. For insulating concrete form walls, the maximum bearing wall height per story as permitted by Section 611 tables plus a height of floor framing not to exceed 16 inches.

Individual walls or walls studs shall be permitted to exceed these limits as permitted by Chapter 6 provisions, provided story heights are not exceeded. An engineered design shall be provided for the wall or wall framing members when they exceed the limits of Chapter 6. Where the story height limits are exceeded, an engineered design shall be provided in accordance with the *International Building Code* for the overall wind and seismic force resisting systems.

R301.4 Dead load. The actual weights of materials and construction shall be used for determining dead load with consideration for the dead load of fixed service equipment.

R301.5 Live load. The minimum uniformly distributed live load shall be as provided in Table R301.5.

R301.6 Roof load. The roof shall be designed for the live load indicated in Table R301.6 or the snow load indicated in Table R301.2(1), whichever is greater.

R301.7 Deflection. The allowable deflection of any structural member under the live load listed in Sections R301.5 and R301.6 shall not exceed the values in Table R301.7.

TABLE R301.5
MINIMUM UNIFORMLY DISTRIBUTED LIVE LOADS
(in pounds per square foot)

USE	LIVE LOAD
Attics with limited storage[b, g, h]	20
Attics without storage[b]	10
Decks[e]	40
Exterior balconies	60
Fire escapes	40
Guardrails and handrails[d]	200[i]
Guardrails in–fill components[f]	50[i]
Passenger vehicle garages[a]	50[a]
Rooms other than sleeping rooms	40
Sleeping rooms	30
Stairs	40[c]

For SI: 1 pound per square foot = 0.0479 kPa, 1 square inch = 645 mm^2, 1 pound = 4.45 N.

a. Elevated garage floors shall be capable of supporting a 2,000-pound load applied over a 20-square-inch area.

b. Attics without storage are those where the maximum clear height between joist and rafter is less than 42 inches, or where there are not two or more adjacent trusses with the same web configuration capable of containing a rectangle 42 inches high by 2 feet wide, or greater, located within the plane of the truss. For attics without storage, this live load need not be assumed to act concurrently with any other live load requirements.

c. Individual stair treads shall be designed for the uniformly distributed live load or a 300-pound concentrated load acting over an area of four square inches, whichever produces the greater stresses.

d. A single concentrated load applied in any direction at any point along the top.

e. See Section R502.2.1 for decks attached to exterior walls.

f. Guard in-fill components (all those except the handrail), balusters and panel fillers shall be designed to withstand a horizontally applied normal load of 50 pounds on an area equal to one square foot. This load need not be assumed to act concurrently with any other live load requirement.

g. For attics with limited storage and constructed with trusses, this live load need be applied only to those portions of the bottom chord where there are two or more adjacent trusses with the same web configuration capable of containing a rectangle 42 inches high or greater by 2 feet wide or greater, located within the plane of the truss. The rectangle shall fit between the top of the bottom chord and the bottom of any other truss member, provided that each of the following criteria is met:

   1. The attic area is accessible by a pull-down stairway or framed opening in accordance with Section R807.1;

   2. The truss has a bottom chord pitch less than 2:12; and

   3. Required insulation depth is less than the bottom chord member depth.

   The bottom chords of trusses meeting the above criteria for limited storage shall be designed for the greater of the actual imposed dead load or ten pounds per square foot, uniformly distributed over the entire span.

h. Attic spaces served by a fixed stair shall be designed to support the minimum live load specified for sleeping rooms.

i. Glazing used in handrail assemblies and guards shall be designed with a safety factor of 4. The safety factor shall be applied to each of the concentrated loads applied to the top of the rail, and to the load on the in-fill components. These loads shall be determined independent of one another, and loads are assumed not to occur with any other live load.

TABLE R301.6
MINIMUM ROOF LIVE LOADS IN POUNDS-FORCE
PER SQUARE FOOT OF HORIZONTAL PROJECTION

ROOF SLOPE	TRIBUTARY LOADED AREA IN SQUARE FEET FOR ANY STRUCTURAL MEMBER		
	0 to 200	201 to 600	Over 600
Flat or rise less than 4 inches per foot (1:3)	20	16	12
Rise 4 inches per foot (1:3) to less than 12 inches per foot (1:1)	16	14	12
Rise 12 inches per foot (1:1) and greater	12	12	12

For SI: 1 square foot = 0.0929 m^2, 1 pound per square foot = 0.0479 kPa, 1 inch per foot = 83.3 mm/m.

TABLE R301.7
ALLOWABLE DEFLECTION OF STRUCTURAL MEMBERS[a,b,c]

STRUCTURAL MEMBER	ALLOWABLE DEFLECTION
Rafters having slopes greater than 3/12 with no finished ceiling attached to rafters	L/180
Interior walls and partitions	H/180
Floors and plastered ceilings	L/360
All other structural members	L/240
Exterior walls with plaster or stucco finish	H/360
Exterior walls—wind loads[a] with brittle finishes	L/240
Exterior walls—wind loads[a] with flexible finishes	L/120

Note: L = span length, H = span height.

a. The wind load shall be permitted to be taken as 0.7 times the Component and Cladding loads for the purpose of the determining deflection limits herein.

b. For cantilever members, L shall be taken as twice the length of the cantilever.

c. For aluminum structural members or panels used in roofs or walls of sunroom additions or patio covers, not supporting edge of glass or sandwich panels, the total load deflection shall not exceed L /60. For sandwich panels used in roofs or walls of sunroom additions or patio covers, the total load deflection shall not exceed L/120.

R301.8 Nominal sizes. For the purposes of this code, where dimensions of lumber are specified, they shall be deemed to be nominal dimensions unless specifically designated as actual dimensions.

SECTION R302
EXTERIOR WALL LOCATION

R302.1 Exterior walls. Construction, projections, openings, and penetrations of exterior walls of dwellings and accessory buildings shall comply with Table 302.1. These provisions shall not apply to walls, projections, openings, or penetrations in walls that are perpendicular to the line used to determine the fire separation distance. Projections beyond the exterior shall not extend more than 12 inches (305 mm) into areas where openings are prohibited.

Exceptions:

   1. Detached garages accessory to a dwelling located within 2 feet (610 mm) of a lot line are permitted to

M
N
M
N
M
N
M

have eave projections not exceeding 4 inches (103 mm).

2. Foundation vents installed in compliance with this code are permitted.

SECTION R303
LIGHT, VENTILATION AND HEATING

R303.1 Habitable rooms. All habitable rooms shall have an aggregate glazing area of not less than 8 percent of the floor area of such rooms. Natural ventilation shall be through windows, doors, louvers or other approved openings to the outdoor air. Such openings shall be provided with ready access or shall otherwise be readily controllable by the building occupants. The minimum openable area to the outdoors shall be 4 percent of the floor area being ventilated.

Exceptions:

1. The glazed areas need not be openable where the opening is not required by Section R310 and an approved mechanical ventilation system capable of producing 0.35 air change per hour in the room is installed or a whole-house mechanical ventilation system is installed capable of supplying outdoor ventilation air of 15 cubic feet per minute (cfm) (78 L/s) per occupant computed on the basis of two occupants for the first bedroom and one occupant for each additional bedroom.

2. The glazed areas need not be installed in rooms where Exception 1 above is satisfied and artificial light is provided capable of producing an average illumination of 6 footcandles (65 lux) over the area of the room at a height of 30 inches (762 mm) above the floor level.

3. Use of sunroom additions and patio covers, as defined in Section R202, shall be permitted for natural ventilation if in excess of 40 percent of the exterior sunroom walls are open, or are enclosed only by insect screening.

R303.2 Adjoining rooms. For the purpose of determining light and ventilation requirements, any room shall be considered as a portion of an adjoining room when at least one-half of the area of the common wall is open and unobstructed and provides an opening of not less than one-tenth of the floor area of the interior room but not less than 25 square feet (2.3 m²).

Exception: Openings required for light and/or ventilation shall be permitted to open into a thermally isolated sunroom addition or patio cover, provided that there is an openable area between the adjoining room and the sunroom addition or patio cover of not less than one-tenth of the floor area of the interior room but not less than 20 square feet (2 m²). The minimum openable area to the outdoors shall be based upon the total floor area being ventilated.

R303.3 Bathrooms. Bathrooms, water closet compartments and other similar rooms shall be provided with aggregate glazing area in windows of not less than 3 square feet (0.3 m²), one-half of which must be openable.

Exception: The glazed areas shall not be required where artificial light and a mechanical ventilation system are provided. The minimum ventilation rates shall be 50 cubic feet per minute (24 L/s) for intermittent ventilation or 20 cubic feet per minute (10 L/s) for continuous ventilation. Ventilation air from the space shall be exhausted directly to the outside.

R303.4 Opening location. Outdoor intake and exhaust openings shall be located in accordance with Sections R303.4.1 and R303.4.2.

R303.4.1 Intake openings. Mechanical and gravity outdoor air intake openings shall be located a minimum of 10 feet (3048 mm) from any hazardous or noxious contaminant, such as vents, chimneys, plumbing vents, streets, alleys, parking lots and loading docks, except as otherwise specified in this code. Where a source of contaminant is located within 10 feet (3048 mm) of an intake opening, such opening shall be located a minimum of 2 feet (610 mm) below the contaminant source.

For the purpose of this section, the exhaust from dwelling unit toilet rooms, bathrooms and kitchens shall not be considered as hazardous or noxious.

TABLE R302.1
EXTERIOR WALLS

EXTERIOR WALL ELEMENT		MINIMUM FIRE-RESISTANCE RATING	MINIMUM FIRE SEPARATION DISTANCE
Walls	(Fire-resistance rated)	1 hour with exposure from both sides	0 feet
	(Not fire-resistance rated)	0 hours	5 feet
Projections	(Fire-resistance rated)	1 hour on the underside[a]	4 feet
	(Not fire-resistance rated)	0 hours	5 feet
Openings	Not allowed	N/A	< 3 feet
	25% Maximum of Wall Area	0 hours	3 feet
	Unlimited	0 hours	5 feet
Penetrations	All	Comply with Section R317.3	< 5 feet
		None required	5 feet

N/A = Not Applicable.

[a]1 hour on the underside equates to one layer of ⁵/₈" type X gypsum sheathing. Openings are not allowed.

M
N

M
N

R303.4.2 Exhaust openings. Outside exhaust openings shall be located so as not to create a nuisance. Exhaust air shall not be directed onto walkways.

R303.5 Outside opening protection. Air exhaust and intake openings that terminate outdoors shall be protected with corrosion-resistant screens, louvers or grilles having a minimum opening size of $^{1}/_{4}$ inch (6 mm) and a maximum opening size of $^{1}/_{2}$ inch (13 mm), in any dimension. Openings shall be protected against local weather conditions. Outdoor air exhaust and intake openings shall meet the provisions for exterior wall opening protectives in accordance with this code.

R303.6 Stairway illumination. All interior and exterior stairways shall be provided with a means to illuminate the stairs, including the landings and treads. Interior stairways shall be provided with an artificial light source located in the immediate vicinity of each landing of the stairway. For interior stairs the artificial light sources shall be capable of illuminating treads and landings to levels not less than 1 foot-candle (11 lux) measured at the center of treads and landings. Exterior stairways shall be provided with an artificial light source located in the immediate vicinity of the top landing of the stairway. Exterior stairways providing access to a basement from the outside grade level shall be provided with an artificial light source located in the immediate vicinity of the bottom landing of the stairway.

Exception: An artificial light source is not required at the top and bottom landing, provided an artificial light source is located directly over each stairway section.

R303.6.1 Light activation. Where lighting outlets are installed in interior stairways, there shall be a wall switch at each floor level to control the lighting outlet where the stairway has six or more risers. The illumination of exterior stairways shall be controlled from inside the dwelling unit.

Exception: Lights that are continuously illuminated or automatically controlled.

R303.7 Required glazed openings. Required glazed openings shall open directly onto a street or public alley, or a yard or court located on the same lot as the building.

R303.7.1 Roofed porches. Required glazed openings may face into a roofed porch where the porch abuts a street, yard or court and the longer side of the porch is at least 65 percent open and unobstructed and the ceiling height is not less than 7 feet (2134 mm).

R303.7.2 Sunroom additions. Required glazed openings shall be permitted to open into sunroom additions or patio covers that abut a street, yard or court if in excess of 40 percent of the exterior sunroom walls are open, or are enclosed only by insect screening, and the ceiling height of the sunroom is not less than 7 feet (2134 mm).

R303.8 Required heating. When the winter design temperature in Table R301.2(1) is below 60°F (16°C), every dwelling unit shall be provided with heating facilities capable of maintaining a minimum room temperature of 68°F (20°C) at a point 3 feet (914 mm) above the floor and 2 feet (610 mm) from exterior walls in all habitable rooms at the design temperature. The

installation of one or more portable space heaters shall not be used to achieve compliance with this section.

SECTION R304
MINIMUM ROOM AREAS

R304.1 Minimum area. Every dwelling unit shall have at least one habitable room that shall have not less than 120 square feet (11 m²) of gross floor area.

R304.2 Other rooms. Other habitable rooms shall have a floor area of not less than 70 square feet (6.5 m²).

Exception: Kitchens.

R304.3 Minimum dimensions. Habitable rooms shall not be less than 7 feet (2134 mm) in any horizontal dimension.

Exception: Kitchens.

R304.4 Height effect on room area. Portions of a room with a sloping ceiling measuring less than 5 feet (1524 mm) or a furred ceiling measuring less than 7 feet (2134 mm) from the finished floor to the finished ceiling shall not be considered as contributing to the minimum required habitable area for that room.

SECTION R305
CEILING HEIGHT

R305.1 Minimum height. Habitable rooms, hallways, corridors, bathrooms, toilet rooms, and basements shall have a ceiling height of not less than 7 feet (2134 mm). The required height shall be measured from the finish floor to the lowest projection from the ceiling. Areas or rooms with ceiling heights less than 7 feet (2134 mm) are considered crawl spaces.

Exceptions:

1. Beams and girders spaced not less than 4 feet (1219 mm) on center may project not more than 6 inches (152 mm) below the required ceiling height.

2. Not more than 50 percent of the required floor area of a room or space is permitted to have a sloped ceiling less than 7 feet (2134 mm) in height with no portion of the required floor area less than 5 feet (1524 mm) in height.

SECTION R306
SANITATION

R306.1 Toilet facilities. Every dwelling unit shall be provided with a water closet, lavatory, and a bathtub or shower.

R306.2 Kitchen. Each dwelling unit shall be provided with a kitchen area and every kitchen area shall be provided with a sink.

R306.3 Sewage disposal. All plumbing fixtures shall be connected to a sanitary sewer or to an approved private sewage disposal system.

R306.4 Water supply to fixtures. All plumbing fixtures shall be connected to an approved water supply. Kitchen sinks, lavatories, bathtubs, showers, bidets, laundry tubs and washing machine outlets shall be provided with hot and cold water.

SECTION R307
TOILET, BATH AND SHOWER SPACES

R307.1 Space required. Fixtures shall be spaced as per Figure R307.1.

R307.2 Bathtub and shower spaces. Bathtub and shower floors and walls above bathtubs with installed shower heads and in shower compartments shall be finished with a nonabsorbent surface. Such wall surfaces shall extend to a height of not less than 6 feet (1829 mm) above the floor.

SECTION R308
GLAZING

R308.1 Identification. Except as indicated in Section R308.1.1 each pane of glazing installed in hazardous locations as defined in Section R308.4 shall be provided with a manufacturer's designation specifying who applied the designation, designating the type of glass and the safety glazing standard with which it complies, which is visible in the final installation. The designation shall be acid etched, sandblasted, ceramic-fired, laser etched, embossed, or be of a type which once applied cannot be removed without being destroyed. A label shall be permitted in lieu of the manufacturer's designation.

Exceptions:

1. For other than tempered glass, manufacturer's designations are not required provided the building official approves the use of a certificate, affidavit or other evidence confirming compliance with this code.

2. Tempered spandrel glass is permitted to be identified by the manufacturer with a removable paper designation.

R308.1.1 Identification of multipane assemblies. Multipane assemblies having individual panes not exceeding 1 square foot (0.09 m²) in exposed area shall have at least one pane in the assembly identified in accordance with Section R308.1. All other panes i-n the assembly shall be labeled "16 CFR 1201."

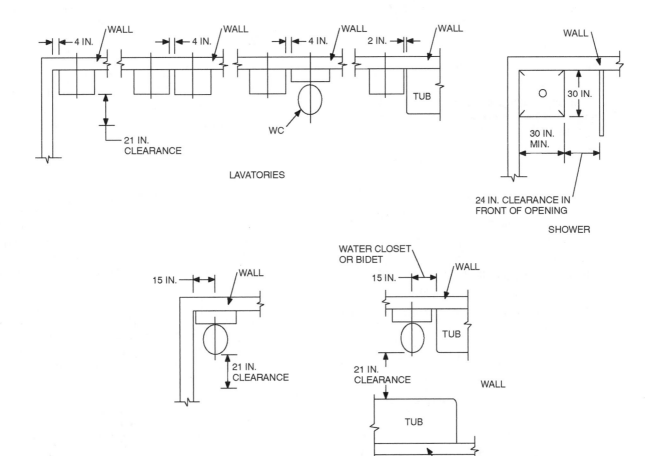

For SI: 1 inch = 25.4 mm.

FIGURE R307.1
MINIMUM FIXTURE CLEARANCES

R308.2 Louvered windows or jalousies. Regular, float, wired or patterned glass in jalousies and louvered windows shall be no thinner than nominal $^3/_{16}$ inch (5 mm) and no longer than 48 inches (1219 mm). Exposed glass edges shall be smooth.

R308.2.1 Wired glass prohibited. Wired glass with wire exposed on longitudinal edges shall not be used in jalousies or louvered windows.

R308.3 Human impact loads. Individual glazed areas, including glass mirrors in hazardous locations such as those indicated as defined in Section R308.4, shall pass the test requirements of CPSC 16 CFR, Part 1201. Glazing shall comply with CPSC 16 CFR, Part 1201 criteria for Category I or Category II as indicated in Table R308.3.

Exception: Louvered windows and jalousies shall comply with Section R308.2.

R308.4 Hazardous locations. The following shall be considered specific hazardous locations for the purposes of glazing:

1. Glazing in swinging doors except jalousies.

2. Glazing in fixed and sliding panels of sliding door assemblies and panels in sliding and bifold closet door assemblies.

3. Glazing in storm doors.

4. Glazing in all unframed swinging doors.

5. Glazing in doors and enclosures for hot tubs, whirlpools, saunas, steam rooms, bathtubs and showers. Glazing in any part of a building wall enclosing these compartments where the bottom exposed edge of the glazing is less than 60 inches (1524 mm) measured vertically above any standing or walking surface.

6. Glazing, in an individual fixed or operable panel adjacent to a door where the nearest vertical edge is within a 24-inch (610 mm) arc of the door in a closed position and whose bottom edge is less than 60 inches (1524 mm) above the floor or walking surface.

7. Glazing in an individual fixed or operable panel, other than those locations described in Items 5 and 6 above, that meets all of the following conditions:

   7.1. Exposed area of an individual pane larger than 9 square feet (0.836 m^2).

   7.2. Bottom edge less than 18 inches (457 mm) above the floor.

   7.3. Top edge more than 36 inches (914 mm) above the floor.

   7.4. One or more walking surfaces within 36 inches (914 mm) horizontally of the glazing.

8. All glazing in railings regardless of an area or height above a walking surface. Included are structural baluster panels and nonstructural infill panels.

9. Glazing in walls and fences enclosing indoor and outdoor swimming pools, hot tubs and spas where the bottom edge of the glazing is less than 60 inches (1524 mm) above a walking surface and within 60 inches (1524 mm) horizontally of the water's edge. This shall apply to single glazing and all panes in multiple glazing.

10. Glazing adjacent to stairways, landings and ramps within 36 inches (914 mm) horizontally of a walking surface when the exposed surface of the glass is less than 60 inches (1524 mm) above the plane of the adjacent walking surface.

11. Glazing adjacent to stairways within 60 inches (1524 mm) horizontally of the bottom tread of a stairway in any direction when the exposed surface of the glass is less than 60 inches (1524 mm) above the nose of the tread.

Exception: The following products, materials and uses are exempt from the above hazardous locations:

1. Openings in doors through which a 3-inch (76 mm) sphere is unable to pass.

2. Decorative glass in Items 1, 6 or 7.

3. Glazing in Section R308.4, Item 6, when there is an intervening wall or other permanent barrier between the door and the glazing.

4. Glazing in Section R308.4, Item 6, in walls perpendicular to the plane of the door in a closed position, other than the wall toward which the door swings when opened, or where access through the door is to a closet or storage area 3 feet (914 mm) or less in depth. Glazing in these applications shall comply with Section R308.4, Item 7.

5. Glazing in Section R308.4, Items 7 and 10, when a protective bar is installed on the accessible side(s) of the glazing 36 inches ± 2 inches (914 mm ± 51 mm) above the floor. The bar shall be capable of withstanding a horizontal load of 50 pounds per linear

TABLE R308.3
MINIMUM CATEGORY CLASSIFICATION OF GLAZING

EXPOSED SURFACE AREA OF ONE SIDE OF ONE LITE	GLAZING IN STORM OR COMBINATION DOORS (Category Class)	GLAZING IN DOORS (Category Class)	GLAZED PANELS REGULATED BY ITEM 7 OF SECTION R308.4 (Category Class)	GLAZED PANELS REGULATED BY ITEM 6 OF SECTION R308.4 (Category Class)	GLAZING IN DOORS AND ENCLOSURES REGULATED BY ITEM 5 OF SECTION R308.4 (Category Class)	SLIDING GLASS DOORS PATIO TYPE (Category Class)
9 sq ft or less	I	I	NR	I	II	II
More than 9 sq ft	II	II	II	II	II	II

For SI: 1 square foot = 0.0929 m^2.
NR means "No Requirement."

foot (730 N/m) without contacting the glass and be a minimum of $1^1/_2$ inches (38 mm) in height.

6. Outboard panes in insulating glass units and other multiple glazed panels in Section R308.4, Item 7, when the bottom edge of the glass is 25 feet (7620 mm) or more above grade, a roof, walking surfaces, or other horizontal [within 45 degrees (0.79 rad) of horizontal] surface adjacent to the glass exterior.

7. Louvered windows and jalousies complying with the requirements of Section R308.2.

8. Mirrors and other glass panels mounted or hung on a surface that provides a continuous backing support.

9. Safety glazing in Section R308.4, Items 10 and 11, is not required where:

　9.1. The side of a stairway, landing or ramp has a guardrail or handrail, including balusters or in-fill panels, complying with the provisions of Sections 1013 and 1607.7 of the *International Building Code*; and

　9.2. The plane of the glass is more than 18 inches (457 mm) from the railing; or

　9.3. When a solid wall or panel extends from the plane of the adjacent walking surface to 34 inches (863 mm) to 36 inches (914 mm) above the floor and the construction at the top of that wall or panel is capable of withstanding the same horizontal load as the protective bar.

10. Glass block panels complying with Section R610.

R308.5 Site built windows. Site built windows shall comply with Section 2404 of the *International Building Code*.

R308.6 Skylights and sloped glazing. Skylights and sloped glazing shall comply with the following sections.

R308.6.1 Definitions.

SKYLIGHTS AND SLOPED GLAZING. Glass or other transparent or translucent glazing material installed at a slope of 15 degrees (0.26 rad) or more from vertical. Glazing materials in skylights, including unit skylights, solariums, sunrooms, roofs and sloped walls are included in this definition.

UNIT SKYLIGHT. A factory assembled, glazed fenestration unit, containing one panel of glazing material, that allows for natural daylighting through an opening in the roof assembly while preserving the weather-resistant barrier of the roof.

R308.6.2 Permitted materials. The following types of glazing may be used:

1. Laminated glass with a minimum 0.015-inch (0.38 mm) polyvinyl butyral interlayer for glass panes 16 square feet (1.5 m²) or less in area located such that the highest point of the glass is not more than 12 feet (3658 mm) above a walking surface or other accessible area; for higher or larger sizes, the minimum interlayer thickness shall be 0.030 inch (0.76 mm).

2. Fully tempered glass.

3. Heat-strengthened glass.

4. Wired glass.

5. Approved rigid plastics.

R308.6.3 Screens, general. For fully tempered or heat-strengthened glass, a retaining screen meeting the requirements of Section R308.6.7 shall be installed below the glass, except for fully tempered glass that meets either condition listed in Section R308.6.5.

R308.6.4 Screens with multiple glazing. When the inboard pane is fully tempered, heat-strengthened or wired glass, a retaining screen meeting the requirements of Section R308.6.7 shall be installed below the glass, except for either condition listed in Section R308.6.5. All other panes in the multiple glazing may be of any type listed in Section R308.6.2.

R308.6.5 Screens not required. Screens shall not be required when fully tempered glass is used as single glazing or the inboard pane in multiple glazing and either of the following conditions are met:

1. Glass area 16 square feet (1.49 m²) or less. Highest point of glass not more than 12 feet (3658 mm) above a walking surface or other accessible area, nominal glass thickness not more than $^3/_{16}$ inch (4.8 mm), and (for multiple glazing only) the other pane or panes fully tempered, laminated or wired glass.

2. Glass area greater than 16 square feet (1.49 m²). Glass sloped 30 degrees (0.52 rad) or less from vertical, and highest point of glass not more than 10 feet (3048 mm) above a walking surface or other accessible area.

R308.6.6 Glass in greenhouses. Any glazing material is permitted to be installed without screening in the sloped areas of greenhouses, provided the greenhouse height at the ridge does not exceed 20 feet (6096 mm) above grade.

R308.6.7 Screen characteristics. The screen and its fastenings shall be capable of supporting twice the weight of the glazing, be firmly and substantially fastened to the framing members, and have a mesh opening of no more than 1 inch by 1 inch (25 mm by 25 mm).

R308.6.8 Curbs for skylights. All unit skylights installed in a roof with a pitch flatter than three units vertical in 12 units horizontal (25-percent slope) shall be mounted on a curb extending at least 4 inches (102 mm) above the plane of the roof unless otherwise specified in the manufacturer's installation instructions.

R308.6.9 Testing and labeling. Unit skylights shall be tested by an approved independent laboratory, and bear a label identifying manufacturer, performance grade rating and approved inspection agency to indicate compliance with the requirements of AAMA/WDMA/CSA 101/I.S.2/A440.

SECTION R309
GARAGES AND CARPORTS

R309.1 Opening protection. Openings from a private garage directly into a room used for sleeping purposes shall not be permitted. Other openings between the garage and residence shall be equipped with solid wood doors not less than $1^3/_8$ inches (35 mm) in thickness, solid or honeycomb core steel doors not less than $1^3/_8$ inches (35 mm) thick, or 20-minute fire-rated doors.

R309.1.1 Duct penetration. Ducts in the garage and ducts penetrating the walls or ceilings separating the dwelling from the garage shall be constructed of a minimum No. 26 gage (0.48 mm) sheet steel or other approved material and shall have no openings into the garage.

R309.1.2 Other penetrations. Penetrations through the separation required in Section R309.2 shall be protected by filling the opening around the penetrating item with approved material to resist the free passage of flame and products of combustion.

R309.2 Separation required. The garage shall be separated from the residence and its attic area by not less than $^1/_2$-inch (12.7 mm) gypsum board applied to the garage side. Garages beneath habitable rooms shall be separated from all habitable rooms above by not less than $^5/_8$-inch (15.9 mm) Type X gypsum board or equivalent. Where the separation is a floor-ceiling assembly, the structure supporting the separation shall also be protected by not less than $^1/_2$-inch (12.7 mm) gypsum board or equivalent. Garages located less than 3 feet (914 mm) from a dwelling unit on the same lot shall be protected with not less than $^1/_2$-inch (12.7 mm) gypsum board applied to the interior side of exterior walls that are within this area. Openings in these walls shall be regulated by Section R309.1. This provision does not apply to garage walls that are perpendicular to the adjacent dwelling unit wall.

R309.3 Floor surface. Garage floor surfaces may be concrete, asphalt, sand, gravel, crushed rock, or natural earth.

R309.4 Carports. Carports shall be open on at least two sides. Carport floor surfaces may be concrete, asphalt, sand, gravel, crushed rock, or natural earth. Carports not open on at least two sides shall be considered a garage and shall comply with the provisions of this section for garages.

R309.5 Flood hazard areas. For buildings located in flood hazard areas as established by Table R301.2(1), garage floors shall be:

1. Elevated to or above the design flood elevation as determined in Section R324; or

2. Located below the design flood elevation provided they are at or above grade on all sides, are used solely for parking, building access, or storage, meet the requirements of Section R324, and are otherwise constructed in accordance with this code.

R309.6 Automatic garage door opening systems. All automatic garage door opening systems that are installed, serviced, or repaired for garages serving residential buildings must comply with the provisions of Minnesota Statutes, sections 325F.82 and 325F.83.

SECTION R310
EMERGENCY ESCAPE AND RESCUE OPENINGS

R310.1 Emergency escape and rescue required. Basements and every sleeping room shall have at least one operable emergency escape and rescue opening. Such opening shall open directly into a public street, public alley, yard or court. Where basements contain one or more sleeping rooms, emergency egress and rescue openings shall be required in each sleeping room, but shall not be required in adjoining areas of the basement. Where emergency escape and rescue openings are provided they shall have a sill height of not more than 44 inches (1118 mm) above the floor. Where a door opening having a threshold below the adjacent ground elevation serves as an emergency escape and rescue opening and is provided with a bulkhead enclosure, the bulkhead enclosure shall comply with Section R310.3. The net clear opening dimensions required by this section shall be obtained by the normal operation of the emergency escape and rescue opening from the inside. Emergency escape and rescue openings with a finished sill height below the adjacent ground elevation shall be provided with a window well in accordance with Section R310.2. Emergency escape and rescue openings shall open directly into a public way, or to a yard or court that opens to a public way.

Exception: Basements used only to house mechanical equipment and not exceeding total floor area of 200 square feet (18.58 m²).

R310.1.1 Minimum opening area. All emergency escape and rescue openings shall have a minimum net clear opening of 5.7 square feet (0.530 m²).

Exception: Grade floor openings shall have a minimum net clear opening of 5 square feet (0.465 m²).

R310.1.2 Minimum opening height. The minimum net clear opening height shall be 24 inches (610 mm).

R310.1.3 Minimum opening width. The minimum net clear opening width shall be 20 inches (508 mm).

R310.1.4 Operational constraints. Emergency escape and rescue openings shall be operational from the inside of the room without the use of keys, tools or special knowledge.

R310.1.5 Replacement windows. Replacement windows installed in buildings meeting the scope of the International Residential Code shall be exempt from the requirements of Sections R310.1, R310.1.1, R310.1.2, and R310.1.3 if the replacement window meets the following conditions:

1. The replacement window is the manufacturer's largest standard size window that will fit within the existing frame or existing rough opening. The replacement window shall be permitted to be of the same operating style as the existing window or a style that provides for a greater window opening area than the existing window;

2. The rooms or areas are not used for any Minnesota state licensed purpose requiring an egress window; and

3. The window is not required to be replaced pursuant to a locally adopted rental housing or rental licensing code.

R310.2 Window wells. The minimum horizontal area of the window well shall be 9 square feet (0.9 m²), with a minimum horizontal projection and width of 36 inches (914 mm). The area of the window well shall allow the emergency escape and rescue opening to be fully opened.

Exception: The ladder or steps required by Section R310.2.1 shall be permitted to encroach a maximum of 6 inches (152 mm) into the required dimensions of the window well.

R310.2.1 Ladder and steps. Window wells with a vertical depth greater than 44 inches (1118 mm) shall be equipped with a permanently affixed ladder or steps usable with the window in the fully open position. Ladders or steps required by this section shall not be required to comply with Sections R311.5 and R311.6. Ladders or rungs shall have an inside width of at least 12 inches (305 mm), shall project at least 3 inches (76 mm) from the wall and shall be spaced not more than 18 inches (457 mm) on center vertically for the full height of the window well.

R310.3 Bulkhead enclosures. Bulkhead enclosures shall provide direct access to the basement. The bulkhead enclosure with the door panels in the fully open position shall provide the minimum net clear opening required by Section R310.1.1. Bulkhead enclosures shall also comply with Section R311.5.8.2.

R310.4 Bars, grilles, covers and screens. Bars, grilles, covers, screens or similar devices are permitted to be placed over emergency escape and rescue openings, bulkhead enclosures, or window wells that serve such openings, provided the minimum net clear opening size complies with Sections R310.1.1 to R310.1.3, and such devices shall be releasable or removable from the inside without the use of a key, tool, special knowledge or force greater than that which is required for normal operation of the escape and rescue opening.

R310.5 Emergency escape windows under decks and porches. Emergency escape windows are allowed to be installed under decks and porches provided the location of the deck allows the emergency escape window to be fully opened and provides a path not less than 36 inches (914 mm) in height to a yard or court.

SECTION R311
MEANS OF EGRESS

R311.1 General. Stairways, ramps, exterior egress balconies, hallways and doors shall comply with this section.

R311.2 Construction.

R311.2.1 Attachment. Required exterior egress balconies, exterior exit stairways and similar means of egress components shall be positively anchored to the primary structure to resist both vertical and lateral forces. Such attachment shall not be accomplished by use of toenails or nails subject to withdrawal.

R311.2.2 Under stair protection. Enclosed accessible space under stairs shall have walls, under stair surface and any soffits protected on the enclosed side with $^1/_2$-inch (13 mm) gypsum board.

R311.3 Hallways. The minimum width of a hallway shall be not less than 3 feet (914 mm).

R311.4 Doors.

R311.4.1 Exit door required. Not less than one exit door conforming to this section shall be provided for each dwelling unit. The required exit door shall provide for direct access from the habitable portions of the dwelling to the exterior without requiring travel through a garage. Access to habitable levels not having an exit in accordance with this section shall be by a ramp in accordance with Section R311.6 or a stairway in accordance with Section R311.5.

R311.4.2 Door type and size. The required exit door shall be a side-hinged door not less than 3 feet (914 mm) in width and 6 feet 8 inches (2032 mm) in height. Other doors shall not be required to comply with these minimum dimensions.

R311.4.3 Landings at doors. Except as provided in this section, there shall be a floor or landing on each side of each exterior door. The width of the landing shall not be less than the door served. The landing shall have a minimum dimension of 36 inches (9114 mm) measured in the direction of travel.

R311.4.3.1 Landings at the exterior exit door required by Section R311.4.1.

1. The floor or landing at the exit door required by Section R311.4.1 shall not be more than 1.5 inches (38 mm) below the top of the threshold, regardless of door swing.

2. The exterior landing shall be up to $7^3/_4$ inches (196 mm) below the top of the threshold, provided the door, other than an exterior storm or screen door, does not swing over the exterior landing.

R311.4.3.2 Landings or floors at exterior doors other than those required by Section R311.4.1.

1. The exterior landing shall be permitted to be no greater than $7^3/_4$ inches (196 mm) below the top of the threshold, provided the door, other than an exterior storm or screen door, does not swing over the exterior landing.

2. Landings in this subsection are not required for the exterior side of a door when a stairway that is less than 30 inches (762 mm) in height is located on the exterior side of the door. The stairway height shall be measured vertically from the interior floor surface to the finished grade.

3. An exterior landing is not required at a doorway when only a storm or screen door is installed which does not swing over the exterior landing.

R311.4.4 Type of lock or latch. All egress doors shall be readily openable from the side from which egress is to be made without the use of a key or special knowledge or effort.

R311.5 Stairways.

R311.5.1 Width. Stairways shall not be less than 36 inches (914 mm) in clear width at all points above the permitted handrail height and below the required headroom height. Handrails shall not project more than 4.5 inches (114 mm) on either side of the stairway and the minimum clear width of the stairway at and below the handrail height, including treads and landings, shall not be less than 31.5 inches (787 mm) where a handrail is installed on one side and 27 inches (698 mm) where handrails are provided on both sides.

Exception: The width of spiral stairways shall be in accordance with Section R311.5.8.

R311.5.2 Headroom. The minimum headroom in all parts of the stairway shall not be less than 6 feet 8 inches (2036 mm) measured vertically from the sloped plane adjoining the tread nosing or from the floor surface of the landing or platform.

R311.5.3 Stair treads and risers.

R311.5.3.1 Riser height. The maximum riser height shall be $7^3/_4$ inches (196 mm). The riser shall be measured vertically between leading edges of the adjacent treads. The greatest riser height within any flight of stairs shall not exceed the smallest by more than $^3/_8$ inch (9.5 mm).

R311.5.3.2 Tread depth. The minimum tread depth shall be 10 inches (254 mm). The tread depth shall be measured horizontally between the vertical planes of the foremost projection of adjacent treads and at a right angle to the tread's leading edge. The greatest tread depth within any flight of stairs shall not exceed the smallest by more than $^3/_8$ inch (9.5 mm). Winder treads shall have a minimum tread depth of 10 inches (254 mm) measured as above at a point 12 inches (305 mm) from the side where the treads are narrower. Winder treads shall have a minimum tread depth of 6 inches (152 mm) at any point. Within any flight of stairs, the largest winder tread depth at the 12 inch (305 mm) walk line shall not exceed the smallest by more than $^3/_8$ inch (9.5 mm).

R311.5.3.3 Profile. The radius of curvature at the leading edge of the tread shall be no greater than $^9/_{16}$ inch (14 mm). A nosing not less than $^3/_4$ inch (19 mm) but not more than $1^1/_4$ inch (32 mm) shall be provided on stairways with solid risers. The greatest nosing projection shall not exceed the smallest nosing projection by more than $^3/_8$ inch (9.5 mm) between two stories, including the nosing at the level of floors and landings. Beveling of nosing shall not exceed $^1/_2$ inch (12.7 mm). Risers shall be vertical or sloped from the underside of the leading edge of the tread above at an angle not more than 30 degrees (0.51 rad) from the vertical. Open risers are permitted, provided that the opening between treads does not permit the passage of a 4-inch diameter (102 mm) sphere.

Exceptions:

1. A nosing is not required where the tread depth is a minimum of 11 inches (279 mm).

2. The opening between adjacent treads is not limited on stairs with a total rise of 30 inches (762 mm) or less.

R311.5.4 Landings for stairways. There shall be a floor or landing at the top and bottom of each stairway.

Exception: A floor or landing is not required at the top of an interior flight of stairs, including stairs in an enclosed garage, provided a door does not swing over the stairs.

A flight of stairs shall not have a vertical rise larger than 12 feet (3658 mm) between floor levels or landings.

The width of each landing shall not be less than the width of the stairway served. Every landing shall have a minimum dimension of 36 inches (914 mm) measured in the direction of travel.

R311.5.5 Stairway walking surface. The walking surface of treads and landings of stairways shall be sloped no steeper than one unit vertical in 48 inches horizontal (2-percent slope).

R311.5.6 Handrails. Handrails shall be provided on at least one side of each continuous run of treads or flight with four or more risers.

R311.5.6.1 Height. Handrail height, measured vertically from the sloped plane adjoining the tread nosing, or finish surface of ramp slope, shall be not less than 34 inches (864 mm) and not more than 38 inches (965 mm).

R311.5.6.2 Continuity. Handrails for stairways shall be continuous for the full length of the flight, from a point directly above the top riser of the flight to a point directly above the lowest riser of the flight. Handrail ends shall be returned or shall terminate in newel posts or safety terminals. Handrails adjacent to a wall shall have a space of not less than $1^1/_2$ inch (38 mm) between the wall and the handrails.

Exceptions:

1. Handrails shall be permitted to be interrupted by a newel post at the turn.

2. The use of a volute, turnout, starting easing or starting newel shall be allowed over the lowest tread.

R311.5.6.3 Handrail grip size. All required handrails shall be of one of the following types or provide equivalent graspability.

1. Type I. Handrails with a circular cross section shall have an outside diameter of at least $1^1/_4$ inches (32 mm) and not greater than 2 inches (51 mm). If the handrail is not circular it shall have a perimeter dimension of at least 4 inches (102 mm) and not greater than $6^1/_4$ inches (160 mm) with a maximum cross section of dimension of $2^1/_4$ inches (57 mm).

2. Type II. Handrails with a perimeter greater than $6^1/_4$ inches (160 mm) shall provide a graspable finger recess area on both sides of the profile. The finger recess shall begin within a distance of $^3/_4$ inch (19 mm) measured vertically from the tallest portion of the profile and achieve a depth of at least $^5/_{16}$ inch (8 mm) within $^7/_8$ inch (22 mm) below the widest portion of the profile. This required depth shall continue for at least $^3/_8$ inch (10 mm) to a level that is not less than $1^3/_4$ inches (45 mm) below the tallest portion of the profile. The minimum width of the handrail above the recess shall be $1^1/_4$ inches (32 mm) to a maximum of $2^3/_4$ inches (70 mm). Edges shall have a minimum radius of 0.01 inch (0.25 mm).

R311.5.7 Illumination. All stairs shall be provided with illumination in accordance with Section R303.6.

R311.5.8 Special stairways. Spiral stairways and bulkhead enclosure stairways shall comply with all requirements of Section R311.5 except as specified below.

R311.5.8.1 Spiral stairways. Spiral stairways are permitted, provided the minimum width shall be 26 inches (660 mm) with each tread having a $7^1/_2$-inches (190 mm) minimum tread depth at 12 inches from the narrower edge. All treads shall be identical, and the rise shall be no more than $9^1/_2$ inches (241 mm). A minimum headroom of 6 feet 6 inches (1982 mm) shall be provided.

R311.5.8.2 Bulkhead enclosure stairways. Stairways serving bulkhead enclosures, not part of the required building egress, providing access from the outside grade level to the basement shall be exempt from the requirements of Sections R311.4.3 and R311.5 where the maximum height from the basement finished floor level to grade adjacent to the stairway does not exceed 8 feet (2438 mm), and the grade level opening to the stairway is covered by a bulkhead enclosure with hinged doors or other approved means.

R311.6 Ramps.

R311.6.1 Maximum slope. Ramps shall have a maximum slope of one unit vertical in twelve units horizontal (8.3-percent slope).

Exception: Where it is technically infeasible to comply because of site constraints, ramps may have a maximum slope of one unit vertical in eight horizontal (12.5 percent slope).

R311.6.2 Landings required. A minimum 3-foot-by-3-foot (914 mm by 914 mm) landing shall be provided:

1. At the top and bottom of ramps.

2. Where doors open onto ramps.

3. Where ramps change direction.

R311.6.3 Handrails required. Handrails shall be provided on at least one side of all ramps exceeding a slope of one unit vertical in 12 units horizontal (8.33-percent slope).

R311.6.3.1 Height. Handrail height, measured above the finished surface of the ramp slope, shall be not less than 34 inches (864 mm) and not more than 38 inches (965 mm).

R311.6.3.2 Handrail grip size. Handrails on ramps shall comply with Section R311.5.6.3.

R311.6.3.3 Continuity. Handrails where required on ramps shall be continuous for the full length of the ramp. Handrail ends shall be returned or shall terminate in newel posts or safety terminals. Handrails adjacent to a wall shall have a space of not less than 1.5 inches (38 mm) between the wall and the handrails.

SECTION R312
GUARDS

R312.1 Guards. Porches, balconies, ramps or raised floor surfaces located more than 30 inches (762 mm) above the floor or grade below shall have guards not less than 36 inches (914 mm) in height. Open sides of stairs with a total rise of more than 30 inches (762 mm) above the floor or grade below shall have guards not less than 34 inches (864 mm) in height measured vertically from the nosing of the treads.

Porches and decks which are enclosed with insect screening shall be equipped with guards where the walking surface is located more than 30 inches (762 mm) above the floor or grade below.

R312.2 Guard opening limitations. Required guards on open sides of stairways, raised floor areas, balconies and porches shall have intermediate rails or ornamental closures which do not allow passage of a sphere 4 inches (102mm) or more in diameter.

Exceptions:

1. The triangular openings formed by the riser, tread and bottom rail of a guard at the open side of a stairway are permitted to be of such a size that a sphere 6 inches (152 mm) cannot pass through.

2. Openings for required guards on the sides of stair treads shall not allow a sphere $4^3/_8$ inches (107 mm) to pass through.

SECTION R313
SMOKE ALARMS

R313.1 Smoke detection and notification. All smoke alarms shall be listed in accordance with UL 217 and installed in accordance with the provisions of this code and the household fire warning equipment provisions of NFPA 72.

Household fire alarm systems installed in accordance with NFPA 72 that include smoke alarms, or a combination of smoke detector and audible notification device installed as required by this section for smoke alarms, shall be permitted. The household fire alarm system shall provide the same level of smoke detection and alarm as required by this section for smoke alarms in the event the fire alarm panel is removed or the system is not connected to a central station.

R313.2 Location. Smoke alarms shall be installed in the following locations:

1. In each sleeping room.

2. Outside each separate sleeping area in the immediate vicinity of the bedrooms.

3. On each additional story of the dwelling, including basements but not including crawl spaces and uninhabitable attics. In dwellings or dwelling units with split levels and without an intervening door between the adjacent levels, a smoke alarm installed on the upper level shall suffice for the adjacent lower level provided that the lower level is less than one full story below the upper level.

When more than one smoke alarm is required to be installed within an individual dwelling unit the alarm devices shall be interconnected in such a manner that the actuation of one alarm will activate all of the alarms in the individual unit.

R313.2.1 Alterations, repairs, or additions. When alterations, repairs, or additions requiring a permit occur, or when one or more sleeping rooms are added or created in existing dwellings, the individual dwelling unit shall be equipped with smoke alarms located as required for new dwellings, and the smoke alarms shall be interconnected and hardwired.

Exceptions:

1. Interconnection and hardwiring of smoke alarms in existing areas shall not be required to be hardwired where the alterations or repairs do not result in the removal of interior wall or ceiling finishes exposing the structure.

2. Work on the exterior surfaces of dwellings, such as the replacement of roofing or siding are exempt from the requirements of this section.

3. Permits involving alterations or repairs to plumbing, electrical, and mechanical are exempt from the requirements of this section.

R313.3 Power source. In new construction, the required smoke alarms shall receive their primary power from the building wiring when such wiring is served from a commercial source, and when primary power is interrupted, shall receive power from a battery. Wiring shall be permanent and without a disconnecting switch other than those required for overcurrent protection. Smoke alarms shall be permitted to be battery operated when installed in buildings without commercial power or in buildings that undergo alterations, repairs or additions regulated by Section R313.2.1.

SECTION R314
FOAM PLASTIC

R314.1 General. The provisions of this section shall govern the materials, design, application, construction and installation of foam plastic materials.

R314.2 Labeling and identification. Packages and containers of foam plastic insulation and foam plastic insulation components delivered to the job site shall bear the label of an approved agency showing the manufacturer's name, the product listing, product identification and information sufficient to determine that the end use will comply with the requirements.

R314.3 Surface burning characteristics. Unless otherwise allowed in Section R314.5 or R314.6, all foam plastic or foam plastic cores used as a component in manufactured assemblies used in building construction shall have a flame spread index of not more than 75 and shall have a smoke-developed index of not more than 450 when tested in the maximum thickness intended for use in accordance with ASTM E 84. Loose-fill-type foam plastic insulation shall be tested as board stock for the flame spread index and smoke-developed index.

Exception: Foam plastic insulation more than 4 inches thick shall have a maximum flame spread index of 75 and a smoke-developed index of 450 where tested at a minimum thickness of 4 inches, provided the end use is approved in accordance with Section R314.6 using the thickness and density intended for use.

R314.4 Thermal barrier. Unless otherwise allowed in Section R314.5 or Section R314.6, foam plastic shall be separated from the interior of a building by an approved thermal barrier of minimum 0.5 inch (12.7 mm) gypsum wallboard or an approved finish material equivalent to a thermal barrier material that will limit the average temperature rise of the unexposed surface to no more than 250°F (139°C) after 15 minutes of fire exposure complying with the ASTM E 119 standard time temperature curve. The thermal barrier shall be installed in such a manner that it will remain in place for 15 minutes based on NFPA 286 with the acceptance criteria of Section R315.4, FM 4880, UL 1040 or UL 1715.

R314.5 Specific requirements. The following requirements shall apply to these uses of foam plastic unless specifically approved in accordance with Section R314.6 or by other sections of the code or the requirements of Sections R314.2 through R314.4 have been met.

R314.5.1 Masonry or concrete construction. The thermal barrier specified in Section R314.4 is not required in a masonry or concrete wall, floor or roof when the foam plastic insulation is separated from the interior of the building by a minimum 1-inch (25 mm) thickness of masonry or concrete.

R314.5.2 Roofing. The thermal barrier specified in Section R314.4 is not required when the foam plastic in a roof assembly or under a roof covering is installed in accordance with the code and the manufacturer's installation instructions and is separated from the interior of the building by tongue-and-groove wood planks or wood structural panel sheathing in accordance with Section R803, not less than $^{15}/_{32}$ inch (11.9 mm) thick bonded with exterior glue and identified as Exposure 1, with edges supported by blocking or tongue-and-groove joints or an equivalent material. The smoke-developed index for roof applications shall not be limited.

R314.5.3 Attics. The thermal barrier specified in Section 314.4 is not required where attic access is required by Section R807.1 and where the space is entered only for service of utilities and when the foam plastic insulation is protected against ignition using one of the following ignition barrier materials:

1. 1.5-inch-thick (38 mm) mineral fiber insulation;

2. 0.25-inch-thick (6.4 mm) wood structural panels;

3. 0.375-inch (9.5 mm) particleboard;

4. 0.25-inch (6.4 mm) hardboard;

5. 0.375-inch (9.5 mm) gypsum board; or

6. Corrosion-resistant steel having a base metal thickness of 0.016 inch (0.406 mm).

The above ignition barrier is not required where the foam plastic insulation has been tested in accordance with Section R314.6.

R314.5.4 Crawl spaces. The thermal barrier specified in Section R314.4 is not required where crawlspace access is required by Section R408.3 and where entry is made only for service of utilities and the foam plastic insulation is protected against ignition using one of the following ignition barrier materials:

1. 1.5-inch-thick (38 mm) mineral fiber insulation;

2. 0.25-inch-thick (6.4 mm) wood structural panels;

3. 0.375-inch (9.5 mm) particleboard;

4. 0.25-inch (6.4 mm) hardboard;

5. 0.375-inch (9.5 mm) gypsum board; or

6. Corrosion-resistant steel having a base metal thickness of 0.016 inch (0.41 mm).

The above ignition barrier is not required where the foam plastic insulation has been tested in accordance with Section R314.6.

R314.5.5 Foam-filled exterior doors. Foam-filled exterior doors are exempt from the requirements of Sections R314.3 and R314.4.

R314.5.6 Foam-filled garage doors. Foam-filled garage doors in attached or detached garages are exempt from the requirements of Sections R314.3 and R314.4.

R314.5.7 Foam backer board. The thermal barrier specified in Section R314.4 is not required where siding backer board foam plastic insulation has a maximum thickness of 0.5 inch (12.7 mm) and a potential heat of not more than 2000 Btu per square foot (22 720 kJ/m^2) when tested in accordance with NFPA 259 provided that:

1. The foam plastic insulation is separated from the interior of the building by not less than 2 inches (51 mm) of mineral fiber insulation or

2. The foam plastic insulation is installed over existing exterior wall finish in conjunction with re-siding or

3. The foam plastic insulation has been tested in accordance with Section R314.6.

R314.5.8 Re-siding. The thermal barrier specified in Section R314.4 is not required where the foam plastic insulation is installed over existing exterior wall finish in conjunction with re-siding provided the foam plastic has a maximum thickness of 0.5 inch (12.7 mm) and a potential heat of not more than 2000 Btu per square foot (22 720 kJ/m^2) when tested in accordance with NFPA 259.

R314.5.9 Interior trim. The thermal barrier specified in Section R314.4 is not required for exposed foam plastic interior trim, provided all of the following are met:

1. The minimum density is 20 pounds per cubic foot (320 kg/m^3).

2. The maximum thickness of the trim is 0.5 inch (12.7 mm) and the maximum width is 8 inches (204 mm).

3. The interior trim shall not constitute more than 10 percent of the aggregate wall and ceiling area of any room or space.

4. The flame spread index does not exceed 75 when tested per ASTM E 84. The smoke-developed index is not limited.

R314.5.10 Interior finish. Foam plastics shall be permitted as interior finish where approved in accordance with R314.6. Foam plastics that are used as interior finish shall also meet the flame spread and smoke-developed requirements of Section R315.

R314.5.11 Sill plate and headers. Foam plastic shall be permitted to be spray-applied to a sill plate and header (rim joist) without thermal barrier subject to all of the following:

1. The maximum thickness of the foam plastic shall not exceed $5^1/_2$ inches (139.5 mm).

2. The foam plastic shall have a flame spread index of 25 or less and an accompanying smoke developed index of 450 or less when tested in accordance with ASTM E 84.

R314.5.12 Sheathing. Foam plastic insulation used as sheathing shall comply with Section R314.3 and Section R314.4. Where the foam plastic sheathing is exposed to the attic space at a gable or kneewall, the provisions of Section R314.5.3 shall apply.

R314.6 Specific approval. Foam plastic not meeting the requirements of Sections R314.3 through R314.5 shall be specifically approved on the basis of one of the following approved tests: NFPA 286 with the acceptance criteria of Section R315.4, FM4880, UL 1040 or UL 1715, or fire tests related to actual end-use configurations. The specific approval shall be based on the actual end use configuration and shall be performed on the finished foam plastic assembly in the maximum thickness intended for use. Assemblies tested shall include seams, joints and other typical details used in the installation of the assembly and shall be tested in the manner intended for use.

R314.7 Termite damage. The use of foam plastics in areas of "very heavy" termite infestation probability shall be in accordance with Section R320.4.

SECTION R315
FLAME SPREAD AND SMOKE DENSITY

R315.1 Wall and ceiling. Wall and ceiling finishes shall have a flame-spread classification of not greater than 200.

Exception: Flame-spread requirements for finishes shall not apply to trim defined as picture molds, chair rails, baseboards and handrails; to doors and windows or their frames; or to materials that are less than $1/_{28}$ inch (0.91 mm) in thickness cemented to the surface of walls or ceilings if these materials have a flame-spread characteristic no greater than paper of this thickness cemented to a noncombustible backing.

R315.2 Smoke-developed index. Wall and ceiling finishes shall have a smoke-developed index of not greater than 450.

R315.3 Testing. Tests shall be made in accordance with ASTM E 84.

R315.4 Alternate test method. As an alternate to having a flame-spread classification of not greater than 200 and a smoke developed index of not greater than 450 when tested in accordance with ASTM E 84, wall and ceiling finishes, other than textiles, shall be permitted to be tested in accordance with NFPA 286. Materials tested in accordance with NFPA 286 shall meet the following criteria:

During the 40 kW exposure, the interior finish shall comply with Item 1. During the 160 kW exposure, the interior finish shall comply with Item 2. During the entire test, the interior finish shall comply with Item 3.

1. During the 40 kW exposure, flames shall not spread to the ceiling.

2. During the 160 kW exposure, the interior finish shall comply with the following:

    2.1. Flame shall not spread to the outer extremity of the sample on any wall or ceiling.

    2.2. Flashover, as defined in NFPA 286, shall not occur.

3. The total smoke released throughout the NFPA 286 test shall not exceed 1,000 m^2.

SECTION R316
INSULATION

R316.1 Insulation. Insulation materials, including facings, such as vapor retarders or vapor permeable membranes installed within floor-ceiling assemblies, roof-ceiling assemblies, wall assemblies, crawl spaces and attics shall have a flame-spread index not to exceed 25 with an accompanying smoke-developed index not to exceed 450 when tested in accordance with ASTM E 84.

Exceptions:

1. When such materials are installed in concealed spaces, the flame-spread and smoke-developed limitations do not apply to the facings, provided that the facing is installed in substantial contact with the unexposed surface of the ceiling, floor or wall finish.

2. Cellulose loose-fill insulation, which is not spray applied, complying with the requirements of Section R316.3, shall only be required to meet the smoke-developed index of not more than 450.

R316.2 Loose-fill insulation. Loose-fill insulation materials that cannot be mounted in the ASTM E 84 apparatus without a screen or artificial supports shall comply with the flame spread and smoke-developed limits of Sections R316.1 and R316.4 when tested in accordance with CAN/ULC S102.2.

Exception: Cellulose loose-fill insulation shall not be required to comply with the flame spread index requirement of CAN/ULC S102.2, provided such insulation complies with the requirements of Section R316.3.

R316.3 Cellulose loose-fill insulation. Cellulose loose-fill insulation shall comply with CPSC 16 CFR, Parts 1209 and 1404. Each package of such insulating material shall be clearly labeled in accordance with CPSC 16 CFR, Parts 1209 and 1404.

R316.4 Exposed attic insulation. All exposed insulation materials installed on attic floors shall have a critical radiant flux not less than 0.12 watt per square centimeter.

R316.5 Testing. Tests for critical radiant flux shall be made in accordance with ASTM E 970.

SECTION R317
DWELLING UNIT SEPARATION

R317.1 Two-family dwellings. Dwelling units in two-family dwellings shall be separated from each other by wall and/or floor assemblies having not less than 1-hour fire-resistance rating when tested in accordance with ASTM E 119. Fire-resistance-rated floor-ceiling and wall assemblies shall extend to and be tight against the exterior wall, and wall assemblies shall extend to and be tight against the exterior wall, and wall assemblies shall extend to the underside of the roof sheathing.

Exceptions:

1. A fire resistance rating of $^1/_2$-hour shall be permitted in buildings equipped throughout with an automatic sprinkler system installed in accordance with NFPA 13.

2. Wall assemblies need not extend through attic spaces when the ceiling is protected by not less than $^5/_8$-inch (15.9 mm) type X gypsum board and an attic draftstop constructed as specified in Section R502.12.1 is provided above and along the wall assembly separating the dwellings. The structural framing supporting the ceiling shall also be protected by not less than $^1/_2$-inch (12.7 mm) gypsum board or equivalent.

R317.1.1 Supporting construction. When floor assemblies are required to be fire-resistance-rated by Section R317.1, the supporting construction of such assemblies shall have an equal or greater fire-resistive rating.

R317.2 Townhouses. Each townhouse shall be considered a separate building and shall be separated by fire-resistance-rated wall assemblies meeting the requirements of Section R302 for exterior walls.

Exception: A common 2-hour fire-resistance-rated wall is permitted for townhouses if such walls do not contain plumbing or mechanical equipment, ducts or vents in the cavity of the common wall. Electrical installations shall be installed in accordance with chapters 33 through 42. Penetrations of electrical outlet boxes shall be in accordance with Section R317.3.

R317.2.1 Continuity. The fire-resistance-rated wall or assembly separating townhouses shall be continuous from the foundation to the underside of the roof sheathing, roof deck, or roof slab and shall extend the full length of the wall including wall extensions through and separating attached accessory structures. Separation shall extend through enclosed soffits, overhangs, and similar projections.

R317.2.2 Parapets. Parapets constructed in accordance with Section R317.2.3 shall be constructed for townhouses as an extension of exterior walls or common walls in accordance with the following:

1. Where roof surfaces adjacent to the wall or walls are at the same elevation, the parapet shall extend not less than 30 inches (762 mm) above the roof surfaces.

2. Where roof surfaces adjacent to the wall or walls are at different elevations and the higher roof is not more than 30 inches (762 mm) above the lower roof, the parapet shall extend not less than 30 inches (762 mm)above the lower roof surface.

   Exception: A parapet is not required in the two cases above when the roof is covered with a minimum class C roof covering, and the roof decking or sheathing is of noncombustible materials or approved fire-retardant-treated wood for a distance of 4 feet (1219 mm) on each side of the wall or walls, or one layer of $^5/_8$-inch (15.9 mm) Type X gypsum board is installed directly beneath the roof decking or sheathing, supported by a minimum of nominal 2-inch (51 mm) ledgers attached to the sides of the roof framing members, for a minimum distance of 4 feet (1220 mm) on each side of the wall or walls.

3. A parapet is not required where roof surfaces adjacent to the wall or walls are at different elevations and the higher roof is more than 30 inches (762 mm) above the lower roof. The common wall construction from the lower roof to the underside of the higher roof deck shall have not less than a 1-hour fire-resistence rating. The wall shall be rated for exposure from both sides.

R317.2.3 Parapet construction. Parapets shall have the same fire-resistance rating as that required for the supporting wall or walls. On any side adjacent to a roof surface, the parapet shall have noncombustible faces for the uppermost 18 inches (457 mm), to include counterflashing and coping materials. Where the roof slopes toward a parapet at slopes greater than two units vertical in 12 units horizontal (16.7-percent slope), the parapet shall extend to the same height as any portion of the roof within a distance of 3 feet (914 mm), but in no case shall the height be less than 30 inches (762 mm).

R317.2.4 Structural independence. Each individual townhouse shall be structurally independent.

Exceptions:

1. Foundations supporting exterior walls or common walls.

2. Structural roof and wall sheathing from each unit may fasten to the common wall framing.

3. Nonstructural wall coverings.

4. Flashing at termination of roof covering over common wall.

5. Townhouses separated by a common 2-hour fire-resistance-rated wall as provided in Section R317.2.

R317.3 Rated penetrations. Penetrations of wall or floor/ceiling assemblies required to be fire-resistance rated in accordance with Section R317.1 or R317.2 shall be protected in accordance with this section.

R317.3.1 Through penetrations. Through penetrations of fire-resistance-rated wall or floor assemblies shall comply with Section R317.3.1.1 or R317.3.1.2.

Exception: Where the penetrating items are steel, ferrous or copper pipes, tubes or conduits, the annular space shall be protected as follows:

1. In concrete or masonry wall or floor assemblies where the penetrating item is a maximum 6 inches (152 mm) nominal diameter and the area of the opening through the wall does not exceed 144 square inches (92 900 mm²), concrete, grout or mortar is permitted where installed to the full thickness of the wall or floor assembly or the thickness required to maintain the fire-resistance rating.

2. The material used to fill the annular space shall prevent the passage of flame and hot gases sufficient to ignite cotton waste where subjected to ASTM E 119 time temperature fire conditions under a minimum positive pressure differential of 0.01 inch of water (3 Pa) at the location of the penetration for the time period equivalent to the fire resistance rating of the construction penetrated.

R317.3.1.1 Fire-resistance-rated assembly. Penetrations shall be installed as tested in the approved fire-resistance-rated assembly.

R317.3.1.2 Penetration firestop system. Penetrations shall be protected by an approved penetration firestop system installed as tested in accordance with ASTM E 814 or UL 1479, with a minimum positive pressure differential of 0.01 inch of water (3 Pa) and shall have an F rating of not less than the required fire-resistance rating of the wall or floor/ceiling assembly penetrated.

R317.3.2 Membrane penetrations. Membrane penetrations shall comply with Section R317.3.1. Where walls are required to have a fire-resistance rating, recessed fixtures shall be so installed such that the required fire resistance will not be reduced.

Exceptions:

1. Membrane penetrations of maximum 2-hour fire-resistance-rated walls and partitions by steel electrical boxes that do not exceed 16 square inches (0.0103 m²) in area provided the aggregate area of the openings through the membrane does not exceed 100 square inches (0.0645 m²) in any 100 square feet (9.29 m²) of wall area. The annular space between the wall membrane and the box shall not exceed $^1/_8$ inch (3.1 mm). Such boxes on opposite sides of the wall shall be separated as follows:

   1.1. By a horizontal distance of not less than 24 inches (610 mm) except at walls or partitions constructed using parallel rows of studs or staggered studs;

1.2. By a horizontal distance of not less than the depth of the wall cavity when the wall cavity is filled with cellulose loose-fill, rockwool or slag mineral wool insulation;

1.3. By solid fire blocking in accordance with Section R602.8.1;

1.4. By protecting both boxes with listed putty pads; or

1.5. By other listed materials and methods.

2. Membrane penetrations by listed electrical boxes of any materials provided the boxes have been tested for use in fire-resistance-rated assemblies and are installed in accordance with the instructions included in the listing. The annular space between the wall membrane and the box shall not exceed $^1/_8$ inch (3.1 mm) unless listed otherwise. Such boxes on opposite sides of the wall shall be separated as follows:

2.1. By a horizontal distance of not less than 24 inches (610 mm) except at walls or partitions constructed using parallel rows of studs or staggered studs;

2.2. By solid fire blocking in accordance with Section R602.8;

2.3. By protecting both boxes with listed putty pads; or

2.4. By other listed materials and methods.

3. The annular space created by the penetration of a fire sprinkler provided it is covered by a metal escutcheon plate.

R317.4 Sound transmission. Wall and floor-ceiling assemblies separating dwelling units, including those separating adjacent townhouse units, shall provide airborne sound insulation for walls, and both airborne and impact sound insulation for floor-ceiling assemblies.

R317.4.1 Airborne sound. Airborne sound insulation for wall and floor-ceiling assemblies shall meet a Sound Transmission Class (STC) rating of 45 when tested in accordance with ASTM E 90. Penetrations or openings in construction assemblies for piping; electrical devices; recessed cabinets; bathtubs; soffits; or heating, ventilating, or exhaust ducts shall be sealed, lined, insulated, or otherwise treated to maintain the required ratings. Dwelling unit entrance doors, which share a common space, shall be tight fitting to the frame and sill.

R317.4.2 Structural-borne sound. Floor/ceiling assemblies between dwelling units or between a dwelling unit and a public or service area within a structure shall have an Impact Insulation Class (IIC) rating of not less than 45 when tested in accordance with ASTM E 492.

R317.4.3 Referenced standards.

R317.4.3.1 ASTM E 90-04 Test Method for Laboratory Measurement of Airborne Sound Transmission Loss of Building Partitions and Elements R317.4.1.

R317.4.3.2 ASTM E 492-04 (1996)e Specification for Laboratory Measurement of Impact Sound Transmission through Floor-Ceiling Assemblies Using the Tapping Machine R317.4.2.

SECTION R318
MOISTURE VAPOR RETARDERS

R318.1 Vapor retarders. In all above grade framed walls, floors, and roof/ceilings comprising elements of the building thermal envelope, a vapor retarder shall be installed on the warm side of the insulation. Vapor retarders installed under a concrete floor slab shall comply with Section R506.2.3.

Exception: In construction where moisture or freezing will not damage the materials.

SECTION R319
PROTECTION AGAINST DECAY

R319.1 Location required. Protection from decay shall be provided in the following locations by the use of naturally durable wood or wood that is preservative treated in accordance with AWPA U1 for the species, product, preservative and end use. Preservatives shall be listed in Section 4 of AWPA U1.

1. Wood joists or the bottom of a wood structural floor when closer than 18 inches (457 mm) or wood girders when closer than 12 inches (305 mm) to the exposed ground in crawl spaces or unexcavated area located within the periphery of the building foundation.

2. All wood framing members that rest on concrete or masonry exterior foundation walls and are less than 8 inches (203 mm) from the exposed ground.

3. Sills and sleepers on a concrete or masonry slab that is in direct contact with the ground unless separated from such slab by an impervious moisture barrier.

4. The ends of wood girders entering exterior masonry or concrete walls having clearances of less than 0.5 inch (12.7 mm) on tops, sides and ends.

5. Wood siding, sheathing and wall framing on the exterior of a building having a clearance of less than 6 inches (152 mm) from the ground.

6. Wood structural members supporting moisture-permeable floors or roofs that are exposed to the weather, such as concrete or masonry slabs, unless separated from such floors or roofs by an impervious moisture barrier.

7. Wood furring strips or other wood framing members attached directly to the interior of exterior masonry walls or concrete walls below grade except where an approved vapor retarder is applied between the wall and the furring strips or framing members.

R319.1.1 Field treatment. Field-cut ends, notches and drilled holes of preservative-treated wood shall be treated in the field in accordance with AWPA M4.

R319.1.2 Ground contact. All wood in contact with the ground, embedded in concrete in direct contact with the ground or embedded in concrete exposed to the weather that supports permanent structures intended for human occupancy shall be approved pressure-preservative-treated wood suitable for ground contact use, except untreated wood may be used where entirely below groundwater level or continuously submerged in fresh water.

R319.1.3 Geographical areas. In geographical areas where experience has demonstrated a specific need, approved naturally durable or pressure-preservative-treated wood shall be used for those portions of wood members that form the structural supports of buildings, balconies, porches or similar permanent building appurtenances when those members are exposed to the weather without adequate protection from a roof, eave, overhang or other covering that would prevent moisture or water accumulation on the surface or at joints between members. Depending on local experience, such members may include:

1. Horizontal members such as girders, joists and decking.

2. Vertical members such as posts, poles and columns.

3. Both horizontal and vertical members.

R319.1.4 Wood columns. Wood columns shall be approved wood of natural decay resistance or approved pressure-preservative-treated wood.

Exceptions:

1. Columns exposed to the weather or in basements when supported by concrete piers or metal pedestals projecting 1 inch (25.4 mm) above a concrete floor or 6 inches (152 mm) above exposed earth and the earth is covered by an approved impervious moisture barrier.

2. Columns in enclosed crawl spaces or unexcavated areas located within the periphery of the building when supported by a concrete pier or metal pedestal at a height more than 8 inches (203mm) from exposed earth and the earth is covered by an impervious moisture barrier.

R319.1.5 Exposed glued-laminated timbers. The portions of glued-laminated timbers that form the structural supports of a building or other structure and are exposed to weather and not properly protected by a roof, eave or similar covering shall be pressure treated with preservative, or be manufactured from naturally durable or preservative-treated wood.

R319.2 Quality mark. Lumber and plywood required to be pressure-preservative-treated in accordance with Section R319.1 shall bear the quality mark of an approved inspection agency that maintains continuing supervision, testing and inspection over the quality of the product and that has been approved by an accreditation body that complies with the requirements of the American Lumber Standard Committee treated wood program.

R319.2.1 Required information. The required quality mark on each piece of pressure-preservative-treated lumber or plywood shall contain the following information:

1. Identification of the treating plant.

2. Type of preservative.

3. The minimum preservative retention.

4. End use for which the product was treated.

5. Standard to which the product was treated.

6. Identity of the approved inspection agency.

7. The designation "Dry," if applicable.

> **Exception:** Quality marks on lumber less than 1 inch (25.4 mm) nominal thickness, or lumber less than nominal 1 inch by 5 inches (25.4 mm by 127 mm) or 2 inches by 4 inches (51 mm by 102 mm) or lumber 36 inches (914 mm) or less in length shall be applied by stamping the faces of exterior pieces or by end labeling not less than 25 percent of the pieces of a bundled unit.

R319.3 Fasteners. Fasteners for pressure-preservative and fire-retardant-treated wood shall be of hot-dipped zinc-coated galvanized steel, stainless steel, silicon bronze or copper. The coating weights for zinc-coated fasteners shall be in accordance with ASTM A 153.

Exceptions:

1. One-half-inch (12.7 mm) diameter or larger steel bolts.

2. Fasteners other than nails and timber rivets shall be permitted to be of mechanically deposited zinc-coated steel with coating weights in accordance with ASTM B 695, Class 55, minimum.

SECTION R320
PROTECTION AGAINST
SUBTERRANEAN TERMITES

R320.1 Subterranean termite control methods. In areas subject to damage from termites as indicated by Table R301.2(1), methods of protection shall be one of the following methods or a combination of these methods:

1. Chemical termiticide treatment, as provided in Section R320.2.

2. Termite baiting system installed and maintained according to the label.

3. Pressure-preservative-treated wood in accordance with the AWPA standards listed in Section R319.1.

4. Naturally termite-resistant wood as provided in Section R320.3.

5. Physical barriers as provided in Section R320.4.

R320.1.1 Quality mark. Lumber and plywood required to be pressure-preservative-treated in accordance with Section R320.1 shall bear the quality mark of an approved inspection agency which maintains continuing supervision, testing and inspection over the quality of the product and which has been approved by an accreditation body which complies with the requirements of the American Lumber Standard Committee treated wood program.

R320.1.2 Field treatment. Field-cut ends, notches, and drilled holes of pressure-preservative-treated wood shall be retreated in the field in accordance with AWPA M4.

R320.2 Chemical termiticide treatment. Chemical termiticide treatment shall include soil treatment and/or field applied wood treatment. The concentration, rate of application and method of treatment of the chemical termiticide shall be in strict accordance with the termiticide label.

R320.3 Naturally resistant wood. Heartwood of redwood and eastern red cedar shall be considered termite resistant.

R320.4 Barriers. Approved physical barriers, such as metal or plastic sheeting or collars specifically designed for termite prevention, shall be installed in a manner to prevent termites from entering the structure. Shields placed on top of an exterior foundation wall are permitted to be used only if in combination with another method of protection.

R320.5 Foam plastic protection. In areas where the probability of termite infestation is "very heavy" as indicated in Figure R301.2(6), extruded and expanded polystyrene, polyisocyanurate and other foam plastics shall not be installed on the exterior face or under interior or exterior foundation walls or slab foundations located below grade. The clearance between foam plastics installed above grade and exposed earth shall be at least 6 inches (152 mm).

Exceptions:

1. Buildings where the structural members of walls, floors, ceilings and roofs are entirely of noncombustible materials or pressure-preservative-treated wood.

2. When in addition to the requirements of Section R320.1, an approved method of protecting the foam plastic and structure from subterranean termite damage is used.

3. On the interior side of basement walls.

SECTION R321
SITE ADDRESS

R321.1 Premises identification. Approved numbers or addresses shall be provided for all new buildings in such a position as to be plainly visible and legible from the street or road fronting the property.

SECTION R322
ACCESSIBILITY

R322.1 Scope. Where there are four or more dwelling units or sleeping units in a single structure, the provisions of Chapter 11 of the *International Building Code* for Group R-3 shall apply.

SECTION R323
ELEVATORS AND PLATFORM LIFTS

R323.1 Elevators. Where provided, passenger elevators, limited-use/limited-application elevators or private residence elevators shall comply with ASME A17.1.

R323.2 Platform lifts. Where provided, platform lifts shall comply with ASME A18.1.

R323.3 Accessibility. Elevators or platform lifts that are part of an accessible route required by Chapter 11 of the *International Building Code*, shall comply with ICC A117.1.

SECTION R324
FLOOD-RESISTANT CONSTRUCTION

R324.1 General. Buildings and structures constructed in whole or in part in flood hazard areas (including A or V Zones) as established in Table R301.2(1) shall be designed and constructed in accordance with the provisions contained in this section.

Exception: Buildings and structures located in whole or in part in identified floodways as established in Table R301.2(1) shall be designed and constructed as stipulated in the *International Building Code*.

R324.1.1 Structural systems. All structural systems of all buildings and structures shall be designed, connected and anchored to resist flotation, collapse or permanent lateral movement due to structural loads and stresses from flooding equal to the design flood elevation.

R324.1.2 Flood-resistant construction. All buildings and structures erected in areas prone to flooding shall be constructed by methods and practices that minimize flood damage.

R324.1.3 Establishing the design flood elevation. The design flood elevation shall be used to define areas prone to flooding, and shall describe, at a minimum, the base flood elevation at the depth of peak elevation of flooding (including wave height) which has a 1 percent (100-year flood) or greater chance of being equaled or exceeded in any given year.

R324.1.3.1 Determination of design flood elevations. If design flood elevations are not specified, the building official is authorized to require the applicant to:

1. Obtain and reasonably use data available from a federal, state or other source; or

2. Determine the design flood elevation in accordance with accepted hydrologic and hydraulic engineering practices used to define special flood hazard areas. Determinations shall be undertaken by a registered design professional who shall document that the technical methods used reflect currently accepted engineering practice. Studies, analyses and computations shall be submitted in sufficient detail to allow thorough review and approval.

R324.1.3.2 Determination of impacts. In riverine flood hazard areas where design flood elevations are specified but floodways have not been designated, the applicant shall demonstrate that the effect of the proposed buildings and structures on design flood elevations, including fill, when combined with all other existing and anticipated flood hazard area encroachments, will not increase the design flood elevation more than 1 foot (305 mm) at any point within the jurisdiction.

R324.1.4 Lowest floor. The lowest floor shall be the floor of the lowest enclosed area, including basement, but excluding any unfinished flood-resistant enclosure that is useable solely for vehicle parking, building access or limited storage provided that such enclosure is not built so as to render the building or structure in violation of this section.

R324.1.5 Protection of mechanical and electrical systems. Electrical systems, equipment and components, and heating, ventilating, air conditioning and plumbing appliances, plumbing fixtures, duct systems, and other service equipment shall be located at or above the design flood elevation. If replaced as part of a substantial improvement, electrical systems, equipment and components, and heating, ventilating, air conditioning, and plumbing appliances, plumbing fixtures, duct systems, and other service equipment shall meet the requirements of this section. Systems, fixtures, and equipment and components shall not be mounted on or penetrate through walls intended to break away under flood loads.

> **Exception:** Electrical systems, equipment and components, and heating, ventilating, air conditioning and plumbing appliances, plumbing fixtures, duct systems, and other service equipment are permitted to be located below the design flood elevation provided that they are designed and installed to prevent water from entering or accumulating within the components and to resist hydrostatic and hydrodynamic loads and stresses, including the effects of buoyancy, during the occurrence of flooding to the design flood elevation in compliance with the flood-resistant construction requirements of the *International Building Code.* Electrical wiring systems are permitted to be located below the design flood elevation provided they conform to the provisions of the electrical part of this code for wet locations.

R324.1.6 Protection of water supply and sanitary sewage systems. New and replacement water supply systems shall be designed to minimize or eliminate infiltration of flood waters into the systems in accordance with the plumbing provisions of this code. New and replacement sanitary sewage systems shall be designed to minimize or eliminate infiltration of floodwaters into systems and discharges from systems into floodwaters in accordance with the plumbing provisions of this code and Chapter 3 of the *International Private Sewage Disposal Code.*

R324.1.7 Flood-resistant materials. Building materials used below the design flood elevation shall comply with the following:

1. All wood, including floor sheathing, shall be pressure-preservative-treated in accordance with AWPA U1 for the species, product, preservative and end use or be the decay-resistant heartwood of redwood, black locust or cedars. Preservatives shall be listed in Section 4 of AWPA U1.

2. Materials and installation methods used for flooring and interior and exterior walls and wall coverings shall conform to the provisions of FEMA/FIA-TB

R324.1.8 Manufactured housing. New or replacement manufactured housing shall be elevated in accordance with Section R324.2 and the anchor and tie-down requirements of Sections AE604 and AE605 of Appendix E shall apply. The foundation and anchorage of manufactured housing to be located in identified flood ways as established in Table R301.2(1) shall be designed and constructed in accordance with the applicable provisions in the *International Building Code.*

R324.1.9 As-built elevation documentation. A registered design professional shall prepare and seal documentation of the elevations specified in Section R324.2 or R324.3.

R324.2 Flood hazard areas (including A Zones). Areas that have been determined to be prone to flooding but not subject to high velocity wave action shall be designated as flood hazard areas. All buildings and structures constructed in whole or in part in flood hazard areas shall be designed and constructed in accordance with Sections R324.2.1 and R324.2.3.

R324.2.1 Elevation requirements.

1. Buildings and structures shall have the lowest floors elevated to or above the design flood elevation.

2. In areas of shallow flooding (AO Zones), buildings and structures shall have the lowest floor (including basement) elevated at least as high above the highest adjacent grade as the depth number specified in feet (mm) on the FIRM, or at least 2 feet (610 mm) if a depth number is not specified.

3. Basement floors that are below grade on all sides shall be elevated to or above the design flood elevation.

Exception: Enclosed areas below the design flood elevation, including basements whose floors are not below grade on all sides, shall meet the requirements of Section R324.2.2.

R324.2.2 Enclosed area below design flood elevation. Enclosed areas, including crawl spaces, that are below the design flood elevation shall:

1. Be used solely for parking of vehicles, building access or storage.

2. Be provided with flood openings that meet the following criteria:

   2.1. There shall be a minimum of two openings on different sides of each enclosed area; if a building has more than one enclosed area below the design flood elevation, each area shall have openings on exterior walls.

   2.2. The total net area of all openings shall be at least 1 square inch (645 mm²) for each square foot (0.093 m²) of enclosed area, or the openings shall be designed and the construction documents shall include a statement that the design and installation will provide for equalization of hydrostatic flood forces on exterior walls by allowing for the automatic entry and exit of floodwaters.

2.3. The bottom of each opening shall be 1 foot (305 mm) or less above the adjacent ground level.

2.4. Openings shall be at least 3 inches (76 mm) in diameter.

2.5. Any louvers, screens or other opening covers shall allow the automatic flow of floodwaters into and out of the enclosed area.

2.6. Openings installed in doors and windows, that meet requirements 2.1 through 2.5, are acceptable; however, doors and windows without installed openings do not meet the requirements of this section.

R324.2.3 Foundation design and construction. Foundation walls for all buildings and structures erected in flood hazard areas shall meet the requirements of Chapter 4.

Exception: Unless designed in accordance with Section R404:

1. The unsupported height of 6-inch (152 mm) plain masonry walls shall be no more than 3 feet (914 mm).

2. The unsupported height of 8-inch (203 mm) plain masonry walls shall be no more than 4 feet (1219 mm).

3. The unsupported height of 8-inch (203 mm) reinforced masonry walls shall be no more than 8 feet (2438 mm).

For the purpose of this exception, unsupported height is the distance from the finished grade of the under-floor space and the top of the wall.

R324.3 Coastal high-hazard areas (including V Zones). Areas that have been determined to be subject to wave heights in excess of 3 feet (914 mm) or subject to high-velocity wave action or wave-induced erosion shall be designated as coastal high-hazard areas. Buildings and structures constructed in whole or in part in coastal high-hazard areas shall be designated and constructed in accordance with Sections R324.3.1 through R324.3.6.

R324.3.1 Location and site preparation.

1. Buildings and structures shall be located landward of the reach of mean high tide.

2. For any alteration of sand dunes and mangrove stands the building official shall require submission of an engineering analysis which demonstrates that the proposed alteration will not increase the potential for flood damage.

R324.3.2 Elevation requirements.

1. All buildings and structures erected within coastal high hazard areas shall be elevated so that the lowest portion of all structural members supporting the lowest floor, with the exception of mat or raft foundations, piling, pile caps, columns, grade beams and

bracing, is located at or above the design flood elevation.

2. Basement floors that are below grade on all sides are prohibited.

3. The use of fill for structural support is prohibited.

4. The placement of fill beneath buildings and structures is prohibited.

Exception: Walls and partitions enclosing areas below the design flood elevation shall meet the requirements of Sections R324.3.4 and R324.3.5.

R324.3.3 Foundations. Buildings and structures erected in coastal high-hazard areas shall be supported on pilings or columns and shall be adequately anchored to those pilings or columns. Pilings shall have adequate soil penetrations to resist the combined wave and wind loads (lateral and uplift). Water loading values used shall be those associated with the design flood. Wind loading values shall be those required by this code. Pile embedment shall include consideration of decreased resistance capacity caused by scour of soil strata surrounding the piling. Pile systems design and installation shall be certified in accordance with Section R324.3.6. Mat, raft or other foundations that support columns shall not be permitted where soil investigations that are required in accordance with Section R401.4 indicate that soil material under the mat, raft or other foundation is subject to scour or erosion from wave-velocity flow conditions. Slabs, pools, pool decks and walkways shall be located and constructed to be structurally independent of buildings and structures and their foundations to prevent transfer of flood loads to the buildings and structures during conditions of flooding, scour or erosion from wave-velocity flow conditions, unless the buildings and structures and their foundation are designed to resist the additional flood load.

R324.3.4 Walls below design flood elevation. Walls and partitions are permitted below the elevated floor, provided that such walls and partitions are not part of the structural support of the building or structure and:

1. Electrical, mechanical, and plumbing system components are not to be mounted on or penetrate through walls that are designed to break away under flood loads; and

2. Are constructed with insect screening or open lattice; or

3. Are designed to break away or collapse without causing collapse, displacement or other structural damage to the elevated portion of the building or supporting foundation system. Such walls, framing and connections shall have a design safe loading resistance of not less than 10 (479 Pa) and no more than 20 pounds per square foot (958 Pa); or

4. Where wind loading values of this code exceed 20 pounds per square foot (958 Pa), the construction documents shall include documentation prepared and sealed by a registered design professional that:

4.1. The walls and partitions below the design flood elevation have been designed to collapse from a water load less than that which would occur during the design flood.

4.2. The elevated portion of the building and supporting foundation system have been designed to withstand the effects of wind and flood loads acting simultaneously on all building components (structural and nonstructural). Water loading values used shall be those associated with the design flood. Wind loading values shall be those required by this code.

R324.3.5 Enclosed areas below design flood elevation. Enclosed areas below the design flood elevation shall be used solely for parking of vehicles, building access or storage.

R324.3.6 Construction documents. The construction documents shall include documentation that is prepared and sealed by a registered design professional that the design and methods of construction to be used meet the applicable criteria of this section.

CHAPTER 4

FOUNDATIONS

SECTION R401
GENERAL

R401.1 Application. The provisions of this chapter shall control the design and construction of the foundation and foundation spaces for all buildings. In addition to the provisions of this chapter, the design and construction of foundations in areas prone to flooding as established by Table R301.2(1) shall meet the provisions of Section R324. Wood foundations shall be designed and installed in accordance with AF&PA Report No. 7.

Exception: The provisions of this chapter shall be permitted to be used for wood foundations only in the following situations:

1. In buildings that have no more than two floors and a roof.

2. When interior basement and foundation walls are constructed at intervals not exceeding 50 feet (15 240 mm).

Wood foundations in Seismic Design Category D_0, D_1 or D_2 shall be designed in accordance with accepted engineering practice.

R401.2 Requirements. Foundation construction shall be capable of accommodating all loads according to Section R301 and of transmitting the resulting loads to the supporting soil. Fill soils that support footings and foundations shall be designed, installed and tested in accordance with accepted engineering practice. Gravel fill used as footings for wood and precast concrete foundations shall comply with Section R403.

R401.3 Drainage. Surface drainage shall be diverted to a storm sewer conveyance or other approved point of collection so as to not create a hazard. Lots shall be graded to drain surface water away from foundation walls. The grade shall fall a minimum of 6 inches (152 mm) within the first 10 feet (3048 mm).

Exception: Where lot lines, walls, slopes or other physical barriers prohibit 6 inches (152 mm) of fall within 10 feet (3048 mm), the final grade shall slope away from the foundation at a minimum slope of 5 percent and the water shall be directed to drains or swales to ensure drainage away from the structure. Swales shall be sloped a minimum of 2 percent when located within 10 feet (3048 mm) of the building foundation. Impervious surfaces within 10 feet (3048 mm) of the building foundation shall be sloped a minimum of 2 percent away from the building.

R401.4 Soil tests. In areas likely to have expansive, compressible, shifting or other unknown soil characteristics, the building official shall determine whether to require a soil test to determine the soil's characteristics at a particular location. This test shall be made by an approved agency using an approved method.

R401.4.1 Geotechnical evaluation. In lieu of a complete geotechnical evaluation, the load-bearing values in Table R401.4.1 shall be assumed.

TABLE R401.4.1
PRESUMPTIVE LOAD–BEARING VALUES OF FOUNDATION MATERIALS[a]

CLASS OF MATERIAL	LOAD-BEARING PRESSURE (pounds per square foot)
Crystalline bedrock	12,000
Sedimentary and foliated rock	4,000
Sandy gravel and/or gravel (GW and GP)	3,000
Sand, silty sand, clayey sand, silty gravel and clayey gravel (SW, SP, SM, SC, GM and GC)	2,000
Clay, sandy clay, silty clay, clayey silt, silt and sandy silt (CL, ML, MH and CH)	1,500[b]

For SI: 1 pound per square foot = 0.0479 kPa.

a. When soil tests are required by Section R401.4, the allowable bearing capacities of the soil shall be part of the recommendations.

b. Where the building official determines that in-place soils with an allowable bearing capacity of less than 1,500 psf are likely to be present at the site, the allowable bearing capacity shall be determined by a soils investigation.

R401.4.2 Compressible or shifting soil. Instead of a complete geotechnical evaluation, when top or subsoils are compressible or shifting, they shall be removed to a depth and width sufficient to assure stable moisture content in each active zone and shall not be used as fill or stabilized within each active zone by chemical, dewatering or presaturation.

SECTION R402
MATERIALS

R402.1 Wood foundations. Wood foundation systems shall be designed and installed in accordance with the provisions of this code.

R402.1.1 Fasteners. Fasteners used below grade to attach plywood to the exterior side of exterior basement or crawlspace wall studs, or fasteners used in knee wall construction, shall be of Type 304 or 316 stainless steel. Fasteners used above grade to attach plywood and all lumber-to-lumber fasteners except those used in knee wall construction shall be of Type 304 or 316 stainless steel, silicon bronze, copper, hot-dipped galvanized (zinc coated) steel nails, or hot-tumbled galvanized (zinc coated) steel nails. Electrogalvanized steel nails and galvanized (zinc coated) steel staples shall not be permitted.

R402.1.2 Wood treatment. All lumber and plywood shall be pressure-preservative treated and dried after treatment in accordance with AWPA U1 (Commodity Specification A, Use Category 4B and Section 5.2), and shall bear the label of an accredited agency. Where lumber and/or plywood is cut or drilled after treatment, the treated surface shall be field treated with copper naphthenate, the concentration of which shall contain a minimum of 2 percent copper metal, by repeated brushing, dipping or soaking until the wood absorbs no more preservative.

R402.2 Concrete. Concrete shall have a minimum specified compressive strength of f'_c, as shown in Table R402.2. Concrete subject to moderate or severe weathering as indicated in Table R301.2(1) shall be air entrained as specified in Table R402.2. The maximum weight of fly ash, other pozzolans, silica fume, slag or blended cements that is included in concrete mixtures for garage floor slabs and for exterior porches, carport slabs and steps that will be exposed to deicing chemicals shall not exceed the percentages of the total weight of cementitious materials specified in Section 4.2.3 of ACI 318. Materials used to produce concrete and testing thereof shall comply with the applicable standards listed in Chapter 3 of ACI 318.

R402.3 Precast concrete. Approved precast concrete foundations shall be designed and installed in accordance with the provisions of this code and the manufacturer's installation instructions.

SECTION R403
FOOTINGS

R403.1 General. All exterior walls shall be supported on continuous solid or fully grouted masonry or concrete footings, wood foundations, or other approved structural systems which shall be of sufficient design to accommodate all loads according to Section R301 and to transmit the resulting loads to the soil within the limitations as determined from the character of the soil. Footings shall be supported on undisturbed natural soils or engineered fill.

TABLE R403.1
MINIMUM WIDTH OF CONCRETE OR MASONRY FOOTINGS
(inches)[a]

	LOAD-BEARING VALUE OF SOIL (psf)			
	1,500	2,000	3,000	≥4,000
Conventional light–frame construction				
1-story	12	12	12	12
2-story	15	12	12	12
3-story	23	17	12	12
4-inch brick veneer over light frame or 8-inch hollow concrete masonry				
1-story	12	12	12	12
2-story	21	16	12	12
3-story	32	24	16	12
8-inch solid or fully grouted masonry				
1-story	16	12	12	12
2-story	29	21	14	12
3-story	42	32	21	16

For SI: 1 inch = 25.4 mm, 1 pound per square foot = 0.0479 kPa.

a. Where minimum footing width is 12 inches, use of a single wythe of solid or fully grouted 12-inch nominal concrete masonry units is permitted.

R403.1.1 Minimum size. Minimum sizes for concrete and masonry footings shall be as set forth in Table R403.1 and Figure R403.1(1). The footing width, W, shall be based on the load-bearing value of the soil in accordance with Table R401.4.1. Spread footings shall be at least 6 inches (152 mm) thick. Footing projections, P, shall be at least 2 inches

TABLE R402.2
MINIMUM SPECIFIED COMPRESSIVE STRENGTH OF CONCRETE

TYPE OR LOCATION OF CONCRETE CONSTRUCTION	MINIMUM SPECIFIED COMPRESSIVE STRENGTH[a] (f'_c)		
	Weathering Potential[b]		
	Negligible	Moderate	Severe
Basement walls, foundations and other concrete not exposed to the weather	2,500	2,500	2,500[c]
Basement slabs and interior slabs on grade, except garage floor slabs	2,500	2,500	2,500[c]
Basement walls, foundation walls, exterior walls and other vertical concrete work exposed to the weather	2,500	3,000[d]	3,000[d]
Porches, carport slabs and steps exposed to the weather, and garage floor slabs	2,500	3,000[d,e,f]	3,500[d,e,f]

For SI: 1 pound per square inch = 6.895 kPa.

a. Strength at 28 days psi.
b. See Table R301.2(1) for weathering potential.
c. Concrete in these locations that may be subject to freezing and thawing during construction shall be air-entrained concrete in accordance with Footnote d.
d. Concrete shall be air-entrained. Total air content (percent by volume of concrete) shall be not less than 5 percent or more than 7 percent.
e. See Section R402.2 for maximum cementitious materials content.
f. For garage floors with a steel troweled finish, reduction of the total air content (percent by volume of concrete) to not less than 3 percent is permitted if the specified compressive strength of the concrete is increased to not less than 4,000 psi.

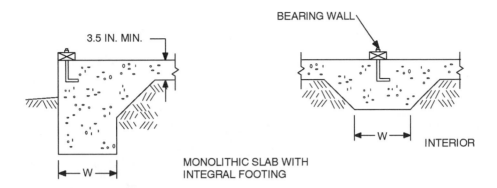

MONOLITHIC SLAB WITH
INTEGRAL FOOTING

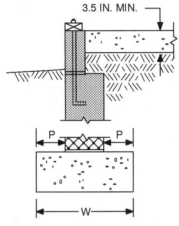

GROUND SUPPORT SLAB
WITH MASONRY WALL
AND SPREAD FOOTING

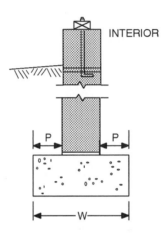

BASEMENT OR CRAWL SPACE
WITH MASONRY WALL AND
SPREAD FOOTING

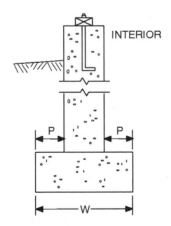

BASEMENT OR CRAWL SPACE
WITH CONCRETE WALL AND
SPREAD FOOTING

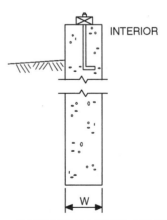

BASEMENT OR CRAWL SPACE
WITH FOUNDATION WALL
BEARING DIRECTLY ON SOIL

For SI: 1 inch = 25.4 mm.

FIGURE R403.1(1)
CONCRETE AND MASONRY FOUNDATION DETAILS

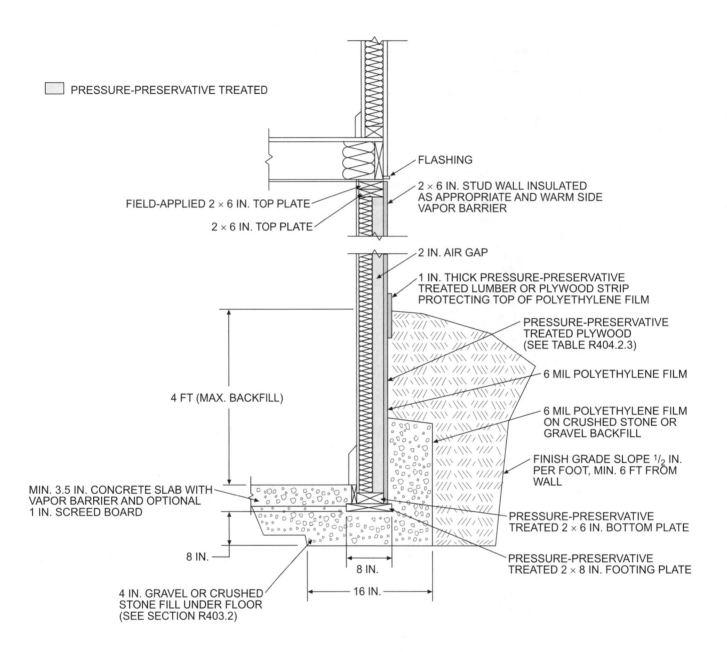

PRESSURE-PRESERVATIVE TREATED

FLASHING

FIELD-APPLIED 2 × 6 IN. TOP PLATE

2 × 6 IN. TOP PLATE

2 × 6 IN. STUD WALL INSULATED AS APPROPRIATE AND WARM SIDE VAPOR BARRIER

2 IN. AIR GAP

1 IN. THICK PRESSURE-PRESERVATIVE TREATED LUMBER OR PLYWOOD STRIP PROTECTING TOP OF POLYETHYLENE FILM

PRESSURE-PRESERVATIVE TREATED PLYWOOD (SEE TABLE R404.2.3)

6 MIL POLYETHYLENE FILM

6 MIL POLYETHYLENE FILM ON CRUSHED STONE OR GRAVEL BACKFILL

FINISH GRADE SLOPE 1/2 IN. PER FOOT, MIN. 6 FT FROM WALL

4 FT (MAX. BACKFILL)

MIN. 3.5 IN. CONCRETE SLAB WITH VAPOR BARRIER AND OPTIONAL 1 IN. SCREED BOARD

PRESSURE-PRESERVATIVE TREATED 2 × 6 IN. BOTTOM PLATE

PRESSURE-PRESERVATIVE TREATED 2 × 8 IN. FOOTING PLATE

8 IN.

8 IN.

16 IN.

4 IN. GRAVEL OR CRUSHED STONE FILL UNDER FLOOR (SEE SECTION R403.2)

For SI: 1 inch 25.4 = mm, 1 foot =304.8, 1 mil =0.0254 mm.

FIGURE R403.1(2)
PERMANENT WOOD FOUNDATION BASEMENT WALL SECTION

(51 mm) and shall not exceed the thickness of the footing. The size of footings supporting piers and columns shall be based on the tributary load and allowable soil pressure in accordance with Table R401.4.1. Footings for wood foundations shall be in accordance with the details set forth in Section R403.2, and Figures R403.1(2) and R403.1(3).

R403.1.2 Continuous footing in Seismic Design Categories D_0, D_1 and D_2. The braced wall panels at exterior walls of buildings located in Seismic Design Categories D_0, D_1

and D_2 shall be supported by continuous footings. All required interior braced wall panels in buildings with plan dimensions greater than 50 feet (15 240 mm) shall also be supported by continuous footings.

R403.1.3 Seismic reinforcing. Concrete footings located in Seismic Design Categories D_0, D_1 and D_2, as established in Table R301.2(1), shall have minimum reinforcement. Bottom reinforcement shall be located a minimum of 3 inches (76 mm) clear from the bottom of the footing.

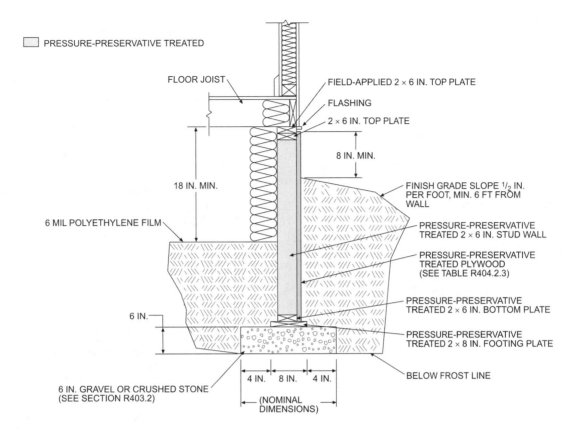

For SI: 1 inch = 25.4 mm, 1 foot = 304.8 mm, 1 mil = 0.0254 mm.

FIGURE R403.1(3)
PERMANENT WOOD FOUNDATION CRAWL SPACE SECTION

In Seismic Design Categories D_0, D_1 and D_2 where a construction joint is created between a concrete footing and a stem wall, a minimum of one No. 4 bar shall be installed at not more than 4 feet (1219 mm) on center. The vertical bar shall extend to 3 inches (76 mm) clear of the bottom of the footing, have a standard hook and extend a minimum of 14 inches (357 mm) into the stem wall.

In Seismic Design Categories D_0, D_1 and D_2 where a grouted masonry stem wall is supported on a concrete footing and stem wall, a minimum of one No. 4 bar shall be installed at not more than 4 feet on center. The vertical bar shall extend to 3 inches (76 mm) clear of the bottom of the footing and have a standard hook.

In Seismic Design Categories D_0, D_1 and D_2 masonry stem walls without solid grout and vertical reinforcing are not permitted.

Exception: In detached one- and two-family dwellings which are three stories or less in height and constructed with stud bearing walls, plain concrete footings without longitudinal reinforcement supporting walls and isolated plain concrete footings supporting columns or pedestals are permitted.

R403.1.3.1 Foundations with stemwalls. Foundations with stem walls shall have installed a minimum of one No. 4 bar within 12 inches (305 mm) of the top of the wall

and one No. 4 bar located 3 inches (76 mm) to 4 inches (102 mm) from the bottom of the footing.

R403.1.3.2 Slabs-on-ground with turned-down footings. Slabs-on-ground with turned-down footings shall have a minimum of one No. 4 bar at the top and bottom of the footing.

Exception: For slabs-on-ground cast monolithically with a footing, one No. 5 bar or two No. 4 bars shall be located in the middle third of the footing depth.

R403.1.4 Minimum depth. All exterior footings shall be placed at least 12 inches (305 mm) below the undisturbed ground surface. Where applicable, the depth of footings shall also conform to Sections R403.1.4.1 through R403.1.4.2.

R403.1.4.1 Frost protection. Except where otherwise protected from frost, foundation walls, piers, and other permanent supports of buildings and structures shall be protected from frost by one or more of the following methods:

1. Extended below the frost line specified in Table R301.2(1);

2. Constructing in accordance with Section R403.3;

3. Constructing in accordance with ASCE 32;

4. Erected on solid rock; or

5. Constructing in accordance with Minnesota Rules, chapter 1303.

Exception: Decks not supported by a dwelling need not be provided with footings that extend below the frost line.

R403.1.4.2 Seismic conditions. In Seismic Design Categories D_0, D_1 and D_2, interior footings supporting bearing or bracing walls and cast monolithically with a slab on grade shall extend to a depth of not less than 12 inches (305 mm) below the top of the slab.

R403.1.5 Slope. The top surface of footings shall be level. The bottom surface of footings shall not have a slope exceeding one unit vertical in 10 units horizontal (10-percent slope). Footings shall be stepped where it is necessary to change the elevation of the top surface of the footings or where the slope of the bottom surface of the footings will exceed one unit vertical in ten units horizontal (10-percent slope).

R403.1.6 Foundation anchorage. When braced wall panels are supported directly on continuous foundations, the wall wood sill plate or cold-formed steel bottom track shall be anchored to the foundation in accordance with this section.

The wood sole plate at exterior walls on monolithic slabs and wood sill plate shall be anchored to the foundation with anchor bolts spaced a maximum of 6 feet (1829 mm) on center. There shall be a minimum of two bolts per plate section with one bolt located not more than 12 inches (305 mm) or less than seven bolt diameters from each end of the plate section. Bolts shall be at least $^1/_2$ inch (12.7 mm) in diameter and shall extend a minimum of 7 inches (178 mm) into masonry or concrete. Interior bearing wall sole plates on monolithic slab foundations shall be positively anchored with approved fasteners. A nut and washer shall be tightened on each bolt to the plate. Sills and sole plates shall be protected against decay and termites where required by Sections R322 and R323. Cold-formed steel framing systems shall be fastened to the wood sill plates or anchored directly to the foundation as required in Section R505.3.1 or R603.1.1. When vertical reinforcing is required by other sections of this code, the foundation anchor bolts shall align with the reinforcing. All anchor bolts installed in masonry shall be grouted in place with at least 1 inch (25 mm) of grout between the bolt and the masonry.

Exceptions:

1. Foundation anchor straps spaced as required to provide equivalent anchorage to $^1/_2$-inch-diameter (12.7 mm) anchor bolts. When vertical reinforcing is required by other sections of this code, the foundation anchor straps shall align with the reinforcing.

2. Walls 24 inches (609.6 mm) total length or shorter connecting offset braced wall panels shall be anchored to the foundation with a minimum of one anchor bolt located in the center third of the plate section and shall be attached to adjacent braced wall panels according to Figure R602.10.5 at corners.

3. Walls 12 inches (304.8 mm) total length or shorter connecting offset braced wall panels shall be permitted to be connected to the foundation without anchor bolts. The wall shall be attached to adjacent braced wall panels according to Figure R602.10.5 at corners.

R403.1.6.1 Foundation anchorage in Seismic Design Categories C, D_0, D_1 and D_2. In addition to the requirements of Section R403.1.6, the following requirements shall apply to wood light-frame structures in Seismic Design Categories D_0, D_1 and D_2 and wood light-frame townhouses in Seismic Design Category C.

1. Plate washers conforming to Section R602.11.1 shall be provided for all anchor bolts over the full length of required braced wall lines. Properly sized cut washers shall be permitted for anchor bolts in wall lines not containing braced wall panels.

2. Interior braced wall plates shall have anchor bolts spaced at not more than 6 feet (1829 mm) on center and located within 12 inches (305 mm) of the ends of each plate section when supported on a continuous foundation.

3. Interior bearing wall sole plates shall have anchor bolts spaced at not more than 6 feet (1829 mm) on center and located within 12 inches (305 mm) of the ends of each plate section when supported on a continuous foundation.

4. The maximum anchor bolt spacing shall be 4 feet (1219 mm) for buildings over two stories in height.

5. Stepped cripple walls shall conform to Section R602.11.3.

6. Where continuous wood foundations in accordance with Section R404.2 are used, the force transfer shall have a capacity equal to or greater than the connections required by Section R602.11.1 or the braced wall panel shall be connected to the wood foundations in accordance with the braced wall panel-to-floor fastening requirements of Table R602.3(1).

R403.1.7 Footings on or adjacent to slopes. The placement of buildings and structures on or adjacent to slopes steeper than 1 unit vertical in 3 units horizontal (33.3-percent slope) shall conform to Sections R403.1.7.1 through R403.1.7.4.

R403.1.7.1 Building clearances from ascending slopes. In general, buildings below slopes shall be set a sufficient distance from the slope to provide protection from slope drainage, erosion and shallow failures. Except as provided in Section R403.1.7.4 and Figure R403.1.7.1, the following criteria will be assumed to provide this protection. Where the existing slope is steeper than one unit vertical in one unit horizontal (100-percent slope), the toe of the slope shall be assumed to be at the intersection of a horizontal plane drawn from the top of the foundation and a plane drawn tangent to the slope at an angle of 45 degrees (0.79 rad) to the horizontal. Where a retaining wall is constructed at the toe of the slope, the height of the slope shall be measured from the top of the wall to the top of the slope.

R403.1.7.2 Footing setback from descending slope surfaces. Footings on or adjacent to slope surfaces shall be founded in material with an embedment and setback from the slope surface sufficient to provide vertical and lateral support for the footing without detrimental settlement. Except as provided for in Section R403.1.7.4 and Figure R403.1.7.1, the following setback is deemed adequate to meet the criteria. Where the slope is steeper than one unit vertical in one unit horizontal (100-percent slope), the required setback shall be measured from an imaginary plane 45 degrees (0.79 rad) to the horizontal, projected upward from the toe of the slope.

R403.1.7.3 Foundation elevation. On graded sites, the top of any exterior foundation shall extend above the elevation of the street gutter at point of discharge or the inlet of an approved drainage device a minimum of 12 inches (305 mm) plus 2 percent. Alternate elevations are permitted subject to the approval of the building official, provided it can be demonstrated that required drainage to the point of discharge and away from the structure is provided at all locations on the site.

R403.1.7.4 Alternate setback and clearances. Alternate setbacks and clearances are permitted, subject to the approval of the building official. The building official is permitted to require an investigation and recommendation of a qualified engineer to demonstrate that the intent of this section has been satisfied. Such an investigation shall include consideration of material, height of slope, slope gradient, load intensity and erosion characteristics of slope material.

R403.1.8 Foundations on expansive soils. Foundation and floor slabs for buildings located on expansive soils shall be designed in accordance with Section 1805.8 of the *International Building Code*.

Exception: Slab-on-ground and other foundation systems which have performed adequately in soil conditions similar to those encountered at the building site are permitted subject to the approval of the building official.

R403.1.8.1 Expansive soils classifications. Soils meeting all four of the following provisions shall be considered expansive, except that tests to show compliance with Items 1, 2 and 3 shall not be required if the test prescribed in Item 4 is conducted:

1. Plasticity Index (PI) of 15 or greater, determined in accordance with ASTM D 4318.

2. More than 10 percent of the soil particles pass a No. 200 sieve (75 mm), determined in accordance with ASTM D 422.

3. More than 10 percent of the soil particles are less than 5 micrometers in size, determined in accordance with ASTM D 422.

4. Expansion Index greater than 20, determined in accordance with ASTM D 4829.

R403.2 Footings for wood foundations. Footings for wood foundations shall be in accordance with Figures R403.1(2) and R403.1(3). Gravel shall be washed and well graded. The maximum size stone shall not exceed $^3/_4$ inch (19.1 mm). Gravel shall be free from organic, clayey or silty soils. Sand shall be coarse, not smaller than $^1/_{16}$-inch (1.6 mm) grains and shall be free from organic, clayey or silty soils. Crushed stone shall have a maximum size of $^1/_2$ inch (12.7 mm).

R403.3 Frost protected shallow foundations. For buildings where the monthly mean temperature of the building is maintained at a minimum of 64°F (18°C), footings are not required to extend below the frost line when protected from frost by insulation in accordance with Figure R403.3(1) and Table R403.3. Foundations protected from frost in accordance with Figure R403.3(1) and Table R403.3 shall not be used for unheated spaces such as porches, utility rooms, garages and carports, and shall not be attached to basements or crawl spaces that are not maintained at a minimum monthly mean temperature of 64°F (18°C).

Materials used below grade for the purpose of insulating footings against frost shall be labeled as complying with ASTM C 578.

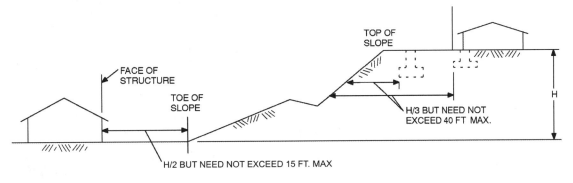

For SI: 1 foot = 304.8 mm.

FIGURE R403.1.7.1
FOUNDATION CLEARANCE FROM SLOPES

TABLE R403.3
MINIMUM INSULATION REQUIREMENTS FOR FROST-PROTECTED FOOTINGS IN HEATED BUILDINGS[a]

AIR FREEZING INDEX (°F-days)[b]	VERTICAL INSULATION R-VALUE[c,d]	HORIZONTAL INSULATION R-VALUE[c,e]		HORIZONTAL INSULATION DIMENSIONS PER FIGURE R403.3(1) (inches)		
		Along walls	At corners	A	B	C
1,500 or less	4.5	Not required	Not required	Not required	Not required	Not required
2,000	5.6	Not required	Not required	Not required	Not required	Not required
2,500	6.7	1.7	4.9	12	24	40
3,000	7.8	6.5	8.6	12	24	40
3,500	9.0	8.0	11.2	24	30	60
4,000	10.1	10.5	13.1	24	36	60

a. Insulation requirements are for protection against frost damage in heated buildings. Greater values may be required to meet energy conservation standards. Interpolation between values is permissible.

b. See Figure R403.3(2) for Air Freezing Index values.

c. Insulation materials shall provide the stated minimum R–values under long-term exposure to moist, below-ground conditions in freezing climates. The following R–values shall be used to determine insulation thicknesses required for this application: Type II expanded polystyrene—2.4R per inch; Type IV extruded polystyrene—4.5R per inch; Type VI extruded polystyrene—4.5R per inch; Type IX expanded polystyrene—3.2R per inch; Type X extruded polystyrene—4.5R per inch.

d. Vertical insulation shall be expanded polystyrene insulation or extruded polystyrene insulation.

e. Horizontal insulation shall be extruded polystyrene insulation.

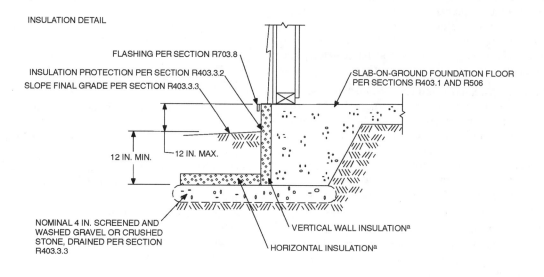

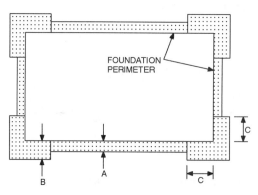

For SI: 1 inch = 25.4 mm.

a. See Table R403.3 for required dimensions and R-values for vertical and horizontal insulation.

FIGURE R403.3(1)
INSULATION PLACEMENT FOR FROST-PROTECTED FOOTINGS IN HEATED BUILDINGS

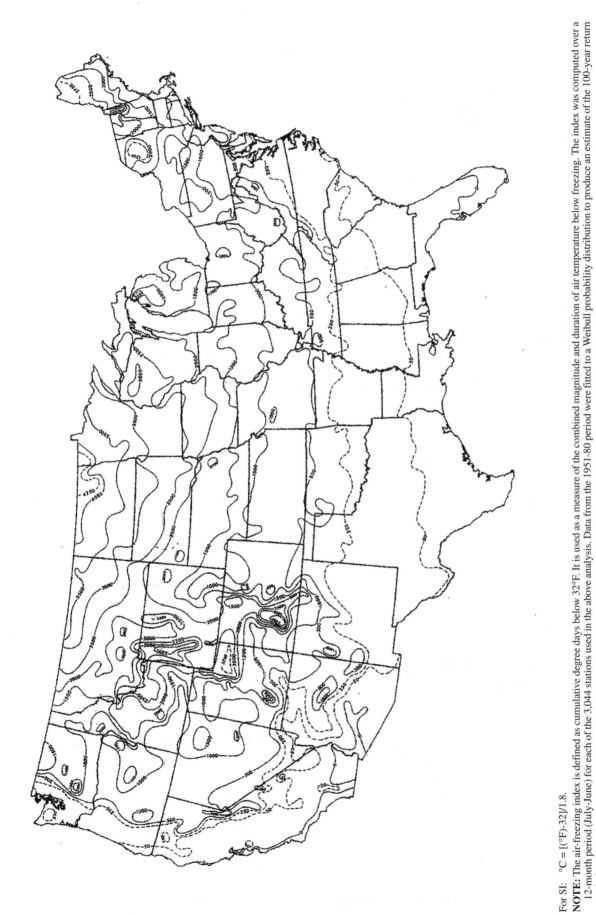

For SI: °C = [(°F)-32]/1.8.

NOTE: The air-freezing index is defined as cumulative degree days below 32°F. It is used as a measure of the combined magnitude and duration of air temperature below freezing. The index was computed over a 12-month period (July-June) for each of the 3,044 stations used in the above analysis. Data from the 1951-80 period were fitted to a Weibull probability distribution to produce an estimate of the 100-year return period.

FIGURE R403.3(2)
AIR–FREEZING INDEX
AN ESTIMATE OF THE 100-YEAR RETURN PERIOD

INSULATION DETAIL

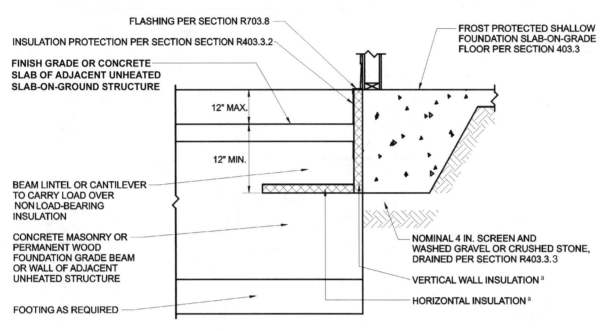

FLASHING PER SECTION R703.8

INSULATION PROTECTION PER SECTION SECTION R403.3.2

FINISH GRADE OR CONCRETE SLAB OF ADJACENT UNHEATED SLAB-ON-GROUND STRUCTURE

FROST PROTECTED SHALLOW FOUNDATION SLAB-ON-GRADE FLOOR PER SECTION 403.3

12" MAX.

12" MIN.

BEAM LINTEL OR CANTILEVER TO CARRY LOAD OVER NON LOAD-BEARING INSULATION

CONCRETE MASONRY OR PERMANENT WOOD FOUNDATION GRADE BEAM OR WALL OF ADJACENT UNHEATED STRUCTURE

NOMINAL 4 IN. SCREEN AND WASHED GRAVEL OR CRUSHED STONE, DRAINED PER SECTION R403.3.3

VERTICAL WALL INSULATION [a]

HORIZONTAL INSULATION [a]

FOOTING AS REQUIRED

HORIZONTAL INSULATION PLAN

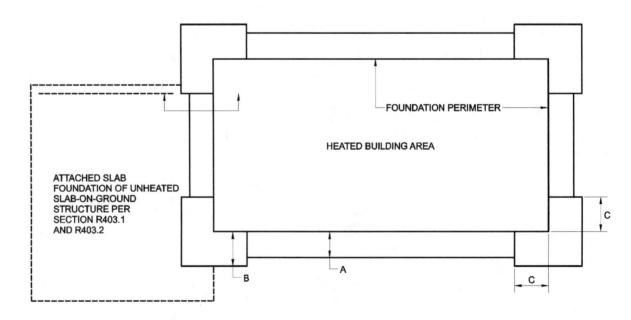

FOUNDATION PERIMETER

HEATED BUILDING AREA

ATTACHED SLAB FOUNDATION OF UNHEATED SLAB-ON-GROUND STRUCTURE PER SECTION R403.1 AND R403.2

C

C

B

A

For SI: 1 inch = 25.4 mm.

a. See Table R403.3 for required dimensions and *R*-values for vertical and horizontal insulation.

FIGURE R403.3(3)
INSULATION PLACEMENT FOR FROST-PROTECTED FOOTINGS

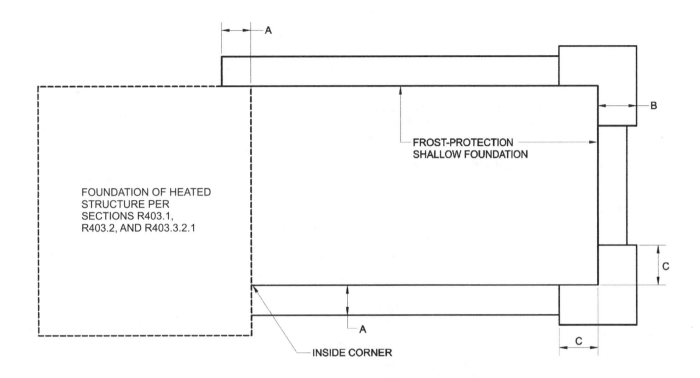

FIGURE R403.3(4)
INSULATION PLACEMENT FOR FROST-PROTECTED
FOOTINGS ADJACENT TO HEATED STRUCTURE

R403.3.1 Foundations adjoining frost protected shallow foundations. Foundations that adjoin frost protected shallow foundations shall be protected from frost in accordance with Section R403.1.4.

R403.3.1.1 Attachment to unheated slab-on-ground structure. Vertical wall insulation and horizontal insulation of frost protected shallow foundations that adjoin a slab-on-ground foundation that does not have a monthly mean temperature maintained at a minimum of 64°F (18°C), shall be in accordance with Figure R403.3(3) and Table R403.3. Vertical wall insulation shall extend between the frost protected shallow foundation and the adjoining slab foundation. Required horizontal insulation shall be continuous under the adjoining slab foundation and through any foundation walls adjoining the frost protected shallow foundation. Where insulation passes through a foundation wall, it shall either be of a type complying with this section and having bearing capacity equal to or greater than the structural loads imposed by the building, or the building shall be designed and constructed using beams, lintels, cantilevers or other means of transferring building loads such that the structural loads of the building do not bear on the insulation.

R403.3.1.2 Attachment to heated structure. Where a frost protected shallow foundation abuts a structure that has a monthly mean temperature maintained at a minimum of 64°F (18°C), horizontal insulation and vertical

wall insulation shall not be required between the frost protected shallow foundation and the adjoining structure. Where the frost protected shallow foundation abuts the heated structure, the horizontal insulation and vertical wall insulation shall extend along the adjoining foundation in accordance with Figure R403.3(4) a distance of not less than Dimension A in Table R403.3.

Exception: Where the frost protected shallow foundation abuts the heated structure to form an inside corner, vertical insulation extending along the adjoining foundation is not required.

R403.3.2 Protection of horizontal insulation below ground. Horizontal insulation placed less than 12 inches (305 mm) below the ground surface or that portion of horizontal insulation extending outward more than 24 inches (610 mm) from the foundation edge shall be protected against damage by use of a concrete slab or asphalt paving on the ground surface directly above the insulation or by cementitious board, plywood rated for below-ground use, or other approved materials placed below ground, directly above the top surface of the insulation.

R403.3.3 Drainage. Final grade shall be sloped in accordance with Section R401.3. In other than Group I Soils, as detailed in Table R405.1, gravel or crushed stone beneath horizontal insulation below ground shall drain to daylight or into an approved sewer system.

R403.3.4 Termite damage. The use of foam plastic in areas of "very heavy" termite infestation probability shall be in accordance with Section R320.5.

SECTION R404
FOUNDATION AND RETAINING WALLS

R404.1 Concrete and masonry foundation walls. Concrete and masonry foundation walls shall be selected and constructed in accordance with the provisions of Section R404 or in accordance with ACI 318, ACI 332, NCMA TR68–A or ACI 530/ASCE 5/TMS 402 or other approved structural standards. When ACI 318, ACI 332 or ACI 530/ASCE 5/TMS 402 or the provisions of Section R404 are used to design concrete or masonry foundation walls, project drawings, typical details and specifications are not required to bear the seal of the architect or engineer responsible for design, unless otherwise required by the state law of the jurisdiction having authority.

Foundation walls that meet all of the following shall be considered laterally supported:

1. Full basement floor shall be 3.5 inches (89 mm) thick concrete slab poured tight against the bottom of the foundation wall.

2. Floor joists and blocking shall be connected to the sill plate at the top of wall by the prescriptive method called out in Table R404.1(1), or; shall be connected with an approved connector with listed capacity meeting Table R404.1(1).

3. Bolt spacing for the sill plate shall be no greater than per Table R404.1(2).

4. Floor shall be blocked perpendicular to the floor joists. Blocking shall be full depth within three joist spaces of the foundation wall.

5. Where foundation walls support unbalanced load on opposite sides of the building, such as a daylight basement, the rim board shall be attached to the sill with a 20 gage metal angle clip at 24 inches on center, with five 8d nails per leg, or an approved connector supplying 230 pounds per linear foot capacity.

R404.1.1 Masonry foundation walls. Concrete masonry and clay masonry foundation walls shall be constructed as set forth in Table 404.1.1(1), R404.1.1(2), R404.1.1(3), or R404.1.1(4) and shall also comply with the provisions of Section R404 and the applicable provisions of Sections R606, R607, and R608. Rubble stone masonry foundation walls shall be constructed in accordance with Sections R404.1.8 and R607.2.2. Cantilevered masonry foundation walls shall be constructed as set forth in Table R404.1.1(6), R404.1.1(7), or R404.1.1(8). Cantilevered means: foundation walls that do not have permanent lateral support at the top.

R404.1.2 Concrete foundation walls. Concrete foundation walls shall be constructed as set forth in Table R404.1.1(5) and shall also comply with the provisions of Section R404 and the applicable provisions of Section R404.2. Cantilevered concrete foundation walls shall be constructed as set forth in Table R404.1.1(6), R404.1.1(7), or R404.1.1(8). Cantilevered means: foundation walls that do not have permanent lateral support at the top.

R404.1.3 Design required. Concrete or masonry foundation walls shall be designed in accordance with accepted engineering practice when either of the following conditions exists:

1. Walls are subject to hydrostatic pressure from groundwater.

2. Walls supporting more than 48 inches (1219 mm) of unbalanced backfill that do not have permanent lateral support at the top or bottom.

> **Exception:** Cantilevered concrete and masonry foundation walls constructed in accordance with Table R404.1.1(6), R404.1.1(7), or R404.1.1(8).

R404.1.4 Seismic Design Categories D_0, D_1 and D_2. In addition to the requirements of Tables R404.1.1(1) and R404.1.1(5), plain concrete and plain masonry foundation walls located in Seismic Design Categories D_0, D_1 and D_2, as established in Table R301.2(1), shall comply with the following.

1. Wall height shall not exceed 8 feet (2438 mm).

2. Unbalanced backfill height shall not exceed 4 feet (1219 mm).

3. Minimum reinforcement for plain concrete foundation walls shall consist of one No. 4 (No. 13) horizontal bar located in the upper 12 inches (305 mm) of the wall.

4. Minimum thickness for plain concrete foundation walls shall be 7.5 inches (191 mm) except that 6 inches (152 mm) is permitted when the maximum height is 4 feet, 6 inches (1372 mm).

5. Minimum nominal thickness for plain masonry foundation walls shall be 8 inches (203 mm).

6. Masonry stem walls shall have a minimum vertical reinforcement of one No. 3 (No. 10) bar located a maximum of 4 feet (1220 mm) on center in grouted cells. Vertical reinforcement shall be tied to the horizontal reinforcement in the footings.

Foundation walls located in Seismic Design Categories D_0, D_1 and D_2, as established in Table R301.2(1), supporting more than 4 feet (1219 mm) of unbalanced backfill or exceeding 8 feet (2438 mm) in height shall be constructed in accordance with Table R404.1.1(2), R404.1.1(3) or R404.1.1(4) for masonry, or Table R404.1.1(5) for concrete. Where Table R404.1.1(5) permits plain concrete walls, not less than No. 4 (No. 13) vertical bars at a spacing not exceeding 48 inches (1219 mm) shall be provided. Insulating concrete form foundation walls shall be reinforced as required in Table R404.4(1), R404.4(2), R404.4(3), R404.4(4) or R404.4(5). Where no vertical reinforcement is required by Table R404.4(2), R404.4(3) or R404.4(4) there shall be a minimum of one No. 4 (No. 13) bar at 48 inches (1220 mm) on center. All concrete and masonry foundation walls shall have two No. 4 (No. 13) horizontal bars located in the upper 12 inches (305 mm) of the wall.

TABLE R404.1(1)
TOP REACTIONS AND PRESCRIPTIVE SUPPORT FOR FOUNDATION WALLS[a]

| MAXIMUM WALL HEIGHT (feet) | MAXIMUM UNBALANCED BACKFILL HEIGHT (feet) | HORIZONTAL REACTION TO TOP (plf) | | |
| | | Soil Classes (Letter indicates connection types[b]) | | |
		GW, GP, SW and SP soils	GM, GC, SM-SC and ML soils	SC, MH, ML-CL and inorganic CL soils
7	4	45.7 A	68.6 A	91.4 A
	5	89.3 A	133.9 B	178.6 B
	6	154.3 B	231.4 C	308.6 C
	7	245.0 C	367.5 C	490.0 D
8	4	40.0 A	60.0 A	80.0 A
	5	78.1 A	117.2 B	156.3 B
	6	135.0 B	202.5 B	270.0 C
	7	214.0 B	321.6 C	428.8 C
	8	320.0 C	480.0 C	640.0 D
9	4	35.6 A	53.3 A	71.1 A
	5	69.4 A	104.2 B	138.9 B
	6	120.0 B	180.0 B	240.0 C
	7	190.6 B	285.8 C	381.1 C
	8	284.4 C	426.7 C	568.9 D
	9	405.0 C	607.5 D	810.0 D

For SI: 1 foot = 304.8 mm, 1 pound = 0.454 kg, 1 plf = pounds per linear foot = 1.488 kg/m.

a. Loads are pounds per linear foot of wall. Prescriptive options are limited to maximum joist and blocking spacing of 24 inches on center.

b. Prescriptive Support Requirements:

Type	Joist/blocking Attachment Requirement
A	3-8d per joist per Table R602.3(1).
B	1-20 gage angle clip each joist with 5-8d per leg.
C	$1\text{-}1/_4$-inch thick steel angle. Horizontal leg attached to sill bolt adjacent to joist/blocking, vertical leg attached to joist/blocking with $1/_2$-inch minimum diameter bolt.
D	$2\text{-}1/_4$-inch thick steel, angles, one on each side of joist/blocking. Attach each angle to adjacent sill bolt through horizontal leg. Bolt to joist/blocking with $1/_2$-inch minimum diameter bolt common to both angles.

TABLE R404.1(2)
MAXIMUM PLATE ANCHOR-BOLT SPACING FOR SUPPORTED FOUNDATION WALL

MAXIMUM WALL HEIGHT (feet)	MAXIMUM UNBALANCED BACKFILL HEIGHT (feet)	SOIL CLASSES	SOIL LOAD (pcf/ft)	TOP OF WALL REACTION (plf)[b]	1/2" DIAMETER ANCHOR BOLT SPACING (inches)[a]
8'-0"	7'-4"	GW, GP, SW and SP	30	250	72
		GM, GC, SM-SC and ML	45	370	72
		SC, HM, ML-CL and I-CL	60	490	48
9'-0"	8'-4"	GW, GP, SW and SP	30	320	72
		GM, GC, SM-SC and ML	45	480	48
		SC, HM, ML-CL and I-CL	60	640	40

For SI: 1 inch = 25.4 mm, 1 foot = 304.8 mm.

a. Sill plate shall be 2 x 6 minimum. Anchor bolt shall be minimum 0.5" diameter cast-in-place with 7" embed. Anchor bolt shall have a 2" diameter by 0.125" thick washer tightened and countersunk 0.25" into the top of the sill plate.

b. Minimum load to be used for sizing of accepted anchors or fasteners if bolts are not used.

TABLE R404.1.1(1)
PLAIN MASONRY FOUNDATION WALLS

MAXIMUM WALL HEIGHT (feet)	MAXIMUM UNBALANCED BACKFILL HEIGHT[c] (feet)	PLAIN MASONRY[a] MINIMUM NOMINAL WALL THICKNESS (inches)		
		Soil classes[b]		
		GW, GP, SW and SP	GM, GC, SM, SM-SC and ML	SC, MH, ML-CL and inorganic CL
5	4	6 solid[d] or 8	6 solid[d] or 8	6 solid[d] or 8
	5	6 solid[d] or 8	8	10
6	4	6 solid[d] or 8	6 solid[d] or 8	6 solid[d] or 8
	5	6 solid[d] or 8	8	10
	6	8	10	12
7	4	6 solid[d] or 8	8	8
	5	6 solid[d] or 8	10	10
	6	10	12	10 solid[d]
	7	12	10 solid[d]	12 solid[d]
8	4	6 solid[d] or 8	6 solid[d] or 8	8
	5	6 solid[d] or 8	10	12
	6	10	12	12 solid[d]
	7	12	12 solid[d]	Footnote e
	8	10 solid[d]	12 solid[d]	Footnote e
9	4	6 solid[d] or 8	6 solid[d] or 8	8
	5	8	10	12
	6	10	12	12 solid[d]
	7	12	12 solid[d]	Footnote e
	8	12 solid[d]	Footnote e	Footnote e
	9	Footnote e	Footnote e	Footnote e

For SI: 1 inch = 25.4 mm, 1 foot = 304.8 mm, 1 pound per square inch = 6.895 Pa.

a. Mortar shall be Type M or S and masonry shall be laid in running bond. Ungrouted hollow masonry units are permitted except where otherwise indicated.

b. Soil classes are in accordance with the Unified Soil Classification System. Refer to Table R405.1.

c. Unbalanced backfill height is the difference in height between the exterior finish ground level and the lower of the top of the concrete footing that supports the foundation wall or the interior finish ground level. Where an interior concrete slab-on-grade is provided and is in contact with the interior surface of the foundation wall, measurement of the unbalanced backfill height from the exterior finish ground level to the top of the interior concrete slab is permitted.

d. Solid grouted hollow units or solid masonry units.

e. Wall construction shall be in accordance with Table R404.1.1(2) or a design shall be provided.

TABLE R404.1.1(2)
8-INCH MASONRY FOUNDATION WALLS WITH REINFORCING
WHERE d > 5 INCHES[a]

WALL HEIGHT	HEIGHT OF UNBALANCED BACKFILL[e]	MINIMUM VERTICAL REINFORCEMENT[b,c]		
		Soil classes and lateral soil load[d] (psf per foot below grade)		
		GW, GP, SW and SP soils 30	GM, GC, SM, SM-SC and ML soils 45	SC, ML-CL and inorganic CL soils 60
6 feet 8 inches	4 feet (or less)	#4 at 48″ o.c.	#4 at 48″ o.c.	#4 at 48″ o.c.
	5 feet	#4 at 48″ o.c.	#4 at 48″ o.c.	#4 at 48″ o.c.
	6 feet 8 inches	#4 at 48″ o.c.	#5 at 48″ o.c.	#6 at 48″ o.c.
7 feet 4 inches	4 feet (or less)	#4 at 48″ o.c.	#4 at 48″ o.c.	#4 at 48″ o.c.
	5 feet	#4 at 48″ o.c.	#4 at 48″ o.c.	#4 at 48″ o.c.
	6 feet	#4 at 48″ o.c.	#5 at 48″ o.c.	#5 at 48″ o.c.
	7 feet 4 inches	#5 at 48″ o.c.	#6 at 48″ o.c.	#6 at 40″ o.c.
8 feet	4 feet (or less)	#4 at 48″ o.c.	#4 at 48″ o.c.	#4 at 48″ o.c.
	5 feet	#4 at 48″ o.c.	#4 at 48″ o.c.	#4 at 48″ o.c.
	6 feet	#4 at 48″ o.c.	#5 at 48″ o.c.	#5 at 48″ o.c.
	7 feet	#5 at 48″ o.c.	#6 at 48″ o.c.	#6 at 40″ o.c.
	8 feet	#5 at 48″ o.c.	#6 at 48″ o.c.	#6 at 32″ o.c.
8 feet 8 inches	4 feet (or less)	#4 at 48″ o.c.	#4 at 48″ o.c.	#4 at 48″ o.c.
	5 feet	#4 at 48″ o.c.	#4 at 48″ o.c.	#5 at 48″ o.c.
	6 feet	#4 at 48″ o.c.	#5 at 48″ o.c.	#6 at 48″ o.c.
	7 feet	#5 at 48″ o.c.	#6 at 48″ o.c.	#6 at 40″ o.c.
	8 feet 8 inches	#6 at 48″ o.c.	#6 at 32″ o.c.	#6 at 24″ o.c.
9 feet 4 inches	4 feet (or less)	#4 at 48″ o.c.	#4 at 48″ o.c.	#4 at 48″ o.c.
	5 feet	#4 at 48″ o.c.	#4 at 48″ o.c.	#5 at 48″ o.c.
	6 feet	#4 at 48″ o.c.	#5 at 48″ o.c.	#6 at 48″ o.c.
	7 feet	#5 at 48″ o.c.	#6 at 48″ o.c.	#6 at 40″ o.c.
	8 feet	#6 at 48″ o.c.	#6 at 40″ o.c.	#6 at 24″ o.c.
	9 feet 4 inches	#6 at 40″ o.c.	#6 at 24″ o.c.	#6 at 16″ o.c.
10 feet	4 feet (or less)	#4 at 48″ o.c.	#4 at 48″ o.c.	#4 at 48″ o.c.
	5 feet	#4 at 48″ o.c.	#4 at 48″ o.c.	#5 at 48″ o.c.
	6 feet	#4 at 48″ o.c.	#5 at 48″ o.c.	#6 at 48″ o.c.
	7 feet	#5 at 48″ o.c.	#6 at 48″ o.c.	#6 at 32″ o.c.
	8 feet	#6 at 48″ o.c.	#6 at 32″ o.c.	#6 at 24″ o.c.
	9 feet	#6 at 40″ o.c.	#6 at 24″ o.c.	#6 at 16″ o.c.
	10 feet	#6 at 32″ o.c.	#6 at 16″ o.c.	#6 at 16″ o.c.

For SI: 1 inch = 25.4 mm, 1 foot = 304.8 mm, 1 pound per square foot per foot = 0.157 kPa/mm.

a. Mortar shall be Type M or S and masonry shall be laid in running bond.

b. Alternative reinforcing bar sizes and spacings having an equivalent cross-sectional area of reinforcement per lineal foot of wall shall be permitted provided the spacing of the reinforcement does not exceed 72 inches.

c. Vertical reinforcement shall be Grade 60 minimum. The distance from the face of the soil side of the wall to the center of vertical reinforcement shall be at least 5 inches.

d. Soil classes are in accordance with the Unified Soil Classification System and design lateral soil loads are for moist conditions without hydrostatic pressure. Refer to Table R405.1.

e. Unbalanced backfill height is the difference in height between the exterior finish ground level and the lower of the top of the concrete footing that supports the foundation wall or the interior finish ground level. Where an interior concrete slab-on-grade is provided and is in contact with the interior surface of the foundation wall, measurement of the unbalanced backfill height from the exterior finish ground level to the top of the interior concrete slab is permitted.

TABLE R404.1.1(3)
10-INCH MASONRY FOUNDATION WALLS WITH REINFORCING
WHERE d > 6.75 INCHES[a]

WALL HEIGHT	HEIGHT OF UNBALANCED BACKFILL[e]	MINIMUM VERTICAL REINFORCEMENT[b, c]		
		Soil classes and later soil load[d] (psf per foot below grade)		
		GW, GP, SW and SP soils 30	GM, GC, SM, SM-SC and ML soils 45	SC, MH, ML-CL and inorganic CL soils 60
6 feet 8 inches	4 feet (or less)	#4 at 56″ o.c.	#4 at 56″ o.c.	#4 at 56″ o.c.
	5 feet	#4 at 56″ o.c.	#4 at 56″ o.c.	#4 at 56″ o.c.
	6 feet 8 inches	#4 at 56″ o.c.	#5 at 56″ o.c.	#5 at 56″ o.c.
7 feet 4 inches	4 feet (or less)	#4 at 56″ o.c.	#4 at 56″ o.c.	#4 at 56″ o.c.
	5 feet	#4 at 56″ o.c.	#4 at 56″ o.c.	#4 at 56″ o.c.
	6 feet	#4 at 56″ o.c.	#4 at 56″ o.c.	#5 at 56″ o.c.
	7 feet 4 inches	#4 at 56″ o.c.	#5 at 56″ o.c.	#6 at 56″ o.c.
8 feet	4 feet (or less)	#4 at 56″ o.c.	#4 at 56″ o.c.	#4 at 56″ o.c.
	5 feet	#4 at 56″ o.c.	#4 at 56″ o.c.	#4 at 56″ o.c.
	6 feet	#4 at 56″ o.c.	#4 at 56″ o.c.	#5 at 56″ o.c.
	7 feet	#4 at 56″ o.c.	#5 at 56″ o.c.	#6 at 56″ o.c.
	8 feet	#5 at 56″ o.c.	#6 at 56″ o.c.	#6 at 48″ o.c.
8 feet 8 inches	4 feet (or less)	#4 at 56″ o.c.	#4 at 56″ o.c.	#4 at 56″ o.c.
	5 feet	#4 at 56″ o.c.	#4 at 56″ o.c.	#4 at 56″ o.c.
	6 feet	#4 at 56″ o.c.	#4 at 56″ o.c.	#5 at 56″ o.c.
	7 feet	#4 at 56″ o.c.	#5 at 56″ o.c.	#6 at 56″ o.c.
	8 feet 8 inches	#5 at 56″ o.c.	#6 at 48″ o.c.	#6 at 32″ o.c.
9 feet 4 inches	4 feet (or less)	#4 at 56″ o.c.	#4 at 56″ o.c.	#4 at 56″ o.c.
	5 feet	#4 at 56″ o.c.	#4 at 56″ o.c.	#4 at 56″ o.c.
	6 feet	#4 at 56″ o.c.	#5 at 56″ o.c.	#5 at 56″ o.c.
	7 feet	#4 at 56″ o.c.	#5 at 56″ o.c.	#6 at 56″ o.c.
	8 feet	#5 at 56″ o.c.	#6 at 56″ o.c.	#6 at 40″ o.c.
	9 feet 4 inches	#6 at 56″ o.c.	#6 at 40″ o.c.	#6 at 24″ o.c.
10 feet	4 feet (or less)	#4 at 56″ o.c.	#4 at 56″ o.c.	#4 at 56″ o.c.
	5 feet	#4 at 56″ o.c.	#4 at 56″ o.c.	#4 at 56″ o.c.
	6 feet	#4 at 56″ o.c.	#5 at 56″ o.c.	#5 at 56″ o.c.
	7 feet	#5 at 56″ o.c.	#6 at 56″ o.c.	#6 at 48″ o.c.
	8 feet	#5 at 56″ o.c.	#6 at 48″ o.c.	#6 at 40″ o.c.
	9 feet	#6 at 56″ o.c.	#6 at 40″ o.c.	#6 at 24″ o.c.
	10 feet	#6 at 48″ o.c.	#6 at 32″ o.c.	#6 at 24″ o.c.

For SI: 1 inch = 25.4 mm, 1 foot = 304.8 mm, 1 pound per square foot per foot = 0.157 kPa/mm.

a. Mortar shall be Type M or S and masonry shall be laid in running bond.

b. Alternative reinforcing bar sizes and spacings having an equivalent cross-sectional area of reinforcement per lineal foot of wall shall be permitted provided the spacing of the reinforcement does not exceed 72 inches.

c. Vertical reinforcement shall be Grade 60 minimum. The distance from the face of the soil side of the wall to the center of vertical reinforcement shall be at least 6.75 inches.

d. Soil classes are in accordance with the Unified Soil Classification System and design lateral soil loads are for moist conditions without hydrostatic pressure. Refer to Table R405.1.

e. Unbalanced backfill height is the difference in height between the exterior finish ground level and the lower of the top of the concrete footing that supports the foundation wall or the interior finish ground level. Where an interior concrete slab-on-grade is provided and is in contact with the interior surface of the foundation wall, measurement of the unbalanced backfill height from the exterior finish ground level to the top of the interior concrete slab is permitted.

2007 MINNESOTA STATE RESIDENTIAL CODE

TABLE R404.1.1(4)
12-INCH MASONRY FOUNDATION WALLS WITH REINFORCING
WHERE d > 8.75 INCHES[a]

WALL HEIGHT	HEIGHT OF UNBALANCED BACKFILL[e]	MINIMUM VERTICAL REINFORCEMENT[b, c]		
		Soil classes and lateral soil load[d] (psf per foot below grade)		
		GW, GP, SW and SP soils 30	GM, GC, SM, SM-SC and ML soils 45	SC, ML-CL and inorganic CL soils 60
6 feet 8 inches	4 feet (or less)	#4 at 72″ o.c.	#4 at 72″ o.c.	#4 at 72″ o.c.
	5 feet	#4 at 72″ o.c.	#4 at 72″ o.c.	#4 at 72″ o.c.
	6 feet 8 inches	#4 at 72″ o.c.	#4 at 72″ o.c.	#5 at 72″ o.c.
7 feet 4 inches	4 feet (or less)	#4 at 72″ o.c.	#4 at 72″ o.c.	#4 at 72″ o.c.
	5 feet	#4 at 72″ o.c.	#4 at 72″ o.c.	#4 at 72″ o.c.
	6 feet	#4 at 72″ o.c.	#4 at 72″ o.c.	#5 at 72″ o.c.
	7 feet 4 inches	#4 at 72″ o.c.	#5 at 72″ o.c.	#6 at 72″ o.c.
8 feet	4 feet (or less)	#4 at 72″ o.c.	#4 at 72″ o.c.	#4 at 72″ o.c.
	5 feet	#4 at 72″ o.c.	#4 at 72″ o.c.	#4 at 72″ o.c.
	6 feet	#4 at 72″ o.c.	#4 at 72″ o.c.	#5 at 72″ o.c.
	7 feet	#4 at 72″ o.c.	#5 at 72″ o.c.	#6 at 72″ o.c.
	8 feet	#5 at 72″ o.c.	#6 at 72″ o.c.	#6 at 64″ o.c.
8 feet 8 inches	4 feet (or less)	#4 at 72″ o.c.	#4 at 72″ o.c.	#4 at 72″ o.c.
	5 feet	#4 at 72″ o.c.	#4 at 72″ o.c.	#4 at 72″ o.c.
	6 feet	#4 at 72″ o.c.	#4 at 72″ o.c.	#5 at 72″ o.c.
	7 feet	#4 at 72″ o.c.	#5 at 72″ o.c.	#6 at 72″ o.c.
	8 feet 8 inches	#5 at 72″ o.c.	#7 at 72″ o.c.	#6 at 48″ o.c.
9 feet 4 inches	4 feet (or less)	#4 at 72″ o.c.	#4 at 72″ o.c.	#4 at 72″ o.c.
	5 feet	#4 at 72″ o.c.	#4 at 72″ o.c.	#4 at 72″ o.c.
	6 feet	#4 at 72″ o.c.	#5 at 72″ o.c.	#5 at 72″ o.c.
	7 feet	#4 at 72″ o.c.	#5 at 72″ o.c.	#6 at 72″ o.c.
	8 feet	#5 at 72″ o.c.	#6 at 72″ o.c.	#6 at 56″ o.c.
	9 feet 4 inches	#6 at 72″ o.c.	#6 at 48″ o.c.	#6 at 40″ o.c.
10 feet	4 feet (or less)	#4 at 72″ o.c.	#4 at 72″ o.c.	#4 at 72″ o.c.
	5 feet	#4 at 72″ o.c.	#4 at 72″ o.c.	#4 at 72″ o.c.
	6 feet	#4 at 72″ o.c.	#5 at 72″ o.c.	#5 at 72″ o.c.
	7 feet	#4 at 72″ o.c.	#6 at 72″ o.c.	#6 at 72″ o.c.
	8 feet	#5 at 72″ o.c.	#6 at 72″ o.c.	#6 at 48″ o.c.
	9 feet	#6 at 72″ o.c.	#6 at 56″ o.c.	#6 at 40″ o.c.
	10 feet	#6 at 64″ o.c.	#6 at 40″ o.c.	#6 at 32″ o.c.

For SI: 1 inch = 25.4 mm, 1 foot = 304.8 mm, 1 pound per square foot per foot = 0.157 kPa/mm.

a. Mortar shall be Type M or S and masonry shall be laid in running bond.

b. Alternative reinforcing bar sizes and spacings having an equivalent cross-sectional area of reinforcement per lineal foot of wall shall be permitted provided the spacing of the reinforcement does not exceed 72 inches.

c. Vertical reinforcement shall be Grade 60 minimum. The distance from the face of the soil side of the wall to the center of vertical reinforcement shall be at least 8.75 inches.

d. Soil classes are in accordance with the Unified Soil Classification System and design lateral soil loads are for moist conditions without hydrostatic pressure. Refer to Table R405.1.

e. Unbalanced backfill height is the difference in height between the exterior finish ground level and the lower of the top of the concrete footing that supports the foundation wall or the interior finish ground levels. Where an interior concrete slab-on-grade is provided and in contact with the interior surface of the foundation wall, measurement of the unbalanced backfill height is permitted to be measured from the exterior finish ground level to the top of the interior concrete slab is permitted.

TABLE R404.1.1(5)
CONCRETE FOUNDATION WALLS[h, i, j, k]

		MINIMUM VERTICAL REINFORCEMENT SIZE AND SPACING[c, d, e, f, l]											
		Soil classes[a] and design lateral soil (psf per foot of depth)											
MAXIMUM WALL HEIGHT (feet)	MAXIMUM UNBALANCED BACKFILL HEIGHT[b] (feet)	GW, GP, SW and SP 30				GM, GC, SM, SM-SC and ML 45				SC, ML-CL and inorganic CL 60			
		Minimum wall thickness (inches)											
		5.5	7.5	9.5	11.5	5.5	7.5	9.5	11.5	5.5	7.5	9.5	11.5
5	4	PC	PC	PC	PC	PC	PC	PC	PC	PC	PC	PC	PC
	5	PC	PC	PC	PC	PC	PC	PC	PC	PC	PC	PC	PC
6	4	PC	PC	PC	PC	PC	PC	PC	PC	PC	PC	PC	PC
	5	PC	PC	PC	PC	PC	PC^g	PC	PC	#4@35"	PC^g	PC	PC
	6	PC	PC	PC	PC	#5@48"	PC	PC	PC	#5@36"	PC	PC	PC
7	4	PC	PC	PC	PC	PC	PC	PC	PC	PC	PC	PC	PC
	5	PC	PC	PC	PC	PC	PC	PC	PC	#5@47"	PC	PC	PC
	6	PC	PC	PC	PC	#5@42"	PC	PC	PC	#6@43"	#5@48"	PC^g	PC
	7	#5@46"	PC	PC	PC	#6@42"	#5@46"	PC^g	PC	#6@34"	#6@48"	PC	PC
8	4	PC	PC	PC	PC	PC	PC	PC	PC	PC	PC	PC	PC
	5	PC	PC	PC	PC	#4@38"	PC^g	PC	PC	#5@43"	PC	PC	PC
	6	#4@37"	PC^g	PC	PC	#5@37"	PC	PC	PC	#6@37"	#5@43"	PC^g	PC
	7	#5@40"	PC	PC	PC	#6@37"	#5@41"	PC	PC	#6@34"	#6@43"	PC	PC
	8	#6@43"	#5@47"	PC^g	PC	#6@34"	#6@43"	PC	PC	#6@27"	#6@32"	#6@44"	PC
9	4	PC	PC	PC	PC	PC	PC	PC	PC	PC	PC	PC	PC
	5	PC	PC	PC	PC	#4@35"	PC^g	PC	PC	#5@40"	PC	PC^e	PC
	6	#4@34"	PC^g	PC	PC	#6@48"	PC	PC	PC	#6@36"	#5@39"	PC^g	PC
	7	#5@36"	PC	PC	PC	#6@34"	#5@37"	PC	PC	#6@33"	#6@38"	#5@37"	PC^g
	8	#6@38"	#5@41"	PC^g	PC	#6@33"	#6@38"	#5@37"	PC^g	#6@24"	#7@39"	#6@39"	#4@48"^h
	9	#6@34"	#6@46"	PC	PC	#6@26"	#7@41"	#6@41"	PC	#6@19"	#7@31"	#7@41"	#6@39"
10	4	PC	PC	PC	PC	PC	PC	PC	PC	PC	PC	PC	PC
	5	PC	PC	PC	PC	#4@33"	PC^g	PC	PC	#5@38"	PC	PC	PC
	6	#5@48"	PC^g	PC	PC	#6@45"	PC	PC	PC	#6@34"	#5@37"	PC	PC
	7	#6@47"	PC	PC	PC	#6@34"	#6@48"	PC	PC	#6@30"	#6@35"	#6@48"	PC^g
	8	#6@34"	#5@38"	PC	PC	#6@30"	#7@47"	#6@47"	PC^g	#6@22"	#7@35"	#7@48"	#6@45"^h
	9	#6@34"	#6@41"	#4@48"	PC^g	#6@23"	#7@37"	#7@48"	#4@48"^h	DR	#6@22"	#7@37"	#7@47"
	10	#6@28"	#7@45"	#6@45"	PC	DR	#7@31"	#7@40"	#6@38"	DR	#6@22"	#7@30"	#7@38"

For SI: 1 inch = 25.4 mm, 1 foot = 304.8 mm, 1 pound per square foot = 0.0479 kPa; 1 pound per square foot per foot = 0.157 kPa/mm.

a. Soil classes are in accordance with the United Soil Classification System. Refer to Table R405.1

b. Unbalanced backfill height is the difference in height of the exterior and interior finish ground levels. Where there is an interior concrete slab, the unbalanced backfill height shall be measured from the exterior finish ground level to the top of the interior concrete slab.

c. The size and spacing of vertical reinforcement shown in the table is based on the use of reinforcement with a minimum yield strength of 60,000 psi. Vertical reinforcement with a minimum yield strength of 40,000 psi or 50,000 psi is permitted, provided the same size bar is used and the spacing shown in the table is reduced by multiplying the spacing by 0.67 or 0.83, respectively.

d. Vertical reinforcement, when required, shall be placed nearest the inside face of the wall a distance d from the outside face (soil side) of the wall. The distance d is equal to the wall thickness, t, minus 1.25 inches plus one-half the bar diameter, db (d = t - (1.25 + db/2). The reinforcement shall be placed within a tolerance of $\pm\,^3/_8$ inch where d is less than or equal to 8 inches, or $\pm\,^1/_2$ inch where d is greater than 8 inches.

e. In lieu of the reinforcement shown, smaller reinforcing bar sizes and closer spacings resulting in an equivalent cross-sectional area of reinforcement per linear foot of wall are permitted.

f. Concrete cover for reinforcement measured from the inside face of the wall shall not be less than $^3/_4$ inch. Concrete cover for reinforcement measured from the outside face of the wall shall not be less than $1^1/_2$ inches for No. 5 bars and smaller, and not less than 2 inches for larger bars.

g. The minimum thickness is permitted to be reduced 2 inches, provided the minimum specified compressive strength of concrete f_c', is 4,000 psi.

(continued)

TABLE R404.1.1(5)—continued
CONCRETE FOUNDATION WALLS[h, l, j, k]

h. A plain concrete wall with a minimum thickness of 11.5 inches is permitted, provided minimum specified compressive strength of concrete, f_c', is 3,500 psi.

i. Concrete shall have a specified compressive strength of not less than 2,500 psi at 28 days, unless a higher strength is required by note g or h.

j. "DR" means design is required in accordance with ACI 318 or ACI 332.

k. "PC" means plain concrete.

l. Where vertical reinforcement is required, horizontal reinforcement shall be provided in accordance with the requirements of Section R404.4.6.2 for ICF foundation walls.

TABLE R404.1.1(6)
CANTILEVERED CONCRETE AND MASONRY FOUNDATION WALLS

MAXIMUM WALL HEIGHT[j] (feet)	MAXIMUM UNBALANCED BACKFILL HEIGHT[e] (feet)	MINIMUM VERTICAL REINFORCEMENT SIZE AND SPACING FOR 8-INCH NOMINAL WALL THICKNESS [a, b, c, e, f, i, k]		
		Soil Classes[d]		
		GW, GP, SW and SP	GM, GC, SM, SM-SC and ML	SC, MH, ML-CL and Inorganic CL
4	3	None required	None required	None required
	4	None required	None required	No. 4@72 in. o.c.
5	3	None required	None required	None required
	4	No. 4@72 in. o.c.	No. 4@56 in. o.c.[h]	No. 4@40 in. o.c.[g]
	5	No. 4@72 in. o.c.	No. 4@56 in. o.c.[h]	No. 4@40 in. o.c.[g]

a. Mortar shall be Type M or S and masonry shall be laid in running bond. Minimum unit compressive strength is 1,900 psi.

b. Alternative reinforcing bar sizes and spacings having an equivalent cross-sectional area of reinforcement per lineal foot of wall shall be permitted provided the spacing of the reinforcement does not exceed 72 inches.

c. Vertical reinforcement shall be Grade 60 minimum. The distance from the face of the soil side of the wall to the center of vertical reinforcement shall be no greater than 2.5 inches.

d. Soil classes are in accordance with the Unified Soil Classification System. Refer to Table R405.1.

e. Interior concrete floor slab-on-grade shall be placed tight to the wall. The exterior grade level shall be 6 inches minimum below the top of wall. Maximum height from top of slab-on-grade to bottom of floor joists is 10 feet, 0 inches. Unbalanced backfill height is the difference in height of the exterior finish ground levels and the top of the interior concrete slab-on-grade.

f. Minimum footing size of 20 inches by 8 inches shall be placed on soil with a bearing capacity of 2,000 psf. Minimum concrete compressive strength of footing shall be 3,000 psi.

g. Provide propped cantilever wall: top of footing shall be 16 inches below the bottom of the concrete floor slab minimum.

h. Provide #5 Grade 60 dowels, 1 foot, 6 inches long, to connect footing to wall. Embed dowel 5 inches into footing. Place dowels in center of wall thickness spaced at 32 inches o.c. maximum. No dowels are required where length of the foundation wall between perpendicular walls is two times the foundation wall height or less.

i. This table is applicable where the length of the foundation wall between perpendicular walls is 35 feet or less, or where the length of the foundation laterally supported on only one end by a perpendicular wall is 17 feet or less.

j. Maximum wall height is measured from top of the foundation wall to the bottom of the interior concrete slab-on-grade.

k. Install foundation anchorage per Section R403.1.6.

TABLE R404.1.1(7)
CANTILEVERED CONCRETE AND MASONRY FOUNDATION WALLS

MAXIMUM WALL HEIGHT[j] (feet)	MAXIMUM UNBALANCED BACKFILL HEIGHT[e] (feet)	MINIMUM VERTICAL REINFORCEMENT SIZE AND SPACING FOR 10-INCH NOMINAL WALL THICKNESS [a, b, c, e, f, i, k]		
		Soil Classes[d]		
		GW, GP, SW and SP	GM, GC, SM, SM-SC and ML	SC, MH, ML-CL and Inorganic CL
4	3	None required	None required	None required
	4	None required	None required	None required
5	3	None required	None required	None required
	4	None required	No. 4@72 in. o.c.	No. 4@64 in. o.c.[g]
	5	No. 4@72 in. o.c.	No. 4@72 in. o.c.	No. 4@56 in. o.c.[g]
6	3	None required	No. 4@72 in. o.c.	No. 4@72 in. o.c.
	4	No. 4@72 in. o.c.	No. 4@72 in. o.c.	No. 4@64 in. o.c.[h]
	5	No. 4@64 in. o.c.[h]	No. 4@40 in. o.c.[g, h]	No. 5@48 in. o.c.[g, h]
	6	No. 4@64 in. o.c.[h]	No. 4@40 in. o.c.[g, h]	No. 5@48 in. o.c.[g, h]

a. Mortar shall be Type M or S and masonry shall be laid in running bond. Minimum unit compressive strength is 1,900 psi.

b. Alternative reinforcing bar sizes and spacings having an equivalent cross-sectional area of reinforcement per lineal foot of wall shall be permitted provided the spacing of the reinforcement does not exceed 72 inches.

c. Vertical reinforcement shall be Grade 60 minimum. The distance from the face of the soil side of the wall to the center of vertical reinforcement shall be no greater than 2.5 inches.

d. Soil classes are in accordance with the Unified Soil Classification System. Refer to Table R405.1.

e. Interior concrete slab-on-grade shall be placed tight to the wall. The exterior grade level shall be 6 inches minimum below the top of wall. Maximum height from top of slab-on-grade to bottom of floor joists is 10 feet, 0 inches. Unbalanced backfill height is the difference in height of the exterior finish ground levels and the top of the interior concrete slab-on-grade.

f. Minimum footing size of 20 inches by 8 inches shall be placed on soil with a bearing capacity of 2,000 psf. Minimum concrete compressive strength of footing shall be 3,000 psi.

g. Provide propped cantilever wall: top of footing shall be 16 inches below the bottom of the concrete floor slab minimum.

h. Provide #5 Grade 60 dowels, 1 foot, 6 inches long, to connect footing to wall. Embed dowel 5 inches into footing. Place dowels in center of wall thickness spaced at 32 inches o.c. maximum. No dowels are required where length of the foundation wall between perpendicular walls is two times the foundation wall height or less.

i. This table is applicable where the length of the foundation wall between perpendicular walls is 35 feet or less, or where the length of the foundation laterally supported on only one end by a perpendicular wall is 17 feet or less.

j. Maximum wall height is measured from top of the foundation wall to the bottom of the interior concrete slab-on-grade.

k. Install foundation anchorage per Section R403.1.6.

TABLE R404.1.1(8)
CANTILEVERED CONCRETE AND MASONRY FOUNDATION WALLS

MAXIMUM WALL HEIGHT[j] (feet)	MAXIMUM UNBALANCED BACKFILL HEIGHT[e] (feet)	MINIMUM VERTICAL REINFORCEMENT SIZE AND SPACING FOR 12-INCH NOMINAL WALL THICKNESS [a, b, c, e, f, i, k]		
		Soil Classes[d]		
		GW, GP, SW and SP	GM, GC, SM, SM-SC and ML	SC, MH, ML-CL and Inorganic CL
4	3	None required	None required	None required
	4	None required	None required	None required
5	3	None required	None required	None required
	4	None required	None required	No. 4@72 in. o.c.
	5	No. 4@72 in. o.c.	No. 4@72 in. o.c.	No. 4@72 in. o.c.
6	3	None required	None required	None required
	4	None required	None required	No. 4@72 in. o.c.
	5	No. 4@72 in. o.c.	No. 4@56 in. o.c.[h]	No. 4@40 in. o.c.[g,]
	6	No. 4@72 in. o.c.	No. 4@56 in. o.c.[g]	No. 4@32 in. o.c.[g, h]
7	3	None required	None required	None required
	4	None required	No. 4@72 in. o.c.	No. 4@72 in. o.c.
	5	No. 4@72 in. o.c.	No. 4@56 in. o.c.[h]	No. 4@40 in. o.c.[g]
	6	No. 4@48 in. o.c.[h]	No. 5@48 in. o.c.[g, h]	No. 6@48 in. o.c.[g, h]
	7	No. 4@48 in. o.c.[h]	No. 5@40 in. o.c.[g, h]	No. 6@48 in. o.c.[g, h]

a. Mortar shall be Type M or S and masonry shall be laid in running bond. Minimum unit compressive strength is 1,900 psi.

b. Alternative reinforcing bar sizes and spacings having an equivalent cross-sectional area of reinforcement per lineal foot of wall shall be permitted provided the spacing of the reinforcement does not exceed 72 inches.

c. Vertical reinforcement shall be Grade 60 minimum. The distance from the face of the soil side of the wall to the center of vertical reinforcement shall be no greater than 3 inches.

d. Soil classes are in accordance with the Unified Soil Classification System. Refer to Table R405.1.

e. Interior concrete slab-on-grade shall be placed tight to the wall. The exterior grade level shall be 6 inches minimum below the top of wall. Maximum height from top of slab-on-grade to bottom of floor joists is 10 feet, 0 inches. Unbalanced backfill height is the difference in height of the exterior finish ground levels and the top of the interior concrete slab-on-grade.

f. Minimum footing size of 20 inches by 8 inches shall be placed on soil with a bearing capacity of 2,000 psf. Minimum concrete compressive strength of footing shall be 3,000 psi.

g. Provide propped cantilever wall: top of footing shall be 16 inches below the bottom of the concrete floor slab minimum.

h. Provide #5 Grade 60 dowels, 1 foot, 6 inches long, to connect footing to wall. Embed dowel 5 inches into footing. Place dowels in center of wall thickness spaced at 32 inches o.c. maximum. No dowels are required where length of the foundation wall between perpendicular walls is two times the foundation wall height or less.

i. This table is applicable where the length of the foundation wall between perpendicular walls is 35 feet or less, or where the length of the foundation laterally supported on only one end by a perpendicular wall is 17 feet or less.

j. vMaximum wall height is measured from top of the foundation wall to the bottom of the interior concrete slab-on-grade.

k. Install foundation anchorage per Section R403.1.6.

R404.1.5 Foundation wall thickness based on walls supported. The thickness of concrete and masonry foundation walls shall not be less than the thickness of the wall supported, except that foundation walls of at least 8-inch (203 mm) nominal thickness shall be permitted under brick-veneered frame walls and under 10-inch-wide (254 mm) cavity walls where the total height of the wall supported, including gables, is not more than 20 feet (6096 mm), provided the requirements of Sections R404.1.1 and R404.1.2 are met.

R404.1.5.1 Pier and curtain wall foundations. Use of Pier and curtain wall foundations shall be permitted to support light-frame construction not more than two stories in height, provided the following requirements are met:

1. All load-bearing walls shall be placed on continuous concrete footings placed integrally with the exterior wall footings.

2. The minimum actual thickness of a load-bearing masonry wall shall be not less than 4 inches (102 mm) nominal or $3^3/_8$ inches (92 mm) actual thickness, and shall be bonded integrally with piers spaced in accordance with Section R606.9.

3. Piers shall be constructed in accordance with Section R606.6 and Section R606.6.1, and shall be bonded into the load-bearing masonry wall in accordance with Section R608.1.1 or Section R608.1.1.2.

4. The maximum height of a 4-inch (102 mm) load-bearing masonry foundation wall supporting wood-frame walls and floors shall not be more than 4 feet (1219 mm).

5. Anchorage shall be in accordance with Section R403.1.6, Figure R404.1.5(1), or as specified by engineered design accepted by the building official.

6. The unbalanced fill for 4-inch (102 mm) foundation walls shall not exceed 24 inches (610 mm) for solid masonry or 12 inches (305 mm) for hollow masonry.

7. In Seismic Design Categories D_0, D_1 and D_2, prescriptive reinforcement shall be provided in the horizontal and vertical direction. Provide minimum horizontal joint reinforcement of two No.9 gage wires spaced not less than 6 inches (152 mm) or one $1/_4$ inch (6.4 mm) diameter wire at 10 inches (254 mm) on center vertically. Provide minimum vertical reinforcement of one No. 4 bar at 48 inches (1220 mm) on center horizontally grouted in place.

R404.1.6 Height above finished grade. Concrete and masonry foundation walls shall extend above the finished grade adjacent to the foundation at all points a minimum of 4 inches (102 mm) where masonry veneer is used and a minimum of 6 inches (152 mm) elsewhere.

R404.1.7 Backfill placement. Backfill shall not be placed against the wall until the wall has sufficient strength and has been anchored to the floor above, or has been sufficiently braced to prevent damage by the backfill.

Exception: Bracing is not required for walls supporting less than 4 feet (1219 mm) of unbalanced backfill.

R404.1.8 Rubble stone masonry. Rubble stone masonry foundation walls shall have a minimum thickness of 16 inches (406 mm), shall not support an unbalanced backfill exceeding 8 feet (2438 mm) in height, shall not support a soil pressure greater than 30 pounds per square foot per foot (4.71 kPa/m), and shall not be constructed in Seismic Design Categories D_0, D_1, D_2 or townhouses in Seismic Design Category C, as established in Figure R301.2(2).

R404.2 Wood foundation walls. Wood foundation walls shall be constructed in accordance with the provisions of Sections R404.2.1 through R404.2.6 and with the details shown in Figures R403.1(2) and R403.1(3).

R404.2.1 Identification. All load-bearing lumber shall be identified by the grade mark of a lumber grading or inspection agency which has been approved by an accreditation body that complies with DOC PS 20. In lieu of a grade mark, a certificate of inspection issued by a lumber grading or inspection agency meeting the requirements of this section shall be accepted. Wood structural panels shall conform to DOC PS 1 or DOC PS 2 and shall be identified by a grade mark or certificate of inspection issued by an approved agency.

R404.2.2 Stud size. The studs used in foundation walls shall be 2-inch by 6-inch (51 mm by 152 mm) members. When spaced 16 inches (406 mm) on center, a wood species with an F_b value of not less than 1,250 pounds per square inch (8612 kPa) as listed in AF&PA/NDS shall be used. When spaced 12 inches (305 mm) on center, an F_b of not less than 875 psi (6029 kPa) shall be required.

R404.2.3 Height of backfill. For wood foundations that are not designed and installed in accordance with AF&PA Report No.7, the height of backfill against a foundation wall shall not exceed 4 feet (1219 mm). When the height of fill is more than 12 inches (305 mm) above the interior grade of a crawl space or floor of a basement, the thickness of the plywood sheathing shall meet the requirements of Table R404.2.3.

R404.2.4 Backfilling. Wood foundation walls shall not be backfilled until the basement floor and first floor have been constructed or the walls have been braced. For crawl space construction, backfill or bracing shall be installed on the interior of the walls prior to placing backfill on the exterior.

R404.2.5 Drainage and dampproofing. Wood foundation basements shall be drained and dampproofed in accordance with Sections R405 and R406, respectively.

R404.2.6 Fastening. Wood structural panel foundation wall sheathing shall be attached to framing in accordance with Table R602.3(1) and Section R402.1.1.

R404.3 Wood sill plates. Wood sill plates shall be a minimum of 2-inch by 4-inch (51 mm by 102 mm) nominal lumber. Sill plate anchorage shall be in accordance with Sections R403.1.6 and R602.11.

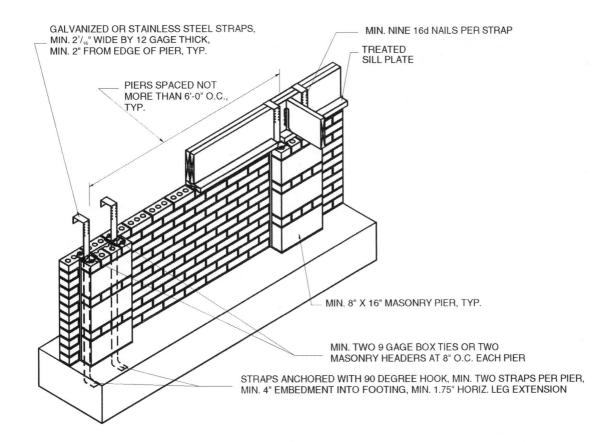

GALVANIZED OR STAINLESS STEEL STRAPS,
MIN. 2$^{1}/_{16}$" WIDE BY 12 GAGE THICK,
MIN. 2" FROM EDGE OF PIER, TYP.

MIN. NINE 16d NAILS PER STRAP

TREATED
SILL PLATE

PIERS SPACED NOT
MORE THAN 6'-0" O.C.,
TYP.

MIN. 8" X 16" MASONRY PIER, TYP.

MIN. TWO 9 GAGE BOX TIES OR TWO
MASONRY HEADERS AT 8" O.C. EACH PIER

STRAPS ANCHORED WITH 90 DEGREE HOOK, MIN. TWO STRAPS PER PIER,
MIN. 4" EMBEDMENT INTO FOOTING, MIN. 1.75" HORIZ. LEG EXTENSION

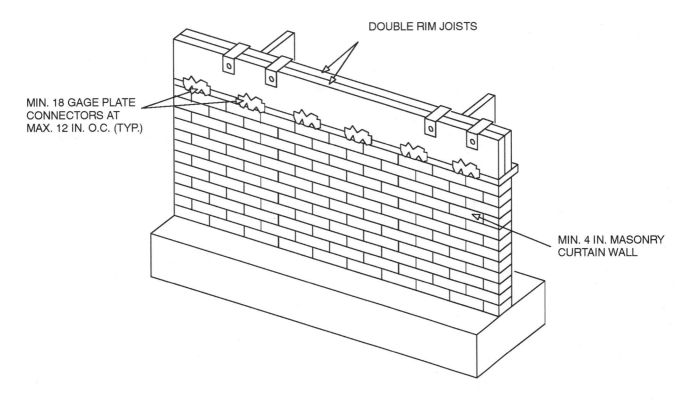

DOUBLE RIM JOISTS

MIN. 18 GAGE PLATE
CONNECTORS AT
MAX. 12 IN. O.C. (TYP.)

MIN. 4 IN. MASONRY
CURTAIN WALL

For SI: 1 inch = 25.4 mm, 1 foot = 304.8 mm, 1 degree = 0.0157 rad.

FIGURE R404.1.5(1)
FOUNDATION WALL CLAY MASONRY CURTAIN WALL WITH CONCRETE MASONRY PIERS

TABLE R404.2.3
PLYWOOD GRADE AND THICKNESS FOR WOOD FOUNDATION CONSTRUCTION
(30 pcf equivalent-fluid weight soil pressure)

HEIGHT OF FILL (inches)	STUD SPACING (inches)	FACE GRAIN ACROSS STUDS			FACE GRAIN PARALLEL TO STUDS		
		Grade[a]	Minimum thickness (inches)	Span rating	Grade[a]	Minimum thickness (inches)[b,c]	Span rating
24	12	B	$^{15}/_{32}$	32/16	A	$^{15}/_{32}$	32/16
					B	$^{15}/_{32}{}^{c}$	32/16
	16	B	$^{15}/_{32}$	32/16	A	$^{15}/_{32}{}^{c}$	32/16
					B	$^{19}/_{32}{}^{c}$ (4, 5 ply)	40/20
36	12	B	$^{15}/_{32}$	32/16	A	$^{15}/_{32}$	32/16
					B	$^{15}/_{32}{}^{c}$ (4, 5 ply)	32/16
					B	$^{19}/_{32}$ (4, 5 ply)	40/20
	16	B	$^{15}/_{32}{}^{c}$	32/16	A	$^{19}/_{32}$	40/20
					B	$^{23}/_{32}$	48/24
48	12	B	$^{15}/_{32}$	32/16	A	$^{15}/_{32}{}^{c}$	32/16
					B	$^{19}/_{32}{}^{c}$ (4, 5 ply)	40/20
	16	B	$^{19}/_{32}$	40/20	A	$^{19}/_{32}{}^{c}$	40/20
					A	$^{23}/_{32}$	48/24

For SI: 1 inch = 25.4 mm, 1 foot = 304.8 mm, 1 pound per cubic foot = 0.1572 kN/m³.

a. Plywood shall be of the following minimum grades in accordance with DOC PS 1 or DOC PS 2:

  1. DOC PS 1 Plywood grades marked:

    1.1. Structural I C-D (Exposure 1)

    1.2. C-D (Exposure 1)

  2. DOC PS 2 Plywood grades marked:

    2.1. Structural I Sheathing (Exposure 1)

    2.2. Sheathing (Exposure 1)

  3. Where a major portion of the wall is exposed above ground and a better appearance is desired, the following plywood grades marked exterior are suitable:

    3.1. Structural I A-C, Structural I B-C or Structural I C-C (Plugged) in accordance with DOC PS 1

    3.2. A-C Group 1, B-C Group 1, C-C (Plugged) Group 1 or MDO Group 1 in accordance with DOC PS 1

    3.3. Single Floor in accordance with DOC PS 1 or DOC PS 2

b. Minimum thickness $^{15}/_{32}$ inch, except crawl space sheathing may be $^{3}/_{8}$ inch for face grain across studs 16 inches on center and maximum 2-foot depth of unequal fill.

c. For this fill height, thickness and grade combination, panels that are continuous over less than three spans (across less than three stud spacings) require blocking 16 inches above the bottom plate. Offset adjacent blocks and fasten through studs with two 16d corrosion-resistant nails at each end.

R404.4 Insulating concrete form foundation walls. Insulating concrete form (ICF) foundation walls shall be designed and constructed in accordance with the provisions of this section or in accordance with the provisions of ACI 318. When ACI 318 or the provisions of this section are used to design insulating concrete form foundation walls, project drawings, typical details and specifications are not required to bear the seal of the architect or engineer responsible for design unless otherwise required by the state law of the jurisdiction having authority.

R404.4.1 Applicability limits. The provisions of this section shall apply to the construction of insulating concrete form foundation walls for buildings not more than 60 feet (18 288 mm) in plan dimensions, and floors not more than 32 feet (9754 mm) or roofs not more than 40 feet (12 192 mm) in clear span. Buildings shall not exceed two stories in height above grade with each story not more than 10 feet (3048 mm) high. Foundation walls constructed in accordance with the provisions of this section shall be limited to buildings subjected to a maximum ground snow load of 70 psf (3.35 kPa) and located in Seismic Design Category A, B or C. In Seismic Design Categories D_0, D_1 and D_2, foundation walls shall comply with Section R404.1.4. Insulating concrete form foundation walls supporting above-grade concrete walls shall be reinforced as required for the above-grade wall immediately above or the requirements in Tables R404.4(1), R404.4(2), R404.4(3), R404.4(4) or R404.4(5), whichever is greater.

R404.4.2 Flat insulating concrete form wall systems. Flat ICF wall systems shall comply with Figure R611.3, shall have a minimum concrete thickness of 5.5 inches (140 mm), and shall have reinforcement in accordance with Table R404.4(1), R404.4(2) or R404.4(3). Alternatively, for 7.5-inch (191 mm) and 9.5-inch (241 mm) flat ICF wall systems, use of Table R404.1.1(5) shall be permitted, provided the vertical reinforcement is of the grade and located within the wall as required by that table.

TABLE R404.4(1)
5.5-INCH THICK FLAT ICF FOUNDATION WALLS[a, b, c, d]

HEIGHT OF BASEMENT WALL (feet)	MAXIMUM UNBALANCED BACKFILL HEIGHT[e] (feet)	MINIMUM VERTICAL REINFORCEMENT SIZE AND SPACING		
		Soil classes[f] and design lateral soil load (psf per foot of depth)		
		GW, GP, SW and SP 30	GM, GC, SM, SM-SC and ML 45	SC, ML-CL and inorganic CL 60
8	4	#4@48″	#4@48″	#4@48″
	5	#4@48″	#3@12″; #4@22″; #5@32″	#3@8″; #4@14″; #5@20″; #6@26″
	6	#3@12″; #4@22″; #5@30″	#3@8″; #4@14″; #5@20″; #6@24″	#3@6″; #4@10″: #5@14″; #6@20″
	7	#3@8″; #4@14″; #5@22″; #6@26″	#3@5″; #4@10″; #5@14″; #6@18″	#3@4″; #4@6″; #5@10″; #6@14″
9	4	#4@48″	#4@48″	#4@48″
	5	#4@48″	#3@12″; #4@20″; #5@28″; #6@36″	#3@8″; #4@14″; #5@20″; #6@22″
	6	#3@10″; #4@20″; #5@28″; #6@34″	#3@6″; #4@12″; #5@18″; #6@20″	#4@8″; #5@14″; #6@16″
	7	#3@8″; #4@14″; #5@20″; #6@22″	#4@8″; #5@12″; #6@16″	#4@6″; #5@10″; #6@12″
	8	#3@6″; #4@10″; #5@14″; #6@16″	#4@6″; #5@10″; #6@12″	#4@4″; #5@6″; #6@8″
10	4	#4@48″	#4@48″	#4@48″
	5	#4@48″	#3@10″; #4@18″; #5@26″; #6@30″	#3@6″; #4@14″; #5@18″; #6@20″
	6	#3@10″; #4@18″; #5@24″; #6@30″	#3@6″; #4@12″; #5@16″; #6@18″	#3@4″; #4@8″; #5@12″; #6@14″
	7	#3@6″; #4@12″; #5@16″; #6@18″	#3@4″; #4@8″; #5@12″	#4@6″; #5@8″; #6@10″
	8	#4@8″; #5@12″; #6@14″	#4@6″; #5@8″; #6@12″	#4@4″; #5@6″; #6@8″
	9	#4@6″; #5@10″; #6@12″	#4@4″; #5@6″; #6@8″	#5@4″; #6@6″

For SI: 1 inch = 25.4 mm, 1 foot = 304.8 mm, 1 pound per square inch = 6.895 kPa, 1 pound per square foot = 0.0479 kPa.

a. This table is based on concrete with a minimum specified concrete strength of 2500 psi, reinforcing steel with a minimum yield strength of 40,000 psi. When reinforcing steel with a minimum yield strength of 60,000 psi is used, the spacing of the reinforcement shall be increased to 1.5 times the spacing value in the table but in no case greater than 48 inches on center.

b. This table is not intended to prohibit the use of an ICF manufacturer's tables based on engineering analysis in accordance with ACI 318.

c. Deflection criteria: L/240.

d. Interpolation between rebar sizes and spacing is not permitted.

e. Unbalanced backfill height is the difference in height of the exterior and interior finished ground. Where an interior concrete slab is provided, the unbalanced backfill height shall be measured from the exterior finished ground level to the top of the interior concrete slab.

f. Soil classes are in accordance with the Unified Soil Classification System. Refer to Table R405.1.

R404.4.3 Waffle-grid insulating concrete form wall systems. Waffle-grid wall systems shall have a minimum nominal concrete thickness of 6 inches (152 mm) for the horizontal and vertical concrete members (cores) and shall be reinforced in accordance with Table R404.4(4). The minimum core dimension shall comply with Table R611.2 and Figure R611.4.

R404.4.4 Screen-grid insulating concrete form wall systems. Screen-grid ICF wall systems shall have a minimum nominal concrete thickness of 6 inches (152 mm) for the horizontal and vertical concrete members (cores). The minimum core dimensions shall comply with Table R611.2 and Figure R611.5. Walls shall have reinforcement in accordance with Table R404.4(5).

TABLE R404.4(2)
7.5-INCH-THICK FLAT ICF FOUNDATION WALLS[a, b, c, d, e]

HEIGHT OF BASEMENT WALL (feet)	MAXIMUM UNBALANCED BACKFILL HEIGHT[f] (feet)	MINIMUM VERTICAL REINFORCEMENT SIZE AND SPACING		
		Soil classes[g] and design lateral soil load (psf per foot of depth)		
		GW, GP, SW and SP 30	GM, GC, SM, SM-SC and ML 45	SC, ML-CL and inorganic CL 60
8	6	N/R	N/R	#3@6"; #4@12"; #5@18"; #6@24"
	7	N/R	#3@8"; #4@14"; #5@20"; #6@28"	#3@6"; #4@10"; #5@16"; #6@20"
9	6	N/R	N/R	#3@8"; #4@14"; #5@20"; #6@28"
	7	N/R	#3@6"; #4@12"; #5@18"; #6@26"	#3@4"; #4@8"; #5@14"; #6@18"
	8	#3@8"; #4@14"; #5@22"; #6@28"	#3@4"; #4@8"; #5@14"; #6@18"	#3@4"; #4@6"; #5@10"; #6@14"
10	6	N/R	N/R	#3@6"; #4@12"; #5@18"; #6@26"
	7	N/R	#3@6"; #4@12"; #5@18"; #6@24"	#3@4"; #4@8"; #5@12"; #6@18"
	8	#3@6"; #4@12"; #5@20"; #6@26"	#3@4"; #4@8"; #5@12"; #6@16"	#3@4"; #4@6"; #5@8"; #6@12"
	9	#3@6"; #4@10"; #5@14"; #6@20"	#3@4"; #4@6"; #5@10"; #6@12"	#4@4"; #5@6"; #6@10"

For SI: 1 inch = 25.4 mm, 1 foot = 304.8 mm, 1 pound per square inch = 6.895 kPa, 1 pound per square foot = 0.0479 kPa.

a. This table is based on concrete with a minimum specified concrete strength of 2500 psi, reinforcing steel with a minimum yield strength of 40,000 psi. When reinforcing steel with a minimum yield strength of 60,000 psi is used, the spacing of the reinforcement shall be increased to 1.5 times the spacing value in the table.

b. This table is not intended to prohibit the use of an ICF manufacturer's tables based on engineering analysis in accordance with ACI 318.

c. N/R denotes "not required."

d. Deflection criteria: L/240.

e. Interpolation between rebar sizes and spacing is not permitted.

f. Unbalanced backfill height is the difference in height of the exterior and interior finished ground. Where an interior concrete slab is provided, the unbalanced backfill height shall be measured from the exterior finished ground level to the top of the interior concrete slab.

g. Soil classes are in accordance with the Unified Soil Classification System. Refer to Table R405.1.

R404.4.5 Concrete material. Ready-mixed concrete for insulating concrete form walls shall be in accordance with Section R402.2. Maximum slump shall not be greater than 6 inches (152 mm) as determined in accordance with ASTM C 143. Maximum aggregate size shall not be larger than $^3/_4$ inch (19.1 mm).

Exception: Concrete mixes conforming to the ICF manufacturer's recommendations.

R404.4.6 Reinforcing steel.

R404.4.6.1 General. Reinforcing steel shall meet the requirements of ASTM A 615, A 706 or A 996. The minimum yield strength of reinforcing steel shall be 40,000 psi (Grade 40) (276 MPa). Vertical and horizontal wall reinforcements shall be placed no closer to the outside face of the wall than one-half the wall thickness. Steel reinforcement for foundation walls shall have concrete cover in accordance with ACI 318.

Exception: Where insulated concrete forms are used and the form remains in place as cover for the con-

crete, the minimum concrete cover for the reinforcing steel is permitted to be reduced to $^3/_4$ inch (19.1 mm).

R404.4.6.2 Horizontal reinforcement. When vertical reinforcement is required, ICF foundation walls shall have horizontal reinforcement in accordance with this section. ICF foundation walls up to 8 feet (2438 mm) in height shall have a minimum of one continuous No. 4 horizontal reinforcing bar placed at 48 inches (1219 mm) on center with one bar located within 12 inches (305 mm) of the top of the wall story. ICF Foundation walls greater than 8 feet (2438 mm) in height shall have a minimum of one continuous No. 4 horizontal reinforcing bar placed at 36 inches (914 mm) on center with one bar located within 12 inches (305 mm) of the top of the wall story.

R404.4.6.3 Wall openings. Vertical wall reinforcement required by Section R404.4.2, R404.4.3 or R404.4.4 that is interrupted by wall openings shall have additional vertical reinforcement of the same size placed within 12 inches (305 mm) of each side of the opening.

TABLE R404.4(3)
9.5-INCH-THICK FLAT ICF FOUNDATION WALLS[a, b, c, d, e]

HEIGHT OF BASEMENT WALL (feet)	MAXIMUM UNBALANCED BACKFILL HEIGHT[f] (feet)	MINIMUM VERTICAL REINFORCEMENT SIZE AND SPACING		
		Soil classes[g] and design lateral soil load (psf per foot of depth)		
		GW, GP, SW and SP 30	GM, GC, SM, SM-SC and ML 45	SC, ML-CL and inorganic CL 60
8	7	N/R	N/R	N/R
9	6	N/R	N/R	N/R
	7	N/R	N/R	#3@6"; #4@12"; #5@18"; #6@26"
	8	N/R	#3@6"; #4@12"; #5@18"; #6@26"	#3@4"; #4@8"; #5@14"; #6@18"
10	5	N/R	N/R	N/R
	6	N/R	N/R	N/R
	7	N/R	N/R	#3@6"; #4@10"; #5@18"; #6@24"
	8	N/R	#3@6"; #4@12"; #5@16"; #6@24"	#3@4"; #4@8"; #5@12"; #6@16"
	9	#3@4"; #4@10"; #5@14"; #6@20"	#3@4"; #4@8"; #5@12"; #6@18"	#3@4"; #4@6"; #5@10"; #6@12"

For SI: 1 inch = 25.4 mm, 1 foot = 304.8 mm, 1 pound per square inch = 6.895 kPa, 1 pound per square foot = 0.0479 kPa.

a. This table is based on concrete with a minimum specified concrete strength of 2500 psi, reinforcing steel with a minimum yield strength of 40,000 psi. When reinforcing steel with a minimum yield strength of 60,000 psi is used, the spacing of the reinforcement shall be increased to 1.5 times the spacing value in the table.

b. This table is not intended to prohibit the use of an ICF manufacturer's tables based on engineering analysis in accordance with ACI 318.

c. N/R denotes "not required."

d. Deflection criteria: $L/240$.

e. Interpolation between rebar sizes and spacing is not permitted.

f. Unbalanced backfill height is the difference in height of the exterior and interior finished ground. Where an interior concrete slab is provided, the unbalanced backfill height shall be measured from the exterior finished ground level to the top of the interior concrete slab.

g. Soil classes are in accordance with the Unified Soil Classification System. Refer to Table R405.1.

R404.4.7 Foam plastic insulation. Foam plastic insulation in insulating concrete foam construction shall comply with this section.

R404.4.7.1 Material. Insulating concrete form material shall meet the surface burning characteristics of Section R314.3. A thermal barrier shall be provided on the building interior in accordance with Section R314.4.

R404.4.7.2 Termite hazards. In areas where hazard of termite damage is very heavy in accordance with Figure R301.2(6), foam plastic insulation shall be permitted below grade on foundation walls in accordance with one of the following conditions:

1. When in addition to the requirements in Section R320.1, an approved method of protecting the foam plastic and structure from subterranean termite damage is provided.

2. The structural members of walls, floors, ceilings and roofs are entirely of noncombustible materials or pressure preservatively treated wood.

3. On the interior side of basement walls.

R404.4.8 Foundation wall thickness based on walls supported. The thickness of ICF foundation walls shall not be less than the thickness of the wall supported above.

R404.4.9 Height above finished ground. ICF foundation walls shall extend above the finished ground adjacent to the foundation at all points a minimum of 4 inches (102 mm) where masonry veneer is used and a minimum of 6 inches (152 mm) elsewhere.

R404.4.10 Backfill placement. Backfill shall be placed in accordance with Section R404.1.7.

R404.4.11 Drainage and dampproofing/waterproofing. ICF foundation basements shall be drained and dampproofed/waterproofed in accordance with Sections R405 and R406.

R404.5 Retaining walls. Retaining walls that are not laterally supported at the top and that retain in excess of 24 inches (610 mm) of unbalanced fill shall be designed to ensure stability against overturning, sliding, excessive foundation pressure and water uplift. Retaining walls shall be designed for a safety factor of 1.5 against lateral sliding and overturning.

TABLE R404.4(4)
WAFFLE GRID ICF FOUNDATION WALLS[a, b, c, d, e]

MINIMUM NOMINAL WALL THICKNESS[f] (inches)	HEIGHT OF BASEMENT WALL (feet)	MAXIMUM UNBALANCED BACKFILL HEIGHT[g] (feet)	MINIMUM VERTICAL REINFORCEMENT SIZE AND SPACING		
			Soil classes[h] and design lateral soil load (psf per foot of depth)		
			GW, GP, SW and SP 30	GM, GC, SM, SM-SC and ML 45	SC, ML-CL and inorganic CL 60
6	8	4	#4@48″	#3@12″; #4@24″	#3@12″
		5	#3@12″; #5@24″	#4@12″	#7@12″
		6	#4@12″	Design required	Design required
		7	#7@12″	Design required	Design required
	9	4	#4@48″	#3@12″; #5@24″	#3@12″
		5	#3@12″	#4@12″	Design required
		6	#5@12″	Design required	Design required
		7	Design required	Design required	Design required
	10	4	#4@48″	#4@12″	#5@12″
		5	#3@12″	Design required	Design required
		6	Design required	Design required	Design required
		7	Design required	Design required	Design required
8	8	4	N/R	N/R	N/R
		5	N/R	#3@12″; #4@24″; #5@36″	#3@12″; #5@24″
		6	#3@12″; #4@24″; #5@36″	#4@12″; #5@24″	#4@12″
		7	#3@12″; #6@24″	#4@12″	#5@12″
	9	4	N/R	N/R	N/R
		5	N/R	#3@12″; #5@24″	#3@12″; #5@24″
		6	#3@12″; #4@24″	#4@12″	#4@12″
		7	#4@12″; #5@24″	#5@12″	#5@12″
		8	#4@12″	#5@12″	#8@12″
	10	4	N/R	#3@12″; #4@24″; #6@36″	#3@12″; #5@24″
		5	N/R	#3@12″; #4@24″; #6@36″	#4@12″; #5@24″
		6	#3@12″; #5@24″	#4@12″	#5@12″
		7	#4@12″	#5@12″	#6@12″
		8	#4@12″	#6@12″	Design required
		9	#5@12″	Design required	Design required

For SI: 1 inch = 25.4 mm, 1 foot = 304.8 mm, 1 pound per square inch = 6.895 kPa, 1 pound per square foot = 0.0479 kPa.

a. This table is based on concrete with a minimum specified concrete strength of 2500 psi, reinforcing steel with a minimum yield strength of 40,000 psi. When reinforcing steel with a minimum yield strength of 60,000 psi is used, the spacing of the reinforcement shall be increased 12 inches but in no case greater than 48 inches on center.

b. This table is not intended to prohibit the use of an ICF manufacturer's tables based on engineering analysis in accordance with ACI 318.

c. N/R denotes "not required."

d. Deflection criteria: $L/240$.

e. Interpolation between rebar sizes and spacing is not permitted.

f. Refer to Table R611.4(2) for wall dimensions.

g. Unbalanced backfill height is the difference in height of the exterior and interior finished ground. Where an interior concrete slab is provided, the unbalanced backfill height shall be measured from the exterior finished ground level to the top of the interior concrete slab.

h. Soil classes are in accordance with the Unified Soil Classification System. Refer to Table R405.1.

TABLE R404.4(5)
SCREEN-GRID ICF FOUNDATION WALLS[a, b, c, d, e]

MINIMUM NOMINAL WALL THICKNESS[f] (inches)	HEIGHT OF BASEMENT WALL (feet)	MAXIMUM UNBALANCED BACKFILL HEIGHT[g] (feet)	MINIMUM VERTICAL REINFORCEMENT SIZE AND SPACING		
			Soil classes[h] and design lateral soil load (psf per foot of depth)		
			GW, GP, SW and SP 30	GM, GC, SM, SM-SC and ML 45	SC, ML-CL and inorganic CL 60
6	8	4	#4@48″	#3@12″; #4@24″; #5@36″	#3@12″; #5@24″
		5	#3@12″; #4@24″	#3@12″	#4@12″
		6	#4@12″	#5@12″	Design required
		7	#4@12″	Design required	Design required
	9	4	#4@48″	#3@12″; #4@24″	#3@12″; #6@24″
		5	#3@12″; #5@24″	#4@12″	#7@12″
		6	#4@12″	Design required	Design required
		7	Design required	Design required	Design required
		8	Design required	Design required	Design required
	10	4	#4@48″	#3@12″; #5@24″	#3@12″
		5	#3@12″	#4@12″	#7@12″
		6	#4@12″	Design required	Design required
		7	Design required	Design required	Design required
		8	Design required	Design required	Design required

For SI: 1 inch = 25.4 mm, 1 foot = 304.8 mm, 1 pound per square inch = 6.895 kPa, 1 pound per square foot = 0.0479 kPa.

a. This table is based on concrete with a minimum specified concrete strength of 2500 psi, reinforcing steel with a minimum yield strength of 40,000 psi. When reinforcing steel with a minimum yield strength of 60,000 psi is used, the spacing of the reinforcement in the shaded cells shall be increased 12 inches.

b. This table is not intended to prohibit the use of an ICF manufacturer's tables based on engineering analysis in accordance with ACI 318.

c. N/R denotes "not required."

d. Deflection criteria: *L*/240.

e. Interpolation between rebar sizes and spacing is not permitted.

f. Refer to Table R611.4(2) for wall dimensions.

g. Unbalanced backfill height is the difference in height of the exterior and interior finished ground. Where an interior concrete slab is provided, the unbalanced backfill height shall be measured from the exterior finished ground level to the top of the interior concrete slab.

h. Soil classes are in accordance with the Unified Soil Classification System. Refer to Table R405.1.

SECTION R405
FOUNDATION DRAINAGE

R405.1 Concrete or masonry foundations. Drains shall be provided around all concrete or masonry foundations that retain earth and enclose habitable or usable spaces located below grade. Drainage tiles, gravel or crushed stone drains, perforated pipe or other approved systems or materials shall be installed at or below the area to be protected and shall discharge by gravity or mechanical means into an approved drainage system. Gravel or crushed stone drains shall extend at least 1 foot (305 mm) beyond the outside edge of the footing and 6 inches (152 mm) above the top of the footing and be covered with an approved filter membrane material. The top of open joints of drain tiles shall be protected with strips of building paper, and the drainage tiles or perforated pipe shall be placed on a minimum of 2 inches (51 mm) of washed gravel or crushed rock at least one sieve size larger than the tile joint opening or perforation and covered with not less than 6 inches (152 mm) of the same material.

> **Exception:** A drainage system is not required when the foundation is installed on well-drained ground or sand-gravel mixture soils according to the Unified Soil

Classification System, Group I Soils, as detailed in Table R405.1.

R405.2 Wood foundations. Wood foundations enclosing habitable or usable spaces located below grade shall be adequately drained in accordance with Sections R405.2.1 through R405.2.3.

R405.2.1 Base. A porous layer of gravel, crushed stone or coarse sand shall be placed to a minimum thickness of 4 inches (102 mm) under the basement floor. Provision shall be made for automatic draining of this layer and the gravel or crushed stone wall footings.

R405.2.2 Moisture barrier. A 6-mil-thick (0.15 mm) polyethylene moisture barrier shall be applied over the porous layer with the basement floor constructed over the polyethylene.

R405.2.3 Drainage system. In other than Group I soils, a sump shall be provided to drain the porous layer and footings. The sump shall be at least 24 inches (610 mm) in diameter or 20 inches square (0.0129 m²), shall extend at least 24 inches (610 mm) below the bottom of the basement floor and shall be capable of positive gravity or mechanical drainage to remove any accumulated water. The drainage system shall discharge into an approved sewer system or to daylight.

SECTION R406
FOUNDATION WATERPROOFING
AND DAMPPROOFING

R406.1 Concrete and masonry foundation dampproofing. Except where required by Section R406.2 to be waterproofed, foundation walls that retain earth and enclose interior spaces and floors below grade shall be dampproofed at a minimum from the top of the footing to the finished grade. Masonry walls shall be parged with not less than $3/8$-inch (9.5 mm) portland cement parging applied to the exterior of the wall. The parging shall be dampproofed in accordance with one of the following:

1. Bituminous coating.

2. 3 pounds per square yard (1.63 kg/m²) of acrylic modified cement.

3. $1/8$-inch (3.2 mm) coat of surface-bonding cement complying with ASTM C 887.

4. Any material permitted for waterproofing in Section R406.2.

5. Other approved methods or materials.

Exception: Parging of unit masonry walls is not required where a material is approved for direct application to the masonry.

Concrete walls shall be dampproofed by applying any one of the above listed dampproofing materials or any one of the waterproofing materials listed in Section R406.2 to the exterior of the wall.

R406.2 Concrete and masonry foundation waterproofing. In all soils groups other than Group 1 soils in accordance with

TABLE R405.1
PROPERTIES OF SOILS CLASSIFIED ACCORDING TO THE UNIFIED SOIL CLASSIFICATION SYSTEM

SOIL GROUP	UNIFIED SOIL CLASSIFICATION SYSTEM SYMBOL	SOIL DESCRIPTION	DRAINAGE CHARACTERISTICS[a]	FROST HEAVE POTENTIAL	VOLUME CHANGE POTENTIAL EXPANSION[b]
Group I	GW	Well-graded gravels, gravel sand mixtures, little or no fines	Good	Low	Low
	GP	Poorly graded gravels or gravel sand mixtures, little or no fines	Good	Low	Low
	SW	Well-graded sands, gravelly sands, little or no fines	Good	Low	Low
	SP	Poorly graded sands or gravelly sands, little or no fines	Good	Low	Low
	GM	Silty gravels, gravel-sand-silt mixtures	Good	Medium	Low
	SM	Silty sand, sand-silt mixtures	Good	Medium	Low
Group II	GC	Clayey gravels, gravel-sand-clay mixtures	Medium	Medium	Low
	SC	Clayey sands, sand-clay mixture	Medium	Medium	Low
	ML	Inorganic silts and very fine sands, rock flour, silty or clayey fine sands or clayey silts with slight plasticity	Medium	High	Low
	CL	Inorganic clays of low to medium plasticity, gravelly clays, sandy clays, silty clays, lean clays	Medium	Medium	Medium to Low
Group III	CH	Inorganic clays of high plasticity, fat clays	Poor	Medium	High
	MH	Inorganic silts, micaceous or diatomaceous fine sandy or silty soils, elastic silts	Poor	High	High
Group IV	OL	Organic silts and organic silty clays of low plasticity	Poor	Medium	Medium
	OH	Organic clays of medium to high plasticity, organic silts	Unsatisfactory	Medium	High
	Pt	Peat and other highly organic soils	Unsatisfactory	Medium	High

For SI: 1 inch = 25.4 mm.

a. The percolation rate for good drainage is over 4 inches per hour, medium drainage is 2 inches to 4 inches per hour, and poor is less than 2 inches per hour.

b. Soils with a low potential expansion typically have a plasticity index (PI) of 0 to 15, soils with a medium potential expansion have a PI of 10 to 35 and soils with a high potential expansion have a PI greater than 20.

Table R405.1, exterior foundation walls that retain earth and enclose interior spaces and floors below grade shall be waterproofed at a minimum from the top of the footing to the finished grade. Walls shall be waterproofed in accordance with one of the following:

1. 2-ply hot-mopped felts.

2. 55 pound (25 kg) roll roofing.

3. 6 mil (0.15 mm) polyvinyl chloride.

4. 6 mil (0.15 mm) polyethylene.

5. 40-mil (1 mm) polymer-modified asphalt.

6. 60-mil (1.5 mm) flexible polymer cement.

7. $^1/_8$-inch cement based, fiber reinforced, waterproof coating.

8. 60-mil (1.5 mm) solvent free liquid applied synthetic rubber.

> **Exception:** Organic solvent-based products such as hydrocarbons, chlorinated hydrocarbons, ketones, and esters shall not be used for ICF walls with expanded polystyrene form material. Plastic roofing cements, acrylic coatings, latex coatings, mortars, and pargings are permitted to be used to seal ICF walls. Cold-setting asphalt or hot asphalt shall conform to Type C of ASTM D 449. Hot asphalt shall be applied at a temperature of less than 200°F (93°C).

All joints in membrane waterproofing shall be lapped and sealed with an adhesive compatible with the membrane.

R406.3 Dampproofing for wood foundations. Wood foundations enclosing habitable or usable spaces located below grade shall be dampproofed in accordance with Sections R406.3.1 through R406.3.4.

R406.3.1 Panel joint sealed. Plywood panel joints in the foundation walls shall be sealed full length with a caulking compound capable of producing a moisture-proof seal under the conditions of temperature and moisture content at which it will be applied and used.

R406.3.2 Below-grade moisture barrier. A 6-mil-thick (0.15 mm) polyethylene film shall be applied over the below-grade portion of exterior foundation walls prior to backfilling. Joints in the polyethylene film shall be lapped 6 inches (152 mm) and sealed with adhesive. The top edge of the polyethylene film shall be bonded to the sheathing to form a seal. Film areas at grade level shall be protected from mechanical damage and exposure by a pressure preservatively treated lumber or plywood strip attached to the wall several inches above finish grade level and extending approximately 9 inches (229 mm) below grade. The joint between the strip and the wall shall be caulked full length prior to fastening the strip to the wall. Other coverings appropriate to the architectural treatment may also be used. The polyethylene film shall extend down to the bottom of the wood footing plate but shall not overlap or extend into the gravel or crushed stone footing.

R406.3.3 Porous fill. The space between the excavation and the foundation wall shall be backfilled with the same material used for footings, up to a height of 1 foot (305 mm)

above the footing for well-drained sites, or one-half the total back-fill height for poorly drained sites. The porous fill shall be covered with strips of 30-pound (13.6 kg) asphalt paper or 6-mil (0.15 mm) polyethylene to permit water seepage while avoiding infiltration of fine soils.

R406.3.4 Backfill. The remainder of the excavated area shall be backfilled with the same type of soil as was removed during the excavation.

SECTION R407
COLUMNS

R407.1 Wood column protection. Wood columns shall be protected against decay as set forth in Section R319.

R407.2 Steel column protection. All surfaces (inside and outside) of steel columns shall be given a shop coat of rust-inhibitive paint, except for corrosion-resistant steel and steel treated with coatings to provide corrosion resistance.

R407.3 Structural requirements. The columns shall be restrained to prevent lateral displacement at the bottom end. Wood columns shall not be less in nominal size than 4 inches by 4 inches (102 mm by 102 mm) and steel columns shall not be less than 3-inch-diameter (76 mm) standard pipe or approved equivalent.

> **Exception:** In Seismic Design Categories A, B and C columns no more than 48 inches (1219 mm) in height on a pier or footing are exempt from the bottom end lateral displacement requirement within underfloor areas enclosed by a continuous foundation.

SECTION R408
UNDER-FLOOR SPACE

R408.1 Ventilation. The under-floor space between the bottom of the floor joists and the earth under any building (except space occupied by a basement) shall have ventilation openings through foundation walls or exterior walls. The minimum net area of ventilation openings shall not be less than 1 square foot (0.0929 m²) for each 150 square feet (14 m²) of under-floor space area. One such ventilating opening shall be within 3 feet (914 mm) of each corner of the building.

R408.2 Openings for under-floor ventilation. The minimum net area of ventilation openings shall not be less than 1 square foot (0.0929 m²) for each 150 square feet (14 m²) of under-floor area. One ventilating opening shall be within 3 feet (914 mm) of each corner of the building. Ventilation openings shall be covered for their height and width with any of the following materials provided that the least dimension of the covering shall not exceed $^1/_4$ inch (6.4 mm):

1. Perforated sheet metal plates not less than 0.070 inch (1.8 mm) thick.

2. Expanded sheet metal plates not less than 0.047 inch (1.2 mm) thick.

3. Cast-iron grill or grating.

4. Extruded load-bearing brick vents.

5. Hardware cloth of 0.035 inch (0.89 mm) wire or heavier.

6. Corrosion-resistant wire mesh, with the least dimension being $^1/_8$ inch (3.2 mm).

R408.3 Unvented crawl space. Ventilation openings in under-floor spaces specified in Sections R408.1 and R408.2 shall not be required where:

1. Exposed earth is covered with a continuous vapor retarder. Joints of the vapor retarder shall overlap by 6 inches (152 mm) and shall be sealed or taped. The edges of the vapor retarder shall extend at least 6 inches (152 mm) up the stem wall and shall be attached and sealed to the stem wall; and

2. One of the following is provided for the under-floor space:

   2.1. Continuously operated mechanical exhaust ventilation at a rate equal to 1 cfm (0.47 L/s) for each 50 ft² (4.7 m²) of crawlspace floor area, including an air pathway to the common area (such as a duct or transfer grille), and perimeter walls insulated in accordance with Section N1102.2.8;

   2.2. Conditioned air supply sized to deliver at a rate equal to 1 cfm (0.47 L/s) for each 50 ft² (4.7 m²) of under-floor area, including a return air pathway to the common area (such as a duct or transfer grille), and perimeter walls insulated in accordance with Section N1102.2.8;

   2.3. Plenum complying with Section M1601.4, if under-floor space is used as a plenum.

R408.4 Access. Access shall be provided to all under-floor spaces. Access openings through the floor shall be a minimum of 18 inches by 24 inches (457 mm by 610 mm). Openings through a perimeter wall shall be not less than 16 inches by 24 inches (407 mm by 610 mm). When any portion of the through-wall access is below grade, an areaway not less than 16 inches by 24 inches (407 mm by 610 mm) shall be provided. The bottom of the areaway shall be below the threshold of the access opening. Through wall access openings shall not be located under a door to the residence. See Section M1305.1.4 for access requirements where mechanical equipment is located under floors.

R408.5 Removal of debris. The under-floor grade shall be cleaned of all vegetation and organic material. All wood forms used for placing concrete shall be removed before a building is occupied or used for any purpose. All construction materials shall be removed before a building is occupied or used for any purpose.

R408.6 Finished grade. The finished grade of under-floor surface may be located at the bottom of the footings; however, where there is evidence that the groundwater table can rise to within 6 inches (152 mm) of the finished floor at the building perimeter or where there is evidence that the surface water does not readily drain from the building site, the grade in the under-floor space shall be as high as the outside finished grade, unless an approved drainage system is provided.

R408.7 Flood resistance. For buildings located in areas prone to flooding as established in Table R301.2(1):

1. Walls enclosing the under-floor space shall be provided with flood openings in accordance with Section R324.2.2.

2. The finished ground level of the under-floor space shall be equal to or higher than the outside finished ground level.

   Exception: Under-floor spaces that meet the requirements of FEMA/FIA TB 11-1.

CHAPTER 5

FLOORS

SECTION R501
GENERAL

R501.1 Application. The provisions of this chapter shall control the design and construction of the floors for all buildings including the floors of attic spaces used to house mechanical or plumbing fixtures and equipment.

R501.2 Requirements. Floor construction shall be capable of accommodating all loads according to Section R301 and of transmitting the resulting loads to the supporting structural elements.

SECTION R502
WOOD FLOOR FRAMING

R502.1 Identification. Load-bearing dimension lumber for joists, beams and girders shall be identified by a grade mark of a lumber grading or inspection agency that has been approved by an accreditation body that complies with DOC PS 20. In lieu of a grade mark, a certificate of inspection issued by a lumber grading or inspection agency meeting the requirements of this section shall be accepted.

R502.1.1 Preservative-treated lumber. Preservative treated dimension lumber shall also be identified as required by Section R319.1.

R502.1.2 Blocking and subflooring. Blocking shall be a minimum of utility grade lumber. Subflooring may be a minimum of utility grade lumber or No. 4 common grade boards.

R502.1.3 End-jointed lumber. Approved end-jointed lumber identified by a grade mark conforming to Section R502.1 may be used interchangeably with solid-sawn members of the same species and grade.

R502.1.4 Prefabricated wood I-joists. Structural capacities and design provisions for prefabricated wood I-joists shall be established and monitored in accordance with ASTM D 5055.

R502.1.5 Structural glued laminated timbers. Glued laminated timbers shall be manufactured and identified as required in AITC A190.1 and ASTM D 3737.

R502.1.6 Structural log members. Stress grading of structural log members of nonrectangular shape, as typically used in log buildings, shall be in accordance with ASTM D 3957. Such structural log members shall be identified by the grade mark of an approved lumber grading or inspection agency. In lieu of a grade mark on the material, a certificate of inspection as to species and grade issued by a lumber-grading or inspection agency meeting the requirements of this section shall be permitted to be accepted.

R502.2 Design and construction. Floors shall be designed and constructed in accordance with the provisions of this chapter, Figure R502.2 and Sections R319 and R320 or in accordance with AF&PA/NDS.

R502.2.1 Framing at braced wall lines. A load path for lateral forces shall be provided between floor framing and braced wall panels located above or below a floor, as specified in Section R602.10.8.

R502.2.2 Decks. Where supported by attachment to an exterior wall, decks shall be positively anchored to the primary structure and designed for both vertical and lateral loads as applicable. Such attachment shall not be accomplished by the use of toenails or nails subject to withdrawal. Where positive connection to the primary building structure cannot be verified during inspection, decks shall be self-supporting. For decks with cantilevered framing members, connections to exterior walls or other framing members, shall be designed and constructed to resist uplift resulting from the full live load specified in Table R301.5 acting on the cantilevered portion of the deck.

R502.3 Allowable joist spans. Spans for floor joists shall be in accordance with Tables R502.3.1(1) and R502.3.1(2). For other grades and species and for other loading conditions, refer to the AF&PA Span Tables for Joists and Rafters.

R502.3.1 Sleeping areas and attic joists. Table R502.3.1(1) shall be used to determine the maximum allowable span of floor joists that support sleeping areas and attics that are accessed by means of a fixed stairway in accordance with Section R311.5 provided that the design live load does not exceed 30 psf (1.44 kPa) and the design dead load does not exceed 20 psf (0.96 kPa). The allowable span of ceiling joists that support attics used for limited storage or no storage shall be determined in accordance with Section R802.4.

R502.3.2 Other floor joists. Table R502.3.1(2) shall be used to determine the maximum allowable span of floor joists that support all other areas of the building, other than sleeping rooms and attics, provided that the design live load does not exceed 40 psf (1.92 kPa) and the design dead load does not exceed 20 psf (0.96 kPa).

R502.3.3 Floor cantilevers. Floor cantilever spans shall not exceed the nominal depth of the wood floor joist. Floor cantilevers constructed in accordance with Table R502.3.3(1) shall be permitted when supporting a light-frame bearing wall and roof only. Floor cantilevers supporting an exterior balcony are permitted to be constructed in accordance with Table R502.3.3(2).

R502.4 Joists under bearing partitions. Joists under parallel bearing partitions shall be of adequate size to support the load. Double joists, sized to adequately support the load, that are separated to permit the installation of piping or vents shall be full depth solid blocked with lumber not less than 2 inches (51 mm) in nominal thickness spaced not more than 4 feet (1219 mm) on center. Bearing partitions perpendicular to joists shall not be offset from supporting girders, walls or partitions more than the joist depth unless such joists are of sufficient size to carry the additional load.

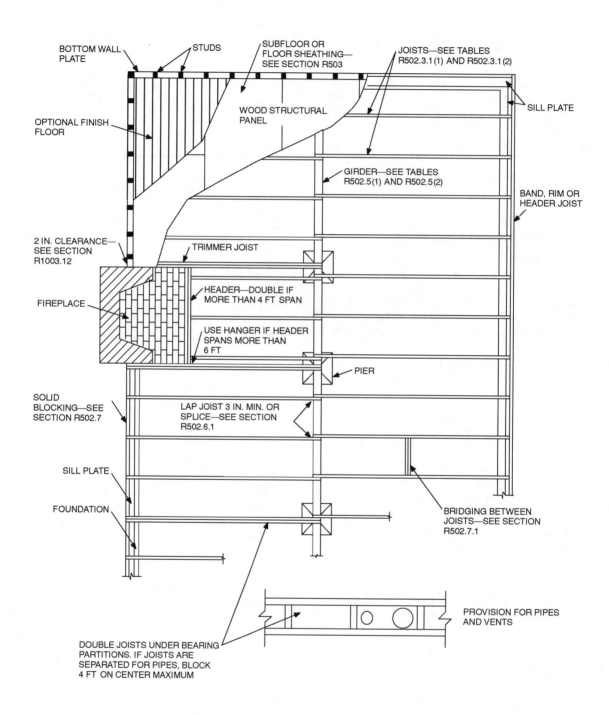

BOTTOM WALL PLATE

STUDS

SUBFLOOR OR FLOOR SHEATHING— SEE SECTION R503

JOISTS—SEE TABLES R502.3.1 (1) AND R502.3.1 (2)

SILL PLATE

OPTIONAL FINISH FLOOR

WOOD STRUCTURAL PANEL

GIRDER—SEE TABLES R502.5(1) AND R502.5(2)

BAND, RIM OR HEADER JOIST

2 IN. CLEARANCE— SEE SECTION R1003.12

TRIMMER JOIST

HEADER—DOUBLE IF MORE THAN 4 FT SPAN

FIREPLACE

USE HANGER IF HEADER SPANS MORE THAN 6 FT

PIER

SOLID BLOCKING—SEE SECTION R502.7

LAP JOIST 3 IN. MIN. OR SPLICE—SEE SECTION R502.6.1

SILL PLATE

FOUNDATION

BRIDGING BETWEEN JOISTS—SEE SECTION R502.7.1

PROVISION FOR PIPES AND VENTS

DOUBLE JOISTS UNDER BEARING PARTITIONS. IF JOISTS ARE SEPARATED FOR PIPES, BLOCK 4 FT ON CENTER MAXIMUM

For SI: 1 inch = 25.4 mm, 1 foot = 304.8 mm.

**FIGURE R502.2
FLOOR CONSTRUCTION**

TABLE R502.3.1(1)
FLOOR JOIST SPANS FOR COMMON LUMBER SPECIES
(Residential sleeping areas, live load = 30 psf, L/Δ = 360)[a]

JOIST SPACING (inches)	SPECIES AND GRADE		DEAD LOAD = 10 psf				DEAD LOAD = 20 psf			
			2×6	2×8	2×10	2×12	2×6	2×8	2×10	2×12
			Maximum floor joist spans							
			(ft - in.)	(ft - in.)	(ft - in.)	(ft - in.)	(ft - in.)	(ft - in.)	(ft - in.)	(ft - in.)
12	Douglas fir-larch	SS	12- 6	16- 6	21- 0	25- 7	12- 6	16- 6	21- 0	25- 7
	Douglas fir-larch	#1	12- 0	15-10	20- 3	24- 8	12- 0	15- 7	19- 0	22- 0
	Douglas fir-larch	#2	11-10	15- 7	19-10	23- 0	11- 6	14- 7	17- 9	20- 7
	Douglas fir-larch	#3	9- 8	12- 4	15- 0	17- 5	8- 8	11- 0	13- 5	15- 7
	Hem-fir	SS	11-10	15- 7	19-10	24- 2	11-10	15- 7	19-10	24- 2
	Hem-fir	#1	11- 7	15- 3	19- 5	23- 7	11- 7	15- 2	18- 6	21- 6
	Hem-fir	#2	11- 0	14- 6	18- 6	22- 6	11- 0	14- 4	17- 6	20- 4
	Hem-fir	#3	9- 8	12- 4	15- 0	17- 5	8- 8	11- 0	13- 5	15- 7
	Southern pine	SS	12- 3	16- 2	20- 8	25- 1	12- 3	16- 2	20- 8	25- 1
	Southern pine	#1	12- 0	15-10	20- 3	24- 8	12- 0	15-10	20- 3	24- 8
	Southern pine	#2	11-10	15- 7	19-10	24- 2	11-10	15- 7	18- 7	21- 9
	Southern pine	#3	10- 5	13- 3	15- 8	18- 8	9- 4	11-11	14- 0	16- 8
	Spruce-pine-fir	SS	11- 7	15- 3	19- 5	23- 7	11- 7	15- 3	19- 5	23- 7
	Spruce-pine-fir	#1	11- 3	14-11	19- 0	23- 0	11- 3	14- 7	17- 9	20- 7
	Spruce-pine-fir	#2	11- 3	14-11	19- 0	23- 0	11- 3	14- 7	17- 9	20- 7
	Spruce-pine-fir	#3	9- 8	12- 4	15- 0	17- 5	8- 8	11- 0	13- 5	15- 7
16	Douglas fir-larch	SS	11- 4	15- 0	19- 1	23- 3	11- 4	15- 0	19- 1	23- 0
	Douglas fir-larch	#1	10-11	14- 5	18- 5	21- 4	10- 8	13- 6	16- 5	19- 1
	Douglas fir-larch	#2	10- 9	14- 1	17- 2	19-11	9-11	12- 7	15- 5	17-10
	Douglas fir-larch	#3	8- 5	10- 8	13- 0	15- 1	7- 6	9- 6	11- 8	13- 6
	Hem-fir	SS	10- 9	14- 2	18- 0	21-11	10- 9	14- 2	18- 0	21-11
	Hem-fir	#1	10- 6	13-10	17- 8	20- 9	10- 4	13- 1	16- 0	18- 7
	Hem-fir	#2	10- 0	13- 2	16-10	19- 8	9-10	12- 5	15- 2	17- 7
	Hem-fir	#3	8- 5	10- 8	13- 0	15- 1	7- 6	9- 6	11- 8	13- 6
	Southern pine	SS	11- 2	14- 8	18- 9	22-10	11- 2	14- 8	18- 9	22-10
	Southern pine	#1	10-11	14- 5	18- 5	22- 5	10-11	14- 5	17-11	21- 4
	Southern pine	#2	10- 9	14- 2	18- 0	21- 1	10- 5	13- 6	16- 1	18-10
	Southern pine	#3	9- 0	11- 6	13- 7	16- 2	8- 1	10- 3	12- 2	14- 6
	Spruce-pine-fir	SS	10- 6	13-10	17- 8	21- 6	10- 6	13-10	17- 8	21- 4
	Spruce-pine-fir	#1	10- 3	13- 6	17- 2	19-11	9-11	12- 7	15- 5	17-10
	Spruce-pine-fir	#2	10- 3	13- 6	17- 2	19-11	9-11	12- 7	15- 5	17-10
	Spruce-pine-fir	#3	8- 5	10- 8	13- 0	15- 1	7- 6	9- 6	11- 8	13- 6
19.2	Douglas fir-larch	SS	10- 8	14- 1	18- 0	21-10	10- 8	14- 1	18- 0	21- 0
	Douglas fir-larch	#1	10- 4	13- 7	16- 9	19- 6	9- 8	12- 4	15- 0	17- 5
	Douglas fir-larch	#2	10- 1	12-10	15- 8	18- 3	9- 1	11- 6	14- 1	16- 3
	Douglas fir-larch	#3	7- 8	9- 9	11-10	13- 9	6-10	8- 8	10- 7	12- 4
	Hem-fir	SS	10- 1	13- 4	17- 0	20- 8	10- 1	13- 4	17- 0	20- 7
	Hem-fir	#1	9-10	13- 0	16- 4	19- 0	9- 6	12- 0	14- 8	17- 0
	Hem-fir	#2	9- 5	12- 5	15- 6	17- 1	8-11	11- 4	13-10	16- 1
	Hem-fir	#3	7- 8	9- 9	11-10	13- 9	6-10	8- 8	10- 7	12- 4
	Southern pine	SS	10- 6	13-10	17- 8	21- 6	10- 6	13-10	17- 8	21- 6
	Southern pine	#1	10- 4	13- 7	17- 4	21- 1	10- 4	13- 7	16- 4	19- 6
	Southern pine	#2	10- 1	13- 4	16- 5	19- 3	9- 6	12- 4	14- 8	17- 2
	Southern pine	#3	8- 3	10- 6	12- 5	14- 9	7- 4	9- 5	11- 1	13- 2
	Spruce-pine-fir	SS	9-10	13- 0	16- 7	20- 2	9-10	13- 0	16- 7	19- 6
	Spruce-pine-fir	#1	9- 8	12- 9	15- 8	18- 3	9- 1	11- 6	14- 1	16- 3
	Spruce-pine-fir	#2	9- 8	12- 9	15- 8	18- 3	9- 1	11- 6	14- 1	16- 3
	Spruce-pine-fir	#3	7- 8	9- 9	11-10	13- 9	6-10	8- 8	10- 7	12- 4
24	Douglas fir-larch	SS	9-11	13- 1	16- 8	20- 3	9-11	13- 1	16- 2	18- 9
	Douglas fir-larch	#1	9- 7	12- 4	15- 0	17- 5	8- 8	11- 0	13- 5	15- 7
	Douglas fir-larch	#2	9- 1	11- 6	14- 1	16- 3	8- 1	10- 3	12- 7	14- 7
	Douglas fir-larch	#3	6-10	8- 8	10- 7	12- 4	6- 2	7- 9	9- 6	11- 0
	Hem-fir	SS	9- 4	12- 4	15- 9	19- 2	9- 4	12- 4	15- 9	18- 5
	Hem-fir	#1	9- 2	12- 0	14- 8	17- 0	8- 6	10- 9	13- 1	15- 2
	Hem-fir	#2	8- 9	11- 4	13-10	16- 1	8- 0	10- 2	12- 5	14- 4
	Hem-fir	#3	6-10	8- 8	10- 7	12- 4	6- 2	7- 9	9- 6	11- 0
	Southern pine	SS	9- 9	12-10	16- 5	19-11	9- 9	12-10	16- 5	19-11
	Southern pine	#1	9- 7	12- 7	16- 1	19- 6	9- 7	12- 4	14- 7	17- 5
	Southern pine	#2	9- 4	12- 4	14- 8	17- 2	8- 6	11- 0	13- 1	15- 5
	Southern pine	#3	7- 4	9- 5	11- 1	13- 2	6- 7	8- 5	9-11	11-10
	Spruce-pine-fir	SS	9- 2	12- 1	15- 5	18- 9	9- 2	12- 1	15- 0	17- 5
	Spruce-pine-fir	#1	8-11	11- 6	14- 1	16- 3	8- 1	10- 3	12- 7	14- 7
	Spruce-pine-fir	#2	8-11	11- 6	14- 1	16- 3	8- 1	10- 3	12- 7	14- 7
	Spruce-pine-fir	#3	6-10	8- 8	10- 7	12- 4	6- 2	7- 9	9- 6	11- 0

For SI: 1 inch = 25.4 mm, 1 foot = 304.8 mm, 1 pound per square foot = 0.0479 kPa.

NOTE: Check sources for availability of lumber in lengths greater than 20 feet.

a. Dead load limits for townhouses in Seismic Design Category C and all structures in Seismic Design Categories D_0, D_1 and D_2 shall be determined in accordance with Section R301.2.2.2.1.

TABLE R502.3.1(2)
FLOOR JOIST SPANS FOR COMMON LUMBER SPECIES
(Residential living areas, live load = 40 psf, L/Δ = 360)[b]

JOIST SPACING (inches)	SPECIES AND GRADE		DEAD LOAD = 10 psf				DEAD LOAD = 20 psf			
			2×6	2×8	2×10	2×12	2×6	2×8	2×10	2×12
			Maximum floor joist spans							
			(ft - in.)	(ft - in.)	(ft - in.)	(ft - in.)	(ft - in.)	(ft - in.)	(ft - in.)	(ft - in.)
12	Douglas fir-larch	SS	11- 4	15- 0	19- 1	23- 3	11- 4	15- 0	19- 1	23- 3
	Douglas fir-larch	#1	10-11	14- 5	18- 5	22- 0	10-11	14- 2	17- 4	20- 1
	Douglas fir-larch	#2	10- 9	14- 2	17- 9	20- 7	10- 6	13- 3	16- 3	18-10
	Douglas fir-larch	#3	8- 8	11- 0	13- 5	15- 7	7-11	10- 0	12- 3	14- 3
	Hem-fir	SS	10- 9	14- 2	18- 0	21-11	10- 9	14- 2	18- 0	21-11
	Hem-fir	#1	10- 6	13-10	17- 8	21- 6	10- 6	13-10	16-11	19- 7
	Hem-fir	#2	10- 0	13- 2	16-10	20- 4	10- 0	13- 1	16- 0	18- 6
	Hem-fir	#3	8- 8	11- 0	13- 5	15- 7	7-11	10- 0	12- 3	14- 3
	Southern pine	SS	11- 2	14- 8	18- 9	22-10	11- 2	14- 8	18- 9	22-10
	Southern pine	#1	10-11	14- 5	18- 5	22- 5	10-11	14- 5	18- 5	22- 5
	Southern pine	#2	10- 9	14- 2	18- 0	21- 9	10- 9	14- 2	16-11	19-10
	Southern pine	#3	9- 4	11-11	14- 0	16- 8	8- 6	10-10	12-10	15- 3
	Spruce-pine-fir	SS	10- 6	13-10	17- 8	21- 6	10- 6	13-10	17- 8	21- 6
	Spruce-pine-fir	#1	10- 3	13- 6	17- 3	20- 7	10- 3	13- 3	16- 3	18-10
	Spruce-pine-fir	#2	10- 3	13- 6	17- 3	20- 7	10- 3	13- 3	16- 3	18-10
	Spruce-pine-fir	#3	8- 8	11- 0	13- 5	15- 7	7-11	10- 0	12- 3	14- 3
16	Douglas fir-larch	SS	10- 4	13- 7	17- 4	21- 1	10- 4	13- 7	17- 4	21- 0
	Douglas fir-larch	#1	9-11	13- 1	16- 5	19- 1	9- 8	12- 4	15- 0	17- 5
	Douglas fir-larch	#2	9- 9	12- 7	15- 5	17-10	9- 1	11- 6	14- 1	16- 3
	Douglas fir-larch	#3	7- 6	9- 6	11- 8	13- 6	6-10	8- 8	10- 7	12- 4
	Hem-fir	SS	9- 9	12-10	16- 5	19-11	9- 9	12-10	16- 5	19-11
	Hem-fir	#1	9- 6	12- 7	16- 0	18- 7	9- 6	12- 0	14- 8	17- 0
	Hem-fir	#2	9- 1	12- 0	15- 2	17- 7	8-11	11- 4	13-10	16- 1
	Hem-fir	#3	7- 6	9- 6	11- 8	13- 6	6-10	8- 8	10- 7	12- 4
	Southern pine	SS	10- 2	13- 4	17- 0	20- 9	10- 2	13- 4	17- 0	20- 9
	Southern pine	#1	9-11	13- 1	16- 9	20- 4	9-11	13- 1	16- 4	19- 6
	Southern pine	#2	9- 9	12-10	16- 1	18-10	9- 6	12- 4	14- 8	17- 2
	Southern pine	#3	8- 1	10- 3	12- 2	14- 6	7- 4	9- 5	11- 1	13- 2
	Spruce-pine-fir	SS	9- 6	12- 7	16- 0	19- 6	9- 6	12- 7	16- 0	19- 6
	Spruce-pine-fir	#1	9- 4	12- 3	15- 5	17-10	9- 1	11- 6	14- 1	16- 3
	Spruce-pine-fir	#2	9- 4	12- 3	15- 5	17-10	9- 1	11- 6	14- 1	16- 3
	Spruce-pine-fir	#3	7- 6	9- 6	11- 8	13- 6	6-10	8- 8	10- 7	12- 4
19.2	Douglas fir-larch	SS	9- 8	12-10	16- 4	19-10	9- 8	12-10	16- 4	19- 2
	Douglas fir-larch	#1	9- 4	12- 4	15- 0	17- 5	8-10	11- 3	13- 8	15-11
	Douglas fir-larch	#2	9- 1	11- 6	14- 1	16- 3	8- 3	10- 6	12-10	14-10
	Douglas fir-larch	#3	6-10	8- 8	10- 7	12- 4	6- 3	7-11	9- 8	11- 3
	Hem-fir	SS	9- 2	12- 1	15- 5	18- 9	9- 2	12- 1	15- 5	18- 9
	Hem-fir	#1	9- 0	11-10	14- 8	17- 0	8- 8	10-11	13- 4	15- 6
	Hem-fir	#2	8- 7	11- 3	13-10	16- 1	8- 2	10- 4	12- 8	14- 8
	Hem-fir	#3	6-10	8- 8	10- 7	12- 4	6- 3	7-11	9- 8	11- 3
	Southern pine	SS	9- 6	12- 7	16- 0	19- 6	9- 6	12- 7	16- 0	19- 6
	Southern pine	#1	9- 4	12- 4	15- 9	19- 2	9- 4	12- 4	14-11	17- 9
	Southern pine	#2	9- 2	12- 1	14- 8	17- 2	8- 8	11- 3	13- 5	15- 8
	Southern pine	#3	7- 4	9- 5	11- 1	13- 2	6- 9	8- 7	10- 1	12- 1
	Spruce-pine-fir	SS	9- 0	11-10	15- 1	18- 4	9- 0	11-10	15- 1	17- 9
	Spruce-pine-fir	#	8- 9	11- 6	14- 1	16- 3	8- 3	10- 6	12-10	14-10
	Spruce-pine-fir	#2	8- 9	11- 6	14- 1	16- 3	8- 3	10- 6	12-10	14-10
	Spruce-pine-fir	#3	6-10	8- 8	10- 7	12- 4	6- 3	7-11	9- 8	11- 3
24	Douglas fir-larch	SS	9- 0	11-11	15- 2	18- 5	9- 0	11-11	14- 9	17- 1
	Douglas fir-larch	#1	8- 8	11- 0	13- 5	15- 7	7-11	10- 0	12- 3	14- 3
	Douglas fir-larch	#2	8- 1	10- 3	12- 7	14- 7	7- 5	9- 5	11- 6	13- 4
	Douglas fir-larch	#3	6- 2	7- 9	9- 6	11- 0	5- 7	7- 1	8- 8	10- 1
	Hem-fir	SS	8- 6	11- 3	14- 4	17- 5	8- 6	11- 3	14- 4	16-10[a]
	Hem-fir	#1	8- 4	10- 9	13- 1	15- 2	7- 9	9- 9	11-11	13-10
	Hem-fir	#2	7-11	10- 2	12- 5	14- 4	7- 4	9- 3	11- 4	13- 1
	Hem-fir	#3	6- 2	7- 9	9- 6	11- 0	5- 7	7- 1	8- 8	10- 1
	Southern pine	SS	8-10	11- 8	14-11	18- 1	8-10	11- 8	14-11	18- 1
	Southern pine	#1	8- 8	11- 5	14- 7	17- 5	8- 8	11- 3	13- 4	15-11
	Southern pine	#2	8- 6	11- 0	13- 1	15- 5	7- 9	10- 0	12- 0	14- 0
	Southern pine	#3	6- 7	8- 5	9-11	11-10	6- 0	7- 8	9- 1	10- 9
	Spruce-pine-fir	SS	8- 4	11- 0	14- 0	17- 0	8- 4	11- 0	13- 8	15-11
	Spruce-pine-fir	#1	8- 1	10- 3	12- 7	14- 7	7- 5	9- 5	11- 6	13- 4
	Spruce-pine-fir	#2	8- 1	10- 3	12- 7	14- 7	7- 5	9- 5	11- 6	13- 4
	Spruce-pine-fir	#3	6- 2	7- 9	9- 6	11- 0	5- 7	7- 1	8- 8	10- 1

For SI: 1 inch = 25.4 mm, 1 foot = 304.8 mm, 1 pound per square foot = 0.0479 kPa.

NOTE: Check sources for availability of lumber in lengths greater than 20 feet.

a. End bearing length shall be increased to 2 inches.

b. Dead load limits for townhouses in Seismic Design Category C and all structures in Seismic Design Categories D_0, D_1, and D_2 shall be determined in accordance with Section R301.2.2.2.1.

TABLE R502.3.3(1)
CANTILEVER SPANS FOR FLOOR JOISTS SUPPORTING LIGHT-FRAME EXTERIOR BEARING WALL AND ROOF ONLY[a, b, c, f, g, h]
(Floor Live Load ≤ 40 psf, Roof Live Load ≤ 20 psf)

Member & Spacing	Maximum Cantilever Span (Uplift Force at Backspan Support in Lbs.)[d, e]											
	Ground Snow Load											
	≤ 20 psf			30 psf			50 psf			70 psf		
	Roof Width			Roof Width			Roof Width			Roof Width		
	24 ft	32 ft	40 ft	24 ft	32 ft	40 ft	24 ft	32 ft	40 ft	24 ft	32 ft	40 ft
2 × 8 @ 12″	20″ (177)	15″ (227)	—	18″ (209)	—	—	—	—	—	—	—	—
2 × 10 @ 16″	29″ (228)	21″ (297)	16″ (364)	26″ (271)	18″ (354)	—	20″ (375)	—	—	—	—	—
2 × 10 @ 12″	36″ (166)	26″ (219)	20″ (270)	34″ (198)	22″ (263)	16″ (324)	26″ (277)	—	—	19″ (356)	—	—
2 × 12 @ 16″	—	32″ (287)	25″ (356)	36″ (263)	29″ (345)	21″ (428)	29″ (367)	20″ (484)	—	23″ (471)	—	—
2 × 12 @ 12″	—	42″ (209)	31″ (263)	—	37″ (253)	27″ (317)	36″ (271)	27″ (358)	17″ (447)	31″ (348)	19″ (462)	—
2 × 12 @ 8″	—	48″ (136)	45″ (169)	—	48″ (164)	38″ (206)	—	40″ (233)	26″ (294)	36″ (230)	29″ (304)	18″ (379)

For SI: 1 inch = 25.4 mm, 1 pound per square foot = 0.0479 kPa.

a. Tabulated values are for clear-span roof supported solely by exterior bearing walls.

b. Spans are based on No. 2 Grade lumber of Douglas fir-larch, hem-fir, southern pine, and spruce-pine-fir for repetitive (3 or more) members.

c. Ratio of backspan to cantilever span shall be at least 3:1.

d. Connections capable of resisting the indicated uplift force shall be provided at the backspan support.

e. Uplift force is for a backspan to cantilever span ratio of 3:1. Tabulated uplift values are permitted to be reduced by multiplying by a factor equal to 3 divided by the actual backspan ratio provided (3/backspan ratio).

f. See Section R301.2.2.2.2, Item 1, for additional limitations on cantilevered floor joists for detached one- and two-family dwellings in Seismic Design Category D_0, D_1, or D_2 and townhouses in Seismic Design Category C, D_0, D_1, or D_2.

g. A full-depth rim joist shall be provided at the cantilevered end of the joists. Solid blocking shall be provided at the cantilever support.

h. Linear interpolation shall be permitted for building widths and ground snow loads other than shown.

TABLE R502.3.3(2)
CANTILEVER SPANS FOR FLOOR JOISTS SUPPORTING EXTERIOR BALCONY[a, b, e, f]

Member Size	Spacing	Maximum Cantilever Span (Uplift Force at Backspan Support in lb)[c, d]		
		Ground Snow Load		
		≤ 30 psf	50 psf	70 psf
2 × 8	12″	42″ (139)	39″ (156)	34″ (165)
2 × 8	16″	36″ (151)	34″ (171)	29″ (180)
2 × 10	12″	61″ (164)	57″ (189)	49″ (201)
2 × 10	16″	53″ (180)	49″ (208)	42″ (220)
2 × 10	24″	43″ (212)	40″ (241)	34″ (255)
2 × 12	16″	72″ (228)	67″ (260)	57″ (268)
2 × 12	24″	58″ (279)	54″ (319)	47″ (330)

For SI: 1 inch = 25.4 mm, 1 pound per square foot = 0.0479 kPa.

a. Spans are based on No. 2 Grade lumber of Douglas fir-larch, hem-fir, southern pine, and spruce-pine-fir for repetitive (3 or more) members.

b. Ratio of backspan to cantilever span shall be at least 2:1.

c. Connections capable of resisting the indicated uplift force shall be provided at the backspan support.

d. Uplift force is for a backspan to cantilever span ratio of 2:1. Tabulated uplift values are permitted to be reduced by multiplying by a factor equal to 2 divided by the actual backspan ratio provided (2/backspan ratio).

e. A full-depth rim joist shall be provided at the cantilevered end of the joists. Solid blocking shall be provided at the cantilevered support.

f. Linear interpolation shall be permitted for ground snow loads other than shown.

TABLE R502.5(1)
GIRDER SPANS[a] AND HEADER SPANS[a] FOR EXTERIOR BEARING WALLS
(Maximum spans for Douglas fir-larch, hem-fir, southern pine and spruce-pine-fir[b] and required number of jack studs)

GIRDERS AND HEADERS SUPPORTING	SIZE	GROUND SNOW LOAD (psf)[e]																	
		30						50						70					
		Building width[c] (feet)																	
		20		28		36		20		28		36		20		28		36	
		Span	NJ[d]	Span	NJ[d]	Span	NJ[d]	Span	NJ[d]	Span	NJ[d]	Span	NJ[d]	Span	NJ[d]	Span	NJ[d]	Span	NJ[d]
Roof and ceiling	2-2×4	3-6	1	3-2	1	2-10	1	3-2	1	2-9	1	2-6	1	2-10	1	2-6	1	2-3	1
	2-2×6	5-5	1	4-8	1	4-2	1	4-8	1	4-1	1	3-8	2	4-2	1	3-8	2	3-3	2
	2-2×8	6-10	1	5-11	2	5-4	2	5-11	2	5-2	2	4-7	2	5-4	2	4-7	2	4-1	2
	2-2×10	8-5	2	7-3	2	6-6	2	7-3	2	6-3	2	5-7	2	6-6	2	5-7	2	5-0	2
	2-2×12	9-9	2	8-5	2	7-6	2	8-5	2	7-3	2	6-6	2	7-6	2	6-6	2	5-10	3
	3-2×8	8-4	1	7-5	1	6-8	1	7-5	1	6-5	2	5-9	2	6-8	1	5-9	2	5-2	2
	3-2×10	10-6	1	9-1	2	8-2	2	9-1	2	7-10	2	7-0	2	8-2	2	7-0	2	6-4	2
	3-2×12	12-2	2	10-7	2	9-5	2	10-7	2	9-2	2	8-2	2	9-5	2	8-2	2	7-4	2
	4-2×8	9-2	1	8-4	1	7-8	1	8-4	1	7-5	1	6-8	1	7-8	1	6-8	1	5-11	2
	4-2×10	11-8	1	10-6	1	9-5	2	10-6	1	9-1	2	8-2	2	9-5	2	8-2	2	7-3	2
	4-2×12	14-1	1	12-2	2	10-11	2	12-2	2	10-7	2	9-5	2	10-11	2	9-5	2	8-5	2
Roof, ceiling and one center-bearing floor	2-2×4	3-1	1	2-9	1	2-5	1	2-9	1	2-5	1	2-2	1	2-7	1	2-3	1	2-0	1
	2-2×6	4-6	1	4-0	1	3-7	2	4-1	1	3-7	2	3-3	2	3-9	2	3-3	2	2-11	2
	2-2×8	5-9	2	5-0	2	4-6	2	5-2	2	4-6	2	4-1	2	4-9	2	4-2	2	3-9	2
	2-2×10	7-0	2	6-2	2	5-6	2	6-4	2	5-6	2	5-0	2	5-9	2	5-1	2	4-7	3
	2-2×12	8-1	2	7-1	2	6-5	2	7-4	2	6-5	2	5-9	3	6-8	2	5-10	3	5-3	3
	3-2×8	7-2	1	6-3	2	5-8	2	6-5	2	5-8	2	5-1	2	5-11	2	5-2	2	4-8	2
	3-2×10	8-9	2	7-8	2	6-11	2	7-11	2	6-11	2	6-3	2	7-3	2	6-4	2	5-8	2
	3-2×12	10-2	2	8-11	2	8-0	2	9-2	2	8-0	2	7-3	2	8-5	2	7-4	2	6-7	2
	4-2×8	8-1	1	7-3	1	6-7	1	7-5	1	6-6	1	5-11	2	6-10	1	6-0	2	5-5	2
	4-2×10	10-1	1	8-10	2	8-0	2	9-1	2	8-0	2	7-2	2	8-4	2	7-4	2	6-7	2
	4-2×12	11-9	2	10-3	2	9-3	2	10-7	2	9-3	2	8-4	2	9-8	2	8-6	2	7-7	2
Roof, ceiling and one clear span floor	2-2×4	2-8	1	2-4	1	2-1	1	2-7	1	2-3	1	2-0	1	2-5	1	2-1	1	1-10	1
	2-2×6	3-11	1	3-5	2	3-0	2	3-10	2	3-4	2	3-0	2	3-6	2	3-1	2	2-9	2
	2-2×8	5-0	2	4-4	2	3-10	2	4-10	2	4-2	2	3-9	2	4-6	2	3-11	2	3-6	2
	2-2×10	6-1	2	5-3	2	4-8	2	5-11	2	5-1	2	4-7	3	5-6	2	4-9	2	4-3	3
	2-2×12	7-1	2	6-1	3	5-5	3	6-10	2	5-11	3	5-4	3	6-4	2	5-6	3	5-0	3
	3-2×8	6-3	2	5-5	2	4-10	2	6-1	2	5-3	2	4-8	2	5-7	2	4-11	2	4-5	2
	3-2×10	7-7	2	6-7	2	5-11	2	7-5	2	6-5	2	5-9	2	6-10	2	6-0	2	5-4	2
	3-2×12	8-10	2	7-8	2	6-10	2	8-7	2	7-5	2	6-8	2	7-11	2	6-11	2	6-3	2
	4-2×8	7-2	1	6-3	2	5-7	2	7-0	1	6-1	2	5-5	2	6-6	1	5-8	2	5-1	2
	4-2×10	8-9	2	7-7	2	6-10	2	8-7	2	7-5	2	6-7	2	7-11	2	6-11	2	6-2	2
	4-2×12	10-2	2	8-10	2	7-11	2	9-11	2	8-7	2	7-8	2	9-2	2	8-0	2	7-2	2
Roof, ceiling and two center-bearing floors	2-2×4	2-7	1	2-3	1	2-0	1	2-6	1	2-2	1	1-11	1	2-4	1	2-0	1	1-9	1
	2-2×6	3-9	2	3-3	2	2-11	2	3-8	2	3-2	2	2-10	2	3-5	2	3-0	2	2-8	2
	2-2×8	4-9	2	4-2	2	3-9	2	4-7	2	4-0	2	3-8	2	4-4	2	3-9	2	3-5	2
	2-2×10	5-9	2	5-1	2	4-7	3	5-8	2	4-11	2	4-5	3	5-3	2	4-7	3	4-2	3
	2-2×12	6-8	2	5-10	3	5-3	3	6-6	2	5-9	3	5-2	3	6-1	3	5-4	3	4-10	3
	3-2×8	5-11	2	5-2	2	4-8	2	5-9	2	5-1	2	4-7	2	5-5	2	4-9	2	4-3	2
	3-2×10	7-3	2	6-4	2	5-8	2	7-1	2	6-2	2	5-7	2	6-7	2	5-9	2	5-3	2
	3-2×12	8-5	2	7-4	2	6-7	2	8-2	2	7-2	2	6-5	3	7-8	2	6-9	2	6-1	3
	4-2×8	6-10	1	6-0	2	5-5	2	6-8	1	5-10	2	5-3	2	6-3	2	5-6	2	4-11	2
	4-2×10	8-4	2	7-4	2	6-7	2	8-2	2	7-2	2	6-5	2	7-7	2	6-8	2	6-0	2
	4-2×12	9-8	2	8-6	2	7-8	2	9-5	2	8-3	2	7-5	2	8-10	2	7-9	2	7-0	2

(continued)

TABLE R502.5(1)—continued
GIRDER SPANS[a] AND HEADER SPANS[a] FOR EXTERIOR BEARING WALLS
(Maximum spans for Douglas fir-larch, hem-fir, southern pine and spruce-pine-fir[b] and required number of jack studs)

GIRDERS AND HEADERS SUPPORTING	SIZE	GROUND SNOW LOAD (psf)[e]																
		30						50						70				
		Building width[c] (feet)																
		20		28		36		20		28		36		20		28		36
		Span	NJ[d]	Span	NJ[d]	Span	NJ[d]	Span	NJ[d]	Span	NJ[d]	Span	NJ[d]	Span	NJ[d]	Span	NJ[d]	Span	NJ[d]
Roof, ceiling, and two clear span floors	2-2×4	2-1	1	1-8	1	1-6	2	2-0	1	1-8	1	1-5	2	2-0	1	1-8	1	1-5	2
	2-2×6	3-1	2	2-8	2	2-4	2	3-0	2	2-7	2	2-3	2	2-11	2	2-7	2	2-3	2
	2-2×8	3-10	2	3-4	2	3-0	3	3-10	2	3-4	2	2-11	3	3-9	2	3-3	2	2-11	3
	2-2×10	4-9	2	4-1	3	3-8	3	4-8	2	4-0	3	3-7	3	4-7	3	4-0	3	3-6	3
	2-2×12	5-6	3	4-9	3	4-3	3	5-5	3	4-8	3	4-2	3	5-4	3	4-7	3	4-1	4
	3-2×8	4-10	2	4-2	2	3-9	2	4-9	2	4-1	2	3-8	2	4-8	2	4-1	2	3-8	2
	3-2×10	5-11	2	5-1	2	4-7	3	5-10	2	5-0	2	4-6	3	5-9	2	4-11	2	4-5	3
	3-2×12	6-10	2	5-11	3	5-4	3	6-9	2	5-10	3	5-3	3	6-8	2	5-9	3	5-2	3
	4-2×8	5-7	2	4-10	2	4-4	2	5-6	2	4-9	2	4-3	2	5-5	2	4-8	2	4-2	2
	4-2×10	6-10	2	5-11	2	5-3	2	6-9	2	5-10	2	5-2	2	6-7	2	5-9	2	5-1	2
	4-2×12	7-11	2	6-10	2	6-2	3	7-9	2	6-9	2	6-0	3	7-8	2	6-8	2	5-11	3

For SI: 1 inch = 25.4 mm, 1 pound per square foot = 0.0479 kPa.

a. Spans are given in feet and inches.
b. Tabulated values assume #2 grade lumber.
c. Building width is measured perpendicular to the ridge. For widths between those shown, spans are permitted to be interpolated.
d. NJ - Number of jack studs required to support each end. Where the number of required jack studs equals one, the header is permitted to be supported by an approved framing anchor attached to the full-height wall stud and to the header.
e. Use 30 psf ground snow load for cases in which ground snow load is less than 30 psf and the roof live load is equal to or less than 20 psf.

R502.5 Allowable girder spans. The allowable spans of girders fabricated of dimension lumber shall not exceed the values set forth in Tables R502.5(1) and R502.5(2).

R502.6 Bearing. The ends of each joist, beam or girder shall have not less than 1.5 inches (38 mm) of bearing on wood or metal and not less than 3 inches (76 mm) on masonry or concrete except where supported on a 1-inch-by-4-inch (25.4 mm by 102 mm) ribbon strip and nailed to the adjacent stud or by the use of approved joist hangers.

R502.6.1 Floor systems. Joists framing from opposite sides over a bearing support shall lap a minimum of 3 inches (76 mm) and shall be nailed together with a minimum three 10d face nails. A wood or metal splice with strength equal to or greater than that provided by the nailed lap is permitted.

R502.6.2 Joist framing. Joists framing into the side of a wood girder shall be supported by approved framing anchors or on ledger strips not less than nominal 2 inches by 2 inches (51 mm by 51 mm).

R502.7 Lateral restraint at supports. Joists shall be supported laterally at the ends by full-depth solid blocking not less than 2 inches (51 mm) nominal in thickness; or by attachment to a full-depth header, band or rim joist, or to an adjoining stud or shall be otherwise provided with lateral support to prevent rotation.

Exception: In Seismic Design Categories D_0, D_1 and D_2, lateral restraint shall also be provided at each intermediate support.

R502.7.1 Bridging. Joists exceeding a nominal 2 inches by 12 inches (51 mm by 305 mm) shall be supported laterally by solid blocking, diagonal bridging (wood or metal), or a continuous 1-inch-by-3-inch (25.4 mm by 76 mm) strip nailed across the bottom of joists perpendicular to joists at intervals not exceeding 8 feet (2438 mm).

R502.8 Drilling and notching. Structural floor members shall not be cut, bored or notched in excess of the limitations specified in this section. See Figure R502.8.

R502.8.1 Sawn lumber. Notches in solid lumber joists, rafters and beams shall not exceed one-sixth of the depth of the member, shall not be longer than one-third of the depth of the member and shall not be located in the middle one-third of the span. Notches at the ends of the member shall not exceed one-fourth the depth of the member. The tension side of members 4 inches (102 mm) or greater in nominal thickness shall not be notched except at the ends of the members. The diameter of holes bored or cut into members shall not exceed one-third the depth of the member. Holes shall not be closer than 2 inches (51 mm) to the top or bottom of the member, or to any other hole located in the member. Where the member is also notched, the hole shall not be closer than 2 inches (51 mm) to the notch.

R502.8.2 Engineered wood products. Cuts, notches and holes bored in trusses, structural composite lumber, structural glue-laminated members or I-joists are prohibited except where permitted by the manufacturer's recommendations or where the effects of such alterations are specifically considered in the design of the member by a registered design professional.

TABLE R502.5(2)
GIRDER SPANS[a] AND HEADER SPANS[a] FOR INTERIOR BEARING WALLS
(Maximum spans for Douglas fir-larch, hem-fir, southern pine and spruce-pine-fir[b] and required number of jack studs)

HEADERS AND GIRDERS SUPPORTING	SIZE	BUILDING WIDTH[c] (feet)					
		20		28		36	
		Span	NJ[d]	Span	NJ[d]	Span	NJ[d]
One floor only	2-2×4	3-1	1	2-8	1	2-5	1
	2-2×6	4-6	1	3-11	1	3-6	1
	2-2×8	5-9	1	5-0	2	4-5	2
	2-2×10	7-0	2	6-1	2	5-5	2
	2-2×12	8-1	2	7-0	2	6-3	2
	3-2×8	7-2	1	6-3	1	5-7	2
	3-2×10	8-9	1	7-7	2	6-9	2
	3-2×12	10-2	2	8-10	2	7-10	2
	4-2×8	9-0	1	7-8	1	6-9	1
	4-2×10	10-1	1	8-9	1	7-10	2
	4-2×12	11-9	1	10-2	2	9-1	2
Two floors	2-2×4	2-2	1	1-10	1	1-7	1
	2-2×6	3-2	2	2-9	2	2-5	2
	2-2×8	4-1	2	3-6	2	3-2	2
	2-2×10	4-11	2	4-3	2	3-10	3
	2-2×12	5-9	2	5-0	3	4-5	3
	3-2×8	5-1	2	4-5	2	3-11	2
	3-2×10	6-2	2	5-4	2	4-10	2
	3-2×12	7-2	2	6-3	2	5-7	3
	4-2×8	6-1	1	5-3	2	4-8	2
	4-2×10	7-2	2	6-2	2	5-6	2
	4-2×12	8-4	2	7-2	2	6-5	2

For SI: 1 inch = 25.4 mm, 1 foot = 304.8 mm.

a. Spans are given in feet and inches.

b. Tabulated values assume #2 grade lumber.

c. Building width is measured perpendicular to the ridge. For widths between those shown, spans are permitted to be interpolated.

d. NJ - Number of jack studs required to support each end. Where the number of required jack studs equals one, the header is permitted to be supported by an approved framing anchor attached to the full-height wall stud and to the header.

R502.9 Fastening. Floor framing shall be nailed in accordance with Table R602.3(1). Where posts and beam or girder construction is used to support floor framing, positive connections shall be provided to ensure against uplift and lateral displacement.

R502.10 Framing of openings. Openings in floor framing shall be framed with a header and trimmer joists. When the header joist span does not exceed 4 feet (1219 mm), the header joist may be a single member the same size as the floor joist. Single trimmer joists may be used to carry a single header joist that is located within 3 feet (914 mm) of the trimmer joist bearing. When the header joist span exceeds 4 feet (1219 mm), the trimmer joists and the header joist shall be doubled and of sufficient cross section to support the floor joists framing into the header. Approved hangers shall be used for the header joist to trimmer joist connections when the header joist span exceeds 6 feet (1829 mm). Tail joists over 12 feet (3658 mm) long shall be supported at the header by framing anchors or on ledger strips not less than 2 inches by 2 inches (51 mm by 51 mm).

R502.11 Wood trusses.

R502.11.1 Design. Wood trusses shall be designed in accordance with approved engineering practice. The design and manufacture of metal plate connected wood trusses shall comply with ANSI/TPI 1. The truss design drawings shall be prepared by a registered professional where required by the statutes of the jurisdiction in which the project is to be constructed in accordance with Section R106.1.

R502.11.2 Bracing. Trusses shall be braced to prevent rotation and provide lateral stability in accordance with the requirements specified in the construction documents for the building and on the individual truss design drawings. In the absence of specific bracing requirements, trusses shall be braced in accordance with the Building Component Safety Information (BCSI 1-03) Guide to Good Practice for Handling, Installing & Bracing of Metal Plate Connected Wood Trusses.

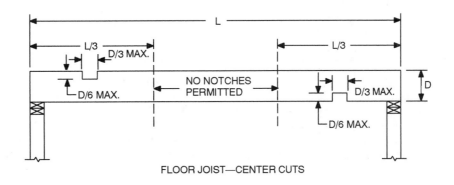

FLOOR JOIST—CENTER CUTS

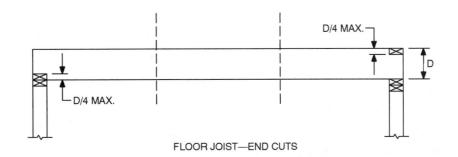

FLOOR JOIST—END CUTS

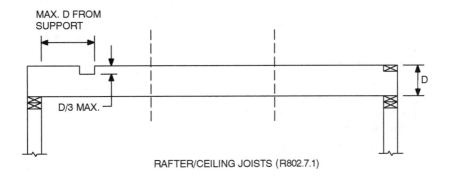

RAFTER/CEILING JOISTS (R802.7.1)

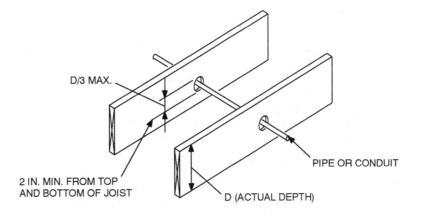

For SI: 1 inch = 25.4 mm.

FIGURE R502.8
CUTTING, NOTCHING AND DRILLING

R502.11.3 Alterations to trusses. Truss members and components shall not be cut, notched, spliced or otherwise altered in any way without the approval of a registered design professional. Alterations resulting in the addition of load (e.g., HVAC equipment, water heater, etc.), that exceed the design load for the truss, shall not be permitted without verification that the truss is capable of supporting the additional loading.

R502.11.4 Truss design drawings. Truss design drawings, prepared in compliance with Section R502.11.1, shall be submitted to the building official and approved prior to installation. Truss design drawings shall be provided with the shipment of trusses delivered to the job site. Truss design drawings shall include, at a minimum, the information specified below:

1. Slope or depth, span and spacing.

2. Location of all joints.

3. Required bearing widths.

4. Design loads as applicable:

    4.1. Top chord live load;

    4.2. Top chord dead load;

    4.3. Bottom chord live load;

    4.4. Bottom chord dead load;

    4.5. Concentrated loads and their points of application; and

    4.6. Controlling wind and earthquake loads.

5. Adjustments to lumber and joint connector design values for conditions of use.

6. Each reaction force and direction.

7. Joint connector type and description, e.g., size, thickness or gauge, and the dimensioned location of each joint connector except where symmetrically located relative to the joint interface.

8. Lumber size, species and grade for each member.

9. Connection requirements for:

    9.1. Truss-to-girder-truss;

    9.2. Truss ply-to-ply; and

    9.3. Field splices.

10. Calculated deflection ratio and/or maximum description for live and total load.

11. Maximum axial compression forces in the truss members to enable the building designer to design the size, connections and anchorage of the permanent continuous lateral bracing. Forces shall be shown on the truss drawing or on supplemental documents.

12. Required permanent truss member bracing location.

R502.12 Draftstopping required. When there is usable space both above and below the concealed space of a floor/ceiling assembly, draftstops shall be installed so that the area of the concealed space does not exceed 1,000 square feet (92.9 m²). Draftstopping shall divide the concealed space into approximately equal areas. Where the assembly is enclosed by a floor membrane above and a ceiling membrane below draftstopping shall be provided in floor/ceiling assemblies under the following circumstances:

1. Ceiling is suspended under the floor framing.

2. Floor framing is constructed of truss-type open-web or perforated members.

R502.12.1 Materials. Draftstopping materials shall not be less than $^1/_2$-inch (12.7 mm) gypsum board, $^3/_8$-inch (9.5 mm) wood structural panels, $^3/_8$-inch (9.5 mm) Type 2-M-W particleboard or other approved materials adequately supported. Draftstopping shall be installed parallel to the floor framing members unless otherwise approved by the building official. The integrity of all draftstops shall be maintained.

R502.13 Fireblocking required. Fireblocking shall be provided in accordance with Section R602.8.

SECTION R503
FLOOR SHEATHING

R503.1 Lumber sheathing. Maximum allowable spans for lumber used as floor sheathing shall conform to Tables R503.1, R503.2.1.1(1) and R503.2.1.1(2).

R503.1.1 End joints. End joints in lumber used as subflooring shall occur over supports unless end-matched lumber is used, in which case each piece shall bear on at least two joists. Subflooring may be omitted when joist spacing does not exceed 16 inches (406 mm) and a 1-inch (25.4 mm) nominal tongue-and-groove wood strip flooring is applied perpendicular to the joists.

TABLE R503.1
MINIMUM THICKNESS OF LUMBER FLOOR SHEATHING

JOIST OR BEAM SPACING (inches)	MINIMUM NET THICKNESS	
	Perpendicular to joist	Diagonal to joist
24	$^{11}/_{16}$	$^3/_4$
16	$^5/_8$	$^5/_8$
48[a]		
54[b]	$1^1/_2$ T & G	N/A
60[c]		

For SI: 1 inch = 25.4 mm, 1 pound per square inch = 6.895 kPa.

a. For this support spacing, lumber sheathing shall have a minimum F_b of 675 and minimum E of 1,100,000 (see AF&PA/NDS).

b. For this support spacing, lumber sheathing shall have a minimum F_b of 765 and minimum E of 1,400,000 (see AF&PA/NDS).

c. For this support spacing, lumber sheathing shall have a minimum F_b of 855 and minimum E of 1,700,000 (see AF&PA/NDS).

R503.2 Wood structural panel sheathing.

R503.2.1 Identification and grade. Wood structural panel sheathing used for structural purposes shall conform to DOC PS 1, DOC PS 2 or, when manufactured in Canada, CSA 0437 or CSA 0325. All panels shall be identified by a grade mark of certificate of inspection issued by an approved agency.

R503.2.1.1 Subfloor and combined subfloor underlayment. Where used as subflooring or combination subfloor underlayment, wood structural panels shall be of one of the grades specified in Table R503.2.1.1(1).

TABLE R503.2.1.1(1)
ALLOWABLE SPANS AND LOADS FOR WOOD STRUCTURAL PANELS FOR ROOF
AND SUBFLOOR SHEATHING AND COMBINATION SUBFLOOR UNDERLAYMENT[a, b, c]

SPAN RATING	MINIMUM NOMINAL PANEL THICKNESS (inch)	ALLOWABLE LIVE LOAD (psf)[h, l]		MAXIMUM SPAN (inches)		LOAD (pounds per square foot, at maximum span)		MAXIMUM SPAN (inches)
		SPAN @ 16" o.c.	SPAN @ 24" o.c.	With edge support[d]	Without edge support	Total load	Live load	
Sheathing[e]				Roof[f]				Subfloor[j]
12/0	$^5/_{16}$	—	—	12	12	40	30	0
16/0	$^5/_{16}$	30	—	16	16	40	30	0
20/0	$^5/_{16}$	50	—	20	20	40	30	0
24/0	$^3/_8$	100	30	24	20[g]	40	30	0
24/16	$^7/_{16}$	100	40	24	24	50	40	16
32/16	$^{15}/_{32}, ^1/_2$	180	70	32	28	40	30	16[h]
40/20	$^{19}/_{32}, ^5/_8$	305	130	40	32	40	30	20[h,i]
48/24	$^{23}/_{32}, ^3/_{48}$	—	175	48	36	45	35	24
60/32	$^7/_8$	—	305	60	48	45	35	32
Underlayment, C-C plugged, single floor[e]				Roof[f]				Combination subfloor underlayment[k]
16 o.c.	$^{19}/_{32}, ^5/_8$	100	40	24	24	50	40	16[i]
20 o.c.	$^{19}/_{32}, ^5/_8$	150	60	32	32	40	30	20[i,j]
24 o.c.	$^{23}/_{32}, ^3/_4$	240	100	48	36	35	25	24
32 o.c.	$^7/_8$	—	185	48	40	50	40	32
48 o.c.	$1^3/_{32}, 1^1/_8$	—	290	60	48	50	40	48

For SI: 1 inch = 25.4 mm, 1 pound per square foot = 0.0479 kPa.

a. The allowable total loads were determined using a dead load of 10 psf. If the dead load exceeds 10 psf, then the live load shall be reduced accordingly.

b. Panels continuous over two or more spans with long dimension perpendicular to supports. Spans shall be limited to values shown because of possible effect of concentrated loads.

c. Applies to panels 24 inches or wider.

d. Lumber blocking, panel edge clips (one midway between each support, except two equally spaced between supports when span is 48 inches), tongue-and-groove panel edges, or other approved type of edge support.

e. Includes Structural 1 panels in these grades.

f. Uniform load deflection limitation: $^1/_{180}$ of span under live load plus dead load, $^1/_{240}$ of span under live load only.

g. Maximum span 24 inches for $^{15}/_{32}$-and $^1/_2$-inch panels.

h. Maximum span 24 inches where $^3/_4$-inch wood finish flooring is installed at right angles to joists.

i. Maximum span 24 inches where 1.5 inches of lightweight concrete or approved cellular concrete is placed over the subfloor.

j. Unsupported edges shall have tongue-and-groove joints or shall be supported with blocking unless minimum nominal $^1/_4$-inch thick underlayment with end and edge joints offset at least 2 inches or 1.5 inches of lightweight concrete or approved cellular concrete is placed over the subfloor, or $^3/_4$-inch wood finish flooring is installed at right angles to the supports. Allowable uniform live load at maximum span, based on deflection of $^1/_{360}$ of span, is 100 psf.

k. Unsupported edges shall have tongue-and-groove joints or shall be supported by blocking unless nominal $^1/_4$-inch-thick underlayment with end and edge joints offset at least 2 inches or $^3/_4$-inch wood finish flooring is installed at right angles to the supports. Allowable uniform live load at maximum span, based on deflection of $^1/_{360}$ of span, is 100 psf, except panels with a span rating of 48 on center are limited to 65 psf total uniform load at maximum span.

l. Allowable live load values at spans of 16" o.c. and 24" o.c taken from reference standard APA E30, APA Engineered Wood Construction Guide. Refer to reference standard for allowable spans not listed in the table.

When sanded plywood is used as combination subfloor underlayment, the grade shall be as specified in Table R503.2.1.1(2).

TABLE R503.2.1.1(2)
ALLOWABLE SPANS FOR SANDED PLYWOOD
COMBINATION SUBFLOOR UNDERLAYMENT[a]

IDENTIFICATION	SPACING OF JOISTS (inches)		
	16	20	24
Species group[b]	—	—	—
1	$^1/_2$	$^5/_8$	$^3/_4$
2, 3	$^5/_8$	$^3/_4$	$^7/_8$
4	$^3/_4$	$^7/_8$	1

For SI: 1 inch = 25.4 mm, 1 pound per square foot = 0.0479 kPa.

a. Plywood continuous over two or more spans and face grain perpendicular to supports. Unsupported edges shall be tongue-and-groove or blocked except where nominal $^1/_4$-inch-thick underlayment or $^3/_4$-inch wood finish floor is used. Allowable uniform live load at maximum span based on deflection of $^1/_{360}$ of span is 100 psf.

b. Applicable to all grades of sanded exterior-type plywood.

R503.2.2 Allowable spans. The maximum allowable span for wood structural panels used as subfloor or combination subfloor underlayment shall be as set forth in Table R503.2.1.1(1), or APA E30. The maximum span for sanded plywood combination subfloor underlayment shall be as set forth in Table R503.2.1.1(2).

R503.2.3 Installation. Wood structural panels used as subfloor or combination subfloor underlayment shall be attached to wood framing in accordance with Table R602.3(1) and shall be attached to cold-formed steel framing in accordance with Table R505.3.1(2).

R503.3 Particleboard.

R503.3.1 Identification and grade. Particleboard shall conform to ANSI A208.1 and shall be so identified by a grade mark or certificate of inspection issued by an approved agency.

R503.3.2 Floor underlayment. Particleboard floor underlayment shall conform to Type PBU and shall not be less than $^1/_4$ inch (6.4 mm) in thickness.

R503.3.3 Installation. Particleboard underlayment shall be installed in accordance with the recommendations of the manufacturer and attached to framing in accordance with Table R602.3(1).

SECTION R504
PRESSURE PRESERVATIVELY TREATED-WOOD FLOORS (ON GROUND)

R504.1 General. Pressure preservatively treated-wood basement floors and floors on ground shall be designed to withstand axial forces and bending moments resulting from lateral soil pressures at the base of the exterior walls and floor live and dead loads. Floor framing shall be designed to meet joist deflection requirements in accordance with Section R301.

R504.1.1 Unbalanced soil loads. Unless special provision is made to resist sliding caused by unbalanced lateral soil loads, wood basement floors shall be limited to applications where the differential depth of fill on opposite exterior foundation walls is 2 feet (610 mm) or less.

R504.1.2 Construction. Joists in wood basement floors shall bear tightly against the narrow face of studs in the foundation wall or directly against a band joist that bears on the studs. Plywood subfloor shall be continuous over lapped joists or over butt joints between in-line joists. Sufficient blocking shall be provided between joists to transfer lateral forces at the base of the end walls into the floor system.

R504.1.3 Uplift and buckling. Where required, resistance to uplift or restraint against buckling shall be provided by interior bearing walls or properly designed stub walls anchored in the supporting soil below.

R504.2 Site preparation. The area within the foundation walls shall have all vegetation, topsoil and foreign material removed, and any fill material that is added shall be free of vegetation and foreign material. The fill shall be compacted to assure uniform support of the pressure preservatively treated-wood floor sleepers.

R504.2.1 Base. A minimum 4-inch-thick (102 mm) granular base of gravel having a maximum size of $^3/_4$ inch (19.1 mm) or crushed stone having a maximum size of $^1/_2$ inch (12.7 mm) shall be placed over the compacted earth.

R504.2.2 Moisture barrier. Polyethylene sheeting of minimum 6-mil (0.15 mm) thickness shall be placed over the granular base. Joints shall be lapped 6 inches (152 mm) and left unsealed. The polyethylene membrane shall be placed over the pressure preservatively treated-wood sleepers and shall not extend beneath the footing plates of the exterior walls.

R504.3 Materials. All framing materials, including sleepers, joists, blocking and plywood subflooring, shall be pressure-preservative treated and dried after treatment in accordance with AWPA U1 (Commodity Specification A, Use Category 4B and section 5.2), and shall bear the label of an accredited agency.

SECTION R505
STEEL FLOOR FRAMING

R505.1 Cold-formed steel floor framing. Elements shall be straight and free of any defects that would significantly affect structural performance. Cold-formed steel floor framing members shall comply with the requirements of this section.

R505.1.1 Applicability limits. The provisions of this section shall control the construction of steel floor framing for buildings not greater than 60 feet (18,288 mm) in length perpendicular to the joist span, not greater than 40 feet (12 192 mm) in width parallel to the joist span, and not greater than two stories in height. Steel floor framing constructed in accordance with the provisions of this section shall be limited to sites subjected to a maximum design wind speed of 110 miles per hour (49 m/s), Exposure A, B, or C, and a maximum ground snow load of 70 psf (3.35 kPa).

R505.1.2 In-line framing. When supported by steel-framed walls in accordance with Section R603, steel floor framing shall be constructed with floor joists located directly in-line with load-bearing studs located below the joists with a maximum tolerance of $^3/_4$ inch (19.1 mm) between the center lines of the joist and the stud.

R505.1.3 Floor trusses. The design, quality assurance, installation and testing of cold-formed steel trusses shall be in accordance with the AISI Standard for Cold-formed Steel Framing-Truss Design (COFS/Truss). Truss members shall not be notched, cut or altered in any manner without an approved design.

R505.2 Structural framing. Load-bearing floor framing members shall comply with Figure R505.2(1) and with the dimensional and minimum thickness requirements specified in Tables R505.2(1) and R505.2(2). Tracks shall comply with Figure R505.2(2) and shall have a minimum flange width of $1^1/_4$ inches (32 mm). The maximum inside bend radius for members shall be the larger of $^3/_{32}$ inch (2.4 mm) or twice the uncoated steel thickness. Holes in joist webs shall comply with all of the following conditions:

1. Holes shall conform to Figure R505.2(3);

2. Holes shall be permitted only along the centerline of the web of the framing member;

3. Holes shall have a center-to-center spacing of not less than 24 inches (610 mm);

4. Holes shall have a web hole width not greater than 0.5 times the member depth, or $2^1/_2$ inches (64.5 mm);

5. Holes shall have a web hole length not exceeding $4^1/_2$ inches (114 mm); and

6. Holes shall have a minimum distance between the edge of the bearing surface and the edge of the web hole of not less than 10 inches (254 mm).

Framing members with web holes not conforming to the above requirements shall be patched in accordance with Section R505.3.6 or designed in accordance with accepted engineering practices.

R505.2.1 Material. Load-bearing members used in steel floor construction shall be cold-formed to shape from structural quality sheet steel complying with the requirements of one of the following:

1. ASTM A 653: Grades 33, 37, 40 and 50 (Class 1 and 3).

2. ASTM A 792: Grades 33, 37, 40 and 50A.

3. ASTM A 875: Grades 33, 37, 40 and 50 (Class 1 and 3).

4. ASTM A 1003: Grades 33, 37, 40 and 50.

R505.2.2 Identification. Load-bearing steel framing members shall have a legible label, stencil, stamp or embossment with the following information as a minimum:

1. Manufacturer's identification.

2. Minimum uncoated steel thickness in inches (mm).

3. Minimum coating designation.

4. Minimum yield strength, in kips per square inch (ksi) (kPa).

R505.2.3 Corrosion protection. Load-bearing steel framing shall have a metallic coating complying with one of the following:

1. A minimum of G 60 in accordance with ASTM A 653.

2. A minimum of AZ 50 in accordance with ASTM A 792.

TABLE R505.2(1)
COLD-FORMED STEEL JOIST SIZES

MEMBER DESIGNATION[a]	WEB DEPTH (inches)	MINIMUM FLANGE WIDTH (inches)	MAXIMUM FLANGE WIDTH (inches)	MINIMUM LIP SIZE (inches)
550S162-t	5.5	1.625	2	0.5
800S162-t	8	1.625	2	0.5
1000S162-t	10	1.625	2	0.5
1200S162-t	12	1.625	2	0.5

For SI: 1 inch = 25.4 mm, 1 mil = 0.0254 mm.

a. The member designation is defined by the first number representing the member depth in 0.01 inch, the letter "S" representing a stud or joist member, the second number representing the flange width in 0.01 inch, and the letter "t" shall be a number representing the minimum base metal thickness in mils [See Table R505.2(2)].

TABLE R505.2(2)
MINIMUM THICKNESS OF COLD-FORMED STEEL MEMBERS

DESIGNATION (mils)	MINIMUM UNCOATED THICKNESS (inches)	REFERENCE GAGE NUMBER
33	0.033	20
43	0.043	18
54	0.054	16
68	0.068	14

For SI: 1 inch = 25.4 mm, 1 mil = 0.0254 mm.

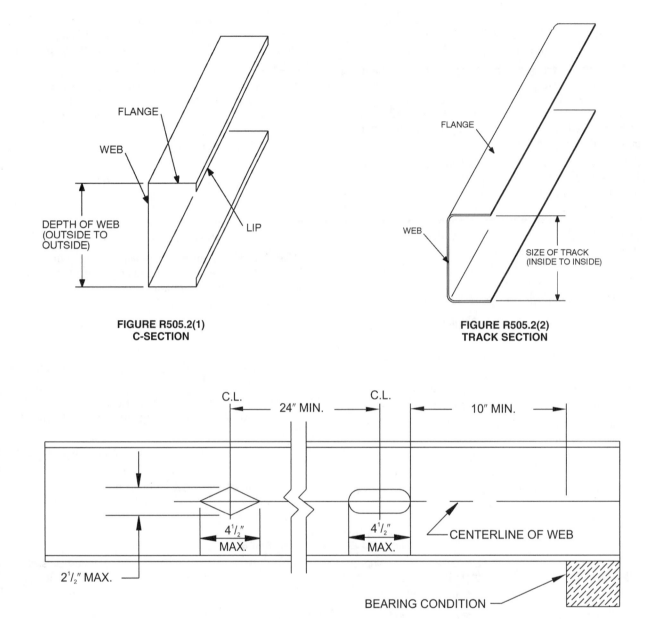

FIGURE R505.2(1)
C-SECTION

FIGURE R505.2(2)
TRACK SECTION

For SI: 1 inch = 25.4 mm.

FIGURE R505.2(3)
FLOOR JOIST WEB HOLES

3. A minimum of GF 60 in accordance with ASTM A 875.

R505.2.4 Fastening requirements. Screws for steel-to-steel connections shall be installed with a minimum edge distance and center-to-center spacing of 0.5 inch (12.7 mm), shall be self-drilling tapping, and shall conform to SAE J78. Floor sheathing shall be attached to steel joists with minimum No. 8 self-drilling tapping screws that conform to SAE J78. Screws attaching floor-sheathing-to-steel joists shall have a minimum head diameter of 0.292 inch (7.4 mm) with countersunk heads and shall be installed with a minimum edge distance of 0.375 inch (9.5 mm). Gypsum board ceilings shall be attached to steel joists with minimum No. 6 screws conforming to ASTM C 954 and shall be installed in accordance with Section R702. For all connections, screws shall extend through the steel a minimum of three exposed threads. All self-drilling tapping screws conforming to SAE J78 shall have a Type II coating in accordance with ASTM B 633.

Where No. 8 screws are specified in a steel to steel connection the required number of screws in the connection is permitted to be reduced in accordance with the reduction factors in Table R505.2.4 when larger screws are used or when one of the sheets of steel being connected is thicker than 33 mils (0.84 mm). When applying the reduction factor the resulting number of screws shall be rounded up.

TABLE R505.2.4
SCREW SUBSTITUTION FACTOR

SCREW SIZE	THINNEST CONNECTED STEEL SHEET (mils)	
	33	43
#8	1.0	0.67
#10	0.93	0.62
#12	0.86	0.56

For SI: 1 mil = 0.0254 mm.

R505.3 Floor construction. Cold-formed steel floors shall be constructed in accordance with this section and Figure R505.3.

R505.3.1 Floor to foundation or bearing wall connections. Cold-formed steel floors shall be anchored to foundations, wood sills or load-bearing walls in accordance with Table R505.3.1(1) and Figure R505.3.1(1), R505.3.1(2), R505.3.1(3), R505.3.1(4), R505.3.1(5) or R505.3.1(6). Continuous steel joists supported by interior load-bearing walls shall be constructed in accordance with Figure R505.3.1(7). Lapped steel joists shall be constructed in accordance with Figure R505.3.1(8). Fastening of steel joists to other framing members shall be in accordance with Table R505.3.1(2).

R505.3.2 Allowable joist spans. The clear span of cold-formed steel floor joists shall not exceed the limits set forth in Tables R505.3.2(1), R505.3.2(2), and R505.3.2(3). Floor joists shall have a minimum bearing length of 1.5 inches (38 mm). When continuous joists are used, the interior bearing supports shall be located within 2 feet (610 mm) of mid span of the steel joists, and the individual spans shall not exceed the span in Tables R505.3.2(2) and R505.3.2(3). Bearing stiffeners shall be installed at each bearing location in accordance with Section R505.3.4 and as shown in Figure R505.3.

Blocking is not required for continuous back-to-back floor joists at bearing supports. Blocking shall be installed between the joists for single continuous floor joists across bearing supports. Blocking shall be spaced at a maximum of 12 feet (3660 mm) on center. Blocking shall consist of C-shape or track section with a minimum thickness of 33 mils (0.84 mm). Blocking shall be fastened to each adjacent joist through a 33-mil (0.84 mm) clip angle, bent web of blocking or flanges of web stiffeners with two No. 8 screws on each side. The minimum depth of the blocking shall be equal to the depth of the joist minus 2 inches (51 mm). The minimum length of the angle shall be equal to the depth of the joist minus 2 inches (51 mm).

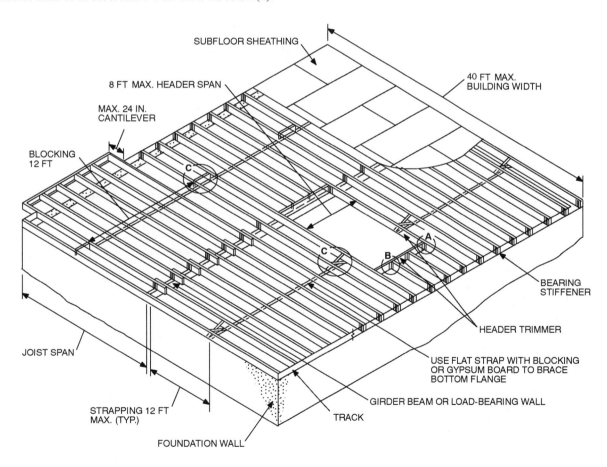

For SI: 1 inch = 25.4 mm, 1 foot = 304.8 mm.

FIGURE R505.3
STEEL FLOOR CONSTRUCTION

(continued)

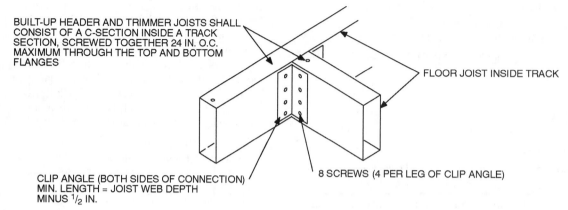

BUILT-UP HEADER AND TRIMMER JOISTS SHALL CONSIST OF A C-SECTION INSIDE A TRACK SECTION, SCREWED TOGETHER 24 IN. O.C. MAXIMUM THROUGH THE TOP AND BOTTOM FLANGES

FLOOR JOIST INSIDE TRACK

CLIP ANGLE (BOTH SIDES OF CONNECTION) MIN. LENGTH = JOIST WEB DEPTH MINUS 1/2 IN.

8 SCREWS (4 PER LEG OF CLIP ANGLE)

BUILT-UP HEADER OR TRIMMER JOIST

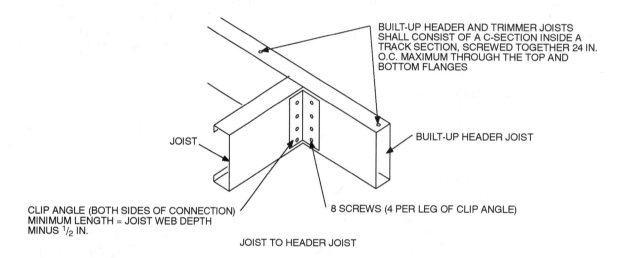

BUILT-UP HEADER AND TRIMMER JOISTS SHALL CONSIST OF A C-SECTION INSIDE A TRACK SECTION, SCREWED TOGETHER 24 IN. O.C. MAXIMUM THROUGH THE TOP AND BOTTOM FLANGES

JOIST

BUILT-UP HEADER JOIST

CLIP ANGLE (BOTH SIDES OF CONNECTION) MINIMUM LENGTH = JOIST WEB DEPTH MINUS 1/2 IN.

8 SCREWS (4 PER LEG OF CLIP ANGLE)

JOIST TO HEADER JOIST

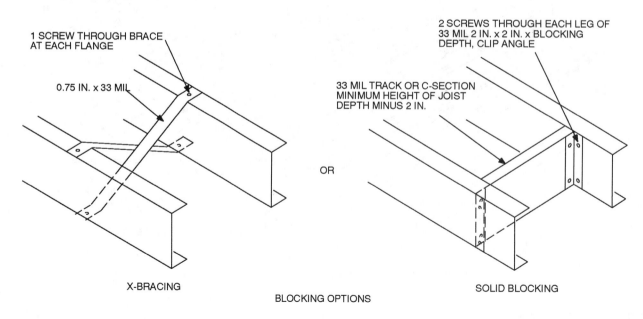

1 SCREW THROUGH BRACE AT EACH FLANGE

0.75 IN. x 33 MIL

2 SCREWS THROUGH EACH LEG OF 33 MIL 2 IN. x 2 IN. x BLOCKING DEPTH, CLIP ANGLE

33 MIL TRACK OR C-SECTION MINIMUM HEIGHT OF JOIST DEPTH MINUS 2 IN.

OR

X-BRACING

SOLID BLOCKING

BLOCKING OPTIONS

For SI: 1 inch = 25.4 mm, 1 mil = 0.0254 mm.

FIGURE R505.3—continued
STEEL FLOOR CONSTRUCTION

TABLE R505.3.1(1)
FLOOR TO FOUNDATION OR BEARING WALL CONNECTION REQUIREMENTS [a, b]

	WIND SPEED (mph) AND EXPOSURE	
FRAMING CONDITION	Up to 110 A/B or 85 C or Seismic Design Categories A, B, C	Up to 110 C
Floor joist to wall track of exterior steel load-bearing wall per Figure R505.3.1(1)	2-No. 8 screws	3-No. 8 screws
Floor joist track to wood sill per Figure R505.3.1(2)	Steel plate spaced at 3' o.c., with 4-No. 8 screws and 4-10d or 6-8d common nails	Steel plate, spaced at 2' o.c., with 4-No. 8 screws and 4-10d or 6-8d common nails
Floor joist track to foundation per Figure R505.3.1(3)	$1/_2''$ minimum diameter anchor bolt and clip angle spaced at 6' o.c. with 8-No. 8 screws	$1/_2''$ minimum diameter anchor bolt and clip angle spaced at 4' o.c. with 8-No. 8 screws
Joist cantilever to wall track per Figure R505.3.1(4)	2-No. 8 screws per stiffener or bent plate	3-No. 8 screws per stiffener or bent plate
Joist cantilever to wood sill per Figure R505.3.1(5)	Steel plate spaced at 3' o.c., with 4-No. 8 screws and 4-10d or 6-8d common nails	Steel plate spaced at 2' o.c., with 4-No. 8 screws and 4-10d or 6-8d common nails
Joist cantilever to foundation per Figure R505.3.1(6)	$1/_2''$ minimum diameter anchor bolt and clip angle spaced at 6' o.c. with 8-No. 8 screws	$1/_2''$ minimum diameter anchor bolt and clip angle spaced at 4' o.c. with 8-No. 8 screws

For SI: 1 inch = 25.4 mm, 1 foot = 304.8 mm, 1 mile per hour = 0.447 m/s.

a. Anchor bolts shall be located not more than 12 inches from corners or the termination of bottom tracks (e.g., at door openings). Bolts shall extend a minimum of 15 inches into masonry or 7 inches into concrete.

b. All screw sizes shown are minimum.

TABLE R505.3.1(2)
FLOOR FASTENING SCHEDULE [a]

DESCRIPTION OF BUILDING ELEMENTS	NUMBER AND SIZE OF FASTENERS	SPACING OF FASTENERS
Floor joist to track of an interior load-bearing wall per Figures R505.3.1(7) and R505.3.1(8)	2 No. 8 screws	Each joist
Floor joist to track at end of joist	2 No. 8 screws	One per flange or two per bearing stiffener
Subfloor to floor joists	No. 8 screws	6" o.c. on edges and 12" o.c. at intermediate supports

For SI: 1 inch = 25.4 mm.

a. All screw sizes shown are minimum.

R505.3.3 Joist bracing. The top flanges of steel joists shall be laterally braced by the application of floor sheathing fastened to the joists in accordance with Table R505.3.1(2). Floor joists with spans that exceed 12 feet (3658 mm) shall have the bottom flanges laterally braced in accordance with one of the following:

1. Gypsum board installed with minimum No. 6 screws in accordance with Section R702.
2. Continuous steel strapping installed in accordance with Figure R505.3. Steel straps shall be at least 1.5 inches (38 mm) in width and 33 mils (0.84 mm) in thickness. Straps shall be fastened to the bottom flange at each joist with at least one No. 8 screw and shall be fastened to blocking with at least two No. 8 screws. Blocking or bridging (X-bracing) shall be installed between joists in-line with straps at a maximum spacing of 12 feet (3658 mm) measured perpendicular to the joist run and at the termination of all straps.

R505.3.4 Bearing stiffeners. Bearing stiffeners shall be installed at all bearing locations for steel floor joists. A bearing stiffener shall be fabricated from a minimum 33 mil (0.84 mm) C-section or 43 mil (1.09 mm) track section. Each stiffener shall be fastened to the web of the joist with a minimum of four No. 8 screws equally spaced as shown in Figure R505.3.4. Stiffeners shall extend across the full depth of the web and shall be installed on either side of the web.

R505.3.5 Cutting and notching. Flanges and lips of load-bearing steel floor framing members shall not be cut or notched.

R505.3.6 Hole patching. Web holes not conforming to the requirements in Section R505.2 shall be designed in accordance with one of the following:

1. Framing members shall be replaced or designed in accordance with accepted engineering practices when web holes exceed the following size limits:
   1.1. The depth of the hole, measured across the web, exceeds 70 percent of the flat width of the web; or
   1.2. The length of the hole measured along the web, exceeds 10 inches (254 mm) or the depth of the web, whichever is greater.
2. Web holes not exceeding the dimensional requirements in Section R505.3.6, Item 1, shall be patched with a solid steel plate, stud section, or track section in accordance with Figure R505.3.6. The steel patch shall, as a minimum, be of the same thickness as the receiving member and shall extend at least 1 inch (25 mm) beyond all edges of the hole. The steel patch shall be fastened to the web of the receiving member with No.8 screws spaced no greater than 1 inch (25 mm) center-to-center along the edges of the patch with minimum edge distance of $1/_2$ inch (13 mm).

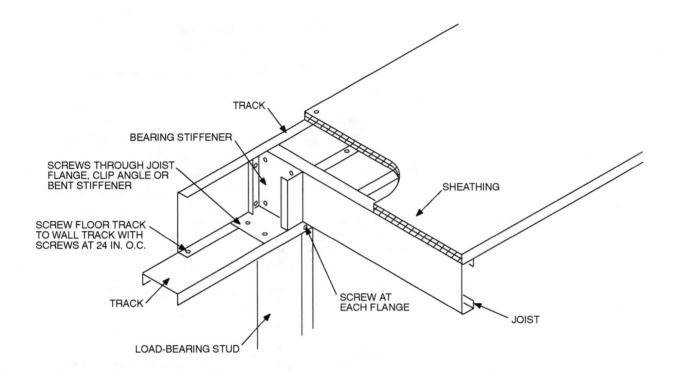

TRACK

BEARING STIFFENER

SCREWS THROUGH JOIST
FLANGE, CLIP ANGLE OR
BENT STIFFENER

SHEATHING

SCREW FLOOR TRACK
TO WALL TRACK WITH
SCREWS AT 24 IN. O.C.

TRACK

SCREW AT
EACH FLANGE

JOIST

LOAD-BEARING STUD

For SI: 1 inch = 25.4 mm, 1 mil = 0.0254 mm.

FIGURE R505.3.1(1)
FLOOR TO LOAD-BEARING WALL STUD CONNECTION

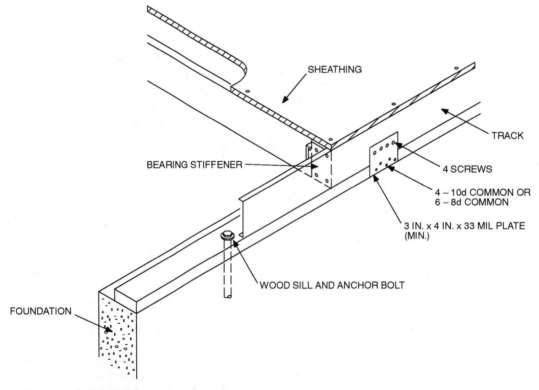

SHEATHING

TRACK

BEARING STIFFENER

4 SCREWS

4 – 10d COMMON OR
6 – 8d COMMON

3 IN. x 4 IN. x 33 MIL PLATE
(MIN.)

WOOD SILL AND ANCHOR BOLT

FOUNDATION

For SI: 1 inch = 25.4 mm, 1 mil = 0.0254 mm.

FIGURE R505.3.1(2)
FLOOR TO WOOD SILL CONNECTION

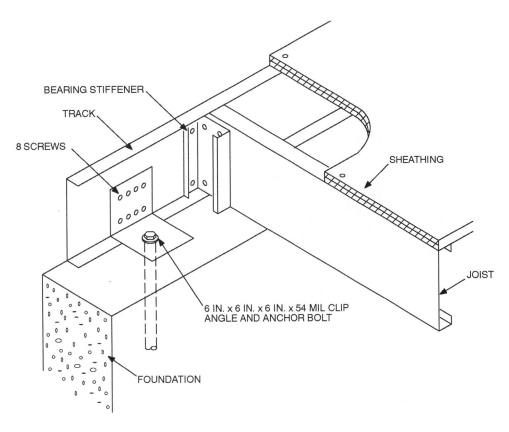

BEARING STIFFENER

TRACK

8 SCREWS

SHEATHING

6 IN. x 6 IN. x 6 IN. x 54 MIL CLIP
ANGLE AND ANCHOR BOLT

JOIST

FOUNDATION

For SI: 1 inch = 25.4 mm, 1 mil = 0.0254 mm.

FIGURE R505.3.1(3)
FLOOR TO FOUNDATION CONNECTION

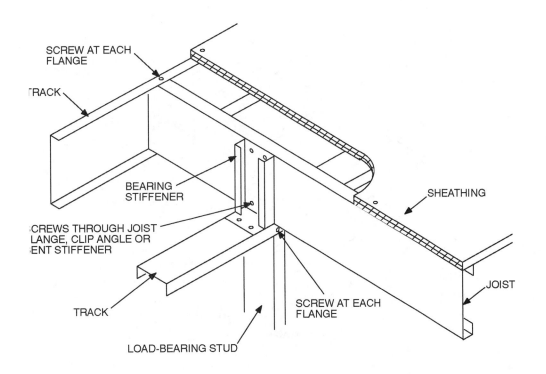

SCREW AT EACH
FLANGE

TRACK

BEARING
STIFFENER

SCREWS THROUGH JOIST
FLANGE, CLIP ANGLE OR
BENT STIFFENER

SHEATHING

JOIST

TRACK

SCREW AT EACH
FLANGE

LOAD-BEARING STUD

FIGURE R505.3.1(4)
FLOOR CANTILEVER TO LOAD-BEARING WALL CONNECTION

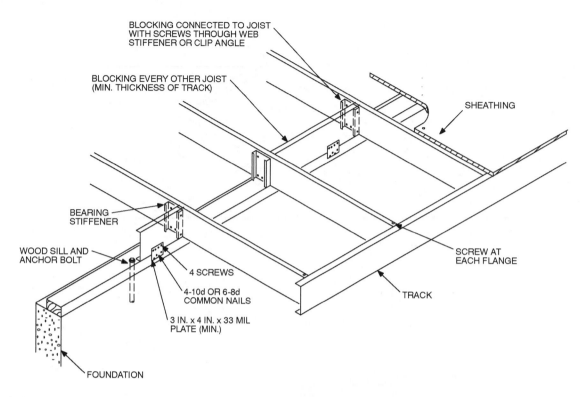

For SI: 1 inch = 25.4 mm, 1 mil = 0.0254.

FIGURE R505.3.1(5)
FLOOR CANTILEVER TO WOOD SILL CONNECTION

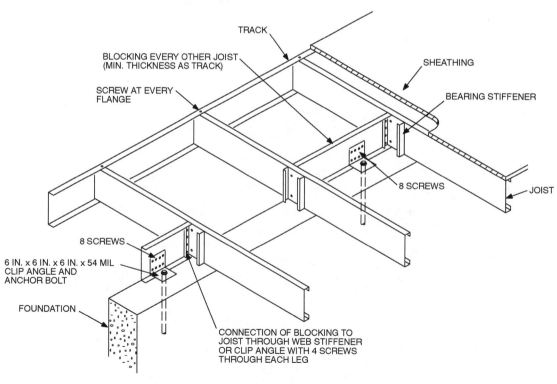

For SI: 1 inch = 25.4 mm, 1 mil = 0.0254.

FIGURE R505.3.1(6)
FLOOR CANTILEVER TO FOUNDATION CONNECTION

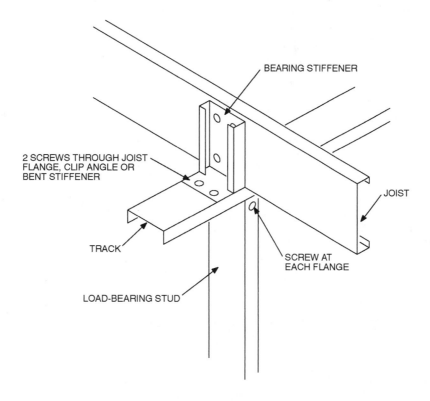

FIGURE R505.3.1(7)
CONTINUOUS JOIST SPAN SUPPORTED ON STUD

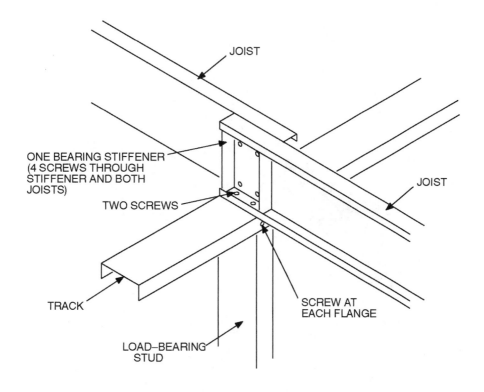

FIGURE R505.3.1(8)
LAPPED JOISTS SUPPORTED ON STUD

TABLE R505.3.2(1)
ALLOWABLE SPANS FOR COLD-FORMED STEEL JOISTS—SINGLE SPANS[a, b] 33 ksi STEEL

JOIST DESIGNATION	30 PSF LIVE LOAD				40 PSF LIVE LOAD			
	Spacing (inches)				Spacing (inches)			
	12	16	19.2	24	12	16	19.2	24
550S162-33	11'-7"	10'-7"	9'-6"	8'-6"	10'-7"	9'-3"	8'-6"	7'-6"
550S162-43	12'-8"	11'-6"	10'-10"	10'-2"	11'-6"	10'-5"	9'-10"	9'-1"
550S162-54	13'-7"	12'-4"	11'-7"	10'-9"	12'-4"	11'-2"	10'-6"	9'-9"
550S162-68	14'-7"	13'-3"	12'-6"	11'-7"	13'-3"	12'-0"	11'-4"	10'-6"
800S162-97	16'-2"	14'-9"	13'-10"	12'-10"	14'-9"	13'-4"	12'-7"	11'-8"
800S162-33	15'-8"	13'-11"	12'-9"	11'-5"	14'-3"	12'-5"	11'-3"	9'-0"
800S162-43	17'-1"	15'-6"	14'-7"	13'-7"	15'-6"	14'-1"	13'-3"	12'-4"
800S162-54	18'-4"	16'-8"	15'-8"	14'-7"	16'-8"	15'-2"	14'-3"	13'-3"
800S162-68	19'-9"	17'-11"	16'-10"	15'-8"	17'-11"	16'-3"	15'-4"	14'-2"
800S162-97	22'-0"	20'-0"	16'-10"	17'-5"	20'-0"	18'-2"	17'-1"	15'-10"
1000S162-43	20'-6"	18'-8"	17'-6"	15'-8"	18'-8"	16'-11"	15'-6"	13'-11"
1000S162-54	22'-1"	20'-0"	18'-10"	17'-6"	20'-0"	18'-2"	17'-2"	15'-11"
1000S162-68	23'-9"	21'-7"	20'-3"	18'-10"	21'-7"	19'-7"	18'-5"	17'-1"
1000S162-97	26'-6"	24'-1"	22'-8"	21'-0"	24'-1"	21'-10"	20'-7"	19'-1"
1200S162-43	23'-9"	20'-10"	19'-0"	16'-8"	21'-5"	18'-6"	16'-6"	13'-2"
1200S162-54	25'-9"	23'-4"	22'-0"	20'-1"	23'-4"	21'-3"	20'-0"	17'-10"
1200S162-68	27'-8"	25'-1"	23'-8"	21'-11"	25'-1"	22'-10"	21'-6"	21'-1"
1200S162-97	30'-11"	28'-1"	26'-5"	24'-6"	28'-1"	25'-6"	24'-0"	22'-3"

For SI: 1 inch = 25.4 mm, 1 foot = 304.8 mm, 1 pound per square foot = 0.0479 kPa.
a. Deflection criteria: $L/480$ for live loads, $L/240$ for total loads.
b. Floor dead load = 10 psf.

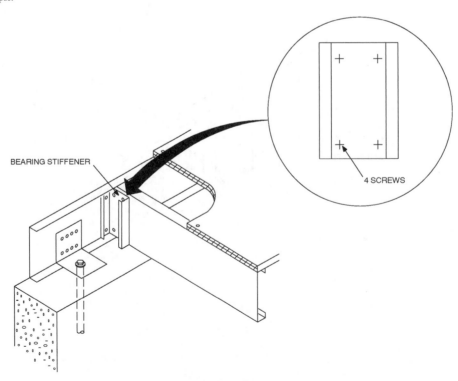

FIGURE R505.3.4
BEARING STIFFENER

TABLE R505.3.2(2)
ALLOWABLE SPANS FOR COLD-FORMED STEEL JOISTS—MULTIPLE SPANS[a, b] 33 ksi STEEL

JOIST DESIGNATION	30 PSF LIVE LOAD				40 PSF LIVE LOAD			
	Spacing (inches)				Spacing (inches)			
	12	16	19.2	24	12	16	19.2	24
550S162-33	12'-1"	10'-5"	9'-6"	8'-6"	10'-9"	9'-3"	8'-6"	7'-6"
550S162-43	14'-5"	12'-5"	11'-4"	10'-2"	12'-9"	11'-11"	10'-1"	9'-0"
550S162-54	16'-3"	14'-1"	12'-10"	11'-6"	14'-5"	12'-6"	11'-5"	10'-2"
550S162-68	19'-7"	17'-9"	16'-9"	15'-6"	17'-9"	16'-2"	15'-2"	14'-1"
800S162-97	21'-9"	19'-9"	18'-7"	17'-3"	19'-9"	17'-11"	16'-10"	15'-4"
800S162-33	14'-8"	11'-10"	10'-4"	8'-8"	12'-4"	9'-11"	8'-7"	7'-2"
800S162-43	20'-0"	17'-4"	15'-9"	14'-1"	17'-9"	15'-4"	14'-0"	12'-0"
800S162-54	23'-7"	20'-5"	18'-8"	16'-8"	21'-0"	18'-2"	16'-7"	14'-10"
800S162-68	26'-5"	23'-1"	21'-0"	18'-10"	23'-8"	20'-6"	18'-8"	16'-9"
800S162-97	29'-6"	26'-10"	25'-3"	22'-8"	26'-10"	24'-4"	22'-6"	20'-2"
1000S162-43	22'-2"	18'-3"	16'-0"	13'-7"	18'-11"	15'-5"	13'-6"	11'-5"
1000S162-54	26'-2"	22'-8"	20'-8"	18'-6"	23'-3"	20'-2"	18'-5"	16'-5"
1000S162-68	31'-5"	27'-2"	24'-10"	22'-2"	27'-11"	24'-2"	22'-1"	19'-9"
1000S162-97	35'-6"	32'-3"	29'-11"	26'-9"	32'-3"	29'-2"	26'-7"	23'-9"
1200S162-43	21'-8"	17'-6"	15'-3"	12'-10"	18'-3"	14'-8"	12'-8"	10'-6[2]
1200S162-54	28'-5"	24'-8"	22'-6"	19'-6"	25'-3"	21'-11"	19'-4"	16'-6"
1200S162-68	33'-7"	29'-1"	26'-6"	23'-9"	29'-10"	25'-10"	23'-7"	21'-1"
1200S162-97	41'-5"	37'-8"	34'-6"	30'-10"	37'-8"	33'-6"	30'-7"	27'-5"

For SI: 1 inch = 25.4 mm, 1 foot = 304.8 mm, 1 pound per square foot = 0.0479 kPa.
a. Deflection criteria: $L/480$ for live loads, $L/240$ for total loads.
b. Floor dead load = 10 psf.

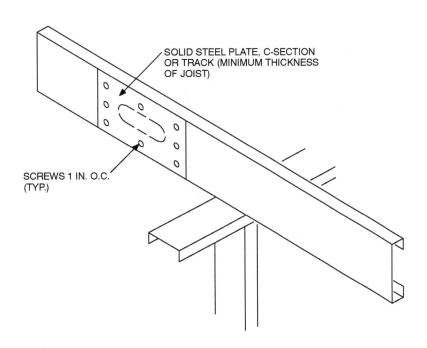

SOLID STEEL PLATE, C-SECTION OR TRACK (MINIMUM THICKNESS OF JOIST)

SCREWS 1 IN. O.C. (TYP.)

For SI: 1 inch = 25.4 mm.

FIGURE R505.3.6
HOLE PATCH

TABLE R505.3.2(3)
ALLOWABLE SPANS FOR COLD-FORMED STEEL JOISTS—MULTIPLE SPANS[a, b] 50 ksi STEEL

JOIST DESIGNATION	30 PSF LIVE LOAD				40 PSF LIVE LOAD			
	Spacing (inches)				Spacing (inches)			
	12	16	19.2	24	12	16	19.2	24
550S162-33	13'-11"	12'-0"	11'-0"	9'-3"	12'-3"	10'-8"	9'-7"	8'-4"
550S162-43	16'-3"	14'-1"	12'-10"	11'-6"	14'-6"	12'-6"	11'-5"	10'-3"
550S162-54	18'-2"	16'-6"	15'-4"	13'-8"	16'-6"	14'-11"	13'-7"	12'-2"
550S162-68	19'-6"	17'-9"	16'-8"	15'-6"	17'-9"	16'-1"	15'-2"	14'-0"
550S162-97	21'-9"	19'-9"	18'-6"	17'-2"	19'-8"	17'-10"	16'-8"	15'-8"
800S162-33	15'-6"	12'-6"	10'-10"	9'-1"	13'-0"	10'-5"	8'-11"	6'-9"
800S162-43	22'-0"	19'-1"	17'-5"	15'-0"	19'-7"	16'-11"	14'-10"	12'-8"
800S162-54	24'-6"	22'-4"	20'-6"	17'-11"	22'-5"	19'-9"	17'-11"	15'-10"
800S162-68	26'-6"	24'-1"	22'-8"	21'-0"	24'-1"	21'-10"	20'-7"	19'-2"
800S162-97	29'-9"	26'-8"	25'-2"	23'-5"	26'-8"	24'-3"	22'-11"	21'-4"
1000S162-43	23'-6"	19'-2"	16'-9"	14'-2"	19'-11"	16'-2"	14'-0"	11'-9"
1000S162-54	28'-2"	23'-10"	21'-7"	18'-11"	24'-8"	20'-11"	18'-9"	18'-4"
1000S162-68	31'-10"	28'-11"	27'-2"	25'-3"	28'-11"	26'-3"	24'-9"	22'-9"
1000S162-97	35'-4"	32'-1"	30'-3"	28'-1"	32'-1"	29'-2"	27'-6"	25'-6"
1200S162-43	22'-11"	18'-5"	16'-0"	13'-4"	19'-2"	15'-4"	13'-2"	10'-6"
1200S162-54	32'-8"	28'-1"	24'-9"	21'-2"	29'-0"	23'-10"	20'-11"	17'-9"
1200S162-68	37'-1"	32'-5"	29'-4"	25'-10"	33'-4"	28'-6"	25'-9"	22'-7"
1200S162-97	41'-2"	37'-6"	35'-3"	32'-9"	37'-6"	34'-1"	32'-1"	29'-9"

For SI: 1 inch = 25.4 mm, 1 foot = 304.8 mm, 1 pound per square foot = 0.0479kPa.
a. Deflection criteria: L/480 for live loads, L/240 for total loads.
b. Floor dead load = 10 psf.

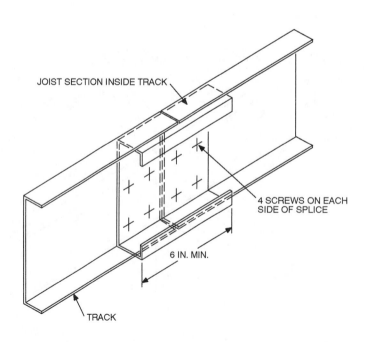

For SI: 1 inch = 25.4 mm.

FIGURE R505.3.8
TRACK SPLICE

R505.3.7 Floor cantilevers. Floor cantilevers shall not exceed 24 inches (610 mm) as illustrated in Figure R505.3. The cantilever back-span shall extend a minimum of 6 feet (1830 mm) within the building, and shall be fastened to a bearing condition in accordance with Section R505.3.1. Floor cantilevers shall be permitted only on the second floor of a two-story building or the first floor of a one-story building. Floor framing that is cantilevered and supports the cantilevered floor only shall consist of single joist members in accordance with Section R505.3.2. Floor framing that is cantilevered and supports the cantilevered floor and the roof framing load above shall consist of double joist members of the same size and material thickness as that for single joist members in accordance with Section R505.3.2, and shall be fastened web-to-web with minimum No. 8 screws at 24 inches (610 mm) maximum on-center spacing top and bottom. Built-up floor framing consisting of a C-section inside a track section, fastened at the top and bottom flanges by minimum No. 8 screws at 24 inches (610 mm) maximum on center spacing, is permitted in lieu of the web-to-web double joist method.

R505.3.8 Splicing. Joists and other structural members shall not be spliced. Splicing of tracks shall conform with Figure R505.3.8.

R505.3.9 Framing of openings. Openings in floor framing shall be framed with header and trimmer joists. Header joist spans shall not exceed 8 feet (2438 mm). Header and trimmer joists shall be fabricated from joist and track sections, which shall be of a minimum size and thickness as the adjacent floor joists and shall be installed in accordance with Figure R505.3. Each header joist shall be connected to trimmer joists with a minimum of four 2-inch-by-2-inch (51 mm by 51 mm) clip angles. Each clip angle shall be fastened to both the header and trimmer joists with four No. 8 screws, evenly spaced, through each leg of the clip angle. The clip angles shall have a steel thickness not less than that of the floor joist.

SECTION R506
CONCRETE FLOORS (ON GROUND)

R506.1 General. Concrete slab-on-ground floors shall be a minimum 3.5 inches (89 mm) thick (for expansive soils, see Section R403.1.8). The specified compressive strength of concrete shall be as set forth in Section R402.2.

R506.2 Site preparation. The area within the foundation walls shall have all vegetation, top soil and foreign material removed.

R506.2.1 Fill. Fill material shall be free of vegetation and foreign material. The fill shall be compacted to assure uniform support of the slab, and except where approved, the fill depths shall not exceed 24 inches (610 mm) for clean sand or gravel and 8 inches (203 mm) for earth.

R506.2.2 Base. A 4-inch-thick (102 mm) base course consisting of clean graded sand, gravel, crushed stone or crushed blast-furnace slag passing a 2-inch (51 mm) sieve shall be placed on the prepared subgrade when the slab is below grade.

> **Exception:** A base course is not required when the concrete slab is installed on well-drained or sand-gravel mixture soils classified as Group I according to the United Soil Classification System in accordance with Table R405.1.

R506.2.3 Vapor retarder. A 6 mil (0.006 inch; 152 μm) polyethylene or approved vapor retarder with joints lapped not less than 6 inches (152 mm) shall be placed between the concrete floor slab and the base course or the prepared subgrade where no base course exists.

> **Exception:** The vapor retarder may be omitted:
>
> 1. From garages, utility buildings and other unheated accessory structures.
> 2. From driveways, walks, patios and other flatwork not likely to be enclosed and heated at a later date.
> 3. Where approved by the building official, based on local site conditions.

R506.2.4 Reinforcement support. Where provided in slabs on ground, reinforcement shall be supported to remain in place from the center to upper one third of the slab for the duration of the concrete placement.

CHAPTER 6

WALL CONSTRUCTION

SECTION R601
GENERAL

R601.1 Application. The provisions of this chapter shall control the design and construction of all walls and partitions for all buildings.

R601.2 Requirements. Wall construction shall be capable of accommodating all loads imposed according to Section R301 and of transmitting the resulting loads to the supporting structural elements.

R601.2.1 Compressible floor-covering materials. Compressible floor-covering materials that compress more than $1/32$ inch (0.8 mm) when subjected to 50 pounds (23 kg) applied over 1 inch square (645 mm) of material and are greater than $1/8$ inch (3 mm) in thickness in the uncompressed state shall not extend beneath walls, partitions or columns, which are fastened to the floor.

SECTION R602
WOOD WALL FRAMING

R602.1 Identification. Load-bearing dimension lumber for studs, plates and headers shall be identified by a grade mark of a lumber grading or inspection agency that has been approved by an accreditation body that complies with DOC PS 20. In lieu of a grade mark, a certification of inspection issued by a lumber grading or inspection agency meeting the requirements of this section shall be accepted.

R602.1.1 End-jointed lumber. Approved end-jointed lumber identified by a grade mark conforming to Section R602.1 may be used interchangeably with solid-sawn members of the same species and grade.

R602.1.2 Structural glued laminated timbers. Glued laminated timbers shall be manufactured and identified as required in AITC A190.1 and ASTM D 3737.

R602.1.3 Structural log members. Stress grading of structural log members of nonrectangular shape, as typically used in log buildings, shall be in accordance with ASTM D 3957. Such structural log members shall be identified by the grade mark of an approved lumber grading or inspection agency. In lieu of a grade mark on the material, a certificate of inspection as to species and grade issued by a lumber-grading or inspection agency meeting the requirements of this section shall be permitted to be accepted.

R602.2 Grade. Studs shall be a minimum No. 3, standard or stud grade lumber.

Exception: Bearing studs not supporting floors and nonbearing studs may be utility grade lumber, provided the studs are spaced in accordance with Table R602.3(5).

R602.3 Design and construction. Exterior walls of wood-frame construction shall be designed and constructed in accordance with the provisions of this chapter and Figures R602.3(1) and R602.3(2) or in accordance with AF&PA's NDS. Components of exterior walls shall be fastened in accordance with Tables R602.3(1) through R602.3(4). Exterior walls covered with foam plastic sheathing shall be braced in accordance with Section R602.10. Structural sheathing shall be fastened directly to structural framing members.

R602.3.1 Stud size, height and spacing. The size, height and spacing of studs shall be in accordance with Table R602.3.(5).

Exceptions:

1. Utility grade studs shall not be spaced more than 16 inches (406 mm) on center, shall not support more than a roof and ceiling, and shall not exceed 8 feet (2438 mm) in height for exterior walls and load-bearing walls or 10 feet (3048 mm) for interior nonload-bearing walls.

2. Studs more than 10 feet (3048 mm) in height which are in accordance with Table R602.3.1.

R602.3.2 Top plate. Wood stud walls shall be capped with a double top plate installed to provide overlapping at corners and intersections with bearing partitions. End joints in top plates shall be offset at least 24 inches (610 mm). Joints in plates need not occur over studs. Plates shall be not less than 2-inches (51 mm) nominal thickness and have a width at least equal to the width of the studs.

Exception: A single top plate may be installed in stud walls, provided the plate is adequately tied at joints, corners and intersecting walls by a minimum 3-inch-by-6-inch by a 0.036-inch-thick (76 mm by 152 mm by 0.914 mm) galvanized steel plate that is nailed to each wall or segment of wall by six 8d nails on each side, provided the rafters or joists are centered over the studs with a tolerance of no more than 1 inch (25 mm). The top plate may be omitted over lintels that are adequately tied to adjacent wall sections with steel plates or equivalent as previously described.

R602.3.3 Bearing studs. Where joists, trusses or rafters are spaced more than 16 inches (406 mm) on center and the bearing studs below are spaced 24 inches (610 mm) on center, such members shall bear within 5 inches (127 mm) of the studs beneath.

Exceptions:

1. The top plates are two 2-inch by 6-inch (38 mm by 140 mm) or two 3-inch by 4-inch (64 mm by 89 mm) members.

2. A third top plate is installed.

3. Solid blocking equal in size to the studs is installed to reinforce the double top plate.

TABLE R602.3(1)
FASTENER SCHEDULE FOR STRUCTURAL MEMBERS

DESCRIPTION OF BUILDING ELEMENTS	NUMBER AND TYPE OF FASTENER[a,b,c]	SPACING OF FASTENERS
Joist to sill or girder, toe nail	3-8d (2-$\frac{1}{2}$″ × 0.113″)	—
1″ × 6″ subfloor or less to each joist, face nail	2-8d (2$\frac{1}{2}$″ × 0.113″) 2 staples, 1$\frac{3}{4}$″	— —
2″ subfloor to joist or girder, blind and face nail	2-16d (3$\frac{1}{2}$″ × 0.135″)	—
Sole plate to joist or blocking, face nail	16d (3$\frac{1}{2}$″ × 0.135″)	16″ o.c.
Top or sole plate to stud, end nail	2-16d (3$\frac{1}{2}$″ × 0.135″)	—
Stud to sole plate, toe nail	3-8d (2$\frac{1}{2}$″ × 0.113″) or 2-16d (3$\frac{1}{2}$″ × 0.135″)	—
Double studs, face nail	10d (3″ × 0.128″)	24″ o.c.
Double top plates, face nail	10d (3″ × 0.128″)	24″ o.c.
Sole plate to joist or blocking at braced wall panels	3-16d (3$\frac{1}{2}$″ × 0.135″)	16″ o.c.
Double top plates, minimum 24-inch offset of end joints, face nail in lapped area	8-16d (3$\frac{1}{2}$″ × 0.135″)	—
Blocking between joists or rafters to top plate, toe nail	3-8d (2$\frac{1}{2}$″ × 0.113″)	—
Rim joist to top plate, toe nail	8d (2$\frac{1}{2}$″ × 0.113″)	6″ o.c.
Top plates, laps at corners and intersections, face nail	2-10d (3″ × 0.128″)	—
Built-up header, two pieces with $\frac{1}{2}$″ spacer	16d (3$\frac{1}{2}$″ × 0.135″)	16″ o.c. along each edge
Continued header, two pieces	16d (3$\frac{1}{2}$″ × 0.135″)	16″ o.c. along each edge
Ceiling joists to plate, toe nail	3-8d (2$\frac{1}{2}$″ × 0.113″)	—
Continuous header to stud, toe nail	4-8d (2$\frac{1}{2}$″ × 0.113″)	—
Ceiling joist, laps over partitions, face nail	3-10d (3″ × 0.128″)	—
Ceiling joist to parallel rafters, face nail	3-10d (3″ × 0.128″)	—
Rafter to plate, toe nail	2-16d (3$\frac{1}{2}$″ × 0.135″)	—
1″ brace to each stud and plate, face nail	2-8d (2$\frac{1}{2}$″ × 0.113″) 2 staples, 1$\frac{3}{4}$″	— —
1″ × 6″ sheathing to each bearing, face nail	2-8d (2$\frac{1}{2}$″ × 0.113″) 2 staples, 1$\frac{3}{4}$″	— —
1″ × 8″ sheathing to each bearing, face nail	2-8d (2$\frac{1}{2}$″ × 0.113″) 3 staples, 1$\frac{3}{4}$″	— —
Wider than 1″ × 8″ sheathing to each bearing, face nail	3-8d (2$\frac{1}{2}$″ × 0.113″) 4 staples, 1$\frac{3}{4}$″	— —
Built-up corner studs	10d (3″ × 0.128″)	24″ o.c.
Built-up girders and beams, 2-inch lumber layers	10d (3″ × 0.128″)	Nail each layer as follows: 32″ o.c. at top and bottom and staggered. Two nails at ends and at each splice.
2″ planks	2-16d (3$\frac{1}{2}$″ × 0.135″)	At each bearing
Roof rafters to ridge, valley or hip rafters: toe nail face nail	4-16d (3$\frac{1}{2}$″ × 0.135″) 3-16d (3$\frac{1}{2}$″ × 0.135″)	— —
Rafter ties to rafters, face nail	3-8d (2$\frac{1}{2}$″ × 0.113″)	—
Collar tie to rafter, face nail, or 1$\frac{1}{4}$″ × 20 gage ridge strap	3-10d (3″ × 0.128″)	—

(continued)

TABLE R602.3(1)—continued
FASTENER SCHEDULE FOR STRUCTURAL MEMBERS

DESCRIPTION OF BUILDING MATERIALS	DESCRIPTION OF FASTENER[b, c, e]	SPACING OF FASTENERS	
		Edges (inches)[i]	Intermediate supports[c,e] (inches)
Wood structural panels, subfloor, roof and wall sheathing to framing, and particleboard wall sheathing to framing			
$5/_{16}$"-$1/_2$"	6d common (2" × 0.113") nail (subfloor, wall) 8d common (2$1/_2$" × 0.131") nail (roof)[f]	6	12[g]
$19/_{32}$"-1"	8d common nail (2$1/_2$" × 0.131")	6	12[g]
$1^1/_8$"-$1^1/_4$"	10d common (3" × 0.148") nail or 8d (2$1/_2$" × 0.131") deformed nail	6	12
Other wall sheathing[h]			
$1/_2$" structural cellulosic fiberboard sheathing	$1^1/_2$" galvanized roofing nail 8d common (2$1/_2$" × 0.131") nail; staple 16 ga., $1^1/_2$" long	3	6
$25/_{32}$" structural cellulosic fiberboard sheathing	$1^3/_4$" galvanized roofing nail 8d common (2$1/_2$" × 0.131") nail; staple 16 ga., $1^3/_4$" long	3	6
$1/_2$" gypsum sheathing[d]	$1^1/_2$" galvanized roofing nail; 6d common (2" x 0.131") nail; staple galvanized $1^1/_2$" long; $1^1/_4$" screws, Type W or S	4	8
$5/_8$" gypsum sheathing[d]	$1^3/_4$" galvanized roofing nail; 8d common (2$1/_2$" × 0.131") nail; staple galvanized $1^5/_8$" long; $1^5/_8$" screws, Type W or S	4	8
Wood structural panels, combination subfloor underlayment to framing			
$3/_4$" and less	6d deformed (2" × 0.120") nail or 8d common (2$1/_2$" × 0.131") nail	6	12
$7/_8$"-1"	8d common (2$1/_2$" × 0.131") nail or 8d deformed (2$1/_2$" × 0.120") nail	6	12
$1^1/_8$"-$1^1/_4$"	10d common (3" × 0.148") nail or 8d deformed (2$1/_2$" × 0.120") nail	6	12

For SI: 1 inch = 25.4 mm, 1 foot = 304.8 mm, 1 mile per hour = 0.447 m/s; 1ksi = 6.895 MPa.

a. All nails are smooth-common, box or deformed shanks except where otherwise stated. Nails used for framing and sheathing connections shall have minimum average bending yield strengths as shown: 80 ksi for shank diameter of 0.192 inch (20d common nail), 90 ksi for shank diameters larger than 0.142 inch but not larger than 0.177 inch, and 100 ksi for shank diameters of 0.142 inch or less.

b. Staples are 16 gage wire and have a minimum $7/_{16}$-inch on diameter crown width.

c. Nails shall be spaced at not more than 6 inches on center at all supports where spans are 48 inches or greater.

d. Four-foot-by-8-foot or 4-foot-by-9-foot panels shall be applied vertically.

e. Spacing of fasteners not included in this table shall be based on Table R602.3(2).

f. For regions having basic wind speed of 110 mph or greater, 8d deformed (2$1/_2$" × 0.120) nails shall be used for attaching plywood and wood structural panel roof sheathing to framing within minimum 48-inch distance from gable end walls, if mean roof height is more than 25 feet, up to 35 feet maximum.

g. For regions having basic wind speed of 100 mph or less, nails for attaching wood structural panel roof sheathing to gable end wall framing shall be spaced 6 inches on center. When basic wind speed is greater than 100 mph, nails for attaching panel roof sheathing to intermediate supports shall be spaced 6 inches on center for minimum 48-inch distance from ridges, eaves and gable end walls; and 4 inches on center to gable end wall framing.

h. Gypsum sheathing shall conform to ASTM C 79 and shall be installed in accordance with GA 253. Fiberboard sheathing shall conform to ASTM C 208.

i. Spacing of fasteners on floor sheathing panel edges applies to panel edges supported by framing members and required blocking and at all floor perimeters only. Spacing of fasteners on roof sheathing panel edges applies to panel edges supported by framing members and required blocking. Blocking of roof or floor sheathing panel edges perpendicular to the framing members need not be provided except as required by other provisions of this code. Floor perimeter shall be supported by framing members or solid blocking.

TABLE R602.3(2)
ALTERNATE ATTACHMENTS

NOMINAL MATERIAL THICKNESS (inches)	DESCRIPTION[a, b] OF FASTENER AND LENGTH (inches)	SPACING[c] OF FASTENERS	
		Edges (inches)	Intermediate supports (inches)
Wood structural panels subfloor, roof and wall sheathing to framing and particleboard wall sheathing to framing[f]			
up to $^1/_2$	Staple 15 ga. $1^3/_4$	4	8
	0.097 - 0.099 Nail $2^1/_4$	3	6
	Staple 16 ga. $1^3/_4$	3	6
$^{19}/_{32}$ and $^5/_8$	0.113 Nail 2	3	6
	Staple 15 and 16 ga. 2	4	8
	0.097 - 0.099 Nail $2^1/_4$	4	8
$^{23}/_{32}$ and $^3/_4$	Staple 14 ga. 2	4	8
	Staple 15 ga. $1^3/_4$	3	6
	0.097 - 0.099 Nail $2^1/_4$	4	8
	Staple 16 ga. 2	4	8
1	Staple 14 ga. $2^1/_4$	4	8
	0.113 Nail $2^1/_4$	3	6
	Staple 15 ga. $2^1/_4$	4	8
	0.097 - 0.099 Nail $2^1/_2$	4	8

NOMINAL MATERIAL THICKNESS (inches)	DESCRIPTION[a,b] OF FASTENER AND LENGTH (inches)	SPACING[c] OF FASTENERS	
		Edges (inches)	Body of panel[d] (inches)
Floor underlayment; plywood-hardboard-particleboard[f]			
Plywood			
$^1/_4$ and $^5/_{16}$	$1^1/_4$ ring or screw shank nail—minimum $12^1/_2$ ga. (0.099″) shank diameter	3	6
	Staple 18 ga., $^7/_8$, $^3/_{16}$ crown width	2	5
$^{11}/_{32}$, $^3/_8$, $^{15}/_{32}$, $^1/_2$ and $^{19}/_{32}$	$1^1/_4$ ring or screw shank nail—minimum $12^1/_2$ ga. (0.099″) shank diameter	6	8[e]
$^5/_8$, $^{23}/_{32}$ and $^3/_4$	$1^1/_2$ ring or screw shank nail—minimum $12^1/_2$ ga. (0.099″) shank diameter	6	8
	Staple 16 ga. $1^1/_2$	6	8
Hardboard[f]			
0.200	$1^1/_2$ long ring-grooved underlayment nail	6	6
	4d cement-coated sinker nail	6	6
	Staple 18 ga., $^7/_8$ long (plastic coated)	3	6
Particleboard			
$^1/_4$	4d ring-grooved underlayment nail	3	6
	Staple 18 ga., $^7/_8$ long, $^3/_{16}$ crown	3	6
$^3/_8$	6d ring-grooved underlayment nail	6	10
	Staple 16 ga., $1^1/_8$ long, $^3/_8$ crown	3	6
$^1/_2$, $^5/_8$	6d ring-grooved underlayment nail	6	10
	Staple 16 ga., $1^5/_8$ long, $^3/_8$ crown	3	6

For SI: 1 inch = 25.4 mm.

a. Nail is a general description and may be T-head, modified round head or round head.

b. Staples shall have a minimum crown width of $^7/_{16}$-inch on diameter except as noted.

c. Nails or staples shall be spaced at not more than 6 inches on center at all supports where spans are 48 inches or greater. Nails or staples shall be spaced at not more than 12 inches on center at intermediate supports for floors.

d. Fasteners shall be placed in a grid pattern throughout the body of the panel.

e. For 5-ply panels, intermediate nails shall be spaced not more than 12 inches on center each way.

f. Hardboard underlayment shall conform to ANSI/AHA A135.4.

TABLE R602.3(3)
WOOD STRUCTURAL PANEL WALL SHEATHING

PANEL SPAN RATING	PANEL NOMINAL THICKNESS (inch)	MAXIMUM STUD SPACING (inches)	
		Siding nailed to:[a]	
		Stud	Sheathing
12/0, 16/0, 20/0, or wall —16 o.c.	$^5/_{16}$, $^3/_8$	16	16[b]
24/0, 24/16, 32/16 or wall—24 o.c.	$^3/_8$, $^7/_{16}$, $^{15}/_{32}$, $^1/_2$	24	24[c]

For SI: 1 inch = 25.4 mm.

a. Blocking of horizontal joints shall not be required.

b. Plywood sheathing $^3/_8$-inch thick or less shall be applied with long dimension across studs.

c. Three-ply plywood panels shall be applied with long dimension across studs.

TABLE R602.3(4)
ALLOWABLE SPANS FOR PARTICLEBOARD WALL SHEATHING[a]

THICKNESS (inch)	GRADE	STUD SPACING (inches)	
		When siding is nailed to studs	When siding is nailed to sheathing
$^3/_8$	M-1 Exterior glue	16	—
$^1/_2$	M-2 Exterior glue	16	16

For SI: 1 inch = 25.4 mm.

a. Wall sheathing not exposed to the weather. If the panels are applied horizontally, the end joints of the panel shall be offset so that four panels corners will not meet. All panel edges must be supported. Leave a $^1/_{16}$-inch gap between panels and nail no closer than $^3/_8$ inch from panel edges.

TABLE R602.3(5)
SIZE, HEIGHT AND SPACING OF WOOD STUDS[a]

STUD SIZE (inches)	BEARING WALLS					NONBEARING WALLS	
	Laterally unsupported stud height[a] (feet)	Maximum spacing when supporting roof and ceiling only (inches)	Maximum spacing when supporting one floor, roof and ceiling (inches)	Maximum spacing when supporting two floors, roof and ceiling (inches)	Maximum spacing when supporting one floor only (inches)	Laterally unsupported stud height[a] (feet)	Maximum spacing (inches)
2 × 3[b]	—	—	—	—	—	10	16
2 × 4	10	24	16	—	24	14	24
3 × 4	10	24	24	16	24	14	24
2 × 5	10	24	24	—	24	16	24
2 × 6	10	24	24	16	24	20	24

For SI: 1 inch = 25.4 mm.

a. Listed heights are distances between points of lateral support placed perpendicular to the plane of the wall. Increases in unsupported height are permitted where justified by analysis.

b. Shall not be used in exterior walls.

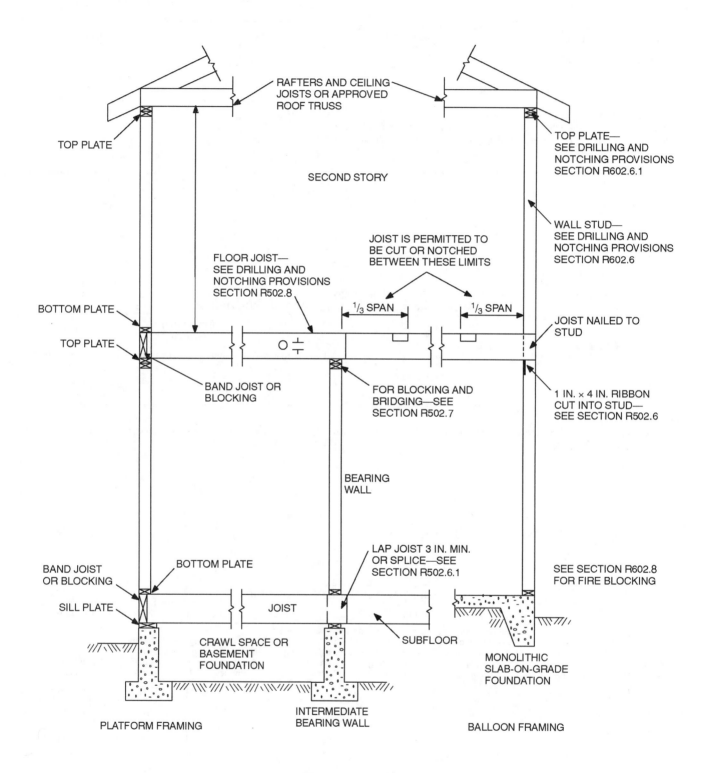

For SI: 1 inch = 25.4 mm.

FIGURE R602.3(1)
TYPICAL WALL, FLOOR AND ROOF FRAMING

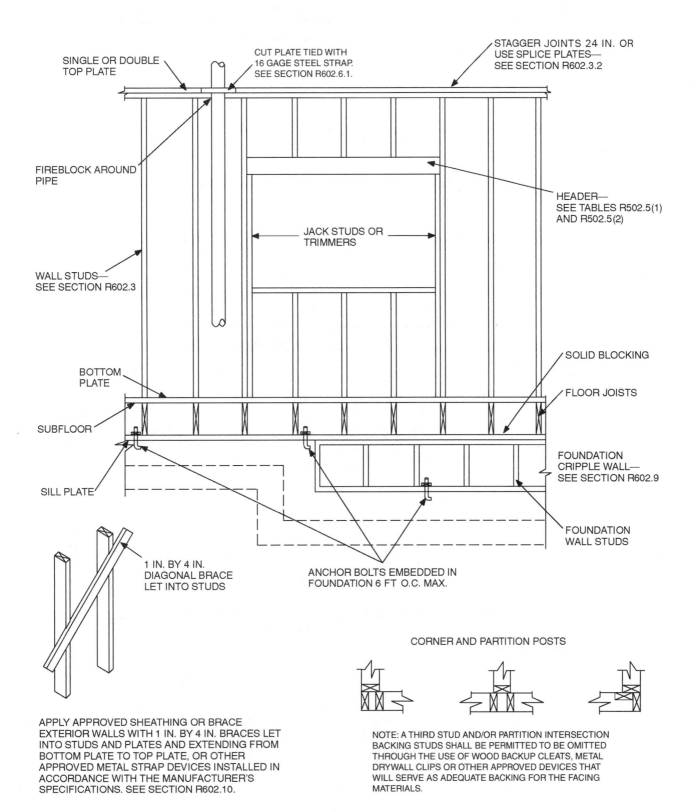

SINGLE OR DOUBLE TOP PLATE

CUT PLATE TIED WITH 16 GAGE STEEL STRAP. SEE SECTION R602.6.1.

STAGGER JOINTS 24 IN. OR USE SPLICE PLATES— SEE SECTION R602.3.2

FIREBLOCK AROUND PIPE

WALL STUDS— SEE SECTION R602.3

JACK STUDS OR TRIMMERS

HEADER— SEE TABLES R502.5(1) AND R502.5(2)

BOTTOM PLATE

SOLID BLOCKING

FLOOR JOISTS

SUBFLOOR

SILL PLATE

FOUNDATION CRIPPLE WALL— SEE SECTION R602.9

FOUNDATION WALL STUDS

1 IN. BY 4 IN. DIAGONAL BRACE LET INTO STUDS

ANCHOR BOLTS EMBEDDED IN FOUNDATION 6 FT O.C. MAX.

APPLY APPROVED SHEATHING OR BRACE EXTERIOR WALLS WITH 1 IN. BY 4 IN. BRACES LET INTO STUDS AND PLATES AND EXTENDING FROM BOTTOM PLATE TO TOP PLATE, OR OTHER APPROVED METAL STRAP DEVICES INSTALLED IN ACCORDANCE WITH THE MANUFACTURER'S SPECIFICATIONS. SEE SECTION R602.10.

CORNER AND PARTITION POSTS

NOTE: A THIRD STUD AND/OR PARTITION INTERSECTION BACKING STUDS SHALL BE PERMITTED TO BE OMITTED THROUGH THE USE OF WOOD BACKUP CLEATS, METAL DRYWALL CLIPS OR OTHER APPROVED DEVICES THAT WILL SERVE AS ADEQUATE BACKING FOR THE FACING MATERIALS.

For SI: 1 inch = 25.4 mm, 1 foot = 304.8 mm.

**FIGURE R602.3(2)
FRAMING DETAILS**

TABLE R602.3.1
MAXIMUM ALLOWABLE LENGTH OF WOOD WALL STUDS EXPOSED TO WIND SPEEDS OF 90 MPH OR LESS[b,c,d,e,f,g,h,i]
Where conditions are not within the parameters of footnotes b, c, d, e, f, g, h, and i, design is required.

ROOF SPANS UP TO 22' SUPPORTING A ROOF ONLY					
MAXIMUM WALL HEIGHT (feet)	**EXPOSURE CATEGORY** [h,i]	**On-Center Spacing (inches)**			
		24	**16**	**12**	**8**
10	B	2 × 6	2 × 4	2 × 4	2 × 4
	C	2 × 6	2 × 6	2 × 4	2 × 4
12	B	2 × 6	2 × 6	2 × 4	2 × 4
	C	2 × 6	2 × 6	2 × 6	2 × 4
14	B	2 × 6	2 × 6	2 × 6	2 × 4
	C	2 × 6	2 × 6	2 × 6	2 × 6
16	B	2 × 8	2 × 6	2 × 6	2 × 6
	C	2 × 8	2 × 6	2 × 6	2 × 6
18	B	2 × 8	2 × 8	2 × 6	2 × 6
	C	2 × 8	2 × 8	2 × 6	2 × 6
20	B	2 × 8	2 × 8	2 × 8	2 × 6
	C	NA[a]	2 × 8	2 × 8	2 × 6
24	B	NA[a]	2 × 8	2 × 8	2 × 8
	C	NA[a]	NA[a]	2 × 8	2 × 8

ROOF SPANS GREATER THAN 22' AND UP TO 26' SUPPORTING A ROOF ONLY					
MAXIMUM WALL HEIGHT (feet)	**EXPOSURE CATEGORY** [h,i]	**On-Center Spacing (inches)**			
		24	**16**	**12**	**8**
10	B	2 × 6	2 × 6	2 × 4	2 × 4
	C	2 × 6	2 × 6	2 × 6	2 × 4
12	B	2 × 6	2 × 6	2 × 6	2 × 4
	C	2 × 6	2 × 6	2 × 6	2 × 6
14	B	2 × 6	2 × 6	2 × 6	2 × 6
	C	2 × 8	2 × 8	2 × 6	2 × 6
16	B	2 × 8	2 × 6	2 × 6	2 × 6
	C	2 × 8	2 × 8	2 × 6	2 × 6
18	B	2 × 8	2 × 8	2 × 6	2 × 6
	C	NA[a]	2 × 8	2 × 8	2 × 6
20	B	NA[a]	2 × 8	2 × 8	2 × 6
	C	NA[a]	NA[a]	2 × 8	2 × 8
24	B	NA[a]	NA[a]	2 × 8	2 × 8
	C	NA[a]	NA[a]	NA[a]	2 × 8

ROOF SPANS GREATER THAN 26' AND UP TO 30' SUPPORTING A ROOF ONLY					
MAXIMUM WALL HEIGHT (feet)	**EXPOSURE CATEGORY** [h,i]	**On-Center Spacing (inches)**			
		24	**16**	**12**	**8**
10	B	2 × 6	2 × 6	2 × 4	2 × 4
	C	2 × 6	2 × 6	2 × 6	2 × 4
12	B	2 × 6	2 × 6	2 × 6	2 × 4
	C	2 × 8	2 × 6	2 × 6	2 × 6
14	B	2 × 8	2 × 6	2 × 6	2 × 6
	C	2 × 8	2 × 8	2 × 6	2 × 6
16	B	2 × 8	2 × 6	2 × 6	2 × 6
	C	2 × 8	2 × 8	2 × 8	2 × 6
18	B	2 × 8	2 × 8	2 × 6	2 × 6
	C	NA[a]	2 × 8	2 × 8	2 × 8
20	B	NA[a]	2 × 8	2 × 8	2 × 6
	C	NA[a]	NA[a]	2 × 8	2 × 8
24	B	NA[a]	NA[a]	2 × 8	2 × 8
	C	NA[a]	NA[a]	NA[a]	2 × 8

(continued)

TABLE R602.3.1
MAXIMUM ALLOWABLE LENGTH OF WOOD WALL STUDS EXPOSED TO WIND SPEEDS OF 90 MPH OR LESS[b,c,d,e,f,g,h,i]
Where conditions are not within the parameters of footnotes b, c, d, e, f, g, h, and i, design is required.

MAXIMUM WALL HEIGHT (feet)	EXPOSURE CATEGORY [h,i]	ROOF SPANS GREATER THAN 30' AND UP TO 34' SUPPORTING A ROOF ONLY			
		On-Center Spacing (inches)			
		24	16	12	8
10	B	2 × 6	2 ×6	2 × 4	2 × 4
	C	2 × 6	2 × 6	2 × 6	2 × 4
12	B	2 × 6	2 × 6	2 × 6	2 × 4
	C	2 × 8	2 × 6	2 × 6	2 × 6
14	B	2 × 8	2 × 6	2 × 6	2 × 6
	C	2 × 8	2 ×8	2 × 6	2 × 6
16	B	2 × 8	2 × 8	2 × 6	2 × 6
	C	NA[a]	2 × 8	2 × 8	2 × 6
18	B	2 × 8	2 × 8	2 × 6	2 × 6
	C	NA[a]	NA[a]	2 × 8	2 × 8
20	B	NA[a]	2 × 8	2 × 8	2 × 6
	C	NA[a]	NA[a]	2 × 8	2 × 8
24	B	NA[a]	NA[a]	2 × 8	2 × 8
	C	NA[a]	NA[a]	NA[a]	2 × 8

a. Design required.

b. Applicability of these tables assumes the following: SPF#2 or better, Ground snow = 60 psf, Roof snow = 42 psf, Component and Cladding Zone 4 - 50 square feet (Exposure B = 14.3 psf, Exposure C = 18.4 psf), eaves not greater than 2.0 feet in dimension.

c. The exterior of the wall shall be continuously sheathed in accordance with one of the methods (2-8) listed in Section R602.10.3.

d. Studs shall be continuous full height.

e. Full depth blocking is required at 10-foot spacing maximum.

f. Utility, standard, stud, and No. 3 grade lumber of any species are not permitted.

g. This table is based on a maximum allowable deflection limit of L/120.

h. Exposure B-Urban and suburban areas, wooded areas, or other terrain with numerous closely spaced obstructions having the size of single-family dwellings or larger. Exposure B shall be assumed unless the site meets the definition of another type exposure.

i. Exposure C - Open terrain with scattered obstructions, including surface undulations or other irregularities, having heights generally less than 30 feet extending more than 1,500 feet from the building site in any quadrant. This category includes flat open country, grasslands, and shorelines in hurricane prone regions. Exposure C shall also apply to any building located within Exposure B type terrain where the building is directly adjacent to open areas of Exposure C type terrain in any quadrant for a distance of more than 600 feet.

R602.3.4 Bottom (sole) plate. Studs shall have full bearing on a nominal 2-by (38 mm) or larger plate or sill having a width at least equal to the width of the studs.

R602.4 Interior load-bearing walls. Interior load-bearing walls shall be constructed, framed and fireblocked as specified for exterior walls.

R602.5 Interior nonbearing walls. Interior nonbearing walls shall be permitted to be constructed with 2-inch-by-3-inch (51 mm by 76 mm) studs spaced 24 inches (610 mm) on center or, when not part of a braced wall line, 2-inch-by-4-inch (51 mm by 102 mm) flat studs spaced at 16 inches (406 mm) on center. Interior nonbearing walls shall be capped with at least a single top plate. Interior nonbearing walls shall be fireblocked in accordance with Section R602.8.

R602.6 Drilling and notching–studs. Drilling and notching of studs shall be in accordance with the following:

1. Notching. Any stud in an exterior wall or bearing partition may be cut or notched to a depth not exceeding 25 percent of its width. Studs in nonbearing partitions may be notched to a depth not to exceed 40 percent of a single stud width.

2. Drilling. Any stud may be bored or drilled, provided that the diameter of the resulting hole is no more than 60 percent of the stud width, the edge of the hole is no more than $5/8$ inch (16 mm) to the edge of the stud, and the hole is not located in the same section as a cut or notch. Studs located in exterior walls or bearing partitions drilled over 40 percent and up to 60 percent shall also be doubled with no more than two successive doubled studs bored. See Figures R602.6(1) and R602.6(2).

   Exception: Use of approved stud shoes is permitted when they are installed in accordance with the manufacturer's recommendations.

R602.6.1 Drilling and notching of top plate. When piping or ductwork is placed in or partly in an exterior wall or interior load-bearing wall, necessitating cutting, drilling or notching of the top plate by more than 50 percent of its width, a galvanized metal tie of not less than 0.054 inch thick (1.37 mm) (16 ga) and $1 1/2$ inches (38 mm) wide shall be fastened across and to the plate at each side of the opening with not less than eight 16d nails at each side or equivalent. See Figure R602.6.1.

   Exception: When the entire side of the wall with the notch or cut is covered by wood structural panel sheathing.

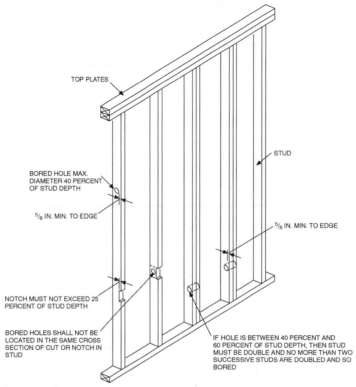

TOP PLATES

STUD

BORED HOLE MAX.
DIAMETER 40 PERCENT
OF STUD DEPTH

$^5/_8$ IN. MIN. TO EDGE

$^5/_8$ IN. MIN. TO EDGE

NOTCH MUST NOT EXCEED 25
PERCENT OF STUD DEPTH

BORED HOLES SHALL NOT BE
LOCATED IN THE SAME CROSS
SECTION OF CUT OR NOTCH IN
STUD

IF HOLE IS BETWEEN 40 PERCENT AND
60 PERCENT OF STUD DEPTH, THEN STUD
MUST BE DOUBLE AND NO MORE THAN TWO
SUCCESSIVE STUDS ARE DOUBLED AND SO
BORED

For SI: 1 inch = 25.4 mm.
NOTE: Condition for exterior and bearing walls.

FIGURE R602.6(1)
NOTCHING AND BORED HOLE LIMITATIONS FOR EXTERIOR WALLS AND BEARING WALLS

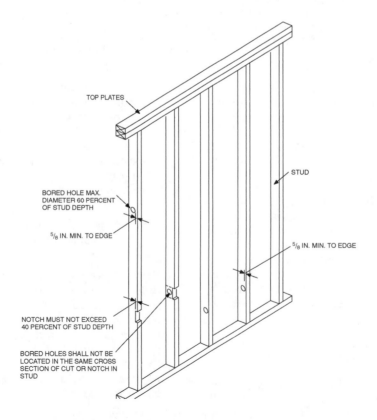

TOP PLATES

STUD

BORED HOLE MAX.
DIAMETER 60 PERCENT
OF STUD DEPTH

$^5/_8$ IN. MIN. TO EDGE

$^5/_8$ IN. MIN. TO EDGE

NOTCH MUST NOT EXCEED
40 PERCENT OF STUD DEPTH

BORED HOLES SHALL NOT BE
LOCATED IN THE SAME CROSS
SECTION OF CUT OR NOTCH IN
STUD

For SI: 1 inch = 25.4 mm.

FIGURE R602.6(2)
NOTCHING AND BORED HOLE LIMITATIONS FOR INTERIOR NONBEARING WALLS

R602.7 Headers. For header spans see Tables R502.5(1) and R502.5(2).

R602.7.1 Wood structural panel box headers. Wood structural panel box headers shall be constructed in accordance with Figure R602.7.2 and Table R602.7.2.

R602.7.2 Nonbearing walls. Load-bearing headers are not required in interior or exterior nonbearing walls. A single flat 2-inch-by-4-inch (51 mm by 102 mm) member may be used as a header in interior or exterior nonbearing walls for openings up to 8 feet (2438 mm) in width if the vertical distance to the parallel nailing surface above is not more than 24 inches (610 mm). For such nonbearing headers, no cripples or blocking are required above the header.

R602.8 Fireblocking required. Fireblocking shall be provided to cut off all concealed draft openings (both vertical and horizon-

tal) and to form an effective fire barrier between stories, and between a top story and the roof space. Fireblocking shall be provided in wood-frame construction in the following locations.

1. In concealed spaces of stud walls and partitions, including furred spaces and parallel rows of studs or staggered studs; as follows:

    1.1. Vertically at the ceiling and floor levels.

    1.2. Horizontally at intervals not exceeding 10 feet (3048 mm).

2. At all interconnections between concealed vertical and horizontal spaces such as occur at soffits, drop ceilings and cove ceilings.

3. In concealed spaces between stair stringers at the top and bottom of the run. Enclosed spaces under stairs shall comply with Section R311.2.2.

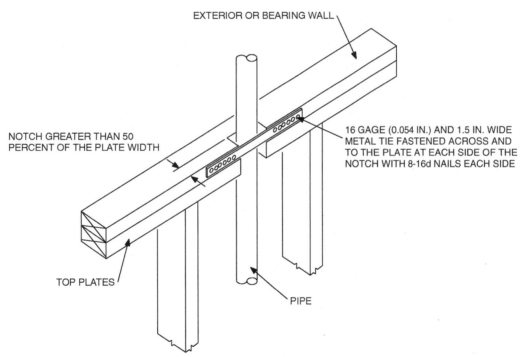

NOTCH GREATER THAN 50 PERCENT OF THE PLATE WIDTH

EXTERIOR OR BEARING WALL

16 GAGE (0.054 IN.) AND 1.5 IN. WIDE METAL TIE FASTENED ACROSS AND TO THE PLATE AT EACH SIDE OF THE NOTCH WITH 8-16d NAILS EACH SIDE

TOP PLATES

PIPE

For SI: 1 inch = 25.4 mm.

FIGURE R602.6.1
TOP PLATE FRAMING TO ACCOMMODATE PIPING

TABLE R602.7.2
MAXIMUM SPANS FOR WOOD STRUCTURAL PANEL BOX HEADERS[a]

HEADER CONSTRUCTION[b]	HEADER DEPTH (inches)	HOUSE DEPTH (feet)				
		24	26	28	30	32
Wood structural panel—one side	9	4	4	3	3	—
	15	5	5	4	3	3
Wood structural panel—both sides	9	7	5	5	4	3
	15	8	8	7	7	6

For SI: 1 inch = 25.4 mm, 1 foot = 304.8 mm.

a. Spans are based on single story with clear-span trussed roof or two-story with floor and roof supported by interior-bearing walls.

b. See Figure R602.7.2 for construction details.

4. At openings around vents, pipes, ducts, cables and wires at ceiling and floor level, with an approved material to resist the free passage of flame and products of combustion.

5. For the fireblocking of chimneys and fireplaces, see Section R1003.19.

6. Fireblocking of cornices of a two-family dwelling is required at the line of dwelling unit separation.

R602.8.1 Materials. Except as provided in Section R602.8, Item 4, fireblocking shall consist of 2-inch (51 mm) nominal lumber, or two thicknesses of 1-inch (25.4 mm) nominal lumber with broken lap joints, or one thickness of $^{23}/_{32}$-inch (19.8 mm) wood structural panels with joints backed by $^{23}/_{32}$-inch (19.8 mm) wood structural panels or one thickness of $^{3}/_{4}$-inch (19.1 mm) particleboard with joints backed by $^{3}/_{4}$-inch (19.1 mm) particleboard, $^{1}/_{2}$-inch (12.7 mm) gypsum board, or $^{1}/_{4}$-inch (6.4 mm) cement-based millboard. Batts or blankets of mineral wool or glass fiber or other approved materials installed in such a manner as to be securely retained in place shall be permitted as an acceptable fire block. Batts or blankets of mineral or glass fiber or other approved nonrigid materials shall be permitted for compliance with the 10 foot horizontal fireblocking in walls constructed using parallel rows of studs or staggered studs. Loose-fill insulation material shall not be used as a fire block unless specifically tested in the form and manner

intended for use to demonstrate its ability to remain in place and to retard the spread of fire and hot gases.

R602.8.1.1 Unfaced fiberglass. Unfaced fiberglass batt insulation used as fireblocking shall fill the entire cross section of the wall cavity to a minimum height of 16 inches (406 mm) measured vertically. When piping, conduit or similar obstructions are encountered, the insulation shall be packed tightly around the obstruction.

R602.8.1.2 Fireblocking integrity. The integrity of all fireblocks shall be maintained.

R602.9 Cripple walls. Foundation cripple walls shall be framed of studs not smaller than the studding above. When exceeding 4 feet (1219 mm) in height, such walls shall be framed of studs having the size required for an additional story.

Cripple walls with a stud height less than 14 inches (356 mm) shall be sheathed on at least one side with a wood structural panel that is fastened to both the top and bottom plates in accordance with Table R602.3(1), or the cripple walls shall be constructed of solid blocking. Cripple walls shall be supported on continuous foundations.

R602.10 Wall bracing. All exterior walls shall be braced in accordance with this section. In addition, interior braced wall lines shall be provided in accordance with Section R602.10.1.1. For buildings in Seismic Design Categories D₀, D₁ and D₂, walls shall be constructed in accordance with the additional requirements of Sections R602.10.9, R602.10.11, and R602.11.

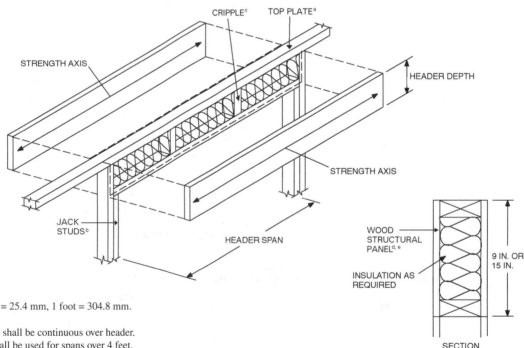

For SI: 1 inch = 25.4 mm, 1 foot = 304.8 mm.

NOTES:

a. The top plate shall be continuous over header.

b. Jack studs shall be used for spans over 4 feet.

c. Cripple spacing shall be the same as for studs.

d. Wood structural panel faces shall be single pieces of $^{15}/_{32}$-inch-thick Exposure 1 (exterior glue) or thicker, installed on the interior or exterior or both sides of the header.

e. Wood structural panel faces shall be nailed to framing and cripples with 8d common or galvanized box nails spaced 3 inches on center, staggering alternate nails $^{1}/_{2}$ inch. Galvanized nails shall be hot-dipped or tumbled.

FIGURE R602.7.2
TYPICAL WOOD STRUCTURAL PANEL BOX HEADER CONSTRUCTION

R602.10.1 Braced wall lines. Braced wall lines shall consist of braced wall panel construction in accordance with Section R602.10.3. The amount and location of bracing shall be in accordance with Table R602.10.1 and the amount of bracing shall be the greater of that required by the seismic design category or the design wind speed. Braced wall panels shall begin no more than 12.5 feet (3810 mm) from each end of a braced wall line. Braced wall panels that are counted as part of a braced wall line shall be in line, except that offsets out-of-plane of up to 4 feet (1219 mm) shall be permitted provided that the total out-to-out offset dimension in any braced wall line is not more than 8 feet (2438 mm).

R602.10.1.1 Spacing. Spacing of braced wall lines shall not exceed 35 feet (10 668 mm) on center in both the longitudinal and transverse directions in each story.

Exception: Spacing of braced wall lines not exceeding 50 feet shall be permitted where:

1. The wall bracing installed equals or exceeds the amount of bracing required by Table R602.10.1 multiplied by a factor equal to the braced wall line spacing divided by 35 feet and

2. The length-to-width ratio for the floor or roof diaphragm does not exceed 3:1.

R602.10.2 Cripple wall bracing.

R602.10.2.1 Seismic design categories other than D$_2$. In Seismic Design Categories other than D$_2$, cripple walls shall be braced with an amount and type of bracing as required for the wall above in accordance with Table R602.10.1 with the following modifications for cripple wall bracing:

1. The percent bracing amount as determined from Table R602.10.1 shall be increased by 15 percent and

2. The wall panel spacing shall be decreased to 18 feet (5486 mm) instead of 25 feet (7620 mm).

R602.10.2.2 Seismic Design Category D$_2$. In Seismic Design Category D$_2$, cripple walls shall be braced in accordance with Table R602.10.1.

R602.10.2.3 Redesignation of cripple walls. In any seismic design category, cripple walls are permitted to be redesignated as the first story walls for purposes of determining wall bracing requirements. If the cripple walls are redesignated, the stories above the redesignated story shall be counted as the second and third stories, respectively.

R602.10.3 Braced wall panel construction methods. The construction of braced wall panels shall be in accordance with one of the following methods:

1. Nominal 1-inch-by-4-inch (25 mm by 102 mm) continuous diagonal braces let in to the top and bottom plates and the intervening studs or approved metal strap devices installed in accordance with the manu-

facturer's specifications. The let-in bracing shall be placed at an angle not more than 60 degrees (1.06 rad) or less than 45 degrees (0.79 rad) from the horizontal.

2. Wood boards of $^5/_8$ inch (16 mm) net minimum thickness applied diagonally on studs spaced a maximum of 24 inches (610 mm). Diagonal boards shall be attached to studs in accordance with Table R602.3(1).

3. Wood structural panel sheathing with a thickness not less than $^5/_{16}$ inch (8 mm) for 16-inch (406 mm) stud spacing and not less than $^3/_8$ inch (9 mm) for 24-inch (610 mm) stud spacing. Wood structural panels shall be installed in accordance with Table R602.3(3).

4. One-half-inch (13 mm) or $^{25}/_{32}$-inch (20 mm) thick structural fiberboard sheathing applied vertically or horizontally on studs spaced a maximum of 16 inches (406 mm) on center. Structural fiberboard sheathing shall be installed in accordance with Table R602.3(1).

5. Gypsum board with minimum $^1/_2$-inch (13 mm) thickness placed on studs spaced a maximum of 24 inches (610 mm) on center and fastened at 7 inches (178 mm) on center with the size nails specified in Table R602.3(1) for sheathing and Table R702.3.5 for interior gypsum board.

6. Particleboard wall sheathing panels installed in accordance with Table R602.3(4).

7. Portland cement plaster on studs spaced a maximum of 16 inches (406 mm) on center and installed in accordance with Section R703.6.

8. Hardboard panel siding when installed in accordance with Table R703.4.

Exception: Alternate braced wall panels constructed in accordance with Section R602.10.6.1 or R602.10.6.2 shall be permitted to replace any of the above methods of braced wall panels.

R602.10.4 Length of braced panels. For Methods 2, 3, 4, 6, 7 and 8 above, each braced wall panel shall be at least 48 inches (1219 mm) in length, covering a minimum of three stud spaces where studs are spaced 16 inches (406 mm) on center and covering a minimum of two stud spaces where studs are spaced 24 inches (610 mm) on center. For Method 5 above, each braced wall panel shall be at least 96 inches (2438 mm) in length where applied to one face of a braced wall panel and at least 48 inches (1219 mm) where applied to both faces.

Exceptions:

1. Lengths of braced wall panels for continuous wood structural panel sheathing shall be in accordance with Section R602.10.5.

2. Lengths of alternate braced wall panels shall be in accordance with Section R602.10.6.1 or Section R602.10.6.2.

TABLE R602.10.1
WALL BRACING

SEISMIC DESIGN CATEGORY OR WIND SPEED	CONDITION	TYPE OF BRACE[b, c]	AMOUNT OF BRACING[a, d, e]
Category A and B ($S_s \leq 0.35g$ and $S_{ds} \leq 0.33g$) or 100 mph or less	One story Top of two or three story	Methods 1, 2, 3, 4, 5, 6, 7 or 8	Located in accordance with Section R602.10 and at least every 25 feet on center but not less than 16% of braced wall line for Methods 2 through 8.
	First story of two story Second story of three story	Methods 1, 2, 3, 4, 5, 6, 7 or 8	Located in accordance with Section R602.10 and at least every 25 feet on center but not less than 16% of braced wall line for Method 3 or 25% of braced wall line for Methods 2, 4, 5, 6, 7 or 8.
	First story of three story	Methods 2, 3, 4, 5, 6, 7 or 8	Located in accordance with Section R602.10 and at least every 25 feet on center but not less than 25% of braced wall line for Method 3 or 35% of braced wall line for Methods 2, 4, 5, 6, 7 or 8.
Category C ($S_s \leq 0.6g$ and $S_{ds} \leq 0.50g$) or less than 110 mph	One story Top of two or three story	Methods 1, 2, 3, 4, 5, 6, 7 or 8	Located in accordance with Section R602.10 and at least every 25 feet on center but not less than 16% of braced wall line for Method 3 or 25% of braced wall line for Methods 2, 4, 5, 6, 7 or 8.
	First story of two story Second story of three story	Methods 2, 3, 4, 5, 6, 7 or 8	Located in accordance with Section R602.10 and at least every 25 feet on center but not less than 30% of braced wall line for Method 3 or 45% of braced wall line for Methods 2, 4, 5, 6, 7 or 8.
	First story of three story	Methods 2, 3, 4, 5, 6, 7 or 8	Located in accordance with Section R602.10 and at least every 25 feet on center but not less than 45% of braced wall line for Method 3 or 60% of braced wall line for Methods 2, 4, 5, 6, 7 or 8.
Categories D_0 and D_1 ($S_s \leq 1.25g$ and $S_{ds} \leq 0.83g$) or less than 110 mph	One story Top of two or three story	Methods 2, 3, 4, 5, 6, 7 or 8	Located in accordance with Section R602.10 and at least every 25 feet on center but not less than 20% of braced wall line for Method 3 or 30% of braced wall line for Methods 2, 4, 5, 6, 7 or 8.
	First story of two story Second story of three story	Methods 2, 3, 4, 5, 6, 7 or 8	Located in accordance with Section R602.10 and at least every 25 feet on center but not less than 45% of braced wall line for Method 3 or 60% of braced wall line for Methods 2, 4, 5, 6, 7 or 8.
	First story of three story	Methods 2, 3, 4, 5, 6, 7 or 8	Located in accordance with Section R602.10 and at least every 25 feet on center but not less than 60% of braced wall line for Method 3 or 85% of braced wall line for Methods 2, 4, 5, 6, 7 or 8.
Category D_2 or less than 110 mph	One story Top of two story	Methods 2, 3, 4, 5, 6, 7 or 8	Located in accordance with Section R602.10 and at least every 25 feet on center but not less than 25% of braced wall line for Method 3 or 40% of braced wall line for Methods 2, 4, 5, 6, 7 or 8.
	First story of two story	Methods 2, 3, 4, 5, 6, 7 or 8	Located in accordance with Section R602.10 and at least every 25 feet on center but not less than 55% of braced wall line for Method 3 or 75% of braced wall line for Methods 2, 4, 5, 6, 7 or 8.
	Cripple walls	Method 3	Located in accordance with Section R602.10 and at least every 25 feet on center but not less than 75% of braced wall line.

For SI: 1 inch = 25.4 mm, 1 foot = 304.8 mm, 1 pound per square foot = 0.0479 kPa, 1 mile per hour = 0.477 m/s.

a. Wall bracing amounts are based on a soil site class "D." Interpolation of bracing amounts between the S_{ds} values associated with the seismic design categories shall be permitted when a site specific S_{ds} value is determined in accordance with Section 1613.5 of the *International Building Code.*

b. Foundation cripple wall panels shall be braced in accordance with Section R602.10.2.

c. Methods of bracing shall be as described in Section R602.10.3. The alternate braced wall panels described in Section R602.10.6.1 or R602.10.6.2 shall also be permitted.

d. The bracing amounts for Seismic Design Categories are based on a 15 psf wall dead load. For walls with a dead load of 8 psf or less, the bracing amounts shall be permitted to be multiplied by 0.85 provided that the adjusted bracing amount is not less than that required for the site's wind speed. The minimum length of braced panel shall not be less than required by Section R602.10.3.

e. When the dead load of the roof/ceiling exceeds 15 psf, the bracing amounts shall be increased in accordance with Section R301.2.2.2.1. Bracing required for a site's wind speed shall not be adjusted.

R602.10.5 Continuous wood structural panel sheathing.
When continuous wood structural panel sheathing is provided in accordance with Method 3 of Section R602.10.3 on all sheathable areas of all exterior walls, and interior braced wall lines, where required, including areas above and below openings, bracing wall panel lengths shall be in accordance with Table R602.10.5. Wood structural panel sheathing shall be installed at corners in accordance with Figure R602.10.5. The bracing amounts in Table R602.10.1 for Method 3 shall be permitted to be multiplied by a factor of 0.9 for wall with a maximum opening height that does not exceed 85 percent of the wall height or a factor of 0.8 for walls with a maximum opening height that does not exceed 67 percent of the wall height.

R602.10.6 Alternate braced wall panel construction methods. Alternate braced wall panels shall be constructed in accordance with Sections R602.10.6.1 and R602.10.6.2.

R602.10.6.1 Alternate braced wall panels. Alternate braced wall lines constructed in accordance with one of the following provisions shall be permitted to replace each 4 feet (1219 mm) of braced wall panel as required by Section R602.10.4. The maximum height and minimum width of each panel shall be in accordance with Table R602.10.6:

1. In one-story buildings, each panel shall be sheathed on one face with $^3/_8$-inch-minimum-thickness (10 mm) wood structural panel sheathing nailed with 8d common or galvanized box nails in accordance with Table R602.3(1) and blocked at all wood structural panel sheathing edges. Two anchor bolts installed in accordance with Figure R403.1(1) shall be provided in each panel. Anchor bolts shall be placed at panel quarter points. Each panel end stud shall have a tie-down device fastened to the foundation, capable of providing an uplift capacity in accordance with Table R602.10.6. The tie down device shall be installed in accordance with the manufacturer's recommendations. The panels shall be supported directly on a foundation or on floor framing supported directly on a foundation which is continuous across the entire length of the braced wall line. This foundation shall be reinforced with not less than one No. 4 bar top and bottom. When the continuous foundation is required to have a depth greater than 12 inches (305 mm), a minimum 12-inch-by-12-inch (305 mm by 305 mm) continuous footing or turned down slab edge is permitted at door openings in the braced wall line. This continuous footing or turned down slab edge shall be reinforced with not less than one No. 4 bar top and bottom. This reinforcement shall be lapped 15 inches (381 mm) with the reinforcement required in the continuous foundation located directly under the braced wall line.

2. In the first story of two-story buildings, each braced wall panel shall be in accordance with Item 1 above, except that the wood structural panel sheathing shall be installed on both faces, sheathing edge nailing spacing shall not exceed 4 inches (102 mm) on center, at least three anchor bolts shall be placed at one-fifth points.

R602.10.6.2 Alternate braced wall panel adjacent to a door or window opening. Alternate braced wall panels constructed in accordance with one of the following provisions are also permitted to replace each 4 feet (1219 mm) of braced wall panel as required by Section R602.10.4 for use adjacent to a window or door opening with a full-length header:

1. In one-story buildings, each panel shall have a length of not less than 16 inches (406 mm) and a height of not more than 10 feet (3048 mm). Each panel shall be sheathed on one face with a single layer of $^3/_8$-inch-minimum-thickness (10 mm) wood structural panel sheathing nailed with 8d common or galvanized box nails in accordance with Figure R602.10.6.2. The wood structural panel sheathing shall extend up over the solid sawn or glued-laminated header and shall be nailed in accordance with Figure R602.10.6.2. Use of a built-up header consisting of at least two 2 x 12s and fastened in accordance with Table R602.3(1)

TABLE R602.10.5
LENGTH REQUIREMENTS FOR BRACED WALL PANELS IN A CONTINUOUSLY SHEATHED WALL[a, b, c]

MINIMUM LENGTH OF BRACED WALL PANEL (inches)			MAXIMUM OPENING HEIGHT NEXT TO THE BRACED WALL PANEL (% of wall height)
8-foot wall	9-foot wall	10-foot wall	
48	54	60	100
32	36	40	85
24	27	30	65

For SI: 1 inch = 25.4 mm, 1 foot = 305 mm, 1 pound per square foot = 0.0479 kPa.

a. Linear interpolation shall be permitted.

b. Full-height sheathed wall segments to either side of garage openings that support light frame roofs only, with roof covering dead loads of 3 psf or less shall be permitted to have a 4:1 aspect ratio.

c. Walls on either or both sides of openings in garages attached to fully sheathed dwellings shall be permitted to be built in accordance with Section R602.10.6.2 and Figure R602.10.6.2 except that a single bottom plate shall be permitted and two anchor bolts shall be placed at 1/3 points. In addition, tie-down devices shall not be required and the vertical wall segment shall have a maximum 6:1 height-to-width ratio (with height being measured from top of header to the bottom of the sill plate). This option shall be permitted for the first story of two-story applications in Seismic Design Categories A through C.

shall be permitted. A spacer, if used, shall be placed on the side of the built-up beam opposite the wood structural panel sheathing. The header shall extend between the inside faces of the first full-length outer studs of each panel. The clear span of the header between the inner studs of each panel shall be not less than 6 feet (1829 mm) and

not more than 18 feet (5486 mm) in length. A strap with an uplift capacity of not less than 1000 pounds (4448 N) shall fasten the header to the side of the inner studs opposite the sheathing. One anchor bolt not less than $^5/_8$-inch-diameter (16 mm) and installed in accordance with Section R403.1.6 shall be installed in the center of each sill

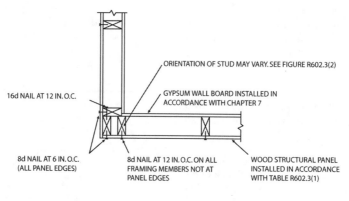

(a) OUTSIDE CORNER DETAIL

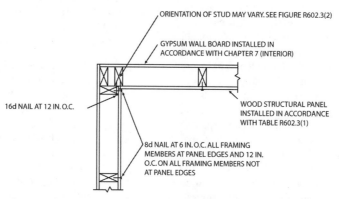

(b) INSIDE CORNER DETAIL

For SI: 1 inch = 25.4 mm.
Gypsum board nails deleted for clarity.

FIGURE R602.10.5
TYPICAL EXTERIOR CORNER FRAMING FOR CONTINUOUS STRUCTURAL
PANEL SHEATHING; SHOWING REQUIRED STUD-TO-STUD NAILING

TABLE R602.10.6
MINIMUM WIDTHS AND TIE-DOWN FORCES OF ALTERNATE BRACED WALL PANELS

SEISMIC DESIGN CATEGORY AND WINDSPEED	TIE-DOWN FORCE (lb)	HEIGHT OF BRACED WALL PANEL				
		Sheathed Width				
		8 ft. 2' - 4"	9 ft. 2' - 8"	10 ft. 2' - 8"	11 ft. 3' - 2"	12 ft. 3' - 6"
SDC A, B, and C Windspeed < 110 mph	R602.10.6.1, Item 1	1800	1800	1800	2000	2200
	R602.10.6.1, Item 2	3000	3000	3000	3300	3600
		Sheathed Width				
		2' - 8"	2' - 8"	2' - 8"	Note a	Note a
SDC D₀, D₁ and D₂ Windspeed < 110 mph	R602.10.6.1, Item 1	1800	1800	1800	—	—
	R602.10.6.1, Item 2	3000	3000	3000	—	—

For SI: 1 inch = 25.4 mm, 1 foot = 304.8 mm.
a. Not permitted because maximum height is 10 feet.

plate. The studs at each end of the panel shall have a tie-down device fastened to the foundation with an uplift capacity of not less than 4,200 pounds (18 683 N).

Where a panel is located on one side of the opening, the header shall extend between the inside face of the first full-length stud of the panel and the bearing studs at the other end of the opening. A strap with an uplift capacity of not less than 1000 pounds (4448 N) shall fasten the header to the bearing studs. The bearing studs shall also have a tie-down device fastened to the foundation with an uplift capacity of not less than 1000 pounds (4448 N).

The tie-down devices shall be an embedded-strap type, installed in accordance with the manufacturer's recommendations. The panels shall be supported directly on a foundation which is continuous across the entire length of the braced wall line. The foundation shall be reinforced with not less than one No. 4 bar top and bottom.

Where the continuous foundation is required to have a depth greater than 12 inches (305 mm), a minimum 12-inch-by-12-inch (305 mm by 305 mm) continuous footing or turned down slab edge is permitted at door openings in the braced wall line. This continuous footing or turned down slab edge shall be reinforced with not less than one No. 4 bar top and bottom. This reinforcement shall be lapped not less than 15 inches (381 mm) with the reinforcement required in the continuous foundation located directly under the braced wall line.

2. In the first story of two-story buildings, each wall panel shall be braced in accordance with Item 1 above, except that each panel shall have a length of not less than 24 inches (610 mm).

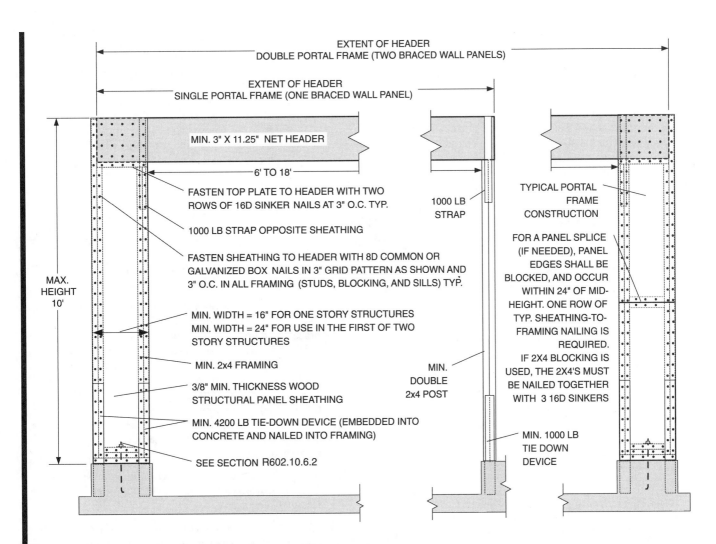

EXTENT OF HEADER
DOUBLE PORTAL FRAME (TWO BRACED WALL PANELS)

EXTENT OF HEADER
SINGLE PORTAL FRAME (ONE BRACED WALL PANEL)

MIN. 3" X 11.25" NET HEADER

6' TO 18'

FASTEN TOP PLATE TO HEADER WITH TWO ROWS OF 16D SINKER NAILS AT 3" O.C. TYP.

1000 LB STRAP OPPOSITE SHEATHING

FASTEN SHEATHING TO HEADER WITH 8D COMMON OR GALVANIZED BOX NAILS IN 3" GRID PATTERN AS SHOWN AND 3" O.C. IN ALL FRAMING (STUDS, BLOCKING, AND SILLS) TYP.

MIN. WIDTH = 16" FOR ONE STORY STRUCTURES
MIN. WIDTH = 24" FOR USE IN THE FIRST OF TWO STORY STRUCTURES

MIN. 2x4 FRAMING

3/8" MIN. THICKNESS WOOD STRUCTURAL PANEL SHEATHING

MIN. 4200 LB TIE-DOWN DEVICE (EMBEDDED INTO CONCRETE AND NAILED INTO FRAMING)

SEE SECTION R602.10.6.2

MAX. HEIGHT 10'

1000 LB STRAP

MIN. DOUBLE 2x4 POST

MIN. 1000 LB TIE DOWN DEVICE

TYPICAL PORTAL FRAME CONSTRUCTION

FOR A PANEL SPLICE (IF NEEDED), PANEL EDGES SHALL BE BLOCKED, AND OCCUR WITHIN 24" OF MID-HEIGHT. ONE ROW OF TYP. SHEATHING-TO-FRAMING NAILING IS REQUIRED. IF 2X4 BLOCKING IS USED, THE 2X4'S MUST BE NAILED TOGETHER WITH 3 16D SINKERS

For SI: 1 inch = 25.4 mm, 1 foot = 304.8 mm, 1 pound = 0.454 kg.

FIGURE R602.10.6.2
ALTERNATE BRACED WALL PANEL ADJACENT TO A DOOR OR WINDOW OPENING

R602.10.7 Panel joints. All vertical joints of panel sheathing shall occur over, and be fastened to, common studs. Horizontal joints in braced wall panels shall occur over, and be fastened to, common blocking of a minimum $1^1/_2$ inch (38 mm) thickness.

Exception: Blocking is not required behind horizontal joints in Seismic Design Categories A and B and detached dwellings in Seismic Design Category C when constructed in accordance with Section R602.10.3, braced-wall-panel construction method 3 and Table R602.10.1, method 3, or where permitted by the manufacturer's installation requirements for the specific sheathing material.

R602.10.8 Connections. Braced wall line sole plates shall be fastened to the floor framing and top plates shall be connected to the framing above in accordance with Table R602.3(1). Sills shall be fastened to the foundation or slab in accordance with Sections R403.1.6 and R602.11. Where joists are perpendicular to the braced wall lines above, blocking shall be provided under and in line with the braced wall panels. Where joists are perpendicular to braced wall lines below, blocking shall be provided over and in line with the braced wall panels. Where joists are parallel to braced wall lines above or below, a rim joist or other parallel framing member shall be provided at the wall to permit fastening per Table R602.3(1).

R602.10.9 Interior braced wall support. In one-story buildings located in Seismic Design Category D_2, interior braced wall lines shall be supported on continuous foundations at intervals not exceeding 50 feet (15 240 mm). In two-story buildings located in Seismic Design Category D_2, all interior braced wall panels shall be supported on continuous foundations.

Exception: Two-story buildings shall be permitted to have interior braced wall lines supported on continuous foundations at intervals not exceeding 50 feet (15 240 mm) provided that:

1. The height of cripple walls does not exceed 4 feet (1219 mm).

2. First-floor braced wall panels are supported on doubled floor joists, continuous blocking or floor beams.

3. The distance between bracing lines does not exceed twice the building width measured parallel to the braced wall line.

R602.10.10 Design of structural elements. Where a building, or portion thereof, does not comply with one or more of the bracing requirements in this section, those portions shall be designed and constructed in accordance with accepted engineering practice.

R602.10.11 Bracing in Seismic Design Categories D_0, D_1 and D_2. Structures located in Seismic Design Categories D_0, D_1 and D_2 shall have exterior and interior braced wall lines.

R602.10.11.1 Braced wall line spacing. Spacing between braced wall lines in each story shall not exceed 25 feet (7620 mm) on center in both the longitudinal and transverse directions.

Exception: In one- and two-story buildings, spacing between two adjacent braced wall lines shall not exceed 35 feet (10 363 mm) on center in order to accommodate one single room not exceeding 900 square feet (84 m²) in each dwelling unit. Spacing between all other braced wall lines shall not exceed 25 feet (7620 mm).

R602.10.11.2 Braced wall panel location. Exterior braced wall lines shall have a braced wall panel at each end of the braced wall line.

Exception: For braced wall panel construction Method 3 of Section R602.10.3, the braced wall panel shall be permitted to begin no more than 8 feet (2438 mm) from each end of the braced wall line provided the following is satisfied:

1. A minimum 24-inch-wide (610 mm) panel is applied to each side of the building corner and the two 24-inch (610 mm) panels at the corner shall be attached to framing in accordance with Figure R602.10.5; or

2. The end of each braced wall panel closest to the corner shall have a tie-down device fastened to the stud at the edge of the braced wall panel closest to the corner and to the foundation or framing below. The tie-down device shall be capable of providing an uplift allowable design value of at least 1,800 pounds (8 kN). The tie-down device shall be installed in accordance with the manufacturer's recommendations.

R602.10.11.3 Collectors. A designed collector shall be provided if a braced wall panel is not located at each end of a braced wall line as indicated in Section R602.10.11.2, or, when using the Section R602.10.11.2 exception, if a braced wall panel is more than 8 feet (2438 mm) from each end of a braced wall line.

R602.10.11.4 Cripple wall bracing. In addition to the requirements of Section R602.10.2, where interior braced wall lines occur without a continuous foundation below, the length of parallel exterior cripple wall bracing shall be one and one-half times the length required by Table R602.10.1. Where cripple walls braced using Method 3 of Section R602.10.3 cannot provide this additional length, the capacity of the sheathing shall be increased by reducing the spacing of fasteners along the perimeter of each piece of sheathing to 4 inches (102 mm) on center.

R602.10.11.5 Sheathing attachment. Adhesive attachment of wall sheathing shall not be permitted in Seismic Design Categories C, D_0, D_1 and D_2.

R602.11 Framing and connections for Seismic Design Categories D_0, D_1 and D_2. The framing and connections details of buildings located in Seismic Design Categories D_0, D_1 and D_2 shall be in accordance with Sections R602.11.1 through R602.11.3.

R602.11.1 Wall anchorage. Braced wall line sills shall be anchored to concrete or masonry foundations in accordance with Sections R403.1.6 and R602.11. For all buildings in Seismic Design Categories D_0, D_1 and D_2 and townhouses in Seismic Design Category C, plate washers, a minimum of 0.229 inch by 3 inches by 3 inches (5.8 mm by 76 mm by 76 mm) in size, shall be installed between the foundation sill plate and the nut. The hole in the plate washer is permitted to be diagonally slotted with a width of up to $^3/_{16}$ inch (5 mm) larger than the bolt diameter and a slot length not to exceed $1^3/_4$ inches (44 mm), provided a standard cut washer is placed between the plate washer and the nut.

R602.11.2 Interior braced wall panel connections. Interior braced wall lines shall be fastened to floor and roof framing in accordance with Table R602.3(1), to required foundations in accordance with Section R602.11.1, and in accordance with the following requirements:

1. Floor joists parallel to the top plate shall be toe-nailed to the top plate with at least 8d nails spaced a maximum of 6 inches (152 mm) on center.

2. Top plate laps shall be face-nailed with at least eight 16d nails on each side of the splice.

R602.11.3 Stepped foundations. Where stepped foundations occur, the following requirements apply:

1. Where the height of a required braced wall panel that extends from foundation to floor above varies more than 4 feet (1220 mm), the braced wall panel shall be constructed in accordance with Figure R602.11.3.

2. Where the lowest floor framing rests directly on a sill bolted to a foundation not less than 8 feet (2440 mm) in length along a line of bracing, the line shall be considered as braced. The double plate of the cripple stud wall beyond the segment of footing that extends to the lowest framed floor shall be spliced by extending the upper top plate a minimum of 4 feet (1219 mm) along the foundation. Anchor bolts shall be located a maximum of 1 foot and 3 feet (305 and 914 mm) from the step in the foundation.

3. Where cripple walls occur between the top of the foundation and the lowest floor framing, the bracing requirements for a story shall apply.

4. Where only the bottom of the foundation is stepped and the lowest floor framing rests directly on a sill bolted to the foundations, the requirements of Section R602.11.1 shall apply.

SECTION R603
STEEL WALL FRAMING

R603.1 General. Elements shall be straight and free of any defects that would significantly affect structural performance. Cold-formed steel wall framing members shall comply with the requirements of this section.

R603.1.1 Applicability limits. The provisions of this section shall control the construction of exterior steel wall framing and interior load-bearing steel wall framing for buildings not more than 60 feet (18 288 mm) long perpendicular to the joist or truss span, not more than 40 feet (12 192 mm) wide parallel to the joist or truss span, and not more than two stories in height. All exterior walls installed in accordance with the provisions of this section shall be considered as load-bearing walls. Steel walls constructed in accordance with the provisions of this section shall be limited to sites subjected to a maximum design wind speed of 110 miles per hour (49 m/s) Exposure A, B or C and a maximum ground snow load of 70 psf (3.35 kPa).

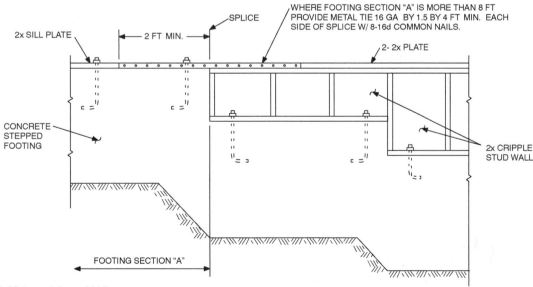

For SI: 1 inch 25.4 mm, 1 foot = 304.8 mm.

Note: Where footing Section "A" is less than 8 feet long in a 25-foot-long wall, install bracing at cripple stud wall.

FIGURE R602.11.3
STEPPED FOUNDATION CONSTRUCTION

R603.1.2 In-line framing. Load-bearing steel studs constructed in accordance with Section R603 shall be located directly in-line with joists, trusses and rafters with a maximum tolerance of $3/_4$ inch (19.1 mm) between their center lines. Interior load-bearing steel stud walls shall be supported on foundations or shall be located directly above load-bearing walls with a maximum tolerance of $3/_4$ inch (19 mm) between the centerline of the studs.

R603.2 Structural framing. Load-bearing steel wall framing members shall comply with Figure R603.2(1) and with the dimensional and minimum thickness requirements specified in Tables R603.2(1) and R603.2(2). Tracks shall comply with Figure R603.2(2) and shall have a minimum flange width of $1^1/_4$ inches (32 mm). The maximum inside bend radius for members shall be the greater of $3/_{32}$ inch (2.4 mm) or twice the uncoated

steel thickness. Holes in wall studs and other structural members shall comply with all of the following conditions:

1. Holes shall conform to Figure R603.2(3);

2. Holes shall be permitted only along the centerline of the web of the framing member;

3. Holes shall have a center-to-center spacing of not less than 24 inches (610 mm);

4. Holes shall have a width not greater than 0.5 times the member depth, or $1^1/_2$ inches (38.1 mm);

5. Holes shall have a length not exceeding $4^1/_2$ inches (114 mm); and

6. Holes shall have a minimum distance between the edge of the bearing surface and the edge of the hole of not less than 10 inches (254 mm).

TABLE R603.2(1)
LOAD-BEARING COLD-FORMED STEEL STUD SIZES

MEMBER DESIGNATION[a]	WEB DEPTH (inches)	MINIMUM FLANGE WIDTH (inches)	MAXIMUM FLANGE WIDTH (inches)	MINIMUM LIP SIZE (inches)
350S162-t	3.5	1.625	2	0.5
550S162-t	5.5	1.625	2	0.5

For SI: 1 inch = 25.4 mm; 1 mil = 0.0254 mm.

a. The member designation is defined by the first number representing the member depth in hundredths of an inch "S" representing a stud or joist member, the second number representing the flange width in hundredths of an inch, and the letter "t" shall be a number representing the minimum base metal thickness in mils [See Table R603.2(2)].

TABLE R603.2(2)
MINIMUM THICKNESS OF COLD-FORMED STEEL STUDS

DESIGNATION (mils)	MINIMUM UNCOATED THICKNESS (inches)	REFERENCE GAGE NUMBER
33	0.033	20
43	0.043	18
54	0.054	16
68	0.068	14

For SI: 1 inch = 25.4 mm, 1 mil = 0.0254 mm.

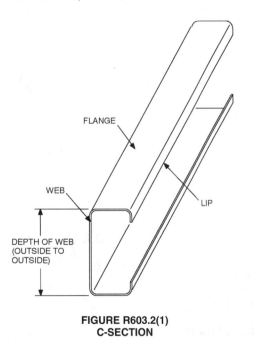

FIGURE R603.2(1)
C-SECTION

FIGURE R603.2(2)
TRACK SECTION

Framing members with web holes violating the above requirements shall be patched in accordance with Section R603.3.5 or designed in accordance with accepted engineering practices.

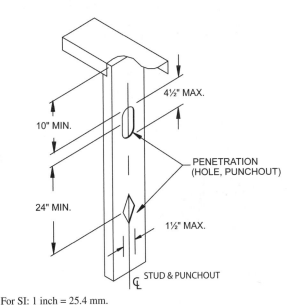

For SI: 1 inch = 25.4 mm.

FIGURE R603.2(3)
WEB HOLES

R603.2.1 Material. Load-bearing steel framing members shall be cold-formed to shape from structural quality sheet steel complying with the requirements of one of the following:

1. ASTM A 653: Grades 33, 37, 40 and 50 (Class 1 and 3).

2. ASTM A 792: Grades 33, 37, 40 and 50A.

3. ASTM A 875: Grades 33, 37, 40 and 50 (Class 1 and 3).

4. ASTM A 1003: Grades 33, 37, 40 and 50.

R603.2.2 Identification. Load-bearing steel framing members shall have a legible label, stencil, stamp or embossment with the following information as a minimum:

1. Manufacturer's identification.

2. Minimum uncoated steel thickness in inches (mm).

3. Minimum coating designation.

4. Minimum yield strength, in kips per square inch (ksi) (kN).

R603.2.3 Corrosion protection. Load-bearing steel framing shall have a metallic coating complying with one of the following:

1. A minimum of G 60 in accordance with ASTM A 653.

2. A minimum of AZ 50 in accordance with ASTM A 792.

3. A minimum of GF 60 in accordance with ASTM A 875.

R603.2.4 Fastening requirements. Screws for steel-to-steel connections shall be installed with a minimum edge distance and center-to-center spacing of $^1/_2$ inch (12.7 mm), shall be self-drilling tapping and shall conform to SAE J 78. Structural sheathing shall be attached to steel studs with minimum No. 8 self-drilling tapping screws that conform to SAE J 78. Screws for attaching structural sheathing to steel wall framing shall have a minimum head diameter of 0.292 inch (7.4 mm) with countersunk heads and shall be installed with a minimum edge distance of $^3/_8$ inch (9.5 mm). Gypsum board shall be attached to steel wall framing with minimum No. 6 screws conforming to ASTM C 954 and shall be installed in accordance with Section R702. For all connections, screws shall extend through the steel a minimum of three exposed threads. All self-drilling tapping screws conforming to SAE J 78 shall have a Type II coating in accordance with ASTM B 633.

Where No. 8 screws are specified in a steel-to-steel connection the required number of screws in the connection is permitted to be reduced in accordance with the reduction factors in Table R603.2.4, when larger screws are used or when one of the sheets of steel being connected is thicker than 33 mils (0.84 mm). When applying the reduction factor the resulting number of screws shall be rounded up.

TABLE R603.2.4
SCREW SUBSTITUTION FACTOR

SCREW SIZE	THINNEST CONNECTED STEEL SHEET (mils)	
	33	43
#8	1.0	0.67
#10	0.93	0.62
#12	0.86	0.56

For SI: 1 mil = 0.0254 mm.

R603.3 Wall construction. All exterior steel framed walls and interior load-bearing steel framed walls shall be constructed in accordance with the provisions of this section and Figure R603.3.

R603.3.1 Wall to foundation or floor connections. Steel framed walls shall be anchored to foundations or floors in accordance with Table R603.3.1 and Figure R603.3.1(1) or R603.3.1(2).

R603.3.2 Load-bearing walls. Steel studs shall comply with Tables R603.3.2(2) through R603.3.2(21). The tabulated stud thickness for structural walls shall be used when the attic load is 10 psf (0.48 kPa) or less. When an attic storage load is greater than 10 psf (0.48 kPa) but less than or equal to 20 psf (0.96 kPa), the next higher snow load column value from Tables R603.3.2(2) through R603.3.2(21) shall be used to select the stud size. The tabulated stud thickness for structural walls supporting one floor, roof and ceiling shall be used when the second floor live load is 30 psf (1.44 kPa). When the second floor live load is greater than 30 psf (1.44 kPa) but less than or equal to 40 psf (1.92 kPa) the design value in the next higher snow load column from Tables R603.2(12) through R603.3.2(21) shall be used to select the stud size.

Fastening requirements shall be in accordance with Section R603.2.4 and Table R603.3.2(1). Tracks shall have the same minimum thickness as the wall studs. Exterior walls with a minimum of $^1/_2$-inch (13 mm) gypsum board installed in accordance with Section R702 on the interior surface and wood structural panels of minimum $^7/_{16}$-inch thick (11mm) oriented-strand board or $^{15}/_{32}$-inch thick (12 mm) plywood installed in accordance with Table R603.3.2(1) on the outside surface shall be permitted to use the next thinner stud from Tables R603.3.2(2) through R603.3.2(13) but not less than 33 mils (0.84 mm). Interior load-bearing walls with a minimum $^1/_2$-inch (13 mm) gypsum board installed in accordance with Section R702 on both sides of the wall shall be permitted to use the next thinner stud from Tables R603.3.2(2) through R603.3.2(13) but not less than 33 mils (0.84 mm).

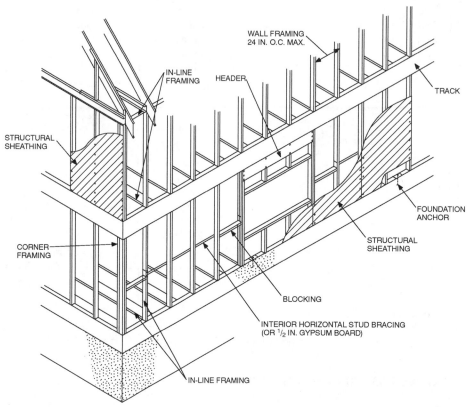

For SI: 1 inch = 25.4 mm.

**FIGURE R603.3
STEEL WALL CONSTRUCTION**

**TABLE R603.3.1
WALL TO FOUNDATION OR FLOOR CONNECTION REQUIREMENTS[a,b,c]**

FRAMING CONDITION	BASIC WIND SPEED (mph) AND EXPOSURE		
	85 A/B or Seismic Design Categories A, B and C	85 C or less than 110 A/B	Less than 110 C
Wall bottom track to floor joist or track	1-No. 8 screw at 12″ o.c.	1-No. 8 screw at 12″o.c.	2-No. 8 screw at 12″ o.c.
Wall bottom track to wood sill per Figure R603.3.1(2)	Steel plate spaced at 4′ o.c., with 4-No. 8 screws and 4-10d or 6-8d common nails	Steel plate spaced at 3′ o.c., with 4-No. 8 screws and 4-10d or 6-8d common nails	Steel plate spaced at 2′ o.c., with 4-No. 8 screws and 4-10d or 6-8d common nails
Wall bottom track to foundation per Figure R603.3.1(1)	$^1/_2$″ minimum diameter anchor bolt at 6′ o.c.	$^1/_2$″ minimum diameter anchor bolt at 6′ o.c.	$^1/_2$″ minimum diameter anchor bolt at 4′ o.c.
Wind uplift connector capacity for 16-inch stud spacing[c]	N/R	N/R	65 lb
Wind uplift connector capacity for 24-inch stud spacing[c]	N/R	N/R	100 lb

For SI: 1 inch = 25.4 mm, 1 foot = 304.8 mm, 1 mile per hour = 0.447 m/s, 1 pound = 4.4 N.

a. Anchor bolts shall be located not more than 12 inches from corners or the termination of bottom tracks (e.g., at door openings or corners). Bolts shall extend a minimum of 7 inches into concrete or masonry.

b. All screw sizes shown are minimum.

c. N/R = uplift connector not required. Uplift connectors are in addition to other connection requirements and shall be applied in accordance with Section R603.8.

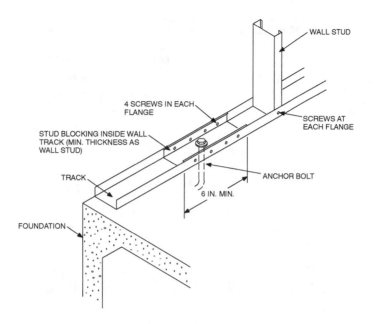

For SI: 1 inch = 25.4 mm.

FIGURE R603.3.1(1)
WALL TO FOUNDATION CONNECTION

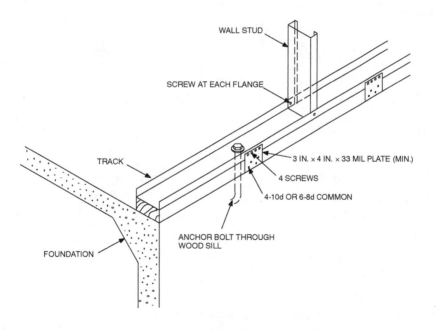

For SI: 1 inch = 25.4 mm.

FIGURE R603.3.1(2)
WALL TO WOOD SILL CONNECTION

TABLE R603.3.2(1)
WALL FASTENING SCHEDULE[a]

DESCRIPTION OF BUILDING ELEMENT	NUMBER AND SIZE OF FASTENERS[a]	SPACING OF FASTENERS
Floor joist to track of load-bearing wall	2-No. 8 screws	Each joist
Wall stud to top or bottom track	2-No. 8 screws	Each end of stud, one per flange
Structural sheathing to wall studs	No. 8 screws	6″ o.c. on edges and 12″ o.c. at intermediate supports
Roof framing to wall	Approved design or tie down in accordance with Section R802.11	

For SI: 1 inch = 25.4 mm.
a. All screw sizes shown are minimum.

TABLE R603.3.2(2)
24-FOOT-WIDE BUILDING SUPPORTING ROOF AND CEILING ONLY[a, b, c]
33 ksi STEEL

WIND SPEED		MEMBER SIZE	STUD SPACING (inches)	MINIMUM STUD THICKNESS (mils)											
				8-Foot Studs				9-Foot Studs				10-Foot Studs			
				Ground Snow Load (psf)											
Exp. A/B	Exp. C			20	30	50	70	20	30	50	70	20	30	50	70
85 mph	—	350S162	16	33	33	33	33	33	33	33	33	33	33	33	33
			24	33	33	33	33	33	33	33	33	33	33	33	43
		550S162	16	33	33	33	33	33	33	33	33	33	33	33	33
			24	33	33	33	33	33	33	33	33	33	33	33	33
90 mph	—	350S162	16	33	33	33	33	33	33	33	33	33	33	33	33
			24	33	33	33	33	33	33	33	33	33	33	33	43
		550S162	16	33	33	33	33	33	33	33	33	33	33	33	33
			24	33	33	33	33	33	33	33	33	33	33	33	33
100 mph	85 mph	350S162	16	33	33	33	33	33	33	33	33	33	33	33	33
			24	33	33	33	33	33	33	33	33	33	33	33	43
		550S162	16	33	33	33	33	33	33	33	33	33	33	33	33
			24	33	33	33	33	33	33	33	33	33	33	33	33
110 mph	90 mph	350S162	16	33	33	33	33	33	33	33	33	33	33	33	33
			24	33	33	33	33	33	33	33	43	33	33	33	43
		550S162	16	33	33	33	33	33	33	33	33	33	33	33	33
			24	33	33	33	33	33	33	33	33	33	33	33	33
—	100 mph	350S162	16	33	33	33	33	33	33	33	33	33	33	33	33
			24	33	33	33	43	33	33	33	43	43	43	43	43
		550S162	16	33	33	33	33	33	33	33	33	33	33	33	33
			24	33	33	33	33	33	33	33	33	33	33	33	33
—	110 mph	350S162	16	33	33	33	33	33	33	33	33	33	33	33	33
			24	33	33	33	43	43	43	43	43	54	54	54	54
		550S162	16	33	33	33	33	33	33	33	33	33	33	33	33
			24	33	33	33	33	33	33	33	33	33	33	33	33

For SI: 1 inch = 25.4 mm, 1 foot = 304.8 mm, 1 mil = 0.0254 mm, 1 mile per hour = 0.447 m/s, 1 pound per square foot = 0.0479 kPa, 1 ksi = 1000 psi = 6.895 MPa.

a. Deflection criterion: $L/240$.
b. Design load assumptions:
   Roof/ceiling dead load is 12 psf.
   Attic live load is 10 psf.
c. Building width is in the direction of horizontal framing members supported by the wall studs.

TABLE R603.3.2(3)
24-FOOT-WIDE BUILDING SUPPORTING ROOF AND CEILING ONLY[a, b, c]
50 ksi STEEL

WIND SPEED		MEMBER SIZE	STUD SPACING (inches)	MINIMUM STUD THICKNESS (mils)											
				8-Foot Studs				9-Foot Studs				10-Foot Studs			
				Ground Snow Load (psf)											
Exp. A/B	Exp. C			20	30	50	70	20	30	50	70	20	30	50	70
85 mph	—	350S162	16	33	33	33	33	33	33	33	33	33	33	33	33
			24	33	33	33	33	33	33	33	33	33	33	33	33
		550S162	16	33	33	33	33	33	33	33	33	33	33	33	33
			24	33	33	33	33	33	33	33	33	33	33	33	33
90 mph	—	350S162	16	33	33	33	33	33	33	33	33	33	33	33	33
			24	33	33	33	33	33	33	33	33	33	33	33	33
		550S162	16	33	33	33	33	33	33	33	33	33	33	33	33
			24	33	33	33	33	33	33	33	33	33	33	33	33
100 mph	85 mph	350S162	16	33	33	33	33	33	33	33	33	33	33	33	33
			24	33	33	33	33	33	33	33	33	33	33	33	33
		550S162	16	33	33	33	33	33	33	33	33	33	33	33	33
			24	33	33	33	33	33	33	33	33	33	33	33	33
110 mph	90 mph	350S162	16	33	33	33	33	33	33	33	33	33	33	33	33
			24	33	33	33	33	33	33	33	33	33	33	33	33
		550S162	16	33	33	33	33	33	33	33	33	33	33	33	33
			24	33	33	33	33	33	33	33	33	33	33	33	33
—	100 mph	350S162	16	33	33	33	33	33	33	33	33	33	33	33	33
			24	33	33	33	33	33	33	33	33	43	43	43	43
		550S162	16	33	33	33	33	33	33	33	33	33	33	33	33
			24	33	33	33	33	33	33	33	33	33	33	33	33
—	110 mph	350S162	16	33	33	33	33	33	33	33	33	33	33	33	33
			24	33	33	33	33	33	33	33	33	54	54	54	54
		550S162	16	33	33	33	33	33	33	33	33	33	33	33	33
			24	33	33	33	33	33	33	33	33	33	33	33	33

For SI: 1 inch = 25.4 mm, 1 foot = 304.8 mm, 1 mil = 0.0254 mm, 1 mile per hour = 0.447 m/s, 1 pound per square foot = 0.0479 kPa,
1 ksi = 1000 psi = 6.895 MPa.

a. Deflection criterion: $L/240$.
b. Design load assumptions:
   Roof/ceiling dead load is 12 psf.
   Attic live load is 10 psf.
c. Building width is in the direction of horizontal framing members supported by the wall studs.

TABLE R603.3.2(4)
28-FOOT-WIDE BUILDING SUPPORTING ROOF AND CEILING ONLY[a, b, c]
33 ksi STEEL

WIND SPEED		MEMBER SIZE	STUD SPACING (inches)	MINIMUM STUD THICKNESS (mils)											
				8-Foot Studs				9-Foot Studs				10-Foot Studs			
				Ground Snow Load (psf)											
Exp. A/B	Exp. C			20	30	50	70	20	30	50	70	20	30	50	70
85 mph	—	350S162	16	33	33	33	33	33	33	33	33	33	33	33	33
			24	33	33	33	43	33	33	33	43	33	33	33	43
		550S162	16	33	33	33	33	33	33	33	33	33	33	33	33
			24	33	33	33	33	33	33	33	33	33	33	33	33
90 mph	—	350S162	16	33	33	33	33	33	33	33	33	33	33	33	33
			24	33	33	33	43	33	33	33	43	33	33	33	43
		550S162	16	33	33	33	33	33	33	33	33	33	33	33	33
			24	33	33	33	33	33	33	33	33	33	33	33	33
100 mph	85 mph	350S162	16	33	33	33	33	33	33	33	33	33	33	33	33
			24	33	33	33	43	33	33	33	43	33	33	43	43
		550S162	16	33	33	33	33	33	33	33	33	33	33	33	33
			24	33	33	33	33	33	33	33	33	33	33	33	33
110 mph	90 mph	350S162	16	33	33	33	33	33	33	33	33	33	33	33	33
			24	33	33	33	43	33	33	33	43	33	33	43	43
		550S162	16	33	33	33	33	33	33	33	33	33	33	33	33
			24	33	33	33	33	33	33	33	33	33	33	33	33
—	100 mph	350S162	16	33	33	33	33	33	33	33	33	33	33	33	33
			24	33	33	33	43	33	33	43	43	43	43	43	43
		550S162	16	33	33	33	33	33	33	33	33	33	33	33	33
			24	33	33	33	33	33	33	33	33	33	33	33	33
—	110 mph	350S162	16	33	33	33	33	33	33	33	33	33	33	33	33
			24	33	33	33	43	43	43	43	43	54	54	54	54
		550S162	16	33	33	33	33	33	33	33	33	33	33	33	33
			24	33	33	33	33	33	33	33	33	33	33	33	33

For SI: 1 inch = 25.4 mm, 1 foot = 304.8 mm, 1 mil = 0.0254 mm, 1 mile per hour = 0.447 m/s, 1 pound per square foot = 0.0479 kPa, 1 ksi = 1000 psi = 6.895 MPa.

a. Deflection criterion: $L/240$.
b. Design load assumptions:
   Roof/ceiling dead load is 12 psf.
   Attic live load is 10 psf.
c. Building width is in the direction of horizontal framing members supported by the wall studs.

TABLE R603.3.2(5)
28-FOOT-WIDE BUILDING SUPPORTING ROOF AND CEILING ONLY[a, b, c]
50 ksi STEEL

WIND SPEED		MEMBER SIZE	STUD SPACING (inches)	MINIMUM STUD THICKNESS (mils)											
				8-Foot Studs				9-Foot Studs				10-Foot Studs			
Exp. A/B	Exp. C			Ground Snow Load (psf)											
				20	30	50	70	20	30	50	70	20	30	50	70
85 mph	—	350S162	16	33	33	33	33	33	33	33	33	33	33	33	33
			24	33	33	33	33	33	33	33	33	33	33	33	43
		550S162	16	33	33	33	33	33	33	33	33	33	33	33	33
			24	33	33	33	33	33	33	33	33	33	33	33	33
90 mph	—	350S162	16	33	33	33	33	33	33	33	33	33	33	33	33
			24	33	33	33	33	33	33	33	33	33	33	33	43
		550S162	16	33	33	33	33	33	33	33	33	33	33	33	33
			24	33	33	33	33	33	33	33	33	33	33	33	33
100 mph	85 mph	350S162	16	33	33	33	33	33	33	33	33	33	33	33	33
			24	33	33	33	33	33	33	33	33	33	33	33	43
		550S162	16	33	33	33	33	33	33	33	33	33	33	33	33
			24	33	33	33	33	33	33	33	33	33	33	33	33
110 mph	90 mph	350S162	16	33	33	33	33	33	33	33	33	33	33	33	33
			24	33	33	33	33	33	33	33	33	33	33	43	43
		550S162	16	33	33	33	33	33	33	33	33	33	33	33	33
			24	33	33	33	33	33	33	33	33	33	33	33	33
—	100 mph	350S162	16	33	33	33	33	33	33	33	33	33	33	33	33
			24	33	33	33	33	33	33	33	33	43	43	43	43
		550S162	16	33	33	33	33	33	33	33	33	33	33	33	33
			24	33	33	33	33	33	33	33	33	33	33	33	33
—	110 mph	350S162	16	33	33	33	33	33	33	33	33	33	33	33	33
			24	33	33	33	43	33	33	33	43	54	54	54	54
		550S162	16	33	33	33	33	33	33	33	33	33	33	33	33
			24	33	33	33	33	33	33	33	33	33	33	33	33

For SI: 1 inch = 25.4 mm, 1 foot = 304.8 mm, 1 mil = 0.0254 mm, 1 mile per hour = 0.447 m/s, 1 pound per square foot = 0.0479 kPa,
1 ksi = 1000 psi = 6.895 MPa.

a. Deflection criterion: $L/240$.
b. Design load assumptions:
   Roof/ceiling dead load is 12 psf.
   Attic live load is 10 psf.
c. Building width is in the direction of horizontal framing members supported by the wall studs.

TABLE R603.3.2(6)
32-FOOT-WIDE BUILDING SUPPORTING ROOF AND CEILING ONLY[a, b, c]
33 ksi STEEL

WIND SPEED		MEMBER SIZE	STUD SPACING (inches)	MINIMUM STUD THICKNESS (mils)											
				8-Foot Studs				9-Foot Studs				10-Foot Studs			
				Ground Snow Load (psf)											
Exp. A/B	Exp. C			20	30	50	70	20	30	50	70	20	30	50	70
85 mph	—	350S162	16	33	33	33	33	33	33	33	33	33	33	33	33
			24	33	33	33	43	33	33	33	43	33	33	43	43
		550S162	16	33	33	33	33	33	33	33	33	33	33	33	33
			24	33	33	33	33	33	33	33	33	33	33	33	33
90 mph	—	350S162	16	33	33	33	33	33	33	33	33	33	33	33	33
			24	33	33	33	43	33	33	33	43	33	33	43	43
		550S162	16	33	33	33	33	33	33	33	33	33	33	33	33
			24	33	33	33	33	33	33	33	33	33	33	33	33
100 mph	85 mph	350S162	16	33	33	33	33	33	33	33	33	33	33	33	33
			24	33	33	33	43	33	33	33	43	33	33	43	43
		550S162	16	33	33	33	33	33	33	33	33	33	33	33	33
			24	33	33	33	33	33	33	33	33	33	33	33	33
110 mph	90 mph	350S162	16	33	33	33	33	33	33	33	33	33	33	33	33
			24	33	33	33	43	33	33	33	43	33	33	43	43
		550S162	16	33	33	33	33	33	33	33	33	33	33	33	33
			24	33	33	33	33	33	33	33	33	33	33	33	33
—	100 mph	350S162	16	33	33	33	33	33	33	33	33	33	33	33	43
			24	33	33	43	43	33	43	43	43	43	43	43	54
		550S162	16	33	33	33	33	33	33	33	33	33	33	33	33
			24	33	33	33	33	33	33	33	33	33	33	33	43
—	110 mph	350S162	16	33	33	33	33	33	33	33	33	33	33	33	43
			24	33	33	43	43	33	43	43	43	54	54	54	54
		550S162	16	33	33	33	33	33	33	33	33	33	33	33	33
			24	33	33	33	33	33	33	33	33	33	33	33	43

For SI: 1 inch = 25.4 mm, 1 foot = 304.8 mm, 1 mil = 0.0254 mm, 1 mile per hour = 0.447 m/s, 1 pound per square foot = 0.0479 kPa,
1 ksi = 1000 psi = 6.895 MPa.

a. Deflection criterion: $L/240$.
b. Design load assumptions:
　　Roof/ceiling dead load is 12 psf.
　　Attic live load is 10 psf.
c. Building width is in the direction of horizontal framing members supported by the wall studs.

TABLE R603.3.2(7)
32-FOOT-WIDE BUILDING SUPPORTING ROOF AND CEILING ONLY[a, b, c]
50 ksi STEEL

WIND SPEED		MEMBER SIZE	STUD SPACING (inches)	MINIMUM STUD THICKNESS (mils)											
				8-Foot Studs				9-Foot Studs				10-Foot Studs			
				Ground Snow Load (psf)											
Exp. A/B	Exp. C			20	30	50	70	20	30	50	70	20	30	50	70
85 mph	—	350S162	16	33	33	33	33	33	33	33	33	33	33	33	33
			24	33	33	33	33	33	33	33	33	33	33	33	43
		550S162	16	33	33	33	33	33	33	33	33	33	33	33	33
			24	33	33	33	33	33	33	33	33	33	33	33	33
90 mph	—	350S162	16	33	33	33	33	33	33	33	33	33	33	33	33
			24	33	33	33	33	33	33	33	33	33	33	33	43
		550S162	16	33	33	33	33	33	33	33	33	33	33	33	33
			24	33	33	33	33	33	33	33	33	33	33	33	33
100 mph	85 mph	350S162	16	33	33	33	33	33	33	33	33	33	33	33	33
			24	33	33	33	43	33	33	33	33	33	33	33	43
		550S162	16	33	33	33	33	33	33	33	33	33	33	33	33
			24	33	33	33	33	33	33	33	33	33	33	33	33
110 mph	90 mph	350S162	16	33	33	33	33	33	33	33	33	33	33	33	33
			24	33	33	33	43	33	33	33	33	33	33	33	43
		550S162	16	33	33	33	33	33	33	33	33	33	33	33	33
			24	33	33	33	33	33	33	33	33	33	33	33	33
—	100 mph	350S162	16	33	33	33	33	33	33	33	33	33	33	33	33
			24	33	33	33	43	33	33	33	43	43	43	43	43
		550S162	16	33	33	33	33	33	33	33	33	33	33	33	33
			24	33	33	33	33	33	33	33	33	33	33	33	33
—	110 mph	350S162	16	33	33	33	33	33	33	33	33	33	33	33	33
			24	33	33	33	43	33	33	33	43	54	54	54	54
		550S162	16	33	33	33	33	33	33	33	33	33	33	33	33
			24	33	33	33	33	33	33	33	33	33	33	33	33

For SI: 1 inch = 25.4 mm, 1 foot = 304.8 mm, 1 mil = 0.0254 mm, 1 mile per hour = 0.447 m/s, 1 pound per square foot = 0.0479 kPa,
1 ksi = 1000 psi = 6.895 MPa.
a. Deflection criterion: $L/240$.
b. Design load assumptions:
   Roof/ceiling dead load is 12 psf.
   Attic live load is 10 psf.
c. Building width is in the direction of horizontal framing members supported by the wall studs.

TABLE R603.3.2(8)
36-FOOT-WIDE BUILDING SUPPORTING ROOF AND CEILING ONLY[a, b, c]
33 ksi STEEL

WIND SPEED		MEMBER SIZE	STUD SPACING (inches)	MINIMUM STUD THICKNESS (mils)											
				8-Foot Studs				9-Foot Studs				10-Foot Studs			
				Ground Snow Load (psf)											
Exp. A/B	Exp. C			20	30	50	70	20	30	50	70	20	30	50	70
85 mph	—	350S162	16	33	33	33	33	33	33	33	33	33	33	33	33
			24	33	33	43	43	33	33	33	43	33	33	43	43
		550S162	16	33	33	33	33	33	33	33	33	33	33	33	33
			24	33	33	33	33	33	33	33	33	33	33	33	33
90 mph	—	350S162	16	33	33	33	33	33	33	33	33	33	33	33	33
			24	33	33	43	43	33	33	33	43	33	33	43	43
		550S162	16	33	33	33	33	33	33	33	33	33	33	33	33
			24	33	33	33	33	33	33	33	33	33	33	33	33
100 mph	85 mph	350S162	16	33	33	33	33	33	33	33	33	33	33	33	33
			24	33	33	33	43	33	33	43	43	33	33	43	54
		550S162	16	33	33	33	33	33	33	33	33	33	33	33	33
			24	33	33	33	33	33	33	33	33	33	33	33	43
110 mph	90 mph	350S162	16	33	33	33	33	33	33	33	33	33	33	33	33
			24	33	33	43	43	33	33	43	43	33	43	43	54
		550S162	16	33	33	33	33	33	33	33	33	33	33	33	33
			24	33	33	33	33	33	33	33	33	33	33	33	43
—	100 mph	350S162	16	33	33	33	33	33	33	33	33	33	33	33	43
			24	33	33	43	43	43	43	43	43	43	43	43	54
		550S162	16	33	33	33	33	33	33	33	33	33	33	33	33
			24	33	33	33	43	33	33	33	43	33	33	33	43
—	110 mph	350S162	16	33	33	33	33	33	33	33	33	33	33	33	43
			24	33	33	43	54	43	43	43	54	54	54	54	54
		550S162	16	33	33	33	33	33	33	33	33	33	33	33	33
			24	33	33	33	43	33	33	33	43	33	33	33	33

For SI: 1 inch = 25.4 mm, 1 foot = 304.8 mm, 1 mil = 0.0254 mm, 1 mile per hour = 0.447 m/s, 1 pound per square foot = 0.0479 kPa, 1 ksi = 1000 psi = 6.895 MPa.

a. Deflection criterion: $L/240$.
b. Design load assumptions:
   Roof/ceiling dead load is 12 psf.
   Attic live load is 10 psf.
c. Building width is in the direction of horizontal framing members supported by the wall studs.

TABLE R603.3.2(9)
36-FOOT-WIDE BUILDING SUPPORTING ROOF AND CEILING ONLY[a, b, c]
50 ksi STEEL

WIND SPEED Exp. A/B	Exp. C	MEMBER SIZE	STUD SPACING (inches)	8-Foot Studs 20	30	50	70	9-Foot Studs 20	30	50	70	10-Foot Studs 20	30	50	70
85 mph	—	350S162	16	33	33	33	33	33	33	33	33	33	33	33	33
			24	33	33	33	43	33	33	33	43	33	33	33	43
		550S162	16	33	33	33	33	33	33	33	33	33	33	33	33
			24	33	33	33	33	33	33	33	33	33	33	33	33
90 mph	—	350S162	16	33	33	33	33	33	33	33	33	33	33	33	33
			24	33	33	33	43	33	33	33	43	33	33	33	43
		550S162	16	33	33	33	33	33	33	33	33	33	33	33	33
			24	33	33	33	33	33	33	33	33	33	33	33	33
100 mph	85 mph	350S162	16	33	33	33	33	33	33	33	33	33	33	33	33
			24	33	33	33	43	33	33	33	43	33	33	33	43
		550S162	16	33	33	33	33	33	33	33	33	33	33	33	33
			24	33	33	33	33	33	33	33	33	33	33	33	33
110 mph	90 mph	350S162	16	33	33	33	33	33	33	33	33	33	33	33	33
			24	33	33	33	43	33	33	33	43	33	33	43	43
		550S162	16	33	33	33	33	33	33	33	33	33	33	33	33
			24	33	33	33	33	33	33	33	33	33	33	33	33
—	100 mph	350S162	16	33	33	33	33	33	33	33	33	33	33	33	33
			24	33	33	33	43	33	33	33	43	43	43	43	43
		550S162	16	33	33	33	33	33	33	33	33	33	33	33	33
			24	33	33	33	33	33	33	33	33	33	33	33	33
—	110 mph	350S162	16	33	33	33	33	33	33	33	33	33	33	33	33
			24	33	33	33	43	33	33	33	43	54	54	54	54
		550S162	16	33	33	33	33	33	33	33	33	33	33	33	33
			24	33	33	33	33	33	33	33	33	33	33	33	33

For SI: 1 inch = 25.4 mm, 1 foot = 304.8 mm, 1 mil = 0.0254 mm, 1 mile per hour = 0.447 m/s, 1 pound per square foot = 0.0479 kPa, 1 ksi = 1000 psi = 6.895 MPa.

a. Deflection criterion: $L/240$.
b. Design load assumptions:
   Roof/ceiling dead load is 12 psf.
   Attic live load is 10 psf.
c. Building width is in the direction of horizontal framing members supported by the wall studs.

TABLE R603.3.2(10)
40-FOOT-WIDE BUILDING SUPPORTING ROOF AND CEILING ONLY[a, b, c]
33 ksi STEEL

WIND SPEED		MEMBER SIZE	STUD SPACING (inches)	MINIMUM STUD THICKNESS (mils)											
				8-Foot Studs				9-Foot Studs				10-Foot Studs			
				Ground Snow Load (psf)											
Exp. A/B	Exp. C			20	30	50	70	20	30	50	70	20	30	50	70
85 mph	—	350S162	16	33	33	33	33	33	33	33	33	33	33	33	43
			24	33	33	43	43	33	33	43	43	33	33	43	54
		550S162	16	33	33	33	33	33	33	33	33	33	33	33	33
			24	33	33	33	43	33	33	33	33	33	33	33	43
90 mph	—	350S162	16	33	33	33	33	33	33	33	33	33	33	33	43
			24	33	33	43	43	33	33	43	43	33	33	43	54
		550S162	16	33	33	33	33	33	33	33	33	33	33	33	33
			24	33	33	33	43	33	33	33	33	33	33	33	43
100 mph	85 mph	350S162	16	33	33	33	33	33	33	33	33	33	33	33	43
			24	33	33	43	43	33	33	43	43	33	33	43	54
		550S162	16	33	33	33	33	33	33	33	33	33	33	33	33
			24	33	33	33	43	33	33	33	43	33	33	33	43
110 mph	90 mph	350S162	16	33	33	33	33	33	33	33	33	33	33	33	43
			24	33	33	43	54	33	33	43	43	43	43	43	54
		550S162	16	33	33	33	33	33	33	33	33	33	33	33	33
			24	33	33	33	43	33	33	33	43	33	33	33	43
—	100 mph	350S162	16	33	33	33	43	33	33	33	43	33	33	33	43
			24	33	33	43	54	43	43	43	54	43	43	43	54
		550S162	16	33	33	33	33	33	33	33	33	33	33	33	33
			24	33	33	33	43	33	33	33	43	33	33	33	43
—	110 mph	350S162	16	33	33	33	43	33	33	33	43	33	33	43	43
			24	33	43	43	54	33	43	43	54	54	54	54	54
		550S162	16	33	33	33	33	33	33	33	33	33	33	33	33
			24	33	33	33	43	33	33	33	43	33	33	33	43

For SI: 1 inch = 25.4 mm, 1 foot = 304.8 mm, 1 mil = 0.0254 mm, 1 mile per hour = 0.447 m/s, 1 pound per square foot = 0.0479 kPa,
1 ksi = 1000 psi = 6.895 MPa.

a. Deflection criterion: $L/240$.
b. Design load assumptions:
Roof/ceiling dead load is 12 psf.
Attic live load is 10 psf.
c. Building width is in the direction of horizontal framing members supported by the wall studs.

TABLE R603.3.2(11)
40-FOOT-WIDE BUILDING SUPPORTING ROOF AND CEILING ONLY[a, b, c]
50 ksi STEEL

WIND SPEED		MEMBER SIZE	STUD SPACING (inches)	MINIMUM STUD THICKNESS (mils)											
				8-Foot Studs				9-Foot Studs				10-Foot Studs			
				Ground Snow Load (psf)											
Exp. A/B	Exp. C			20	30	50	70	20	30	50	70	20	30	50	70
85 mph	—	350S162	16	33	33	33	33	33	33	33	33	33	33	33	33
			24	33	33	33	43	33	33	33	43	33	33	43	43
		550S162	16	33	33	33	33	33	33	33	33	33	33	33	33
			24	33	33	33	33	33	33	33	33	33	33	33	33
90 mph	—	350S162	16	33	33	33	33	33	33	33	33	33	33	33	33
			24	33	33	33	43	33	33	33	43	33	33	43	43
		550S162	16	33	33	33	33	33	33	33	33	33	33	33	33
			24	33	33	33	33	33	33	33	33	33	33	33	33
100 mph	85 mph	350S162	16	33	33	33	33	33	33	33	33	33	33	33	33
			24	33	33	33	43	33	33	33	43	33	33	43	43
		550S162	16	33	33	33	33	33	33	33	33	33	33	33	33
			24	33	33	33	33	33	33	33	33	33	33	33	33
110 mph	90 mph	350S162	16	33	33	33	33	33	33	33	33	33	33	33	33
			24	33	33	33	43	33	33	33	43	33	33	43	43
		550S162	16	33	33	33	33	33	33	33	33	33	33	33	33
			24	33	33	33	33	33	33	33	33	33	33	33	33
—	100 mph	350S162	16	33	33	33	33	33	33	33	33	33	33	33	33
			24	33	33	43	43	33	33	33	43	43	43	43	54
		550S162	16	33	33	33	33	33	33	33	33	33	33	33	33
			24	33	33	33	33	33	33	33	33	33	33	33	33
—	110 mph	350S162	16	33	33	33	33	33	33	33	33	33	33	33	43
			24	33	33	43	43	33	33	43	43	54	54	54	54
		550S162	16	33	33	33	33	33	33	33	33	33	33	33	33
			24	33	33	33	33	33	33	33	33	33	33	33	33

For SI: 1 inch = 25.4 mm, 1 foot = 304.8 mm, 1 mil = 0.0254 mm, 1 mile per hour = 0.447 m/s, 1 pound per square foot = 0.0479 kPa, 1 ksi = 1000 psi = 6.895 MPa.

a. Deflection criterion: $L/240$.
b. Design load assumptions:
   Roof/ceiling dead load is 12 psf.
   Attic live load is 10 psf.
c. Building width is in the direction of horizontal framing members supported by the wall studs.

TABLE R603.3.2(12)
24-FOOT-WIDE BUILDING SUPPORTING ONE FLOOR, ROOF AND CEILING[a, b, c]
33 ksi STEEL

WIND SPEED		MEMBER SIZE	STUD SPACING (inches)	MINIMUM STUD THICKNESS (mils)											
				8-Foot Studs				9-Foot Studs				10-Foot Studs			
				Ground Snow Load (psf)											
Exp. A/B	Exp. C			20	30	50	70	20	30	50	70	20	30	50	70
85 mph	—	350S162	16	33	33	33	33	33	33	33	33	33	33	33	33
			24	33	33	33	43	33	33	33	43	43	43	43	43
		550S162	16	33	33	33	33	33	33	33	33	33	33	33	33
			24	33	33	33	33	33	33	33	33	33	33	33	33
90 mph	—	350S162	16	33	33	33	33	33	33	33	33	33	33	33	33
			24	33	33	33	43	33	33	33	43	43	43	43	43
		550S162	16	33	33	33	33	33	33	33	33	33	33	33	33
			24	33	33	33	33	33	33	33	33	33	33	33	33
100 mph	85 mph	350S162	16	33	33	33	33	33	33	33	33	33	33	33	33
			24	33	33	33	43	33	33	43	43	43	43	43	43
		550S162	16	33	33	33	33	33	33	33	33	33	33	33	33
			24	33	33	33	33	33	33	33	33	33	33	33	33
110 mph	90 mph	350S162	16	33	33	33	33	33	33	33	33	33	33	33	33
			24	33	33	43	43	43	43	43	43	43	43	43	43
		550S162	16	33	33	33	33	33	33	33	33	33	33	33	33
			24	33	33	33	33	33	33	33	33	33	33	33	33
—	100 mph	350S162	16	33	33	33	33	33	33	33	33	33	33	43	43
			24	43	43	43	43	43	43	43	43	43	43	54	54
		550S162	16	33	33	33	33	33	33	33	33	33	33	33	33
			24	33	33	33	33	33	33	33	33	33	33	33	33
—	110 mph	350S162	16	33	33	33	33	33	33	33	33	43	43	43	43
			24	43	43	43	43	43	43	43	43	54	54	54	54
		550S162	16	33	33	33	33	33	33	33	33	33	33	33	33
			24	33	33	33	33	33	33	33	33	33	33	33	43

For SI: 1 inch = 25.4 mm, 1 foot = 304.8 mm, 1 mil = 0.0254 mm, 1 mile per hour = 0.447 m/s, 1 pound per square foot = 0.0479 kPa,
1 ksi = 1000 psi = 6.895 MPa.

a. Deflection criterion: *L*/240.
b. Design load assumptions:
    Second floor dead load is 10 psf.
    Second floor live load is 30 psf.
    Roof/ceiling dead load is 12 psf.
    Attic live load is 10 psf.
c. Building width is in the direction of horizontal framing members supported by the wall studs.

TABLE R603.3.2(13)
24-FOOT-WIDE BUILDING SUPPORTING ONE FLOOR, ROOF AND CEILING[a, b, c]
50 ksi STEEL

WIND SPEED		MEMBER SIZE	STUD SPACING (inches)	MINIMUM STUD THICKNESS (mils)											
				8-Foot Studs				9-Foot Studs				10-Foot Studs			
Exp. A/B	Exp. C			Ground Snow Load (psf)											
				20	30	50	70	20	30	50	70	20	30	50	70
85 mph	—	350S162	16	33	33	33	33	33	33	33	33	33	33	33	33
			24	33	33	33	33	33	33	33	33	33	33	33	43
		550S162	16	33	33	33	33	33	33	33	33	33	33	33	33
			24	33	33	33	33	33	33	33	33	33	33	33	33
90 mph	—	350S162	16	33	33	33	33	33	33	33	33	33	33	33	33
			24	33	33	33	33	33	33	33	33	33	33	33	43
		550S162	16	33	33	33	33	33	33	33	33	33	33	33	33
			24	33	33	33	33	33	33	33	33	33	33	33	33
100 mph	85 mph	350S162	16	33	33	33	33	33	33	33	33	33	33	33	33
			24	33	33	33	33	33	33	33	33	33	33	33	43
		550S162	16	33	33	33	33	33	33	33	33	33	33	33	33
			24	33	33	33	33	33	33	33	33	33	33	33	33
110 mph	90 mph	350S162	16	33	33	33	33	33	33	33	33	33	33	33	33
			24	33	33	33	33	33	33	33	33	33	33	43	43
		550S162	16	33	33	33	33	33	33	33	33	33	33	33	33
			24	33	33	33	33	33	33	33	33	33	33	33	33
—	100 mph	350S162	16	33	33	33	33	33	33	33	33	33	33	33	33
			24	33	33	33	43	33	33	33	43	43	43	43	43
		550S162	16	33	33	33	33	33	33	33	33	33	33	33	33
			24	33	33	33	33	33	33	33	33	33	33	33	33
—	110 mph	350S162	16	33	33	33	33	33	33	33	33	33	33	33	33
			24	33	33	33	43	33	43	43	43	54	54	54	54
		550S162	16	33	33	33	33	33	33	33	33	33	33	33	33
			24	33	33	33	33	33	33	33	33	33	33	33	33

For SI: 1 inch = 25.4 mm, 1 foot = 304.8 mm, 1 mil = 0.0254 mm, 1 mile per hour = 0.447 m/s, 1 pound per square foot = 0.0479 kPa, 1 ksi = 1000 psi = 6.895 MPa.

a. Deflection criterion: $L/240$.
b. Design load assumptions:
   Second floor dead load is 10 psf.
   Second floor live load is 30 psf.
   Roof/ceiling dead load is 12 psf.
   Attic live load is 10 psf.
c. Building width is in the direction of horizontal framing members supported by the wall studs.

TABLE R603.3.2(14)
28-FOOT-WIDE BUILDING SUPPORTING ONE FLOOR, ROOF AND CEILING[a, b, c]
33 ksi STEEL

WIND SPEED		MEMBER SIZE	STUD SPACING (inches)	MINIMUM STUD THICKNESS (mils)											
				8-Foot Studs				9-Foot Studs				10-Foot Studs			
				Ground Snow Load (psf)											
Exp. A/B	Exp. C			20	30	50	70	20	30	50	70	20	30	50	70
85 mph	—	350S162	16	33	33	33	33	33	33	33	33	33	33	33	33
			24	33	43	43	43	33	33	43	43	43	43	43	43
		550S162	16	33	33	33	33	33	33	33	33	33	33	33	33
			24	33	33	33	33	33	33	33	33	33	33	33	33
90 mph	—	350S162	16	33	33	33	33	33	33	33	33	33	33	33	33
			24	33	43	43	43	33	33	43	43	43	43	43	43
		550S162	16	33	33	33	33	33	33	33	33	33	33	33	33
			24	33	33	33	33	33	33	33	33	33	33	33	33
100 mph	85 mph	350S162	16	33	33	33	33	33	33	33	33	33	33	33	33
			24	33	43	43	43	43	43	43	43	43	43	43	43
		550S162	16	33	33	33	33	33	33	33	33	33	33	33	33
			24	33	33	33	33	33	33	33	33	33	33	33	33
110 mph	90 mph	350S162	16	33	33	33	33	33	33	33	33	33	33	33	33
			24	43	43	43	43	43	43	43	43	43	43	43	54
		550S162	16	33	33	33	33	33	33	33	33	33	33	33	33
			24	33	33	33	33	33	33	33	33	33	33	33	33
—	100 mph	350S162	16	33	33	33	33	33	33	33	33	43	43	43	43
			24	43	43	43	43	43	43	43	43	54	54	54	54
		550S162	16	33	33	33	33	33	33	33	33	33	33	33	33
			24	33	33	33	33	33	33	33	33	33	33	33	43
—	110 mph	350S162	16	33	33	33	33	33	33	33	43	43	43	43	43
			24	43	43	43	43	43	43	54	54	54	54	54	54
		550S162	16	33	33	33	33	33	33	33	33	33	33	33	33
			24	33	33	33	33	33	33	33	33	33	43	43	43

For SI: 1 inch = 25.4 mm, 1 foot = 304.8 mm, 1 mil = 0.0254 mm, 1 mile per hour = 0.447 m/s, 1 pound per square foot = 0.0479 kPa, 1 ksi = 1000 psi = 6.895 MPa.

a. Deflection criterion: $L/240$.

b. Design load assumptions:
   Second floor dead load is 10 psf.
   Second floor live load is 30 psf.
   Roof/ceiling dead load is 12 psf.
   Attic live load is 10 psf.

c. Building width is in the direction of horizontal framing members supported by the wall studs.

TABLE R603.3.2(15)
28-FOOT-WIDE BUILDING SUPPORTING ONE FLOOR, ROOF AND CEILING[a, b, c]
50 ksi STEEL

WIND SPEED		MEMBER SIZE	STUD SPACING (inches)	MINIMUM STUD THICKNESS (mils)											
				8-Foot Studs				9-Foot Studs				10-Foot Studs			
Exp. A/B	Exp. C			Ground Snow Load (psf)											
				20	30	50	70	20	30	50	70	20	30	50	70
85 mph	—	350S162	16	33	33	33	33	33	33	33	33	33	33	33	33
			24	33	33	33	43	33	33	33	33	33	33	33	43
		550S162	16	33	33	33	33	33	33	33	33	33	33	33	33
			24	33	33	33	33	33	33	33	33	33	33	33	33
90 mph	—	350S162	16	33	33	33	33	33	33	33	33	33	33	33	33
			24	33	33	33	43	33	33	33	33	33	33	33	43
		550S162	16	33	33	33	33	33	33	33	33	33	33	33	33
			24	33	33	33	33	33	33	33	33	33	33	33	33
100 mph	85 mph	350S162	16	33	33	33	33	33	33	33	33	33	33	33	33
			24	33	33	33	43	33	33	33	33	33	33	43	43
		550S162	16	33	33	33	33	33	33	33	33	33	33	33	33
			24	33	33	33	33	33	33	33	33	33	33	33	33
110 mph	90 mph	350S162	16	33	33	33	33	33	33	33	33	33	33	33	33
			24	33	33	33	43	33	33	33	43	43	43	43	43
		550S162	16	33	33	33	33	33	33	33	33	33	33	33	33
			24	33	33	33	33	33	33	33	33	33	33	33	33
—	100 mph	350S162	16	33	33	33	33	33	33	33	33	33	33	33	33
			24	33	33	43	43	33	33	43	43	43	43	43	43
		550S162	16	33	33	33	33	33	33	33	33	33	33	33	33
			24	33	33	33	33	33	33	33	33	33	33	33	33
—	110 mph	350S162	16	33	33	33	33	33	33	33	33	33	33	33	43
			24	33	43	43	43	43	43	43	43	54	54	54	54
		550S162	16	33	33	33	33	33	33	33	33	33	33	33	33
			24	33	33	33	33	33	33	33	33	33	33	33	33

For SI: 1 inch = 25.4 mm, 1 foot = 304.8 mm, 1 mil = 0.0254 mm, 1 mile per hour = 0.447 m/s, 1 pound per square foot = 0.0479 kPa, 1 ksi = 1000 psi = 6.895 MPa.

a. Deflection criterion: $L/240$.
b. Design load assumptions:
   Second floor dead load is 10 psf.
   Second floor live load is 30 psf.
   Roof/ceiling dead load is 12 psf.
   Attic live load is 10 psf.
c. Building width is in the direction of horizontal framing members supported by the wall studs.

TABLE R603.3.2(16)
32-FOOT-WIDE BUILDING SUPPORTING ONE FLOOR, ROOF AND CEILING[a, b, c]
33 ksi STEEL

WIND SPEED		MEMBER SIZE	STUD SPACING (inches)	MINIMUM STUD THICKNESS (mils)											
				8-Foot Studs				9-Foot Studs				10-Foot Studs			
				Ground Snow Load (psf)											
Exp. A/B	Exp. C			20	30	50	70	20	30	50	70	20	30	50	70
85 mph	—	350S162	16	33	33	33	33	33	33	33	33	33	33	33	33
			24	43	43	43	43	43	43	43	43	43	43	43	54
		550S162	16	33	33	33	33	33	33	33	33	33	33	33	33
			24	33	33	33	43	33	33	33	33	33	33	33	43
90 mph	—	350S162	16	33	33	33	33	33	33	33	33	33	33	33	33
			24	43	43	43	43	43	43	43	43	43	43	43	54
		550S162	16	33	33	33	33	33	33	33	33	33	33	33	33
			24	33	33	33	43	33	33	33	33	33	33	33	43
100 mph	85 mph	350S162	16	33	33	33	33	33	33	33	33	33	33	33	43
			24	43	43	43	43	43	43	43	43	43	43	43	54
		550S162	16	33	33	33	33	33	33	33	33	33	33	33	33
			24	33	33	33	43	33	33	33	33	33	33	33	43
110 mph	90 mph	350S162	16	33	33	33	33	33	33	33	33	33	33	33	43
			24	43	43	43	43	43	43	43	43	43	43	43	54
		550S162	16	33	33	33	33	33	33	33	33	33	33	33	33
			24	33	33	33	43	33	33	33	33	33	33	33	43
—	100 mph	350S162	16	33	33	33	33	33	33	33	33	43	43	43	43
			24	43	43	43	54	43	43	43	54	54	54	54	54
		550S162	16	33	33	33	33	33	33	33	33	33	33	33	33
			24	33	33	33	43	33	33	33	43	33	33	43	43
—	110 mph	350S162	16	33	33	33	43	33	33	43	43	43	43	43	43
			24	43	43	43	54	43	54	54	54	54	54	54	68
		550S162	16	33	33	33	33	33	33	33	33	33	33	33	33
			24	33	33	33	43	33	33	33	43	43	43	43	43

For SI: 1 inch = 25.4 mm, 1 foot = 304.8 mm, 1 mil = 0.0254 mm, 1 mile per hour = 0.447 m/s, 1 pound per square foot = 0.0479 kPa,
1 ksi = 1000 psi = 6.895 MPa.
a. Deflection criterion: $L/240$.
b. Design load assumptions:
Second floor dead load is 10 psf.
Second floor live load is 30 psf.
Roof/ceiling dead load is 12 psf.
Attic live load is 10 psf.
c. Building width is in the direction of horizontal framing members supported by the wall studs.

TABLE R603.3.2(17)
32-FOOT-WIDE BUILDING SUPPORTING ONE FLOOR, ROOF AND CEILING[a, b, c]
50 ksi STEEL

WIND SPEED		MEMBER SIZE	STUD SPACING (inches)	MINIMUM STUD THICKNESS (mils)											
				8-Foot Studs				9-Foot Studs				10-Foot Studs			
				Ground Snow Load (psf)											
Exp. A/B	Exp. C			20	30	50	70	20	30	50	70	20	30	50	70
85 mph	—	350S162	16	33	33	33	33	33	33	33	33	33	33	33	33
			24	33	43	43	43	33	33	33	43	33	33	43	43
		550S162	16	33	33	33	33	33	33	33	33	33	33	33	33
			24	33	33	33	33	33	33	33	33	33	33	33	33
90 mph	—	350S162	16	33	33	33	33	33	33	33	33	33	33	33	33
			24	33	43	43	43	33	33	33	43	33	33	43	43
		550S162	16	33	33	33	33	33	33	33	33	33	33	33	33
			24	33	33	33	33	33	33	33	33	33	33	33	33
100 mph	85 mph	350S162	16	33	33	33	33	33	33	33	33	33	33	33	33
			24	33	43	43	43	33	33	33	43	43	43	43	43
		550S162	16	33	33	33	33	33	33	33	33	33	33	33	33
			24	33	33	33	33	33	33	33	33	33	33	33	33
110 mph	90 mph	350S162	16	33	33	33	33	33	33	33	33	33	33	33	33
			24	33	43	43	43	33	33	33	43	43	43	43	54
		550S162	16	33	33	33	33	33	33	33	33	33	33	33	33
			24	33	33	33	33	33	33	33	33	33	33	33	33
—	100 mph	350S162	16	33	33	33	33	33	33	33	33	33	33	33	33
			24	33	43	43	43	43	43	43	43	43	43	43	54
		550S162	16	33	33	33	33	33	33	33	33	33	33	33	33
			24	33	33	33	33	33	33	33	33	33	33	33	33
—	110 mph	350S162	16	33	33	33	33	33	33	33	33	33	33	33	43
			24	43	43	43	43	43	43	43	43	54	54	54	54
		550S162	16	33	33	33	33	33	33	33	33	33	33	33	33
			24	33	33	33	33	33	33	33	33	33	33	33	33

For SI: 1 inch = 25.4 mm, 1 foot = 304.8 mm, 1 mil = 0.0254 mm, 1 mile per hour = 0.447 m/s, 1 pound per square foot = 0.0479 kPa, 1 ksi = 1000 psi = 6.895 MPa.

a. Deflection criterion: L/240.
b. Design load assumptions:
   Second floor dead load is 10 psf.
   Second floor live load is 30 psf.
   Roof/ceiling dead load is 12 psf.
   Attic live load is 10 psf.
c. Building width is in the direction of horizontal framing members supported by the wall studs.

TABLE R603.3.2(18)
36-FOOT-WIDE BUILDING SUPPORTING ONE FLOOR, ROOF AND CEILING[a, b, c]
33 ksi STEEL

WIND SPEED		MEMBER SIZE	STUD SPACING (inches)	MINIMUM STUD THICKNESS (mils)											
				8-Foot Studs				9-Foot Studs				10-Foot Studs			
				Ground Snow Load (psf)											
Exp. A/B	Exp. C			20	30	50	70	20	30	50	70	20	30	50	70
85 mph	—	350S162	16	33	33	33	33	33	33	33	33	33	33	33	43
			24	43	43	43	54	43	43	43	43	43	43	43	54
		550S162	16	33	33	33	33	33	33	33	33	33	33	33	33
			24	43	43	43	43	33	33	33	43	33	33	33	43
90 mph	—	350S162	16	33	33	33	33	33	33	33	33	33	33	33	43
			24	43	43	43	54	43	43	43	43	43	43	43	54
		550S162	16	33	33	33	33	33	33	33	33	33	33	33	33
			24	43	43	43	43	33	33	33	43	33	33	43	43
100 mph	85 mph	350S162	16	33	33	33	33	33	33	33	33	33	33	33	43
			24	43	43	43	54	43	43	43	54	43	43	54	54
		550S162	16	33	33	33	33	33	33	33	33	33	33	33	33
			24	43	43	43	43	33	33	33	43	33	33	43	43
110 mph	90 mph	350S162	16	33	33	33	43	33	33	33	33	33	33	43	43
			24	43	43	43	54	43	43	43	54	43	43	54	54
		550S162	16	33	33	33	33	33	33	33	33	33	33	33	33
			24	43	43	43	43	33	33	33	43	33	33	43	43
—	100 mph	350S162	16	33	33	33	43	33	33	43	43	43	43	43	43
			24	43	43	43	54	43	43	54	54	54	54	54	54
		550S162	16	33	33	33	33	33	33	33	33	33	33	33	33
			24	43	43	43	43	33	33	33	43	43	43	43	43
—	110 mph	350S162	16	33	33	33	43	33	33	43	43	43	43	43	43
			24	43	43	43	54	43	54	54	54	54	54	54	68
		550S162	16	33	33	33	33	33	33	33	33	33	33	33	33
			24	33	33	33	43	33	33	33	43	43	43	43	43

For SI: 1 inch = 25.4 mm, 1 foot = 304.8 mm, 1 mil = 0.0254 mm, 1 mile per hour = 0.447 m/s, 1 pound per square foot = 0.0479 kPa,
          1 ksi = 1000 psi = 6.895 MPa.
a. Deflection criterion: $L/240$.
b. Design load assumptions:
     Second floor dead load is 10 psf.
     Second floor live load is 30 psf.
     Roof/ceiling dead load is 12 psf.
     Attic live load is 10 psf.
c. Building width is in the direction of horizontal framing members supported by the wall studs.

TABLE R603.3.2(19)
36-FOOT-WIDE BUILDING SUPPORTING ONE FLOOR, ROOF AND CEILING[a, b, c]
50 ksi STEEL

WIND SPEED Exp. A/B	Exp. C	MEMBER SIZE	STUD SPACING (inches)	8-Foot Studs 20	30	50	70	9-Foot Studs 20	30	50	70	10-Foot Studs 20	30	50	70
85 mph	—	350S162	16	33	33	33	33	33	33	33	33	33	33	33	33
			24	43	43	43	43	33	33	43	43	43	43	43	43
		550S162	16	33	33	33	33	33	33	33	33	33	33	33	33
			24	33	33	33	43	33	33	33	33	33	33	33	33
90 mph	—	350S162	16	33	33	33	33	33	33	33	33	33	33	33	33
			24	43	43	43	43	33	33	43	43	43	43	43	43
		550S162	16	33	33	33	33	33	33	33	33	33	33	33	33
			24	33	43	33	43	33	33	33	33	33	33	33	33
100 mph	85 mph	350S162	16	33	33	33	33	33	33	33	33	33	33	33	33
			24	43	43	43	43	33	33	43	43	43	43	43	43
		550S162	16	33	33	33	33	33	33	33	33	33	33	33	33
			24	33	33	33	43	33	33	33	33	33	33	33	33
110 mph	90 mph	350S162	16	33	33	33	33	33	33	33	33	33	33	33	33
			24	43	43	43	43	33	33	43	43	43	43	43	54
		550S162	16	33	33	33	33	33	33	33	33	33	33	33	33
			24	43	33	33	43	33	33	33	33	33	33	33	33
—	100 mph	350S162	16	33	33	33	33	33	33	33	33	33	33	33	43
			24	43	43	43	43	43	43	43	43	43	43	54	54
		550S162	16	33	33	33	33	33	33	33	33	33	33	33	33
			24	33	33	33	43	33	33	33	33	33	33	33	43
—	110 mph	350S162	16	33	33	33	33	33	33	33	33	33	33	43	43
			24	43	43	43	54	43	43	43	43	54	54	54	54
		550S162	16	33	33	33	33	33	33	33	33	33	33	33	33
			24	33	33	33	33	33	33	33	33	33	33	33	43

For SI: 1 inch = 25.4 mm, 1 foot = 304.8 mm, 1 mil = 0.0254 mm, 1 mile per hour = 0.447 m/s 1 pound per square foot = 0.0479 kPa, 1 ksi = 1000 psi = 6.895 MPa.

a. Deflection criterion: $L/240$.

b. Design load assumptions:
   Second floor dead load is 10 psf.
   Second floor live load is 30 psf.
   Roof/ceiling dead load is 12 psf.
   Attic live load is 10 psf.

c. Building width is in the direction of horizontal framing members supported by the wall studs.

TABLE R603.3.2(20)
40-FOOT-WIDE BUILDING SUPPORTING ONE FLOOR, ROOF AND CEILING[a, b, c]
33 ksi STEEL

WIND SPEED		MEMBER SIZE	STUD SPACING (inches)	MINIMUM STUD THICKNESS (mils)											
				8-Foot Studs				9-Foot Studs				10-Foot Studs			
Exp. A/B	Exp. C			Ground Snow Load (psf)											
				20	30	50	70	20	30	50	70	20	30	50	70
85 mph	—	350S162	16	33	33	33	43	33	33	33	43	33	33	33	43
			24	43	54	54	54	43	43	43	54	43	43	54	54
		550S162	16	33	33	33	33	33	33	33	33	33	33	33	33
			24	43	43	43	43	43	43	43	43	33	43	43	43
90 mph	—	350S162	16	33	33	33	43	33	33	33	43	33	33	33	43
			24	43	54	54	54	43	43	43	54	43	43	54	54
		550S162	16	33	33	33	33	33	33	33	33	33	33	33	33
			24	43	43	43	43	43	43	43	43	33	43	43	43
100 mph	85 mph	350S162	16	33	33	33	43	33	33	33	43	33	33	43	43
			24	43	54	54	54	43	43	43	54	43	43	54	54
		550S162	16	33	33	33	33	33	33	33	33	33	33	33	33
			24	43	43	43	43	43	43	43	43	33	43	43	43
110 mph	90 mph	350S162	16	33	33	33	43	33	33	33	43	33	43	43	43
			24	43	54	54	54	43	43	43	54	43	54	54	54
		550S162	16	33	33	33	33	33	33	33	33	33	33	33	33
			24	43	43	43	43	43	43	43	43	33	43	43	43
—	100 mph	350S162	16	33	33	33	43	33	33	43	43	33	43	43	43
			24	43	54	54	54	54	54	54	54	43	54	54	68
		550S162	16	33	33	33	33	33	33	33	33	33	33	33	33
			24	43	43	43	43	43	43	43	43	33	43	43	43
—	110 mph	350S162	16	33	33	43	43	43	43	43	43	33	43	43	43
			24	54	54	54	54	54	54	54	54	54	68	68	68
		550S162	16	33	33	33	33	33	33	33	33	33	33	33	33
			24	43	43	43	43	43	43	43	43	33	43	43	43

For SI: 1 inch = 25.4 mm, 1 foot = 304.8 mm, 1 mil = 0.0254 mm, 1 mile per hour = 0.447 m/s, 1 pound per square foot = 0.0479 kPa, 1 ksi = 1000 psi = 6.895 MPa.

a. Deflection criterion: $L/240$.
b. Design load assumptions:
   Second floor dead load is 10 psf.
   Second floor live load is 30 psf.
   Roof/ceiling dead load is 12 psf.
   Attic live load is 10 psf.
c. Building width is in the direction of horizontal framing members supported by the wall studs.

TABLE R603.3.2(21)
40-FOOT-WIDE BUILDING SUPPORTING ONE FLOOR, ROOF AND CEILING[a, b, c]
50 ksi STEEL

WIND SPEED Exp. A/B	Exp. C	MEMBER SIZE	STUD SPACING (inches)	8-Foot Studs				9-Foot Studs				10-Foot Studs			
				20	30	50	70	20	30	50	70	20	30	50	70
85 mph	—	350S162	16	33	33	33	33	33	33	33	33	33	33	33	33
			24	43	43	43	54	43	43	43	43	43	43	43	54
		550S162	16	33	33	33	33	33	33	33	33	33	33	33	33
			24	33	33	43	43	33	33	33	33	33	33	33	43
90 mph	—	350S162	16	33	33	33	33	33	33	33	33	33	33	33	33
			24	43	43	43	54	43	43	43	43	43	43	43	54
		550S162	16	33	33	33	33	33	33	33	33	33	33	33	33
			24	33	33	43	43	33	33	33	33	33	33	33	43
100 mph	85 mph	350S162	16	33	33	33	33	33	33	33	33	33	33	33	33
			24	43	43	43	54	43	43	43	43	43	43	43	54
		550S162	16	33	33	33	33	33	33	33	33	33	33	33	33
			24	33	33	43	43	33	33	33	33	33	33	33	43
110 mph	90 mph	350S162	16	33	33	33	33	33	33	33	33	33	33	33	43
			24	43	43	43	54	43	43	43	43	43	43	43	54
		550S162	16	33	33	33	33	33	33	33	33	33	33	33	33
			24	33	33	43	43	33	33	33	33	33	33	33	43
—	100 mph	350S162	16	33	33	33	33	33	33	33	33	33	33	33	43
			24	43	43	43	54	43	43	43	43	43	54	54	54
		550S162	16	33	33	33	33	33	33	33	33	33	33	33	33
			24	33	33	43	43	33	33	33	33	33	33	33	43
—	110 mph	350S162	16	33	33	33	43	33	33	33	43	33	43	43	43
			24	43	43	43	54	43	43	43	54	54	54	54	54
		550S162	16	33	33	33	33	33	33	33	33	33	33	33	33
			24	33	33	43	43	33	33	43	43	33	33	43	43

For SI: 1 inch = 25.4 mm, 1 foot = 304.8 mm, 1 mil = 0.0254 mm, 1 mile per hour = 0.447 m/s, 1 pound per square foot = 0.0479 kPa, 1 ksi = 1000 psi = 6.895 MPa.

a. Deflection criterion: $L/240$.
b. Design load assumptions:
    Second floor dead load is 10 psf.
    Second floor live load is 30 psf.
    Roof/ceiling dead load is 12 psf.
    Attic live load is 10 psf.
c. Building width is in the direction of horizontal framing members supported by the wall studs.

R603.3.3 Stud bracing. The flanges of steel studs shall be laterally braced in accordance with one of the following:

1. Gypsum board installed with minimum No. 6 screws in accordance with Section R702 or structural sheathing installed in accordance with Table R603.3.2(1).

2. Horizontal steel strapping installed in accordance with Figure R603.3 at mid-height for 8-foot (2438 mm) walls, and one-third points for 9-foot and 10-foot (2743 mm and 3048 mm) walls. Steel straps shall be at least 1.5 inches in width and 33 mils in thickness (38 mm by 0.84 mm). Straps shall be attached to the flanges of studs with at least one No. 8 screw. In-line blocking shall be installed between studs at the termination of all straps. Straps shall be fastened to the blocking with at least two No. 8 screws.

3. Sheathing on one side and strapping on the other side. Sheathing shall be installed in accordance with Method #1 above. Steel straps shall be installed in accordance with Method #2 above.

R603.3.4 Cutting and notching. Flanges and lips of steel studs and headers shall not be cut or notched.

R603.3.5 Hole patching. Web holes violating the requirements in Section R603.2 shall be designed in accordance with one of the following:

1. Framing members shall be replaced or designed in accordance with accepted engineering practices when web holes exceed the following size limits:

    1.1. The depth of the hole, measured across the web, exceeds 70 percent of the flat width of the web; or

    1.2. The length of the hole measured along the web exceeds 10 inches (254 mm) or the depth of the web, whichever is greater.

2. Web holes not exceeding the dimensional requirements in R603.3.5(1) shall be patched with a solid steel plate, stud section, or track section in accordance with Figure R603.3.5. The steel patch shall be as a minimum the same thickness as the receiving member and shall extend at least 1 inch (25 mm) beyond all edges of the hole. The steel patch shall be fastened to the web of the receiving member with No. 8 screws spaced no more than 1 inch (25 mm) center-to-center along the edges of the patch with a minimum edge distance of $\frac{1}{2}$ inch (13 mm).

R603.3.6 Splicing. Steel studs and other structural members shall not be spliced. Tracks shall be spliced in accordance with Figure R603.3.6.

R603.4 Corner framing. Corner studs and the top tracks shall be installed in accordance with Figure R603.4.

R603.5 Exterior wall covering. The method of attachment of exterior wall covering materials to cold-formed steel stud wall framing shall conform to the manufacturer's installation instructions.

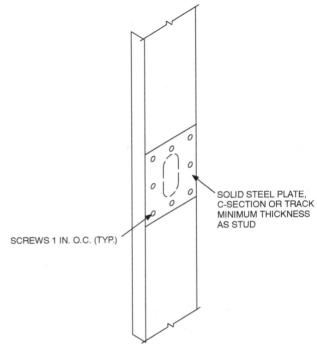

SOLID STEEL PLATE, C-SECTION OR TRACK MINIMUM THICKNESS AS STUD

SCREWS 1 IN. O.C. (TYP.)

For SI: 1 inch = 25.4 mm.

FIGURE R603.3.5
HOLE PATCH

R603.6 Headers. Headers shall be installed above wall openings in all exterior walls and interior load-bearing walls in accordance with Figure R603.6 and Tables R603.6(1) through R603.6(8), or shall be designed in accordance with the AISI Standard for Cold-formed Steel Framing–Header Design (COFS/Header Design).

R603.6.1 Jack and king studs, and head track. The number of jack and king studs shall comply with Table R603.6(9). King and jack studs shall be of the same dimension and thickness as the adjacent wall studs. Headers constructed of C-shape framing members shall be connected to king studs in accordance with Table R603.6.(10). One-half the total number of screws shall be applied to the header and one-half to the king stud by use of a minimum 2-inch by 2-inch (51 mm by 51 mm) clip angle or 4-inch-wide (102 mm) steel plate. The clip angle or plate shall extend the depth of the header minus $\frac{1}{2}$ inch (13 mm) and shall have a minimum thickness of the header members or the wall studs, whichever is thicker.

Head track spans shall comply with Table R603.6(11) and shall be in accordance with Figures R603.3 and R603.6. Increasing the head track tabular value shall not be prohibited when in accordance with one of the following:

1. For openings less than 4 feet (1219 mm) in height that have a top and bottom head track, multiply the tabular value by 1.75; or

2. For openings less than 6 feet (1829 mm) in height that have a top and bottom head track, multiply the tabular value by 1.50.

TABLE R603.6(1)
BOX-BEAM HEADER SPANS
Headers supporting roof and ceiling only (33 ksi steel)[a, b, c]

MEMBER DESIGNATION	GROUND SNOW LOAD (20 psf)					GROUND SNOW LOAD (30 psf)				
	Building width[c]					Building width[c]				
	24'	28'	32'	36'	40'	24'	28'	32'	36'	40'
2-350S162-33	3'-10"	3'-5"	3'-0"	2'-6"	2'-2"	3'-3"	2'-9"	2'-4"	—	—
2-350S162-43	5'-1"	4'-8"	4'-4"	4'-0"	3'-7"	4'-6"	4'-2"	3'-8"	3'-4"	2'-11"
2-350S162-54	5'-9"	5'-4"	5'-0"	4'-9"	4'-5"	5'-3"	4'-10"	4'-6"	4'-2"	3'-10"
2-350S162-68	6'-7"	6'-1"	5'-9"	5'-5"	5'-1"	6'-0"	5'-6"	5'-2"	4'-10"	4'-7"
2-350S162-97	8'-0"	7'-5"	7'-0"	6'-6"	6'-3"	7'-3"	6'-9"	6'-4"	6'-0"	5'-7"
2-550S162-33	5'-8"	5'-0"	4'-5"	3'-11"	3'-4"	4'-9"	4'-1"	3'-6"	2'-11"	—
2-550S162-43	7'-2"	6'-8"	6'-3"	5'-8"	5'-2"	6'-6"	5'-11"	5'-3"	4'-9"	4'-3"
2-550S162-54	8'-2"	7'-7"	7'-2"	6'-9"	6'-5"	7'-5"	6'-11"	6'-6"	6'-0"	5'-6"
2-550S162-68	9'-3"	8'-7"	8'-0"	7'-8"	7'-3"	8'-5"	7'-10"	7'-4"	7'-0"	6'-7"
2-550S162-97	11'-2"	10'-5"	9'-10"	9'-3"	8'-11"	10'-2"	9'-6"	9'-1"	8'-5"	8'-0"
2-800S162-33	6'-9"	5'-11"	5'-2"	4'-6"	3'-10"	5'-6"	4'-6"	4'-0"	—	—
2-800S162-43	9'-0"	8'-5"	7'-8"	7'-0"	6'-4"	8'-1"	7'-3"	6'-6"	5'-9"	5'-2"
2-800S162-54	10'-9"	10'-0"	9'-5"	8'-11"	8'-4"	9'-9"	9'-1"	8'-6"	7'-9"	7'-1"
2-800S162-68	12'-2"	11'-4"	10'-8"	10'-2"	9'-7"	11'-1"	10'-4"	9'-9"	9'-3"	8'-9"
2-800S162-97	14'-9"	13'-9"	13'-0"	12'-3"	11'-7"	13'-5"	12'-6"	11'-10"	11'-2"	10'-7"
2-1000S162-43	10'-0"	9'-2"	8'-4"	7'-6"	6'-9"	8'-9"	7'-10"	7'-0"	6'-2"	5'-5"
2-1000S162-54	12'-0"	11'-2"	10'-6"	9'-11"	9'-2"	10'-11"	10'-2"	9'-3"	8'-6"	7'-9"
2-1000S162-68	14'-5"	13'-6"	12'-8"	12'-0"	11'-5"	13'-2"	12'-3"	11'-6"	11'-0"	10'-4"
2-1000S162-97	17'-5"	16'-4"	15'-4"	14'-6"	13'-11"	16'-0"	14'-11"	14'-0"	13'-3"	12'-7"
2-1200S162-43	10'-10"	9'-9"	8'-9"	7'-11"	7'-1"	9'-3"	8'-2"	7'-2"	6'-4"	5'-6"
2-1200S162-54	13'-0"	12'-2"	11'-6"	10'-7"	9'-9"	11'-11"	11'-0"	10'-0"	9'-0"	8'-2"
2-1200S162-68	15'-5"	14'-5"	13'-6"	12'-11"	12'-3"	14'-0"	13'-2"	12'-4"	11'-9"	10'-11"
2-1200S162-97	20'-1"	18'-9"	17'-9"	16'-9"	16'-0"	18'-4"	17'-2"	16'-2"	15'-3"	14'-7"

For SI: 1 inch = 25.4 mm, 1 foot = 304.8 mm, 1 pound per square foot = 0.0479 kPa, 1 pound per square inch = 6.895 kPa.

a. Deflection criteria: $L/360$ for live loads, $L/240$ for total loads.

b. Design load assumptions:
    Roof/Ceiling dead load is 12 psf.
    Attic dead load is 10 psf.

c. Building width is in the direction of horizontal framing members supported by the header.

TABLE R603.6(2)
BOX-BEAM HEADER SPANS
Headers supporting roof and ceiling only (33 ksi steel)[a, b, c]

MEMBER DESIGNATION	GROUND SNOW LOAD (50 psf)					GROUND SNOW LOAD (70 psf)				
	Building width[c]					Building width[c]				
	24'	28'	32'	36'	40'	24'	28'	32'	36'	40'
2-350S162-33	—	—	—	—	—	—	—	—	—	—
2-350S162-43	3'-2"	2'-7"	2'-2"	—	—	2'-0"	—	—	—	—
2-350S162-54	4'-1"	3'-6"	3'-1"	2'-8"	2'-3"	3'-0"	2'-6"	—	—	—
2-350S162-68	4'-9"	4'-5"	4'-0"	3'-7"	3'-3"	4'-0"	3'-4"	3'-0"	2'-6"	2'-1"
2-350S162-97	5'-10"	5'-5"	5'-1"	4'-9"	4'-6"	5'-0"	4'-7"	4'-4"	4'-0"	3'-9"
2-550S162-33	2'-9"	—	—	—	—	—	—	—	—	—
2-550S162-43	4'-7"	3'-11"	3'-3"	—	—	3'-2"	—	—	—	—
2-550S162-54	5'-10"	5'-2"	4'-6"	4'-0"	3'-6"	4'-5"	3'-9"	3'-1"	—	—
2-550S162-68	6'-10"	6'-4"	5'-9"	5'-3"	4'-9"	5'-7"	5'-0"	4'-4"	3'-9"	3'-3"
2-550S162-97	8'-4"	7'-9"	7'-3"	6'-10"	6'-6"	7'-2"	6'-8"	6'-3"	5'-11"	5'-7"
2-800S162-33	—	—	—	—	—	—	—	—	—	—
2-800S162-43	5'-7"	4'-9"	3'-11"	—	—	—	—	—	—	—
2-800S162-54	7'-7"	6'-8"	5'-11"	5'-2"	4'-6"	5'-9"	4'-10"	—	—	—
2-800S162-68	9'-1"	8'-4"	7'-6"	6'-10"	6'-3"	7'-4"	6'-6"	5'-9"	5'-0"	4'-4"
2-800S162-97	11'-0"	10'-4"	9'-8"	9'-2"	8'-9"	9'-6"	8'-11"	8'-4"	7'-11"	7'-6"
2-1000S162-43	6'-0"	4'-11"	—	—	—	—	—	—	—	—
2-1000S162-54	8'-4"	7'-4"	6'-4"	5'-7"	4'-9"	6'-3"	5'-2"	—	—	—
2-1000S162-68	10'-9"	9'-9"	8'-10"	8'-0"	7'-3"	8'-7"	7'-7"	6'-7"	5'-9"	5'-0"
2-1000S162-97	13'-1"	12'-3"	11'-6"	10'-11"	10'-4"	11'-4"	10'-7"	10'-0"	9'-5"	8'-11"
2-1200S162-43	6'-1"	—	—	—	—	—	—	—	—	—
2-1200S162-54	8'-9"	7'-8"	6'-7"	5'-9"	—	6'-6"	—	—	—	—
2-1200S162-68	11'-6"	10'-4"	9'-4"	8'-4"	7'-7"	9'-1"	8'-0"	6'-11"	6'-0"	—
2-1200S162-97	15'-1"	14'-1"	13'-3"	12'-7"	12'-0"	13'-1"	12'-3"	11'-6"	11'-0"	10'-2"

For SI: 1 inch = 25.4 mm, 1 foot = 304.8 mm, 1 pound per square foot = 0.0479 kPa, 1 pound per square inch = 6.895 kPa.

a. Deflection criteria: L/360 for live loads, L/240 for total loads.

b. Design load assumptions:
   Roof/Ceiling dead load is 12 psf.
   Attic dead load is 10 psf.

c. Building width is in the direction of horizontal framing members supported by the header.

TABLE R603.6(3)
BOX-BEAM HEADER SPANS
Headers supporting one floor, roof and ceiling (33 ksi steel)[a, b, c]

MEMBER DESIGNATION	GROUND SNOW LOAD (20 psf)					GROUND SNOW LOAD (30 psf)				
	Building width[c]					Building width[c]				
	24'	28'	32'	36'	40'	24'	28'	32'	36'	40'
2-350S162-33	—	—	—	—	—	—	—	—	—	—
2-350S162-43	2'-6"	—	—	—	—	2'-5"	—	—	—	—
2-350S162-54	3'-6"	3'-0"	2'-6"	—	—	3'-4"	2'-10"	2'-4"	—	—
2-350S162-68	4'-4"	3'-11"	3'-5"	3'-0"	2'-7"	4'-3"	3'-9"	3'-3"	2'-10"	2'-6"
2-350S162-97	5'-4"	5'-0"	4'-7"	4'-4"	4'-1"	5'-4"	4'-11"	4'-6"	4'-3"	4'-0"
2-550S162-33	—	—	—	—	—	—	—	—	—	—
2-550S162-43	3'-9"	3'-0"	—	—	—	3'-7"	2'-11"	—	—	—
2-550S162-54	5'-0"	4'-4"	3'-9"	3'-2"	—	4'-10"	4'-2"	3'-6"	3'-0"	—
2-550S162-68	6'-3"	5'-6"	5'-0"	4'-5"	4'-0"	6'-1"	5'-5"	4'-9"	4'-3"	3'-9"
2-550S162-97	7'-8"	7'-2"	6'-8"	6'-4"	6'-0"	7'-6"	7'-0"	6'-6"	6'-2"	5'-10"
2-800S162-33	—	—	—	—	—	—	—	—	—	—
2-800S162-43	4'-6"	—	—	—	—	4'-4"	—	—	—	—
2-800S162-54	6'-6"	5'-7"	4'-10"	4'-1"	—	6'-4"	5'-5"	4'-7"	—	—
2-800S162-68	8'-2"	7'-3"	6'-6"	5'-10"	5'-2"	8'-0"	7'-0"	6'-4"	5'-6"	5'-0"
2-800S162-97	10'-1"	9'-6"	8'-11"	8'-6"	8'-0"	10'-0"	9'-4"	8'-9"	8'-3"	7'-11"
2-1000S162-43	4'-9"	—	—	—	—	—	—	—	—	—
2-1000S162-54	7'-1"	6'-0"	5'-2"	—	—	6'-10"	5'-10"	4'-11"	—	—
2-1000S162-68	9'-7"	8'-6"	7'-7"	6'-9"	6'-0"	9'-4"	8'-4"	7'-4"	6'-6"	5'-9"
2-1000S162-97	12'-0"	11'-3"	10'-7"	10'-0"	9'-6"	11'-11"	11'-1"	10'-5"	9'-11"	9'-5"
2-1200S162-43	—	—	—	—	—	—	—	—	—	—
2-1200S162-54	7'-6"	6'-4"	—	—	—	7'-2"	6'-0"	—	—	—
2-1200S162-68	10'-1"	9'-0"	8'-0"	7'-0"	6'-2"	9'-11"	8'-9"	7'-9"	6'-9"	6'-0"
2-1200S162-97	14'-0"	13'-0"	12'-3"	11'-7"	11'-0"	13'-9"	12'-10"	12'-0"	11'-6"	10'-11"

For SI: 1 inch = 25.4 mm, 1 foot = 304.8 mm, 1 pound per square foot = 0.0479kPa, 1 pound per square inch = 6.895 kPa.

a. Deflection criteria: $L/360$ for live loads, $L/240$ for total loads.

b. Design load assumptions:
    Roof/Ceiling dead load is 12 psf.
    Attic dead load is 10 psf.

c. Building width is in the direction of horizontal framing members supported by the header.

TABLE R603.6(4)
BOX-BEAM HEADER SPANS
Headers supporting one floor, roof and ceiling (33 ksi steel)[a, b, c]

MEMBER DESIGNATION	GROUND SNOW LOAD (50 psf)					GROUND SNOW LOAD (70 psf)				
	Building width[c]					Building width[c]				
	24'	28'	32'	36'	40'	24'	28'	32'	36'	40'
2-350S162-33	—	—	—	—	—	—	—	—	—	—
2-350S162-43	—	—	—	—	—	—	—	—	—	—
2-350S162-54	2'-6"	2'-1"	—	—	—	—	—	—	—	—
2-350S162-68	3'-6"	3'-0"	2'-6"	2'-2"	—	2'-9"	2'-2"	—	—	—
2-350S162-97	4'-9"	4'-5"	4'-1"	3'-10"	3'-7"	4'-2"	3'-11"	3'-7"	3'-4"	2'-11"
2-550S162-33	—	—	—	—	—	—	—	—	—	—
2-550S162-43	—	—	—	—	—	—	—	—	—	—
2-550S162-54	3'-11"	3'-4"	—	—	—	2'-10"	—	—	—	—
2-550S162-68	5'-2"	4'-6"	3'-11"	3'-4"	2'-10"	4'-1"	3'-5"	2'-9"	—	—
2-550S162-97	6'-10"	6'-4"	6'-0"	5'-7"	5'-4"	6'-1"	5'-7"	5'-4"	4'-9"	4'-4"
2-800S162-33	—	—	—	—	—	—	—	—	—	—
2-800S162-43	—	—	—	—	—	—	—	—	—	—
2-800S162-54	5'-1"	4'-2"	—	—	—	—	—	—	—	—
2-800S162-68	6'-9"	6'-1"	5'-2"	4'-5"	—	5'-5"	4'-6"	—	—	—
2-800S162-97	9'-1"	8'-6"	8'-0"	7'-6"	7'-1"	8'-2"	7'-7"	7'-0"	6'-5"	5'-10"
2-1000S162-43	—	—	—	—	—	—	—	—	—	—
2-1000S162-54	5'-6"	—	—	—	—	—	—	—	—	—
2-1000S162-68	7'-10"	6'-11"	6'-0"	5'-2"	—	6'-4"	5'-4"	—	—	—
2-1000S162-97	10'-10"	10'-1"	9'-6"	9'-0"	8'-4"	9'-9"	9'-2"	8'-4"	7'-7"	7'-0"
2-1200S162-43	—	—	—	—	—	—	—	—	—	—
2-1200S162-54	5'-7"	—	—	—	—	—	—	—	—	—
2-1200S162-68	8'-4"	7'-2"	6'-2"	—	—	6'-6"	—	—	—	—
2-1200S162-97	12'-6"	11'-8"	11'-0"	10'-4"	9'-6"	11'-3"	10'-6"	9'-6"	8'-8"	8'-0"

For SI: 1 inch = 25.4 mm, 1 foot = 304.8 mm, 1 pound per square foot = 0.0479 kPa, 1 pound per square inch = 6.895 kPa.

a. Deflection criteria: L/360 for live loads, L/240 for total loads.
b. Design load assumptions:
    Roof/Ceiling dead load is 12 psf.
    Attic dead load is 10 psf.
c. Building width is in the direction of horizontal framing members supported by the header.

TABLE R603.6(5)
BACK-TO-BACK HEADER SPANS
Headers supporting roof and ceiling only (33 ksi steel)[a, b, c]

MEMBER DESIGNATION	GROUND SNOW LOAD (20 psf)					GROUND SNOW LOAD (30 psf)				
	Building width[c]					Building width[c]				
	24'	28'	32'	36'	40'	24'	28'	32'	36'	40'
2-350S162-33	3'-7"	3'-1"	2'-8"	2'-4"	—	2'-11"	2'-6"	—	—	—
2-350S162-43	5'-0"	4'-8"	4'-4"	3'-10"	3'-7"	4'-6"	4'-0"	3'-8"	3'-4"	2'-11"
2-350S162-54	5'-9"	5'-5"	5'-0"	4'-9"	4'-6"	5'-3"	4'-10"	4'-6"	4'-4"	3'-11"
2-350S162-68	6'-7"	6'-2"	5'-9"	5'-5"	5'-2"	5'-11"	5'-7"	5'-2"	4'-10"	4'-7"
2-350S162-97	7'-11"	7'-6"	6'-11"	6'-7"	6'-6"	7'-4"	6'-9"	6'-4"	5'-11"	5'-8"
2-550S162-33	5'-5"	4'-9"	4'-4"	3'-9"	3'-5"	4'-7"	3'-11"	3'-5"	2'-11"	—
2-550S162-43	7'-3"	6'-8"	6'-2"	5'-8"	5'-4"	6'-6"	5'-10"	5'-5"	4'-10"	4'-6"
2-550S162-54	8'-2"	7'-8"	7'-2"	6'-9"	6'-5"	7'-5"	6'-10"	6'-6"	6'-1"	5'-9"
2-550S162-68	9'-4"	8'-8"	8'-7"	7'-8"	7'-4"	8'-6"	7'-10"	7'-5"	6'-11"	6'-7"
2-550S162-97	11'-3"	10'-6"	9'-11"	9'-4"	8'-10"	10'-3"	9'-6"	8'-11"	8'-6"	8'-0"
2-800S162-33	6'-9"	5'-11"	5'-5"	4'-9"	4'-4"	6'-9"	5'-0"	4'-5"	3'-9"	—
2-800S162-43	9'-1"	8'-6"	7'-9"	7'-3"	6'-8"	8'-3"	7'-6"	6'-9"	6'-3"	5'-8"
2-800S162-54	10'-9"	10'-1"	9'-6"	8'-11"	8'-6"	9'-9"	9'-2"	8'-7"	8'-2"	7'-8"
2-800S162-68	12'-3"	11'-5"	10'-9"	10'-2"	9'-8"	11'-2"	10'-5"	9'-9"	9'-4"	8'-9"
2-800S162-97	14'-9"	13'-9"	13'-0"	12'-4"	11'-8"	13'-6"	12'-7"	11'-10"	11'-2"	10'-8"
2-1000S162-43	10'-1"	9'-5"	8'-8"	8'-0"	7'-6"	9'-1"	8'-4"	7'-7"	6'-11"	6'-5"
2-1000S162-54	12'-0"	11'-5"	10'-7"	10'-0"	9'-6"	11'-0"	10'-3"	9'-7"	9'-1"	8'-6"
2-1000S162-68	14'-6"	13'-6"	12'-8"	12'-0"	11'-6"	13'-2"	12'-4"	11'-7"	10'-11"	10'-6"
2-1000S162-97	17'-6"	16'-5"	15'-5"	14'-7"	13'-10"	16'-0"	14'-10"	14'-0"	13'-4"	12'-8"
2-1200S162-43	11'-0"	10'-4"	9'-6"	8'-9"	8'-2"	10'-0"	9'-1"	8'-4"	7'-7"	7'-0"
2-1200S162-54	13'-1"	12'-3"	11'-6"	10'-10"	10'-5"	11'-10"	11'-1"	10'-6"	9'-10"	9'-4"
2-1200S162-68	15'-6"	14'-6"	13'-7"	12'-10"	12'-3"	14'-1"	13'-2"	12'-5"	11'-9"	11'-2"
2-1200S162-97	20'-2"	18'-9"	17'-9"	16'-9"	16'-0"	18'-4"	17'-2"	16'-2"	15'-5"	14'-7"

For SI: 1 inch = 25.4 mm, 1 foot = 304.8 mm, 1 pound per square foot = 0.0479 kPa, 1 pound per square inch = 6.895 kPa.
a. Deflection criteria: $L/360$ for live loads, $L/240$ for total loads.
b. Design load assumptions:
   Roof/Ceiling dead load is 12 psf.
   Attic dead load is 10 psf.
c. Building width is in the direction of horizontal framing members supported by the header.

TABLE R603.6(6)
BACK-TO-BACK HEADER SPANS
Headers supporting roof and ceiling only (33 ksi steel)[a, b, c]

MEMBER DESIGNATION	GROUND SNOW LOAD (50 psf)					GROUND SNOW LOAD (70 psf)				
	Building width[c]					Building width[c]				
	24'	28'	32'	36'	40'	24'	28'	32'	36'	40'
2-350S162-33	—	—	—	—	—	—	—	—	—	—
2-350S162-43	3'-2"	2'-8"	2'-4"	—	—	2'-3"	—	—	—	—
2-350S162-54	4'-3"	3'-8"	3'-5"	2'-11"	2'-8"	3'-4"	2'-9"	2'-5"	2'-0"	1'-7"
2-350S162-68	4'-9"	4'-6"	4'-2"	3'-10"	3'-7"	4'-1"	3'-9"	3'-5"	3'-1"	2'-8"
2-350S162-97	5'-10"	5'-6"	5'-2"	4'-10"	4'-7"	5'-0"	4'-8"	4'-5"	4'-2"	3'-10"
2-550S162-33	2'-9"	—	—	—	—	—	—	—	—	—
2-550S162-43	4'-9"	4'-2"	3'-8"	3'-3"	2'-8"	3'-6"	2'-10"	—	—	—
2-550S162-54	6'-0"	5'-6"	4'-11"	4'-6"	4'-1"	4'-10"	4'-4"	3'-10"	3'-6"	2'-11"
2-550S162-68	6'-10"	6'-5"	5'-11"	5'-8"	5'-4"	5'-11"	5'-6"	4'-11"	4'-7"	4'-3"
2-550S162-97	8'-5"	7'-7"	4'-4"	6'-10"	6'-7"	7'-3"	6'-8"	6'-4"	5'-11"	5'-8"
2-800S162-33	3'-8"	—	—	—	—	—	—	—	—	—
2-800S162-43	6'-1"	5'-5"	4'-9"	4'-2"	3'-8"	4'-7"	3'-9"	—	—	—
2-800S162-54	8'-0"	7'-4"	6'-8"	6'-1"	5'-7"	6'-6"	5'-8"	5'-3"	4'-8"	4'-3"
2-800S162-68	9'-1"	8'-6"	7'-11"	7'-7"	7'-1"	7'-10"	7'-5"	6'-9"	6'-3"	5'-9"
2-800S162-97	11'-1"	10'-4"	9'-8"	9'-2"	8'-9"	9'-8"	8'-11"	8'-5"	7'-11"	7'-7"
2-1000S162-43	6'-9"	6'-0"	5'-5"	4'-9"	4'-2"	5'-2"	4'-5"	—	—	—
2-1000S162-54	8'-11"	8'-2"	7'-6"	6'-10"	6'-6"	7'-4"	6'-7"	5'-10"	5'-4"	4'-9"
2-1000S162-68	10'-9"	10'-1"	9'-6"	8'-11"	8'-6"	9'-5"	8'-9"	8'-1"	7'-6"	6'-10"
2-1000S162-97	13'-1"	12'-4"	11'-6"	10'-10"	10'-5"	11'-5"	10'-7"	9'-11"	9'-6"	8'-11"
2-1200S162-43	7'-6"	6'-7"	5'-10"	5'-2"	4'-7"	5'-8"	4'-10"	—	—	—
2-1200S162-54	9'-9"	8'-10"	8'-1"	7'-6"	6'-10"	7'-11"	7'-2"	6'-6"	5'-9"	5'-3"
2-1200S162-68	11'-7"	10'-9"	10'-2"	9'-7"	9'-1"	10'-2"	9'-6"	8'-7"	7'-11"	7'-5"
2-1200S162-97	15'-1"	14'-1"	13'-4"	12'-7"	12'-0"	13'-2"	12'-4"	11'-7"	10'-11"	10'-6"

For SI: 1 inch = 25.4 mm, 1 foot = 304.8 mm, 1 pound per square foot = 0.0479kPa, 1 pound per square inch = 6.895 kPa.

a. Deflection criteria: L/360 for live loads, L/240 for total loads.

b. Design load assumptions:
    Roof/Ceiling dead load is 12 psf.
    Attic dead load is 10 psf.

c. Building width is in the direction of horizontal framing members supported by the header.

TABLE R603.6(7)
BACK-TO-BACK HEADER SPANS
Headers supporting one floor, roof and ceiling (33 ksi steel)[a, b, c]

MEMBER DESIGNATION	GROUND SNOW LOAD (20 psf) Building width[c]					GROUND SNOW LOAD (30 psf) Building width[c]				
	24'	28'	32'	36'	40'	24'	28'	32'	36'	40'
2-350S162-33	—	—	—	—	—	—	—	—	—	—
2-350S162-43	2'-7"	2'-1"	—	—	—	2'-6"	—	—	—	—
2-350S162-54	3'-8"	3'-3"	2'-9"	2'-6"	2'-1"	3'-7"	3'-1"	2'-8"	2'-5"	1'-11"
2-350S162-68	4'-5"	4'-0"	3'-9"	3'-6"	3'-1"	4'-4"	3'-11"	3'-8"	3'-5"	3'-0"
2-350S162-97	5'-5"	4'-11"	4'-8"	4'-5"	4'-1"	5'-4"	4'-10"	4'-7"	4'-4"	4'-0"
2-550S162-33	—	—	—	—	—	—	—	—	—	—
2-550S162-43	4'-1"	3'-6"	2'-10"	2'-5"	—	3'-11"	3'-5"	2'-9"	—	—
2-550S162-54	5'-5"	4'-9"	4'-4"	3'-10"	3'-6"	5'-3"	4'-8"	4'-3"	3'-9"	3'-5"
2-550S162-68	6'-6"	5'-10"	5'-6"	5'-1"	4'-8"	6'-2"	5'-9"	5'-5"	4'-11"	4'-7"
2-550S162-97	7'-8"	7'-2"	6'-8"	6'-5"	5'-11"	7'-7"	7'-0"	6'-7"	6'-3"	5'-10"
2-800S162-33	—	—	—	—	—	—	—	—	—	—
2-800S162-43	5'-4"	4'-7"	3'-10"	3'-4"	—	5'-1"	4'-5"	3'-9"	—	—
2-800S162-54	7'-3"	6'-6"	5'-10"	5'-4"	4'-9"	6'-11"	6'-4"	5'-8"	5'-3"	4'-8"
2-800S162-68	8'-5"	7'-9"	7'-5"	6'-9"	6'-5"	8'-4"	7'-8"	7'-3"	6'-8"	6'-3"
2-800S162-97	10'-2"	9'-6"	8'-11"	8'-6"	8'-1"	10'-0"	9'-5"	8'-9"	8'-5"	7'-10"
2-1000S162-43	5'-9"	5'-1"	4'-5"	3'-9"	—"	5'-8"	4'-11"	4'-4"	—	—
2-1000S162-54	7'-11"	7'-3"	6'-7"	5'-11"	5'-5"	7'-9"	7'-1"	6'-5"	5'-9"	5'-4"
2-1000S162-68	9'-11"	9'-4"	8'-9"	8'-1"	7'-7"	9'-10"	9'-2"	8'-7"	7'-11"	7'-5"
2-1000S162-97	12'-1"	11'-4"	10'-8"	10'-0"	9'-7"	11'-11"	11'-1"	10'-6"	9'-10"	9'-6"
2-1200S162-43	6'-6"	5'-8"	4'-10"	4'-2"	—	6'-4"	5'-6"	4'-8"	—	—
2-1200S162-54	8'-8"	7'-10"	7'-2"	6'-6"	5'-11"	8'-6"	7'-8"	6'-11"	6'-5"	5'-9"
2-1200S162-68	10'-8"	9'-11"	9'-5"	8'-8"	8'-1"	10'-6"	9'-9"	9'-3"	8'-6"	7'-11"
2-1200S162-97	13'-11"	13'-0"	12'-4"	11'-7"	11'-1"	13'-9"	12'-10"	12'-1"	11'-6"	10'-10"

For SI: 1 inch = 25.4 mm, 1 foot = 304.8 mm, 1 pound per square foot = 0.0479 kPa, 1 pound per square inch = 6.895 kPa.

a. Deflection criteria: $L/360$ for live loads, $L/240$ for total loads.

b. Design load assumptions:
　　Second floor dead load is 10 psf.
　　Roof/Ceiling dead load is 12 psf.
　　Second floor live load is 30 psf.
　　Roof/ceiling load is 12 psf.
　　Attic dead load is 10 psf.

c. Building width is in the direction of horizontal framing members supported by the header.

TABLE R603.6(8)
BACK-TO-BACK HEADER SPANS
Headers supporting one floor, roof and ceiling (33 ksi steel)[a, b, c]

MEMBER DESIGNATION	GROUND SNOW LOAD (50 psf)					GROUND SNOW LOAD (70 psf)				
	Building width[c]					Building width[c]				
	24'	28'	32'	36'	40'	24'	28'	32'	36'	40'
2-350S162-33	—	—	—	—	—	—	—	—	—	—
2-350S162-43	—	—	—	—	—	—	—	—	—	—
2-350S162-54	2'-11"	2'-6"	2'-2"	—	—	2'-4"	—	—	—	—
2-350S162-68	3'-10"	3'-6"	3'-2"	2'-9"	2'-6"	3'-4"	2'-10"	2'-6"	2'-3"	1'-10"
2-350S162-97	4'-9"	4'-5"	4'-2"	3'-10"	3'-8"	4'-3"	3'-10"	3'-8"	3'-5"	3'-2"
2-550S162-33	—	—	—	—	—	—	—	—	—	—
2-550S162-43	3'-1"	2'-5"	—	—	—	—	—	—	—	—
2-550S162-54	4'-6"	3'-10"	3'-6"	3'-0"	2'-7"	3'-8"	3'-1"	2'-7"	2'-1"	—
2-550S162-68	5'-7"	5'-1"	4'-8"	4'-4"	3'-11"	4'-10"	4'-5"	3'-10"	3'-6"	3'-3"
2-550S162-97	6'-10"	6'-5"	5'-11"	5'-8"	5'-5"	6'-2"	5'-8"	5'-5"	3'-1"	4'-9"
2-800S162-33	—	—	—	—	—	—	—	—	—	—
2-800S162-43	4'-1"	3'-5"	—	—	—	—	—	—	—	—
2-800S162-54	6'-0"	5'-5"	4'-9"	4'-4"	3'-9"	4'-11"	4'-5"	3'-9"	3'-2"	—
2-800S162-68	7'-6"	6'-10"	6'-5"	5'-10"	5'-5"	6'-7"	5'-10"	5'-5"	4'-10"	4'-6"
2-800S162-97	9'-1"	8'-6"	8'-0"	7'-7"	7'-4"	8'-3"	7'-8"	7'-3"	6'-9"	6'-6"
2-1000S162-43	4'-8"	3'-10"	—	—	—	—	—	—	—	—
2-1000S162-54	6'-9"	6'-0"	5'-5"	4'-10"	4'-4"	5'-8"	4'-10"	4'-4"	3'-8"	—
2-1000S162-68	8'-10"	8'-3"	7'-7"	6'-11"	6'-6"	7'-9"	7'-1"	6'-6"	5'-10"	5'-5"
2-1000S162-97	10'-10"	10'-3"	9'-7"	9'-1"	8'-8"	9'-9"	9'-3"	8'-7"	8'-3"	7'-9"
2-1200S162-43	5'-1"	4'-4²	—	—	—	—	—	—	—	—
2-1200S162-54	7'-5"	6'-6"	5'-10"	5'-4"	4'-9"	6'-3"	5'-5"	4'-8"	4'-1"	—
2-1200S162-68	9'-7"	8'-9"	8'-1"	7'-6"	6'-11"	8'-8"	7'-7"	6'-11"	6'-4"	5'-9"
2-1200S162-97	12'-6"	11'-8"	11'-1"	10'-6"	9'-11"	11'-4"	10'-7"	10'-0"	9'-6"	9'-0"

For SI: 1 inch = 25.4 mm, 1 foot = 304.8 mm, 1 pound per square foot = 0.0479 kPa, 1 pound per square inch = 6.895 kPa.

a. Deflection criteria: $L/360$ for live loads, $L/240$ for total loads.

b. Design load assumptions:
   Second floor dead load is 10 psf.
   Roof/Ceiling dead load is 12 psf.
   Second floor live load is 30 psf.
   Roof/ceiling dead load is 12 psf.
   Attic dead load is 10 psf.

c. Building width is in the direction of horizontal framing members supported by the header.

TABLE R603.6(9)
TOTAL NUMBER OF JACK AND KING STUDS REQUIRED AT EACH END OF AN OPENING

SIZE OF OPENING (feet-inches)	24" O.C. STUD SPACING		16" O.C. STUD SPACING	
	No. of jack studs	No. of king studs	No. of jack studs	No. of king studs
Up to 3'-6"	1	1	1	1
> 3'-6" to 5'-0"	1	2	1	2
> 5'-0" to 5'-6"	1	2	2	2
> 5'-6" to 8'-0"	1	2	2	2
> 8'-0" to 10'-6"	2	2	2	3
> 10'-6" to 12'-0"	2	2	3	3
> 12'-0" to 13'-0"	2	3	3	3
> 13'-0" to 14'-0"	2	3	3	4
> 14'-0" to 16'-0"	2	3	3	4
> 16'-0" to 18'-0"	3	3	4	4

For SI: 1 inch = 25.4 mm, 1 foot = 304.8 mm.

TABLE R603.6(10)
HEADER TO KING STUD CONNECTION REQUIREMENTS[a, b, c, d]

HEADER SPAN (feet)	BASIC WIND SPEED (mph), EXPOSURE		
	85 A/B or Seismic Design Categories A, B, C, D$_0$, D$_1$ and D$_2$	85 C or less than 110 A/B	Less than 110 C
≤ 4'	4-No. 8 screws	4-No. 8 screws	6-No. 8 screws
> 4' to 8'	4-No. 8 screws	4-No. 8 screws	8-No. 8 screws
> 8' to 12'	4-No. 8 screws	6-No. 8 screws	10-No. 8 screws
> 12'to 16'	4-No. 8 screws	8-No. 8 screws	12-No. 8 screws

For SI: 1 inch = 25.4 mm, 1 foot = 304.8 mm, 1 mile per hour = 0.447 m/s, 1 pound = 4.448 N.

a. All screw sizes shown are minimum.

b. For headers located on the first floor of a two-story building, the total number of screws may be reduced by two screws, but the total number of screws shall be no less than four.

c. For roof slopes of 6:12 or greater, the required number of screws may be reduced by half, but the total number of screws shall be no less than four.

d. Screws can be replaced by an uplift connector which has a capacity of the number of screws multiplied by 164 pounds (e.g., 12-No. 8 screws can be replaced by an uplift connector whose capacity exceeds 12 × 164 pounds = 1,968 pounds).

TABLE R603.6(11)
HEAD TRACK SPAN (33 ksi Steel)

BASIC WIND SPEED (mph)		ALLOWABLE HEAD TRACK SPAN[a, b] (ft-in)					
Exposure		Track Designation					
A/B	C	350T125-33	350T125-43	350T125-54	550T125-33	550T125-43	550T125-54
85		5'-0"	5'-7"	6'-2"	5'-10"	6'-8"	7'-0"
90		4'-10"	5'-5"	6'-0"	5'-8"	6'-3"	6'-10"
100	85	4'-6"	5'-1"	5'-8"	5'-4"	5'-11"	6'-5"
110	90	4'-2"	4'-9"	5'-4"	5'-1"	5'-7"	6'-1"
	100	3'-11"	4'-6"	5'-0"	4'-10"	5'-4"	5'-10"
	110	3'-8"	4'-2"	4'-9"	4'-1"	5'-1"	5'-7"

For SI: 1 inch = 25.4 mm, 1 foot = 304.8 mm, 1 mile per hour = 0.447 m/s.

a. Deflection Limit: L/240

b. Head track spans are based on components and cladding wind speeds and a 49-inch tributary span.

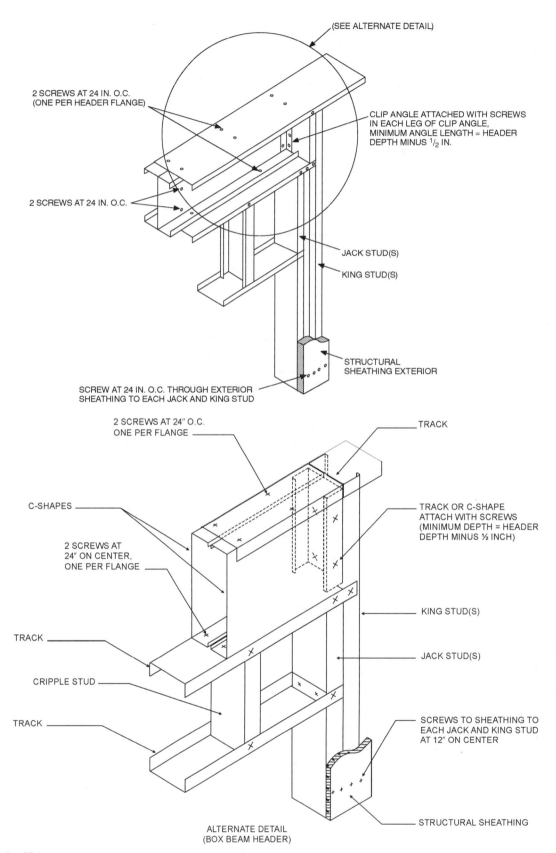

2 SCREWS AT 24 IN. O.C.
(ONE PER HEADER FLANGE)

(SEE ALTERNATE DETAIL)

CLIP ANGLE ATTACHED WITH SCREWS
IN EACH LEG OF CLIP ANGLE,
MINIMUM ANGLE LENGTH = HEADER
DEPTH MINUS $^1/_2$ IN.

2 SCREWS AT 24 IN. O.C.

JACK STUD(S)

KING STUD(S)

STRUCTURAL
SHEATHING EXTERIOR

SCREW AT 24 IN. O.C. THROUGH EXTERIOR
SHEATHING TO EACH JACK AND KING STUD

2 SCREWS AT 24″ O.C.
ONE PER FLANGE

TRACK

C-SHAPES

TRACK OR C-SHAPE
ATTACH WITH SCREWS
(MINIMUM DEPTH = HEADER
DEPTH MINUS ½ INCH)

2 SCREWS AT
24″ ON CENTER,
ONE PER FLANGE

KING STUD(S)

TRACK

JACK STUD(S)

CRIPPLE STUD

TRACK

SCREWS TO SHEATHING TO
EACH JACK AND KING STUD
AT 12″ ON CENTER

STRUCTURAL SHEATHING

ALTERNATE DETAIL
(BOX BEAM HEADER)

For SI: 1 inch = 25.4 mm.

**FIGURE R603.6
HEADER DETAIL**

R603.7 Structural sheathing. In areas where the basic wind speed is less than 110 miles per hour (49 m/s), wood structural panel sheathing shall be installed on all exterior walls of buildings in accordance with this section. Wood structural panel sheathing shall consist of minimum $^7/_{16}$-inch-thick (11 mm) oriented-strand board or $^{15}/_{32}$-inch-thick (12 mm) plywood and shall be installed on all exterior wall surfaces in accordance with Section R603.7.1 and Figure R603.3. The minimum length of full height sheathing on exterior walls shall be determined in accordance with Table R603.7, but shall not be less than 20 percent of the braced wall length in any case. The minimum percentage of full height sheathing in Table R603.7 shall include only those sheathed wall sections, uninterrupted by openings, which are a minimum of 48 inches (1120 mm) wide. The minimum percentage of full-height structural sheathing shall be multiplied by 1.10 for 9-foot-high (2743 mm) walls and multiplied by 1.20 for 10-foot-high (3048 mm) walls. In addition, structural sheathing shall:

1. Be installed with the long dimension parallel to the stud framing and shall cover the full vertical height of studs, from the bottom of the bottom track to the top of the top track of each story.

2. Be applied to each end (corners) of each of the exterior walls with a minimum 48-inch-wide (1219 mm) panel.

R603.7.1 Structural sheathing fastening. All edges and interior areas of wood structural panel sheathing shall be fastened to a framing member and tracks in accordance with Table R603.3.2(1).

R603.7.2 Hold-down requirements. Multiplying the percentage of structural sheathing required in Table R603.7 by 0.6 is permitted where a hold-down anchor with a capacity of 4,300 pounds (19 kN) is provided at each end of exterior walls. Installations of a single hold-down anchor at wall corners is permitted.

SECTION R604
WOOD STRUCTURAL PANELS

R604.1 Identification and grade. Wood structural panels shall conform to DOC PS 1 or DOC PS 2. All panels shall be identified by a grade mark or certificate of inspection issued by an approved agency.

R604.2 Allowable spans. The maximum allowable spans for wood structural panel wall sheathing shall not exceed the values set forth in Table R602.3(3).

R604.3 Installation. Wood structural panel wall sheathing shall be attached to framing in accordance with Table R602.3(1). Wood structural panels marked Exposure 1 or Exterior are considered water-repellent sheathing under the code.

SECTION R605
PARTICLEBOARD

R605.1 Identification and grade. Particleboard shall conform to ANSI A208.1 and shall be so identified by a grade mark or certificate of inspection issued by an approved agency. Particleboard shall comply with the grades specified in Table R602.3(4).

SECTION R606
GENERAL MASONRY CONSTRUCTION

R606.1 General. Masonry construction shall be designed and constructed in accordance with the provisions of this section or in accordance with the provisions of ACI 530/ASCE 5/TMS 402.

R606.1.1 Professional registration not required. When the empirical design provisions of ACI 530/ASCE 5/TMS 402 Chapter 5 or the provisions of this section are used to design masonry, project drawings, typical details and speci-

TABLE R603.7
MINIMUM PERCENTAGE OF FULL HEIGHT STRUCTURAL SHEATHING ON EXTERIOR WALLS[a, b, c, d, e]

WALL SUPPORTING	ROOF SLOPE	WIND SPEED (mph) AND EXPOSURE				
		85 A/B	100 A/B	110 A/B or 85 C	100 C	110 C
Roof and ceiling only	3:12	8	9	12	16	20
	6:12	12	15	20	26	35
	9:12	21	25	30	50	58
	12:12	30	35	40	66	75
One story, roof and ceiling	3:12	24	30	35	50	66
	6:12	25	30	40	58	74
	9:12	35	40	55	74	91
	12:12	40	50	65	100	115

For SI: 1 mile per hour = 0.447 m/s.

a. Linear interpolation shall be permitted.

b. Bracing amount shall not be less than 20 percent of the wall length after all applicable adjustments are made.

c. Minimum percentages are based on a building aspect ratio of 1:1. Minimum percentages for the shorter walls of a building shall be multiplied by a factor of 1.5 and 2.0 for building aspect ratios of 1.5:1 and 2:1 respectively.

d. For hip roofed homes with continuous structural sheathing, the amount of bracing shall be permitted to be multiplied by a factor of 0.95 for roof slopes not exceeding 7:12 and a factor of 0.9 for roof slopes greater than 7:12.

e. Sheathing percentages are permitted to be reduced in accordance with Section R603.7.2.

fications are not required to bear the seal of the architect or engineer responsible for design, unless otherwise required by the state law of the jurisdiction having authority.

R606.2 Thickness of masonry. The nominal thickness of masonry walls shall conform to the requirements of Sections R606.2.1 through R606.2.4.

R606.2.1 Minimum thickness. The minimum thickness of masonry bearing walls more than one story high shall be 8 inches (203 mm). Solid masonry walls of one-story dwellings and garages shall not be less than 6 inches (152 mm) in thickness when not greater than 9 feet (2743 mm) in height, provided that when gable construction is used, an additional 6 feet (1829 mm) is permitted to the peak of the gable. Masonry walls shall be laterally supported in either the horizontal or vertical direction at intervals as required by Section R606.9.

R606.2.2 Rubble stone masonry wall. The minimum thickness of rough, random or coursed rubble stone masonry walls shall be 16 inches (406 mm).

R606.2.3 Change in thickness. Where walls of masonry of hollow units or masonry-bonded hollow walls are decreased in thickness, a course of solid masonry shall be constructed between the wall below and the thinner wall above, or special units or construction shall be used to transmit the loads from face shells or wythes above to those below.

R606.2.4 Parapet walls. Unreinforced solid masonry parapet walls shall not be less than 8 inches (203 mm) thick and their height shall not exceed four times their thickness. Unreinforced hollow unit masonry parapet walls shall be not less than 8 inches (203 mm) thick, and their height shall not exceed three times their thickness. Masonry parapet walls in areas subject to wind loads of 30 pounds per square foot (1.44 kPa) located in Seismic Design Category D_0, D_1 or D_2, or on townhouses in Seismic Design Category C shall be reinforced in accordance with Section R606.12.

R606.3 Corbeled masonry. Solid masonry units shall be used for corbeling. The maximum corbeled projection beyond the face of the wall shall not be more than one-half of the wall thickness or one-half the wythe thickness for hollow walls; the maximum projection of one unit shall not exceed one-half the height of the unit or one-third the thickness at right angles to the wall. When corbeled masonry is used to support floor or roof-framing members, the top course of the corbel shall be a header course or the top course bed joint shall have ties to the vertical wall. The hollow space behind the corbeled masonry shall be filled with mortar or grout.

R606.4 Support conditions. Bearing and support conditions shall be in accordance with Sections R606.4.1 and R606.4.2.

R606.4.1 Bearing on support. Each masonry wythe shall be supported by at least two-thirds of the wythe thickness.

R606.4.2 Support at foundation. Cavity wall or masonry veneer construction may be supported on an 8-inch (203 mm) foundation wall, provided the 8-inch (203 mm) wall is corbeled with solid masonry to the width of the wall system above. The total horizontal projection of the corbel shall not exceed 2 inches (51 mm) with individual corbels projecting not more than one-third the thickness of the unit or one-half the height of the unit.

R606.5 Allowable stresses. Allowable compressive stresses in masonry shall not exceed the values prescribed in Table R606.5. In determining the stresses in masonry, the effects of all loads and conditions of loading and the influence of all

TABLE R606.5
ALLOWABLE COMPRESSIVE STRESSES FOR EMPIRICAL DESIGN OF MASONRY

CONSTRUCTION; COMPRESSIVE STRENGTH OF UNIT, GROSS AREA	ALLOWABLE COMPRESSIVE STRESSES[a] GROSS CROSS-SECTIONAL AREA[b]	
	Type M or S mortar	Type N mortar
Solid masonry of brick and other solid units of clay or shale; sand-lime or concrete brick:		
8,000 + psi	350	300
4,500 psi	225	200
2,500 psi	160	140
1,500 psi	115	100
Grouted[c] masonry, of clay or shale; sand-lime or concrete:		
4,500+ psi	225	200
2,500 psi	160	140
1,500 psi	115	100
Solid masonry of solid concrete masonry units:		
3,000+ psi	225	200
2,000 psi	160	140
1,200 psi	115	100
Masonry of hollow load-bearing units:		
2,000+ psi	140	120
1,500 psi	115	100
1,000 psi	75	70
700 psi	60	55
Hollow walls (cavity or masonry bonded[d]) solid units:		
2,500+ psi	160	140
1,500 psi	115	100
Hollow units	75	70
Stone ashlar masonry:		
Granite	720	640
Limestone or marble	450	400
Sandstone or cast stone	360	320
Rubble stone masonry:		
Coarse, rough or random	120	100

For SI: 1 pound per square inch = 6.895 kPa.

a. Linear interpolation shall be used for determining allowable stresses for masonry units having compressive strengths that are intermediate between those given in the table.

b. Gross cross-sectional area shall be calculated on the actual rather than nominal dimensions.

c. See Section R608.

d. Where floor and roof loads are carried upon one wythe, the gross cross-sectional area is that of the wythe under load; if both wythes are loaded, the gross cross-sectional area is that of the wall minus the area of the cavity between the wythes. Walls bonded with metal ties shall be considered as cavity walls unless the collar joints are filled with mortar or grout.

forces affecting the design and strength of the several parts shall be taken into account.

R606.5.1 Combined units. In walls or other structural members composed of different kinds or grades of units, materials or mortars, the maximum stress shall not exceed the allowable stress for the weakest of the combination of units, materials and mortars of which the member is composed. The net thickness of any facing unit that is used to resist stress shall not be less than 1.5 inches (38 mm).

R606.6 Piers. The unsupported height of masonry piers shall not exceed ten times their least dimension. When structural clay tile or hollow concrete masonry units are used for isolated piers to support beams and girders, the cellular spaces shall be filled solidly with concrete or Type M or S mortar, except that unfilled hollow piers may be used if their unsupported height is not more than four times their least dimension. Where hollow masonry units are solidly filled with concrete or Type M, S or N mortar, the allowable compressive stress shall be permitted to be increased as provided in Table R606.5.

R606.6.1 Pier cap. Hollow piers shall be capped with 4 inches (102 mm) of solid masonry or concrete or shall have cavities of the top course filled with concrete or grout or other approved methods.

R606.7 Chases. Chases and recesses in masonry walls shall not be deeper than one-third the wall thickness, and the maximum length of a horizontal chase or horizontal projection shall not exceed 4 feet (1219 mm), and shall have at least 8 inches (203 mm) of masonry in back of the chases and recesses and between adjacent chases or recesses and the jambs of openings. Chases and recesses in masonry walls shall be designed and constructed so as not to reduce the required strength or required fire resistance of the wall and in no case shall a chase or recess be permitted within the required area of a pier. Masonry directly above chases or recesses wider than 12 inches (305 mm) shall be supported on noncombustible lintels.

R606.8 Stack bond. In unreinforced masonry where masonry units are laid in stack bond, longitudinal reinforcement consisting of not less than two continuous wires each with a minimum aggregate cross-sectional area of 0.017 square inch (11 mm²) shall be provided in horizontal bed joints spaced not more than 16 inches (406 mm) on center vertically.

R606.9 Lateral support. Masonry walls shall be laterally supported in either the horizontal or the vertical direction. The maximum spacing between lateral supports shall not exceed the distances in Table R606.9. Lateral support shall be provided by cross walls, pilasters, buttresses or structural frame members when the limiting distance is taken horizontally, or by floors or roofs when the limiting distance is taken vertically.

R606.9.1 Horizontal lateral support. Lateral support in the horizontal direction provided by intersecting masonry walls shall be provided by one of the methods in Section R606.9.1.1 or Section R606.9.1.2.

R606.9.1.1 Bonding pattern. Fifty percent of the units at the intersection shall be laid in an overlapping masonry bonding pattern, with alternate units having a bearing of not less than 3 inches (76 mm) on the unit below.

TABLE R606.9
SPACING OF LATERAL SUPPORT FOR MASONRY WALLS

CONSTRUCTION	MAXIMUM WALL LENGTH TO THICKNESS OR WALL HEIGHT TO THICKNESS[a,b]
Bearing walls:	
Solid or solid grouted	20
All other	18
Nonbearing walls:	
Exterior	18
Interior	36

For SI: 1 foot = 304.8 mm.

a. Except for cavity walls and cantilevered walls, the thickness of a wall shall be its nominal thickness measured perpendicular to the face of the wall. For cavity walls, the thickness shall be determined as the sum of the nominal thicknesses of the individual wythes. For cantilever walls, except for parapets, the ratio of height to nominal thickness shall not exceed 6 for solid masonry, or 4 for hollow masonry. For parapets, see Section R606.2.4.

b. An additional unsupported height of 6 feet is permitted for gable end walls.

R606.9.1.2 Metal reinforcement. Interior nonload- bearing walls shall be anchored at their intersections, at vertical intervals of not more than 16 inches (406 mm) with joint reinforcement of at least 9 gage [0.148 in. (4mm)], or $1/4$ inch (6 mm) galvanized mesh hardware cloth. Intersecting masonry walls, other than interior nonloadbearing walls, shall be anchored at vertical intervals of not more than 8 inches (203 mm) with joint reinforcement of at least 9 gage and shall extend at least 30 inches (762 mm) in each direction at the intersection. Other metal ties, joint reinforcement or anchors, if used, shall be spaced to provide equivalent area of anchorage to that required by this section.

R606.9.2 Vertical lateral support. Vertical lateral support of masonry walls in Seismic Design Category A, B or C shall be provided in accordance with one of the methods in Section R606.9.2.1 or Section R606.9.2.2.

R606.9.2.1 Roof structures. Masonry walls shall be anchored to roof structures with metal strap anchors spaced in accordance with the manufacturer's instructions, $1/2$-inch (13 mm) bolts spaced not more than 6 feet (1829 mm) on center, or other approved anchors. Anchors shall be embedded at least 16 inches (406 mm) into the masonry, or be hooked or welded to bond beam reinforcement placed not less than 6 inches (152 mm) from the top of the wall.

R606.9.2.2 Floor diaphragms. Masonry walls shall be anchored to floor diaphragm framing by metal strap anchors spaced in accordance with the manufacturer's instructions, $1/2$-inch-diameter (13 mm) bolts spaced at intervals not to exceed 6 feet (1829 mm) and installed as shown in Figure R606.11(1), or by other approved methods.

R606.10 Lintels. Masonry over openings shall be supported by steel lintels, reinforced concrete or masonry lintels or masonry arches, designed to support load imposed.

R606.11 Anchorage. Masonry walls shall be anchored to floor and roof systems in accordance with the details shown in Figure R606.11(1), R606.11(2) or R606.11(3). Footings may be considered as points of lateral support.

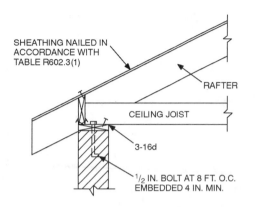

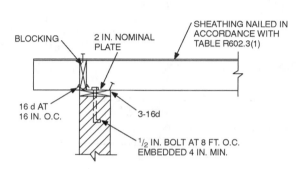

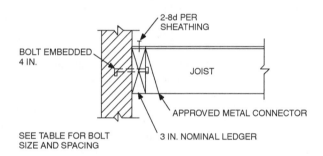

**LEDGER BOLT
SIZE AND SPACING**

JOIST SPAN	BOLT SIZE AND SPACING	
	ROOF	FLOOR
10 FT.	$1/2$ AT 2 FT. 6 IN. $7/8$ AT 3 FT. 6 IN.	$1/2$ AT 2 FT. 0 IN. $7/8$ AT 2 FT. 9 IN.
10–15 FT.	$1/2$ AT 1 FT. 9 IN. $7/8$ AT 2 FT. 6 IN.	$1/2$ AT 1 FT. 4 IN. $7/8$ AT 2 FT. 0 IN.
15-20 FT.	$1/2$ AT 1 FT. 3 IN. $7/8$ AT 2 FT. 0 IN.	$1/2$ AT 1 FT. 0 IN. $7/8$ AT 1 FT. 6 IN.

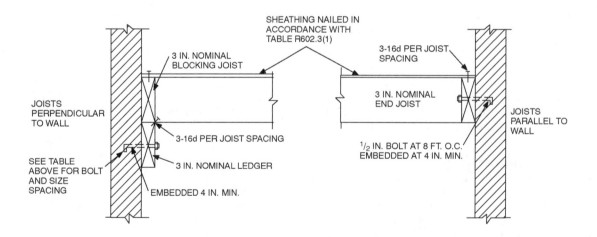

NOTE: Where bolts are located in hollow masonry, the cells in the courses receiving the bolt shall be grouted solid.

For SI: 1 inch = 25.4 mm, 1 foot = 304.8 mm, 1 pound per square foot = 0.0479 kPa.

**FIGURE R606.11(1)
ANCHORAGE REQUIREMENTS FOR MASONRY WALLS LOCATED IN SEISMIC DESIGN CATEGORY
A, B OR C AND WHERE WIND LOADS ARE LESS THAN 30 PSF**

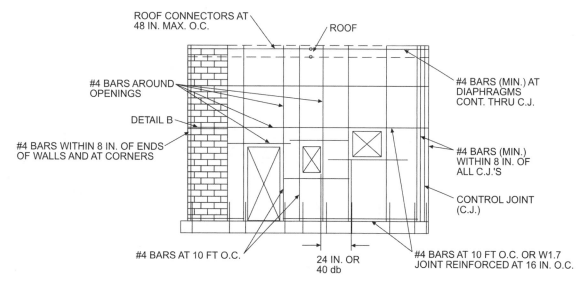

ROOF CONNECTORS AT 48 IN. MAX. O.C.

ROOF

#4 BARS AROUND OPENINGS

DETAIL B

#4 BARS WITHIN 8 IN. OF ENDS OF WALLS AND AT CORNERS

#4 BARS (MIN.) AT DIAPRHAGMS CONT. THRU C.J.

#4 BARS (MIN.) WITHIN 8 IN. OF ALL C.J.'S

CONTROL JOINT (C.J.)

#4 BARS AT 10 FT O.C.

24 IN. OR 40 db

#4 BARS AT 10 FT O.C. OR W1.7 JOINT REINFORCED AT 16 IN. O.C.

MINIMUM REINFORCEMENT FOR MASONRY WALLS

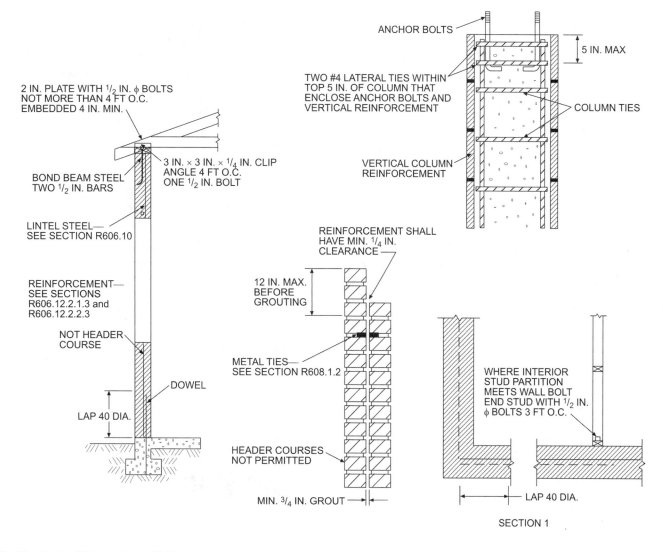

2 IN. PLATE WITH 1/2 IN. φ BOLTS NOT MORE THAN 4 FT O.C. EMBEDDED 4 IN. MIN.

BOND BEAM STEEL TWO 1/2 IN. BARS

3 IN. × 3 IN. × 1/4 IN. CLIP ANGLE 4 FT O.C. ONE 1/2 IN. BOLT

LINTEL STEEL— SEE SECTION R606.10

REINFORCEMENT— SEE SECTIONS R606.12.2.1.3 and R606.12.2.2.3

NOT HEADER COURSE

DOWEL

LAP 40 DIA.

ANCHOR BOLTS

5 IN. MAX

TWO #4 LATERAL TIES WITHIN TOP 5 IN. OF COLUMN THAT ENCLOSE ANCHOR BOLTS AND VERTICAL REINFORCEMENT

COLUMN TIES

VERTICAL COLUMN REINFORCEMENT

REINFORCEMENT SHALL HAVE MIN. 1/4 IN. CLEARANCE

12 IN. MAX. BEFORE GROUTING

METAL TIES— SEE SECTION R608.1.2

HEADER COURSES NOT PERMITTED

MIN. 3/4 IN. GROUT

WHERE INTERIOR STUD PARTITION MEETS WALL BOLT END STUD WITH 1/2 IN. φ BOLTS 3 FT O.C.

LAP 40 DIA.

SECTION 1

For SI: 1 inch = 25.4 mm, 1 foot = 304.8 mm.

FIGURE R606.11(2)
REQUIREMENTS FOR REINFORCED GROUTED MASONRY CONSTRUCTION IN SEISMIC DESIGN CATEGORY C

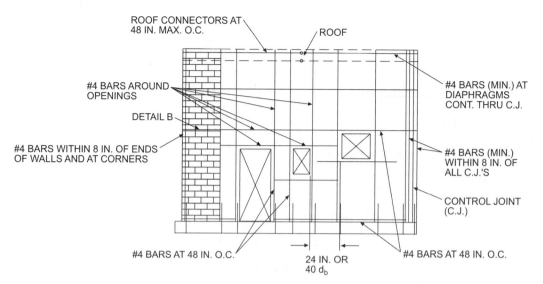

MINIMUM REINFORCEMENT FOR MASONRY WALLS

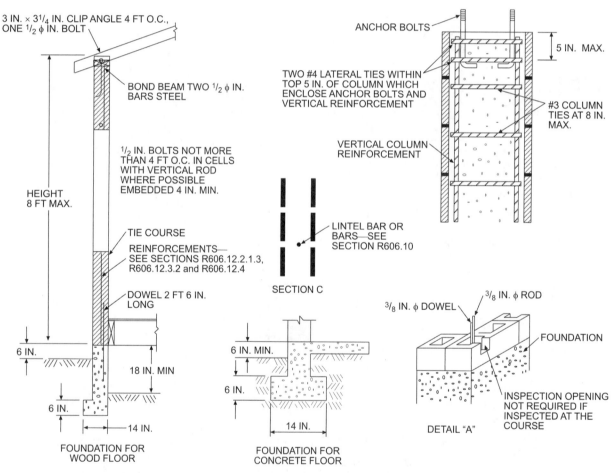

Note: A full bed joint must be provided. All cells containing vertical bars are to be filled to the top of wall and provide inspection opening as shown on detail "A." Horizontal bars are to be laid as shown on detail "B." Lintel bars are to be laid as shown on Section C.

NOTE: A full bed joint must be provided. All cells containing vertical bars are to be filled to the top of wall and provide inspection opening as shown on detail "A." Horizontal bars are to be laid as shown on detail "B." Lintel bars are to be laid as shown on Section C.

For SI: 1 inch = 25.4 mm, 1 foot = 304.8 mm.

FIGURE R606.11(3)
REQUIREMENTS FOR REINFORCED MASONRY CONSTRUCTION IN SEISMIC DESIGN CATEGORY D_0, D_1 OR D_2

R606.12 Seismic requirements. The seismic requirements of this section shall apply to the design of masonry and the construction of masonry building elements located in Seismic Design Category D_0, D_1 or D_2. Townhouses in Seismic Design Category C shall comply with the requirements of Section R606.12.2. These requirements shall not apply to glass unit masonry conforming to Section R610 or masonry veneer conforming to Section R703.7.

R606.12.1 General. Masonry structures and masonry elements shall comply with the requirements of Sections R606.12.2 through R606.12.4 based on the seismic design category established in Table R301.2(1). Masonry structures and masonry elements shall comply with the requirements of Section R606.12 and Figures R606.11(1), R606.11(2) and R606.11(3) or shall be designed in accordance with ACI 530/ASCE 5/TMS 402.

R606.12.1.1 Floor and roof diaphragm construction. Floor and roof diaphragms shall be constructed of wood structural panels attached to wood framing in accordance with Table R602.3(1) or to cold-formed steel floor framing in accordance with Table R505.3.1(2) or to cold-formed steel roof framing in accordance with Table R804.3. Additionally, sheathing panel edges perpendicular to framing members shall be backed by blocking, and sheathing shall be connected to the blocking with fasteners at the edge spacing. For Seismic Design Categories C, D_0, D_1 and D_2, where the width-to-thickness dimension of the diaphragm exceeds 2-to-1, edge spacing of fasteners shall be 4 inches (102 mm) on center.

R606.12.2 Seismic Design Category C. Townhouses located in Seismic Design Category C shall comply with the requirements of this section.

R606.12.2.1 Design of elements not part of the lateral force-resisting system.

R606.12.2.1.1 Load-bearing frames or columns. Elements not part of the lateral-force-resisting system shall be analyzed to determine their effect on the response of the system. The frames or columns shall be adequate for vertical load carrying capacity and induced moment caused by the design story drift.

R606.12.2.1.2 Masonry partition walls. Masonry partition walls, masonry screen walls and other masonry elements that are not designed to resist vertical or lateral loads, other than those induced by their own weight, shall be isolated from the structure so that vertical and lateral forces are not imparted to these elements. Isolation joints and connectors between these elements and the structure shall be designed to accommodate the design story drift.

R606.12.2.1.3 Reinforcement requirements for masonry elements. Masonry elements listed in Section R606.12.2.1.2 shall be reinforced in either the horizontal or vertical direction as shown in Figure R606.11(2) and in accordance with the following:

1. Horizontal reinforcement. Horizontal joint reinforcement shall consist of at least two longitudinal W1.7 wires spaced not more than 16 inches (406 mm) for walls greater than 4 inches (102 mm) in width and at least one longitudinal W1.7 wire spaced not more than 16 inches (406 mm) for walls not exceeding 4 inches (102 mm) in width; or at least one No. 4 bar spaced not more than 48 inches (1219 mm). Where two longitudinal wires of joint reinforcement are used, the space between these wires shall be the widest that the mortar joint will accommodate. Horizontal reinforcement shall be provided within 16 inches (406 mm) of the top and bottom of these masonry elements.

2. Vertical reinforcement. Vertical reinforcement shall consist of at least one No. 4 bar spaced not more than 48 inches (1219 mm). Vertical reinforcement shall be located within 16 inches (406 mm) of the ends of masonry walls.

R606.12.2.2 Design of elements part of the lateral-force-resisting system.

R606.12.2.2.1 Connections to masonry shear walls. Connectors shall be provided to transfer forces between masonry walls and horizontal elements in accordance with the requirements of Section 2.1.8 of ACI 530/ASCE 5/TMS 402. Connectors shall be designed to transfer horizontal design forces acting either perpendicular or parallel to the wall, but not less than 200 pounds per linear foot (2919 N/m) of wall. The maximum spacing between connectors shall be 4 feet (1219 mm). Such anchorage mechanisms shall not induce tension stresses perpendicular to grain in ledgers or nailers.

R606.12.2.2.2 Connections to masonry columns. Connectors shall be provided to transfer forces between masonry columns and horizontal elements in accordance with the requirements of Section 2.1.8 of ACI 530/ASCE 5/TMS 402. Where anchor bolts are used to connect horizontal elements to the tops of columns, the bolts shall be placed within lateral ties. Lateral ties shall enclose both the vertical bars in the column and the anchor bolts. There shall be a minimum of two No. 4 lateral ties provided in the top 5 inches (127 mm) of the column.

R606.12.2.2.3 Minimum reinforcement requirements for masonry shear walls. Vertical reinforcement of at least one No. 4 bar shall be provided at corners, within 16 inches (406 mm) of each side of openings, within 8 inches (203 mm) of each side of movement joints, within 8 inches (203 mm) of the ends of walls, and at a maximum spacing of 10 feet (3048 mm).

Horizontal joint reinforcement shall consist of at least two wires of W1.7 spaced not more than 16 inches (406 mm); or bond beam reinforcement of at least one No. 4 bar spaced not more than 10 feet (3048 mm) shall be provided. Horizontal reinforcement shall also be provided at the bottom and top of wall openings and shall extend not less than 24 inches (610 mm) nor less than 40 bar diameters past the opening; continuously at structurally connected roof and floor levels; and within 16 inches (406 mm) of the top of walls.

R606.12.3 Seismic Design Category D₀ or D₁. Structures in Seismic Design Category D_0 or D_1 shall comply with the requirements of Seismic Design Category C and the additional requirements of this section.

R606.12.3.1 Design requirements. Masonry elements other than those covered by Section R606.12.2.1.2 shall be designed in accordance with the requirements of Chapter 1 and Sections 2.1 and 2.3 of ACI 530/ASCE 5/TMS 402 and shall meet the minimum reinforcement requirements contained in Sections R606.12.3.2 and R606.12.3.2.1.

Exception: Masonry walls limited to one story in height and 9 feet (2743 mm) between lateral supports need not be designed provided they comply with the minimum reinforcement requirements of Sections R606.12.3.2 and R606.12.3.2.1.

R606.12.3.2 Minimum reinforcement requirements for masonry walls. Masonry walls other than those covered by Section R606.12.2.1.3 shall be reinforced in both the vertical and horizontal direction. The sum of the cross-sectional area of horizontal and vertical reinforcement shall be at least 0.002 times the gross cross-sectional area of the wall, and the minimum cross-sectional area in each direction shall be not less than 0.0007 times the gross cross-sectional area of the wall. Reinforcement shall be uniformly distributed. Table R606.12.3.2 shows the minimum reinforcing bar sizes required for varying thicknesses of masonry walls. The maximum spacing of reinforcement shall be 48 inches (1219 mm) provided that the walls are solid grouted and constructed of hollow open-end units, hollow units laid with full head joints or two wythes of solid units. The maximum spacing of reinforcement shall be 24 inches (610 mm) for all other masonry.

R606.12.3.2.1 Shear wall reinforcement requirements. The maximum spacing of vertical and horizontal reinforcement shall be the smaller of one-third the length of the shear wall, one-third the height of the shear wall, or 48 inches (1219 mm). The minimum cross-sectional area of vertical reinforcement shall be one-third of the required shear reinforcement. Shear

reinforcement shall be anchored around vertical reinforcing bars with a standard hook.

R606.12.3.3 Minimum reinforcement for masonry columns. Lateral ties in masonry columns shall be spaced not more than 8 inches (203 mm) on center and shall be at least $^3/_8$ inch (9.5 mm) diameter. Lateral ties shall be embedded in grout.

R606.12.3.4 Material restrictions. Type N mortar or masonry cement shall not be used as part of the lateral-force-resisting system.

R606.12.3.5 Lateral tie anchorage. Standard hooks for lateral tie anchorage shall be either a 135-degree (2.4 rad) standard hook or a 180-degree (3.2 rad) standard hook.

R606.12.4 Seismic Design Category D₂. All structures in Seismic Design Category D_2 shall comply with the requirements of Seismic Design Category D_1 and to the additional requirements of this section.

R606.12.4.1 Design of elements not part of the lateral-force-resisting system. Stack bond masonry that is not part of the lateral-force-resisting system shall have a horizontal cross-sectional area of reinforcement of at least 0.0015 times the gross cross-sectional area of masonry. Table R606.12.4.1 shows minimum reinforcing bar sizes for masonry walls. The maximum spacing of horizontal reinforcement shall be 24 inches (610 mm). These elements shall be solidly grouted and shall be constructed of hollow open-end units or two wythes of solid units.

TABLE R606.12.4.1
MINIMUM REINFORCING FOR STACKED BONDED MASONRY WALLS IN SEISMIC DESIGN CATEGORY D₂

NOMINAL WALL THICKNESS (inches)	MINIMUM BAR SIZE SPACED AT 24 INCHES
6	#4
8	#5
10	#5
12	#6

For SI: 1 inch = 25.4 mm.

R606.12.4.2 Design of elements part of the lateral-force-resisting system. Stack bond masonry that is part of the lateral-force-resisting system shall have a horizontal cross-sectional area of reinforcement of at least 0.0025 times the gross cross-sectional area of masonry. Table R606.12.4.2 shows minimum reinforcing bar sizes

TABLE R606.12.3.2
MINIMUM DISTRIBUTED WALL REINFORCEMENT FOR BUILDING ASSIGNED TO SEISMIC DESIGN CATEGORY D₀ or D₁

NOMINAL WALL THICKNESS (inches)	MINIMUM SUM OF THE VERTICAL AND HORIZONTAL REINFORCEMENT AREAS[a] (square inches per foot)	MINIMUM REINFORCEMENT AS DISTRIBUTED IN BOTH HORIZONTAL AND VERTICAL DIRECTIONS[b] (square inches per foot)	MINIMUM BAR SIZE FOR REINFORCEMENT SPACED AT 48 INCHES
6	0.135	0.047	#4
8	0.183	0.064	#5
10	0.231	0.081	#6
12	0.279	0.098	#6

For SI: 1 inch = 25.4 mm, 1 foot = 304.8 mm, 1 square inch per foot = 2064 mm²/m.

a. Based on the minimum reinforcing ratio of 0.002 times the gross cross-sectional area of the wall.

b. Based on the minimum reinforcing ratio each direction of 0.0007 times the gross cross-sectional area of the wall.

for masonry walls. The maximum spacing of horizontal reinforcement shall be 16 inches (406 mm). These elements shall be solidly grouted and shall be constructed of hollow open-end units or two wythes of solid units.

TABLE R606.12.4.2
MINIMUM REINFORCING FOR STACKED BONDED MASONRY WALLS IN SEISMIC DESIGN CATEGORY D₂

NOMINAL WALL THICKNESS (inches)	MINIMUM BAR SIZE SPACED AT 16 INCHES
6	#4
8	#5
10	#5
12	#6

For SI: 1 inch = 25.4 mm.

R606.13 Protection for reinforcement. Bars shall be completely embedded in mortar or grout. Joint reinforcement embedded in horizontal mortar joints shall not have less than $^5/_8$-inch (15.9 mm) mortar coverage from the exposed face. All other reinforcement shall have a minimum coverage of one bar diameter over all bars, but not less than $^3/_4$ inch (19 mm), except where exposed to weather or soil, in which case the minimum coverage shall be 2 inches (51 mm).

R606.14 Beam supports. Beams, girders or other concentrated loads supported by a wall or column shall have a bearing of at least 3 inches (76 mm) in length measured parallel to the beam upon solid masonry not less than 4 inches (102 mm) in thickness, or upon a metal bearing plate of adequate design and dimensions to distribute the load safely, or upon a continuous reinforced masonry member projecting not less than 4 inches (102 mm) from the face of the wall.

R606.14.1 Joist bearing. Joists shall have a bearing of not less than $1^1/_2$ inches (38 mm), except as provided in Section R606.14, and shall be supported in accordance with Figure R606.11(1).

R606.15 Metal accessories. Joint reinforcement, anchors, ties and wire fabric shall conform to the following: ASTM A 82 for wire anchors and ties; ASTM A 36 for plate, headed and bent-bar anchors; ASTM A 510 for corrugated sheet metal anchors and ties; ASTM A 951 for joint reinforcement; ASTM B 227 for copper-clad steel wire ties; or ASTM A 167 for stainless steel hardware.

R606.15.1 Corrosion protection. Minimum corrosion protection of joint reinforcement, anchor ties and wire fabric for use in masonry wall construction shall conform to Table R606.15.1.

SECTION R607
UNIT MASONRY

R607.1 Mortar. Mortar for use in masonry construction shall comply with ASTM C 270. The type of mortar shall be in accordance with Sections R607.1.1, R607.1.2 and R607.1.3 and shall meet the proportion specifications of Table R607.1 or the property specifications of ASTM C 270.

TABLE R606.15.1
MINIMUM CORROSION PROTECTION

MASONRY METAL ACCESSORY	STANDARD
Joint reinforcement, interior walls	ASTM A 641, Class 1
Wire ties or anchors in exterior walls completely embedded in mortar or grout	ASTM A 641, Class 3
Wire ties or anchors in exterior walls not completely embedded in mortar or grout	ASTM A 153, Class B-2
Joint reinforcement in exterior walls or interior walls exposed to moist environment	ASTM A 153, Class B-2
Sheet metal ties or anchors exposed to weather	ASTM A 153, Class B-2
Sheet metal ties or anchors completely embedded in mortar or grout	ASTM A 653, Coating Designation G60
Stainless steel hardware for any exposure	ASTM A 167, Type 304

R607.1.1 Foundation walls. Masonry foundation walls constructed as set forth in Tables R404.1.1(1) through R404.1.1(4) and mortar shall be Type M or S.

R607.1.2 Masonry in Seismic Design Categories A, B and C. Mortar for masonry serving as the lateral-force-resisting system in Seismic Design Categories A, B and C shall be Type M, S or N mortar.

R607.1.3 Masonry in Seismic Design Categories D₀, D₁ and D₂. Mortar for masonry serving as the lateral-force-resisting system in Seismic Design Categories D₀, D₁ and D₂ shall be Type M or S portland cement-lime or mortar cement mortar.

R607.2 Placing mortar and masonry units.

R607.2.1 Bed and head joints. Unless otherwise required or indicated on the project drawings, head and bed joints shall be $^3/_8$ inch (10 mm) thick, except that the thickness of the bed joint of the starting course placed over foundations shall not be less than $^1/_4$ inch (7 mm) and not more than $^3/_4$ inch (19 mm).

R607.2.1.1 Mortar joint thickness tolerance. Mortar joint thickness shall be within the following tolerances from the specified dimensions:

1. Bed joint: + $^1/_8$ inch (3 mm).

2. Head joint: $^1/_4$ inch (7 mm), + $^3/_8$ inch (10 mm).

3. Collar joints: $^1/_4$ inch (7 mm), + $^3/_8$ inch (10 mm).

Exception: Nonload-bearing masonry elements and masonry veneers designed and constructed in accordance with Section R703.7 are not required to meet these tolerances.

R607.2.2 Masonry unit placement. The mortar shall be sufficiently plastic and units shall be placed with sufficient pressure to extrude mortar from the joint and produce a tight joint. Deep furrowing of bed joints that produces voids shall not be permitted. Any units disturbed to the extent that initial bond is broken after initial placement shall be removed and relaid in fresh mortar. Surfaces to be in contact with mortar shall be clean and free of deleterious materials.

R607.2.2.1 Solid masonry. Solid masonry units shall be laid with full head and bed joints and all interior vertical joints that are designed to receive mortar shall be filled.

R607.2.2.2 Hollow masonry. For hollow masonry units, head and bed joints shall be filled solidly with mortar for a distance in from the face of the unit not less than the thickness of the face shell.

R607.3 Installation of wall ties. The installation of wall ties shall be as follows:

1. The ends of wall ties shall be embedded in mortar joints. Wall tie ends shall engage outer face shells of hollow units by at least $^1/_2$ inch (13 mm). Wire wall ties shall be embedded at least $1^1/_2$ inches (38 mm) into the mortar bed of solid masonry units or solid grouted hollow units.

2. Wall ties shall not be bent after being embedded in grout or mortar.

SECTION R608
MULTIPLE WYTHE MASONRY

R608.1 General. The facing and backing of multiple wythe masonry walls shall be bonded in accordance with Section R608.1.1, R608.1.2 or R608.1.3. In cavity walls, neither the facing nor the backing shall be less than 3 inches (76 mm) nominal in thickness and the cavity shall not be more than 4 inches (102 mm) nominal in width. The backing shall be at least as thick as the facing.

Exception: Cavities shall be permitted to exceed the 4-inch (102 mm) nominal dimension provided tie size and tie spacing have been established by calculation.

R608.1.1 Bonding with masonry headers. Bonding with solid or hollow masonry headers shall comply with Sections R608.1.1.1 and R608.1.1.2.

R608.1.1.1 Solid units. Where the facing and backing (adjacent wythes) of solid masonry construction are bonded by means of masonry headers, no less than 4 percent of the wall surface of each face shall be composed of headers extending not less than 3 inches (76 mm) into the backing. The distance between adjacent full-length headers shall not exceed 24 inches (610 mm) either vertically or horizontally. In walls in which a single header does not extend through the wall, headers from the opposite sides shall overlap at least 3 inches (76 mm), or headers from opposite sides shall be covered with another header course overlapping the header below at least 3 inches (76 mm).

R608.1.1.2 Hollow units. Where two or more hollow units are used to make up the thickness of a wall, the stretcher courses shall be bonded at vertical intervals not exceeding 34 inches (864 mm) by lapping at least 3 inches (76 mm) over the unit below, or by lapping at vertical intervals not exceeding 17 inches (432 mm) with units that are at least 50 percent thicker than the units below.

TABLE R607.1
MORTAR PROPORTIONS[a, b]

MORTAR	TYPE	Portland cement or blended cement	Mortar cement			Masonry cement			Hydrated lime[c] or lime putty	Aggregate ratio (measured in damp, loose conditions)
			M	S	N	M	S	N		
Cement-lime	M	1	—	—	—	—	—	—	$^1/_4$	
	S	1	—	—	—	—	—	—	over $^1/_4$ to $^1/_2$	
	N	1	—	—	—	—	—	—	over $^1/_2$ to $1^1/_4$	
	O	1	—	—	—	—	—	—	over $1^1/_4$ to $2^1/_2$	
Mortar cement	M	1	—	—	1	—	—	—	—	Not less than $2^1/_4$ and not more than 3 times the sum of separate volumes of lime, if used, and cement
	M	—	1	—	—	—	—	—		
	S	$^1/_2$	—	—	1	—	—	—		
	S	—	—	1	—	—	—	—		
	N	—	—	1	—	—	—	—		
	O	—	—	—	1	—	—	—		
Masonry cement	M	1				—	—	1	—	
	M	—				1	—	—		
	S	$^1/_2$				—	—	1		
	S	—				—	1	—		
	N	—				—	—	1		
	O	—				—	—	1		

For SI: 1 cubic foot = 0.0283 m³, 1 pound = 0.454 kg.

a. For the purpose of these specifications, the weight of 1 cubic foot of the respective materials shall be considered to be as follows:

Portland Cement	94 pounds	Masonry Cement	Weight printed on bag
Mortar Cement	Weight printed on bag	Hydrated Lime	40 pounds
Lime Putty (Quicklime)	80 pounds	Sand, damp and loose	80 pounds of dry sand

b. Two air-entraining materials shall not be combined in mortar.

c. Hydrated lime conforming to the requirements of ASTM C 207.

R608.1.2 Bonding with wall ties or joint reinforcement.
Bonding with wall ties or joint reinforcement shall comply with Sections R608.1.2.1 through R608.1.2.3.

R608.1.2.1 Bonding with wall ties. Bonding with wall ties, except as required by Section R610, where the facing and backing (adjacent wythes) of masonry walls are bonded with $^3/_{16}$-inch-diameter (5 mm) wall ties embedded in the horizontal mortar joints, there shall be at least one metal tie for each 4.5 square feet (0.418 m^2) of wall area. Ties in alternate courses shall be staggered. The maximum vertical distance between ties shall not exceed 24 inches (610 mm), and the maximum horizontal distance shall not exceed 36 inches (914 mm). Rods or ties bent to rectangular shape shall be used with hollow masonry units laid with the cells vertical. In other walls, the ends of ties shall be bent to 90-degree (0.79 rad) angles to provide hooks no less than 2 inches (51 mm) long. Additional bonding ties shall be provided at all openings, spaced not more than 3 feet (914 mm) apart around the perimeter and within 12 inches (305 mm) of the opening.

R608.1.2.2 Bonding with adjustable wall ties. Where the facing and backing (adjacent wythes) of masonry are bonded with adjustable wall ties, there shall be at least one tie for each 2.67 square feet (0.248 m^2) of wall area. Neither the vertical nor the horizontal spacing of the adjustable wall ties shall exceed 24 inches (610 mm). The maximum vertical offset of bed joints from one wythe to the other shall be 1.25 inches (32 mm). The maximum clearance between connecting parts of the ties shall be $^1/_{16}$ inch (2 mm). When pintle legs are used, ties shall have at least two $^3/_{16}$-inch-diameter (5 mm) legs.

R608.1.2.3 Bonding with prefabricated joint reinforcement. Where the facing and backing (adjacent wythes) of masonry are bonded with prefabricated joint reinforcement, there shall be at least one cross wire serving as a tie for each 2.67 square feet (0.248 m^2) of wall area. The vertical spacing of the joint reinforcement shall not exceed 16 inches (406 mm). Cross wires on prefabricated joint reinforcement shall not be smaller than No. 9 gage. The longitudinal wires shall be embedded in the mortar.

R608.1.3 Bonding with natural or cast stone. Bonding with natural and cast stone shall conform to Sections R608.1.3.1 and R608.1.3.2.

R608.1.3.1 Ashlar masonry. In ashlar masonry, bonder units, uniformly distributed, shall be provided to the extent of not less than 10 percent of the wall area. Such bonder units shall extend not less than 4 inches (102 mm) into the backing wall.

R608.1.3.2 Rubble stone masonry. Rubble stone masonry 24 inches (610 mm) or less in thickness shall have bonder units with a maximum spacing of 3 feet (914 mm) vertically and 3 feet (914 mm) horizontally, and if the masonry is of greater thickness than 24 inches (610 mm), shall have one bonder unit for each 6 square feet (0.557 m^2) of wall surface on both sides.

R608.2 Masonry bonding pattern. Masonry laid in running and stack bond shall conform to Sections R608.2.1 and R608.2.2.

R608.2.1 Masonry laid in running bond. In each wythe of masonry laid in running bond, head joints in successive courses shall be offset by not less than one-fourth the unit length, or the masonry walls shall be reinforced longitudinally as required in Section R608.2.2.

R608.2.2 Masonry laid in stack bond. Where unit masonry is laid with less head joint offset than in Section R607.2.1, the minimum area of horizontal reinforcement placed in mortar bed joints or in bond beams spaced not more than 48 inches (1219 mm) apart, shall be 0.0007 times the vertical cross-sectional area of the wall.

SECTION R609
GROUTED MASONRY

R609.1 General. Grouted multiple-wythe masonry is a form of construction in which the space between the wythes is solidly filled with grout. It is not necessary for the cores of masonry units to be filled with grout. Grouted hollow unit masonry is a form of construction in which certain cells of hollow units are continuously filled with grout.

R609.1.1 Grout. Grout shall consist of cementitious material and aggregate in accordance with ASTM C 476 and the proportion specifications of Table R609.1.1. Type M or Type S mortar to which sufficient water has been added to produce pouring consistency can be used as grout.

R609.1.2 Grouting requirements. Maximum pour heights and the minimum dimensions of spaces provided for grout placement shall conform to Table R609.1.2. If the work is stopped for one hour or longer, the horizontal construction joints shall be formed by stopping all tiers at the same elevation and with the grout 1 inch (25 mm) below the top.

TABLE R609.1.1
GROUT PROPORTIONS BY VOLUME FOR MASONRY CONSTRUCTION

TYPE	PORTLAND CEMENT OR BLENDED CEMENT SLAG CEMENT	HYDRATED LIME OR LIME PUTTY	AGGREGATE MEASURED IN A DAMP, LOOSE CONDITION	
			Fine	Coarse
Fine	1	0 to 1/10	$2^1/_4$ to 3 times the sum of the volume of the cementitious materials	—
Coarse	1	0 to 1/10	$2^1/_4$ to 3 times the sum of the volume of the cementitious materials	1 to 2 times the sum of the volumes of the cementitious materials

TABLE R609.1.2
GROUT SPACE DIMENSIONS AND POUR HEIGHTS

GROUT TYPE	GROUT POUR MAXIMUM HEIGHT (feet)	MINIMUM WIDTH OF GROUT SPACES[a,b] (inches)	MINIMUM GROUT[b,c] SPACE DIMENSIONS FOR GROUTING CELLS OF HOLLOW UNITS (inches x inches)
Fine	1	0.75	1.5×2
	5	2	2×3
	12	2.5	2.5×3
	24	3	3×3
Coarse	1	1.5	1.5×3
	5	2	2.5×3
	12	2.5	3×3
	24	3	3×4

For SI: 1 inch = 25.4 mm, 1 foot = 304.8 mm.

a. For grouting between masonry wythes.

b. Grout space dimension is the clear dimension between any masonry protrusion and shall be increased by the horizontal projection of the diameters of the horizontal bars within the cross section of the grout space.

c. Area of vertical reinforcement shall not exceed 6 percent of the area of the grout space.

R609.1.3 Grout space (cleaning). Provision shall be made for cleaning grout space. Mortar projections that project more than 0.5 inch (13 mm) into grout space and any other foreign matter shall be removed from grout space prior to inspection and grouting.

R609.1.4 Grout placement. Grout shall be a plastic mix suitable for pumping without segregation of the constituents and shall be mixed thoroughly. Grout shall be placed by pumping or by an approved alternate method and shall be placed before any initial set occurs and in no case more than $1^1/_2$ hours after water has been added. Grouting shall be done in a continuous pour, in lifts not exceeding 5 feet (1524 mm). It shall be consolidated by puddling or mechanical vibrating during placing and reconsolidated after excess moisture has been absorbed but before plasticity is lost.

R609.1.4.1 Grout pumped through aluminum pipes. Grout shall not be pumped through aluminum pipes.

R609.1.5 Cleanouts. Where required by the building official, cleanouts shall be provided as specified in this section. The cleanouts shall be sealed before grouting and after inspection.

R609.1.5.1 Grouted multiple-wythe masonry. Cleanouts shall be provided at the bottom course of the exterior wythe at each pour of grout where such pour exceeds 5 feet (1524 mm) in height.

R609.1.5.2 Grouted hollow unit masonry. Cleanouts shall be provided at the bottom course of each cell to be grouted at each pour of grout, where such pour exceeds 4 feet (1219 mm) in height.

R609.2 Grouted multiple-wythe masonry. Grouted multiple-wythe masonry shall conform to all the requirements specified in Section R609.1 and the requirements of this section.

R609.2.1 Bonding of backup wythe. Where all interior vertical spaces are filled with grout in multiple-wythe construction, masonry headers shall not be permitted. Metal wall ties shall be used in accordance with Section R608.1.2

to prevent spreading of the wythes and to maintain the vertical alignment of the wall. Wall ties shall be installed in accordance with Section R608.1.2 when the backup wythe in multiple-wythe construction is fully grouted.

R609.2.2 Grout spaces. Fine grout shall be used when interior vertical space to receive grout does not exceed 2 inches (51 mm) in thickness. Interior vertical spaces exceeding 2 inches (51 mm) in thickness shall use coarse or fine grout.

R609.2.3 Grout barriers. Vertical grout barriers or dams shall be built of solid masonry across the grout space the entire height of the wall to control the flow of the grout horizontally. Grout barriers shall not be more than 25 feet (7620 mm) apart. The grouting of any section of a wall between control barriers shall be completed in one day with no interruptions greater than one hour.

R609.3 Reinforced grouted multiple-wythe masonry. Reinforced grouted multiple-wythe masonry shall conform to all the requirements specified in Sections R609.1 and R609.2 and the requirements of this section.

R609.3.1 Construction. The thickness of grout or mortar between masonry units and reinforcement shall not be less than $1/_4$ inch (7 mm), except that $1/_4$-inch (7 mm) bars may be laid in horizontal mortar joints at least $1/_2$ inch (13 mm) thick, and steel wire reinforcement may be laid in horizontal mortar joints at least twice the thickness of the wire diameter.

R609.4 Reinforced hollow unit masonry. Reinforced hollow unit masonry shall conform to all the requirements of Section R609.1 and the requirements of this section.

R609.4.1 Construction. Requirements for construction shall be as follows:

1. Reinforced hollow-unit masonry shall be built to preserve the unobstructed vertical continuity of the cells to be filled. Walls and cross webs forming cells to be filled shall be full-bedded in mortar to prevent leakage of grout. Head and end joints shall be solidly filled

with mortar for a distance in from the face of the wall or unit not less than the thickness of the longitudinal face shells. Bond shall be provided by lapping units in successive vertical courses.

2. Cells to be filled shall have vertical alignment sufficient to maintain a clear, unobstructed continuous vertical cell of dimensions prescribed in Table R609.1.2.

3. Vertical reinforcement shall be held in position at top and bottom and at intervals not exceeding 200 diameters of the reinforcement.

4. Cells containing reinforcement shall be filled solidly with grout. Grout shall be poured in lifts of 8-foot (2438 mm) maximum height. When a total grout pour exceeds 8 feet (2438 mm) in height, the grout shall be placed in lifts not exceeding 5 feet (1524 mm) and special inspection during grouting shall be required.

5. Horizontal steel shall be fully embedded by grout in an uninterrupted pour.

SECTION R610
GLASS UNIT MASONRY

R610.1 General. Panels of glass unit masonry located in load-bearing and nonload-bearing exterior and interior walls shall be constructed in accordance with this section.

R610.2 Materials. Hollow glass units shall be partially evacuated and have a minimum average glass face thickness of $3/_{16}$ inch (5 mm). The surface of units in contact with mortar shall be treated with a polyvinyl butyral coating or latex-based paint. The use of reclaimed units is prohibited.

R610.3 Units. Hollow or solid glass block units shall be standard or thin units.

R610.3.1 Standard units. The specified thickness of standard units shall be at least $3^7/_8$ inches (98 mm).

R610.3.2 Thin units. The specified thickness of thin units shall be at least $3^1/_8$ inches (79 mm) for hollow units and at least 3 inches (76 mm) for solid units.

R610.4 Isolated panels. Isolated panels of glass unit masonry shall conform to the requirements of this section.

R610.4.1 Exterior standard-unit panels. The maximum area of each individual standard-unit panel shall be 144 square feet (13.4 m^2) when the design wind pressure is 20 psf (958 Pa). The maximum area of such panels subjected to design wind pressures other than 20 psf (958 Pa) shall be in accordance with Figure R610.4.1. The maximum panel dimension between structural supports shall be 25 feet (7620 mm) in width or 20 feet (6096 mm) in height.

R610.4.2 Exterior thin-unit panels. The maximum area of each individual thin-unit panel shall be 85 square feet (7.9 m^2). The maximum dimension between structural supports shall be 15 feet (4572 mm) in width or 10 feet (3048 mm) in height. Thin units shall not be used in applications where the design wind pressure as stated in Table R301.2(1) exceeds 20 psf (958 Pa).

R610.4.3 Interior panels. The maximum area of each individual standard-unit panel shall be 250 square feet (23.2 m^2). The maximum area of each thin-unit panel shall be 150 square feet (13.9 m^2). The maximum dimension between structural supports shall be 25 feet (7620 mm) in width or 20 feet (6096 mm) in height.

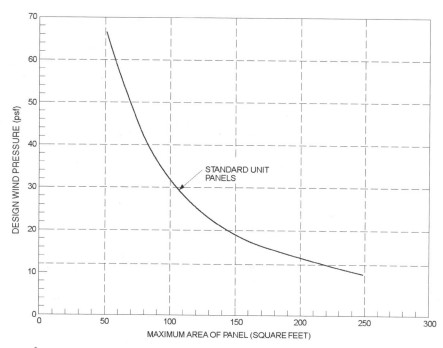

For SI: 1 square foot = 0.0929 m^2, 1 pound per square foot = 0.0479 kPa.

FIGURE R610.4.1
GLASS UNIT MASONRY DESIGN WIND LOAD RESISTANCE

R610.4.4 Curved panels. The width of curved panels shall conform to the requirements of Sections R610.4.1, R610.4.2 and R610.4.3, except additional structural supports shall be provided at locations where a curved section joins a straight section, and at inflection points in multicurved walls.

R610.5 Panel support. Glass unit masonry panels shall conform to the support requirements of this section.

R610.5.1 Deflection. The maximum total deflection of structural members that support glass unit masonry shall not exceed $^1/_{600}$.

R610.5.2 Lateral support. Glass unit masonry panels shall be laterally supported along the top and sides of the panel. Lateral supports for glass unit masonry panels shall be designed to resist a minimum of 200 pounds per lineal feet (2918 N/m) of panel, or the actual applied loads, whichever is greater. Except for single unit panels, lateral support shall be provided by panel anchors along the top and sides spaced a maximum of 16 inches (406 mm) on center or by channel-type restraints. Single unit panels shall be supported by channel-type restraints.

Exceptions:

1. Lateral support is not required at the top of panels that are one unit wide.

2. Lateral support is not required at the sides of panels that are one unit high.

R610.5.2.1 Panel anchor restraints. Panel anchors shall be spaced a maximum of 16 inches (406 mm) on center in both jambs and across the head. Panel anchors shall be embedded a minimum of 12 inches (305 mm) and shall be provided with two fasteners so as to resist the loads specified in Section R610.5.2.

R610.5.2.2 Channel-type restraints. Glass unit masonry panels shall be recessed at least 1 inch (25 mm) within channels and chases. Channel-type restraints shall be oversized to accommodate expansion material in the opening, packing and sealant between the framing restraints, and the glass unit masonry perimeter units.

R610.6 Sills. Before bedding of glass units, the sill area shall be covered with a water base asphaltic emulsion coating. The coating shall shall be a minimum of $^1/_8$ inch (3 mm) thick.

R610.7 Expansion joints. Glass unit masonry panels shall be provided with expansion joints along the top and sides at all structural supports. Expansion joints shall be a minimum of $^3/_8$ inch (10 mm) in thickness and shall have sufficient thickness to accommodate displacements of the supporting structure. Expansion joints shall be entirely free of mortar and other debris and shall be filled with resilient material.

R610.8 Mortar. Glass unit masonry shall be laid with Type S or N mortar. Mortar shall not be retempered after initial set. Mortar unused within $1^1/_2$ hours after initial mixing shall be discarded.

R610.9 Reinforcement. Glass unit masonry panels shall have horizontal joint reinforcement spaced a maximum of 16 inches (406 mm) on center located in the mortar bed joint. Horizontal joint reinforcement shall extend the entire length of the panel but shall not extend across expansion joints. Longitudinal wires shall be lapped a minimum of 6 inches (152 mm) at splices. Joint reinforcement shall be placed in the bed joint immediately below and above openings in the panel. The reinforcement shall have not less than two parallel longitudinal wires of size W1.7 or greater, and have welded cross wires of size W1.7 or greater.

R610.10 Placement. Glass units shall be placed so head and bed joints are filled solidly. Mortar shall not be furrowed. Head and bed joints of glass unit masonry shall be $^1/_4$ inch (6.4 mm) thick, except that vertical joint thickness of radial panels shall not be less than $^1/_8$ inch (3 mm) or greater than $^5/_8$ inch (16 mm). The bed joint thickness tolerance shall be minus $^1/_{16}$ inch (1.6 mm) and plus $^1/_8$ inch (3 mm). The head joint thickness tolerance shall be plus or minus $^1/_8$ inch (3 mm).

SECTION R611
INSULATING CONCRETE FORM
WALL CONSTRUCTION

R611.1 General. Insulating Concrete Form (IFC) walls shall be designed and constructed in accordance with the provisions of this section or in accordance with the provisions of ACI 318. When ACI 318 or the provisions of this section are used to design insulating concrete form walls, project drawings, typical details and specifications are not required to bear the seal of the architect or engineer responsible for design, unless otherwise required by the state law of the jurisdiction having authority.

R611.2 Applicability limits. The provisions of this section shall apply to the construction of insulating concrete form walls for buildings not greater than 60 feet (18 288 mm) in plan dimensions, and floors not greater than 32 feet (9754 mm) or roofs not greater than 40 feet (12 192 mm) in clear span. Buildings shall not exceed two stories in height above-grade. ICF walls shall comply with the requirements in Table R611.2. Walls constructed in accordance with the provisions of this section shall be limited to buildings subjected to a maximum design wind speed of 150 miles per hour (67 m/s), and Seismic Design Categories A, B, C, D_0, D_1 and D_2. The provisions of this section shall not apply to the construction of ICF walls for buildings or portions of buildings considered irregular as defined in Section R301.2.2.2.2.

For townhouses in Seismic Design Category C and all buildings in Seismic Design Category D_0, D_1 or D_2, the provisions of this section shall apply only to buildings meeting the following requirements.

1. Rectangular buildings with a maximum building aspect ratio of 2:1. The building aspect ratio shall be determined by dividing the longest dimension of the building by the shortest dimension of the building.

2. Walls are aligned vertically with the walls below.

3. Cantilever and setback construction shall not be permitted.

4. The weight of interior and exterior finishes applied to ICF walls shall not exceed 8 psf (380 Pa).

5. The gable portion of ICF walls shall be constructed of light-frame construction.

R611.3 Flat insulating concrete form wall systems. Flat ICF wall systems shall comply with Figure R611.3 and shall have reinforcement in accordance with Tables R611.3(1) and R611.3(2) and Section R611.7.

R611.4 Waffle-grid insulating concrete form wall systems. Waffle-grid wall systems shall comply with Figure R611.4 and shall have reinforcement in accordance with Tables R611.3(1) and R611.4(1) and Section R611.7. The minimum core dimensions shall comply with Table R611.2.

R611.5 Screen-grid insulating concrete form wall systems. Screen-grid ICF wall systems shall comply with Figure R611.5 and shall have reinforcement in accordance with Tables

R611.3(1) and R611.5 and Section R611.7. The minimum core dimensions shall comply with Table R611.2.

R611.6 Material. Insulating concrete form wall materials shall comply with this section.

R611.6.1 Concrete material. Ready-mixed concrete for insulating concrete form walls shall be in accordance with Section R402.2. Maximum slump shall not be greater than 6 inches (152 mm) as determined in accordance with ASTM C 143. Maximum aggregate size shall not be larger than $3/4$ inch (19 mm).

Exception: Concrete mixes conforming to the ICF manufacturer's recommendations.

In Seismic Design Categories D_0, D_1 and D_2, the minimum concrete compressive strength shall be 3,000 psi (20.5 MPa).

TABLE R611.2
REQUIREMENTS FOR ICF WALLS[b]

WALL TYPE AND NOMINAL SIZE	MAXIMUM WALL WEIGHT (psf)[c]	MINIMUM WIDTH OF VERTICAL CORE (inches)[a]	MINIMUM THICKNESS OF VERTICAL CORE (inches)[a]	MAXIMUM SPACING OF VERTICAL CORES (inches)	MAXIMUM SPACING OF HORIZONTAL CORES (inches)	MINIMUM WEB THICKNESS (inches)
3.5″ Flat[d]	44[d]	N/A	N/A	N/A	N/A	N/A
5.5″ Flat	69	N/A	N/A	N/A	N/A	N/A
7.5″ Flat	94	N/A	N/A	N/A	N/A	N/A
9.5″ Flat	119	N/A	N/A	N/A	N/A	N/A
6″ Waffle-Grid	56	6.25	5	12	16	2
8″ Waffle-Grid	76	7	7	12	16	2
6″ Screen-Grid	53	5.5	5.5	12	12	N/A

For SI: 1 inch = 25.4 mm; 1 pound per cubic foot = 16.018 kg/m³; 1 pound per square foot = 0.0479 kPa.

a. For width "W", thickness "T", spacing, and web thickness, refer to Figures R611.4 and R611.5.

b. N/A indicates not applicable.

c. Wall weight is based on a unit weight of concrete of 150 pcf. The tabulated values do not include any allowance for interior and exterior finishes.

d. For all buildings in Seismic Design Category A or B, and detached one- and two-family dwellings in Seismic Design Category C the actual wall thickness is permitted to be up to 1 inch thicker than shown and the maximum wall weight to be 56 psf. Construction requirements and other limitations within Section R611 for 3.5-inch flat ICF walls shall apply. Interpolation between provisions for 3.5-inch and 5.5-inch flat ICF walls is not permitted.

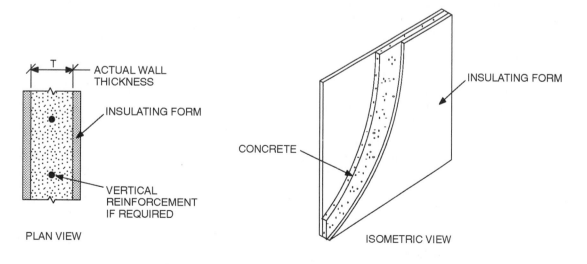

FIGURE R611.3
FLAT ICF WALL SYSTEM

WIND SPEED (mph)[e]	DESIGN WIND PRESSURE (psf)					
	Enclosed[b]			Partially Enclosed[b]		
	Exposure[c]			Exposure[c]		
	B	C	D	B	C	D
85	18	24	29	23	31	37
90	20	27	32	25	35	41
100	24	34	39	31	43	51
110	29	41	48	38	52	61
120	35	48	57	45	62	73
130	41	56	66	53	73	85[d]
140	47	65	77	61	84[d]	99[d]
150	54	75	88[d]	70	96[d]	114[d]

For SI: 1 pound per square foot = 0.0479 kPa; 1 mile per hour = 0.447 m/s; 1 foot = 304.8 mm; 1 square foot = 0.0929 m².

a. This table is based on ASCE 7-98 components and cladding wind pressures using a mean roof height of 35 ft and a tributary area of 10 ft².

b. Buildings in wind-borne debris regions as defined in Section R202 shall be considered as "Partially Enclosed" unless glazed openings are protected in accordance with Section R301.2.1.2, in which case the building shall be considered as "Enclosed." All other buildings shall be classified as "Enclosed."

c. Exposure Categories shall be determined in accordance with Section R301.2.1.4.

d. For wind pressures greater than 80 psf, design is required in accordance with ACI 318 and approved manufacturer guidelines.

e. Interpolation is permitted between wind speeds.

R611.6.2 Reinforcing steel. Reinforcing steel shall meet the requirements of ASTM A 615, A 706, or A 996. Except in Seismic Design Categories D_0, D_1 and D_2, the minimum yield strength of reinforcing steel shall be 40,000 psi (Grade 40) (276 MPa). In Seismic Design Categories D_0, D_1 and D_2, reinforcing steel shall meet the requirements of ASTM A 706 for low-alloy steel with a minimum yield strength of 60,000 psi (Grade 60) (414 Mpa).

R611.6.3 Insulation materials. Insulating concrete forms material shall meet the surface burning characteristics of Section R314.3. A thermal barrier shall be provided on the building interior in accordance with Section R314.4 or Section R702.3.4.

R611.7 Wall construction. Insulating concrete form walls shall be constructed in accordance with the provisions of this section and Figure R611.7(1).

R611.7.1 Reinforcement.

R611.7.1.1 Location. Vertical and horizontal wall reinforcement shall be placed within the middle third of the wall. Steel reinforcement shall have a minimum concrete cover in accordance with ACI 318.

Exception: Where insulated concrete forms are used and the form remains in place as cover for the concrete, the minimum concrete cover for the reinforcing steel is permitted to be reduced to $^3/_4$ inch (19 mm).

R611.7.1.2 Vertical steel. Above-grade concrete walls shall have reinforcement in accordance with Sections R611.3, R611.4, or R611.5 and R611.7.2. Where the design wind pressure exceeds 40 psf (1.92 kPa) in accordance with Table R611.3(1) or for townhouses in Seismic Design Category C and all buildings in Seismic Design Categories D_0, D_1 and D_2, vertical wall reinforcement in

the top-most ICF story shall terminate with a 90-degree (1.57 rad) standard hook in accordance with Section R611.7.1.5. The free end of the hook shall be within 4 inches (102 mm) of the top of the ICF wall and shall be oriented parallel to the horizontal steel in the top of the wall.

For townhouses in Seismic Design Category C, the minimum vertical reinforcement shall be one No. 5 bar at 24 inches (610 mm) on center or one No. 4 at 16 inches (407 mm) on center. For all buildings in Seismic Design Categories D_0, D_1 and D_2, the minimum vertical reinforcement shall be one No. 5 bar at 18 inches (457 mm) on center or one No. 4 at 12 inches (305 mm) on center.

Above-grade ICF walls shall be supported on concrete foundations reinforced as required for the above-grade wall immediately above, or in accordance with Tables R404.4(1) through R404.4(5), whichever requires the greater amount of reinforcement.

Vertical reinforcement shall be continuous from the bottom of the foundation wall to the roof. Lap splices, if required, shall comply with Section R611.7.1.4. Where vertical reinforcement in the above-grade wall is not continuous with the foundation wall reinforcement, dowel bars with a size and spacing to match the vertical ICF wall reinforcement shall be embedded 40 d_b into the foundation wall and shall be lap spliced with the above-grade wall reinforcement. Alternatively, for No. 6 and larger bars, the portion of the bar embedded in the foundation wall shall be embedded 24 inches in the foundation wall and shall have a standard hook.

R611.7.1.3 Horizontal reinforcement. Concrete walls with a minimum thickness of 4 inches (102 mm) shall have a minimum of one continuous No. 4 horizontal reinforcing bar placed at 32 inches (812 mm) on center with one bar within 12 inches (305 mm) of the top of the wall story. Concrete walls 5.5 inches (140 mm) thick or more shall have a minimum of one continuous No. 4 horizontal reinforcing bar placed at 48 inches (1219 mm) on center with one bar located within 12 inches (305 mm) of the top of the wall story.

For townhouses in Seismic Design Category C, the minimum horizontal reinforcement shall be one No. 5 bar at 24 inches (610 mm) on center or one No. 4 at 16 inches (407 mm) on center. For all buildings in Seismic Design Categories D_0, D_1 and D_2, the minimum horizon-

tal reinforcement shall be one No. 5 bar at 18 inches (457 mm) on center or one No. 4 at 12 inches (305 mm) on center.

Horizontal reinforcement shall be continuous around building corners using corner bars or by bending the bars. In either case, the minimum lap splice shall be 24 inches (610 mm). For townhouses in Seismic Design Category C and for all buildings in Seismic Design Categories D_0, D_1 and D_2, each end of all horizontal reinforcement shall terminate with a standard hook or lap splice.

TABLE R611.3(2)
MINIMUM VERTICAL WALL REINFORCEMENT FOR FLAT ICF ABOVE-GRADE WALLS[a, b, c, d]

Design Wind Pressure [Table R611.3(1)] (psf)	Maximum Unsupported Wall Height (feet)	Minimum Vertical Reinforcement[d, e, f]					
		Nonload-Bearing Wall or Supporting Roof		Supporting Light-Framed Second Story and Roof		Supporting ICF Second Story and Roof	
		Minimum Wall Thickness (inches)					
		3.5[g]	5.5	3.5[g]	5.5	3.5[g]	5.5
20	8	#4@48	#4@48	#4@48	#4@48	#4@48	#4@48
	9	#4@48	#4@48	#4@48	#4@48	#4@48	#4@48
	10	#4@38	#4@48	#4@40	#4@48	#4@42	#4@48
30	8	#4@42	#4@48	#4@46	#4@48	#4@48	#4@48
	9	#4@32; #5@48	#4@48	#4@34; #5@48	#4@48	#4@34; #5@48	#4@48
	10	Design Required	#4@48	Design Required	#4@48	Design Required	#4@48
40	8	#4@30; #5@48	#4@48	#4@30; #5@48	#4@48	#4@32; #5@48	#4@48
	9	Design Required	#4@42	Design Required	#4@46	Design Required	#4@48
	10	Design Required	#4@32; #5@48	Design Required	#4@34; #5@48	Design Required	#4@38
50	8	#4@20; #5@30	#4@42	#4@22; #5@34	#4@46	#4@24; #5@36	#4@48
	9	Design Required	#4@34; #5@48	Design Required	#4@34; #5@48	Design Required	#4@38
	10	Design Required	#4@26; #5@38	Design Required	#4@26; #5@38	Design Required	#4@28; #5@46
60	8	Design Required	#4@34; #5@48	Design Required	#4@36	Design Required	#4@40
	9	Design Required	#4@26; #5@38	Design Required	#4@28; #5@46	Design Required	#4@34; #5@48
	10	Design Required	#4@22; #5@34	Design Required	#4@22; #5@34	Design Required	#4@26; #5@38
70	8	Design Required	#4@28; #5@46	Design Required	#4@30; #5@48	Design Required	#4@34; #5@48
	9	Design Required	#4@22; #5@34	Design Required	#4@22; #5@34	Design Required	#4@24; #5@36
	10	Design Required	#4@16; #5@26	Design Required	#4@18; #5@28	Design Required	#4@20; #5@30
80	8	Design Required	#4@26; #5@38	Design Required	#4@26; #5@38	Design Required	#4@28; #5@46
	9	Design Required	#4@20; #5@30	Design Required	#4@20; #5@30	Design Required	#4@21; #5@34
	10	Design Required	#4@14; #5@24	Design Required	#4@14; #5@24	Design Required	#4@16; #5@26

For SI: 1 inch = 25.4 mm; 1 foot = 304.8 mm; 1 mile per hour = 0.447 m/s; 1 pound per square inch = 6.895 kPa.

a. This table is based on reinforcing bars with a minimum yield strength of 40,000 psi and concrete with a minimum specified compressive strength of 2,500 psi. For Seismic Design Categories D_0, D_1 and D_2, reinforcing bars shall have a minimum yield strength of 60,000 psi. See Section R611.6.2.

b. Deflection criterion is $L/240$, where L is the height of the wall story in inches.

c. Interpolation shall not be permitted.

d. Reinforcement spacing for 3.5 inch walls shall be permitted to be multiplied by 1.6 when reinforcing steel with a minimum yield strength of 60,000 psi is used. Reinforcement shall not be less than one #4 bar at 48 inches (1.2 m) on center.

e. Reinforcement spacing for 5.5 inch (139.7 mm) walls shall be permitted to be multiplied by 1.5 when reinforcing steel with a minimum yield strength of 60,000 psi is used. Reinforcement shall not be less than one #4 bar at 48 inches on center.

f. See Section R611.7.1.2 for limitations on maximum spacing of vertical reinforcement in Seismic Design Categories C, D_0, D_1 and D_2.

g. A 3.5-inch wall shall not be permitted if wood ledgers are used to support floor or roof loads. See Section R611.8.

TABLE R611.4(1)
MINIMUM VERTICAL WALL REINFORCEMENT FOR WAFFLE-GRID ICF ABOVE-GRADE WALLS[a, b, c]

Design Wind Pressure [Table R611.3(1)] (psf)	Maximum Unsupported Wall Height (feet)	Nonload-Bearing Wall or Supporting Roof		Supporting Light-Framed Second Story and Roof		Supporting ICF Second Story and Roof	
		6	8	6	8	6	8
20	8	#4@48	#4@48	#4@48	#4@48	#4@48	#4@48
	9	#4@48	#4@48	#4@48	#4@48	#4@48	#4@48
	10	#4@48	#4@48	#4@48	#4@48	#4@48	#4@48
30	8	#4@48	#4@48	#4@48	#4@48	#4@48	#4@48
	9	#4@48	#4@48	#4@48	#4@48	#4@48	#4@48
	10	#4@36; #5@48	#4@48	#4@36; #5@48	#4@48	#4@36; #5@48	#4@48
40	8	#4@36; #5@48	#4@48	#4@48	#4@48	#4@48	#4@48
	9	#4@36; #5@48	#4@48	#4@36; #5@48	#4@48	#4@36; #5@48	#4@48
	10	#4@24; #5@36	#4@36; #5@48	#4@24; #5@36	#4@48	#4@24; #5@36	#4@48
50	8	#4@36; #5@48	#4@48	#4@36; #5@48	#4@48	#4@36; #5@48	#4@48
	9	#4@24; #5@36	#4@36; #5@48	#4@24; #5@36	#4@48	#4@24; #5@48	#4@48
	10	Design Required	#4@36; #5@48	Design Required	#4@36; #5@48	Design Required	#4@36; #5@48
60	8	#4@24; #5@36	#4@48	#4@24; #5@36	#4@48	#4@24; #5@48	#4@48
	9	Design Required	#4@36; #5@48	Design Required	#4@36; #5@48	Design Required	#4@36; #5@48
	10	Design Required	#4@24; #5@36	Design Required	#4@24; #5@36	Design Required	#4@24; #5@48
70	8	#4@24; #5@36	#4@36; #5@48	#4@24; #5@36	#4@36; #5@48	#4@24; #5@36	#4@48
	9	Design Required	#4@24; #5@36	Design Required	#4@24; #5@48	Design Required	#4@24; #5@48
	10	Design Required	#4@12; #5@36	Design Required	#4@24; #5@36	Design Required	#4@24; #5@36
80	8	#4@12; #5@24	#4@24; #5@48	#4@12; #5@24	#4@24; #5@48	#4@12; #5@24	#4@36; #5@48
	9	Design Required	#4@24; #5@36	Design Required	#4@24; #5@36	Design Required	#4@24; #5@36
	10	Design Required	#4@12; #5@24	Design Required	#4@12; #5@24	Design Required	#4@12; #5@24

For SI: 1 foot = 304.8 mm; 1 inch = 25.4 mm; 1 mile per hour = 0.447 m/s; 1 pound per square inch = 6.895 MPa.

a. This table is based on reinforcing bars with a minimum yield strength of 40,000 psi and concrete with a minimum specified compressive strength of 2,500 psi. For Seismic Design Categories D_0, D_1 and D_2, reinforcing bars shall have a minimum yield strength of 60,000 psi. See Section R611.6.2.

b. Deflection criterion is $L/240$, where L is the height of the wall story in inches.

c. Interpolation shall not be permitted.

d. Increasing reinforcement spacing by 12 inches shall be permitted when reinforcing steel with a minimum yield strength of 60,000 psi is used or substitution of No. 4 reinforcing bars for #5 bars shall be permitted when reinforcing steel with a minimum yield strength of 60,000 psi is used at the same spacing required for #5 bars. Reinforcement shall not be less than one #4 bar at 48 inches on center.

e. See Section R611.7.1.2 for limitations on maximum spacing of vertical reinforcement in Seismic Design Categories C, D_0, D_1 and D_2.

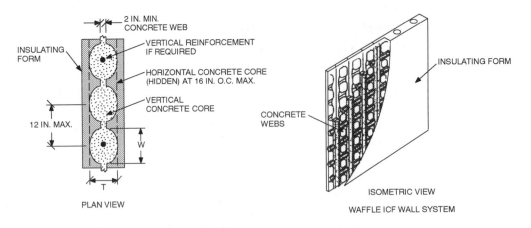

PLAN VIEW

ISOMETRIC VIEW
WAFFLE ICF WALL SYSTEM

FIGURE R611.4
WAFFLE-GRID ICF WALL SYSTEM

TABLE R611.5
MINIMUM VERTICAL WALL REINFORCEMENT FOR SCREEN-GRID ICF ABOVE-GRADE WALLS[a, b, c]

DESIGN WIND PRESSURE [TABLE R611.3(1)] (psf)	MAXIMUM UNSUPPORTED WALL HEIGHT (feet)	MINIMUM VERTICAL REINFORCEMENT[d,e]		
		Nonload-Bearing Wall or Supporting Roof	Supporting Light-Framed Second Story and Roof	Supporting ICF Second Story and Roof
20	8	#4@48	#4@48	#4@48
	9	#4@48	#4@48	#4@48
	10	#4@48	#4@48	#4@48
30	8	#4@48	#4@48	#4@48
	9	#4@48	#4@48	#4@48
	10	#4@36; #5@48	#4@48	#4@48
40	8	#4@48	#4@48	#4@48
	9	#4@36; #5@48	#4@36; #5@48	#4@48
	10	#4@24; #5@48	#4@24; #5@48	#4@24; #5@48
50	8	#4@36; #5@48	#4@36; #5@48	#4@48
	9	#4@24; #5@48	#4@24; #5@48	#4@24; #5@48
	10	Design Required	Design Required	Design Required
60	8	#4@24; #5@48	#4@24; #5@48	#4@36; #5@48
	9	#4@24; #5@36	#4@24; #5@36	#4@24; #5@36
	10	Design Required	Design Required	Design Required
70	8	#4@24; #5@36	#4@24; #5@36	#4@24; #5@36
	9	Design Required	Design Required	Design Required
	10	Design Required	Design Required	Design Required
080	8	#4@12; #5@36	#4@24; #5@36	#4@24; #5@36
	9	Design Required	Design Required	Design Required
	10	Design Required	Design Required	Design Required

For SI: 1 inch = 25.4 mm, 1 foot = 304.8 mm, 1 mile per hour = 0.447 m/s; 1 pound per square inch = 6.895 kPa.

a. This table is based on reinforcing bars with a minimum yield strength of 40,000 psi and concrete with a minimum specified compressive strength of 2,500 psi. For Seismic Design Categories D_0, D_1 and D_2, reinforcing bars shall have a minimum yield strength of 60,000 psi. See Section R611.6.2.

b. Deflection criterion is $L/240$, where L is the height of the wall story in inches.

c. Interpolation shall not be permitted.

d. Increasing reinforcement spacing by 12 inches shall be permitted when reinforcing steel with a minimum yield strength of 60,000 psi is used. Reinforcement shall not be less than one #4 bar at 48 inches on center.

e. See Section R611.7.1.2 for limitations on maximum spacing of vertical reinforcement in Seismic Design Categories C, D_0, D_1 and D_2.

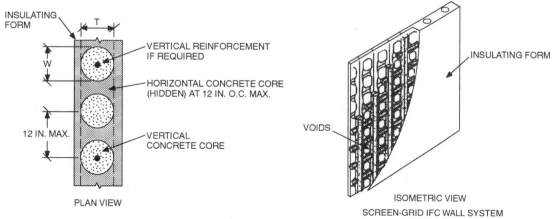

For SI: 1 inch = 25.4 mm.

FIGURE R611.5
SCREEN-GRID IFC WALL SYSTEM

TABLE R611.7(1)
MINIMUM WALL OPENING REINFORCEMENT REQUIREMENTS IN ICF WALLS[a]

WALL TYPE AND OPENING WIDTH (L) (feet)	MINIMUM HORIZONTAL OPENING REINFORCEMENT	MINIMUM VERTICAL OPENING REINFORCEMENT
Flat, Waffle-, and Screen-Grid: $L < 2$	None required	None required
Flat, Waffle-, and Screen-Grid: $L \geq 2$	Provide lintels in accordance with Section R611.7.3. Provide one No. 4 bar within 12 inches from the bottom of the opening. Top and bottom lintel reinforcement shall extend a minimum of 24 inches beyond the limits of the opening.	In locations with wind speeds less than or equal to 110 mph or in Seismic Design Categories A and B, provide one No. 4 bar for the full height of the wall story within 12 inches of each side of the opening. In locations with wind speeds greater than 110 mph, townhouses in Seismic Design Category C, or all buildings in Seismic Design Categories D_0, D_1 and D_2, provide two No. 4 bars or one No. 5 bar for the full height of the wall story within 12 inches of each side of the opening.

For SI: 1 inch = 25.4 mm, 1 foot = 304.8 mm, 1 mile per hour = 0.447 m/s; 1 pound per square inch = 6.895 kPa.

a. This table is based on concrete with a minimum specified compressive strength of 2,500 psi, reinforcing steel with a minimum yield strength of 40,000 psi and an assumed equivalent rectangular cross section. This table is not intended to prohibit the use of ICF manufacturer's tables based on engineering analysis in accordance with ACI 318.

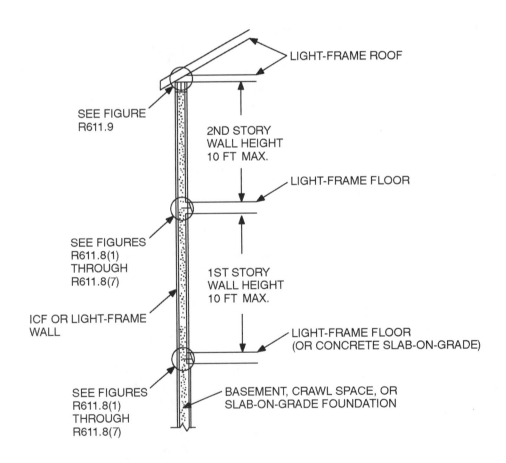

For SI: 1 foot = 304.8 mm.
NOTE: Section cut through flat wall or vertical core of waffle- or screen-grid walls.

FIGURE R611.7(1)
ICF WALL CONSTRUCTION

TABLE R611.7(2)
MAXIMUM ALLOWABLE CLEAR SPANS FOR ICF LINTELS FOR FLAT LOAD-BEARING WALLS[a, b, c, d, f]
NO. 4 BOTTOM BAR SIZE

MINIMUM LINTEL THICKNESS, T (inches)	LINTEL DEPTH, D (inches)	MAXIMUM CLEAR SPAN, (feet-inches) (Number is Middle of Span, A)[e]					
		Supporting Roof Only		Supporting Light-Framed 2nd Story and Roof		Supporting ICF Second Story and Roof	
		Ground Snow Load					
		30 psf	70 psf	30 psf	70 psf	30 psf	70 psf
3.5	8	4-9 (1-2)	4-2 (0-9)	3-10 (0-8)	3-4 (0-6)	3-5 (0-6)	3-1 (0-5)
	12	6-8 (1-11)	5-5 (1-3)	5-0 (1-1)	4-5 (0-10)	4-6 (0-10)	4-0 (0-8)
	16	7-11 (2-9)	6-5 (1-9)	6-0 (1-6)	5-3 (1-2)	5-4 (1-2)	4-10 (1-0)
	20	8-11 (3-5)	7-4 (2-3)	6-9 (1-11)	6-0 (1-6)	6-1 (1-7)	5-6 (1-3)
	24	9-10 (4-1)	8-1 (2-9)	7-6 (2-4)	6-7 (1-10)	6-9 (1-11)	6-1 (1-6)
5.5	8	5-2 (1-10)	4-2 (1-2)	3-10 (1-0)	3-5 (0-9)	3-5 (0-10)	3-1 (0-8)
	12	6-8 (3-0)	5-5 (2-0)	5-0 (1-9)	4-5 (1-4)	4-6 (1-4)	4-1 (1-1)
	16	7-10 (4-1)	6-5 (2-9)	6-0 (2-5)	5-3 (1-10)	5-4 (1-11)	4-10 (1-7)
	20	8-10 (5-3)	7-3 (3-6)	6-9 (3-1)	6-0 (2-4)	6-1 (2-5)	5-6 (2-0)
	24	9-8 (6-3)	8-0 (4-3)	7-5 (3-8)	6-7 (2-11)	6-8 (3-0)	6-0 (2-5)
7.5	8	5-2 (2-6)	4-2 (1-8)	3-11 (1-5)	3-5 (1-1)	3-6 (1-1)	3-2 (0-11)
	12	6-7 (4-0)	5-5 (2-8)	5-0 (2-4)	4-5 (1-10)	4-6 (1-10)	4-1 (1-6)
	16	7-9 (5-5)	6-5 (3-8)	5-11 (3-3)	5-3 (2-6)	5-4 (2-7)	4-10 (2-2)
	20	8-8 (6-10)	7-2 (4-8)	6-8 (4-2)	5-11 (3-3)	6-0 (3-4)	5-5 (2-9)
	24	9-6 (8-2)	7-11 (5-8)	7-4 (5-1)	6-6 (3-11)	6-7 (4-1)	6-0 (3-4)
9.5	8	5-2 (3-1)	4-2 (2-1)	3-11 (1-9)	3-5 (1-5)	3-6 (1-5)	3-2 (1-2)
	12	6-7 (5-0)	5-5 (3-4)	5-0 (3-0)	4-5 (2-4)	4-6 (2-5)	4-1 (1-11)
	16	7-8 (6-9)	6-4 (4-7)	5-11 (4-2)	5-3 (3-3)	5-4 (3-4)	4-10 (2-8)

For SI: 1 inch = 25.4 mm, 1 foot = 304.8 mm, 1 pound per square inch = 6.895 kPa, 1 pound per square foot = 0.0479 kPa.

a. This table is based on concrete with a minimum specified compressive strength of 2,500 psi, reinforcing steel with a minimum yield strength of 40,000 psi and an assumed equivalent rectangular cross section. When reinforcement with a minimum yield strength of 60,000 psi is used, the span lengths in the shaded cells shall be increased by 1.2 times the table values.

b. This table is not intended to prohibit the use of ICF manufacturer's tables based on engineering analysis in accordance with ACI 318.

c. Deflection criterion: $L/240$.

d. Design load assumptions:

    Floor dead load is 10 psf   Attic live load is 20 psf
    Floor live load is 30 psf   Roof dead load is 15 psf
    Building width is 32 feet   ICF wall dead load is 69 psf
    Light-framed wall dead load is 10 psf

e. No. 3 stirrups are required at $d/2$ spacing except no stirrups are required for the distance, (A), shown in the middle portion of the span in accordance with Figure R611.7(2) and Section R611.7.3.2.

f. Interpolation is permitted between ground snow loads and between lintel depths.

TABLE R611.7(3)
MAXIMUM ALLOWABLE CLEAR SPANS FOR ICF LINTELS FOR FLAT LOAD-BEARING WALLS[a, b, c, d, f]
NO. 5 BOTTOM BAR SIZE

MINIMUM LINTEL THICKNESS, T (inches)	LINTEL DEPTH, D (inches)	MAXIMUM CLEAR SPAN, (feet-inches) (Number is Middle of Span, A)[e]					
		Supporting Roof		Supporting Light-Framed 2nd Story and Roof		Supporting ICF Second Story and Roof	
		Ground Snow Load					
		30 psf	70 psf	30 psf	70 psf	30 psf	70 psf
3.5	8	4-9 (1-2)	4-2 (0-9)	3-11 (0-8)	3-7 (0-6)	3-7 (0-6)	3-5 (0-5)
	12	7-2 (1-11)	6-3 (1-3)	5-11 (1-1)	5-5 (0-10)	5-5 (0-10)	5-0 (0-8)
	16	9-6 (2-9)	8-0 (1-9)	7-4 (1-6)	6-6 (1-2)	6-7 (1-2)	5-11 (1-0)
	20	11-1 (3-5)	9-1 (2-3)	8-4 (1-11)	7-5 (1-6)	7-6 (1-7)	6-9 (1-3)
	24	12-2 (4-1)	10-0 (2-9)	9-3 (2-4)	8-2 (1-10)	8-4 (1-11)	7-6 (1-6)
5.5	8	5-6 (1-10)	4-10 (1-2)	4-7 (1-0)	4-2 (0-9)	4-2 (0-10)	3-10 (0-8)
	12	8-3 (3-0)	6-9 (2-0)	6-3 (1-9)	5-6 (1-4)	5-7 (1-4)	5-0 (1-1)
	16	9-9 (4-1)	8-0 (2-9)	7-5 (2-5)	6-6 (1-10)	6-7 (1-11)	6-0 (1-7)
	20	10-11 (5-3)	9-0 (3-6)	8-4 (3-1)	7-5 (2-4)	7-6 (2-5)	6-9 (2-0)
	24	12-0 (6-3)	9-11 (4-3)	9-3 (3-8)	8-2 (2-11)	8-3 (3-0)	7-6 (2-5)
7.5	8	6-1 (2-6)	5-2 (1-8)	4-9 (1-5)	4-3 (1-1)	4-3 (1-1)	3-10 (0-11)
	12	8-2 (4-0)	6-9 (2-8)	6-3 (2-4)	5-6 (1-10)	5-7 (1-10)	5-0 (1-6)
	16	9-7 (5-5)	7-11 (3-8)	7-4 (3-3)	6-6 (2-6)	6-7 (2-7)	6-0 (2-2)
	20	10-10 (6-10)	8-11 (4-8)	8-4 (4-2)	7-4 (3-3)	7-6 (3-4)	6-9 (2-9)
	24	11-10 (8-2)	9-10 (5-8)	9-2 (5-1)	8-1 (3-11)	8-3 (4-1)	7-5 (3-4)
9.5	8	6-4 (3-1)	5-2 (2-1)	4-10 (1-9)	4-3 (1-5)	4-4 (1-5)	3-11 (1-2)
	12	8-2 (5-0)	6-8 (3-4)	6-2 (3-0)	5-6 (2-4)	5-7 (2-5)	5-0 (1-11)
	16	9-6 (6-9)	7-11 (4-7)	7-4 (4-2)	6-6 (3-3)	6-7 (3-4)	5-11 (2-8)
	20	10-8 (8-4)	8-10 (5-10)	8-3 (5-4)	7-4 (4-2)	7-5 (4-3)	6-9 (3-6)
	24	11-7 (10-0)	9-9 (6-11)	9-0 (6-5)	8-1 (5-0)	8-2 (5-2)	7-5 (4-3)

For SI: 1 inch = 25.4 mm, 1 foot = 304.8 mm, 1 pound per square inch = 6.895 kPa, 1 pound per square foot = 0.0479 kPa.

a. This table is based on concrete with a minimum specified compressive strength of 2,500 psi, reinforcing steel with a minimum yield strength of 40,000 psi and an assumed equivalent rectangular cross section. When reinforcement with a minimum yield strength of 60,000 psi is used the span lengths in the shaded cells shall be increased by 1.2 times the table values.

b. This table is not intended to prohibit the use of ICF manufacturer's tables based on engineering analysis in accordance with ACI 318.

c. Deflection criterion: $L/240$.

d. Design load assumptions:

Floor dead load is 10 psf	Attic live load is 20 psf
Floor live load is 30 psf	Roof dead load is 15 psf
Building width is 32 feet	ICF wall dead load is 69 psf
Light-framed wall dead load is 10 psf	

e. No. 3 stirrups are required at $d/2$ spacing except no stirrups are required for the distance, (A), shown in the middle portion of the span in accordance with Figure R611.7(2) and Section R611.7.3.2.

f. Interpolation is permitted between ground snow loads and between lintel depths.

TABLE R611.7(4)
MAXIMUM ALLOWABLE CLEAR SPANS FOR WAFFLE-GRID ICF WALL LINTELS[a, b, c, d, f]
NO. 4 BOTTOM BAR SIZE

NOMINAL LINTEL THICKNESS T[g,h] (inches)	LINTEL DEPTH D (inches)	MAXIMUM CLEAR SPAN (feet-inches) (Number is Middle of Span, A)[e]					
		Supporting Roof		Supporting Light-Framed 2nd Story and Roof		Supporting ICF Second Story and Roof	
		Ground Snow Load					
		30 psf	70 psf	30 psf	70 psf	30 psf	70 psf
6	8	5-2 (0-10)	4-2 (0-7)	3-10 (0-6)	3-5 (0-4)	3-6 (0-5)	3-2 (0-4)
	12	6-8 (1-5)	5-5 (0-11)	5-0 (0-9)	4-5 (0-7)	4-7 (0-8)	4-2 (0-6)
	16	7-11 (1-11)	6-6 (1-4)	6-0 (1-1)	5-3 (0-10)	5-6 (0-11)	4-11 (0-9)
	20	8-11 (2-6)	7-4 (1-8)	6-9 (1-5)	6-0 (1-1)	6-3 (1-2)	5-7 (0-11)
	24	9-10 (3-0)	8-1 (2-0)	7-6 (1-9)	6-7 (1-4)	6-10 (1-5)	6-2 (1-2)
8	8	5-2 (0-10)	4-3 (0-7)	3-11 (0-6)	3-5 (0-4)	3-7 (0-5)	3-2 (0-4)
	12	6-8 (1-5)	5-5 (0-11)	5-1 (0-9)	4-5 (0-7)	4-8 (0-8)	4-2 (0-6)
	16	7-10 (1-11)	6-5 (1-4)	6-0 (1-1)	5-3 (0-10)	5-6 (0-11)	4-11 (0-9)
	20	8-10 (2-6)	7-3 (1-8)	6-9 (1-5)	6-0 (1-1)	6-2 (1-2)	5-7 (0-11)
	24	9-8 (3-0)	8-0 (2-0)	7-5 (1-9)	6-7 (1-4)	6-10 (1-5)	6-2 (1-2)

For SI: 1 inch = 25.4 mm, 1 foot = 304.8 mm, 1 psi = 6.895 kPa, 1 psf = 0.0479 kPa.

a. This table is based on concrete with a minimum specified compressive strength of 2,500 psi, reinforcing steel with a minimum yield strength of 40,000 psi and an assumed equivalent rectangular cross section. When reinforcement with a minimum yield strength of 60,000 psi is used the span lengths in the shaded cells shall be increased by 1.2 times the table values.

b. This table is not intended to prohibit the use of ICF manufacturer's tables based on engineering analysis in accordance with ACI 318.

c. Deflection criterion: $L/240$.

d. Design load assumptions:

Floor dead load is 10 psf   Attic live load is 20 psf
Floor live load is 30 psf   Roof dead load is 15 psf
Building width is 32 feet   ICF wall dead load is 55 psf
Light-framed wall dead load is 10 psf

e. No. 3 stirrups are required at $d/2$ spacing except no stirrups are required for the distance, (A), shown in the middle portion of the span in accordance with Figure R611.7(2) and Section R611.7.3.2.

f. Interpolation is permitted between ground snow loads and between lintel depths.

g. For actual wall lintel width, refer to Table R611.2.

h. Lintel width corresponds to the nominal waffle-grid ICF wall thickness with a minimum thickness of 2 inches.

TABLE R611.7(5)
MAXIMUM ALLOWABLE CLEAR SPANS FOR WAFFLE-GRID ICF WALL LINTELS[a, b, c, d, f]
NO. 5 BOTTOM BAR SIZE

NOMINAL LINTEL THICKNESS, T[g, h] (inches)	LINTEL DEPTH D (inches)	MAXIMUM CLEAR SPAN (feet-inches) (Number is Middle of Span, A)[e]					
		Supporting Roof		Supporting Light-Framed 2nd Story and Roof		Supporting ICF Second Story and Roof	
		Ground Snow Load					
		30 psf	70 psf	30 psf	70 psf	30 psf	70 psf
6	8	5-4 (0-10)	4-8 (0-7)	4-5 (0-6)	4-1 (0-4)	4-5 (0-5)	3-10 (0-4)
	12	8-0 (1-5)	6-9 (0-11)	6-3 (0-9)	5-6 (0-7)	6-3 (0-8)	5-1 (0-6)
	16	9-9 (1-11)	8-0 (1-4)	7-5 (1-1)	6-6 (0-10)	7-5 (0-11)	6-1 (0-9)
	20	11-0 (2-6)	9-1 (1-8)	8-5 (1-5)	7-5 (1-1)	8-5 (1-2)	6-11 (0-11)
	24	12-2 (3-0)	10-0 (2-0)	9-3 (1-9)	8-2 (1-4)	9-3 (1-5)	7-8 (1-2)
8	8	6-0 (0-10)	5-2 (0-7)	4-9 (0-6)	4-3 (0-4)	4-9 (0-5)	3-11 (0-4)
	12	8-3 (1-5)	6-9 (0-11)	6-3 (0-9)	5-6 (0-7)	6-3 (0-8)	5-2 (0-6)
	16	9-9 (1-11)	8-0 (1-4)	7-5 (1-1)	6-6 (0-10)	7-5 (0-11)	6-1 (0-9)
	20	10-11 (2-6)	9-0 (1-8)	8-4 (1-5)	7-5 (1-1)	8-4 (1-2)	6-11 (0-11)
	24	12-0 (3-0)	9-11 (2-0)	9-2 (1-9)	8-2 (1-4)	9-2 (1-5)	7-8 (1-2)

For SI: 1 inch = 25.4 mm, 1 foot = 304.8 mm, 1 psi = 6.895 kPa, 1 psf = 0.0479 kPa.

a. This table is based on concrete with a minimum specified compressive strength of 2,500 psi, reinforcing steel with a minimum yield strength of 40,000 psi and an assumed equivalent rectangular cross section. When reinforcement with a minimum yield strength of 60,000 psi is used the span lengths in the shaded cells shall be increased by 1.2 times the table values.

b. This table is not intended to prohibit the use of ICF manufacturer's tables based on engineering analysis in accordance with ACI 318.

c. Deflection criterion: $L/240$.

d. Design load assumptions:

 Floor dead load is 10 psf   Attic live load is 20 psf
 Floor live load is 30 psf   Roof dead load is 15 psf
 Building width is 32 feet   ICF wall dead load is 53 psf
 Light-framed wall dead load is 10 psf

e. No. 3 stirrups are required at $d/2$ spacing except no stirrups are required for the distance, (A), shown in the middle portion of the span in accordance with Figure R611.7(2) and Section R611.7.3.2.

f. Interpolation is permitted between ground snow loads and between lintel depths.

g. For actual wall lintel width, refer to Table R611.2.

h. Lintel width corresponds to the nominal waffle-grid ICF wall thickness with a minimum thickness of 2 inches.

TABLE R611.7(6)
MAXIMUM ALLOWABLE CLEAR SPANS FOR SCREEN-GRID ICF LINTELS IN LOAD-BEARING WALLS[a, b, c, d,e, f, g]
NO. 4 BOTTOM BAR SIZE

MINIMUM LINTEL THICKNESS, T (inches)[h,i]	MINIMUM LINTEL DEPTH, D (inches)	MAXIMUM CLEAR SPAN (feet-inches)					
		Supporting Roof		Supporting Light-Framed Second Story and Roof		Supporting ICF Second Story and Roof	
		Maximum Ground Snow Load (psf)					
		30	70	30	70	30	70
6	12	3-7	2-10	2-5	2-0	2-0	NA
	24	9-10	8-1	7-6	6-7	6-11	6-2

For SI: 1 inch = 25.4 mm, 1 foot = 304.8 mm, 1 psi = 6.895 kPa, 1 psf = 0.0479 kPa.

a. This table is based on concrete with a minimum specified compressive strength of 2,500 psi, reinforcing steel with a minimum yield strength of 40,000 psi and an assumed equivalent rectangular cross section. When reinforcement with a minimum yield strength of 60,000 psi is used the span lengths in the shaded cells shall be increased by 1.2 times the table values.

b. This table is not intended to prohibit the use of ICF manufacturer's tables based on engineering analysis in accordance with ACI 318.

c. Deflection criterion: $L/240$.

d Design load assumptions:

    Floor dead load is 10 psf   Attic live load is 20 psf
    Floor live load is 30 psf   Roof dead load is 15 psf
    Maximum floor clear span is 32 ft   ICF wall dead load is 53 psf
    Light-frame wall dead load is 10 psf

e. Stirrup requirements:
    Stirrups are not required for lintels 12 inches deep.
    One No. 3 stirrup is required in each vertical core for lintels 24 inches deep.

f. Interpolation is permitted between ground snow loads.

g. Flat ICF lintels may be used in lieu of screen-grid lintels.

h. For actual wall lintel width, refer to Table R611.2.

i. Lintel width corresponds to the nominal screen-grid ICF wall thickness.

TABLE R611.7(7)
MAXIMUM ALLOWABLE CLEAR SPANS FOR SCREEN-GRID ICF LINTELS IN LOAD-BEARING WALLS[a, b, c, d, e, f, g]
NO. 5 BOTTOM BAR SIZE

MINIMUM LINTEL THICKNESS, T (inches)[h,i]	MINIMUM LINTEL DEPTH, D (inches)	MAXIMUM CLEAR SPAN (feet-inches)					
		Supporting Roof		Supporting Light-Framed Second Story and Roof		Supporting ICF Second Story and Roof	
		Maximum Ground Snow Load (psf)					
		30	70	30	70	30	70
6	12	3-7	2-10	2-5	2-0	2-0	NA
	24	12-3	10-0	9-3	8-3	8-7	7-8

For SI: 1 inch = 25.4 mm, 1 foot = 304.8 mm, 1 pound per square inch = 6.895 kPa, 1 pound per square foot = 0.0479 kPa.

a. This table is based on concrete with a minimum specified compressive strength of 2,500 psi, reinforcing steel with a minimum yield strength of 40,000 psi and an assumed equivalent rectangular cross section. When reinforcement with a minimum yield strength of 60,000 psi is used the span lengths in the shaded cells shall be increased by 1.2 times the table values.

b. This table is not intended to prohibit the use of ICF manufacturer's tables based on engineering analysis in accordance with ACI 318.

c. Deflection criterion: $L/240$.

d.   Design load assumptions:

    Floor dead load is 10 psf   Attic live load is 20 psf
    Floor live load is 30 psf   Roof dead load is 15 psf
    Maximum floor clear span is 32 ft   ICF wall dead load is 53 psf
    Light-frame wall dead load is 10 psf

e. Stirrup requirements:
    Stirrups are not required for lintels 12 inches deep.
    One No. 3 stirrup is required in each vertical core for lintels 24 inches deep.

f. Interpolation is permitted between ground snow loads.

g. Flat ICF lintels may be used in lieu of screen-grid lintels.

h. For actual wall lintel width, refer to Table R611.2.

i. Lintel width corresponds to the nominal screen-grid ICF wall thickness.

TABLE R611.7(8)
MAXIMUM ALLOWABLE CLEAR SPANS FOR ICF LINTELS WITHOUT STIRRUPS IN LOAD-BEARING WALLS[a, b, c, d, e, f, g, h]
(NO. 4 OR NO. 5) BOTTOM BAR SIZE

MINIMUM LINTEL THICKNESS, T (inches)	MINIMUM LINTEL DEPTH, D (inches)	MAXIMUM CLEAR SPAN (feet-inches)					
		Supporting Roof Only		Supporting Light-Framed Second Story and Roof		Supporting ICF Second Story and Roof	
		MAXIMUM GROUND SNOW LOAD (psf)					
		30	70	30	70	30	70
Flat ICF Lintel							
3.5	8	2-6	2-6	2-6	2-4	2-5	2-2
	12	4-2	4-2	4-1	3-10	3-10	3-7
	16	4-11	4-8	4-6	4-2	4-2	3-11
	20	6-3	5-3	4-11	4-6	4-6	4-3
	24	7-7	6-4	6-0	5-6	5-6	5-2
5.5	8	2-10	2-6	2-6	2-5	2-6	2-2
	12	4-8	4-4	4-3	3-11	3-10	3-7
	16	6-5	5-1	4-8	4-2	4-3	3-11
	20	8-2	6-6	6-0	5-4	5-5	5-0
	24	9-8	7-11	7-4	6-6	6-7	6-1
7.5	8	3-6	2-8	2-7	2-5	2-5	2-2
	12	5-9	4-5	4-4	4-0	3-10	3-7
	16	7-9	6-1	5-7	4-10	4-11	4-5
	20	8-8	7-2	6-8	5-11	6-0	5-5
	24	9-6	7-11	7-4	6-6	6-7	6-0
9.5	8	4-2	3-1	2-9	2-5	2-5	2-2
	12	6-7	5-1	4-7	3-11	4-0	3-7
	16	7-10	6-4	5-11	5-3	5-4	4-10
	20	8-7	7-2	6-8	5-11	6-0	5-5
	24	9-4	7-10	7-3	6-6	6-7	6-0
Waffle-Grid ICF Lintel							
6 or 8	8	2-6	2-6	2-6	2-4	2-4	2-2
	12	4-2	4-2	4-1	3-8	3-9	3-7
	16	5-9	5-8	5-7	5-1	5-2	4-8
	20	7-6	7-4	6-9	6-0	6-3	5-7
	24	9-2	8-1	7-6	6-7	6-10	6-2

For SI: 1 inch = 25.4 mm; 1 foot = 304.8 mm; 1 pound per square foot = 0.0479 kPa; 1 pound per square inch = 6.895 kPa.

a. Table values are based on tensile reinforcement with a minimum yield strength of 40,000 psi (276 MPa), concrete with a minimum specified compressive strength of 2,500 psi, and a building width (clear span) of 32 feet.

b. Spans located in shaded cells shall be permitted to be multiplied by 1.05 when concrete with a minimum compressive strength of 3,000 psi is used or by 1.1 when concrete with a minimum compressive strength of 4,000 psi is used.

c. Deflection criterion is $L/240$, where L is the clear span of the lintel in inches.

d. Linear interpolation shall be permitted between ground snow loads and between lintel depths.

e. Lintel depth, D, shall be permitted to include the available height of ICF wall located directly above the lintel, provided that the increased lintel depth spans the entire length of the opening.

f. Spans shall be permitted to be multiplied by 1.05 for a building width (clear span) of 28 feet.

g. Spans shall be permitted to be multiplied by 1.1 for a building width (clear span) of 24 feet or less.

h. ICF wall dead load is 69 psf.

TABLE R611.7(9)
MINIMUM BOTTOM BAR ICF LINTEL REINFORCEMENT FOR LARGE CLEAR SPANS IN LOAD-BEARING WALLS[a, b, c, d, e, f, h]

MINIMUM LINTEL THICKNESS, T[e,g] (inches)	MINIMUM LINTEL DEPTH, D (inches)	MINIMUM BOTTOM LINTEL REINFORCEMENT					
		Supporting Light-Frame Roof Only		Supporting Light-Framed Second Story and Roof		Supporting ICF Second Story and Light-Frame Roof	
		Maximum Ground Snow Load (psf)					
		30	70	30	70	30	70
Flat ICF Lintel, 12 feet- 3 inches Maximum Clear Span							
3.5	24	1 #5	1 #7	D/R	D/R	D/R	D/R
5.5	20	1 #6	1 #7	D/R	D/R	D/R	D/R
	24	1 #5	1 #7	1 #7	1 #8	1 #8	D/R
7.5	16	1 #7; 2 #5	D/R	D/R	D/R	D/R	D/R
	20	1 #6; 2 #4	1#7; 2 #5	1 #8; 2 #6	D/R	D/R	D/R
	24	1 #6; 2 #4	1 #7; 2 #5	1 #7; 2 #5	1 #8; 2 #6	1 #8; 2 #6	1 #8; 2 #6
9.5	16	1 #7; 2 #5	D/R	D/R	D/R	D/R	D/R
	20	1 #6; 2 #4	1 #7; 2 #5	1 #8; 2 #6	1 #8; 2 #6	1 #8; 2 #6	1 #9; 2 #6
	24	1 #6; 2 #4	1 #7; 2 #5	1 #7; 2 #5	1 #7; 2 #6	1 #8; 2 #6	1 #9; 2 #6
Flat ICF Lintel, 16 feet-3 inches Maximum Clear Span							
5.5	24	1 #7	D/R	D/R	D/R	D/R	D/R
7.5	24	1 #7; 2 #5	D/R	D/R	D/R	D/R	D/R
9.5	24	1 #7; 2 #5	1 #9; 2 #6	1 #9; 2 #6	D/R	D/R	D/R
Waffle-Grid ICF Lintel, 12 feet-3 inches Maximum Clear Span							
6	20	1 #6	D/R	D/R	D/R	D/R	D/R
	24	1 #5	1 #7; 2 #5	1 #7; 2 #5	1 #8; 2 #6	1 #8; 2 #6	D/R
8	16	1 #7; 2 #5	D/R	D/R	D/R	D/R	D/R
	20	1 #6; 2 #4	1 #7; 2 #5	1 #8; 2 #6	D/R	D/R	D/R
	24	1 #5	1 #7; 2 #5	1 #7; 2 #5	1 #8; 2 #6	1 #8; 2 #6	1 #8; 2 #6
Screen-Grid ICF Lintel, 12 feet-3 inches Maximum Clear Span							
6	24	1 #5	1 #7	D/R	D/R	D/R	D/R

For SI: 1 inch = 25.4 mm, 1 foot = 304.8 mm, 1 psi = 6.895 kPa, 1 psf = 0.0479 kPa.

a. This table is based on concrete with a minimum specified compressive strength of 2,500 psi, reinforcing steel with a minimum yield strength of 40,000 psi and an assumed equivalent rectangular cross section. When reinforcement with a minimum yield strength of 60,000 psi is used the span lengths in the shaded cells shall be increased by 1.2 times the table values.

b. This table is not intended to prohibit the use of ICF manufacturers tables based on engineering analysis in accordance with ACI 318.

c. D/R indicates design is required.

d. Deflection criterion: L/240.

e. Interpolation is permitted between ground snow loads and between lintel depths.

f. No. 3 stirrups are required a maximum d/2 spacing for spans greater than 4 feet.

g. Actual thickness is shown for flat lintels; nominal thickness is given for waffle-grid and screen-grid lintels. Lintel thickness corresponds to the nominal waffle-grid and screen-grid ICF wall thickness. Refer to Table R611.2 for actual wall thickness.

h. ICF wall dead load varies based on wall thickness using 150 pcf concrete density.

TABLE R611.7(9A)
MINIMUM SOLID END WALL LENGTH REQUIREMENTS FOR FLAT ICF WALLS (WIND PERPENDICULAR TO RIDGE)[a, b, c]

WALL CATEGORY	BUILDING SIDE WALL LENGTH, L (feet)	Roof Slope	WIND VELOCITY PRESSURE FROM TABLE R611.7.4 (psf)							
			20	25	30	35	40	45	50	60
			Minimum Solid Wall Length on Building End Wall (feet)							
One-Story or Top Story of Two-Story	16	≤ 1:12	4.00	4.00	4.00	4.00	4.00	4.00	4.00	4.00
		5:12	4.00	4.00	4.00	4.00	4.00	4.00	4.25	4.50
		7:12[d]	4.00	4.25	4.25	4.50	4.75	4.75	5.00	5.50
		12:12[d]	4.25	4.50	4.75	5.00	5.25	5.50	5.75	6.25
	24	≤ 1:12	4.00	4.00	4.00	4.00	4.00	4.00	4.25	4.50
		5:12	4.00	4.00	4.00	4.25	4.25	4.50	4.50	4.75
		7:12[d]	4.25	4.50	4.75	5.00	5.25	5.50	5.75	6.25
		12:12[d]	4.75	5.00	5.25	5.75	6.00	6.50	6.75	7.50
	32	≤ 1:12	4.00	4.00	4.00	4.00	4.25	4.25	4.50	4.75
		5:12	4.00	4.00	4.25	4.50	4.50	4.75	5.00	5.25
		7:12[d]	4.50	5.00	5.25	5.50	6.00	6.25	6.50	7.25
		12:12[d]	5.00	5.50	6.00	6.50	7.00	7.25	7.75	8.75
	40	≤ 1:12	4.00	4.00	4.25	4.25	4.50	4.50	4.75	5.00
		5:12	4.00	4.25	4.50	4.75	4.75	5.00	5.25	5.50
		7:12[d]	4.75	5.25	5.75	6.00	6.50	7.00	7.25	8.00
		12:12[d]	5.50	6.00	6.50	7.25	7.75	8.25	8.75	10.0
	50	≤ 1:12	4.00	4.25	4.25	4.50	4.75	4.75	5.00	5.50
		5:12	4.25	4.50	4.75	5.00	5.25	5.50	5.75	6.00
		7:12[d]	5.25	5.75	6.25	6.75	7.25	7.75	8.25	9.25
		12:12[d]	6.00	6.75	7.50	8.00	8.75	9.50	10.25	11.5
	60	≤ 1:12	4.00	4.25	4.50	4.75	5.00	5.25	5.25	5.75
		5:12	4.50	4.75	5.00	5.25	5.50	5.75	6.00	6.75
		7:12[d]	5.50	6.25	6.75	7.50	8.00	8.50	9.25	10.25
		12:12[d]	6.50	7.25	8.25	9.00	9.75	10.5	11.5	13.0
First Story of Two-Story	16	≤ 1:12	4.00	4.25	4.50	4.75	5.00	5.25	5.25	5.75
		5:12	4.50	4.75	5.00	5.25	5.50	5.75	6.00	6.75
		7:12[d]	4.50	5.00	5.25	5.75	6.00	6.25	6.75	7.25
		12:12[d]	5.00	5.25	5.75	6.25	6.50	7.00	7.25	8.25
	24	≤ 1:12	4.50	4.75	5.00	5.25	5.50	5.75	6.00	6.75
		5:12	4.75	5.25	5.50	6.00	6.25	6.75	7.00	7.75
		7:12[d]	5.25	5.75	6.25	6.75	7.00	7.50	8.00	9.00
		12:12[d]	5.50	6.25	6.75	7.25	8.00	8.50	9.00	10.25
	32	≤ 1:12	4.75	5.00	5.50	5.75	6.25	6.50	6.75	7.50
		5:12	5.25	5.75	6.25	6.75	7.25	7.50	8.00	9.00
		7:12[d]	5.75	6.50	7.00	7.75	8.25	9.00	9.50	10.75
		12:12[d]	6.25	7.00	7.75	8.50	9.25	10.0	10.75	12.25
	40	≤ 1:12	5.00	5.50	5.75	6.25	6.75	7.25	7.50	8.50
		5:12	5.50	6.25	6.75	7.25	8.00	8.50	9.00	10.25
		7:12[d]	6.25	7.00	7.75	8.75	9.50	10.25	11.0	12.5
		12:12[d]	7.00	8.00	8.75	9.75	10.75	11.5	12.5	14.25
	50	≤ 1:12	5.50	6.00	6.50	7.00	7.50	8.00	8.50	9.50
		5:12	6.00	6.75	7.50	8.25	9.00	9.75	10.5	11.75
		7:12[d]	7.00	8.00	9.00	10.0	10.75	11.75	12.75	14.5
		12:12[d]	7.75	9.00	10.0	11.25	12.25	13.50	14.75	17.0
	60	≤ 1:12	5.75	6.50	7.00	7.50	8.25	8.75	9.50	10.75
		5:12	6.75	7.50	8.25	9.25	10.0	10.75	11.75	13.25
		7:12[d]	7.75	9.00	10.0	11.0	12.25	13.25	14.5	16.75
		12:12[d]	8.75	10.0	11.5	12.75	14.0	15.5	16.75	19.5

(continued)

Footnotes to Table R611.7 (9A)

For SI: 1 foot = 304.8 mm; 1 inch = 25.4 mm; 1 pound per square foot = 0.0479 kPa.

a. Table values are based on a 3.5 in thick flat wall. For a 5.5 in thick flat wall, multiply the table values by 0.9. The adjusted values shall not result in solid wall lengths less than 4ft.

b. Table values are based on a maximum unsupported wall height of 10 ft.

c. Linear interpolation shall be permitted.

d. The minimum solid wall lengths shown in the table are based on a building with an end wall length "W" of 60 feet and a roof slope of less than 7:12. For roof slopes of 7:12 or greater and end wall length "W" greater than 30 feet, the minimum solid wall length determined from the table shall be multiplied by:

$1 + 0.4[(W-30)/30]$.

TABLE R611.7(9B)
MINIMUM SOLID SIDEWALL LENGTH REQUIREMENTS FOR FLAT ICF WALLS (WIND PARALLEL TO RIDGE) [a, b, c, d]

WALL CATEGORY	BUILDING END WALL WIDTH, *W* (feet)	WIND VELOCITY PRESSURE FROM TABLE R611.7.4 (psf)							
		20	25	30	35	40	45	50	60
		Minimum Solid Wall Length on Building Side Wall (feet)							
One-Story or Top Story of Two-Story	16	4.00	4.00	4.00	4.00	4.25	4.25	4.50	4.75
	24	4.00	4.25	4.50	4.75	4.75	5.00	5.25	5.50
	32	4.50	4.75	5.00	5.25	5.50	6.00	6.25	6.75
	40	5.00	5.50	5.75	6.25	6.75	7.00	7.50	8.25
	50	5.75	6.25	7.00	7.50	8.25	8.75	9.50	10.75
	60	6.50	7.50	8.25	9.25	10.0	10.75	11.75	13.25
First Story of Two-Story	16	4.25	4.50	4.75	5.00	5.25	5.50	5.75	6.50
	24	4.75	5.25	5.50	6.00	6.25	6.75	7.00	8.00
	32	5.50	6.00	6.50	7.00	7.50	8.00	8.75	9.75
	40	6.25	7.00	7.50	8.25	9.00	9.75	10.5	12.0
	50	7.25	8.25	9.25	10.25	11.25	12.25	13.25	15.25
	60	8.50	9.75	11.0	12.25	13.5	15.0	16.25	18.75

For SI: 1 foot = 304.8 mm; 1 inch = 25.4 mm; 1 pound per square foot = 0.0479 kPa.

a. Table values are based on a 3.5 in thick flat wall. For a 5.5 in thick flat wall, multiply the table values by 0.9. The adjusted values shall not result in solid wall lengths less than 4ft.

b. Table values are based on a maximum unsupported wall height of 10 ft.

c. Table values are based on a maximum 12:12 roof pitch.

d. Linear interpolation shall be permitted.

TABLE R611.7(10)
MAXIMUM ALLOWABLE CLEAR SPANS FOR ICF LINTELS IN NONLOAD-BEARING WALLS WITHOUT STIRRUPS[a,b,c,d]
NO. 4 BOTTOM BAR

MINIMUM LINTEL THICKNESS, T (inches)	MINIMUM LINTEL DEPTH, D (inches)	MAXIMUM CLEAR SPAN	
		Supporting Light-Framed Nonbearing Wall (feet-inches)	Supporting ICF Second Story and Nonbearing Wall (feet-inches)
Flat ICF Lintel			
3.5	8	11-1	3-1
	12	15-11	5-1
	16	16-3	6-11
	20	16-3	8-8
	24	16-3	10-5
5.5	8	16-3	4-4
	12	16-3	7-0
	16	16-3	9-7
	20	16-3	12-0
	24	16-3	14-3
7.5	8	16-3	5-6
	12	16-3	8-11
	16	16-3	12-2
	20	16-3	15-3
	24	16-3	16-3
9.5	8	16-3	6-9
	12	16-3	10-11
	16	16-3	14-10
	20	16-3	16-3
	24	16-3	16-3
Waffle-Grid ICF Lintel			
6 or 8	8	9-1	2-11
	12	13-4	4-10
	16	16-3	6-7
	20	16-3	8-4
	24	16-3	9-11
Screen-Grid Lintel			
6	12	5-8	4-1
	24	16-3	9-1

For SI: 1 foot = 304.8 mm; 1 inch = 25.4 mm; 1 pounds per square foot = 0.0479 kPa.

a. This table is based on concrete with a minimum specified compressive strength of 2,500 psi, reinforcing steel with a minimum yield strength of 40,000 psi and an assumed equivalent rectangular cross section.

b. This table is not intended to prohibit the use of ICF manufacturers tables based on engineering analysis in accordance with ACI 318.

c. Deflection criterion is $L/240$, where L is the clear span of the lintel in inches.

d. Linear interpolation is permitted between lintel depths.

TABLE R611.7(10A)
MINIMUM SOLID END WALL LENGTH REQUIREMENTS FOR WAFFLE AND
SCREEN-GRID ICF WALLS (WIND PERPENDICULAR TO RIDGE)[a, b, c]

WALL CATEGORY	BUILDING SIDE WALL LENGTH, L (feet)	ROOF SLOPE	WIND VELOCITY PRESSURE FROM TABLE R611.7.4							
			20	25	30	35	40	45	50	60
			Minimum Solid Wall Length on Building End Wall (feet)							
One-Story or Top Story of Two-Story	16	≤1:12	4.00	4.00	4.00	4.00	4.00	4.00	4.00	4.25
		5:12	4.00	4.00	4.00	4.00	4.00	4.25	4.25	4.50
		7:12[d]	4.00	4.25	4.50	4.75	5.00	5.25	5.50	6.00
		12:12[d]	4.25	4.75	5.00	5.50	5.75	6.00	6.50	7.00
	24	≤1:12	4.00	4.00	4.00	4.00	4.00	4.25	4.25	4.50
		5:12	4.00	4.00	4.00	4.25	4.50	4.50	4.75	5.00
		7:12[d]	4.50	4.75	5.00	5.50	5.75	6.25	6.50	7.25
		12:12[d]	5.00	5.50	6.00	6.50	7.00	7.25	7.75	8.75
	32	≤1:12	4.00	4.00	4.00	4.25	4.25	4.50	4.75	5.00
		5:12	4.00	4.00	4.25	4.50	4.75	5.00	5.25	5.75
		7:12[d]	4.75	5.25	5.75	6.25	6.50	7.00	7.50	8.50
		12:12[d]	5.50	6.25	6.75	7.50	8.00	8.75	9.25	10.5
	40	≤1:12	4.00	4.00	4.25	4.50	4.50	4.75	5.00	5.50
		5:12	4.00	4.25	4.50	5.00	5.25	5.50	5.75	6.25
		7:12[d]	5.25	5.75	6.25	7.00	7.50	8.00	8.50	9.75
		12:12[d]	6.00	6.75	7.75	8.50	9.25	10.0	10.75	12.25
	50	≤1:12	4.00	4.25	4.50	4.75	5.00	5.25	5.50	6.00
		5:12	4.25	4.75	5.00	5.25	5.50	6.00	6.25	7.00
		7:12[d]	5.75	6.50	7.00	7.75	8.50	9.25	9.75	11.25
		12:12[d]	6.75	7.75	8.75	9.75	10.75	11.5	12.5	14.5
	60	≤1:12	4.25	4.50	4.75	5.00	5.25	5.50	5.75	6.50
		5:12	4.50	5.00	5.25	5.75	6.00	6.50	6.75	7.75
		7:12[d]	6.25	7.00	8.00	8.75	9.50	10.25	11.25	12.75
		12:12[d]	7.50	8.75	9.75	11.0	12.0	13.25	14.25	16.5
First Story of Two-Story	16	≤1:12	4.25	4.50	4.75	5.00	5.25	5.50	5.75	6.50
		5:12	4.50	5.00	5.25	5.75	6.00	6.50	6.75	7.75
		7:12[d]	4.75	5.25	5.75	6.25	6.75	7.25	7.75	8.75
		12:12[d]	5.25	5.75	6.50	7.00	7.50	8.00	8.75	9.75
	24	≤1:12	4.50	5.00	5.25	5.75	6.25	6.50	7.00	7.75
		5:12	5.00	5.75	6.25	6.75	7.25	7.75	8.25	9.25
		7:12[d]	5.75	6.25	7.00	7.75	8.25	9.00	9.75	11.0
		12:12[d]	6.25	7.00	7.75	8.50	9.50	10.25	11.0	12.75
	32	≤1:12	5.00	5.50	6.00	6.50	7.00	7.50	8.00	9.00
		5:12	5.75	6.25	7.00	7.75	8.25	9.00	9.75	11.0
		7:12[d]	6.50	7.25	8.25	9.00	10.0	10.75	11.75	13.5
		12:12[d]	7.25	8.25	9.25	10.25	11.25	12.5	13.5	15.5
	40	≤1:12	5.50	6.00	6.50	7.25	7.75	8.50	9.00	10.25
		5:12	6.25	7.00	7.75	8.75	9.50	10.25	11.0	12.75
		7:12[d]	7.25	8.25	9.25	10.5	11.5	12.5	13.75	15.75
		12:12[d]	8.00	9.50	10.75	12.0	13.25	14.5	15.75	18.25

(continued)

TABLE R611.7(10A)—continued
MINIMUM SOLID END WALL LENGTH REQUIREMENTS FOR WAFFLE AND
SCREEN-GRID ICF WALLS (WIND PERPENDICULAR TO RIDGE)[a, b, c]

WALL CATEGORY	BUILDING SIDE WALL LENGTH, L (feet)	ROOF SLOPE	WIND VELOCITY PRESSURE FROM TABLE R611.7.4							
			20	25	30	35	40	45	50	60
			Minimum Solid Wall Length on Building End Wall (feet)							
First Story of Two-Story	50	≤ 1:12	6.00	6.75	7.50	8.00	8.75	9.50	10.25	11.75
		5:12	7.00	8.00	9.00	10.0	11.0	12.0	13.0	14.75
		7:12[d]	8.25	9.50	10.75	12.25	13.5	14.75	16.0	18.75
		12:12[d]	9.25	11.0	12.5	14.0	15.5	17.25	18.75	22.0
	60	≤ 1:12	6.50	7.25	8.25	9.00	10.0	10.75	11.75	13.25
		5:12	7.75	8.75	10.0	11.25	12.25	13.5	14.75	17.0
		7:12[d]	9.25	10.75	12.25	14.0	15.5	17.0	18.5	21.75
		12:12[d]	10.5	12.25	14.25	16.25	18.0	20.0	21.75	25.5

For SI: 1 foot = 304.8 mm; 1 inch = 25.4 mm; 1 pound per square foot = 0.0479 kPa.

a. Table values are based on a 6 in (152.4 mm) thick nominal waffle-grid wall. For a 8 in thick nominal waffle-grid wall, multiply the table values by 0.90.

b. Table values are based on a maximum unsupported wall height of 10 ft.

c. Linear interpolation is permitted.

d. The minimum solid wall lengths shown in the table are based on a building with an end wall length "W" of 60 feet and a roof slope of less than 7:12. For roof slopes of 7:12 or greater and end wall length "W" greater than 30 feet, the minimum solid wall length determined from the table shall be multiplied by: 1 + 0.4 [(W-30)/30].

TABLE R611.7(10B)
MINIMUM SOLID SIDE WALL LENGTH REQUIREMENTS FOR 6-INCH WAFFLE AND
SCREEN-GRID ICF WALLS (WIND PARALLEL TO RIDGE)[a, b, c, d]

WALL CATEGORY	BUILDING END WALL WIDTH, W (feet)	WIND VELOCITY PRESSURE FROM TABLE R611.7.4 (psf)							
		20	25	30	35	40	45	50	60
		Minimum Solid Wall Length on Building Side Wall (feet)							
One-Story or Top Story of Two-Story	16	4.00	4.00	4.00	4.25	4.25	4.50	4.75	5.00
	24	4.00	4.25	4.50	5.00	5.25	5.50	5.75	6.25
	32	4.50	5.00	5.50	5.75	6.25	6.75	7.00	8.00
	40	5.25	6.00	6.50	7.00	7.75	8.25	8.75	10.0
	50	6.50	7.25	8.00	9.00	9.75	10.75	11.5	13.25
	60	7.75	8.75	10.0	11.25	12.25	13.5	14.5	17.0
First Story of Two-Story	16	4.50	4.75	5.25	5.50	5.75	6.25	6.50	7.25
	24	5.00	5.75	6.25	6.75	7.25	7.75	8.25	9.50
	32	6.00	6.75	7.50	8.25	9.00	9.75	10.5	12.0
	40	7.00	8.00	9.00	10.0	11.0	12.0	13.0	15.0
	50	8.50	9.75	11.25	12.5	14.0	15.25	16.75	19.5
	60	10.25	12.0	13.75	15.5	17.25	19.0	21.0	24.5

For SI: 1 foot = 304.8 mm; 1 inch = 25.4 mm; 1 pound per square foot = 0.0479 kPa.

a. Table values are based on a 6 in thick nominal waffle-grid wall. For a 8 in thick nominal waffle-grid wall, multiply the table values by 0.90.

b. Table values are based on a maximum unsupported wall height of 10 ft.

c. Table values are based on a maximum 12:12 roof pitch.

d. Linear interpolation shall be permitted.

R611.7.1.4 Lap splices. Where lap splicing of vertical or horizontal reinforcing steel is necessary, the lap splice shall be in accordance with Figure R611.7.1.4 and a minimum of 40 d_b, where d_b is the diameter of the smaller bar. The maximum distance between noncontact parallel bars at a lap splice shall not exceed 8 d_b.

R611.7.1.5 Standard hook. Where the free end of a reinforcing bar is required to have a standard hook, the hook shall be a 180-degree bend plus 4 d_b extension but not less than $2^1/_2$ inches, or a 90-degree bend plus 12 d_b extension.

R611.7.2 Wall openings. Wall openings shall have a minimum of 8 inches (203 mm) of depth of concrete for flat and waffle-grid ICF walls and 12 inches (305 mm) for screen-grid walls over the length of the opening. When the depth of concrete above the opening is less than 12 inches for flat or waffle-grid walls, lintels in accordance with Section

R611.7.3 shall be provided. Reinforcement around openings shall be provided in accordance with Table R611.7(1) and Figure R611.7(2). Reinforcement placed horizontally above or below an opening shall extend a minimum of 24 inches (610 mm) beyond the limits of the opening. Wall opening reinforcement shall be provided in addition to the reinforcement required by Sections R611.3, R611.4, R611.5 and R611.7.1. The perimeter of all wall openings shall be framed with a minimum 2-inch by 4-inch plate, anchored to the wall with $^1/_2$-inch (13 mm) diameter anchor bolts spaced a maximum of 24 inches (610 mm) on center. The bolts shall be embedded into the concrete a minimum of 4 inches (102 mm) and have a minimum of $1^1/_2$ inches (38 mm) of concrete cover to the face of the wall.

Exception: The 2-inch by 4-inch plate is not required where the wall is formed to provide solid concrete around the perimeter of the opening with a minimum depth of 4 inches (102 mm) for the full thickness of the wall.

TABLE R611.7(11)
MINIMUM PERCENTAGE OF SOLID WALL LENGTH ALONG EXTERIOR WALL LINES FOR TOWNHOUSES IN SEISMIC DESIGN CATEGORY C AND ALL BUILDINGS IN SEISMIC DESIGN CATEGORIES D_0, D_1 AND D_2[a, b]

	MINIMUM SOLID WALL LENGTH (percent)		
SEISMIC DESIGN CATEGORY (SDC)	**One-Story or Top Story of Two-Story**	**Wall Supporting Light-Framed Second Story and Roof**	**Wall Supporting ICF Second Story and Roof**
Townhouses in SDC C[c]	20 percent	25 percent	35 percent
D_1[d]	25 percent	30 percent	40 percent
D_2[d]	30 percent	35 percent	45 percent

For SI: 1 inch = 25.4 mm; 1 mile per hour = 0.447 m/s.

a. Base percentages are applicable for maximum unsupported wall height of 10-feet, light-frame gable construction, and all ICF wall types. These percentages assume that the maximum weight of the interior and exterior wall finishes applied to ICF walls do not exceed 8 psf.

b. For all walls, the minimum required length of solid walls shall be based on the table percent value multiplied by the minimum dimension of a rectangle inscribing the overall building plan.

c. Walls shall be reinforced with a minimum No. 5 bar (Grade 40 or 60) spaced a maximum of 24 inches on center each way or a No. 4 bar spaced a maximum of 16 inches on center each way. (Grade 40 or 60) spaced at a maximum of 16 inches on center each way.

d. Walls shall be constructed with a minimum concrete compressive strength of 3,000 psi and reinforced with minimum #5 rebar (Grade 60 ASTM A 706) spaced a maximum of 18 inches on center each way or No. 4 rebar (Grade 60 ASTM A706) spaced at a maximum of 12 inches (304.8 mm) on center each way. The minimum thickness of flat ICF walls shall be 5.5 inches.

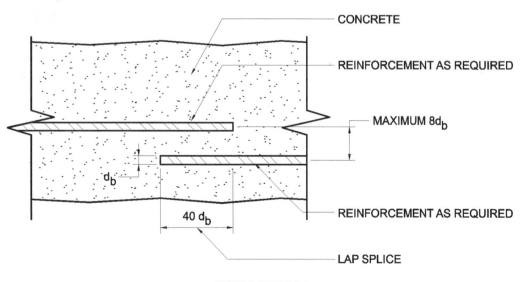

FIGURE R611.7.1.4
LAP SPLICES

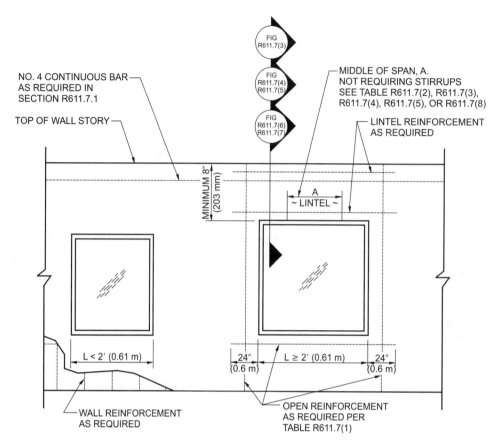

FIGURE R611.7(2)
REINFORCEMENT OF OPERNINGS

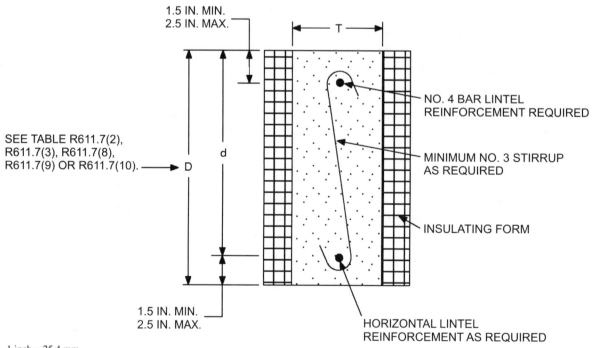

For SI: 1 inch = 25.4 mm.
NOTE: Section cut through flat wall.

FIGURE R611.7(3)
ICF LINTELS FOR FLAT AND SCREEN-GRID WALLS

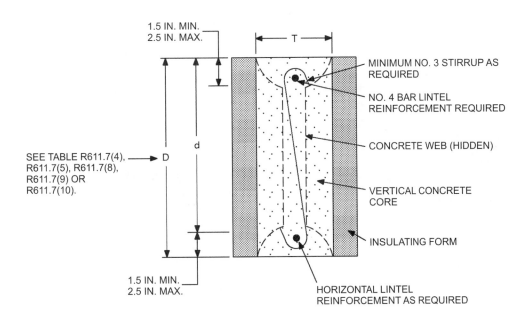

For SI: 1 inch = 25.4 mm.
NOTE: Section cut through vertical core of a waffle-grid lintel.

FIGURE R611.7(4)
SINGLE FORM HEIGHT WAFFLE-GRID LINTEL

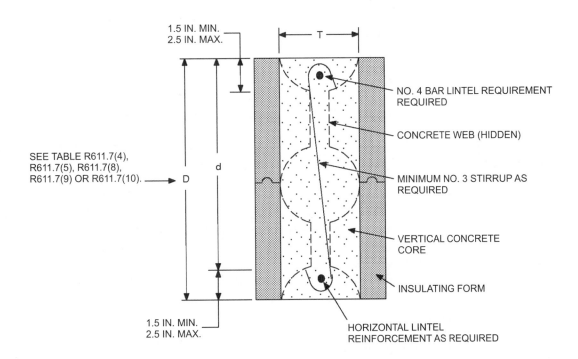

For SI: 1 inch = 25.4 mm.
NOTE: Section cut through vertical core of a waffle-grid lintel.

FIGURE R611.7(5)
DOUBLE FORM HEIGHT WAFFLE-GRID LINTEL

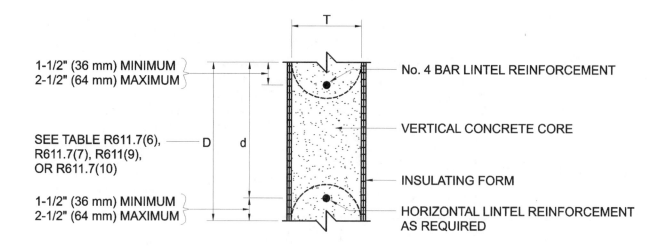

FIGURE R611.7(6)
SINGLE FORM HEIGHT SCREEN-GRID LINTEL

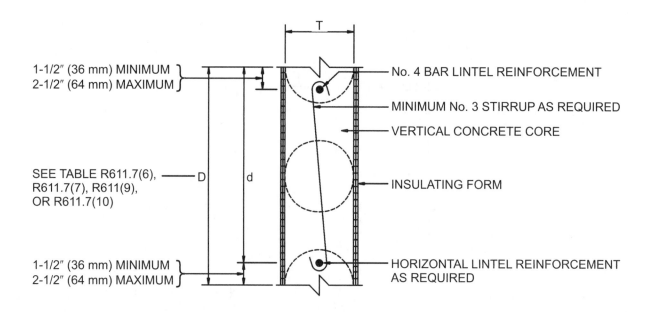

FIGURE R611.7(7)
DOUBLE FORM HEIGHT SCREEN-GRID LINTEL

R611.7.3 Lintels.

R611.7.3.1 General requirements. Lintels shall be provided over all openings greater than or equal to 2 feet (610 mm) in width. Lintels for flat ICF walls shall be constructed in accordance with Figure R611.7(3) and Table R611.7(2) or R611.7(3). Lintels for waffle-grid ICF walls shall be constructed in accordance with Figure R611.7(4) or Figure R611.7(5) and Table R611.7(4) or R611.7(5). Lintels for screen-grid ICF walls shall be constructed in accordance with Figure R611.7(6) or Figure R611.7(7). Lintel construction in accordance with Figure R611.7(3) shall be permitted with waffle-grid and screen-grid ICF wall construction.

Lintel depths are permitted to be increased by the height of the ICF wall located directly above the opening, provided that the lintel depth spans the entire length of the opening.

R611.7.3.2 Stirrups. Where required, No. 3 stirrups shall be installed in flat, waffle-grid and screen-grid wall lintels in accordance with the following:

1. For flat walls the stirrups shall be spaced at a maximum spacing of $d/2$ where d equals the depth of the lintel (D) minus the bottom cover of concrete as shown in Figure R611.7(3). Stirrups shall not be required in the middle portion of the span (A) per Figure R611.7(2), for flat walls for a length

not to exceed the values shown in parenthesis in Tables R611.7(2) and R611.7(3) or for spans in accordance with Table R611.7(8).

2. For waffle-grid walls a minimum of two No. 3 stirrups shall be placed in each vertical core of waffle-grid lintels. Stirrups shall not be required in the middle portion of the span (A) per Figure R611.7(2), for waffle-grid walls for a length not to exceed the values shown in parenthesis in Tables R611.7(4) and R611.7(5) or for spans in accordance with Table R611.7(8).

3. For screen-grid walls one No. 3 stirrup shall be placed in each vertical core of screen-grid lintels.

> **Exception:** Stirrups are not required in screen-grid lintels meeting the following requirements:
>
> 1. Lintel Depth (D) = 12 inches (305 mm) - spans less than or equal 3 feet 7 inches.
>
> 2. Lintel Depth (D) = 24 inches (610 mm) - spans less than or equal 4 feet 4 inches.

R611.7.3.3 Horizontal reinforcement. One No. 4 horizontal bar shall be provided in the top of the lintel. Horizontal reinforcement placed within 12 inches (305 mm) of the top of the wall in accordance with Section R611.7.1.3 shall be permitted to serve as the top or bottom reinforcement in the lintel provided the reinforcement meets the location requirements in Figure R611.7(2), R611.7(3), R611.7(4), R611.7(5), R611.7(6), or R611.7(7), and the size requirements in Tables R611.7(2), R611.7(3), R611.7(4), R611.7(5), R611.7(6), R611.7(7), or R611.7(8).

R611.7.3.4 Load-bearing walls. Lintels in flat ICF load-bearing walls shall comply with Table R611.7(2), Table RR611.7(3) or Table R611.7(8). Lintels in waffle-grid ICF load-bearing walls shall comply with Table R611.7(4), Table R611.7(5) or Table R611.7(8). Lintels in screen-grid ICF load-bearing walls shall comply with Table R611.7(6) or Table R611.7(7).

Where spans larger than those permitted in Table R611.7(2), Table R611.7(3), Table R611.7(4), Table R611.7(5), R611.7(6), R611.7(7) or R611.7(8) are required, the lintels shall comply with Table R611.7 (9).

R611.7.3.5 Nonload-bearing walls. Lintels in nonload-bearing flat, waffle-grid and screen-grid ICF walls shall comply with Table R611.7 (10). Stirrups are not required.

R611.7.4 Minimum length of wall without openings. The wind velocity pressures of Table R611.7.4 shall be used to determine the minimum amount of solid wall length in accordance with Tables R611.7(9A) through R611.7(10B) and Figure R611.7.4. Table R611.7(11) shall be used to determine the minimum amount of solid wall length for townhouses in Seismic Design Category C, and all buildings in Seismic Design Categories D_0, D_1 and D_2 for all types of ICF walls. The greater amount of solid wall length required by wind loading or seismic loading shall apply.

The minimum percentage of solid wall length shall include only those solid wall segments that are a minimum of 24 inches (610 mm) in length. The maximum distance between wall segments included in determining solid wall length shall not exceed 18 feet (5486 mm). A minimum length of 24 inches (610 mm) of solid wall segment, extending the full height of each wall story, shall occur at all interior and exterior corners of exterior walls.

TABLE R611.7.4
WIND VELOCITY PRESSURE FOR DETERMINATION OF MINIMUM SOLID WALL LENGTH[a]

WIND SPEED (mph) [d]	VELOCITY PRESSURE (psf)		
	Exposure [b]		
	B	C	D
85	14	19	23
90	16	21	25
100	19	26	31
110	23	32	37
120	27	38	44
130	32	44	52
140	37	51	60
150	43	59	69[c]

For SI: 1 pound per square foot = 0.0479 kPa; 1 mile per hour = 0.447 m/s.

a. Table values are based on ASCE 7-98 Figure 6-4 using a mean roof height of 35 ft.

b. Exposure Categories shall be determined in accordance with Section R301.2.1.4.

c. Design is required in accordance with ACI 318 and approved manufacturer guidelines.

d. Interpolation is permitted between wind speeds.

R611.8 ICF wall-to-floor connections.

R611.8.1 Top bearing. Floors bearing on the top of ICF foundation walls in accordance with Figure R611.8(1) shall have the wood sill plate anchored to the ICF wall with minimum $^1/_2$-inch (13 mm) diameter bolts embedded a minimum of 7 inches (178 mm) and placed at a maximum spacing of 6 feet (1829 mm) on center and not more than 12 inches (305 mm) from corners. Anchor bolts for waffle-grid and screen-grid walls shall be located in the cores. In conditions where wind speeds are in excess of 90 miles per hour (40 m/s), the $^1/_2$-inch (13 mm) diameter anchor bolts shall be placed at a maximum spacing of 4 feet (1219 mm) on center. Bolts shall extend a minimum of 7 inches (178 mm) into concrete. Sill plates shall be protected against decay where required by Section R319. Cold-formed steel framing systems shall be anchored to the concrete in accordance with Section R505.3.1 or Section R603.3.1.

R611.8.1.1 Top bearing requirements for Seismic Design Categories C, D_0, D_1 and D_2. For townhouses in Seismic Design Category C, wood sill plates attached to ICF walls shall be anchored with Grade A 307, $^3/_8$-inch-diameter (10 mm) headed anchor bolts embedded a minimum of 7 inches (178 mm) and placed at a maximum spacing of 36 inches (914 mm) on center. For all buildings in Seismic Design Category D_0 or D_1, wood sill plates attached to ICF walls shall be anchored with ASTM A 307, Grade A, $^3/_8$-inch-diameter (10 mm) headed anchor bolts embedded a minimum of 7 inches (178 mm) and placed at a maximum spacing of 24 inches (610 mm) on center. For all buildings in Seismic Design Category D_2, wood sill plates attached to ICF walls shall be anchored with ASTM A 307, Grade A, $^3/_8$-inch-diameter (10 mm) headed anchor bolts embedded a minimum of 7 inches (178 mm) and placed at a maximum spacing of 16 inches (406 mm) on center. Larger diameter bolts than specified herein shall not be used.

For townhouses in Seismic Design Category C, each floor joist perpendicular to an ICF wall shall be attached to the sill plate with an 18-gage [(0.0478 in.) (1.2 mm)] angle bracket using 3 - 8d common nails per leg in accordance with Figure R611.8(1). For all buildings in Seismic Design Category D_0 or D_1, each floor joist perpendicular to an ICF wall shall be attached to the sill plate with an 18-gage [(0.0478 in.) (1.2 mm)] angle bracket using 4 - 8d common nails per leg in accordance with Figure R611.8(1). For all buildings in Seismic Design Category D_2, each floor joist perpendicular to an ICF wall shall be attached to the sill plate with an 18-gage

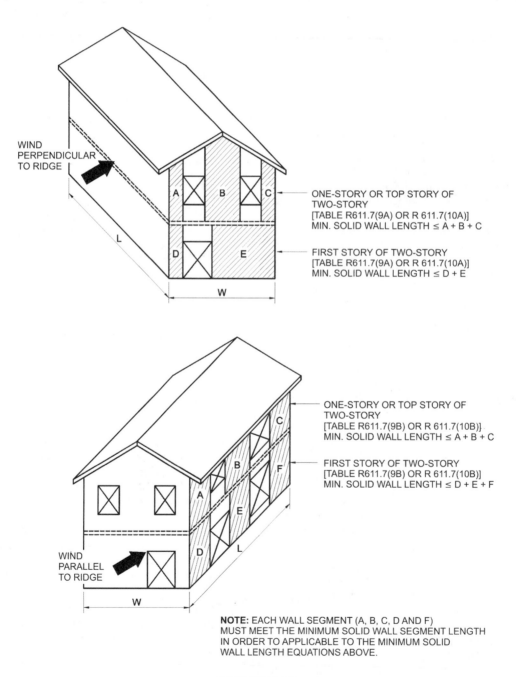

NOTE: EACH WALL SEGMENT (A, B, C, D AND F) MUST MEET THE MINIMUM SOLID WALL SEGMENT LENGTH IN ORDER TO APPLICABLE TO THE MINIMUM SOLID WALL LENGTH EQUATIONS ABOVE.

FIGURE R611.7.4
MINIMUM SOLID WALL LENGTH

[(0.0478 in.) (1.2 mm)] angle bracket using 6 - 8d common nails per leg in accordance with Figure R611.8(1).

For ICF walls parallel to floor framing in townhouses in Seismic Design Category C, full depth blocking shall be placed at 24 inches (610 mm) on center and shall be attached to the sill plate with an 18-gage [(0.0478 in.) (1.2 mm)] angle bracket using 5 - 8d common nails per leg in accordance with Figure R611.8(6). For ICF walls parallel to floor framing for all buildings in Seismic Design Category D_0 or D_1, full depth blocking shall be placed at 24 inches (610 mm) on center and shall be attached to the sill plate with an 18-gage [(0.0478 in.) (1.2 mm)] angle bracket using 6 - 8d common nails per

TABLE R611.8(1)
FLOOR LEDGER-ICF WALL CONNECTION (SIDE-BEARING CONNECTION) REQUIREMENTS[a, b, c]

MAXIMUM FLOOR CLEAR SPAN[d] (feet)	MAXIMUM ANCHOR BOLT SPACING[e] (inches)			
	Staggered $1/2$-inch-diameter anchor bolts	Staggered $5/8$-inch-diameter anchor bolts	Two $1/2$-inch-diameter anchor bolts[f]	Two $5/8$-inch-diameter anchor bolts[f]
8	18	20	36	40
10	16	18	32	36
12	14	18	28	36
14	12	16	24	32
16	10	14	20	28
18	9	13	18	26
20	8	11	16	22
22	7	10	14	20
24	7	9	14	18
26	6	9	12	18
28	6	8	12	16
30	5	8	10	16
32	5	7	10	14

For SI: 1 inch = 25.4 mm, 1 foot = 304.8 mm.

a. Minimum ledger board nominal depth shall be 8 inches. The thickness of the ledger board shall be a minimum of 2 inches. Thickness of ledger board is in nominal lumber dimensions. Ledger board shall be minimum No. 2 Grade.

b. Minimum edge distance shall be 2 inches for $1/2$-inch-diameter anchor bolts and 2.5 inches for $5/8$-inch-diameter anchor bolts.

c. Interpolation is permitted between floor spans.

d. Floor span corresponds to the clear span of the floor structure (i.e., joists or trusses) spanning between load-bearing walls or beams.

e. Anchor bolts shall extend through the ledger to the center of the flat ICF wall thickness or the center of the horizontal or vertical core thickness of the waffle-grid or screen-grid ICF wall system.

f. Minimum vertical distance between bolts shall be 1.5 inches for $1/2$-inch-diameter anchor bolts and 2 inches for $5/8$-inch-diameter anchor bolts.

TABLE R611.8(2)
DESIGN VALUES (PLF) FOR FLOOR JOIST-TO-WALL ANCHORS REQUIRED FOR TOWNHOUSES
IN SEISMIC DESIGN CATEGORY C AND ALL BUILDINGS IN SEISMIC DESIGN CATEGORIES D_0, D_1 AND D_2[a, b]

WALL TYPE	SEISMIC DESIGN CATEGORY		
	C	D_0 or D_1	D_2
Flat 3.5	193	NP	NP
Flat 5.5	303	502	708
Flat 7.5	413	685	965
Flat 9.5	523	867	1,223
Waffle 6	246	409	577
Waffle 8	334	555	782
Screen 6	233	387	546

For SI: 1pound per linear foot = 1.488 kg/m.

NP = Not Permitted

a. Table values are based on IBC Equation 16–64 using a tributary wall height of 11 feet. Table values shall be permitted to be reduced for tributary wall heights less than 11 feet by multiplying the table values by X/11, where X is the tributary wall height.

b. Values may be reduced by 30 percent when used for ASD.

leg in accordance with Figure R611.8(6). For ICF walls parallel to floor framing for all buildings in Seismic Design Category D_2, full depth blocking shall be placed at 24 inches (610 mm) on center and shall be attached to the sill plate with an 18-gage [(0.0478 in.) (1.2 mm)] angle bracket using 9 - 8d common nails per leg in accordance with Figure R611.8(6).

R611.8.2 Ledger bearing. Wood ledger boards supporting bearing ends of joists or trusses shall be anchored to flat ICF walls with minimum thickness of 5.5 inches (140 mm) and to waffle- or screen-grid ICF walls with minimum nominal thickness of 6 inches (152 mm) in accordance with Figure R611.8(2), R611.8(3), R611.8(4) or R611.8(5) and Table R611.8(1). Wood ledger boards supporting bearing ends of joists or trusses shall be anchored to flat ICF walls with minimum thickness of 3.5 inches (140 mm) in accordance with Figure R611.8(5) and Table R611.8(1). The ledger shall be a minimum 2 by 8, No. 2 Southern Yellow Pine or No. 2 Douglas Fir. Ledgers anchored to nonload-bearing walls to support floor or roof sheathing shall be attached with $1/_2$ inch (12.7 mm) diameter or headed anchor bolts spaced a maximum of 6 feet (1829 mm) on center. Anchor bolts shall be embedded a minimum of 4 inches (102 mm) into the concrete measured from the inside face of the insulating form. For insulating forms with a face shell thickness of 1.5 inches (38 mm) or less, the hole in the form shall be a minimum of 4 inches (102 mm) in diameter. For insulating forms with a face shell thicker than 1.5 inches (38 mm), the diameter of the hole in the form shall be increased by 1 inch (25 mm) for each $1/_2$ inch (13 mm) of additional insulating form face shell thickness. The ledger board shall be in direct contact with the concrete at each bolt location.

R611.8.2.1 Ledger bearing requirements for Seismic Design Categories C, D_0, D_1 and D_2. Additional anchorage mechanisms connecting the wall to the floor system shall be installed at a maximum spacing of 6 feet (1829 mm) on center for townhouses in Seismic Design Category C and 4 feet (1220 mm) on center for all buildings in Seismic Design Categories D_0, D_1 and D_2. The additional anchorage mechanisms shall be attached to the ICF wall reinforcement and joist rafters or blocking in accordance with Figures R611.8(1) through R611.8(7). The additional anchorage shall be installed through an oversized hole in the ledger board that is $1/_2$ inch (13 mm) larger than the anchorage mechanism diameter to prevent combined tension and shear in the mechanism. The blocking shall be attached to floor or roof sheathing in accordance with edge fastener spacing. Such additional anchorage shall not be accomplished by the use of toe nails or nails subject to withdrawal nor shall such anchorage mechanisms induce tension stresses perpendicular to grain in ledgers or nailers. The capacity of such anchors shall result in connections capable of resisting the design values listed in Table R611.8(2).The diaphragm sheathing fasteners applied directly to a ledger shall not be considered effective in providing the additional anchorage required by this section.

Where the additional anchorage mechanisms consist of threaded rods with hex nuts or headed bolts complying with ASTM A 307, Grade A or ASTM F 1554, Grade 36, the design tensile strengths shown in Table R611.9 shall be equal to or greater than the product of the design values listed in Table R611.8(2) and the spacing of the bolts in feet (mm). Anchor bolts shall be embedded as indicated in Table R611.9. Bolts with hooks shall not be used.

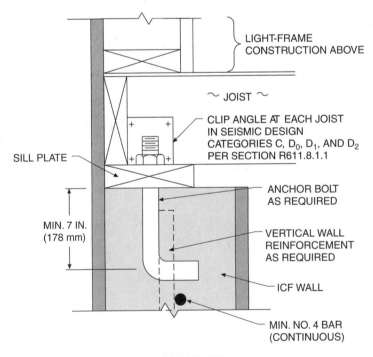

FIGURE R611.8(1)
SECTION CUT THROUGH FLAT WALL OR VERTICAL CORE
OF WAFFLE- OR SCREEN-GRID WALL

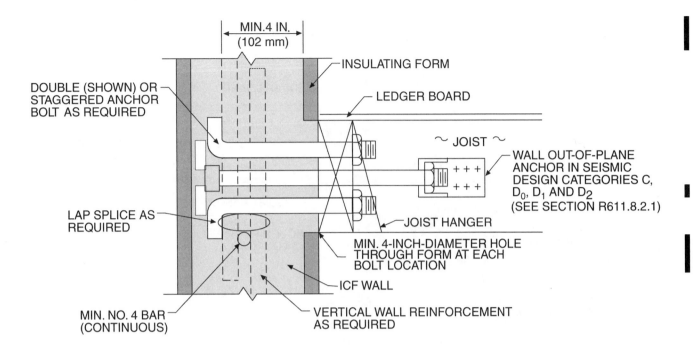

For SI: 1 inch = 25.4 mm.
NOTE: Section cut through flat wall or vertical core of a waffle- or screen-grid wall.

FIGURE R611.8(2)
FLOOR LEDGER—ICF WALL CONNECTION (SIDE-BEARING CONNECTION)

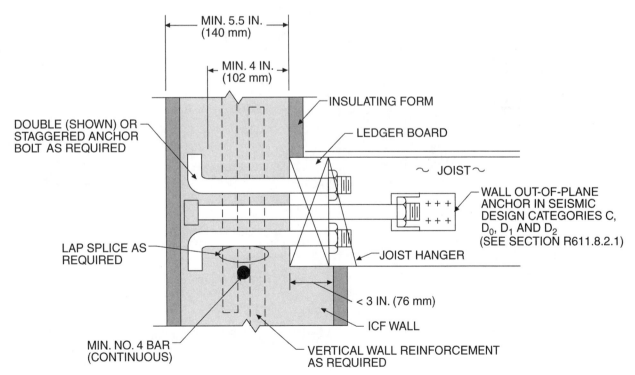

For SI: 1 inch = 25.4 mm.
NOTE: Section cut through flat wall or vertical core of a waffle- or screen-grid wall.

FIGURE R611.8(3)
FLOOR LEDGER—ICF WALL CONNECTION (LEDGE-BEARING CONNECTION)

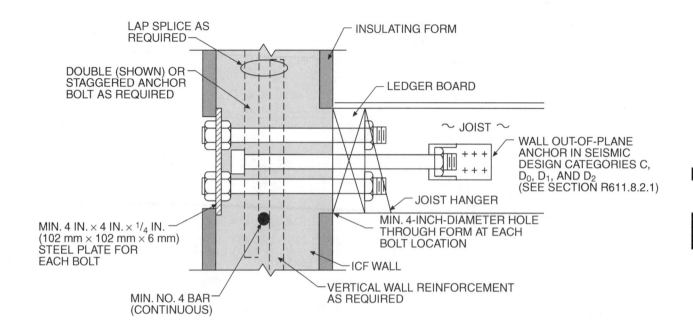

LAP SPLICE AS REQUIRED

INSULATING FORM

DOUBLE (SHOWN) OR STAGGERED ANCHOR BOLT AS REQUIRED

LEDGER BOARD

~ JOIST ~

WALL OUT-OF-PLANE ANCHOR IN SEISMIC DESIGN CATEGORIES C, D_0, D_1, AND D_2 (SEE SECTION R611.8.2.1)

JOIST HANGER

MIN. 4 IN. × 4 IN. × 1/4 IN. (102 mm × 102 mm × 6 mm) STEEL PLATE FOR EACH BOLT

MIN. 4-INCH-DIAMETER HOLE THROUGH FORM AT EACH BOLT LOCATION

ICF WALL

VERTICAL WALL REINFORCEMENT AS REQUIRED

MIN. NO. 4 BAR (CONTINUOUS)

For SI: 1 inch = 25.4 mm.
NOTE: Section cut through flat wall.

FIGURE R611.8(4)
WOOD FLOOR LEDGER—ICF WALL SYSTEM CONNECTION
(THROUGH-BOLT SIDE-BEARING CONNECTION)

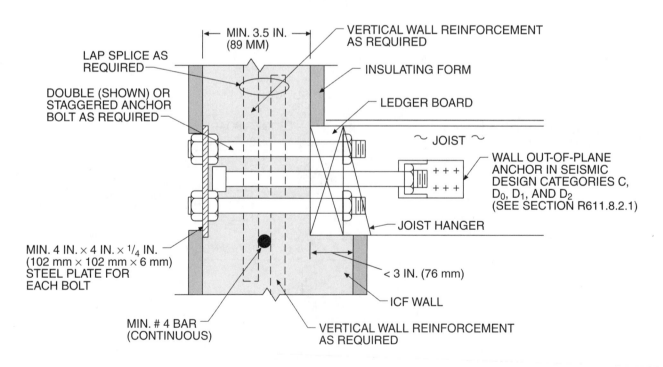

MIN. 3.5 IN. (89 MM)

VERTICAL WALL REINFORCEMENT AS REQUIRED

LAP SPLICE AS REQUIRED

INSULATING FORM

DOUBLE (SHOWN) OR STAGGERED ANCHOR BOLT AS REQUIRED

LEDGER BOARD

~ JOIST ~

WALL OUT-OF-PLANE ANCHOR IN SEISMIC DESIGN CATEGORIES C, D_0, D_1, AND D_2 (SEE SECTION R611.8.2.1)

JOIST HANGER

MIN. 4 IN. × 4 IN. × 1/4 IN. (102 mm × 102 mm × 6 mm) STEEL PLATE FOR EACH BOLT

< 3 IN. (76 mm)

ICF WALL

MIN. # 4 BAR (CONTINUOUS)

VERTICAL WALL REINFORCEMENT AS REQUIRED

For SI: 1 inch = 25.4 mm.
NOTE: Section cut through flat wall.

FIGURE R611.8(5)
FLOOR LEDGER—ICF WALL CONNECTION

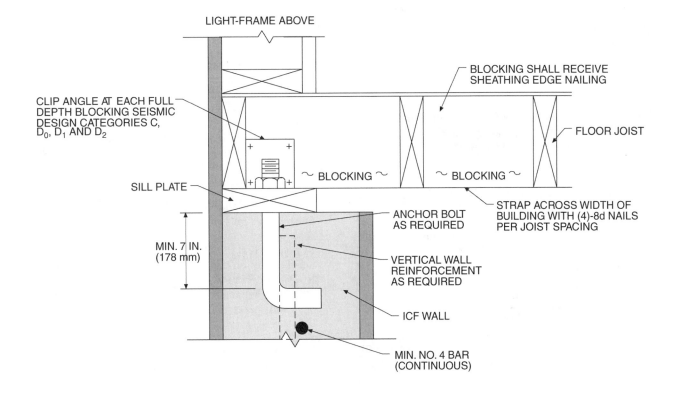

LIGHT-FRAME ABOVE

BLOCKING SHALL RECEIVE
SHEATHING EDGE NAILING

CLIP ANGLE AT EACH FULL
DEPTH BLOCKING SEISMIC
DESIGN CATEGORIES C,
D_0, D_1 AND D_2

FLOOR JOIST

~ BLOCKING ~   ~ BLOCKING ~

SILL PLATE

STRAP ACROSS WIDTH OF
BUILDING WITH (4)-8d NAILS
PER JOIST SPACING

ANCHOR BOLT
AS REQUIRED

MIN. 7 IN.
(178 mm)

VERTICAL WALL
REINFORCEMENT
AS REQUIRED

ICF WALL

MIN. NO. 4 BAR
(CONTINUOUS)

FIGURE R611.8(6)
ANCHORAGE REQUIREMENTS FOR TOP BEARING WALLS FOR TOWNHOUSES IN SEISMIC DESIGN CATEGORY C
AND ALL BUILDINGS IN SEISMIC DESIGN CATEGORIES D_0, D_1, AND D_2 FOR FLOOR FRAMING PARALLEL TO WALL

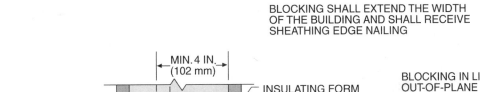

BLOCKING SHALL EXTEND THE WIDTH
OF THE BUILDING AND SHALL RECEIVE
SHEATHING EDGE NAILING

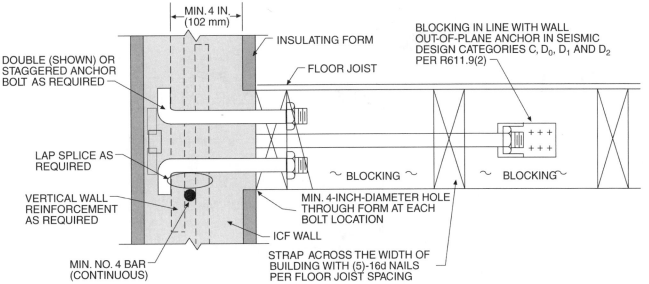

MIN. 4 IN.
(102 mm)

INSULATING FORM

BLOCKING IN LINE WITH WALL
OUT-OF-PLANE ANCHOR IN SEISMIC
DESIGN CATEGORIES C, D_0, D_1 AND D_2
PER R611.9(2)

DOUBLE (SHOWN) OR
STAGGERED ANCHOR
BOLT AS REQUIRED

FLOOR JOIST

LAP SPLICE AS
REQUIRED

~ BLOCKING ~   ~ BLOCKING ~

VERTICAL WALL
REINFORCEMENT
AS REQUIRED

MIN. 4-INCH-DIAMETER HOLE
THROUGH FORM AT EACH
BOLT LOCATION

ICF WALL

MIN. NO. 4 BAR
(CONTINUOUS)

STRAP ACROSS THE WIDTH OF
BUILDING WITH (5)-16d NAILS
PER FLOOR JOIST SPACING

FIGURE R611.8(7)
ANCHORAGE REQUIREMENTS FOR LEDGER BEARING WALLS FOR TOWNHOUSES IN SEISMIC DESIGN CATEGORY C AND ALL
BUILDINGS IN SEISMIC DESIGN CATEGORIES D_0, D_1 AND D_2 FOR FLOOR FRAMING PARALLEL TO WALL

R611.8.3 Floor and roof diaphragm construction. Floor and roof diaphragms shall be constructed of wood structural panel sheathing attached to wood framing in accordance with Table R602.3(1) or Table R602.3(2) or to cold-formed steel floor framing in accordance with Table R505.3.1(2) or to cold-formed steel roof framing in accordance with Table R804.3.

R611.8.3.1 Floor and roof diaphragm construction requirements in Seismic Design Categories D_0, D_1 and D_2. The requirements of this section shall apply in addition to those required by Section R611.8.3. Edge spacing of fasteners in floor and roof sheathing shall be 4 inches (102 mm) on center for Seismic Design Category D_0 or D_1 and 3 inches (76 mm) on center for Seismic Design Category D_2. In Seismic Design Categories D_0, D_1 and D_2, all sheathing edges shall be attached to framing or blocking. Minimum sheathing fastener size shall be 0.113 inch (3 mm) diameter with a minimum penetration of $1^3/_8$-inches (35 mm) into framing members supporting the sheathing. Minimum wood structural panel thickness shall be $^7/_{16}$ inch (11 mm) for roof sheathing and $^{23}/_{32}$ inch (18 mm) for

floor sheathing. Vertical offsets in floor framing shall not be permitted.

R611.9 ICF wall to top sill plate (roof) connections. Wood sill plates attaching roof framing to ICF walls shall be anchored with minimum $^1/_2$ inch (13 mm) diameter anchor bolt embedded a minimum of 7 inches (178 mm) and placed at 6 feet (1829 mm) on center in accordance with Figure R611.9. Anchor bolts shall be located in the cores of waffle-grid and screen-grid ICF walls. Roof assemblies subject to wind uplift pressure of 20 pounds per square foot (1.44 kPa) or greater as established in Table R301.2(2) shall have rafter or truss ties provided in accordance with Table R802.11.

R611.9.1 ICF wall to top sill plate (roof) connections for Seismic Design Categories C, D_0, D_1 and D_2. The requirements of this section shall apply in addition to those required by Section R611.9. The top of an ICF wall at a gable shall be attached to an attic floor in accordance with Section R611.8.1.1. For townhouses in Seismic Design Category C, attic floor diaphragms shall be constructed of structural wood sheathing panels attached to wood framing in accordance

TABLE R611.9
DESIGN TENSILE STRENGTH OF HEADED BOLTS CAST IN CONCRETE[a]

DIAMETER OF BOLT (inches)	MINIMUM EMBEDMENT DEPTH (inches)	DESIGN TENSILE STRENGTH[b] (pounds)
$^1/_4$	2	1040
$^3/_8$ with washer[c]	$2^3/_4$[d]	2540
$^1/_2$ with washer[c]	4[d]	4630

For SI: 1 pound per square inch = 6.895 kPa.

a. Applicable to concrete of all strengths. See Notes (c) and (d).

b. Values are based on ASTM F 1554, Grade 36 bolts. Where ASTM A 307, Grade A headed bolts are used, the strength shall be increased by 1.034.

c. A hardened washer shall be installed at the nut embedded in the concrete or head of the bolt to increase the bearing area. The washer is not required where the concrete strength is 4000 psi or more.

d. Embedment depth shall be permitted to be reduced $^1/_4$-inch where 4000 psi concrete is used.

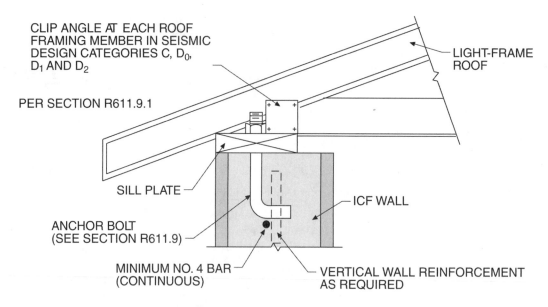

NOTE: Section cut through flat wall or vertical core of a waffle- or screen-grid wall.

FIGURE R611.9
ROOF SILL PLATE—ICF WALL CONNECTION

with Table R602.3(1) or Table R602.3(2). Edge spacing of fasteners in attic floor sheathing shall be 4 inches (102 mm) on center for Seismic Design Category D_0 or D_1 and 3 inches (76 mm) on center for Seismic Design Category D_2. In Seismic Design Categories D_0, D_1 and D_2, all sheathing edges shall be attached to framing or blocking. Minimum sheathing fastener size shall be 0.113 inch (2.8 mm) diameter with a minimum penetration of $1^3/_8$ inches (35 mm) into framing members supporting the sheathing. Minimum wood structural panel thickness shall be $^7/_{16}$ inch (11 mm) for the attic floor sheathing. Where hipped roof construction is used, the use of a structural attic floor is not required.

For townhouses in Seismic Design Category C, wood sill plates attached to ICF walls shall be anchored with ASTM A 307, Grade A, $^3/_8$-inch (10 mm) diameter anchor bolts embedded a minimum of 7 inches (178 mm) and placed at a maximum spacing of 36 inches (914 mm) on center. For all buildings in Seismic Design Category D_0 or D_1, wood sill plates attached to ICF walls shall be anchored with ASTM A 307, Grade A, $^3/_8$-inch (10 mm) diameter anchor bolts embedded a minimum of 7 inches (178 mm) and placed at a maximum spacing of 16 inches (406 mm) on center. For all buildings in Seismic Design Category D_2, wood sill plates attached to ICF walls shall be anchored with ASTM A 307, Grade A, $^3/_8$-inch (10 mm) diameter anchor bolts embedded a minimum of 7 inches (178 mm) and placed at a maximum spacing of 16 inches (406 mm) on center.

For townhouses in Seismic Design Category C, each floor joist shall be attached to the sill plate with an 18-gage [(0.0478 in.) (1.2 mm)] angle bracket using 3 - 8d common nails per leg in accordance with Figure R611.8(1). For all buildings in Seismic Design Category D_0 or D_1, each floor joist shall be attached to the sill plate with an 18-gage [(0.0478 in.) (1.2 mm)] angle bracket using 4 - 8d common nails per leg in accordance with Figure R611.8(1). For all buildings in Seismic Design Category D_2, each floor joist shall be attached to the sill plate with an 18-gage [(0.0478 in.) (1.2 mm)] angle bracket using 6-8d common nails per leg in accordance with Figure R611.8(1).

Where hipped roof construction is used without an attic floor, the following shall apply. For townhouses in Seismic Design Category C, each rafter shall be attached to the sill plate with an 18-gage [(0.0478 in.) (1.2 mm)] angle bracket using 3 - 8d common nails per leg in accordance with Figure R611.9. For all buildings in Seismic Design Category D_0 or D_1, each rafter shall be attached to the sill plate with an 18-gage [(0.0478 in.) (1.2 mm)] angle bracket using 4 - 8d common nails per leg in accordance with Figure R611.9. For all buildings in Seismic Design Category D_2, each rafter shall be attached to the sill plate with an 18-gage [(0.0478 in.) (1.2 mm)] angle bracket using 6-8d common nails per leg in accordance with Figure R611.9.

SECTION R612
CONVENTIONALLY FORMED CONCRETE WALL CONSTRUCTION

R612.1 General. Conventionally formed concrete walls with flat surfaces shall be designed and constructed in accordance

with the provisions of Section R611 for Flat ICF walls or in accordance with the provisions of ACI 318.

SECTION R613
EXTERIOR WINDOWS AND GLASS DOORS

R613.1 General. This section prescribes performance and construction requirements for exterior window systems installed in wall systems. Windows and doors shall be installed in accordance with the manufacturer's installation instructions. Installation instructions shall be provided by the manufacturer for each exterior window or door type.

R613.3 Performance. Exterior windows and doors shall be designed to resist the design wind loads specified in Table R301.2(2) adjusted for height and exposure per Table R301.2(3).

R613.4 Testing and labeling. Exterior windows and sliding doors shall be tested by an approved independent laboratory, and bear a label identifying manufacturer, performance characteristics and approved inspection agency to indicate compliance with AAMA/WDMA/CSA 101/I.S.2/A440. Exterior side-hinged doors shall be tested and labeled as conforming to AAMA/WDMA/CSA 101/I.S.2/A440 or comply with Section R613.6.

Exception: Decorative glazed openings.

R613.4.1 Comparative analysis. Structural wind load design pressures for window and door units smaller than the size tested in accordance with Section R613.4 shall be permitted to be higher than the design value of the tested unit provided such higher pressures are determined by accepted engineering analysis. All components of the small unit shall be the same as those of the tested unit. Where such calculated design pressures are used, they shall be validated by an additional test of the window or door unit having the highest allowable design pressure.

R613.5 Vehicular access doors. Vehicular access doors shall be tested in accordance with either ASTM E 330 or ANSI/DASMA 108, and shall meet the acceptance criteria of ANSI/DASMA 108.

R613.6 Other exterior window and door assemblies. Exterior windows and door assemblies not included within the scope of Section R613.4 or Section R613.5 shall be tested in accordance with ASTM E 330. Glass in assemblies covered by this exception shall comply with Section R308.5.

R613.7 Wind-borne debris protection. Protection of exterior windows and glass doors in buildings located in wind-borne debris regions shall be in accordance with Section R301.2.1.2.

R613.7.1 Fenestration testing and labeling. Fenestration shall be tested by an approved independent laboratory, listed by an approved entity, and bear a label identifying manufacturer, performance characteristics, and approved inspection agency to indicate compliance with the requirements of the following specification:

1. ASTM E 1886 and ASTM E 1996; or
2. AAMA 506.

R613.8 Anchorage methods. The methods cited in this section apply only to anchorage of window and glass door assemblies to the main force-resisting system.

R613.8.1 Anchoring requirements. Window and glass door assemblies shall be anchored in accordance with the published manufacturer's recommendations to achieve the design pressure specified. Substitute anchoring systems used for substrates not specified by the fenestration manufacturer shall provide equal or greater anchoring performance as demonstrated by accepted engineering practice.

R613.8.2 Anchorage details. Products shall be anchored in accordance with the minimum requirements illustrated in Figures R613.8(1), R613.8(2), R613.8(3), R613.8(4), R613.8(5), R613.8(6), R613.8(7) and R613.8(8).

R613.8.2.1 Masonry, concrete or other structural substrate. Where the wood shim or buck thickness is less than $1^1/_2$ inches (38 mm), window and glass door assemblies shall be anchored through the jamb, or by jamb clip and anchors shall be embedded directly into the masonry, concrete or other substantial substrate material.

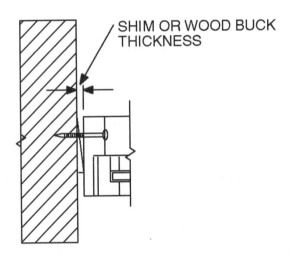

FIGURE R613.8(1)
THROUGH THE FRAME

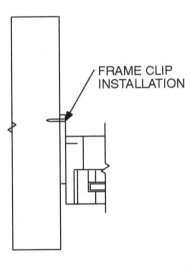

APPLY FRAME CLIP TO WINDOW OR DOOR IN ACCORDANCE WITH PUBLISHED MANUFACTURER'S RECOMMENDATIONS.

FIGURE R613.8(2)
FRAME CLIP

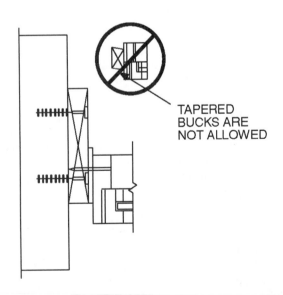

THROUGH THE FRAME ANCHORING METHOD. ANCHORS SHALL BE PROVIDED TO TRANSFER LOAD FROM THE WINDOW OR DOOR FRAME INTO THE ROUGH OPENING SUBSTRATE.

FIGURE R613.8(3)
THROUGH THE FRAME

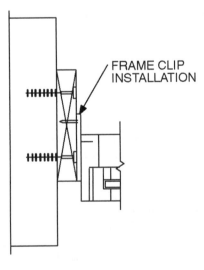

APPLY FRAME CLIP TO WINDOW OR DOOR FRAME IN ACCORDANCE WITH PUBLISHED MANUFACTURER'S RECOMMENDATIONS. ANCHORS SHALL BE PROVIDED TO TRANSFER LOAD FROM THE FRAME CLIP INTO THE ROUGH OPENING SUBSTRATE.

FIGURE R613.8(4)
FRAME CLIP

Anchors shall adequately transfer load from the window or door frame into the rough opening substrate [see Figures R613.8(1) and R613.8(2).]

Where the wood shim or buck thickness is 1$^1/_2$ inches (38 mm) or more, the buck is securely fastened to the masonry, concrete or other substantial substrate, and the buck extends beyond the interior face of the window or door frame, window and glass door assemblies shall be anchored through the jamb, or by jamb clip, or through the flange to the secured wood buck. Anchors shall be embedded into the secured wood buck to adequately transfer load from the window or door frame assembly [Figures R613.8(3), R613.8(4) and R613.8(5)].

R613.8.2.2 Wood or other approved framing material. Where the framing material is wood or other approved framing material, window and glass door assemblies shall be anchored through the frame, or by frame clip, or through the flange. Anchors shall be embedded into the frame construction to adequately transfer load [Figures R613.8(6), R613.8(7) and R613.8(8)].

R613.9 Mullions occurring between individual window and glass door assemblies.

R613.9.1 Mullions. Mullions shall be tested by an approved testing laboratory in accordance with AAMA 450, or be engineered in accordance with accepted engineering practice. Mullions tested as stand-alone units or qualified by engineering shall use performance criteria cited in Sections R613.9.2, R613.9.3 and R613.9.4. Mullions

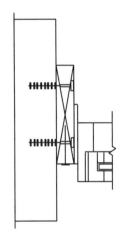

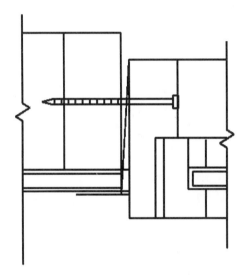

APPLY ANCHORS THROUGH FLANGE IN ACCORDANCE WITH PUBLISHED MANUFACTURER'S RECOMMENDATIONS.

FIGURE R613.8(5)
THROUGH THE FLANGE

FIGURE R613.8(6)
THROUGH THE FRAME

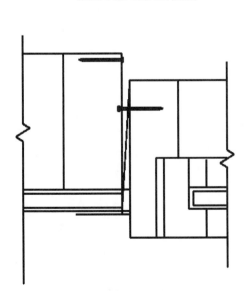

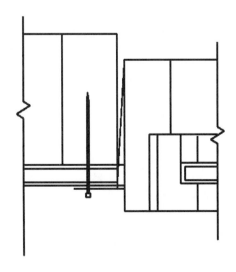

FIGURE R613.8(7)
FRAME CLIP

FIGURE R613.8(8)
THROUGH THE FLANGE

qualified by an actual test of an entire assembly shall comply with Sections R613.9.2 and R613.9.4.

R613.9.2 Load transfer. Mullions shall be designed to transfer the design pressure loads applied by the window and door assemblies to the rough opening substrate.

R613.9.3 Deflection. Mullions shall be capable of resisting the design pressure loads applied by the window and door assemblies to be supported without deflecting more than $L/175$, where L is the span of the mullion in inches.

R613.9.4 Structural safety factor. Mullions shall be capable of resisting a load of 1.5 times the design pressure loads applied by the window and door assemblies to be supported without exceeding the appropriate material stress levels. If tested by an approved laboratory, the 1.5 times the design pressure load shall be sustained for 10 seconds, and the permanent deformation shall not exceed 0.4 percent of the mullion span after the 1.5 times design pressure load is removed.

CHAPTER 7
WALL COVERING

SECTION R701
GENERAL

R701.1 Application. The provisions of this chapter shall control the design and construction of the interior and exterior wall covering for all buildings.

R701.2 Installation. Products sensitive to adverse weather shall not be installed until adequate weather protection for the installation is provided. Exterior sheathing shall be dry before applying exterior cover.

SECTION R702
INTERIOR COVERING

R702.1 General. Interior coverings or wall finishes shall be installed in accordance with this chapter and Table R702.1(1), Table R702.1(2), Table R702.1(3) and Table R702.3.5. Interior masonry veneer shall comply with the requirements of Section R703.7.1 for support and Section R703.7.4 for anchorage, except an air space is not required. Interior finishes and materials shall conform to the flame spread and smoke-density requirements of Section R315.

TABLE R702.1(1)
THICKNESS OF PLASTER

PLASTER BASE	FINISHED THICKNESS OF PLASTER FROM FACE OF LATH, MASONRY, CONCRETE (inches)	
	Gypsum plaster	Portland cement mortar
Expanded metal lath	$^5/_8$, minimum[a]	$^5/_8$, minimum[a]
Wire lath	$^5/_8$, minimum[a]	$^3/_4$, minimum (interior)[b] $^7/_8$, minimum (exterior)[b]
Gypsum lath[g]	$^1/_2$, minimum	$^3/_4$, minimum (interior)[b]
Masonry walls[c]	$^1/_2$, minimum	$^1/_2$, minimum
Monolithic concrete walls[c,d]	$^5/_8$, maximum	$^7/_8$, maximum
Monolithic concrete ceilings[c,d]	$^3/_8$, maximum[e]	$^1/_2$, maximum
Gypsum veneer base[f,g]	$^1/_{16}$, minimum	$^3/_4$, minimum (interior)[b]
Gypsum sheathing[g]	—	$^3/_4$, minimum (interior)[b] $^7/_8$, minimum (exterior)[b]

For SI: 1 inch = 25.4 mm.

a. When measured from back plane of expanded metal lath, exclusive of ribs, or self-furring lath, plaster thickness shall be $^3/_4$ inch minimum.

b. When measured from face of support or backing.

c. Because masonry and concrete surfaces may vary in plane, thickness of plaster need not be uniform.

d. When applied over a liquid bonding agent, finish coat may be applied directly to concrete surface.

e. Approved acoustical plaster may be applied directly to concrete or over base coat plaster, beyond the maximum plaster thickness shown.

f. Attachment shall be in accordance with Table R702.3.5.

g. Where gypsum board is used as a base for portland cement plaster, weather-resistant sheathing paper complying with Section R703.2 shall be provided.

TABLE R702.1(2)
GYPSUM PLASTER PROPORTIONS[a]

NUMBER	COAT	PLASTER BASE OR LATH	MAXIMUM VOLUME AGGREGATE PER 100 POUNDS NEAT PLASTER[b] (cubic feet)	
			Damp loose sand[a]	Perlite or vermiculite[c]
Two-coat work	Base coat	Gypsum lath	2.5	2
	Base coat	Masonry	3	3
Three-coat work	First coat	Lath	2[d]	2
	Second coat	Lath	3[d]	2[e]
	First and second coats	Masonry	3	3

For SI: 1 inch = 25.4 mm, 1 cubic foot = 0.0283 m³, 1 pound = 0.454 kg.

a. Wood-fibered gypsum plaster may be mixed in the proportions of 100 pounds of gypsum to not more than 1 cubic foot of sand where applied on masonry or concrete.

b. When determining the amount of aggregate in set plaster, a tolerance of 10 percent shall be allowed.

c. Combinations of sand and lightweight aggregate may be used, provided the volume and weight relationship of the combined aggregate to gypsum plaster is maintained.

d. If used for both first and second coats, the volume of aggregate may be 2.5 cubic feet.

e. Where plaster is 1 inch or more in total thickness, the proportions for the second coat may be increased to 3 cubic feet.

TABLE R702.1(3)
PORTLAND CEMENT PLASTER

	MAXIMUM VOLUME AGGREGATE PER VOLUME CEMENTITIOUS MATERIAL[a]					
	Portland cement plaster[b] maximum volume aggregate per volume cement	Portland cement-lime plaster[c]			MINIMUM PERIOD MOIST COATS	MINIMUM INTERVAL BETWEEN
Coat		Maximum volume lime per volume cement	Maximum volume sand per volume cement and lime	Approximate minimum thickness[d] curing (inches)		
First	4	$^3/_4$	4	$^3/_8$[e]	48 Hours[f]	48 Hours[g]
Second	5	$^3/_4$	5	First and second coats	48 Hours	7 Days[h]
Finish	3[i]	—	3[i]	$^1/_8$	—	Note h

For SI: 1 inch = 25.4 mm, 1 pound = 0.454 kg.

a. When determining the amount of aggregate in set plaster, a tolerance of 10 percent may be allowed.
b. From 10 to 20 pounds of dry hydrated lime (or an equivalent amount of lime putty) may be added as a plasticizing agent to each sack of Type I and Type II standard portland cement in base coat plaster.
c. No plasticizing agents shall be added.
d. See Table R702.1(1).
e. Measured from face of support or backing to crest of scored plaster.
f. Twenty-four-hour minimum period for moist curing of interior portland cement plaster.
g. Twenty-four hour minimum interval between coats of interior portland cement plaster.
h. Finish coat plaster may be applied to interior portland cement base coats after a 48-hour period.
i. For finish coat, plaster up to an equal part of dry hydrated lime by weight (or an equivalent volume of lime putty) may be added to Type I, Type II and Type III standard portland cement.

R702.2 Interior plaster. Gypsum plaster or portland cement plastering materials shall conform to ASTM C 5, C 28, C 35, C 37, C 59, C 61, C 587, C 588, C 631, C 847, C 897, C 933, C 1032 and C 1047, and shall be installed or applied in conformance with ASTM C 843, C 844 and C 1063. Plaster shall not be less than three coats when applied over metal lath and not less than two coats when applied over other bases permitted by this section, except that veneer plaster may be applied in one coat not to exceed $^3/_{16}$ inch (5 mm) thickness, provided the total thickness is as set forth in Table R702.1(1).

R702.2.1 Support. Support spacing for gypsum or metal lath on walls or ceilings shall not exceed 16 inches (406 mm) for $^3/_8$ inch thick (10 mm) or 24 inches (610 mm) for $^1/_2$-inch-thick (13 mm) plain gypsum lath. Gypsum lath shall be installed at right angles to support framing with end joints in adjacent courses staggered by at least one framing space.

R702.3 Gypsum board.

R702.3.1 Materials. All gypsum board materials and accessories shall conform to ASTM C 36, C 79, C 475, C 514, C 630, C 931, C 960, C 1002, C 1047, C 1177, C 1178, C 1278, C 1395 or C 1396 and shall be installed in accordance with the provisions of this section. Adhesives for the installation of gypsum board shall conform to ASTM C 557.

R702.3.2 Wood framing. Wood framing supporting gypsum board shall not be less than 2 inches (51 mm) nominal thickness in the least dimension except that wood furring strips not less than 1-inch-by-2 inch (25 mm by 51 mm) nominal dimension may be used over solid backing or framing spaced not more than 24 inches (610 mm) on center.

R702.3.3 Steel framing. Steel framing supporting gypsum board shall not be less than 1.25 inches (32 mm) wide in the least dimension. Light-gage nonload-bearing steel framing shall comply with ASTM C 645. Load-bearing steel framing and steel framing from 0.033 inch to 0.112 inch (1 mm to 3 mm) thick shall comply with ASTM C 955.

R702.3.4 Insulating concrete form walls. Foam plastics for insulating concrete form walls constructed in accordance with Sections R404.4 and R611 on the interior of habitable spaces shall be covered in accordance with Section R314.4. Use of adhesives in conjunction with mechanical fasteners is permitted. Adhesives used for interior and exterior finishes shall be compatible with the insulating form materials.

R702.3.5 Application. Maximum spacing of supports and the size and spacing of fasteners used to attach gypsum board shall comply with Table R702.3.5. Gypsum sheathing shall be attached to exterior walls in accordance with Table R602.3(1). Gypsum board shall be applied at right angles or parallel to framing members. All edges and ends of gypsum board shall occur on the framing members, except those edges and ends that are perpendicular to the framing members. Interior gypsum board shall not be installed where it is directly exposed to the weather or to water.

R702.3.6 Fastening. Screws for attaching gypsum board to wood framing shall be Type W or Type S in accordance with ASTM C 1002 and shall penetrate the wood not less than $^5/_8$ inch (16 mm). Screws for attaching gypsum board to light-gage steel framing shall be Type S in accordance with ASTM C 1002 and shall penetrate the steel not less than $^3/_8$ inch (10 mm). Screws for attaching gypsum board to steel framing 0.033 inch to 0.112 inch (1 mm to 3 mm) thick shall comply with ASTM C 954.

TABLE R702.3.5
MINIMUM THICKNESS AND APPLICATION OF GYPSUM BOARD

THICKNESS OF GYPSUM BOARD (inches)	APPLICATION	ORIENTATION OF GYPSUM BOARD TO FRAMING	MAXIMUM SPACING OF FRAMING MEMBERS (inches o.c.)	MAXIMUM SPACING OF FASTENERS (inches)		SIZE OF NAILS FOR APPLICATION TO WOOD FRAMING[c]
				Nails[a]	Screws[b]	
Application without adhesive						
$^3/_8$	Ceiling[d]	Perpendicular	16	7	12	13 gage, $1^1/_4''$ long, $^{19}/_{64}''$ head; 0.098″ diameter, $1^1/_4''$ long, annular-ringed; or 4d cooler nail, 0.080″ diameter, $1^3/_8''$ long, $^7/_{32}''$ head.
	Wall	Either direction	16	8	16	
$^1/_2$	Ceiling	Either direction	16	7	12	13 gage, $1^3/_8''$ long, $^{19}/_{64}''$ head; 0.098″ diameter, $1^1/_4''$ long, annular-ringed; 5d cooler nail, 0.086″ diameter, $1^5/_8''$ long, $^{15}/_{64}''$ head; or gypsum board nail, 0.086″ diameter, $1^5/_8''$ long, $^9/_{32}''$ head.
	Ceiling[d]	Perpendicular	24	7	12	
	Wall	Either direction	24	8	12	
	Wall	Either direction	16	8	16	
$^5/_8$	Ceiling	Either direction	16	7	12	13 gage, $1^5/_8''$ long, $^{19}/_{64}''$ head; 0.098″ diameter, $1^3/_8''$ long, annular-ringed; 6d cooler nail, 0.092″ diameter, $1^7/_8''$ long, $^1/_4''$ head; or gypsum board nail, 0.0915″ diameter, $1^7/_8''$ long, $^{19}/_{64}''$ head.
	Ceiling[e]	Perpendicular	24	7	12	
	Wall	Either direction	24 .	8	12	
	Wall	Either direction	16	8	16	
Application with adhesive						
$^3/_8$	Ceiling[d]	Perpendicular	16	16	16	Same as above for $^3/_8''$ gypsum board
	Wall	Either direction	16	16	24	
$^1/_2$ or $^5/_8$	Ceiling	Either direction	16	16	16	Same as above for $^1/_2''$ and $^5/_8''$ gypsum board, respectively
	Ceiling[d]	Perpendicular	24	12	16	
	Wall	Either direction	24	16	24	
Two $^3/_8$ layers	Ceiling	Perpendicular	16	16	16	Base ply nailed as above for $^1/_2''$ gypsum board; face ply installed with adhesive
	Wall	Either direction	24	24	24	

For SI: 1 inch = 25.4 mm.

a. For application without adhesive, a pair of nails spaced not less than 2 inches apart or more than $2^1/_2$ inches apart may be used with the pair of nails spaced 12 inches on center.

b. Screws shall be Type S or W per ASTM C 1002 and shall be sufficiently long to penetrate wood framing not less than $^5/_8$ inch and metal framing not less than $^3/_8$ inch.

c. Where metal framing is used with a clinching design to receive nails by two edges of metal, the nails shall be not less than $^5/_8$ inch longer than the gypsum board thickness and shall have ringed shanks. Where the metal framing has a nailing groove formed to receive the nails, the nails shall have barbed shanks or be 5d, $13^1/_2$ gage, $1^5/_8$ inches long, $^{15}/_{64}$-inch head for $^1/_2$-inch gypsum board; and 6d, 13 gage, $1^7/_8$ inches long, $^{15}/_{64}$-inch head for $^5/_8$-inch gypsum board.

d. Three-eighths-inch-thick single-ply gypsum board shall not be used on a ceiling where a water-based textured finish is to be applied, or where it will be required to support insulation above a ceiling. On ceiling applications to receive a water-based texture material, either hand or spray applied, the gypsum board shall be applied perpendicular to framing. When applying a water-based texture material, the minimum gypsum board thickness shall be increased from $^3/_8$ inch to $^1/_2$ inch for 16-inch on center framing, and from $^1/_2$ inch to $^5/_8$ inch for 24-inch on center framing or $^1/_2$-inch sag-resistant gypsum ceiling board shall be used.

e. Type X gypsum board for garage ceilings beneath habitable rooms shall be installed perpendicular to the ceiling framing and shall be fastened at maximum 6 inches o.c. by minimum $1^7/_8$ inches 6d coated nails or equivalent drywall screws.

R702.3.7 Horizontal gypsum board diaphragm ceilings. Use of gypsum board shall be permitted on wood joists to create a horizontal diaphragm in accordance with Table R702.3.7. Gypsum board shall be installed perpendicular to ceiling framing members. End joints of adjacent courses of board shall not occur on the same joist. The maximum allowable diaphragm proportions shall be $1^1/_2$:1 between shear resisting elements. Rotation or cantilever conditions shall not be permitted. Gypsum board shall not be used in diaphragm ceilings to resist lateral forces imposed by masonry or concrete construction. All perimeter edges shall be blocked using wood members not less than 2-inch (51 mm) by 6-inch (152 mm) nominal dimension. Blocking material shall be installed flat over the top plate of the wall to provide a nailing surface not less than 2 inches (51 mm) in width for the attachment of the gypsum board.

R702.3.8 Water-resistant gypsum backing board. Gypsum board used as the base or backer for adhesive application of ceramic tile or other required nonabsorbent finish material shall conform to ASTM C 630 or C 1178. Use of water-resistant gypsum backing board shall be permitted on ceilings where framing spacing does not exceed 12 inches (305 mm) on center for $^1/_2$-inch-thick (13 mm) or 16 inches (406 mm) for $^5/_8$-inch-thick (16 mm) gypsum board. Water-resistant gypsum board shall not be installed over a vapor retarder in a shower or tub compartment. Cut or exposed edges, including those at wall intersections, shall be sealed as recommended by the manufacturer.

R702.3.8.1 Limitations. Water resistant gypsum backing board shall not be used where there will be direct exposure to water, or in areas subject to continuous high humidity.

TABLE R702.3.7
SHEAR CAPACITY FOR HORIZONTAL WOOD-FRAMED
GYPSUM BOARD DIAPHRAGM CEILING ASSEMBLIES

MATERIAL	THICKNESS OF MATERIAL (min.) (in.)	SPACING OF FRAMING MEMBERS (max.) (in.)	SHEAR VALUE[a, b] (plf of ceiling)	MINIMUM FASTENER SIZE[c, d]
Gypsum Board	$^1/_2$	16 o.c.	90	5d cooler or wallboard nail; $1^5/_8$-inch long; 0.086- inch shank; $^{15}/_{64}$-inch head
Gypsum Board	$^1/_2$	24 o.c.	70	5d cooler or wallboard nail; $1^5/_8$-inch long; 0.086- inch shank; $^{15}/_{64}$-inch head

For SI: 1 inch = 25.4 mm, 1 pound per linear foot = 1.488 kg/m.

a. Values are not cumulative with other horizontal diaphragm values and are for short-term loading caused by wind or seismic loading. Values shall be reduced 25 per-cent for normal loading.

b. Values shall be reduced 50 percent in Seismic Design Categories D_0, D_1, D_2 and E.

c. $1^1/_4$", #6 Type S or W screws may be substituted for the listed nails.

d. Fasteners shall be spaced not more than 7 inches on center at all supports, including perimeter blocking, and not less than $^3/_8$ inch from the edges and ends of the gypsum board.

R702.4 Ceramic tile.

R702.4.1 General. Ceramic tile surfaces shall be installed in accordance with ANSI A108.1, A108.4, A108.5, A108.6, A108.11, A118.1, A118.3, A136.1 and A137.1.

R702.4.2 Cement, fiber-cement and glass mat gypsum backers. Cement, fiber-cement or glass mat gypsum back-ers in compliance with ASTM C 1288, C 1325 or C 1178 and installed in accordance with manufacturers' recommen-dations shall be used as backers for wall tile in tub and shower areas and wall panels in shower areas.

R702.5 Other finishes. Wood veneer paneling and hardboard paneling shall be placed on wood or cold-formed steel fram-ing spaced not more than 16 inches (406 mm) on center. Wood veneer and hard board paneling less than $^1/_4$ inch (6 mm) nom-inal thickness shall not have less than a $^3/_8$-inch (10 mm) gyp-sum board backer. Wood veneer paneling not less than $^1/_4$-inch (6 mm) nominal thickness shall conform to ANSI/HPVA HP-1. Hardboard paneling shall conform to ANSI/AHA A135.5.

R702.6 Wood shakes and shingles. Wood shakes and shingles shall conform to CSSB *Grading Rules for Wood Shakes and Shingles* and shall be permitted to be installed directly to the studs with maximum 24 inches (610 mm) on-center spacing.

R702.6.1 Attachment. Nails, staples or glue are permitted for attaching shakes or shingles to the wall, and attachment of the shakes or shingles directly to the surface shall be per-mitted provided the fasteners are appropriate for the type of wall surface material. When nails or staples are used, two fasteners shall be provided and shall be placed so that they are covered by the course above.

R702.6.2 Furring strips. Where furring strips are used, they shall be 1 inch by 2 inches or 1 inch by 3 inches (25 mm by 51 mm or 25 mm by 76 mm), spaced a distance on center equal to the desired exposure, and shall be attached to the wall by nailing through other wall material into the studs.

SECTION R703
EXTERIOR COVERING

R703.1 General. Exterior walls shall provide the building with a weather-resistant exterior wall envelope. The exterior wall envelope shall include flashing as described in Section R703.8. The exterior wall envelope shall be designed and constructed in a manner that prevents the accumulation of water within the wall assembly by providing a water-resistant barrier behind the exterior veneer as required by Section R703.2. and a means of draining water that enters the assem-bly to the exterior. Protection against condensation in the exterior wall assembly shall be provided in accordance with Chapter 11 of this code.

Exceptions:

1. A weather-resistant exterior wall envelope shall not be required over concrete or masonry walls designed in accordance with Chapter 6 and flashed according to Section R703.7 or R703.8.

2. Compliance with the requirements for a means of drainage, and the requirements of Section R703.2 and Section R703.8, shall not be required for an exterior wall envelope that has been demonstrated to resist wind-driven rain through testing of the exterior wall envelope, including joints, penetrations and intersec-tions with dissimilar materials, in accordance with ASTM E 331 under the following conditions:

    2.1. Exterior wall envelope test assemblies shall include at least one opening, one control joint, one wall/eave interface and one wall sill. All tested openings and penetrations shall be rep-resentative of the intended end-use configura-tion.

    2.2. Exterior wall envelope test assemblies shall be at least 4 feet (1219 mm) by 8 feet (2438 mm) in size.

2.3. Exterior wall assemblies shall be tested at a minimum differential pressure of 6.24 pounds per square foot (299 Pa).

2.4. Exterior wall envelope assemblies shall be subjected to a minimum test exposure duration of 2 hours.

The exterior wall envelope design shall be considered to resist wind-driven rain where the results of testing indicate that water did not penetrate: control joints in the exterior wall envelope; joints at the perimeter of openings penetration; or intersections of terminations with dissimilar materials.

R703.2 Water-resistive barrier. One layer of No. 15 asphalt felt, free from holes and breaks, complying with ASTM D 226 for Type 1 felt or other approved water-resistive barrier shall be applied over studs or sheathing of all exterior walls. Such felt or material shall be applied horizontally, with the upper layer lapped over the lower layer not less than 2 inches (51 mm). Where joints occur, felt shall be lapped not less than 6 inches (152 mm). The felt or other approved material shall be continuous to the top of walls and terminated at penetrations and building appendages in a manner to meet the requirements of the exterior wall envelope as described in Section R703.1.

Exception: Omission of the water-resistive barrier is permitted in the following situations:

1. In detached accessory buildings.

2. Under exterior wall finish materials as permitted in Table R703.4.

3. Under paperbacked stucco lath when the paper backing is an approved weather-resistive sheathing paper.

R703.3 Wood, hardboard and wood structural panel siding.

R703.3.1 Panel siding. Joints in wood, hardboard or wood structural panel siding shall be made as follows unless otherwise approved. Vertical joints in panel siding shall occur over framing members, unless wood or wood structural panel sheathing is used, and shall be shiplapped or covered with a batten. Horizontal joints in panel siding shall be lapped a minimum of 1 inch (25 mm) or shall be shiplapped or shall be flashed with Z-flashing and occur over solid blocking, wood or wood structural panel sheathing.

R703.3.2 Horizontal siding. Horizontal lap siding shall be lapped a minimum of 1 inch (25 mm), or 0.5 inch (13 mm) if rabbeted, and shall have the ends caulked, covered with a batten, or sealed and installed over a strip of flashing.

R703.4 Attachments. Unless specified otherwise, all wall coverings shall be securely fastened in accordance with Table R703.4 or with other approved aluminum, stainless steel, zinc-coated or other approved corrosion-resistant fasteners. Where the basic wind speed per Figure R301.2(4) is 110 miles per hour (49 m/s) or higher, the attachment of wall coverings shall be designed to resist the component and cladding loads specified in Table R301.2(2), adjusted for height and exposure in accordance with Table R301.2(3).

R703.5 Wood shakes and shingles. Wood shakes and shingles shall conform to CSSB *Grading Rules for Wood Shakes and Shingles.*

R703.5.1 Application. Wood shakes or shingles shall be applied either single-course or double-course over nominal $^1/_2$-inch (13 mm) wood-based sheathing or to furring strips over $^1/_2$-inch (13 mm) nominal nonwood sheathing . A permeable water-resistive barrier shall be provided over all sheathing, with horizontal overlaps in the membrane of not less than 2 inches (51mm) and vertical overlaps of not less than 6 inches (152 mm). Where furring strips are used, they shall be 1 inch by 3 inches or 1 inch by 4 inches (25 mm by 76 mm or 25 mm by 102 mm) and shall be fastened horizontally to the studs with 7d or 8d box nails and shall be spaced a distance on center equal to the actual weather exposure of the shakes or shingles, not to exceed the maximum exposure specified in Table R703.5.2. The spacing between adjacent shingles to allow for expansion shall not exceed $^1/_4$ inch (6 mm), and between adjacent shakes, it shall not exceed $^1/_2$ inch (13 mm). The offset spacing between joints in adjacent courses shall be a minimum of $1^1/_2$ inches (38 mm).

R703.5.2 Weather exposure. The maximum weather exposure for shakes and shingles shall not exceed that specified in Table R703.5.2.

R703.5.3 Attachment. Each shake or shingle shall be held in place by two hot-dipped zinc-coated, stainless steel, or aluminum nails or staples. The fasteners shall be long enough to penetrate the sheathing or furring strips by a minimum of $^1/_2$ inch (13 mm) and shall not be overdriven.

R703.5.3.1 Staple attachment. Staples shall not be less than 16 gage and shall have a crown width of not less than $^7/_{16}$ inch (11 mm), and the crown of the staples shall be parallel with the butt of the shake or shingle. In single-course application, the fasteners shall be concealed by the course above and shall be driven approximately 1 inch (25 mm) above the butt line of the succeeding course and $^3/_4$ inch (19 mm) from the edge. In double-course applications, the exposed shake or shingle shall be face-nailed with two casing nails, driven approximately 2 inches (51 mm) above the butt line and $^3/_4$ inch (19 mm) from each edge. In all applications, staples shall be concealed by the course above. With shingles wider than 8 inches (203 mm) two additional nails shall be required and shall be nailed approximately 1 inch (25 mm) apart near the center of the shingle.

R703.5.4 Bottom courses. The bottom courses shall be doubled.

R703.6 Exterior plaster. Installation of these materials shall be in compliance with ASTM C 926-98a and ASTM C 1063-03 and provisions of this code.

R703.6.1 Lath. All lath and lath attachments shall be of corrosion-resistant materials. Expanded metal or woven wire lath shall be attached with 11 gage nails having a $^7/_{16}$-inch (11.1 mm) head or 16 gage staples, spaced at no more than 6 inches (152 mm) or as otherwise approved. Nails or staples shall penetrate wood framing support members not less than $^3/_4$-inch (19 mm).

TABLE R703.4
WEATHER–RESISTANT SIDING ATTACHMENT AND MINIMUM THICKNESS

SIDING MATERIAL		NOMINAL THICKNES[a] (inches)	JOINT TREATMENT	WATER-RESISTIVE BARRIER REQUIRED	TYPE OF SUPPORTS FOR THE SIDING MATERIAL AND FASTENERS[b,c,d]					Number or spacing of fasteners
					Wood or wood structural panel sheathing	Fiberboard sheathing into stud	Gypsum sheathing into stud	Foam plastic sheathing into stud	Direct to studs	
Horizontal aluminum[e]	Without insulation	0.019[f]	Lap	Yes	0.120 nail 1¹/₂″ long	0.120 nail 2″ long	0.120 nail 2″ long	0.120 nail[y]	Not allowed	Same as stud spacing
		0.024	Lap	Yes	0.120 nail 1¹/₂″ long	0.120 nail 2″ long	0.120 nail 2″ long	0.120 nail[y]	Not allowed	
	With insulation	0.019	Lap	Yes	0.120 nail 1¹/₂″ long	0.120 nail 2¹/₂″ long	0.120 nail 2¹/₂″ long	0.120 nail[y]	0.120 nail 1¹/₂″ long	
Brick veneer[z] Concrete masonry veneer[z]		2 2	Section R703	Yes (Note l)	See Section R703 and Figure R703.7[g]					
Hardboard[k] Panel siding-vertical		⁷/₁₆	—	Yes	Note n	Note n	Note n	Note n	Note n	6″ panel edges 12″ inter. sup.[o]
Hardboard[k] Lap-siding-horizontal		⁷/₁₆	Note q	Yes	Note p	Note p	Note p	Note p	Note p	Same as stud spacing 2 per bearing
Steel[h]		29 ga.	Lap	Yes	0.113 nail 1³/₄″ Staple–1³/₄″	0.113 nail 2³/₄″ Staple–2¹/₂″	0.113 nail 2¹/₂″ Staple–2¹/₄″	0.113 nail[y] Staple[y]	Not allowed	Same as stud spacing
Stone veneer		2	Section R703	Yes (Note l)	See Section R703 and Figure R703.7[g]					
Particleboard panels		³/₈ – ¹/₂	—	Yes	6d box nail (2″ × 0.099″)	6d box nail (2″ × 0.099″)	6d box nail (2″ × 0.099″)	box nail[y]	6d box nail (2″ × 0.099″), ³/₈ not allowed	6″ panel edge, 12″ inter. sup.
		⁵/₈	—	Yes	6d box nail (2″ × 0.099″)	8d box nail (2¹/₂″ × 0.113″)	8d box nail (2¹/₂″ × 0.113″)	box nail[y]	6d box nail (2″ × 0.099″)	
Plywood panel[i] (exterior grade)		³/₈	—	Yes	0.099 nail–2″	0.113 nail–2¹/₂″	0.099 nail–2″	0.113 nail[y]	0.099 nail–2″	6″ on edges, 12″ inter. sup.
Vinyl siding[m]		0.035	Lap	Yes	0.120 nail 1¹/₂″ Staple–1³/₄″	0.120 nail 2″ Staple–2¹/₂″	0.120 nail 2″ Staple–2¹/₂″	0.120 nail[y] Staple[y]	Not allowed	Same as stud spacing
Wood[j] rustic, drop		³/₈ Min	Lap	Yes	Fastener penetration into stud–1″				0.113 nail– 2¹/₂″ Staple–2″	Face nailing up to 6″ widths, 1 nail per bearing; 8″ widths and over, 2 nails per bearing
Shiplap		¹⁹/₃₂ Average	Lap	Yes						
Bevel		⁷/₁₆								
Butt tip		³/₁₆	Lap	Yes						
Fiber cement panel siding[r]		⁵/₁₆	Note s	Yes Note x	6d corrosion-resistant nail[t]	6d corrosion-resistant nail[t]	6d corrosion-resistant nail[t]	6d corrosion-resistant nail[t,y]	4d corrosion-resistant nail[u]	6″ o.c. on edges, 12″ o.c. on intermed. studs
Fiber cement lap siding[r]		⁵/₁₆	Note v	Yes Note x	6d corrosion-resistant nail[t]	6d corrosion-resistant nail[t]	6d corrosion-resistant nail[t]	6d corrosion-resistant nail[t,y]	6d corrosion-resistant nail[w]	Note w

For SI: 1 inch = 25.4 mm.

a. Based on stud spacing of 16 inches on center where studs are spaced 24 inches, siding shall be applied to sheathing approved for that spacing.

b. Nail is a general description and shall be T-head, modified round head, or round head with smooth or deformed shanks.

c. Staples shall have a minimum crown width of ⁷/₁₆-inch outside diameter and be manufactured of minimum 16 gage wire.

d. Nails or staples shall be aluminum, galvanized, or rust-preventative coated and shall be driven into the studs for fiberboard or gypsum backing.

e. Aluminum nails shall be used to attach aluminum siding.

f. Aluminum (0.019 inch) shall be unbacked only when the maximum panel width is 10 inches and the maximum flat area is 8 inches. The tolerance for aluminum siding shall be +0.002 inch of the nominal dimension.

g. All attachments shall be coated with a corrosion-resistant coating.

h. Shall be of approved type.

(continued)

Footnotes to Table R703.4—continued

i. Three-eighths-inch plywood shall not be applied directly to studs spaced more than 16 inches on center when long dimension is parallel to studs. Plywood $^1/_2$-inch or thinner shall not be applied directly to studs spaced more than 24 inches on center. The stud spacing shall not exceed the panel span rating provided by the manufacturer unless the panels are installed with the face grain perpendicular to the studs or over sheathing approved for that stud spacing.

j. Wood board sidings applied vertically shall be nailed to horizontal nailing strips or blocking set 24 inches on center. Nails shall penetrate $1^1/_2$ inches into studs, studs and wood sheathing combined, or blocking. A weather-resistive membrane shall be installed weatherboard fashion under the vertical siding unless the siding boards are lapped or battens are used.

k. Hardboard siding shall comply with AHA A135.6.

l. For masonry veneer, a weather-resistive sheathing paper is not required over a sheathing that performs as a weather-resistive barrier when a 1-inch air space is provided between the veneer and the sheathing. When the 1-inch space is filled with mortar, a weather-resistive sheathing paper is required over studs or sheathing.

m. Vinyl siding shall comply with ASTM D 3679.

n. Minimum shank diameter of 0.092 inch, minimum head diameter of 0.225 inch, and nail length must accommodate sheathing and penetrate framing $1^1/_2$ inches.

o. When used to resist shear forces, the spacing must be 4 inches at panel edges and 8 inches on interior supports.

p. Minimum shank diameter of 0.099 inch, minimum head diameter of 0.240 inch, and nail length must accommodate sheathing and penetrate framing $1^1/_2$ inches.

q. Vertical end joints shall occur at studs and shall be covered with a joint cover or shall be caulked.

r. Fiber cement siding shall comply with the requirements of ASTM C 1186.

s. See Section R703.10.1.

t. Minimum 0.102″ smooth shank, 0.255″ round head.

u. Minimum 0.099″ smooth shank, 0.250″ round head.

v. See Section R703.10.2.

w. Face nailing: 2 nails at each stud. Concealed nailing: one 11 gage $1^1/_2$ galv. roofing nail (0.371″ head diameter, 0.120″ shank) or 6d galv. box nail at each stud.

x. See Section R703.2 exceptions.

y. Minimum nail length must accommodate sheathing and penetrate framing $1^1/_2$ inches.

z. Adhered masonry veneer shall comply with the requirements in Sections 6.1 and 6.3 of ACI 530/ASCE 5/TMS-402.

TABLE R703.5.2
MAXIMUM WEATHER EXPOSURE FOR WOOD SHAKES AND SHINGLES ON EXTERIOR WALLS[a,b,c]
(Dimensions are in inches)

LENGTH	EXPOSURE FOR SINGLE COURSE	EXPOSURE FOR DOUBLE COURSE
Shingles[a]		
16	$7^1/_2$	12[b]
18	$8^1/_2$	14[c]
24	$11^1/_2$	16
Shakes[a]		
18	$8^1/_2$	14
24	$11^1/_2$	18

For SI: 1 inch = 25.4 mm.

a. Dimensions given are for No. 1 grade.

b. A maximum 10-inch exposure is permitted for No. 2 grade.

c. A maximum 11-inch exposure is permitted for No. 2 grade.

R703.6.1.1 Reserved.

R703.6.1.2 Reserved.

R703.6.1.3 Control joints and expansion joints. Provisions for the control of expansion shall be determined by the exterior plaster application designer. ASTM C 1063-03 sections 7.11.4 - 7.11.4.4 do not apply.

R703.6.2 Plaster. Plastering with portland cement plaster shall be not less than three coats when applied over metal lath or wire lath and shall be not less than two coats when applied over masonry, concrete, pressure-preservative treated wood or decay-resistant wood as specified in Section R319.1 or gypsum backing. If the plaster surface is completely covered by veneer or other facing material or is completely concealed, plaster application need be only two coats, provided the total thickness is as set forth in Table R702.1(1).

On wood-frame construction with an on-grade floor slab system, exterior plaster shall be applied to cover, but not extend below, lath, paper and screed.

The proportion of aggregate to cementitious materials shall be as set forth in Table R702.1(3).

R703.6.2.1 Weep screeds. A minimum 0.019-inch (No. 26 galvanized sheet gage), corrosion-resistant weep screed or plastic weep screed, with a minimum vertical attachment flange of $3^1/_2$ inches (89 mm) shall be provided at or below the foundation plate line on exterior stud walls in accordance with ASTM C 1063-03. The weep screed shall be placed a minimum of 4 inches (102 mm) above the earth or 2 inches (51 mm) above paved areas and shall be of a type that will allow trapped water to drain to the exterior of the building. The weather-resistant barrier shall lap the attachment flange. The exterior lath shall cover and terminate on the attachment flange of the weep screed.

R703.6.3 Water-resistive barriers. Water-resistive barriers shall be installed as required in Section R703.2 and, where applied over wood-based sheathing, shall include two layers of a water-resistive vapor-permeable barrier. Each layer shall meet both of the following requirements:

1. A water resistance not less than that of 60-minute Grade D paper; or a minimum hydrostatic head of 60.9 cm when tested in accordance with hydrostatic pressure test method AATCC 127-1998; or a mini-

mum water transudation time of 60 minutes when tested in accordance with ASTM D-779.

2. A water vapor permeance not less than that of no. 15 felt; or a minimum permeance rating of 8.5 gr/h.ft.² in Hg (US perm) (4.9 x 1010 kg/Pa · s · m²) when tested in accordance with Procedure B of ASTM E 96.

Exception: One layer of water-resistive barrier complying with R703.2 is permitted when a drainage space that allows bulk water to flow freely behind the cladding is provided.

R703.7 Stone and masonry veneer, general. Stone and masonry veneer shall be installed in accordance with this chapter, Table R703.4 and Figure R703.7. These veneers installed over a backing of wood or cold-formed steel shall be limited to the first story above-grade and shall not exceed 5 inches (127 mm) in thickness.

For structures in 90 mph wind speed region apply Seismic Design Category A limitations and requirements of Exception 1 and Table R703.7(1).

Exceptions:

1. For all buildings in Seismic Design Categories A, B and C, exterior stone or masonry veneer, as specified in Table R703.7(1), with a backing of wood or steel framing shall be permitted to the height specified in Table R703.7(1) above a noncombustible foundation. Wall bracing at exterior and interior braced wall lines shall be in accordance with Section R602.10 or R603.7, and the additional requirements of Table R703.7(1).

2. For detached one- or two-family dwellings in Seismic Design Categories D_0, D_1 and D_2, exterior stone or masonry veneer, as specified in Table R703.7(2), with a backing of wood framing shall be permitted to the height specified in Table R703.7(2) above a noncombustible foundation. Wall bracing and hold downs at exterior and interior braced wall lines shall be in accordance with Sections R602.10 and R602.11 and the additional requirements of Table R703.7(2). In Seismic Design Categories D_0, D_1 and D_2, cripple walls shall not be permitted, and required interior braced wall lines shall be supported on continuous foundations.

R703.7.1 Interior veneer support. Veneers used as interior wall finishes shall be permitted to be supported on wood or cold-formed steel floors that are designed to support the loads imposed.

R703.7.2 Exterior veneer support. Except in Seismic Design Categories D_0, D_1 and D_2, exterior masonry veneers having an installed weight of 40 pounds per square foot (195 kg/m²) or less shall be permitted to be supported on wood or cold-formed steel construction. When masonry veneer supported by wood or cold-formed steel construction adjoins masonry veneer supported by the foundation, there shall be a movement joint between the veneer supported by the wood or cold-formed steel construction and the veneer supported by the foundation. The wood or cold-formed steel construction supporting the masonry veneer shall be

designed to limit the deflection to $^1/_{600}$ of the span for the supporting members. The design of the wood or cold-formed steel construction shall consider the weight of the veneer and any other loads.

R703.7.2.1 Support by steel angle. A minimum 6 inches by 4 inches by $^5/_{16}$ inch (152 mm by 102 mm by 8 mm) steel angle, with the long leg placed vertically, shall be anchored to double 2 inches by 4 inches (51 mm by 102 mm) wood studs at a maximum on-center spacing of 16 inches (406 mm). Anchorage of the steel angle at every double stud spacing shall be a minimum of two $^7/_{16}$ inch (11 mm) diameter by 4 inch (102 mm) lag screws. The steel angle shall have a minimum clearance to underlying construction of $^1/_{16}$ inch (2 mm). A minimum of two-thirds the width of the masonry veneer thickness shall bear on the steel angle. Flashing and weep holes shall be located in the masonry veneer wythe in accordance with Figure R703.7.2.1. The maximum height of masonry veneer above the steel angle support shall be 12 feet, 8 inches (3861 mm). The air space separating the masonry veneer from the wood backing shall be in accordance with Sections R703.7.4 and R703.7.4.2. The method of support for the masonry veneer on wood construction shall be constructed in accordance with Figure R703.7.2.1.

The maximum slope of the roof construction without stops shall be 7:12. Roof construction with slopes greater than 7:12 but not more than 12:12 shall have stops of a minimum 3 inch × 3 inch × $^1/_4$ inch (76 mm × 76 mm × 6 mm) steel plate welded to the angle at 24 inches (610 mm) on center along the angle or as approved by the building official.

R703.7.2.2 Support by roof construction. A steel angle shall be placed directly on top of the roof construction. The roof supporting construction for the steel angle shall consist of a minimum of three 2-inch by 6-inch (51 mm by 152 mm) wood members. The wood member abutting the vertical wall stud construction shall be anchored with a minimum of three $^5/_8$-inch (16 mm) diameter by 5-inch (127 mm) lag screws to every wood stud spacing. Each additional roof member shall be anchored by the use of two 10d nails at every wood stud spacing. A minimum of two-thirds the width of the masonry veneer thickness shall bear on the steel angle. Flashing and weep holes shall be located in the masonry veneer wythe in accordance with Figure R703.7.2.2. The maximum height of the masonry veneer above the steel angle support shall be 12 feet, 8 inches (3861 mm). The air space separating the masonry veneer from the wood backing shall be in accordance with Sections R703.7.4 and R703.7.4.2. The support for the masonry veneer on wood construction shall be constructed in accordance with Figure R703.7.2.2.

The maximum slope of the roof construction without stops shall be 7:12. Roof construction with slopes greater than 7:12 but not more than 12:12 shall have stops of a minimum 3 inch × 3 inch × $^1/_4$ inch (76 mm × 76 mm × 6 mm) steel plate welded to the angle at 24 inches (610 mm) on center along the angle or as approved by the building official.

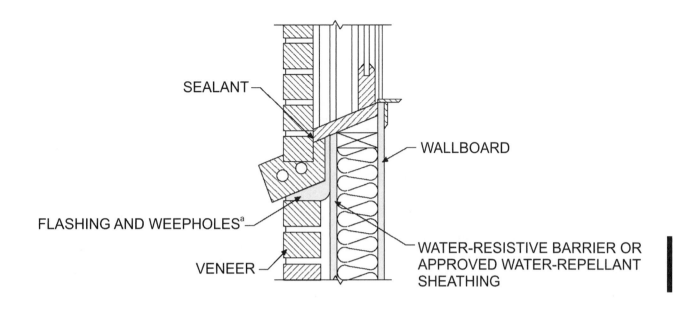

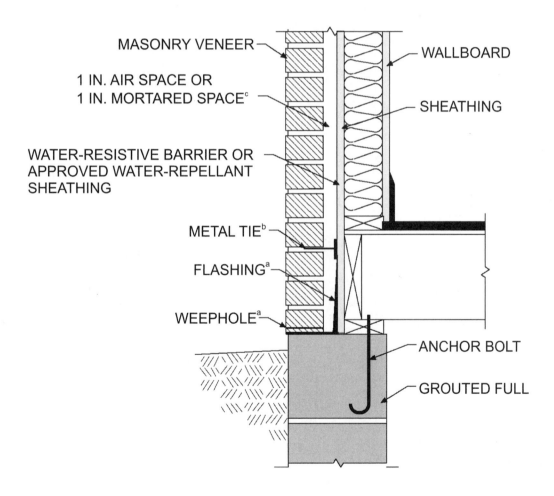

SEALANT

WALLBOARD

FLASHING AND WEEPHOLES[a]

VENEER

WATER-RESISTIVE BARRIER OR
APPROVED WATER-REPELLANT
SHEATHING

MASONRY VENEER

1 IN. AIR SPACE OR
1 IN. MORTARED SPACE[c]

WATER-RESISTIVE BARRIER OR
APPROVED WATER-REPELLANT
SHEATHING

METAL TIE[b]

FLASHING[a]

WEEPHOLE[a]

WALLBOARD

SHEATHING

ANCHOR BOLT

GROUTED FULL

For SI: 1 inch = 25.4 mm.

FIGURE R703.7
MASONRY VENEER WALL DETAILS

(continued)

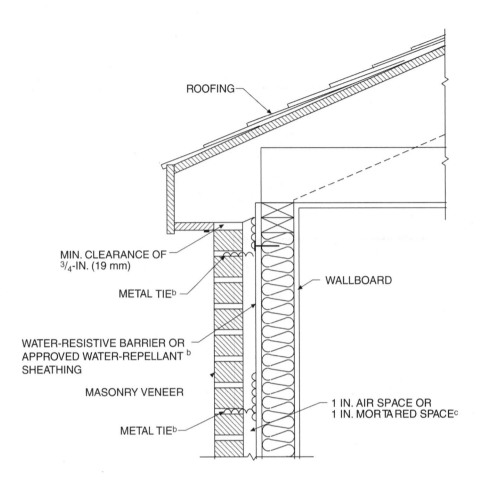

ROOFING

MIN. CLEARANCE OF
³/₄-IN. (19 mm)

METAL TIE[b]

WATER-RESISTIVE BARRIER OR
APPROVED WATER-REPELLANT [b]
SHEATHING

MASONRY VENEER

METAL TIE[b]

WALLBOARD

1 IN. AIR SPACE OR
1 IN. MORTARED SPACE[c]

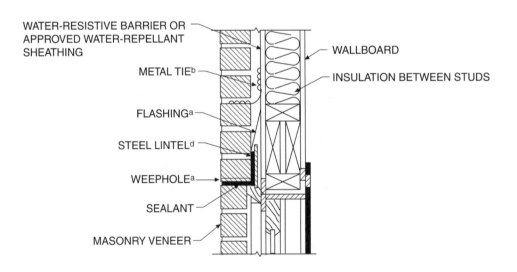

WATER-RESISTIVE BARRIER OR
APPROVED WATER-REPELLANT
SHEATHING

METAL TIE[b]

FLASHING[a]

STEEL LINTEL[d]

WEEPHOLE[a]

SEALANT

MASONRY VENEER

WALLBOARD

INSULATION BETWEEN STUDS

For SI: 1 inch = 25.4 mm.
a. See Sections R703.7.5, R703.7.6 and R703.8.
b. See Sections R703.2 and R703.7.4.
c. See Sections R703.7.4.2 and R703.7.4.3.
d. See Section R703.7.3.

FIGURE R703.7—continued
MASONRY VENEER WALL DETAILS

R703.7.3 Lintels. Masonry veneer shall not support any vertical load other than the dead load of the veneer above. Veneer above openings shall be supported on lintels of noncombustible materials and the allowable span shall not exceed the value set forth in Table R703.7.3. The lintels shall have a length of bearing not less than 4 inches (102 mm).

R703.7.4 Anchorage. Masonry veneer shall be anchored to the supporting wall with corrosion-resistant metal ties. Where veneer is anchored to wood backings by corrugated sheet metal ties, the distance separating the veneer from the sheathing material shall be a maximum of a nominal 1 inch (25 mm). Where the veneer is anchored to wood backings

using metal strand wire ties, the distance separating the veneer from the sheathing material shall be a maximum of $4^1/_2$ inches (114 mm). Where the veneer is anchored to cold-formed steel backings, adjustable metal strand wire ties shall be used. Where veneer is anchored to cold-formed steel backings, the distance separating the veneer from the sheathing material shall be a maximum of $4^1/_2$ inches (114 mm).

R703.7.4.1 Size and spacing. Veneer ties, if strand wire, shall not be less in thickness than No. 9 U.S. gage [(0.148 in.) (4 mm)] wire and shall have a hook embedded in the mortar joint, or if sheet metal, shall be not less than No. 22 U.S. gage by [(0.0299 in.)(0.76 mm)] $^7/_8$ inch (22 mm)

TABLE R703.7(1)
STONE OR MASONRY VENEER LIMITATIONS AND REQUIREMENTS, WOOD
OR STEEL FRAMING, SEISMIC DESIGN CATEGORIES A, B AND C

SEISMIC DESIGN CATEGORY	NUMBER OF WOOD OR STEEL FRAMED STORIES	MAXIMUM HEIGHT OF VENEER ABOVE NONCOMBUSTIBLE FOUNDATION[a] (feet)	MAXIMUM NOMINAL THICKNESS OF VENEER (inches)	MAXIMUM WEIGHT OF VENEER (psf)[b]	WOOD OR STEEL FRAMED STORY	MINIMUM SHEATHING AMOUNT (percent of braced wall line length)[c]
A or B	Steel: 1 or 2 Wood: 1, 2 or 3	30	5	50	all	Table R602.10.1 or Table R603.7
C	1	30	5	50	1 only	Table R602.10.1 or Table R603.7
	2	30	5	50	top	Table R602.10.1 or Table R603.7
					bottom	1.5 times length required by Table R602.10.1 or 1.5 times length required by Table R603.7
	Wood only: 3	30	5	50	top	Table R602.10.1
					middle	1.5 times length required by Table R602.10.1
					bottom	1.5 times length required by Table R602.10.1

For SI: 1 inch = 25.4 mm, 1 foot = 304.8 mm, 1 pound per square foot = 0.479 kPa.
a. An Additional 8 feet is permitted for gable end walls. See also story height limitations of Section R301.3.
b. Maximum weight is installed weight and includes weight of mortar, grout, lath and other materials used for installation. Where veneer is placed on both faces of a wall, the combined weight shall not exceed that specified in this table.
c. Applies to exterior and interior braced wall lines.

TABLE R703.7.3
ALLOWABLE SPANS FOR LINTELS SUPPORTING MASONRY VENEER[a, b, c]

SIZE OF STEEL ANGLE[a, c] (inches)	NO STORY ABOVE	ONE STORY ABOVE	TWO STORIES ABOVE	NO. OF $^1/_2$″ OR EQUIVALENT REINFORCING BARS[b]
$3 \times 3 \times ^1/_4$	6′-0″	4′-6″	3′-0″	1
$4 \times 3 \times ^1/_4$	8′-0″	6′-0″	4′-6″	1
$5 \times 3^1/_2 \times ^5/_{16}$	10′-0″	8′-0″	6′-0″	2
$6 \times 3^1/_2 \times ^5/_{16}$	14′-0″	9′-6″	7′-0″	2
$2-6 \times 3^1/_2 \times ^5/_{16}$	20′-0″	12′-0″	9′-6″	4

For SI: 1 inch = 25.4 mm, 1 foot =304.8 mm.
a. Long leg of the angle shall be placed in a vertical position.
b. Depth of reinforced lintels shall not be less than 8 inches and all cells of hollow masonry lintels shall be grouted solid. Reinforcing bars shall extend not less than 8 inches into the support.
c. Steel members indicated are adequate typical examples; other steel members meeting structural design requirements may be used.

corrugated. Each tie shall be spaced not more than 24 inches (610 mm) on center horizontally and vertically and shall support not more than 2.67 square feet (0.25 m²) of wall area.

Exception: In Seismic Design Category D_0, D_1 or D_2 or townhouses in Seismic Design Category C or in wind areas of more than 30 pounds per square foot pressure (1.44 kPa), each tie shall support not more than 2 square feet (0.2 m²) of wall area.

R703.7.4.1.1 Veneer ties around wall openings. Veneer ties around wall openings. Additional metal ties shall be provided around all wall openings greater than 16 inches (406 mm) in either dimension. Metal ties around the perimeter of openings shall be spaced not more than 3 feet (9144 mm) on center and placed within 12 inches (305 mm) of the wall opening.

R703.7.4.2 Air space. The veneer shall be separated from the sheathing by an air space of a minimum of a nominal 1 inch (25 mm) but nor more than $4^{1}/_{2}$ inches (114 mm).

Exception: One layer of water-resistive barrier complying with Section R703.2 is permitted when a drainage space that allows bulk water to flow freely behind the cladding is provided.

R703.7.4.3 Mortar or grout fill. As an alternate to the air space required by Section R703.7.4.2, mortar or grout shall be permitted to fill the air space. When the 1-inch (25.4 mm) space is filled with mortar, a weather-resistant membrane or building paper as described in Section R703.2 or R703.6.3 is required over studs or sheathing. When filling the air space, it is permitted to replace the sheathing and weather-resistant membrane or

TABLE R703.7(2)
STONE OR MASONRY VENEER LIMITATIONS AND REQUIREMENTS, ONE- AND TWO-FAMILY DETACHED DWELLINGS, WOOD FRAMING, SEISMIC DESIGN CATEGORIES D_0, D_1 AND D_2

SEISMIC DESIGN CATEGORY	NUMBER OF WOOD FRAMED STORIES[a]	MAXIMUM HEIGHT OF VENEER ABOVE NONCOMBUSTIBLE FOUNDATION OR FOUNDATION WALL (feet)	MAXIMUM NOMINAL THICKNESS OF VENEER (inches)	MAXIMUM WEIGHT OF VENEER (psf)[b]	WOOD FRAMED STORY	MINIMUM SHEATHING AMOUNT (percent of braced wall line length)[c]	MINIMUM SHEATHING THICKNESS AND FASTENING	SINGLE STORY HOLD DOWN FORCE (lb)[d]	CUMULATIVE HOLD DOWN FORCE (lb)[e]
D_0	1	20[f]	4	40	1 only	35	$^7/_{16}$-inch wood structural panel sheathing with 8d common nails spaced at 4 inches on center at panel edges, 12 inches on center at intermediate supports. 8d common nails at 4 inches on center at braced wall panel end posts with hold down attached.	N/A	—
	2	20[f]	4	40	top	35		1900	—
					bottom	45		3200	5100
	3	30[g]	4	40	top	40		1900	—
					middle	45		3500	5400
					bottom	60		3500	8900
D_1	1	20[f]	4	40	1 only	45		2100	—
	2	20[f]	4	40	top	45		2100	—
					bottom	45		3700	5800
	3	20[f]	4	40	top	45		2100	—
					middle	45		3700	5800
					bottom	60		3700	9500
D_2	1	20[f]	3	30	1 only	55		2300	—
	2	20[f]	3	30	top	55		2300	—
					bottom	55		3900	6200

For SI: 1 inch = 25.4 mm, 1 foot = 304.8 mm, 1 pound per square foot = 0.479 kPa, 1 pound-force = 4.448 N.

a. Cripple walls are not permitted in Seismic Design Categories D_0, D_1 and D_2.

b. Maximum weight is installed weight and includes weight of mortar, grout and lath, and other materials used for installation.

c. Applies to exterior and interior braced wall lines.

d. Hold down force is minimum allowable stress design load for connector providing uplift tie from wall framing at end of braced wall panel at the noted story to wall framing at end of braced wall panel at the story below, or to foundation or foundation wall. Use single story hold down force where edges of braced wall panels do not align; a continuous load path to the foundation shall be maintained. [See Figure R703.7(1)(b)].

e. Where hold down connectors from stories above align with stories below, use cumulative hold down force to size middle and bottom story hold down connectors. [See Figure R703.7(1)(a)].

f. The veneer shall not exceed 20 feet in height above a noncombustible foundation, with an additional 8 feet permitted for gable end walls, or 30 feet in height with an additional 8 feet for gable end walls where the lower 10 feet has a backing of concrete or masonry wall. See also story height limitations of Section R301.3.

g. The veneer shall not exceed 30 feet in height above a noncombustible foundation, with an additional 8 feet permitted for gable end walls. See also story height limitations of Section R301.3.

asphalt-saturated felt paper with a wire mesh and approved paper or an approved paper-backed reinforcement attached directly to the studs.

R703.7.4.4 Masonry veneer on sheathed substrates. On sheathed substrates, a corrosion-resistant, self-furring expanded metal lath shall be installed over the weather-resistant membrane or building paper with appropriate fasteners as described in Section R703.6.1. Fasteners shall penetrate wood supports a minimum of one inch.

R703.7.5 Flashing. Flashing shall be located beneath the first course of masonry above finished ground level above the foundation wall or slab and at other points of support, including structural floors, shelf angles and lintels when masonry veneers are designed in accordance with Section R703.7. See Section R703.8 for additional requirements.

R703.7.6 Weepholes. Weepholes shall be provided in the outside wythe of masonry walls at a maximum spacing of 33 inches (838 mm) on center. Weepholes shall not be less than $^3/_{16}$ inch (5 mm) in diameter. Weepholes shall be located immediately above the flashing.

R703.8 Flashing. Approved corrosion-resistant flashing shall be applied shingle-fashion in such a manner as to prevent entry of water into the wall cavity or penetration of water to the building structural framing components. The flashing shall extend to the surface of the exterior wall finish. Approved corrosion-resistant flashing shall be installed at all of the following locations:

1. Exterior window and door openings. Flashing at exterior window and door openings shall extend to the surface of the exterior wall finish or to the water-resistive barrier for subsequent drainage.

2. At the intersection of chimneys or other masonry construction with frame or stucco walls, with projecting lips on both sides under stucco copings.

3. Under and at the ends of masonry, wood, or metal copings and sills.

4. Continuously above all projecting wood trim.

5. Where exterior porches, decks, or stairs attach to a wall or floor assembly of wood-frame construction.

6. At wall and roof intersections.

7. At built-in gutters.

8. Where exterior material meets in other than a vertical line.

9. Where the lower portion of a sloped roof stops within the plane of an intersecting wall cladding in such a manner as to divert or kick out water away from the assembly.

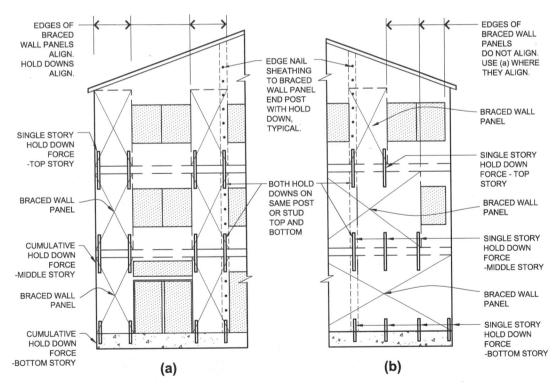

(a) Braced wall panels stacked (aligned story to story). Use cumulative hold down force.
(b) Braced wall panels not stacked. Use single story hold down force.

FIGURE R703.7(1)
HOLD DOWNS AT EXTERIOR AND INTERIOR BRACED WALL PANELS
WHEN USING STONE OR MASONRY VENEER

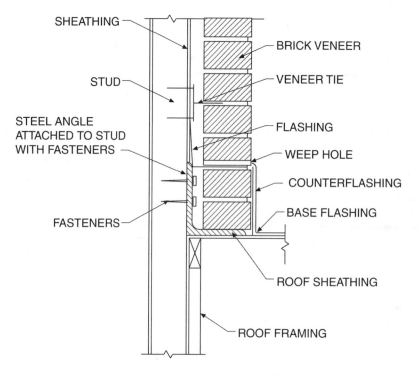

SUPPORT BY STEEL ANGLE

FIGURE R703.7.2.1
EXTERIOR MASONRY VENEER SUPPORT BY STEEL ANGLES

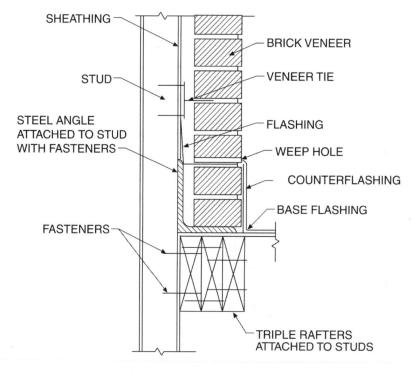

SUPPORT BY ROOF MEMBERS

FIGURE R703.7.2.2
EXTERIOR MASONRY VENEER SUPPORT BY ROOF MEMBERS

MN

R703.8.1 Pan flashing of windows and doors. A pan flashing shall be provided under all exterior windows and doors. Pan flashing shall be (a) sloped to drain water to the exterior surface of a weather-resistive barrier or flat with sealed back dam and side dams to prevent re-entry of water into the wall cavity or onto interior finishes, and (b) maintain the thermal envelope of the building. Pan flashing made from metal must be thermally isolated from interior surfaces.

Exceptions:

1. Windows or doors installed in accordance with the manufacturer's installation instructions which include an alternate flashing method.

2. Windows or doors in detached accessory structures.

3. Skylights, bow or bay windows.

4. Doors required to meet accessibility requirements that would prevent the installation of pan flashing.

5. Repairs or replacement of existing windows and doors.

6. When a method is provided by a registered design professional.

R703.9 Exterior insulation finish systems, general. All Exterior Insulation Finish Systems (EIFS) shall be installed in accordance with the manufacturer's installation instructions and the requirements of this section. Decorative trim shall not be face nailed through the EIFS. The EIFS shall terminate not less than 6 inches (152 mm) above the finished ground level.

R703.9.1 Water-resistive barrier. All EIFS shall have a water-resistive barrier applied between the underlying water-sensitive building components and the exterior insulation, and a means of draining water to the exterior of the veneer. A water-resistive barrier shall be compliant with ASTM D 226 Type I asphalt saturated felt or equivalent, shall be applied horizontally with the upper layer lapped over the lower layer not less than 2 inches (51 mm), and shall have all vertical joints lapped not less than 6 inches (152 mm).

R703.9.2 Flashing, general. Flashing of EIFS shall be provided in accordance with the requirements of Section R703.8.

R703.10 Fiber cement siding.

R703.10.1 Panel siding. Panels shall be installed with the long dimension parallel to framing. Vertical joints shall occur over framing members and shall be sealed with caulking or covered with battens. Horizontal joints shall be flashed with Z-flashing and blocked with solid wood framing.

R703.10.2 Horizontal lap siding. Lap siding shall be lapped a minimum of $1^1/_4$ inches (32 mm) and shall have the ends sealed with caulking, covered with an H-section joint cover, or located over a strip of flashing. Lap siding courses may be installed with the fastener heads exposed or concealed, according to approved manufacturers' installation instructions.

R703.11 Vinyl siding. Vinyl siding shall be certified and labeled as conforming to the requirements of ASTM D 3679 by an approved quality control agency.

R703.11.1 Installation. Vinyl siding, soffit and accessories shall be installed in accordance with the manufacturer's installation instructions.

CHAPTER 8

ROOF-CEILING CONSTRUCTION

SECTION R801
GENERAL

R801.1 Application. The provisions of this chapter shall control the design and construction of the roof-ceiling system for all buildings.

R801.2 Requirements. Roof and ceiling construction shall be capable of accommodating all loads imposed according to Section R301 and of transmitting the resulting loads to the supporting structural elements.

R801.3 Roof drainage. In areas where expansive or collapsible soils are known to exist, all dwellings shall have a controlled method of water disposal from roofs that will collect and discharge roof drainage to the ground surface at least 5 feet (1524 mm) from foundation walls or to an approved drainage system.

SECTION R802
WOOD ROOF FRAMING

R802.1 Identification. Load-bearing dimension lumber for rafters, trusses and ceiling joists shall be identified by a grade mark of a lumber grading or inspection agency that has been approved by an accreditation body that complies with DOC PS 20. In lieu of a grade mark, a certificate of inspection issued by a lumber grading or inspection agency meeting the requirements of this section shall be accepted.

R802.1.1 Blocking. Blocking shall be a minimum of utility grade lumber.

R802.1.2 End-jointed lumber. Approved end-jointed lumber identified by a grade mark conforming to Section R802.1 may be used interchangeably with solid-sawn members of the same species and grade.

R802.1.3 Fire-retardant-treated wood. Fire-retardant-treated wood (FRTW) is any wood product which, when impregnated with chemicals by a pressure process or other means during manufacture, shall have, when tested in accordance with ASTM E 84, a listed flame spread index of 25 or less and shows no evidence of significant progressive combustion when the test is continued for an additional 20-minute period. In addition, the flame front shall not progress more than 10.5 feet (3200 mm) beyond the center line of the burners at any time during the test.

R802.1.3.1 Labeling. Fire-retardant-treated lumber and wood structural panels shall be labeled. The label shall contain:

1. The identification mark of an approved agency in accordance with Section 1703.5 of the *International Building Code*.

2. Identification of the treating manufacturer.

3. The name of the fire-retardant treatment.

4. The species of wood treated.

5. Flame spread and smoke-developed rating.

6. Method of drying after treatment.

7. Conformance to appropriate standards in accordance with Sections R802.1.3.2 through R802.1.3.5.

8. For FRTW exposed to weather, or a damp or wet location, the words "No increase in the listed classification when subjected to the Standard Rain Test" (ASTM D 2898).

R802.1.3.2 Strength adjustments. Design values for untreated lumber and wood structural panels as specified in Section R802.1 shall be adjusted for fire-retardant-treated wood. Adjustments to design values shall be based upon an approved method of investigation which takes into consideration the effects of the anticipated temperature and humidity to which the fire-retardant-treated wood will be subjected, the type of treatment and redrying procedures.

R802.1.3.2.1 Wood structural panels. The effect of treatment and the method of redrying after treatment, and exposure to high temperatures and high humidities on the flexure properties of fire-retardant-treated softwood plywood shall be determined in accordance with ASTM D 5516. The test data developed by ASTM D 5516 shall be used to develop adjustment factors, maximum loads and spans, or both for untreated plywood design values in accordance with ASTM D 6305. Each manufacturer shall publish the allowable maximum loads and spans for service as floor and roof sheathing for their treatment.

R802.1.3.2.2 Lumber. For each species of wood treated, the effect of the treatment and the method of redrying after treatment and exposure to high temperatures and high humidities on the allowable design properties of fire-retardant-treated lumber shall be determined in accordance with ASTM D 5664. The test data developed by ASTM D 5664 shall be used to develop modification factors for use at or near room temperature and at elevated temperatures and humidity in accordance with ASTM D 6841. Each manufacturer shall publish the modification factors for service at temperatures of not less than 80°F (27°C) and for roof framing. The roof framing modification factors shall take into consideration the climatological location.

R802.1.3.3 Exposure to weather. Where fire-retardant-treated wood is exposed to weather or damp or wet locations, it shall be identified as "Exterior" to indicate there is no increase in the listed flame spread index as defined in Section R802.1.3 when subjected to ASTM D 2898.

R802.1.3.4 Interior applications. Interior fire-retardant-treated wood shall have a moisture content of not over 28 percent when tested in accordance with ASTM D 3201 procedures at 92 percent relative humidity. Interior fire-retardant-treated wood shall be tested in accordance with Section R802.1.3.2.1 or R802.1.3.2.2. Interior fire-retardant-treated wood designated as Type A shall be tested in accordance with the provisions of this section.

R802.1.3.5 Moisture content. Fire-retardant-treated wood shall be dried to a moisture content of 19 percent or less for lumber and 15 percent or less for wood structural panels before use. For wood kiln dried after treatment (KDAT) the kiln temperatures shall not exceed those used in kiln drying the lumber and plywood submitted for the tests described in Section R802.1.3.2.1 for plywood and R802.1.3.2.2 for lumber.

R802.1.4 Structural glued laminated timbers. Glued laminated timbers shall be manufactured and identified as required in AITC A190.1 and ASTM D 3737.

R802.1.5 Structural log members. Stress grading of structural log members of nonrectangular shape, as typically used in log buildings, shall be in accordance with ASTM D 3957. Such structural log members shall be identified by the grade mark of an approved lumber grading or inspection agency. In lieu of a grade mark on the material, a certificate of inspection as to species and grade issued by a lumber-grading or inspection agency meeting the requirements of this section shall be permitted to be accepted.

R802.2 Design and construction. The framing details required in Section R802 apply to roofs having a minimum slope of three units vertical in 12 units horizontal (25-percent slope) or greater. Roof-ceilings shall be designed and constructed in accordance with the provisions of this chapter and Figures R606.11(1), R606.11(2) and R606.11(3) or in accordance with AFPA/NDS. Components of roof-ceilings shall be fastened in accordance with Table R602.3(1).

R802.3 Framing details. Rafters shall be framed to ridge board or to each other with a gusset plate as a tie. Ridge board shall be at least 1-inch (25 mm) nominal thickness and not less in depth than the cut end of the rafter. At all valleys and hips there shall be a valley or hip rafter not less than 2-inch (51 mm) nominal thickness and not less in depth than the cut end of the rafter. Hip and valley rafters shall be supported at the ridge by a brace to a bearing partition or be designed to carry and distribute the specific load at that point. Where the roof pitch is less than three units vertical in 12 units horizontal (25-percent slope), structural members that support rafters and ceiling joists, such as ridge beams, hips and valleys, shall be designed as beams.

R802.3.1 Ceiling joist and rafter connections. Ceiling joists and rafters shall be nailed to each other in accordance with Table R802.5.1(9), and the rafter shall be nailed to the top wall plate in accordance with Table R602.3(1). Ceiling joists shall be continuous or securely joined in accordance with Table R802.5.1(9) where they meet over interior partitions and are nailed to adjacent rafters to provide a continu-ous tie across the building when such joists are parallel to the rafters.

Where ceiling joists are not connected to the rafters at the top wall plate, joists connected higher in the attic shall be installed as rafter ties, or rafter ties shall be installed to provide a continuous tie. Where ceiling joists are not parallel to rafters, rafter ties shall be installed. Rafter ties shall be a minimum of 2-inch by 4-inch (51 mm by 102 mm) (nominal), installed in accordance with the connection requirements in Table R802.5.1(9), or connections of equivalent capacities shall be provided. Where ceiling joists or rafter ties are not provided, the ridge formed by these rafters shall be supported by a wall or girder designed in accordance with accepted engineering practice.

Collar ties or ridge straps to resist wind uplift shall be connected in the upper third of the attic space in accordance with Table R602.3(1).

Collar ties shall be a minimum of 1-inch by 4-inch (25 mm by 102 mm) (nominal), spaced not more than 4 feet (1219 mm) on center.

R802.3.2 Ceiling joists lapped. Ends of ceiling joists shall be lapped a minimum of 3 inches (76 mm) or butted over bearing partitions or beams and toenailed to the bearing member. When ceiling joists are used to provide resistance to rafter thrust, lapped joists shall be nailed together in accordance with Table R602.3(1) and butted joists shall be tied together in a manner to resist such thrust.

R802.4 Allowable ceiling joist spans. Spans for ceiling joists shall be in accordance with Tables R802.4(1) and R802.4(2). For other grades and species and for other loading conditions, refer to the AF&PA Span Tables for Joists and Rafters.

R802.5 Allowable rafter spans. Spans for rafters shall be in accordance with Tables R802.5.1(1) through R802.5.1(8). For other grades and species and for other loading conditions, refer to the AF&PA Span Tables for Joists and Rafters. The span of each rafter shall be measured along the horizontal projection of the rafter.

R802.5.1 Purlins. Installation of purlins to reduce the span of rafters is permitted as shown in Figure R802.5.1. Purlins shall be sized no less than the required size of the rafters that they support. Purlins shall be continuous and shall be supported by 2-inch by 4-inch (51 mm by 102 mm) braces installed to bearing walls at a slope not less than 45 degrees from the horizontal. The braces shall be spaced not more than 4 feet (1219 mm) on center and the unbraced length of braces shall not exceed 8 feet (2438 mm).

R802.6 Bearing. The ends of each rafter or ceiling joist shall have not less than $1^1/_2$ inches (38 mm) of bearing on wood or metal and not less than 3 inches (76 mm) on masonry or concrete.

R802.6.1 Finished ceiling material. If the finished ceiling material is installed on the ceiling prior to the attachment of the ceiling to the walls, such as in construction at a factory, a compression strip of the same thickness as the finish ceiling material shall be installed directly above the top plate of bearing walls if the compressive strength of the finish ceiling material is less than the loads it will be required to withstand. The compression strip shall cover the entire length of such top plate and shall be at least one-half the width of the top plate. It shall be of material capable of transmitting the loads transferred through it.

R802.7 Cutting and notching. Structural roof members shall not be cut, bored or notched in excess of the limitations specified in this section.

R802.7.1 Sawn lumber. Notches in solid lumber joists, rafters and beams shall not exceed one-sixth of the depth of the member, shall not be longer than one-third of the depth of the member and shall not be located in the middle one-third of the span. Notches at the ends of the member shall not exceed one-fourth the depth of the member. The tension side of members 4 inches (102 mm) or greater in nominal thickness shall not be notched except at the ends of the members. The diameter of the holes bored or cut into members shall not exceed one-third the depth of the member. Holes shall not be closer than 2 inches (51 mm) to the top or bottom of the member, or to any other hole located in the member. Where the member is also notched, the hole shall not be closer than 2 inches (51 mm) to the notch.

> **Exception:** Notches on cantilevered portions of rafters are permitted provided the dimension of the remaining portion of the rafter is not less than 4-inch nominal (102 mm) and the length of the cantilever does not exceed 24 inches (610 mm).

R802.7.2 Engineered wood products. Cuts, notches and holes bored in trusses, structural composite lumber, structural glue-laminated members or I-joists are prohibited except where permitted by the manufacturer's recommendations or where the effects of such alterations are specifically considered in the design of the member by a registered design professional.

R802.8 Lateral support. Rafters and ceiling joists having a depth-to-thickness ratio exceeding 5 to 1 based on nominal dimensions shall be provided with lateral support at points of bearing to prevent rotation.

R802.8.1 Bridging. Rafters and ceiling joists having a depth-to-thickness ratio exceeding 6 to 1 based on nominal dimensions shall be supported laterally by solid blocking, diagonal bridging (wood or metal) or a continuous 1-inch by 3-inch (25 mm by 76 mm) wood strip nailed across the rafters or ceiling joists at intervals not exceeding 8 feet (2438 mm).

R802.9 Framing of openings. Openings in roof and ceiling framing shall be framed with header and trimmer joists. When the header joist span does not exceed 4 feet (1219 mm), the header joist may be a single member the same size as the ceiling joist or rafter. Single trimmer joists may be used to carry a single header joist that is located within 3 feet (914 mm) of the trimmer joist bearing. When the header joist span exceeds 4 feet (1219 mm), the trimmer joists and the header joist shall be doubled and of sufficient cross section to support the ceiling joists or rafter framing into the header. Approved hangers shall be used for the header joist to trimmer joist connections when the header joist span exceeds 6 feet (1829 mm). Tail joists over 12 feet (3658 mm) long shall be supported at the header by

framing anchors or on ledger strips not less than 2 inches by 2 inches (51 mm by 51 mm).

R802.10 Wood trusses.

R802.10.1 Truss design drawings. Truss design drawings, prepared in conformance to Section R802.10.1, shall be provided to the building official and approved prior to installation. Truss design drawings shall include, at a minimum, the information specified below. Truss design drawing shall be provided with the shipment of trusses delivered to the jobsite.

1. Slope or depth, span and spacing.

2. Location of all joints.

3. Required bearing widths.

4. Design loads as applicable.

> 4.1. Top chord live load (as determined from Section R301.6).
>
> 4.2. Top chord dead load.
>
> 4.3. Bottom chord live load.
>
> 4.4. Bottom chord dead load.
>
> 4.5. Concentrated loads and their points of application.
>
> 4.6. Controlling wind and earthquake loads.

5. Adjustments to lumber and joint connector design values for conditions of use.

6. Each reaction force and direction.

7. Joint connector type and description (e.g., size, thickness or gage) and the dimensioned location of each joint connector except where symmetrically located relative to the joint interface.

8. Lumber size, species and grade for each member.

9. Connection requirements for:

> 9.1. Truss to girder-truss.
>
> 9.2. Truss ply to ply.
>
> 9.3. Field splices.

10. Calculated deflection ratio and/or maximum description for live and total load.

11. Maximum axial compression forces in the truss members to enable the building designer to design the size, connections and anchorage of the permanent continuous lateral bracing. Forces shall be shown on the truss design drawing or on supplemental documents.

12. Required permanent truss member bracing location.

R802.10.2 Design. Wood trusses shall be designed in accordance with accepted engineering practice. The design and manufacture of metal-plate-connected wood trusses shall comply with ANSI/TPI 1. The truss design drawings shall be prepared by a registered professional where required by the statutes of the jurisdiction in which the project is to be constructed in accordance with Section R106.1.

TABLE R802.4(1)
CEILING JOIST SPANS FOR COMMON LUMBER SPECIES
(Uninhabitable attics without storage, live load = 10 psf, L/Δ = 240)

CEILING JOIST SPACING (inches)	SPECIES AND GRADE		DEAD LOAD = 5 psf			
			2 × 4	2 × 6	2 × 8	2 × 10
			Maximum ceiling joist spans			
			(feet - inches)	(feet - inches)	(feet - inches)	(feet - inches)
12	Douglas fir-larch	SS	13-2	20-8	Note a	Note a
	Douglas fir-larch	#1	12-8	19-11	Note a	Note a
	Douglas fir-larch	#2	12-5	19-6	25-8	Note a
	Douglas fir-larch	#3	10-10	15-10	20-1	24-6
	Hem-fir	SS	12-5	19-6	25-8	Note a
	Hem-fir	#1	12-2	19-1	25-2	Note a
	Hem-fir	#2	11-7	18-2	24-0	Note a
	Hem-fir	#3	10-10	15-10	20-1	24-6
	Southern pine	SS	12-11	20-3	Note a	Note a
	Southern pine	#1	12-8	19-11	Note a	Note a
	Southern pine	#2	12-5	19-6	25-8	Note a
	Southern pine	#3	11-6	17-0	21-8	25-7
	Spruce-pine-fir	SS	12-2	19-1	25-2	Note a
	Spruce-pine-fir	#1	11-10	18-8	24-7	Note a
	Spruce-pine-fir	#2	11-10	18-8	24-7	Note a
	Spruce-pine-fir	#3	10-10	15-10	20-1	24-6
16	Douglas fir-larch	SS	11-11	18-9	24-8	Note a
	Douglas fir-larch	#1	11-6	18-1	23-10	Note a
	Douglas fir-larch	#2	11-3	17-8	23-0	Note a
	Douglas fir-larch	#3	9-5	13-9	17-5	21-3
	Hem-fir	SS	11-3	17-8	23-4	Note a
	Hem-fir	#1	11-0	17-4	22-10	Note a
	Hem-fir	#2	10-6	16-6	21-9	Note a
	Hem-fir	#3	9-5	13-9	17-5	21-3
	Southern pine	SS	11-9	18-5	24-3	Note a
	Southern pine	#1	11-6	18-1	23-1	Note a
	Southern pine	#2	11-3	17-8	23-4	Note a
	Southern pine	#3	10-0	14-9	18-9	22-2
	Spruce-pine-fir	SS	11-0	17-4	22-10	Note a
	Spruce-pine-fir	#1	10-9	16-11	22-4	Note a
	Spruce-pine-fir	#2	10-9	16-11	22-4	Note a
	Spruce-pine-fir	#3	9-5	13-9	17-5	21-3
19.2	Douglas fir-larch	SS	11-3	17-8	23-3	Note a
	Douglas fir-larch	#1	10-10	17-0	22-5	Note a
	Douglas fir-larch	#2	10-7	16-7	21-0	25-8
	Douglas fir-larch	#3	8-7	12-6	15-10	19-5
	Hem-fir	SS	10-7	16-8	21-11	Note a
	Hem-fir	#1	10-4	16-4	21-6	Note a
	Hem-fir	#2	9-11	15-7	20-6	25-3
	Hem-fir	#3	8-7	12-6	15-10	19-5
	Southern -pine	SS	11-0	17-4	22-10	Note a
	Southern pine	#1	10-10	17-0	22-5	Note a
	Southern pine	#2	10-7	16-8	21-11	Note a
	Southern pine	#3	9-1	13-6	17-2	20-3
	Spruce-pine-fir	SS	10-4	16-4	21-6	Note a
	Spruce-pine-fir	#1	10-2	15-11	21-0	25-8
	Spruce-pine-fir	#2	10-2	15-11	21-0	25-8
	Spruce-pine-fir	#3	8-7	12-6	15-10	19-5

(continued)

TABLE R802.4(1)—continued
CEILING JOIST SPANS FOR COMMON LUMBER SPECIES
(Uninhabitable attics without storage, live load = 10 psf, L/Δ = 240)

CEILING JOIST SPACING (inches)	SPECIES AND GRADE		DEAD LOAD = 5 psf			
			2 × 4	2 × 6	2 × 8	2 × 10
			Maximum ceiling joist spans			
			(feet - inches)	(feet - inches)	(feet - inches)	(feet - inches)
24	Douglas fir-larch	SS	10-5	16-4	21-7	Note a
	Douglas fir-larch	#1	10-0	15-9	20-1	24-6
	Douglas fir-larch	#2	9-10	14-10	18-9	22-11
	Douglas fir-larch	#3	7-8	11-2	14-2	17-4
	Hem-fir	SS	9-10	15-6	20-5	Note a
	Hem-fir	#1	9-8	15-2	19-7	23-11
	Hem-fir	#2	9-2	14-5	18-6	22-7
	Hem-fir	#3	7-8	11-2	14-2	17-4
	Southern pine	SS	10-3	16-1	21-2	Note a
	Southern pine	#1	10-0	15-9	20-10	Note a
	Southern pine	#2	9-10	15-6	20-1	23-11
	Southern pine	#3	8-2	12-0	15-4	18-1
	Spruce-pine-fir	SS	9-8	15-2	19-11	25-5
	Spruce-pine-fir	#1	9-5	14-9	18-9	22-11
	Spruce-pine-fir	#2	9-5	14-9	18-9	22-11
	Spruce-pine-fir	#3	7-8	11-2	14-2	17-4

Check sources for availability of lumber in lengths greater than 20 feet.

For SI: 1 inch = 25.4 mm, 1 foot = 304.8 mm, 1 pound per square foot = 0.0479 kPa.

a. Span exceeds 26 feet in length.

TABLE R802.4(2)
CEILING JOIST SPANS FOR COMMON LUMBER SPECIES
(Uninhabitable attics with limited storage, live load = 20 psf, L/Δ = 240)

CEILING JOIST SPACING (inches)	SPECIES AND GRADE		DEAD LOAD = 10 psf			
			2 × 4	2 × 6	2 × 8	2 × 10
			Maximum ceiling joist spans			
			(feet - inches)	(feet - inches)	(feet - inches)	(feet - inches)
12	Douglas fir-larch	SS	10-5	16-4	21-7	Note a
	Douglas fir-larch	#1	10-0	15-9	20-1	24-6
	Douglas fir-larch	#2	9-10	14-10	18-9	22-11
	Douglas fir-larch	#3	7-8	11-2	14-2	17-4
	Hem-fir	SS	9-10	15-6	20-5	Note a
	Hem-fir	#1	9-8	15-2	19-7	23-11
	Hem-fir	#2	9-2	14-5	18-6	22-7
	Hem-fir	#3	7-8	11-2	14-2	17-4
	Southern pine	SS	10-3	16-1	21-2	Note a
	Southern pine	#1	10-0	15-9	20-10	Note a
	Southern pine	#2	9-10	15-6	20-1	23-11
	Southern pine	#3	8-2	12-0	15-4	18-1
	Spruce-pine-fir	SS	9-8	15-2	19-11	25-5
	Spruce-pine-fir	#1	9-5	14-9	18-9	22-11
	Spruce-pine-fir	#2	9-5	14-9	18-9	22-11
	Spruce-pine-fir	#3	7-8	11-2	14-2	17-4
16	Douglas fir-larch	SS	9-6	14-11	19-7	25-0
	Douglas fir-larch	#1	9-1	13-9	17-5	21-3
	Douglas fir-larch	#2	8-9	12-10	16-3	19-10
	Douglas fir-larch	#3	6-8	9-8	12-4	15-0
	Hem-fir	SS	8-11	14-1	18-6	23-8
	Hem-fir	#1	8-9	13-5	16-10	20-8
	Hem-fir	#2	8-4	12-8	16-0	19-7
	Hem-fir	#3	6-8	9-8	12-4	15-0
	Southern pine	SS	9-4	14-7	19-3	24-7
	Southern pine	#1	9-1	14-4	18-11	23-1
	Southern pine	#2	8-11	13-6	17-5	20-9
	Southern pine	#3	7-1	10-5	13-3	15-8
	Spruce-pine-fir	SS	8-9	13-9	18-1	23-1
	Spruce-pine-fir	#1	8-7	12-10	16-3	19-10
	Spruce-pine-fir	#2	8-7	12-10	16-3	19-10
	Spruce-pine-fir	#3	6-8	9-8	12-4	15-0
19.2	Douglas fir-larch	SS	8-11	14-0	18-5	23-4
	Douglas fir-larch	#1	8-7	12-6	15-10	19-5
	Douglas fir-larch	#2	8-0	11-9	14-10	18-2
	Douglas fir-larch	#3	6-1	8-10	11-3	13-8
	Hem-fir	SS	8-5	13-3	17-5	22-3
	Hem-fir	#1	8-3	12-3	15-6	18-11
	Hem-fir	#2	7-10	11-7	14-8	17-10
	Hem-fir	#3	6-1	8-10	11-3	13-8
	Southern pine	SS	8-9	13-9	18-1	23-1
	Southern pine	#1	8-7	13-6	17-9	21-1
	Southern pine	#2	8-5	12-3	15-10	18-11
	Southern pine	#3	6-5	9-6	12-1	14-4
	Spruce-pine-fir	SS	8-3	12-11	17-1	21-8
	Spruce-pine-fir	#1	8-0	11-9	14-10	18-2
	Spruce-pine-fir	#2	8-0	11-9	14-10	18-2
	Spruce-pine-fir	#3	6-1	8-10	11-3	13-8

(continued)

TABLE R802.4(2)—continued
CEILING JOIST SPANS FOR COMMON LUMBER SPECIES
(Uninhabitable attics with limited storage, live load = 20 psf, L/Δ = 240)

CEILING JOIST SPACING (inches)	SPECIES AND GRADE		DEAD LOAD = 10 psf			
			2 × 4	2 × 6	2 × 8	2 × 10
			Maximum Ceiling Joist Spans			
			(feet - inches)	(feet - inches)	(feet - inches)	(feet - inches)
24	Douglas fir-larch	SS	8-3	13-0	17-1	20-11
	Douglas fir-larch	#1	7-8	11-2	14-2	17-4
	Douglas fir-larch	#2	7-2	10-6	13-3	16-3
	Douglas fir-larch	#3	5-5	7-11	10-0	12-3
	Hem-fir	SS	7-10	12-3	16-2	20-6
	Hem-fir	#1	7-6	10-11	13-10	16-11
	Hem-fir	#2	7-1	10-4	13-1	16-0
	Hem-fir	#3	5-5	7-11	10-0	12-3
	Southern pine	SS	8-1	12-9	16-10	21-6
	Southern pine	#1	8-0	12-6	15-10	18-10
	Southern pine	#2	7-8	11-0	14-2	16-11
	Southern pine	#3	5-9	8-6	10-10	12-10
	Spruce-pine-fir	SS	7-8	12-0	15-10	19-5
	Spruce-pine-fir	#1	7-2	10-6	13-3	16-3
	Spruce-pine-fir	#2	7-2	10-6	13-3	16-3
	Spruce-pine-fir	#3	5-5	7-11	10-0	12-3

Check sources for availability of lumber in lengths greater than 20 feet.

For SI: 1 inch = 25.4 mm, 1 foot = 304.8 mm, 1 pound per square foot = 0.0479kPa.

a. Span exceeds 26 feet in length.

TABLE R802.5.1(1)
RAFTER SPANS FOR COMMON LUMBER SPECIES
(Roof live load=20 psf, ceiling not attached to rafters, L/Δ = 180)

RAFTER SPACING (inches)	SPECIES AND GRADE		DEAD LOAD = 10 psf					DEAD LOAD = 20 psf				
			2 × 4	2 × 6	2 × 8	2 × 10	2 × 12	2 × 4	2 × 6	2 × 8	2 × 10	2 × 12
			Maximum rafter spans[a]									
			(feet - inches)	(feet - inches)	(feet - inches)	(feet - inches)	(feet - inches)	(feet - inches)	(feet - inches)	(feet - inches)	(feet - inches)	(feet - inches)
12	Douglas fir-larch	SS	11-6	18-0	23-9	Note b	Note b	11-6	18-0	23-5	Note b	Note b
	Douglas fir-larch	#1	11-1	17-4	22-5	Note b	Note b	10-6	15-4	19-5	23-9	Note b
	Douglas fir-larch	#2	10-1	16-7	21-0	25-8	Note b	9-10	14-4	18-2	22-3	25-9
	Douglas fir-larch	#3	8-7	12-6	15-10	19-5	22-6	7-5	10-10	13-9	16-9	19-6
	Hem-fir	SS	10-10	17-0	22-5	Note b	Note b	10-10	17-0	22-5	Note b	Note b
	Hem-fir	#1	10-7	16-8	21-10	Note b	Note b	10-3	14-11	18-11	23-2	Note b
	Hem-fir	#2	10-1	15-11	20-8	25-3	Note b	9-8	14-2	17-11	21-11	25-5
	Hem-fir	#3	8-7	12-6	15-10	19-5	22-6	7-5	10-10	13-9	16-9	19-6
	Southern pine	SS	11-3	17-8	23-4	Note b	Note b	11-3	17-8	23-4	Note b	Note b
	Southern pine	#1	11-1	17-4	22-11	Note b	Note b	11-1	17-3	21-9	25-10	Note b
	Southern pine	#2	10-10	17-0	22-5	Note b	Note b	10-6	15-1	19-5	23-2	Note b
	Southern pine	#3	9-1	13-6	17-2	20-3	24-1	7-11	11-8	14-10	17-6	20-11
	Spruce-pine-fir	SS	10-7	16-8	21-11	Note b	Note b	10-7	16-8	21-9	Note b	Note b
	Spruce-pine-fir	#1	10-4	16-3	21-0	25-8	Note b	9-10	14-4	18-2	22-3	25-9
	Spruce-pine-fir	#2	10-4	16-3	21-0	25-8	Note b	9-10	14-4	18-2	22-3	25-9
	Spruce-pine-fir	#3	8-7	12-6	15-10	19-5	22-6	7-5	10-10	13-9	16-9	19-6
16	Douglas fir-larch	SS	10-5	16-4	21-7	Note b	Note b	10-5	16-0	20-3	24-9	Note b
	Douglas fir-larch	#1	10-0	15-4	19-5	23-9	Note b	9-1	13-3	16-10	20-7	23-10
	Douglas fir-larch	#2	9-10	14-4	18-2	22-3	25-9	8-6	12-5	15-9	19-3	22-4
	Douglas fir-larch	#3	7-5	10-10	13-9	16-9	19-6	6-5	9-5	11-11	14-6	16-10
	Hem-fir	SS	9-10	15-6	20-5	Note b	Note b	9-10	15-6	19-11	24-4	Note b
	Hem-fir	#1	9-8	14-11	18-11	23-2	Note b	8-10	12-11	16-5	20-0	23-3
	Hem-fir	#2	9-2	14-2	17-11	21-11	25-5	8-5	12-3	15-6	18-11	22-0
	Hem-fir	#3	7-5	10-10	13-9	16-9	19-6	6-5	9-5	11-11	14-6	16-10
	Southern pine	SS	10-3	16-1	21-2	Note b	Note b	10-3	16-1	21-2	Note b	Note b
	Southern pine	#1	10-0	15-9	20-10	25-10	Note b	10-0	15-0	18-10	22-4	Note b
	Southern pine	#2	9-10	15-1	19-5	23-2	Note b	9-1	13-0	16-10	20-1	23-7
	Southern pine	#3	7-11	11-8	14-10	17-6	20-11	6-10	10-1	12-10	15-2	18-1
	Spruce-pine-fir	SS	9-8	15-2	19-11	25-5	Note b	9-8	14-10	18-10	23-0	Note b
	Spruce-pine-fir	#1	9-5	14-4	18-2	22-3	25-9	8-6	12-5	15-9	19-3	22-4
	Spruce-pine-fir	#2	9-5	14-4	18-2	22-3	25-9	8-6	12-5	15-9	19-3	22-4
	Spruce-pine-fir	#3	7-5	10-10	13-9	16-9	19-6	6-5	9-5	11-11	14-6	16-10
19.2	Douglas fir-larch	SS	9-10	15-5	20-4	25-11	Note b	9-10	14-7	18-6	22-7	Note b
	Douglas fir-larch	#1	9-5	14-0	17-9	21-8	25-2	8-4	12-2	15-4	18-9	21-9
	Douglas fir-larch	#2	8-11	13-1	16-7	20-3	23-6	7-9	11-4	14-4	17-7	20-4
	Douglas fir-larch	#3	6-9	9-11	12-7	15-4	17-9	5-10	8-7	10-10	13-3	15-5
	Hem-fir	SS	9-3	14-7	19-2	24-6	Note b	9-3	14-4	18-2	22-3	25-9
	Hem-fir	#1	9-1	13-8	17-4	21-1	24-6	8-1	11-10	15-0	18-4	21-3
	Hem-fir	#2	8-8	12-11	16-4	20-0	23-2	7-8	11-2	14-2	17-4	20-1
	Hem-fir	#3	6-9	9-11	12-7	15-4	17-9	5-10	8-7	10-10	13-3	15-5
	Southern pine	SS	9-8	15-2	19-11	25-5	Note b	9-8	15-2	19-11	25-5	Note b
	Southern pine	#1	9-5	14-10	19-7	23-7	Note b	9-3	13-8	17-2	20-5	24-4
	Southern pine	#2	9-3	13-9	17-9	21-2	24-10	8-4	11-11	15-4	18-4	21-6
	Southern pine	#3	7-3	10-8	13-7	16-0	19-1	6-3	9-3	11-9	13-10	16-6
	Spruce-pine-fir	SS	9-1	14-3	18-9	23-11	Note b	9-1	13-7	17-2	21-0	24-4
	Spruce-pine-fir	#1	8-10	13-1	16-7	20-3	23-6	7-9	11-4	14-4	17-7	20-4
	Spruce-pine-fir	#2	8-10	13-1	16-7	20-3	23-6	7-9	11-4	14-4	17-7	20-4
	Spruce-pine-fir	#3	6-9	9-11	12-7	15-4	17-9	5-10	8-7	10-10	13-3	15-5

(continued)

TABLE R802.5.1(1)—continued
RAFTER SPANS FOR COMMON LUMBER SPECIES
(Roof live load=20 psf, ceiling not attached to rafters, L/Δ = 180)

RAFTER SPACING (inches)	SPECIES AND GRADE		DEAD LOAD = 10 psf					DEAD LOAD = 20 psf				
			2 × 4	2 × 6	2 × 8	2 × 10	2 × 12	2 × 4	2 × 6	2 × 8	2 × 10	2 × 12
			Maximum rafter spans[a]									
			(feet - inches)	(feet - inches)	(feet - inches)	(feet - inches)	(feet - inches)	(feet - inches)	(feet - inches)	(feet - inches)	(feet - inches)	(feet - inches)
24	Douglas fir-larch	SS	9-1	14-4	18-10	23-4	Note b	8-11	13-1	16-7	20-3	23-5
	Douglas fir-larch	#1	8-7	12-6	15-10	19-5	22-6	7-5	10-10	13-9	16-9	19-6
	Douglas fir-larch	#2	8-0	11-9	14-10	18-2	21-0	6-11	10-2	12-10	15-8	18-3
	Douglas fir-larch	#3	6-1	8-10	11-3	13-8	15-11	5-3	7-8	9-9	11-10	13-9
	Hem-fir	SS	8-7	13-6	17-10	22-9	Note b	8-7	12-10	16-3	19-10	23-0
	Hem-fir	#1	8-4	12-3	15-6	18-11	21-11	7-3	10-7	13-5	16-4	19-0
	Hem-fir	#2	7-11	11-7	14-8	17-10	20-9	6-10	10-0	12-8	15-6	17-11
	Hem-fir	#3	6-1	8-10	11-3	13-8	15-11	5-3	7-8	9-9	11-10	13-9
	Southern pine	SS	8-11	14-1	18-6	23-8	Note b	8-11	14-1	18-6	22-11	Note b
	Southern pine	#1	8-9	13-9	17-9	21-1	25-2	8-3	12-3	15-4	18-3	21-9
	Southern pine	#2	8-7	12-3	15-10	18-11	22-2	7-5	10-8	13-9	16-5	19-3
	Southern pine	#3	6-5	9-6	12-1	14-4	17-1	5-7	8-3	10-6	12-5	14-9
	Spruce-pine-fir	SS	8-5	13-3	17-5	21-8	25-2	8-4	12-2	15-4	18-9	21-9
	Spruce-pine-fir	#1	8-0	11-9	14-10	18-2	21-0	6-11	10-2	12-10	15-8	18-3
	Spruce-pine-fir	#2	8-0	11-9	14-10	18-2	21-0	6-11	10-2	12-10	15-8	18-3
	Spruce-pine-fir	#3	6-1	8-10	11-3	13-8	15-11	5-3	7-8	9-9	11-10	13-9

Check sources for availability of lumber in lengths greater than 20 feet.

For SI: 1 inch = 25.4 mm, 1 foot = 304.8 mm, 1 pound per square foot = 0.0479 kPa.

a. The tabulated rafter spans assume that ceiling joists are located at the bottom of the attic space or that some other method of resisting the outward push of the rafters on the bearing walls, such as rafter ties, is provided at that location. When ceiling joists or rafter ties are located higher in the attic space, the rafter spans shall be multiplied by the factors given below:

H_C/H_R	Rafter Span Adjustment Factor
1/3	0.67
1/4	0.76
1/5	0.83
1/6	0.90
1/7.5 or less	1.00

where:

H_C = Height of ceiling joists or rafter ties measured vertically above the top of the rafter support walls.

H_R = Height of roof ridge measured vertically above the top of the rafter support walls.

b. Span exceeds 26 feet in length.

TABLE R802.5.1(2)
RAFTER SPANS FOR COMMON LUMBER SPECIES
(Roof live load=20 psf, ceiling attached to rafters, L/Δ = 240)

RAFTER SPACING (inches)	SPECIES AND GRADE		DEAD LOAD = 10 psf					DEAD LOAD = 20 psf				
			2 × 4	2 × 6	2 × 8	2 × 10	2 × 12	2 × 4	2 × 6	2 × 8	2 × 10	2 × 12
			Maximum rafter spans[a]									
			(feet - inches)	(feet - inches)	(feet - inches)	(feet - inches)	(feet - inches)	(feet - inches)	(feet - inches)	(feet - inches)	(feet - inches)	(feet - inches)
12	Douglas fir-larch	SS	10-5	16-4	21-7	Note b	Note b	10-5	16-4	21-7	Note b	Note b
	Douglas fir-larch	#1	10-0	15-9	20-10	Note b	Note b	10-0	15-4	19-5	23-9	Note b
	Douglas fir-larch	#2	9-10	15-6	20-5	25-8	Note b	9-10	14-4	18-2	22-3	25-9
	Douglas fir-larch	#3	8-7	12-6	15-10	19-5	22-6	7-5	10-10	13-9	16-9	19-6
	Hem-fir	SS	9-10	15-6	20-5	Note b	Note b	9-10	15-6	20-5	Note b	Note b
	Hem-fir	#1	9-8	15-2	19-11	25-5	Note b	9-8	14-11	18-11	23-2	Note b
	Hem-fir	#2	9-2	14-5	19-0	24-3	Note b	9-2	14-2	17-11	21-11	25-5
	Hem-fir	#3	8-7	12-6	15-10	19-5	22-6	7-5	10-10	13-9	16-9	19-6
	Southern pine	SS	10-3	16-1	21-2	Note b	Note b	10-3	16-1	21-2	Note b	Note b
	Southern pine	#1	10-0	15-9	20-10	Note b	Note b	10-0	15-9	20-10	25-10	Note b
	Southern pine	#2	9-10	15-6	20-5	Note b	Note b	9-10	15-1	19-5	23-2	Note b
	Southern pine	#3	9-1	13-6	17-2	20-3	24-1	7-11	11-8	14-10	17-6	20-11
	Spruce-pine-fir	SS	9-8	15-2	19-11	25-5	Note b	9-8	15-2	19-11	25-5	Note b
	Spruce-pine-fir	#1	9-5	14-9	19-6	24-10	Note b	9-5	14-4	18-2	22-3	25-9
	Spruce-pine-fir	#2	9-5	14-9	19-6	24-10	Note b	9-5	14-4	18-2	22-3	25-9
	Spruce-pine-fir	#3	8-7	12-6	15-10	19-5	22-6	7-5	10-10	13-9	16-9	19-6
16	Douglas fir-larch	SS	9-6	14-11	19-7	25-0	Note b	9-6	14-11	19-7	24-9	Note b
	Douglas fir-larch	#1	9-1	14-4	18-11	23-9	Note b	9-1	13-3	16-10	20-7	23-10
	Douglas fir-larch	#2	8-11	14-1	18-2	22-3	25-9	8-6	12-5	15-9	19-3	22-4
	Douglas fir-larch	#3	7-5	10-10	13-9	16-9	19-6	6-5	9-5	11-11	14-6	16-10
	Hem-fir	SS	8-11	14-1	18-6	23-8	Note b	8-11	14-1	18-6	23-8	Note b
	Hem-fir	#1	8-9	13-9	18-1	23-1	Note b	8-9	12-11	16-5	20-0	23-3
	Hem-fir	#2	8-4	13-1	17-3	21-11	25-5	8-4	12-3	15-6	18-11	22-0
	Hem-fir	#3	7-5	10-10	13-9	16-9	19-6	6-5	9-5	11-11	14-6	16-10
	Southern pine	SS	9-4	14-7	19-3	24-7	Note b	9-4	14-7	19-3	24-7	Note b
	Southern pine	#1	9-1	14-4	18-11	24-1	Note b	9-1	14-4	18-10	22-4	Note b
	Southern pine	#2	8-11	14-1	18-6	23-2	Note b	8-11	13-0	16-10	20-1	23-7
	Southern pine	#3	7-11	11-8	14-10	17-6	20-11	6-10	10-1	12-10	15-2	18-1
	Spruce-pine-fir	SS	8-9	13-9	18-1	23-1	Note b	8-9	13-9	18-1	23-0	Note b
	Spruce-pine-fir	#1	8-7	13-5	17-9	22-3	25-9	8-6	12-5	15-9	19-3	22-4
	Spruce-pine-fir	#2	8-7	13-5	17-9	22-3	25-9	8-6	12-5	15-9	19-3	22-4
	Spruce-pine-fir	#3	7-5	10-10	13-9	16-9	19-6	6-5	9-5	11-11	14-6	16-10
19.2	Douglas fir-larch	SS	8-11	14-0	18-5	23-7	Note b	8-11	14-0	18-5	22-7	Note b
	Douglas fir-larch	#1	8-7	13-6	17-9	21-8	25-2	8-4	12-2	15-4	18-9	21-9
	Douglas fir-larch	#2	8-5	13-1	16-7	20-3	23-6	7-9	11-4	14-4	17-7	20-4
	Douglas fir-larch	#3	6-9	9-11	12-7	15-4	17-9	5-10	8-7	10-10	13-3	15-5
	Hem-fir	SS	8-5	13-3	17-5	22-3	Note b	8-5	13-3	17-5	22-3	25-9
	Hem-fir	#1	8-3	12-11	17-1	21-1	24-6	8-1	11-10	15-0	18-4	21-3
	Hem-fir	#2	7-10	12-4	16-3	20-0	23-2	7-8	11-2	14-2	17-4	20-1
	Hem-fir	#3	6-9	9-11	12-7	15-4	17-9	5-10	8-7	10-10	13-3	15-5
	Southern pine	SS	8-9	13-9	18-1	23-1	Note b	8-9	13-9	18-1	23-1	Note b
	Southern pine	#1	8-7	13-6	17-9	22-8	Note b	8-7	13-6	17-2	20-5	24-4
	Southern pine	#2	8-5	13-3	17-5	21-2	24-10	8-4	11-11	15-4	18-4	21-6
	Southern pine	#3	7-3	10-8	13-7	16-0	19-1	6-3	9-3	11-9	13-10	16-6
	Spruce-pine-fir	SS	8-3	12-11	17-1	21-9	Note b	8-3	12-11	17-1	21-0	24-4
	Spruce-pine-fir	#1	8-1	12-8	16-7	20-3	23-6	7-9	11-4	14-4	17-7	20-4
	Spruce-pine-fir	#2	8-1	12-8	16-7	20-3	23-6	7-9	11-4	14-4	17-7	20-4
	Spruce-pine-fir	#3	6-9	9-11	12-7	15-4	17-9	5-10	8-7	10-10	13-3	15-5

(continued)

TABLE R802.5.1(2)—continued
RAFTER SPANS FOR COMMON LUMBER SPECIES
(Roof live load=20 psf, ceiling attached to rafters, L/Δ = 240)

RAFTER SPACING (inches)	SPECIES AND GRADE		DEAD LOAD = 10 psf					DEAD LOAD = 20 psf				
			2 × 4	2 × 6	2 × 8	2 × 10	2 × 12	2 × 4	2 × 6	2 × 8	2 × 10	2 × 12
			Maximum rafter spans[a]									
			(feet - inches)	(feet - inches)	(feet - inches)	(feet - inches)	(feet - inches)	(feet - inches)	(feet - inches)	(feet - inches)	(feet - inches)	(feet - inches)
24	Douglas fir-larch	SS	8-3	13-0	17-2	21-10	Note b	8-3	13-0	16-7	20-3	23-5
	Douglas fir-larch	#1	8-0	12-6	15-10	19-5	22-6	7-5	10-10	13-9	16-9	19-6
	Douglas fir-larch	#2	7-10	11-9	14-10	18-2	21-0	6-11	10-2	12-10	15-8	18-3
	Douglas fir-larch	#3	6-1	8-10	11-3	13-8	15-11	5-3	7-8	9-9	11-10	13-9
	Hem-fir	SS	7-10	12-3	16-2	20-8	25-1	7-10	12-3	16-2	19-10	23-0
	Hem-fir	#1	7-8	12-0	15-6	18-11	21-11	7-3	10-7	13-5	16-4	19-0
	Hem-fir	#2	7-3	11-5	14-8	17-10	20-9	6-10	10-0	12-8	15-6	17-11
	Hem-fir	#3	6-1	8-10	11-3	13-8	15-11	5-3	7-8	9-9	11-10	13-9
	Southern pine	SS	8-1	12-9	16-10	21-6	Note b	8-1	12-9	16-10	21-6	Note b
	Southern pine	#1	8-0	12-6	16-6	21-1	25-2	8-0	12-3	15-4	18-3	21-9
	Southern pine	#2	7-10	12-3	15-10	18-11	22-2	7-5	10-8	13-9	16-5	19-3
	Southern pine	#3	6-5	9-6	12-1	14-4	17-1	5-7	8-3	10-6	12-5	14-9
	Spruce-pine-fir	SS	7-8	12-0	15-10	20-2	24-7	7-8	12-0	15-4	18-9	21-9
	Spruce-pine-fir	#1	7-6	11-9	14-10	18-2	21-0	6-11	10-2	12-10	15-8	18-3
	Spruce-pine-fir	#2	7-6	11-9	14-10	18-2	21-0	6-11	10-2	12-10	15-8	18-3
	Spruce-pine-fir	#3	6-1	8-10	11-3	13-8	15-11	5-3	7-8	9-9	11-10	13-9

Check sources for availability of lumber in lengths greater than 20 feet.

For SI: 1 inch = 25.4 mm, 1 foot = 304.8 mm, 1 pound per square foot = 0.0479kPa.

a. The tabulated rafter spans assume that ceiling joists are located at the bottom of the attic space or that some other method of resisting the outward push of the rafters on the bearing walls, such as rafter ties, is provided at that location. When ceiling joists or rafter ties are located higher in the attic space, the rafter spans shall be multiplied by the factors given below:

H_C/H_R	Rafter Span Adjustment Factor
1/3	0.67
1/4	0.76
1/5	0.83
1/6	0.90
1/7.5 or less	1.00

where:

H_C = Height of ceiling joists or rafter ties measured vertically above the top of the rafter support walls.

H_R = Height of roof ridge measured vertically above the top of the rafter support walls.

b. Span exceeds 26 feet in length.

TABLE R802.5.1(3)
RAFTER SPANS FOR COMMON LUMBER SPECIES
(Ground snow load=30 psf, ceiling not attached to rafters, L/Δ = 180)

RAFTER SPACING (inches)	SPECIES AND GRADE		DEAD LOAD = 10 psf					DEAD LOAD = 20 psf				
			2 × 4	2 × 6	2 × 8	2 × 10	2 × 12	2 × 4	2 × 6	2 × 8	2 × 10	2 × 12
			Maximum rafter spans[a]									
			(feet - inches)	(feet - inches)	(feet - inches)	(feet - inches)	(feet - inches)	(feet - inches)	(feet - inches)	(feet - inches)	(feet - inches)	(feet - inches)
12	Douglas fir-larch	SS	10-0	15-9	20-9	Note b	Note b	10-0	15-9	20-1	24-6	Note b
	Douglas fir-larch	#1	9-8	14-9	18-8	22-9	Note b	9-0	13-2	16-8	20-4	23-7
	Douglas fir-larch	#2	9-5	13-9	17-5	21-4	24-8	8-5	12-4	15-7	19-1	22-1
	Douglas fir-larch	#3	7-1	10-5	13-2	16-1	18-8	6-4	9-4	11-9	14-5	16-8
	Hem-fir	SS	9-6	14-10	19-7	25-0	Note b	9-6	14-10	19-7	24-1	Note b
	Hem-fir	#1	9-3	14-4	18-2	22-2	25-9	8-9	12-10	16-3	19-10	23-0
	Hem-fir	#2	8-10	13-7	17-2	21-0	24-4	8-4	12-2	15-4	18-9	21-9
	Hem-fir	#3	7-1	10-5	13-2	16-1	18-8	6-4	9-4	11-9	14-5	16-8
	Southern pine	SS	9-10	15-6	20-5	Note b	Note b	9-10	15-6	20-5	Note b	Note b
	Southern pine	#1	9-8	15-2	20-0	24-9	Note b	9-8	14-10	18-8	22-2	Note b
	Southern pine	#2	9-6	14-5	18-8	22-3	Note b	9-0	12-11	16-8	19-11	23-4
	Southern pine	#3	7-7	11-2	14-3	16-10	20-0	6-9	10-0	12-9	15-1	17-11
	Spruce-pine-fir	SS	9-3	14-7	19-2	24-6	Note b	9-3	14-7	18-8	22-9	Note b
	Spruce-pine-fir	#1	9-1	13-9	17-5	21-4	24-8	8-5	12-4	15-7	19-1	22-1
	Spruce-pine-fir	#2	9-1	13-9	17-5	21-4	24-8	8-5	12-4	15-7	19-1	22-1
	Spruce-pine-fir	#3	7-1	10-5	13-2	16-1	18-8	6-4	9-4	11-9	14-5	16-8
16	Douglas fir-larch	SS	9-1	14-4	18-10	23-9	Note b	9-1	13-9	17-5	21-3	24-8
	Douglas fir-larch	#1	8-9	12-9	16-2	19-9	22-10	7-10	11-5	14-5	17-8	20-5
	Douglas fir-larch	#2	8-2	11-11	15-1	18-5	21-5	7-3	10-8	13-6	16-6	19-2
	Douglas fir-larch	#3	6-2	9-0	11-5	13-11	16-2	5-6	8-1	10-3	12-6	14-6
	Hem-fir	SS	8-7	13-6	17-10	22-9	Note b	8-7	13-6	17-1	20-10	24-2
	Hem-fir	#1	8-5	12-5	15-9	19-3	22-3	7-7	11-1	14-1	17-2	19-11
	Hem-fir	#2	8-0	11-9	14-11	18-2	21-1	7-2	10-6	13-4	16-3	18-10
	Hem-fir	#3	6-2	9-0	11-5	13-11	16-2	5-6	8-1	10-3	12-6	14-6
	Southern pine	SS	8-11	14-1	18-6	23-8	Note b	8-11	14-1	18-6	23-8	Note b
	Southern pine	#1	8-9	13-9	18-1	21-5	25-7	8-8	12-10	16-2	19-2	22-10
	Southern pine	#2	8-7	12-6	16-2	19-3	22-7	7-10	11-2	14-5	17-3	20-2
	Southern pine	#3	6-7	9-8	12-4	14-7	17-4	5-10	8-8	11-0	13-0	15-6
	Spruce-pine-fir	SS	8-5	13-3	17-5	22-1	25-7	8-5	12-9	16-2	19-9	22-10
	Spruce-pine-fir	#1	8-2	11-11	15-1	18-5	21-5	7-3	10-8	13-6	16-6	19-2
	Spruce-pine-fir	#2	8-2	11-11	15-1	18-5	21-5	7-3	10-8	13-6	16-6	19-2
	Spruce-pine-fir	#3	6-2	9-0	11-5	13-11	16-2	5-6	8-1	10-3	12-6	14-6
19.2	Douglas fir-larch	SS	8-7	13-6	17-9	21-8	25-2	8-7	12-6	15-10	19-5	22-6
	Douglas fir-larch	#1	7-11	11-8	14-9	18-0	20-11	7-1	10-5	13-2	16-1	18-8
	Douglas fir-larch	#2	7-5	10-11	13-9	16-10	19-6	6-8	9-9	12-4	15-1	17-6
	Douglas fir-larch	#3	5-7	8-3	10-5	12-9	14-9	5-0	7-4	9-4	11-5	13-2
	Hem-fir	SS	8-1	12-9	16-9	21-4	24-8	8-1	12-4	15-7	19-1	22-1
	Hem-fir	#1	7-9	11-4	14-4	17-7	20-4	6-11	10-2	12-10	15-8	18-2
	Hem-fir	#2	7-4	10-9	13-7	16-7	19-3	6-7	9-7	12-2	14-10	17-3
	Hem-fir	#3	5-7	8-3	10-5	12-9	14-9	5-0	7-4	9-4	11-5	13-2
	Southern pine	SS	8-5	13-3	17-5	22-3	Note b	8-5	13-3	17-5	22-0	25-9
	Southern pine	#1	8-3	13-0	16-6	19-7	23-4	7-11	11-9	14-9	17-6	20-11
	Southern pine	#2	7-11	11-5	14-9	17-7	20-7	7-1	10-2	13-2	15-9	18-5
	Southern pine	#3	6-0	8-10	11-3	13-4	15-10	5-4	7-11	10-1	11-11	14-2
	Spruce-pine-fir	SS	7-11	12-5	16-5	20-2	23-4	7-11	11-8	14-9	18-0	20-11
	Spruce-pine-fir	#1	7-5	10-11	13-9	16-10	19-6	6-8	9-9	12-4	15-1	17-6
	Spruce-pine-fir	#2	7-5	10-11	13-9	16-10	19-6	6-8	9-9	12-4	15-1	17-6
	Spruce-pine-fir	#3	5-7	8-3	10-5	12-9	14-9	5-0	7-4	9-4	11-5	13-2

(continued)

TABLE R802.5.1(3)—continued
RAFTER SPANS FOR COMMON LUMBER SPECIES
(Ground snow load=30 psf, ceiling not attached to rafters, L/Δ = 180)

RAFTER SPACING (inches)	SPECIES AND GRADE		DEAD LOAD = 10 psf					DEAD LOAD = 20 psf				
			2 × 4	2 × 6	2 × 8	2 × 10	2 × 12	2 × 4	2 × 6	2 × 8	2 × 10	2 × 12
			Maximum rafter spans[a]									
			(feet - inches)	(feet - inches)	(feet - inches)	(feet - inches)	(feet - inches)	(feet - inches)	(feet - inches)	(feet - inches)	(feet - inches)	(feet - inches)
24	Douglas fir-larch	SS	7-11	12-6	15-10	19-5	22-6	7-8	11-3	14-2	17-4	20-1
	Douglas fir-larch	#1	7-1	10-5	13-2	16-1	18-8	6-4	9-4	11-9	14-5	16-8
	Douglas fir-larch	#2	6-8	9-9	12-4	15-1	17-6	5-11	8-8	11-0	13-6	15-7
	Douglas fir-larch	#3	5-0	7-4	9-4	11-5	13-2	4-6	6-7	8-4	10-2	11-10
	Hem-fir	SS	7-6	11-10	15-7	19-1	22-1	7-6	11-0	13-11	17-0	19-9
	Hem-fir	#1	6-11	10-2	12-10	15-8	18-2	6-2	9-1	11-6	14-0	16-3
	Hem-fir	#2	6-7	9-7	12-2	14-10	17-3	5-10	8-7	10-10	13-3	15-5
	Hem-fir	#3	5-0	7-4	9-4	11-5	13-2	4-6	6-7	8-4	10-2	11-10
	Southern pine	SS	7-10	12-3	16-2	20-8	25-1	7-10	12-3	16-2	19-8	23-0
	Southern pine	#1	7-8	11-9	14-9	17-6	20-11	7-1	10-6	13-2	15-8	18-8
	Southern pine	#2	7-1	10-2	13-2	15-9	18-5	6-4	9-2	11-9	14-1	16-6
	Southern pine	#3	5-4	7-11	10-1	11-11	14-2	4-9	7-1	9-0	10-8	12-8
	Spruce-pine-fir	SS	7-4	11-7	14-9	18-0	20-11	7-1	10-5	13-2	16-1	18-8
	Spruce-pine-fir	#1	6-8	9-9	12-4	15-1	17-6	5-11	8-8	11-0	13-6	15-7
	Spruce-pine-fir	#2	6-8	9-9	12-4	15-1	17-6	5-11	8-8	11-0	13-6	15-7
	Spruce-pine-fir	#3	5-0	7-4	9-4	11-5	13-2	4-6	6-7	8-4	10-2	11-10

Check sources for availability of lumber in lengths greater than 20 feet.

For SI: 1 inch = 25.4 mm, 1 foot = 304.8 mm, 1 pound per square foot = 0.0479 kPa.

a. The tabulated rafter spans assume that ceiling joists are located at the bottom of the attic space or that some other method of resisting the outward push of the rafters on the bearing walls, such as rafter ties, is provided at that location. When ceiling joists or rafter ties are located higher in the attic space, the rafter spans shall be multiplied by the factors given below:

H_C/H_R	Rafter Span Adjustment Factor
1/3	0.67
1/4	0.76
1/5	0.83
1/6	0.90
1/7.5 or less	1.00

where:

H_C = Height of ceiling joists or rafter ties measured vertically above the top of the rafter support walls.

H_R = Height of roof ridge measured vertically above the top of the rafter support walls.

b. Span exceeds 26 feet in length.

TABLE R802.5.1(4)
RAFTER SPANS FOR COMMON LUMBER SPECIES
(Ground snow load=50 psf, ceiling not attached to rafters, L/Δ = 180)

RAFTER SPACING (inches)	SPECIES AND GRADE		DEAD LOAD = 10 psf					DEAD LOAD = 20 psf				
			2 × 4	2 × 6	2 × 8	2 × 10	2 × 12	2 × 4	2 × 6	2 × 8	2 × 10	2 × 12
			Maximum rafter spans[a]									
			(feet - inches)	(feet - inches)	(feet - inches)	(feet - inches)	(feet - inches)	(feet - inches)	(feet - inches)	(feet - inches)	(feet - inches)	(feet - inches)
12	Douglas fir-larch	SS	8-5	13-3	17-6	22-4	26-0	8-5	13-3	17-0	20-9	24-0
	Douglas fir-larch	#1	8-2	12-0	15-3	18-7	21-7	7-7	11-2	14-1	17-3	20-0
	Douglas fir-larch	#2	7-8	11-3	14-3	17-5	20-2	7-1	10-5	13-2	16-1	18-8
	Douglas fir-larch	#3	5-10	8-6	10-9	13-2	15-3	5-5	7-10	10-0	12-2	14-1
	Hem-fir	SS	8-0	12-6	16-6	21-1	25-6	8-0	12-6	16-6	20-4	23-7
	Hem-fir	#1	7-10	11-9	14-10	18-1	21-0	7-5	10-10	13-9	16-9	19-5
	Hem-fir	#2	7-5	11-1	14-0	17-2	19-11	7-0	10-3	13-0	15-10	18-5
	Hem-fir	#3	5-10	8-6	10-9	13-2	15-3	5-5	7-10	10-0	12-2	14-1
	Southern pine	SS	8-4	13-0	17-2	21-11	Note b	8-4	13-0	17-2	21-11	Note b
	Southern pine	#1	8-2	12-10	16-10	20-3	24-1	8-2	12-6	15-9	18-9	22-4
	Southern pine	#2	8-0	11-9	15-3	18-2	21-3	7-7	10-11	14-1	16-10	19-9
	Southern pine	#3	6-2	9-2	11-8	13-9	16-4	5-9	8-5	10-9	12-9	15-2
	Spruce-pine-fir	SS	7-10	12-3	16-2	20-8	24-1	7-10	12-3	15-9	19-3	22-4
	Spruce-pine-fir	#1	7-8	11-3	14-3	17-5	20-2	7-1	10-5	13-2	16-1	18-8
	Spruce-pine-fir	#2	7-8	11-3	14-3	17-5	15-2	7-1	10-5	13-2	16-1	18-8
	Spruce-pine-fir	#3	5-10	8-6	10-9	13-2	20-3	5-5	7-10	10-0	12-2	14-1
16	Douglas fir-larch	SS	7-8	12-1	15-10	19-5	22-6	7-8	11-7	14-8	17-11	20-10
	Douglas fir-larch	#1	7-1	10-5	13-2	16-1	18-8	6-7	9-8	12-2	14-11	17-3
	Douglas fir-larch	#2	6-8	9-9	12-4	15-1	17-6	6-2	9-0	11-5	13-11	16-2
	Douglas fir-larch	#3	5-0	7-4	9-4	11-5	13-2	4-8	6-10	8-8	10-6	12-3
	Hem-fir	SS	7-3	11-5	15-0	19-1	22-1	7-3	11-5	14-5	17-8	20-5
	Hem-fir	#1	6-11	10-2	12-10	15-8	18-2	6-5	9-5	11-11	14-6	16-10
	Hem-fir	#2	6-7	9-7	12-2	14-10	17-3	6-1	8-11	11-3	13-9	15-11
	Hem-fir	#3	5-0	7-4	9-4	11-5	13-2	4-8	6-10	8-8	10-6	12-3
	Southern pine	SS	7-6	11-10	15-7	19-11	24-3	7-6	11-10	15-7	19-11	23-10
	Southern pine	#1	7-5	11-7	14-9	17-6	20-11	7-4	10-10	13-8	16-2	19-4
	Southern pine	#2	7-1	10-2	13-2	15-9	18-5	6-7	9-5	12-2	14-7	17-1
	Southern pine	#3	5-4	7-11	10-1	11-11	14-2	4-11	7-4	9-4	11-0	13-1
	Spruce-pine-fir	SS	7-1	11-2	14-8	18-0	20-11	7-1	10-9	13-8	15-11	19-4
	Spruce-pine-fir	#1	6-8	9-9	12-4	15-1	17-6	6-2	9-0	11-5	13-11	16-2
	Spruce-pine-fir	#2	6-8	9-9	12-4	15-1	17-6	6-2	9-0	11-5	13-11	16-2
	Spruce-pine-fir	#3	5-0	7-4	9-4	11-5	13-2	4-8	6-10	8-8	10-6	12-3
19.2	Douglas fir-larch	SS	7-3	11-4	14-6	17-8	20-6	7-3	10-7	13-5	16-5	19-0
	Douglas fir-larch	#1	6-6	9-6	12-0	14-8	17-1	6-0	8-10	11-2	13-7	15-9
	Douglas fir-larch	#2	6-1	8-11	11-3	13-9	15-11	5-7	8-3	10-5	12-9	14-9
	Douglas fir-larch	#3	4-7	6-9	8-6	10-5	12-1	4-3	6-3	7-11	9-7	11-2
	Hem-fir	SS	6-10	10-9	14-2	17-5	20-2	6-10	10-5	13-2	16-1	18-8
	Hem-fir	#1	6-4	9-3	11-9	14-4	16-7	5-10	8-7	10-10	13-3	15-5
	Hem-fir	#2	6-0	8-9	11-1	13-7	15-9	5-7	8-1	10-3	12-7	14-7
	Hem-fir	#3	4-7	6-9	8-6	10-5	12-1	4-3	6-3	7-11	9-7	11-2
	Southern pine	SS	7-1	11-2	14-8	18-9	22-10	7-1	11-2	14-8	18 7	21-9
	Southern pine	#1	7-0	10-8	13-5	16-0	19-1	6-8	9-11	12-5	14-10	17-8
	Southern pine	#2	6-6	9-4	12-0	14-4	16-10	6-0	8-8	11-2	13-4	15-7
	Southern pine	#3	4-11	7-3	9-2	10-10	12-11	4-6	6-8	8-6	10-1	12-0
	Spruce-pine-fir	SS	6-8	10-6	13-5	16-5	19-1	6-8	9-10	12-5	15-3	17-8
	Spruce-pine-fir	#1	6-1	8-11	11-3	13-9	15-11	5-7	8-3	10-5	12-9	14-9
	Spruce-pine-fir	#2	6-1	8-11	11-3	13-9	15-11	5-7	8-3	10-5	12-9	14-9
	Spruce-pine-fir	#3	4-7	6-9	8-6	10-5	12-1	4-3	6-3	7-11	9-7	11-2

(continued)

TABLE R802.5.1(4)—continued
RAFTER SPANS FOR COMMON LUMBER SPECIES
(Ground snow load=50 psf, ceiling not attached to rafters, L/Δ = 180)

RAFTER SPACING (inches)	SPECIES AND GRADE		DEAD LOAD = 10 psf					DEAD LOAD = 20 psf				
			2 × 4	2 × 6	2 × 8	2 × 10	2 × 12	2 × 4	2 × 6	2 × 8	2 × 10	2 × 12
			Maximum rafter spans[a]									
			(feet - inches)	(feet - inches)	(feet - inches)	(feet - inches)	(feet - inches)	(feet - inches)	(feet - inches)	(feet - inches)	(feet - inches)	(feet - inches)
24	Douglas fir-larch	SS	6-8	10-	13-0	15-10	18-4	6-6	9-6	12-0	14-8	17-0
	Douglas fir-larch	#1	5-10	8-6	10-9	13-2	15-3	5-5	7-10	10-0	12-2	14-1
	Douglas fir-larch	#2	5-5	7-11	10-1	12-4	14-3	5-0	7-4	9-4	11-5	13-2
	Douglas fir-larch	#3	4-1	6-0	7-7	9-4	10-9	3-10	5-7	7-1	8-7	10-0
	Hem-fir	SS	6-4	9-11	12-9	15-7	18-0	6-4	9-4	11-9	14-5	16-8
	Hem-fir	#1	5-8	8-3	10-6	12-10	14-10	5-3	7-8	9-9	11-10	13-9
	Hem-fir	#2	5-4	7-10	9-11	12-1	14-1	4-11	7-3	9-2	11-3	13-0
	Hem-fir	#3	4-1	6-0	7-7	9-4	10-9	3-10	5-7	7-1	8-7	10-0
	Southern pine	SS	6-7	10-4	13-8	17-5	21-0	6-7	10-4	13-8	16-7	19-5
	Southern pine	#1	6-5	9-7	12-0	14-4	17-1	6-0	8-10	11-2	13-3	15-9
	Southern pine	#2	5-10	8-4	10-9	12-10	15-1	5-5	7-9	10-0	11-11	13-11
	Southern pine	#3	4-4	6-5	8-3	9-9	11-7	4-1	6-0	7-7	9-0	10-8
	Spruce-pine-fir	SS	6-2	9-6	12-0	14-8	17-1	6-0	8-10	11-2	13-7	15-9
	Spruce-pine-fir	#1	5-5	7-11	10-1	12-4	14-3	5-0	7-4	9-4	11-5	13-2
	Spruce-pine-fir	#2	5-5	7-11	10-1	12-4	14-3	5-0	7-4	9-4	11-5	13-2
	Spruce-pine-fir	#3	4-1	6-0	7-7	9-4	10-9	3-10	5-7	7-1	8-7	10-0

Check sources for availability of lumber in lengths greater than 20 feet.

For SI: 1 inch = 25.4 mm, 1 foot = 304.8 mm, 1 pound per square foot = 0.0479kPa.

a. The tabulated rafter spans assume that ceiling joists are located at the bottom of the attic space or that some other method of resisting the outward push of the rafters on the bearing walls, such as rafter ties, is provided at that location. When ceiling joists or rafter ties are located higher in the attic space, the rafter spans shall be multiplied by the factors given below:

H_C/H_R	Rafter Span Adjustment Factor
1/3	0.67
1/4	0.76
1/5	0.83
1/6	0.90
1/7.5 or less	1.00

where:

H_C = Height of ceiling joists or rafter ties measured vertically above the top of the rafter support walls.

H_R = Height of roof ridge measured vertically above the top of the rafter support walls.

b. Span exceeds 26 feet in length.

TABLE R802.5.1(5)
RAFTER SPANS FOR COMMON LUMBER SPECIES
(Ground snow load=30 psf, ceiling attached to rafters, L/Δ = 240)

RAFTER SPACING (inches)	SPECIES AND GRADE		DEAD LOAD = 10 psf					DEAD LOAD = 20 psf				
			2 × 4	2 × 6	2 × 8	2 × 10	2 × 12	2 × 4	2 × 6	2 × 8	2 × 10	2 × 12
			Maximum rafter spans[a]									
			(feet - inches)	(feet - inches)	(feet - inches)	(feet - inches)	(feet - inches)	(feet - inches)	(feet - inches)	(feet - inches)	(feet - inches)	(feet - inches)
12	Douglas fir-larch	SS	9-1	14-4	18-10	24-1	Note b	9-1	14-4	18-10	24-1	Note b
	Douglas fir-larch	#1	8-9	13-9	18-2	22-9	Note b	8-9	13-2	16-8	20-4	23-7
	Douglas fir-larch	#2	8-7	13-6	17-5	21-4	24-8	8-5	12-4	15-7	19-1	22-1
	Douglas fir-larch	#3	7-1	10-5	13-2	16-1	18-8	6-4	9-4	11-9	14-5	16-8
	Hem-fir	SS	8-7	13-6	17-10	22-9	Note b	8-7	13-6	17-10	22-9	Note b
	Hem-fir	#1	8-5	13-3	17-5	22-2	25-9	8-5	12-10	16-3	19-10	23-0
	Hem-fir	#2	8-0	12-7	16-7	21-0	24-4	8-0	12-2	15-4	18-9	21-9
	Hem-fir	#3	7-1	10-5	13-2	16-1	18-8	6-4	9-4	11-9	14-5	16-8
	Southern pine	SS	8-11	14-1	18-6	23-8	Note b	8-11	14-1	18-6	23-8	Note b
	Southern pine	#1	8-9	13-9	18-2	23-2	Note b	8-9	13-9	18-2	22-2	Note b
	Southern pine	#2	8-7	13-6	17-10	22-3	Note b	8-7	12-11	16-8	19-11	23-4
	Southern pine	#3	7-7	11-2	14-3	16-10	20-0	6-9	10-0	12-9	15-1	17-11
	Spruce-pine-fir	SS	8-5	13-3	17-5	22-3	Note b	8-5	13-3	17-5	22-3	Note b
	Spruce-pine-fir	#1	8-3	12-11	17-0	21-4	24-8	8-3	12-4	15-7	19-1	22-1
	Spruce-pine-fir	#2	8-3	12-11	17-0	21-4	24-8	8-3	12-4	15-7	19-1	22-1
	Spruce-pine-fir	#3	7-1	10-5	13-2	16-1	18-8	6-4	9-4	11-9	14-5	16-8
16	Douglas fir-larch	SS	8-3	13-0	17-2	21-10	Note b	8-3	13-0	17-2	21-3	24-8
	Douglas fir-larch	#1	8-0	12-6	16-2	19-9	22-10	7-10	11-5	14-5	17-8	20-5
	Douglas fir-larch	#2	7-10	11-11	15-1	18-5	21-5	7-3	10-8	13-6	16-6	19-2
	Douglas fir-larch	#3	6-2	9-0	11-5	13-11	16-2	5-6	8-1	10-3	12-6	14-6
	Hem-fir	SS	7-10	12-3	16-2	20-8	25-1	7-10	12-3	16-2	20-8	24-2
	Hem-fir	#1	7-8	12-0	15-9	19-3	22-3	7-7	11-1	14-1	17-2	19-11
	Hem-fir	#2	7-3	11-5	14-11	18-2	21-1	7-2	10-6	13-4	16-3	18-10
	Hem-fir	#3	6-2	9-0	11-5	13-11	16-2	5-6	8-1	10-3	12-6	14-6
	Southern pine	SS	8-1	12-9	16-10	21-6	Note b	8-1	12-9	16-10	21-6	Note b
	Southern pine	#1	8-0	12-6	16-6	21-1	25-7	8-0	12-6	16-2	19-2	22-10
	Southern pine	#2	7-10	12-3	16-2	19-3	22-7	7-10	11-2	14-5	17-3	20-2
	Southern pine	#3	6-7	9-8	12-4	14-7	17-4	5-10	8-8	11-0	13-0	15-6
	Spruce-pine-fir	SS	7-8	12-0	15-10	20-2	24-7	7-8	12-0	15-10	19-9	22-10
	Spruce-pine-fir	#1	7-6	11-9	15-1	18-5	21-5	7-3	10-8	13-6	16-6	19-2
	Spruce-pine-fir	#2	7-6	11-9	15-1	18-5	21-5	7-3	10-8	13-6	16-6	19-2
	Spruce-pine-fir	#3	6-2	9-0	11-5	13-11	16-2	5-6	8-1	10-3	12-6	14-6
19.2	Douglas fir-larch	SS	7-9	12-3	16-1	20-7	25-0	7-9	12-3	15-10	19-5	22-6
	Douglas fir-larch	#1	7-6	11-8	14-9	18-0	20-11	7-1	10-5	13-2	16-1	18-8
	Douglas fir-larch	#2	7-4	10-11	13-9	16-10	19-6	6-8	9-9	12-4	15-1	17-6
	Douglas fir-larch	#3	5-7	8-3	10-5	12-9	14-9	5-0	7-4	9-4	11-5	13-2
	Hem-fir	SS	7-4	11-7	15-3	19-5	23-7	7-4	11-7	15-3	19-1	22-1
	Hem-fir	#1	7-2	11-4	14-4	17-7	20-4	6-11	10-2	12-10	15-8	18-2
	Hem-fir	#2	6-10	10-9	13-7	16-7	19-3	6-7	9-7	12-2	14-10	17-3
	Hem-fir	#3	5-7	8-3	10-5	12-9	14-9	5-0	7-4	9-4	11-5	13-2
	Southern pine	SS	7-8	12-0	15-10	20-2	24-7	7-8	12-0	15-10	20-2	24-7
	Southern pine	#1	7-6	11-9	15-6	19-7	23-4	7-6	11-9	14-9	17-6	20-11
	Southern pine	#2	7-4	11-5	14-9	17-7	20-7	7-1	10-2	13-2	15-9	18-5
	Southern pine	#3	6-0	8-10	11-3	13-4	15-10	5-4	7-11	10-1	11-11	14-2
	Spruce-pine-fir	SS	7-2	11-4	14-11	19-0	23-1	7-2	11-4	14-9	18-0	20-11
	Spruce-pine-fir	#1	7-0	10-11	13-9	16-10	19-6	6-8	9-9	12-4	15-1	17-6
	Spruce-pine-fir	#2	7-0	10-11	13-9	16-10	19-6	6-8	9-9	12-4	15-1	17-6
	Spruce-pine-fir	#3	5-7	8-3	10-5	12-9	14-9	5-0	7-4	9-4	11-5	13-2

(continued)

TABLE R802.5.1(5)—continued
RAFTER SPANS FOR COMMON LUMBER SPECIES
(Ground snow load=30 psf, ceiling attached to rafters, L/Δ = 240)

RAFTER SPACING (inches)	SPECIES AND GRADE		DEAD LOAD = 10 psf					DEAD LOAD = 20 psf				
			2 × 4	2 × 6	2 × 8	2 × 10	2 × 12	2 × 4	2 × 6	2 × 8	2 × 10	2 × 12
			Maximum rafter spans[a]									
			(feet-inches)	(feet-inches)	(feet-inches)	(feet-inches)	(feet-inches)	(feet-inches)	(feet-inches)	(feet-inches)	(feet-inches)	(feet-inches)
24	Douglas fir-larch	SS	7-3	11-4	15-0	19-1	22-6	7-3	11-3	14-2	17-4	20-1
	Douglas fir-larch	#1	7-0	10-5	13-2	16-1	18-8	6-4	9-4	11-9	14-5	16-8
	Douglas fir-larch	#2	6-8	9-9	12-4	15-1	17-6	5-11	8-8	11-0	13-6	15-7
	Douglas fir-larch	#3	5-0	7-4	9-4	11-5	13-2	4-6	6-7	8-4	10-2	11-10
	Hem-fir	SS	6-10	10-9	14-2	18-0	21-11	6-10	10-9	13-11	17-0	19-9
	Hem-fir	#1	6-8	10-2	12-10	15-8	18-2	6-2	9-1	11-6	14-0	16-3
	Hem-fir	#2	6-4	9-7	12-2	14-10	17-3	5-10	8-7	10-10	13-3	15-5
	Hem-fir	#3	5-0	7-4	9-4	11-5	13-2	4-6	6-7	8-4	10-2	11-10
	Southern pine	SS	7-1	11-2	14-8	18-9	22-10	7-1	11-2	14-8	18-9	22-10
	Southern pine	#1	7-0	10-11	14-5	17-6	20-11	7-0	10-6	13-2	15-8	18-8
	Southern pine	#2	6-10	10-2	13-2	15-9	18-5	6-4	9-2	11-9	14-1	16-6
	Southern pine	#3	5-4	7-11	10-1	11-11	14-2	4-9	7-1	9-0	10-8	12-8
	Spruce-pine-fir	SS	6-8	10-6	13-10	17-8	20-11	6-8	10-5	13-2	16-1	18-8
	Spruce-pine-fir	#1	6-6	9-9	12-4	15-1	17-6	5-11	8-8	11-0	13-6	15-7
	Spruce-pine-fir	#2	6-6	9-9	12-4	15-1	17-6	5-11	8-8	11-0	13-6	15-7
	Spruce-pine-fir	#3	5-0	7-4	9-4	11-5	13-2	4-6	6-7	8-4	10-2	11-10

Check sources for availability of lumber in lengths greater than 20 feet.

For SI: 1 inch = 25.4 mm, 1 foot = 304.8 mm, 1 pound per square foot = 0.0479kPa.

a. The tabulated rafter spans assume that ceiling joists are located at the bottom of the attic space or that some other method of resisting the outward push of the rafters on the bearing walls, such as rafter ties, is provided at that location. When ceiling joists or rafter ties are located higher in the attic space, the rafter spans shall be multiplied by the factors given below:

H_C/H_R	Rafter Span Adjustment Factor
1/3	0.67
1/4	0.76
1/5	0.83
1/6	0.90
1/7.5 or less	1.00

where:

H_C = Height of ceiling joists or rafter ties measured vertically above the top of the rafter support walls.

H_R = Height of roof ridge measured vertically above the top of the rafter support walls.

b. Span exceeds 26 feet in length.

TABLE R802.5.1(6)
RAFTER SPANS FOR COMMON LUMBER SPECIES
(Ground snow load=50 psf, ceiling attached to rafters, L/Δ = 240)

RAFTER SPACING (inches)	SPECIES AND GRADE		DEAD LOAD = 10 psf					DEAD LOAD = 20 psf				
			2 × 4	2 × 6	2 × 8	2 × 10	2 × 12	2 × 4	2 × 6	2 × 8	2 × 10	2 × 12
			Maximum rafter spans[a]									
			(feet-inches)	(feet-inches)	(feet-inches)	(feet-inches)	(feet-inches)	(feet-inches)	(feet-inches)	(feet-inches)	(feet-inches)	(feet-inches)
12	Douglas fir-larch	SS	7-8	12-1	15-11	20-3	24-8	7-8	12-1	15-11	20-3	24-0
	Douglas fir-larch	#1	7-5	11-7	15-3	18-7	21-7	7-5	11-2	14-1	17-3	20-0
	Douglas fir-larch	#2	7-3	11-3	14-3	17-5	20-2	7-1	10-5	13-2	16-1	18-8
	Douglas fir-larch	#3	5-10	8-6	10-9	13-2	15-3	5-5	7-10	10-0	12-2	14-1
	Hem-fir	SS	7-3	11-5	15-0	19-2	23-4	7-3	11-5	15-0	19-2	23-4
	Hem-fir	#1	7-1	11-2	14-8	18-1	21-0	7-1	10-10	13-9	16-9	19-5
	Hem-fir	#2	6-9	10-8	14-0	17-2	19-11	6-9	10-3	13-0	15-10	18-5
	Hem-fir	#3	5-10	8-6	10-9	13-2	15-3	5-5	7-10	10-0	12-2	14-1
	Southern pine	SS	7-6	11-10	15-7	19-11	24-3	7-6	11-10	15-7	19-11	24-3
	Southern pine	#1	7-5	11-7	15-4	19-7	23-9	7-5	11-7	15-4	18-9	22-4
	Southern pine	#2	7-3	11-5	15-0	18-2	21-3	7-3	10-11	14-1	16-10	19-9
	Southern pine	#3	6-2	9-2	11-8	13-9	16-4	5-9	8-5	10-9	12-9	15-2
	Spruce-pine-fir	SS	7-1	11-2	14-8	18-9	22-10	7-1	11-2	14-8	18-9	22-4
	Spruce-pine-fir	#1	6-11	10-11	14-3	17-5	20-2	6-11	10-5	13-2	16-1	18-8
	Spruce-pine-fir	#2	6-11	10-11	14-3	17-5	20-2	6-11	10-5	13-2	16-1	18-8
	Spruce-pine-fir	#3	5-10	8-6	10-9	13-2	15-3	5-5	7-10	10-0	12-2	14-1
16	Douglas fir-larch	SS	7-0	11-0	14-5	18-5	22-5	7-0	11-0	14-5	17-11	20-10
	Douglas fir-larch	#1	6-9	10-5	13-2	16-1	18-8	6-7	9-8	12-2	14-11	17-3
	Douglas fir-larch	#2	6-7	9-9	12-4	15-1	17-6	6-2	9-0	11-5	13-11	16-2
	Douglas fir-larch	#3	5-0	7-4	9-4	11-5	13-2	4-8	6-10	8-8	10-6	12-3
	Hem-fir	SS	6-7	10-4	13-8	17-5	21-2	6-7	10-4	13-8	17-5	20-5
	Hem-fir	#1	6-5	10-2	12-10	15-8	18-2	6-5	9-5	11-11	14-6	16-10
	Hem-fir	#2	6-2	9-7	12-2	14-10	17-3	6-1	8-11	11-3	13-9	15-11
	Hem-fir	#3	5-0	7-4	9-4	11-5	13-2	4-8	6-10	8-8	10-6	12-3
	Southern pine	SS	6-10	10-9	14-2	18-1	22-0	6-10	10-9	14-2	18-1	22-0
	Southern pine	#1	6-9	10-7	13-11	17-6	20-11	6-9	10-7	13-8	16-2	19-4
	Southern pine	#2	6-7	10-2	13-2	15-9	18-5	6-7	9-5	12-2	14-7	17-1
	Southern pine	#3	5-4	7-11	10-1	11-11	14-2	4-11	7-4	9-4	11-0	13-1
	Spruce-pine-fir	SS	6-5	10-2	13-4	17-0	20-9	6-5	10-2	13-4	16-8	19-4
	Spruce-pine-fir	#1	6-4	9-9	12-4	15-1	17-6	6-2	9-0	11-5	13-11	16-2
	Spruce-pine-fir	#2	6-4	9-9	12-4	15-1	17-6	6-2	9-0	11-5	13-11	16-2
	Spruce-pine-fir	#3	5-0	7-4	9-4	11-5	13-2	4-8	6-10	8-8	10-6	12-3
19.2	Douglas fir-larch	SS	6-7	10-4	13-7	17-4	20-6	6-7	10-4	13-5	16-5	19-0
	Douglas fir-larch	#1	6-4	9-6	12-0	14-8	17-1	6-0	8-10	11-2	13-7	15-9
	Douglas fir-larch	#2	6-1	8-11	11-3	13-9	15-11	5-7	8-3	10-5	12-9	14-9
	Douglas fir-larch	#3	4-7	6-9	8-6	10-5	12-1	4-3	6-3	7-11	9-7	11-2
	Hem-fir	SS	6-2	9-9	12-10	16-5	19-11	6-2	9-9	12-10	16-1	18-8
	Hem-fir	#1	6-1	9-3	11-9	14-4	16-7	5-10	8-7	10-10	13-3	15-5
	Hem-fir	#2	5-9	8-9	11-1	13-7	15-9	5-7	8-1	10-3	12-7	14-7
	Hem-fir	#3	4-7	6-9	8-6	10-5	12-1	4-3	6-3	7-11	9-7	11-2
	Southern pine	SS	6-5	10-2	13-4	17-0	20-9	6-5	10-2	13-4	17-0	20-9
	Southern pine	#1	6-4	9-11	13-1	16-0	19-1	6-4	9-11	12-5	14-10	17-8
	Southern pine	#2	6-2	9-4	12-0	14-4	16-10	6-0	8-8	11-2	13-4	15-7
	Southern pine	#3	4-11	7-3	9-2	10-10	12-11	4-6	6-8	8-6	10-1	12-0
	Spruce-pine-fir	SS	6-1	9-6	12-7	16-0	19-1	6-1	9-6	12-5	15-3	17-8
	Spruce-pine-fir	#1	5-11	8-11	11-3	13-9	15-11	5-7	8-3	10-5	12-9	14-9
	Spruce-pine-fir	#2	5-11	8-11	11-3	13-9	15-11	5-7	8-3	10-5	12-9	14-9
	Spruce-pine-fir	#3	4-7	6-9	8-6	10-5	12-1	4-3	6-3	7-11	9-7	11-2

(continued)

TABLE R802.5.1(6)—continued
RAFTER SPANS FOR COMMON LUMBER SPECIES
(Ground snow load=50 psf, ceiling attached to rafters, L/Δ = 240)

RAFTER SPACING (inches)	SPECIES AND GRADE		DEAD LOAD = 10 psf					DEAD LOAD = 20 psf				
			2 × 4	2 × 6	2 × 8	2 × 10	2 × 12	2 × 4	2 × 6	2 × 8	2 × 10	2 × 12
			Maximum rafter spans[a]									
			(feet-inches)	(feet-inches)	(feet-inches)	(feet-inches)	(feet-inches)	(feet-inches)	(feet-inches)	(feet-inches)	(feet-inches)	(feet-inches)
24	Douglas fir-larch	SS	6-1	9-7	12-7	15-10	18-4	6-1	9-6	12-0	14-8	17-0
	Douglas fir-larch	#1	5-10	8-6	10-9	13-2	15-3	5-5	7-10	10-0	12-2	14-1
	Douglas fir-larch	#2	5-5	7-11	10-1	12-4	14-3	5-0	7-4	9-4	11-5	13-2
	Douglas fir-larch	#3	4-1	6-0	7-7	9-4	10-9	3-10	5-7	7-1	8-7	10-0
	Hem-fir	SS	5-9	9-1	11-11	15-2	18-0	5-9	9-1	11-9	14-5	15-11
	Hem-fir	#1	5-8	8-3	10-6	12-10	14-10	5-3	7-8	9-9	11-10	13-9
	Hem-fir	#2	5-4	7-10	9-11	12-1	14-1	4-11	7-3	9-2	11-3	13-0
	Hem-fir	#3	4-1	6-0	7-7	9-4	10-9	3-10	5-7	7-1	8-7	10-0
	Southern pine	SS	6-0	9-5	12-5	15-10	19-3	6-0	9-5	12-5	15-10	19-3
	Southern pine	#1	5-10	9-3	12-0	14-4	17-1	5-10	8-10	11-2	13-3	15-9
	Southern pine	#2	5-9	8-4	10-9	12-10	15-1	5-5	7-9	10-0	11-11	13-11
	Southern pine	#3	4-4	6-5	8-3	9-9	11-7	4-1	6-0	7-7	9-0	10-8
	Spruce-pine-fir	SS	5-8	8-10	11-8	14-8	17-1	5-8	8-10	11-2	13-7	15-9
	Spruce-pine-fir	#1	5-5	7-11	10-1	12-4	14-3	5-0	7-4	9-4	11-5	13-2
	Spruce-pine-fir	#2	5-5	7-11	10-1	12-4	14-3	5-0	7-4	9-4	11-5	13-2
	Spruce-pine-fir	#3	4-1	6-0	7-7	9-4	10-9	3-10	5-7	7-1	8-7	10-0

Check sources for availability of lumber in lengths greater than 20 feet.

For SI: 1 inch = 25.4 mm, 1 foot = 304.8 mm, 1 pound per square foot = 0.0479 kPa.

a. The tabulated rafter spans assume that ceiling joists are located at the bottom of the attic space or that some other method of resisting the outward push of the rafters on the bearing walls, such as rafter ties, is provided at that location. When ceiling joists or rafter ties are located higher in the attic space, the rafter spans shall be multiplied by the factors given below:

H_C/H_R	Rafter Span Adjustment Factor
1/3	0.67
1/4	0.76
1/5	0.83
1/6	0.90
1/7.5 or less	1.00

where:

H_C = Height of ceiling joists or rafter ties measured vertically above the top of the rafter support walls.

H_R = Height of roof ridge measured vertically above the top of the rafter support walls.

TABLE R802.5.1(7)
RAFTER SPANS FOR 70 PSF GROUND SNOW LOAD
(Ceiling not attached to rafters, L/Δ = 180)

RAFTER SPACING (inches)	SPECIES AND GRADE		DEAD LOAD = 10 psf					DEAD LOAD = 20 psf				
			2 × 4	2 × 6	2 × 8	2 × 10	2 × 12	2 × 4	2 × 6	2 × 8	2 × 10	2 × 12
			Maximum Rafter Spans[a]									
			(feet-inches)	(feet-inches)	(feet-inches)	(feet-inches)	(feet-inches)	(feet-inches)	(feet-inches)	(feet-inches)	(feet-inches)	(feet-inches)
12	Douglas fir-larch	SS	7-7	11-10	15-8	19-5	22-6	7-7	11-10	15-0	18-3	21-2
	Douglas fir-larch	#1	7-1	10-5	13-2	16-1	18-8	6-8	9-10	12-5	15-2	17-7
	Douglas fir-larch	#2	6-8	9-9	12-4	15-1	17-6	6-3	9-2	11-8	14-2	16-6
	Douglas fir-larch	#3	5-0	7-4	9-4	11-5	13-2	4-9	6-11	8-9	10-9	12-5
	Hem-fir	SS	7-2	11-3	14-9	18-10	22-1	7-2	11-3	14-8	18-0	20-10
	Hem-fir	#1	6-11	10-2	12-10	15-8	18-2	6-6	9-7	12-1	14-10	17-2
	Hem-fir	#2	6-7	9-7	12-2	14-10	17-3	6-2	9-1	11-5	14-0	16-3
	Hem-fir	#3	5-0	7-4	9-4	11-5	13-2	4-9	6-11	8-9	10-9	12-5
	Southern pine	SS	7-5	11-8	15-4	19-7	23-10	7-5	11-8	15-4	19-7	23-10
	Southern pine	#1	7-3	11-5	14-9	17-6	20-11	7-3	11-1	13-11	16-6	19-8
	Southern pine	#2	7-1	10-2	13-2	15-9	18-5	6-8	9-7	12-5	14-10	17-5
	Southern pine	#3	5-4	7-11	10-1	11-11	14-2	5-1	7-5	9-6	11-3	13-4
	Spruce-pine-fir	SS	7-0	11-0	14-6	18-0	20-11	7-0	11-0	13-11	17-0	19-8
	Spruce-pine-fir	#1	6-8	9-9	12-4	15-1	17-6	6-3	9-2	11-8	14-2	16-6
	Spruce-pine-fir	#2	6-8	9-9	12-4	15-1	17-6	6-3	9-2	11-8	14-2	16-6
	Spruce-pine-fir	#3	5-0	7-4	9-4	11-5	13-2	4-9	6-11	8-9	10-9	12-5
16	Douglas fir-larch	SS	6-10	10-9	13-9	16-10	19-6	6-10	10-3	13-0	15-10	18-4
	Douglas fir-larch	#1	6-2	9-0	11-5	13-11	16-2	5-10	8-6	10-9	13-2	15-3
	Douglas fir-larch	#2	5-9	8-5	10-8	13-1	15-2	5-5	7-11	10-1	12-4	14-3
	Douglas fir-larch	#3	4-4	6-4	8-1	9-10	11-5	4-1	6-0	7-7	9-4	10-9
	Hem-fir	SS	6-6	10-2	13-5	16-6	19-2	6-6	10-1	12-9	15-7	18-0
	Hem-fir	#1	6-0	8-9	11-2	13-7	15-9	5-8	8-3	10-6	12-10	14-10
	Hem-fir	#2	5-8	8-4	10-6	12-10	14-11	5-4	7-10	9-11	12-1	14-1
	Hem-fir	#3	4-4	6-4	8-1	9-10	11-5	4-1	6-0	7-7	9-4	10-9
	Southern pine	SS	6-9	10-7	14-0	17-10	21-8	6-9	10-7	14-0	17-10	21-0
	Southern pine	#1	6-7	10-2	12-9	15-2	18-1	6-5	9-7	12-0	14-4	17-1
	Southern pine	#2	6-2	8-10	11-5	13-7	16-0	5-10	8-4	10-9	12-10	15-1
	Southern pine	#3	4-8	6-10	8-9	10-4	12-3	4-4	6-5	8-3	9-9	11-7
	Spruce-pine-fir	SS	6-4	10-0	12-9	15-7	18-1	6-4	9-6	12-0	14-8	17-1
	Spruce-pine-fir	#1	5-9	8-5	10-8	13-1	15-2	5-5	7-11	10-1	12-4	14-3
	Spruce-pine-fir	#2	5-9	8-5	10-8	13-1	15-2	5-5	7-11	10-1	12-4	14-3
	Spruce-pine-fir	#3	4-4	6-4	8-1	9-10	11-5	4-1	6-0	7-7	9-4	10-9
19.2	Douglas fir-larch	SS	6-5	9-11	12-7	15-4	17-9	6-5	9-4	11-10	14-5	16-9
	Douglas fir-larch	#1	5-7	8-3	10-5	12-9	14-9	5-4	7-9	9-10	12-0	13-11
	Douglas fir-larch	#2	5-3	7-8	9-9	11-11	13-10	5-0	7-3	9-2	11-3	13-0
	Douglas fir-larch	#3	4-0	5-10	7-4	9-0	10-5	3-9	5-6	6-11	8-6	9-10
	Hem-fir	SS	6-1	9-7	12-4	15-1	17-4	6-1	9-2	11-8	14-2	15-5
	Hem-fir	#1	5-6	8-0	10-2	12-5	14-5	5-2	7-7	9-7	11-8	13-7
	Hem-fir	#2	5-2	7-7	9-7	11-9	13-7	4-11	7-2	9-1	11-1	12-10
	Hem-fir	#3	4-0	5-10	7-4	9-0	10-5	3-9	5-6	6-11	8-6	9-10
	Southern pine	SS	6-4	10-0	13-2	16-9	20-4	6-4	10-0	13-2	16-5	19-2
	Southern pine	#1	6-3	9-3	11-8	13-10	16-6	5-11	8-9	11-0	13-1	15-7
	Southern pine	#2	5-7	8-1	10-5	12-5	14-7	5-4	7-7	9-10	11-9	13-9
	Southern pine	#3	4-3	6-3	8-0	9-5	11-2	4-0	5-11	7-6	8-10	10-7
	Spruce-pine-fir	SS	6-0	9-2	11-8	14-3	16-6	5-11	8-8	11-0	13-5	15-7
	Spruce-pine-fir	#1	5-3	7-8	9-9	11-11	13-10	5-0	7-3	9-2	11-3	13-0
	Spruce-pine-fir	#2	5-3	7-8	9-9	11-11	13-10	5-0	7-3	9-2	11-3	13-0
	Spruce-pine-fir	#3	4-0	5-10	7-4	9-0	10-5	3-9	5-6	6-11	8-6	9-10

(continued)

TABLE R802.5.1(7)—continued
RAFTER SPANS FOR 70 PSF GROUND SNOW LOAD
(Ceiling not attached to rafters, L/Δ = 180)

RAFTER SPACING (inches)	SPECIES AND GRADE		DEAD LOAD = 10 psf					DEAD LOAD = 20 psf				
			2 × 4	2 × 6	2 × 8	2 × 10	2 × 12	2 × 4	2 × 6	2 × 8	2 × 10	2 × 12
			Maximum rafter spans[a]									
			(feet-inches)	(feet-inches)	(feet-inches)	(feet-inches)	(feet-inches)	(feet-inches)	(feet-inches)	(feet-inches)	(feet-inches)	(feet-inches)
24	Douglas fir-larch	SS	6-0	8-10	11-3	13-9	15-11	5-9	8-4	10-7	12-11	15-0
	Douglas fir-larch	#1	5-0	7-4	9-4	11-5	13-2	4-9	6-11	8-9	10-9	12-5
	Douglas fir-larch	#2	4-8	6-11	8-9	10-8	12-4	4-5	6-6	8-3	10-0	11-8
	Douglas fir-larch	#3	3-7	5-2	6-7	8-1	9-4	3-4	4-11	6-3	7-7	8-10
	Hem-fir	SS	5-8	8-8	11-0	13-6	13-11	5-7	8-3	10-5	12-4	12-4
	Hem-fir	#1	4-11	7-2	9-1	11-1	12-10	4-7	6-9	8-7	10-6	12-2
	Hem-fir	#2	4-8	6-9	8-7	10-6	12-2	4-4	6-5	8-1	9-11	11-6
	Hem-fir	#3	3-7	5-2	6-7	8-1	9-4	3-4	4-11	6-3	7-7	8-10
	Southern pine	SS	5-11	9-3	12-2	15-7	18-2	5-11	9-3	12-2	14-8	17-2
	Southern pine	#1	5-7	8-3	10-5	12-5	14-9	5-3	7-10	9-10	11-8	13-11
	Southern pine	#2	5-0	7-3	9-4	11-1	13-0	4-9	6-10	8-9	10-6	12-4
	Southern pine	#3	3-9	5-7	7-1	8-5	10-0	3-7	5-3	6-9	7-11	9-5
	Spruce-pine-fir	SS	5-6	8-3	10-5	12-9	14-9	5-4	7-9	9-10	12-0	12-11
	Spruce-pine-fir	#1	4-8	6-11	8-9	10-8	12-4	4-5	6-6	8-3	10-0	11-8
	Spruce-pine-fir	#2	4-8	6-11	8-9	10-8	12-4	4-5	6-6	8-3	10-0	11-8
	Spruce-pine-fir	#3	3-7	5-2	6-7	8-1	9-4	3-4	4-11	6-3	7-7	8-10

Check sources for availability of lumber in lengths greater than 20 feet.

For SI: 1 inch = 25.4 mm, 1 foot = 304.8 mm, 1 pound per square foot = 0.0479kPa.

a. The tabulated rafter spans assume that ceiling joists are located at the bottom of the attic space or that some other method of resisting the outward push of the rafters on the bearing walls, such as rafter ties, is provided at that location. When ceiling joists or rafter ties are located higher in the attic space, the rafter spans shall be multiplied by the factors given below:

H_C/H_R	Rafter Span Adjustment Factor
1/3	0.67
1/4	0.76
1/5	0.83
1/6	0.90
1/7.5 or less	1.00

where:

H_C = Height of ceiling joists or rafter ties measured vertically above the top of the rafter support walls.

H_R = Height of roof ridge measured vertically above the top of the rafter support walls.

TABLE R802.5.1(8)
RAFTER SPANS FOR 70 PSF GROUND SNOW LOAD
(Ceiling attached to rafters, L/Δ = 240)

RAFTER SPACING (inches)	SPECIES AND GRADE		DEAD LOAD = 10 psf					DEAD LOAD = 20 psf				
			2 × 4	2 × 6	2 × 8	2 × 10	2 × 12	2 × 4	2 × 6	2 × 8	2 × 10	2 × 12
			Maximum rafter spans[a]									
			(feet - inches)	(feet - inches)	(feet - inches)	(feet - inches)	(feet - inches)	(feet - inches)	(feet - inches)	(feet - inches)	(feet - inches)	(feet - inches)
12	Douglas fir-larch	SS	6-10	10-9	14-3	18-2	22-1	6-10	10-9	14-3	18-2	21-2
	Douglas fir-larch	#1	6-7	10-5	13-2	16-1	18-8	6-7	9-10	12-5	15-2	17-7
	Douglas fir-larch	#2	6-6	9-9	12-4	15-1	17-6	6-3	9-2	11-8	14-2	16-6
	Douglas fir-larch	#3	5-0	7-4	9-4	11-5	13-2	4-9	6-11	8-9	10-9	12-5
	Hem-fir	SS	6-6	10-2	13-5	17-2	20-10	6-6	10-2	13-5	17-2	20-10
	Hem-fir	#1	6-4	10-0	12-10	15-8	18-2	6-4	9-7	12-1	14-10	17-2
	Hem-fir	#2	6-1	9-6	12-2	14-10	17-3	6-1	9-1	11-5	14-0	16-3
	Hem-fir	#3	5-0	7-4	9-4	11-5	13-2	4-9	6-11	8-9	10-9	12-5
	Southern pine	SS	6-9	10-7	14-0	17-10	21-8	6-9	10-7	14-0	17-10	21-8
	Southern pine	#1	6-7	10-5	13-8	17-6	20-11	6-7	10-5	13-8	16-6	19-8
	Southern pine	#2	6-6	10-2	13-2	15-9	18-5	6-6	9-7	12-5	14-10	17-5
	Southern pine	#3	5-4	7-11	10-1	11-11	14-2	5-1	7-5	9-6	11-3	13-4
	Spruce-pine-fir	SS	6-4	10-0	13-2	16-9	20-5	6-4	10-0	13-2	16-9	19-8
	Spruce-pine-fir	#1	6-2	9-9	12-4	15-1	17-6	6-2	9-2	11-8	14-2	16-6
	Spruce-pine-fir	#2	6-2	9-9	12-4	15-1	17-6	6-2	9-2	11-8	14-2	16-6
	Spruce-pine-fir	#3	5-0	7-4	9-4	11-5	13-2	4-9	6-11	8-9	10-9	12-5
16	Douglas fir-larch	SS	6-3	9-10	12-11	16-6	19-6	6-3	9-10	12-11	15-10	18-4
	Douglas fir-larch	#1	6-0	9-0	11-5	13-11	16-2	5-10	8-6	10-9	13-2	15-3
	Douglas fir-larch	#2	5-9	8-5	10-8	13-1	15-2	5-5	7-11	10-1	12-4	14-3
	Douglas fir-larch	#3	4-4	6-4	8-1	9-10	11-5	4-1	6-0	7-7	9-4	10-9
	Hem-fir	SS	5-11	9-3	12-2	15-7	18-11	5-11	9-3	12-2	15-7	18-0
	Hem-fir	#1	5-9	8-9	11-2	13-7	15-9	5-8	8-3	10-6	12-10	14-10
	Hem-fir	#2	5-6	8-4	10-6	12-10	14-11	5-4	7-10	9-11	12-1	14-1
	Hem-fir	#3	4-4	6-4	8-1	9-10	11-5	4-1	6-0	7-7	9-4	10-9
	Southern pine	SS	6-1	9-7	12-8	16-2	19-8	6-1	9-7	12-8	16-2	19-8
	Southern pine	#1	6-0	9-5	12-5	15-2	18-1	6-0	9-5	12-0	14-4	17-1
	Southern pine	#2	5-11	8-10	11-5	13-7	16-0	5-10	8-4	10-9	12-10	15-1
	Southern pine	#3	4-8	6-10	8-9	10-4	12-3	4-4	6-5	8-3	9-9	11-7
	Spruce-pine-fir	SS	5-9	9-1	11-11	15-3	18-1	5-9	9-1	11-11	14-8	17-1
	Spruce-pine-fir	#1	5-8	8-5	10-8	13-1	15-2	5-5	7-11	10-1	12-4	14-3
	Spruce-pine-fir	#2	5-8	8-5	10-8	13-1	15-2	5-5	7-11	10-1	12-4	14-3
	Spruce-pine-fir	#3	4-4	6-4	8-1	9-10	11-5	4-1	6-0	7-7	9-4	10-9
19.2	Douglas fir-larch	SS	5-10	9-3	12-2	15-4	17-9	5-10	9-3	11-10	14-5	16-9
	Douglas fir-larch	#1	5-7	8-3	10-5	12-9	14-9	5-4	7-9	9-10	12-0	13-11
	Douglas fir-larch	#2	5-3	7-8	9-9	11-11	13-10	5-0	7-3	9-2	11-3	13-0
	Douglas fir-larch	#3	4-0	5-10	7-4	9-0	10-5	3-9	5-6	6-11	8-6	9-10
	Hem-fir	SS	5-6	8-8	11-6	14-8	17-4	5-6	8-8	11-6	14-2	15-5
	Hem-fir	#1	5-5	8-0	10-2	12-5	14-5	5-2	7-7	9-7	11-8	13-7
	Hem-fir	#2	5-2	7-7	9-7	11-9	13-7	4-11	7-2	9-1	11-1	12-10
	Hem-fir	#3	4-0	5-10	7-4	9-0	10-5	3-9	5-6	6-11	8-6	9-10
	Southern pine	SS	5-9	9-1	11-11	15-3	18-6	5-9	9-1	11-11	15-3	18-6
	Southern pine	#1	5-8	8-11	11-8	13-10	16-6	5-8	8-9	11-0	13-1	15-7
	Southern pine	#2	5-6	8-1	10-5	12-5	14-7	5-4	7-7	9-10	11-9	13-9
	Southern pine	#3	4-3	6-3	8-0	9-5	11-2	4-0	5-11	7-6	8-10	10-7
	Spruce-pine-fir	SS	5-5	8-6	11-3	14-3	16-6	5-5	8-6	11-0	13-5	15-7
	Spruce-pine-fir	#1	5-3	7-8	9-9	11-11	13-10	5-0	7-3	9-2	11-3	13-0
	Spruce-pine-fir	#2	5-3	7-8	9-9	11-11	13-10	5-0	7-3	9-2	11-3	13-0
	Spruce-pine-fir	#3	4-0	5-10	7-4	9-0	10-5	3-9	5-6	6-11	8-6	9-10

(continued)

TABLE R802.5.1(8)—continued
RAFTER SPANS FOR 70 PSF GROUND SNOW LOAD[a]
(Ceiling attached to rafters, L/Δ = 240)

RAFTER SPACING (inches)	SPECIES AND GRADE		DEAD LOAD = 10 psf					DEAD LOAD = 20 psf				
			2 × 4	2 × 6	2 × 8	2 × 10	2 × 12	2 × 4	2 × 6	2 × 8	2 × 10	2 × 12
			Maximum rafter spans[a]									
			(feet - inches)	(feet - inches)	(feet - inches)	(feet - inches)	(feet - inches)	(feet - inches)	(feet - inches)	(feet - inches)	(feet - inches)	(feet - inches)
24	Douglas fir-larch	SS	5-5	8-7	11-3	13-9	15-11	5-5	8-4	10-7	12-11	15-0
	Douglas fir-larch	#1	5-0	7-4	9-4	11-5	13-2	4-9	6-11	8-9	10-9	12-5
	Douglas fir-larch	#2	4-8	6-11	8-9	10-8	12-4	4-5	6-6	8-3	10-0	11-8
	Douglas fir-larch	#3	3-7	5-2	6-7	8-1	9-4	3-4	4-11	6-3	7-7	8-10
	Hem-fir	SS	5-2	8-1	10-8	13-6	13-11	5-2	8-1	10-5	12-4	12-4
	Hem-fir	#1	4-11	7-2	9-1	11-1	12-10	4-7	6-9	8-7	10-6	12-2
	Hem-fir	#2	4-8	6-9	8-7	10-6	12-2	4-4	6-5	8-1	9-11	11-6
	Hem-fir	#3	3-7	5-2	6-7	8-1	9-4	3-4	4-11	6-3	7-7	8-10
	Southern pine	SS	5-4	8-5	11-1	14-2	17-2	5-4	8-5	11-1	14-2	17-2
	Southern pine	#1	5-3	8-3	10-5	12-5	14-9	5-3	7-10	9-10	11-8	13-11
	Southern pine	#2	5-0	7-3	9-4	11-1	13-0	4-9	6-10	8-9	10-6	12-4
	Southern pine	#3	3-9	5-7	7-1	8-5	10-0	3-7	5-3	6-9	7-11	9-5
	Spruce-pine-fir	SS	5-0	7-11	10-5	12-9	14-9	5-0	7-9	9-10	12-0	12-11
	Spruce-pine-fir	#1	4-8	6-11	8-9	10-8	12-4	4-5	6-6	8-3	10-0	11-8
	Spruce-pine-fir	#2	4-8	6-11	8-9	10-8	12-4	4-5	6-6	8-3	10-0	11-8
	Spruce-pine-fir	#3	3-7	5-2	6-7	8-1	9-4	3-4	4-11	6-3	7-7	8-10

Check sources for availability of lumber in lengths greater than 20 feet.

For SI: 1 inch = 25.4 mm, 1 foot = 304.8 mm, 1 pound per square foot = 0.0479kPa.

a. The tabulated rafter spans assume that ceiling joists are located at the bottom of the attic space or that some other method of resisting the outward push of the rafters on the bearing walls, such as rafter ties, is provided at that location. When ceiling joists or rafter ties are located higher in the attic space, the rafter spans shall be multiplied by the factors given below:

H_C/H_R	Rafter Span Adjustment Factor
1/3	0.67
1/4	0.76
1/5	0.83
1/6	0.90
1/7.5 or less	1.00

where:

H_C = Height of ceiling joists or rafter ties measured vertically above the top of the rafter support walls.

H_R = Height of roof ridge measured vertically above the top of the rafter support walls.

TABLE R802.5.1(9)
RAFTER/CEILING JOIST HEEL JOINT CONNECTIONS[a, b, c, d, e, f, g]

RAFTER SLOPE	RAFTER SPACING (inches)	GROUND SNOW LOAD (psf)											
		30				50				70			
		Roof span (feet)											
		12	20	28	36	12	20	28	36	12	20	28	36
		Required number of 16d common nails[a,b] per heel joint splices[c,d,e,f]											
3:12	12	4	6	8	11	5	8	12	15	6	11	15	20
	16	5	8	11	14	6	11	15	20	8	14	20	26
	24	7	11	16	21	9	16	23	30	12	21	30	39
4:12	12	3	5	6	8	4	6	9	11	5	8	12	15
	16	4	6	8	11	5	8	12	15	6	11	15	20
	24	5	9	12	16	7	12	17	22	9	16	23	29
5:12	12	3	4	5	7	3	5	7	9	4	7	9	12
	16	3	5	7	9	4	7	9	12	5	9	12	16
	24	4	7	10	13	6	10	14	18	7	13	18	23
7:12	12	3	3	4	5	3	4	5	7	3	5	7	9
	16	3	4	5	6	3	5	7	9	4	6	9	11
	24	3	5	7	9	4	7	10	13	5	9	13	17
9:12	12	3	3	3	4	3	3	4	5	3	4	5	7
	16	3	3	4	5	3	4	5	7	3	5	7	9
	24	3	4	6	7	3	6	8	10	4	7	10	13
12:12	12	3	3	3	3	3	3	3	4	3	3	4	5
	16	3	3	3	4	3	3	4	5	3	4	5	7
	24	3	3	4	6	3	4	6	8	3	6	8	10

For SI: 1 inch = 25.4 mm, 1 foot = 304.8 mm, 1 pound per square foot = 0.0479 kPa.

a. 40d box nails shall be permitted to be substituted for 16d common nails.

b. Nailing requirements shall be permitted to be reduced 25 percent if nails are clinched.

c. Heel joint connections are not required when the ridge is supported by a load-bearing wall, header or ridge beam.

d. When intermediate support of the rafter is provided by vertical struts or purlins to a loadbearing wall, the tabulated heel joint connection requirements shall be permitted to be reduced proportionally to the reduction in span.

e. Equivalent nailing patterns are required for ceiling joist to ceiling joist lap splices.

f. When rafter ties are substituted for ceiling joists, the heel joint connection requirement shall be taken as the tabulated heel joint connection requirement for two-thirds of the actual rafter-slope.

g. Tabulated heel joint connection requirements assume that ceiling joists or rafter ties are located at the bottom of the attic space. When ceiling joists or rafter ties are located higher in the attic, heel joint connection requirements shall be increased by the following factors:

H_C/H_R	Heel Joint Connection Adjustment Factor
1/3	1.5
1/4	1.33
1/5	1.25
1/6	1.2
1/10 or less	1.11

where:

H_C = Height of ceiling joists or rafter ties measured vertically above the top of the rafter support walls.

H_R = Height of roof ridge measured vertically above the top of the rafter support walls.

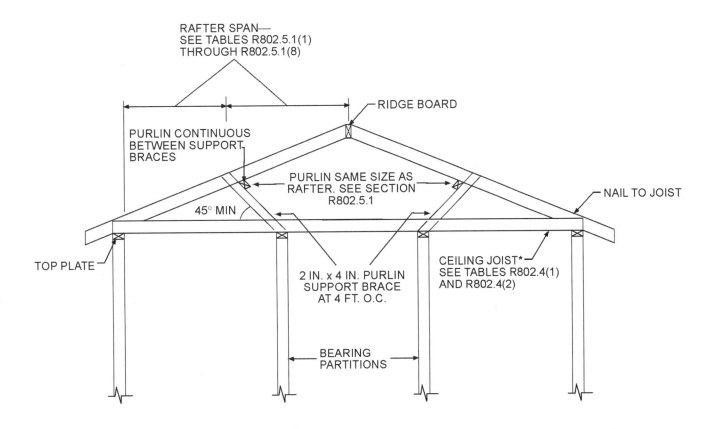

For SI: 1 inch = 25.4 mm, 1 foot = 304.8 mm, 1 degree = 0.018 rad.
NOTE: Where ceiling joints run perpendicular to the rafters, rafter ties shall be nailed to each rafter near the top of the ceiling joist.

FIGURE R802.5.1
BRACED RAFTER CONSTRUCTION

R802.10.2.1 Applicability limits. The provisions of this section shall control the design of truss roof framing when snow controls for buildings not greater than 60 feet (18 288 mm) in length perpendicular to the joist, rafter or truss span, not greater than 36 feet (10 973 mm) in width parallel to the joist span or truss, not greater than two stories in height with each story not greater than 10 feet (3048 mm) high, and roof slopes not smaller than 3:12 (25-percent slope) or greater than 12:12 (100-percent slope). Truss roof framing constructed in accordance with the provisions of this section shall be limited to sites subjected to a maximum design wind speed of 110 miles per hour (49 m/s), Exposure A, B or C, and a maximum ground snow load of 70 psf (3352 Pa). Roof snow load is to be computed as: $0.7\,p_g$.

R802.10.3 Bracing. Trusses shall be braced to prevent rotation and provide lateral stability in accordance with the requirements specified in the construction documents for the building and on the individual truss design drawings. In the absence of specific bracing requirements, trusses shall be braced in accordance with the Building Component Safety Information (BCSI 1-03) Guide to Good Practice for Handling, Installing & Bracing of Metal Plate Connected Wood Trusses.

R802.10.4 Alterations to trusses. Truss members shall not be cut, notched, drilled, spliced or otherwise altered in any way without the approval of a registered design professional. Alterations resulting in the addition of load (e.g., HVAC equipment, water heater) that exceeds the design load for the truss shall not be permitted without verification that the truss is capable of supporting such additional loading.

R802.10.5 Truss to wall connection. Trusses shall be connected to wall plates by the use of fasteners or connectors having a resistance to uplift of not less than the value listed on the truss design drawings.

R802.11 Roof tie-down.

R802.11.1 Uplift resistance. Roof assemblies which are subject to wind uplift pressures of 20 pounds per square foot (960 Pa) or greater shall have roof rafters or trusses attached to their supporting wall assemblies by connections capable of providing the resistance required in Table R802.11. Wind uplift pressures shall be determined using an effective wind area of 100 square feet (9.3 m²) and Zone 1 in Table R301.2(2), as adjusted for height and exposure per Table R301.2(3).

A continuous load path shall be designed to transmit the uplift forces from the rafter or truss ties to the foundation.

TABLE R802.11
REQUIRED STRENGTH OF TRUSS OR RAFTER CONNECTIONS TO RESIST WIND UPLIFT FORCES[a, b, c, e, f]
(Pounds per connection)

BASIC WIND SPEED (mph) (3–second gust)	ROOF SPAN (feet)							OVERHANGS[d] (pounds/foot)
	12	20	24	28	32	36	40	
85	-72	-120	-145	-169	-193	-217	-241	-38.55
90	-91	-151	-181	-212	-242	-272	-302	-43.22
100	-131	-218	-262	-305	-349	-393	-436	-53.36
110	-175	-292	-351	-409	-467	-526	-584	-64.56

For SI: 1 inch = 25.4 mm, 1 foot = 305 mm, 1 mph = 0.447 m/s, 1 pound/foot = 14.5939 N/m, 1 pound = 0.454 kg.

a. The uplift connection requirements are based on a 30 foot mean roof height located in Exposure B. For Exposures C and D and for other mean roof heights, multiply the above loads by the Adjustment Coefficients in Table R301.2(3).

b. The uplift connection requirements are based on the framing being spaced 24 inches on center. Multiply by 0.67 for framing spaced 16 inches on center and multiply by 0.5 for framing spaced 12 inches on center.

c. The uplift connection requirements include an allowance for 10 pounds of dead load.

d. The uplift connection requirements do not account for the effects of overhangs. The magnitude of the above loads shall be increased by adding the overhang loads found in the table. The overhang loads are also based on framing spaced 24 inches on center. The overhang loads given shall be multiplied by the overhang projection and added to the roof uplift value in the table.

e. The uplift connection requirements are based on wind loading on end zones as defined in Figure 6-2 of ASCE 7. Connection loads for connections located a distance of 20% of the least horizontal dimension of the building from the corner of the building are permitted to be reduced by multiplying the table connection value by 0.7 and multiplying the overhang load by 0.8.

f. For wall-to-wall and wall-to-foundation connections, the capacity of the uplift connector is permitted to be reduced by 100 pounds for each full wall above. (For example, if a 600-pound rated connector is used on the roof framing, a 500-pound rated connector is permitted at the next floor level down).

SECTION R803
ROOF SHEATHING

R803.1 Lumber sheathing. Allowable spans for lumber used as roof sheathing shall conform to Table R803.1. Spaced lumber sheathing for wood shingle and shake roofing shall conform to the requirements of Sections R905.7 and R905.8. Spaced lumber sheathing is not allowed in Seismic Design Category D_2.

TABLE R803.1
MINIMUM THICKNESS OF LUMBER ROOF SHEATHING

RAFTER OR BEAM SPACING (inches)	MINIMUM NET THICKNESS (inches)
24	$^5/_8$
48[a]	
60[b]	$1^1/_2$ T & G
72[c]	

For SI: 1 inch = 25.4 mm.
a. Minimum 270 F_b, 340,000 E.
b. Minimum 420 F_b, 660,000 E.
c. Minimum 600 F_b, 1,150,000 E.

R803.2 Wood structural panel sheathing.

R803.2.1 Identification and grade. Wood structural panels shall conform to DOC PS 1, DOC PS 2 or, when manufactured in Canada, CSA 0437, and shall be identified by a grade mark or certificate of inspection issued by an approved agency. Wood structural panels shall comply with the grades specified in Table R503.2.1.1(1).

R803.2.1.1 Exposure durability. All wood structural panels, when designed to be permanently exposed in outdoor applications, shall be of an exterior exposure durability. Wood structural panel roof sheathing exposed to the underside may be of interior type bonded with exterior glue, identified as Exposure 1.

R803.2.1.2 Fire-retardant-treated plywood. The allowable unit stresses for fire-retardant-treated plywood, including fastener values, shall be developed from an approved method of investigation that considers the effects of anticipated temperature and humidity to which the fire-retardant-treated plywood will be subjected, the type of treatment and redrying process. The fire-retardant-treated plywood shall be graded by an approved agency.

R803.2.2 Allowable spans. The maximum allowable spans for wood structural panel roof sheathing shall not exceed the values set forth in Table R503.2.1.1(1), or APA E30.

R803.2.3 Installation. Wood structural panel used as roof sheathing shall be installed with joints staggered or not staggered in accordance with Table R602.3(1), or APA E30 for wood roof framing or with Table R804.3 for steel roof framing.

SECTION R804
STEEL ROOF FRAMING

R804.1 General. Elements shall be straight and free of any defects that would significantly affect their structural performance. Cold-formed steel roof framing members shall comply with the requirements of this section.

R804.1.1 Applicability limits. The provisions of this section shall control the construction of steel roof framing for buildings not greater than 60 feet (18 288 mm) perpendicular to the joist, rafter or truss span, not greater than 40 feet (12 192 mm) in width parallel to the joist span or truss, not greater than two stories in height and roof slopes not smaller than 3:12 (25-percent slope) or greater than 12:12 (100 percent slope). Steel roof framing constructed in accordance with the provisions of this section shall be limited to sites subjected to a maximum design wind speed of 110 miles per hour (49 m/s), Exposure A, B, or C, and a maximum ground snow load of 70 pounds per square foot (3350 Pa).

R804.1.2 In-line framing. Steel roof framing constructed in accordance with Section R804 shall be located directly in line with load-bearing studs below with a maximum tolerance of $^3/_4$ inch (19 mm) between the centerline of the stud and the roof joist/rafter.

R804.1.3 Roof trusses. The design, quality assurance, installation and testing of cold-formed steel trusses shall be in accordance with the AISI Standard for Cold-formed Steel Framing-Truss Design (COFS/Truss). Truss members shall not be notched, cut or altered in any manner without an approved design.

R804.2 Structural framing. Load-bearing steel roof framing members shall comply with Figure R804.2(1) and with the dimensional and minimum thickness requirements specified in Tables R804.2(1) and R804.2(2). Tracks shall comply with Figure R804.2(2) and shall have a minimum flange width of $1^1/_4$ inches (32 mm). The maximum inside bend radius for load-bearing members shall be the greater of $^3/_{32}$ inch (2.4 mm) or twice the uncoated steel thickness. Holes in roof framing members shall comply with all of the following conditions:

1. Holes shall conform to Figure R804.2(3);

2. Holes shall be permitted only along the centerline of the web of the framing member;

3. Holes shall have a center-to-center spacing of not less than 24 inches (610 mm);

4. Holes shall have a width not greater than 0.5 times the member depth, or $2^1/_2$ inches (64 mm);

5. Holes shall have a length not exceeding $4^1/_2$ inches (114 mm); and

6. Holes shall have a minimum distance between the edge of the bearing surface and the edge of the hole of not less than 10 inches (254 mm).

Framing members with web holes not conforming to these requirements shall be patched in accordance with Section R804.3.6 or designed in accordance with accepted engineering practices.

R804.2.1 Material. Load-bearing steel framing members shall be cold-formed to shape from structural quality sheet steel complying with the requirements of one of the following:

1. ASTM A 653: Grades 33, 37, 40 and 50 (Class 1 and 3).

2. ASTM A 792: Grades 33, 37, 40 and 50A.

3. ASTM A 875: Grades 33, 37, 40 and 50 (Class 1 and 3).

4. ASTM A 1003: Grades 33, 37, 40 and 50.

R804.2.2 Identification. Load-bearing steel framing members shall have a legible label, stencil, stamp or embossment with the following information as a minimum:

1. Manufacturer's identification.

2. Minimum uncoated steel thickness in inches (mm).

3. Minimum coating designation.

4. Minimum yield strength, in kips per square inch (ksi).

R804.2.3 Corrosion protection. Load-bearing steel framing shall have a metallic coating complying with one of the following:

1. A minimum of G 60 in accordance with ASTM A 653.

TABLE R804.2(1)
LOAD-BEARING COLD-FORMED STEEL MEMBER SIZES

NOMINAL MEMBER SIZE MEMBER DESIGNATION[a]	WEB DEPTH (inches)	MINIMUM FLANGE WIDTH (inches)	MAXIMUM FLANGE WIDTH (inches)	MINIMUM LIP SIZE (inches)
350S162-t	3.5	1.625	2	0.5
550S162-t	5.5	1.625	2	0.5
800S162-t	8	1.625	2	0.5
1000S162-t	10	1.625	2	0.5
1200S162-t	12	1.625	2	0.5

For SI: 1 inch = 25.4 mm.

a. The member designation is defined by the first number representing the member depth in hundredths of an inch, the letter "s" representing a stud or joist member, the second number representing the flange width in hundredths of an inch, and the letter "t" shall be a number representing the minimum base metal thickness in mils [see Table R804.2(2)].

TABLE R804.2(2)
MINIMUM THICKNESS OF COLD-FORMED STEEL ROOF FRAMING MEMBERS

DESIGNATION (mils)	MINIMUM UNCOATED THICKNESS (inches)	REFERENCED GAGE NUMBER
33	0.033	20
43	0.043	18
54	0.054	16
68	0.068	14

For SI: 1 inch = 25.4 mm, 1 mil = 0.0254 mm.

2. A minimum of AZ 50 in accordance with ASTM A 792.

3. A minimum of GF 60 in accordance with ASTM A 875.

R804.2.4 Fastening requirements. Screws for steel-to-steel connections shall be installed with a minimum edge distance and center-to-center spacing of $^1/_2$ inch (13 mm), shall be self-drilling tapping, and shall conform to SAE J78. Structural sheathing shall be attached to roof rafters with minimum No. 8 self-drilling tapping screws that conform to SAE J78. Screws for attaching structural sheathing to steel roof framing shall have a minimum head diameter of 0.292 inch (7.4 mm) with countersunk heads and shall be installed with a minimum edge distance of $^3/_8$ inch (10 mm). Gypsum board ceilings shall be attached to steel joists with minimum No. 6 screws conforming to ASTM C 954 and shall be installed in accordance with Section R805. For all connections, screws shall extend through the steel a minimum of three exposed threads. All self-drilling tapping screws con-

forming to SAE J78 shall have a minimum Type II coating in accordance with ASTM B 633.

Where No. 8 screws are specified in a steel-to-steel connection, reduction of the required number of screws in the connection is permitted in accordance with the reduction factors in Table R804.2.4 when larger screws are used or when one of the sheets of steel being connected is thicker that 33 mils (0.84 mm). When applying the reduction factor, the resulting number of screws shall be rounded up.

TABLE R804.2.4
SCREW SUBSTITUTION FACTOR

SCREW SIZE	THINNEST CONNECTED STEEL SHEET (mils)	
	33	43
#8	1.0	0.67
#10	0.93	0.62
#12	0.86	0.56

For SI: 1 mil = 0.0254 mm.

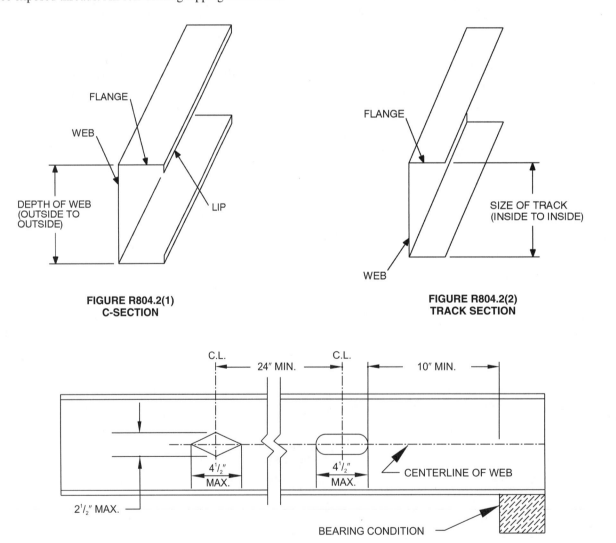

FIGURE R804.2(1)
C-SECTION

FIGURE R804.2(2)
TRACK SECTION

For SI: 1 inch = 25.4 mm.

FIGURE R804.2(3)
WEB HOLES

R804.3 Roof construction. Steel roof systems constructed in accordance with the provisions of this section shall consist of both ceiling joists and rafters in accordance with Figure R804.3 and fastened in accordance with Table R804.3.

R804.3.1 Allowable ceiling joist spans. The clear span of cold-formed steel ceiling joists shall not exceed the limits set forth in Tables R804.3.1(1) through R804.3.1(8). Ceiling joists shall have a minimum bearing length of 1.5 inches (38 mm) and shall be connected to rafters (heel joint) in accordance with Figure R804.3.1(1) and Table R804.3.1. When continuous joists are framed across interior bearing supports, the interior bearing supports shall be located within 24 inches (610 mm) of midspan of the ceiling joist, and the individual spans shall not exceed the applicable spans in Tables R804.3.1(2), R804.3.1(4), R804.3.1(6), R804.3.1(8). Where required in Tables R804.3.1(1) through R804.3.1(8), bearing stiffeners shall be installed at each bearing location in accordance with Section R804.3.8 and Figure R804.3.8. When the attic is to be used as an occupied space, the ceiling joists shall be designed in accordance with Section R505.

TABLE R804.3
ROOF FRAMING FASTENING SCHEDULE[a,b]

DESCRIPTION OF BUILDING ELEMENTS	NUMBER AND SIZE OF FASTENERS	SPACING OF FASTENERS
Ceiling joist to top track of load-bearing wall	2 No. 10 screws	Each joist
Roof sheathing (oriented strand board or plywood) to rafters	No. 8 screws	6″ o.c. on edges and 12″ o.c. at interior supports. 6″ o.c. at gable end truss
Truss to bearing wall[a]	2 No. 10 screws	Each truss
Gable end truss to endwall top track	No. 10 screws	12″ o.c.
Rafter to ceiling joist	Minimum No. 10 screws, per Table R804.3.1	Evenly spaced, not less than $^1/_2$″ from all edges.

For SI: 1 inch = 25.4 mm, 1 foot = 304.8 mm, 1 pound per square foot = 0.0479 kPa, 1 mil = 0.0254 mm.

a. Screws shall be applied through the flanges of the truss or ceiling joist or a 54 mil clip angle shall be used with two No. 10 screws in each leg. See Section R804.4 for additional requirements to resist uplift forces.

b. Spacing of fasteners on roof sheathing panel edges applies to panel edges supported by framing members and at all roof plane perimeters. Blocking of roof sheathing panel edges perpendicular to the framing members shall not be required except at the intersection of adjacent roof planes. Roof perimeter shall be supported by framing members or cold-formed blocking of the same depth and gage as the floor members.

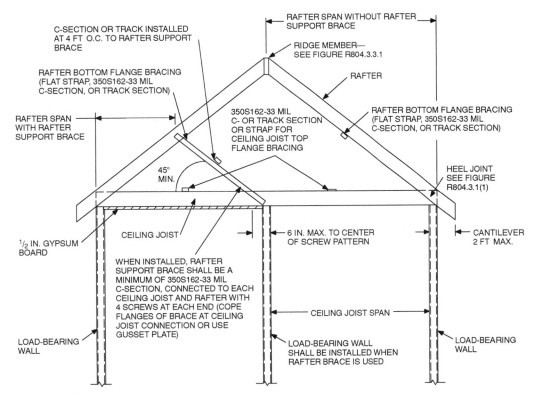

For SI: 1 inch = 25.4 mm, 1 foot = 304.8 mm, 1 mil = 0.0254 mm.

FIGURE R804.3
STEEL ROOF CONSTRUCTION

TABLE R804.3.1(1)
CEILING JOIST SPANS
SINGLE SPANS WITH BEARING STIFFENERS
10 lb per sq ft LIVE LOAD (NO ATTIC STORAGE)[a, b, c] **33 ksi STEEL**

MEMBER DESIGNATION	ALLOWABLE SPAN (feet-inches)					
	Lateral Support of Top (Compression) Flange					
	Unbraced		Mid-Span Bracing		Third-Point Bracing	
	Ceiling Joist Spacing (inches)					
	16	24	16	24	16	24
350S162-33	9'-5"	8'-6"	12'-2"	10'-4"	12'-2"	10'-7"
350S162-43	10'-3"	9'-2"	12'-10"	11'-2"	12'-10"	11'-2"
350S162-54	11'-1"	9'-11"	13'-9"	12'-0"	13'-9"	12'-0"
350S162-68	12'-1"	10'-9"	14'-8"	12'-10"	14'-8"	12'-10"
350S162-97	14'-4"	12'-7"	16'-4"	14'-3"	16'-4"	14'-3"
550S162-33	10'-7"	9'-6"	14'-10"	12'-10"	15'-11"	13'-4"
550S162-43	11'-8"	10'-6"	16'-4"	14'-3"	17'-10"	15'-3"
550S162-54	12'-6"	11'-2"	17'-7"	15'-7"	19'-5"	16'-10"
550S162-68	13'-6"	12'-1"	19'-2"	17'-1"	21'-0"	18'-4"
550S162-97	15'-9"	13'-11"	21'-8"	19'-3"	23'-5"	20'-5"
800S162-33	12'-2"	10'-11"	17'-8"	15'-10"	19'-10"	17'-1"
800S162-43	13'-0"	11'-9"	18'-10"	17'-0"	21'-6"	19'-1"
800S162-54	13'-10"	12'-5"	20'-0"	18'-0"	22'-9"	20'-4"
800S162-68	14'-11"	13'-4"	21'-3"	19'-1"	24'-1"	21'-8"
800S162-97	17'-1"	15'-2"	23'-10"	21'-3"	26'-7"	23'-10"
1000S162-43	13'-11"	12'-6"	20'-2"	18'-3"	23'-1"	20'-9"
1000S162-54	14'-9"	13'-3"	21'-4"	19'-3"	24'-4"	22'-0"
1000S162-68	15'-10"	14'-2"	22'-8"	20'-5"	25'-9"	23'-2"
1000S162-97	18'-0"	16'-0"	25'-3"	22'-7"	28'-3"	25'-4"
1200S162-43	14'-8"	13'-3"	21'-4"	19'-3"	24'-5"	21'-8"
1200S162-54	15'-7"	14'-0"	22'-6"	20'-4"	25'-9"	23'-2"
1200S162-68	16'-8"	14'-11"	23'-11"	21'-6"	27'-2"	24'-6"
1000S162-97	18'-9"	16'-9"	26'-6"	23'-8"	29'-9"	26'-9"

For SI: 1 inch = 25.4 mm, 1 foot = 304.8 mm, 1 pound per square foot = 0.0479 kPa.

a. Deflection criterion: $L/240$ for total loads.

b. Ceiling dead load = 5 psf.

c. Bearing stiffeners are required at all bearing points and concentrated load locations.

TABLE R804.3.1(2)
CEILING JOIST SPANS
TWO EQUAL SPANS WITH BEARING STIFFENERS
10 lb per sq ft LIVE LOAD (NO ATTIC STORAGE)[a, b, c] 33 ksi STEEL

MEMBER DESIGNATION	ALLOWABLE SPAN (feet-inches)					
	Lateral Support of Top (Compression) Flange					
	Unbraced		Mid-Span Bracing		Third-Point Bracing	
	Ceiling Joist Spacing (inches)					
	16	24	16	24	16	24
350S162-33	12'-11"	10'-11"	13'-5"	10'-11"	13'-5"	10'-11"
350S162-43	14'-2"	12'-8"	15'-10"	12'-11"	15'-10"	12'-11"
350S162-54	15'-6"	13'-10"	17'-1"	14'-6"	17'-9"	14'-6"
350S162-68	17'-3"	15'-3"	18'-6"	16'-1"	19'-8"	16'-1"
350S162-97	20'-10"	18'-4"	21'-5"	18'-10"	21'-11"	18'-10"
550S162-33	14'-4"	12'-11"	16'-7"	14'-1"	17'-3"	14'-1"
550S162-43	16'-0"	14'-1"	17'-11"	16'-1"	20'-7"	16'-10"
550S162-54	17'-4"	15'-6"	19'-5"	17'-6"	23'-2"	19'-0"
550S162-68	19'-1"	16'-11"	20'-10"	18'-8"	25'-2"	21'-5"
550S162-97	22'-8"	19'-9"	23'-6"	20'-11"	27'-11"	25'-1"
800S162-33	16'-5"	14'-10"	19'-2"	17'-3"	23'-1"	18'-3"
800S162-43	17'-9"	15'-11"	20'-6"	18'-5"	25'-0"	22'-6"
800S162-54	19'-1"	17'-1"	21'-8"	19'-6"	26'-4"	23'-9"
800S162-68	20'-9"	18'-6"	23'-1"	20'-9"	28'-0"	25'-2"
800S162-97	24'-5"	21'-6"	26'-0"	23'-2"	31'-1"	27'-9"
1000S162-43	18'-11"	17'-0"	21'-11"	19'-9"	26'-8"	24'-1"
1000S162-54	20'-3"	18'-2"	23'-2"	20'-10"	28'-2"	25'-5"
1000S162-68	21'-11"	19'-7"	24'-7"	22'-2"	29'-10"	26'-11"
1000S162-97	25'-7"	22'-7"	27'-6"	24'-6"	33'-0"	29'-7"
1200S162-43	19'-11"	17'-11"	23'-1"	20'-10"	28'-3"	25'-6"
1200S162-54	21'-3"	19'-1"	24'-5"	22'-0"	29'-9"	26'-10"
1200S162-68	23'-0"	20'-7"	25'-11"	23'-4"	31'-6"	28'-4"
1000S162-97	26'-7"	23'-6"	28'-9"	25'-10"	34'-8"	31'-1"

For SI: 1 inch = 25.4 mm, 1 foot = 304.8 mm, 1 pound per square foot = 0.0479 kPa.

a. Deflection criterion: $L/240$ for total loads.
b. Ceiling dead load = 5 psf.
c. Bearing stiffeners are required at all bearing points and concentrated load locations.

TABLE R804.3.1(3)
CEILING JOIST SPANS
SINGLE SPANS WITH BEARING STIFFENERS
20 lb per sq ft LIVE LOAD (LIMITED ATTIC STORAGE)[a, b, c] 33 ksi STEEL

MEMBER DESIGNATION	ALLOWABLE SPAN (feet-inches)					
	Lateral Support of Top (Compression) Flange					
	Unbraced		Mid-Span Bracing		Third-Point Bracing	
	Ceiling Joist Spacing (inches)					
	16	24	16	24	16	24
350S162-33	8'-2"	7'-2"	9'-9"	8'-1"	9'-11"	8'-1"
350S162-43	8'-10"	7'-10"	11'-0"	9'-5"	11'-0"	9'-7"
350S162-54	9'-6"	8'-6"	11'-9"	10'-3"	11'-9"	10'-3"
350S162-68	10'-4"	9'-2"	12'-7"	11'-0"	12'-7"	11'-0"
350S162-97	12'-1"	10'-8"	14'-0"	12'-0"	14'-0"	12'-0"
550S162-33	9'-2"	8'-3"	12'-2"	10'-2"	12'-6"	10'-5"
550S162-43	10'-1"	9'-1"	13'-7"	11'-7"	14'-5"	12'-2"
550S162-54	10'-9"	9'-8"	14'-10"	12'-10"	15'-11"	13'-6"
550S162-68	11'-7"	10'-4"	16'-4"	14'-0"	17'-5"	14'-11"
550S162-97	13'-4"	11'-10"	18'-5"	16'-2"	20'-1"	17'-1"
800S162-33	10'-7"	9'-6"	15'-1"	13'-0"	16'-2"	13'-7"
800S162-43	11'-4"	10'-2"	16'-5"	14'-6"	18'-2"	15'-9"
800S162-54	12'-0"	10'-9"	17'-4"	15'-6"	19'-6"	17'-0"
800S162-68	12'-10"	11'-6"	18'-5"	16'-6"	20'-10"	18'-3"
800S162-97	14'-7"	12'-11"	20'-5"	18'-3"	22'-11"	20'-5"
1000S162-43	12'-1"	10'-11"	17'-7"	15'-10"	19'-11"	17'-3"
1000S162-54	12'-10"	11'-6"	18'-7"	16'-9"	21'-2"	18'-10"
1000S162-68	13'-8"	12'-3"	19'-8"	17'-8"	22'-4"	20'-1"
1000S162-97	15'-4"	13'-8"	21'-8"	19'-5"	24'-5"	21'-11"
1200S162-43	12'-9"	11'-6"	18'-7"	16'-6"	20'-9"	18'-2"
1200S162-54	13'-6"	12'-2"	19'-7"	17'-8"	22'-5"	20'-2"
1200S162-68	14'-4"	12'-11"	20'-9"	18'-8"	23'-7"	21'-3"
1000S162-97	16'-1"	14'-4"	22'-10"	20'-6"	25'-9"	23'-2"

For SI: 1 inch = 25.4 mm, 1 foot = 304.8 mm, 1 pound per square foot = 0.0479 kPa.
a. Deflection criterion: $L/240$ for total loads.
b. Ceiling dead load = 5 psf.
c. Bearing stiffeners are required at all bearing points and concentrated load locations.

TABLE R804.3.1(4)
CEILING JOIST SPANS
TWO EQUAL SPANS WITH BEARING STIFFENERS
20 lb per sq ft LIVE LOAD (LIMITED ATTIC STORAGE)[a, b, c] 33 ksi STEEL

MEMBER DESIGNATION	ALLOWABLE SPAN (feet-inches)					
	Lateral Support of Top (Compression) Flange					
	Unbraced		Mid-Span Bracing		Third-Point Bracing	
	Ceiling Joist Spacing (inches)					
	16	24	16	24	16	24
350S162-33	10'-2"	8'-4"	10'-2"	8'-4"	10'-2"	8'-4"
350S162-43	12'-1"	9'-10"	12'-1"	9'-10"	12'-1"	9'-10"
350S162-54	13'-3"	11'-0"	13'-6"	11'-0"	13'-6"	11'-0"
350S162-68	14'-7"	12'-3"	15'-0"	12'-3"	15'-0"	12'-3"
350S162-97	17'-6"	14'-3"	17'-6"	14'-3"	17'-6"	14'-3"
550S162-33	12'-5"	10'-9"	13'-2"	10'-9"	13'-2"	10'-9"
550S162-43	13'-7"	12'-1"	15'-6"	12'-9"	15'-8"	12'-9"
550S162-54	14'-11"	13'-4"	16'-10"	14'-5"	17'-9"	14'-5"
550S162-68	16'-3"	14'-5"	18'-0"	16'-1"	20'-0"	16'-4"
550S162-97	19'-1"	16'-10"	20'-3"	18'-0"	23'-10"	19'-5"
800S162-33	14'-3"	12'-4"	16'-7"	12'-4"	16'-7"	12'-4"
800S162-43	15'-4"	13'-10"	17'-9"	16'-0"	21'-8"	17'-9"
800S162-54	16'-5"	14'-9"	18'-10"	16'-11"	22'-11"	20'-6"
800S162-68	17'-9"	15'-11"	20'-0"	18'-0"	24'-3"	21'-10"
800S162-97	20'-8"	18'-3"	22'-3"	19'-11"	26'-9"	24'-0"
1000S162-43	16'-5"	14'-9"	19'-0"	17'-2"	23'-3"	18'-11"
1000S162-54	17'-6"	15'-8"	20'-1"	18'-1"	24'-6"	22'-1"
1000S162-68	18'-10"	16'-10"	21'-4"	19'-2"	25'-11"	23'-4"
1000S162-97	21'-8"	19'-3"	23'-7"	21'-2"	28'-5"	25'-6"
1200S162-43	17'-3"	15'-7"	20'-1"	18'-2"	24'-6"	18'-3"
1200S162-54	18'-5"	16'-6"	21'-3"	19'-2"	25'-11"	23'-5"
1200S162-68	19'-9"	17'-8"	22'-6"	20'-3"	27'-4"	24'-8"
1000S162-97	22'-7"	20'-1"	24'-10"	22'-3"	29'-11"	26'-11"

For SI: 1 inch = 25.4 mm, 1 foot = 304.8 mm, 1 pound per square foot = 0.0479 kPa.
a. Deflection criterion: $L/240$ for total loads.
b. Ceiling dead load = 5 psf.
c. Bearing stiffeners are required at all bearing points and concentrated load locations.

TABLE R804.3.1(5)
CEILING JOIST SPANS
SINGLE SPANS WITHOUT BEARING STIFFENERS
10 lb per sq ft LIVE LOAD (NO ATTIC STORAGE)[a, b] 33 ksi STEEL

MEMBER DESIGNATION	ALLOWABLE SPAN (feet-inches)					
	Lateral Support of Top (Compression) Flange					
	Unbraced		Mid-Span Bracing		Third-Point Bracing	
	Ceiling Joist Spacing (inches)					
	16	24	16	24	16	24
350S162-33	9'-5"	8'-6"	12'-2"	10'-4"	12'-2"	10'-7"
350S162-43	10'-3"	9'-12"	13'-2"	11'-6"	13'-2"	11'-6"
350S162-54	11'-1"	9'-11"	13'-9"	12'-0"	13'-9"	12'-0"
350S162-68	12'-1"	10'-9"	14'-8"	12'-10"	14'-8"	12'-10"
350S162-97	14'-4"	12'-7"	16'-10"	14'-3"	16'-4"	14'-3"
550S162-33	10'-7"	9'-6"	14'-10"	12'-10"	15'-11"	13'-4"
550S162-43	11'-8"	10'-6"	16'-4"	14'-3"	17'-10"	15'-3"
550S162-54	12'-6"	11'-2"	17'-7"	15'-7"	19'-5"	16'-10"
550S162-68	13'-6"	12'-1"	19'-2"	17'-0"	21'-0"	18'-4"
550S162-97	15'-9"	13'-11"	21'-8"	19'-3"	23'-5"	20'-5"
800S162-33	—	—	—	—	—	—
800S162-43	13'-0"	11'-9"	18'-10"	17'-0"	21'-6"	19'-0"
800S162-54	13'-10"	12'-5"	20'-0"	18'-0"	22'-9"	20'-4"
800S162-68	14'-11"	13'-4"	21'-3"	19'-1"	24'-1"	21'-8"
800S162-97	17'-1"	15'-2"	23'-10"	21'-3"	26'-7"	23'-10"
1000S162-43	—	—	—	—	—	—
1000S162-54	14'-9"	13'-3"	21'-4"	19'-3"	24'-4"	22'-0"
1000S162-68	15'-10"	14'-2"	22'-8"	20'-5"	25'-9"	23'-2"
1000S162-97	18'-0"	16'-0"	25'-3"	22'-7"	28'-3"	25'-4"
1200S162-43	—	—	—	—	—	—
1200S162-54	—	—	—	—	—	—
1200S162-68	16'-8"	14'-11"	23'-11"	21'-6"	27'-2"	24'-6"
1000S162-97	18'-9"	16'-9"	26'-6"	23'-8"	29'-9"	26'-9"

For SI: 1 inch = 25.4 mm, 1 foot = 304.8 mm, 1 pound per square foot = 0.0479 kPa.

a. Deflection criterion: $L/240$ for total loads.

b. Ceiling dead load = 5 psf.

TABLE R804.3.1(6)
CEILING JOIST SPANS
TWO EQUAL SPANS WITHOUT BEARING STIFFENERS
10 lb per sq ft LIVE LOAD (NO ATTIC STORAGE)[a, b] 33 ksi STEEL

MEMBER DESIGNATION	ALLOWABLE SPAN (feet-inches)					
	Lateral Support of Top (Compression) Flange					
	Unbraced		Mid-Span Bracing		Third-Point Bracing	
	Ceiling Joist Spacing (inches)					
	16	24	16	24	16	24
350S162-33	11'-9"	8'-11"	11'-9"	8'-11"	11'-9"	8'-11"
350S162-43	14'-2"	11'-7"	14'-11"	11'-7"	14'-11"	11'-7"
350S162-54	15'-6"	13'-10"	17'-1"	13'-10"	17'-7"	13'-10"
350S162-68	17'-3"	15'-3"	18'-6"	16'-1"	19'-8"	16'-1"
350S162-97	20'-10"	18'-4"	21'-5"	18'-9"	21'-11"	18'-9"
550S162-33	13'-4"	9'-11"	13'-4"	9'-11"	13'-4"	9'-11"
550S162-43	16'-0"	13'-6"	17'-9"	13'-6"	17'-9"	13'-6"
550S162-54	17'-4"	15'-6"	19'-5"	16'-10"	21'-9"	16'-10"
550S162-68	19'-1"	16'-11"	20'-10"	18'-8"	24'-11"	20'-6"
550S162-97	22'-8"	20'-0"	23'-9"	21'-1"	28'-2"	25'-1"
800S162-33	—	—	—	—	—	—
800S162-43	17'-9"	15'-7"	20'-6"	15'-7"	21'-0"	15'-7"
800S162-54	19'-1"	17'-1"	21'-8"	19'-6"	26'-4"	23'-10"
800S162-68	20'-9"	18'-6"	23'-1"	20'-9"	28'-0"	25'-2"
800S162-97	24'-5"	21'-6"	26'-0"	23'-2"	31'-1"	27'-9"
1000S162-43	—	—	—	—	—	—
1000S162-54	20'-3"	18'-2"	23'-2"	20'-10"	28'-2"	21'-2"
1000S162-68	21'-11"	19'-7"	24'-7"	22'-2"	29'-10"	26'-11"
1000S162-97	25'-7"	22'-7"	27'-6"	24'-6"	33'-0"	29'-7"
1200S162-43	—	—	—	—	—	—
1200S162-54	—	—	—	—	—	—
1200S162-68	23'-0"	20'-7"	25'-11"	23'-4"	31'-6"	28'-4"
1000S162-97	26'-7"	23'-6"	28'-9"	25'-10"	34'-8"	31'-1"

For SI: 1 inch = 25.4 mm, 1 foot = 304.8 mm, 1 pound per square foot = 0.0479 kPa.
a. Deflection criterion: L/240 for total loads.
b. Ceiling dead load = 5 psf.

TABLE R804.3.1(7)
CEILING JOIST SPANS
SINGLE SPANS WITHOUT BEARING STIFFENERS
20 lb per sq ft LIVE LOAD (LIMITED ATTIC STORAGE)[a, b] 33 ksi STEEL

MEMBER DESIGNATION	ALLOWABLE SPAN (feet-inches)					
	Lateral Support of Top (Compression) Flange					
	Unbraced		Mid-Span Bracing		Third-Point Bracing	
	Ceiling Joist Spacing (inches)					
	16	24	16	24	16	24
350S162-33	8'-2"	6'-10"	9'-9"	6'-10"	9'-11"	6'-10"
350S162-43	8'-10"	7'-10"	11'-0"	9'-5"	11'-0"	9'-7"
350S162-54	9'-6"	8'-6"	11'-9"	10'-3"	11'-9"	10'-3"
350S162-68	10'-4"	9'-2"	12'-7"	11'-0"	12'-7"	11'-0"
350S162-97	12'-10"	10'-8"	13'-9"	12'-0"	13'-9"	12'-0"
550S162-33	9'-2"	8'-3"	12'-2"	8'-5"	12'-6"	8'-5"
550S162-43	10'-1"	9'-1"	13'-7"	11'-8"	14'-5"	12'-2"
550S162-54	10'-9"	9'-8"	14'-10"	12'-10"	15'-11"	13'-6"
550S162-68	11'-7"	10'-4"	16'-4"	14'-0"	17'-5"	14'-11"
550S162-97	13'-4"	11'-10"	18'-5"	16'-2"	20'-1"	17'-4"
800S162-33	—	—	—	—	—	—
800S162-43	11'-4"	10'-1"	16'-5"	13'-6"	18'-1"	13'-6"
800S162-54	20'-0"	10'-9"	17'-4"	15'-6"	19'-6"	27'-0"
800S162-68	12'-10"	11'-6"	18'-5"	16'-6"	20'-10"	18'-3"
800S162-97	14'-7"	12'-11"	20'-5"	18'-3"	22'-11"	20'-5"
1000S162-43	—	—	—	—	—	—
1000S162-54	12'-10"	11'-6"	18'-7"	16'-9"	21'-2"	15'-5"
1000S162-68	13'-8"	12'-3"	19'-8"	17'-8"	22'-4"	20'-1"
1000S162-97	15'-4"	13'-8"	21'-8"	19'-5"	24'-5"	21'-11"
1200S162-43	—	—	—	—	—	—
1200S162-54	—	—	—	—	—	—
1200S162-68	14'-4"	12'-11"	20'-9"	18'-8"	23'-7"	21'-3"
1000S162-97	16'-1"	14'-4"	22'-10"	20'-6"	25'-9"	23'-2"

For SI: 1 inch = 25.4 mm, 1 foot = 304.8 mm, 1 pound per square foot = 0.0479 kPa.

a. Deflection criterion: $L/240$ for total loads.

b. Ceiling dead load = 5 psf.

TABLE R804.3.1(8)
CEILING JOIST SPANS
TWO EQUAL SPANS WITHOUT BEARING STIFFENERS
20 lb per sq ft LIVE LOAD (LIMITED ATTIC STORAGE)[a, b] 33 ksi STEEL

MEMBER DESIGNATION	ALLOWABLE SPAN (feet-inches)					
	Lateral Support of Top (Compression) Flange					
	Unbraced		Mid-Span Bracing		Third-Point Bracing	
	Ceiling Joist Spacing (inches)					
	16	24	16	24	16	24
350S162-33	8'-1"	6'-1"	8'-1"	6'-1"	8'-1"	6'-1"
350S162-43	10'-7"	8'-1"	10'-7"	8'-1"	10'-7"	8'-1"
350S162-54	12'-8"	9'-10"	12'-8"	9'-10"	12'-8"	9'-10"
350S162-68	14'-7"	11'-10"	14'-11"	11'-10"	14'-11"	11'-10"
350S162-97	17'-6"	14'-3"	17'-6"	14'-3"	17'-6"	14'-3"
550S162-33	8'-11"	6'-8"	8'-11"	6'-8"	8'-11"	6'-8"
550S162-43	12'-3"	9'-2"	12'-3"	9'-2"	12'-3"	9'-2"
550S162-54	14'-11"	11'-8"	15'-4"	11'-8"	15'-4"	11'-8"
550S162-68	16'-3"	14'-5"	18'-0"	15'-8"	18'-10"	14'-7"
550S162-97	19'-1"	16'-10"	20'-3"	18'-0"	23'-9"	19'-5"
800S162-33	—	—	—	—	—	—
800S162-43	13'-11"	9'-10"	13'-11"	9'-10"	13'-11"	9'-10"
800S162-54	16'-5"	13'-9"	18'-8"	13'-9"	18'-8"	13'-9"
800S162-68	17'-9"	15'-11"	20'-0"	18'-0"	24'-1"	18'-3"
800S162-97	20'-8"	18'-3"	22'-3"	19'-11"	26'-9"	24'-0"
1000S162-43	—	—	—	—	—	—
1000S162-54	17'-6"	13'-11"	19'-1"	13'-11"	19'-1"	13'-11"
1000S162-68	18'-10"	16'-10"	21'-4"	19'-2"	25'-11"	19'-7"
1000S162-97	21'-8"	19'-3"	23'-7"	21'-2"	28'-5"	25'-6"
1200S162-43	—	—	—	—	—	—
1200S162-54	—	—	—	—	—	—
1200S162-68	19'-9"	17'-8"	22'-6"	19'-8"	26'-8"	19'-8"
1000S162-97	22'-7"	20'-1"	24'-10"	22'-3"	29'-11"	26'-11"

For SI: 1 inch = 25.4 mm, 1 foot = 304.8 mm, 1 pound per square foot = 0.0479 kPa.

a. Deflection criterion: *L*/240 for total loads.

b. Ceiling dead load = 5 psf.

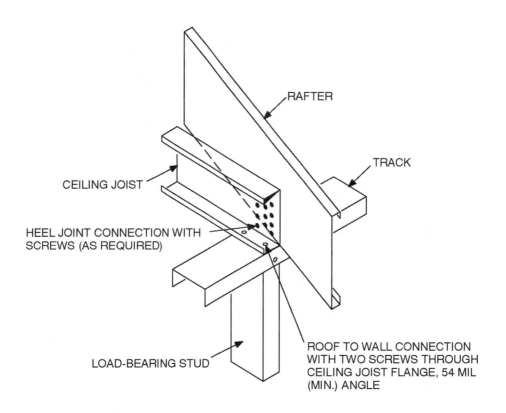

For SI: 1 mil = 0.0254 mm.

FIGURE R804.3.1(1)
JOIST TO RAFTER CONNECTION

TABLE R804.3.1
NUMBER OF SCREWS REQUIRED FOR CEILING JOIST TO RAFTER CONNECTION[a]

ROOF SLOPE	NUMBER OF SCREWS																			
	Building width (feet)																			
	24				28				32				36				40			
	Ground snow load (psf)																			
	20	30	50	70	20	30	50	70	20	30	50	70	20	30	50	70	20	30	50	70
3/12	5	6	9	11	5	7	10	13	6	8	11	15	7	8	13	17	8	9	14	19
4/12	4	5	7	9	4	5	8	10	5	6	9	12	5	7	10	13	6	7	11	14
5/12	3	4	6	7	4	4	6	8	4	5	7	10	5	5	8	11	5	6	9	12
6/12	3	3	5	6	3	4	6	7	4	4	6	8	4	5	7	9	4	5	8	10
7/12	3	3	4	6	3	3	5	7	3	4	6	7	4	4	6	8	4	5	7	9
8/12	2	3	4	5	3	3	5	6	3	4	5	7	3	4	6	8	4	4	6	8
9/12	2	3	4	5	3	3	4	6	3	3	5	6	3	4	5	7	3	4	6	8
10/12	2	2	4	5	2	3	4	5	3	3	5	6	3	3	5	7	3	4	6	7
11/12	2	2	3	4	2	3	4	5	3	3	4	6	3	3	5	6	3	4	5	7
12/12	2	2	3	4	2	3	4	5	2	3	4	5	3	3	5	6	3	4	5	7

For SI: 1 inch = 25.4 mm, 1 foot = 304.8 mm, 1 pound per square foot = 0.0479 kPa.
a. Screws shall be No. 10.

R804.3.2 Ceiling joist bracing. The bottom flanges of steel ceiling joists shall be laterally braced in accordance with Section R702. The top flanges of steel ceiling joists shall be laterally braced with a minimum of 33 mil (0.84 mm) C-section, 33 mil (0.84 mm) track section or 1¹/₂ inch by 33 mil (38 mm by 0.84 mm) continuous steel strapping as required in Tables R804.3.1(1) through R804.3.1(8). Lateral bracing shall be installed in accordance with Figure R804.3. C-section, tracks or straps shall be fastened to the top flange at each joist with at least one No. 8 screw and shall be fastened to blocking with at least two No. 8 screws. Blocking or bridging (X-bracing) shall be installed between joists in line with strap bracing at a maximum spacing of 12 feet (3658 mm) measured perpendicular to the joists, and at the termination of all straps. The third-point bracing span values from Tables R804.3.1(1) through R804.3.1(8) shall be used for straps installed at closer spacings than third-point bracing, or when sheathing is applied to the top of the ceiling joists.

R804.3.3 Allowable rafter spans. The horizontal projection of the rafter span, as shown in Figure R804.3, shall not exceed the limits set forth in Table R804.3.3(1). Wind speeds shall be converted to equivalent ground snow loads in accordance with Table R804.3.3(2). Rafter spans shall be selected based on the higher of the ground snow load or the equivalent snow load converted from the wind speed. When required, a rafter support brace shall be a minimum of 350S162-33 C-section with maximum length of 8 feet (2438 mm) and shall be connected to a ceiling joist and rafter with four No. 10 screws at each end.

R804.3.3.1 Rafter framing. Rafters shall be connected to a parallel ceiling joist to form a continuous tie between exterior walls in accordance with Figures R804.3 and R804.3.1(1) and Table R804.3.1. Rafters shall be connected to a ridge member with a minimum 2-inch by 2-inch (51 mm by 51 mm) clip angle fastened with minimum No. 10 screws to the ridge member in accordance with Figure R804.3.3.1 and Table R804.3.3.1. The clip angle shall have a minimum steel thickness as the rafter member and shall extend the full depth of the rafter member. The ridge member shall be fabricated from a C-section and a track section, which shall be of a minimum size and steel thickness as the adjacent rafters and shall be installed in accordance with Figure R804.3.3.1.

TABLE R804.3.3(1)
ALLOWABLE HORIZONTAL RAFTER SPANS[a, b, c] 33 ksi STEEL

MEMBER DESIGNATION	ALLOWABLE SPAN MEASURED HORIZONTALLY (feet-inches)							
	Ground Snow Load							
	20 psf		30 psf		50 psf		70 psf	
	Rafter spacing (in)							
	16	24	16	24	16	24	16	24
550S162-33	14'-0"	11'-5"	11'-10"	9'-8"	9'-5"	7'-8"	8'-1"	6'-7"
550S162-43	16'-6"	13'-10"	14'-4"	11'-9"	11'-5"	9'-4"	9'-10"	8'-0"
550S162-54	17'-9"	15'-6"	15'-6"	13'-2"	12'-11"	10'-6"	11'-1"	9'-0"
550S162-68	19'-0"	16'-7"	16'-8"	14'-7"	14'-1"	11'-10"	12'-5"	10'-2"
550S162-97	21'-2"	18'-6"	18'-7"	16'-2"	15'-8"	13'-8"	14'-0"	12'-2"
800S162-33	17'-0"	13'-11"	14'-5"	11'-9"	11'-6"	7'-9"	8'-6"	5'-8"
800S162-43	21'-1"	17'-3"	17'-10"	14'-7"	14'-3"	11'-7"	12'-2"	9'-11"
800S162-54	23'-11"	20'-4"	21'-0"	17'-3"	16'-10"	13'-9"	14'-5"	11'-9"
800S162-68	25'-9"	22'-6"	22'-7"	19'-5"	19'-0"	15'-6"	16'-3"	13'-3"
800S162-97	28'-9"	25'-1"	25'-2"	22'-0"	21'-3"	18'-7"	19'-0"	16'-0"
1000S162-43	23'-4"	19'-1"	19'-9"	16'-2"	15'-9"	12'-11"	13'-6"	10'-0"
1000S162-54	27'-8"	22'-7"	23'-5"	19'-1"	18'-8"	15'-3"	16'-0"	13'-1"
1000S162-68	30'-11"	27'-0"	27'-2"	22'-11"	22'-5"	18'-3"	19'-2"	15'-8"
1000S162-97	34'-7"	30'-2"	30'-4"	26'-6"	25'-7"	22'-1"	22'-10"	18'-11"
1200S162-43	25'-5"	20'-9"	21'-6"	17'-6"	17'-1"	11'-5"	12'-6"	8'-6"
1200S162-54	30'-0"	24'-6"	25'-5"	20'-9"	20'-3"	16'-7"	17'-5"	14'-2"
1200S162-68	35'-5"	28'-11"	30'-0"	24'-6"	23'-11"	19'-6"	20'-6"	16'-9"
1200S162-97	40'-4"	35'-3"	35'-5"	30'-11"	29'-10"	25'-5"	26'-8"	21'-9"

For SI: 1 inch = 25.4 mm, 1 foot = 304.8 mm, 1 pound per square foot = 0.0479kPa.

a. Table provides maximum horizontal rafter spans in feet and inches for slopes between 3:12 and 12:12.

b. Deflection criterion: $L/240$ for live loads and $L/180$ for total loads.

c. Roof dead load = 12 psf.

R804.3.3.2 Roof cantilevers. Roof cantilevers shall not exceed 24 inches (610 mm) in accordance with Figure R804.3. Roof cantilevers shall be supported by a header in accordance with Section R603.6 or shall be supported by the floor framing in accordance with Section R505.3.7.

R804.3.4 Rafter bottom flange bracing. The bottom flanges of steel rafters shall be continuously braced with a minimum 33-mil (0.84 mm) C-section, 33-mil (0.84 mm) track section, or a 1½-inch by 33-mil (38 mm by 0.84 mm) steel strapping at a maximum spacing of 8 feet (2438 mm) as measured parallel to the rafters. Bracing shall be installed in accordance with Figure R804.3. The C-section, track section, or straps shall be fastened to blocking with at least two No. 8 screws. Blocking or bridging (X-bracing) shall be installed between rafters in-line with the continuous bracing at a maximum spacing of 12 feet (3658 mm) measured perpendicular to the rafters and at the termination of all straps. The ends of continuous bracing shall be fastened to blocking with at least two No. 8 screws.

TABLE R804.3.3(2)
BASIC WIND SPEED TO EQUIVALENT SNOW LOAD CONVERSION

BASIC WIND SPEED AND EXPOSURE		EQUIVALENT GROUND SNOW LOAD (psf)									
		Roof slope									
Exp. A/B	Exp. C	3:12	4:12	5:12	6:12	7:12	8:12	9:12	10:12	11:12	12:12
85 mph	—	20	20	20	20	20	20	30	30	30	30
100 mph	85 mph	20	20	20	20	30	30	30	30	50	50
110 mph	100 mph	20	20	20	20	30	50	50	50	50	50
—	110 mph	30	30	30	50	50	50	70	70	70	—

For SI: 1 mile per hour = 0.447 m/s, 1 pound per square foot = 0.0479 kPa.

TABLE R804.3.3.1
NUMBER OF SCREWS REQUIRED AT EACH LEG OF CLIP ANGLE FOR RAFTER TO RIDGE MEMBER CONNECTION[a]

BUILDING WIDTH (feet)	NUMBER OF SCREWS			
	Ground snow load (psf)			
	0 to 20	21 to 30	31 to 50	51 to 70
24	2	2	3	4
28	2	3	4	5
32	2	3	4	5
36	3	3	5	6
40	3	4	5	7

For SI: 1 inch = 25.4 mm, 1 foot = 304.8 mm, 1 pound per square foot = 0.0479 kPa.
a. Screws shall be No. 10 minimum.

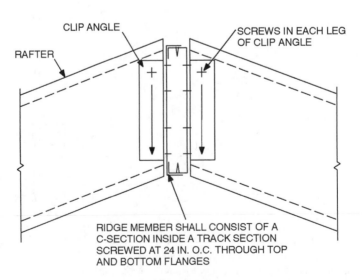

For SI: 1 inch = 25.4 mm.

FIGURE R804.3.3.1
RIDGE BOARD CONNECTION

R804.3.5 Cutting and notching. Flanges and lips of load-bearing steel roof framing members shall not be cut or notched. Holes in webs shall be in accordance with Section R804.2.

R804.3.6 Hole patching. Web holes not conforming to the requirements in Section R804.2 shall be designed in accordance with one of the following:

1. Framing members shall be replaced or designed in accordance with accepted engineering practices when web holes exceed the following size limits:

    1.1. The depth of the hole, measured across the web, exceeds 70 percent of the flat width of the web; or,

    1.2. The length of the hole, measured along the web, exceeds 10 inches (254 mm) or the depth of the web, whichever is greater.

2. Web holes not exceeding the dimensional requirements in Section R804.3.6, Item 1 shall be patched with a solid steel plate, stud section, or track section in accordance with Figure R804.3.6. The steel patch shall be of a minimum thickness as the receiving member and shall extend at least 1 inch (25 mm) beyond all edges of the hole. The steel patch shall be fastened to the web of the receiving member with No. 8 screws spaced no greater than 1 inch (25 mm) center-to-center along the edges of the patch with minimum edge distance of $^1/_2$ inch (13 mm).

R804.3.7 Splicing. Rafters and other structural members, except ceiling joists, shall not be spliced. Splices in ceiling joists shall only be permitted at interior bearing points and shall be constructed in accordance with Figure R804.3.7(1).

Spliced ceiling joists shall be connected with the same number and size of screws on connection. Splicing of tracks shall conform to Figure R804.3.7(2).

R804.3.8 Bearing stiffener. A bearing stiffener shall be fabricated from a minimum 33-mil (0.84 mm) C-section or track section. Each stiffener shall be fastened to the web of the ceiling joist with a minimum of four No. 8 screws equally spaced as shown in Figure R804.3.8. Stiffeners shall extend across the full depth of the web and shall be installed on either side of the web.

R804.3.9 Headers. Roof-ceiling framing above wall openings shall be supported on headers. The allowable spans for headers in bearing walls shall not exceed the values set forth in Table R603.6(1).

R804.3.10 Framing of opening. Openings in roof and ceiling framing shall be framed with headers and trimmers between ceiling joists or rafters. Header joist spans shall not exceed 4 feet (1219 mm). Header and trimmer joists shall be fabricated from joist and track sections, which shall be of a minimum size and thickness in accordance with Figures R804.3.10(1) and R804.3.10(2). Each header joist shall be connected to a trimmer joist with a minimum of four 2-inch by 2-inch (51 by 51 mm) clip angles. Each clip angle shall be fastened to both the header and trimmer joists with four No. 8 screws, evenly spaced, through each leg of the clip angle. The clip angles shall have a steel thickness not less than that of the floor joist.

R804.4 Roof tie-down. Roof assemblies subject to wind uplift pressures of 20 pounds per square foot (0.96 kN/m²) or greater, as established in Table R301.2(2), shall have rafter-to-bearing wall ties provided in accordance with Table R802.11.

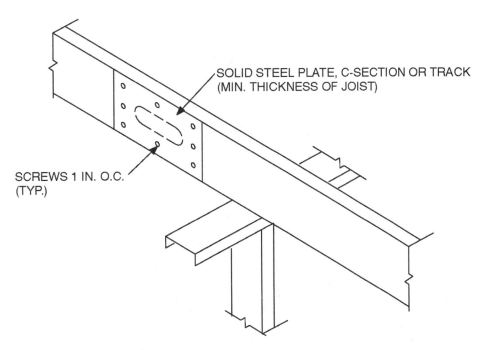

SOLID STEEL PLATE, C-SECTION OR TRACK
(MIN. THICKNESS OF JOIST)

SCREWS 1 IN. O.C.
(TYP.)

For SI: 1 inch = 25.4 mm.

FIGURE R804.3.6
HOLE PATCHING

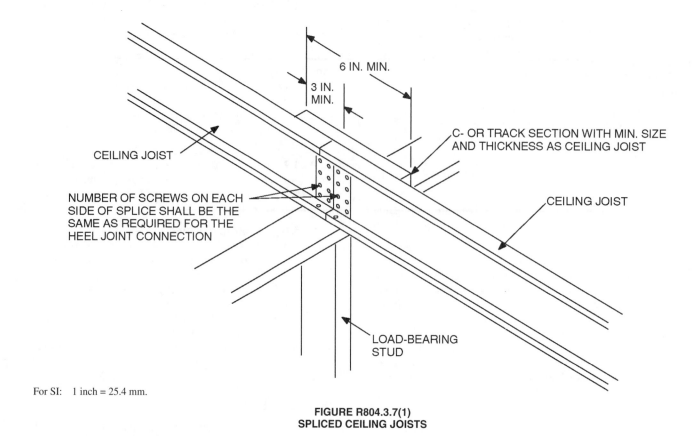

CEILING JOIST

NUMBER OF SCREWS ON EACH
SIDE OF SPLICE SHALL BE THE
SAME AS REQUIRED FOR THE
HEEL JOINT CONNECTION

6 IN. MIN.

3 IN.
MIN.

C- OR TRACK SECTION WITH MIN. SIZE
AND THICKNESS AS CEILING JOIST

CEILING JOIST

LOAD-BEARING
STUD

For SI: 1 inch = 25.4 mm.

FIGURE R804.3.7(1)
SPLICED CEILING JOISTS

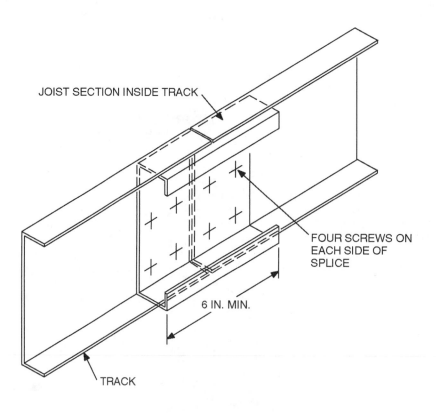

JOIST SECTION INSIDE TRACK

FOUR SCREWS ON
EACH SIDE OF
SPLICE

6 IN. MIN.

TRACK

For SI: 1 inch = 25.4 mm.

FIGURE R804.3.7(2)
TRACK SPLICE

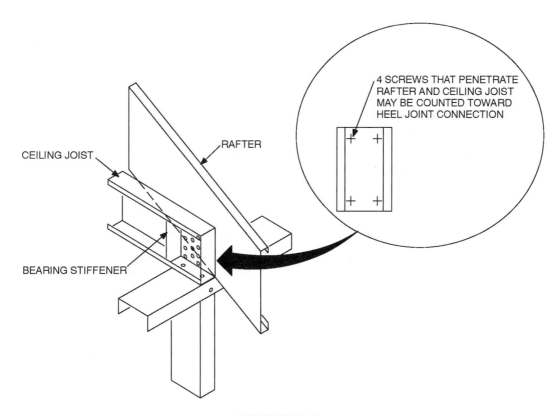

FIGURE R804.3.8
BEARING STIFFENER

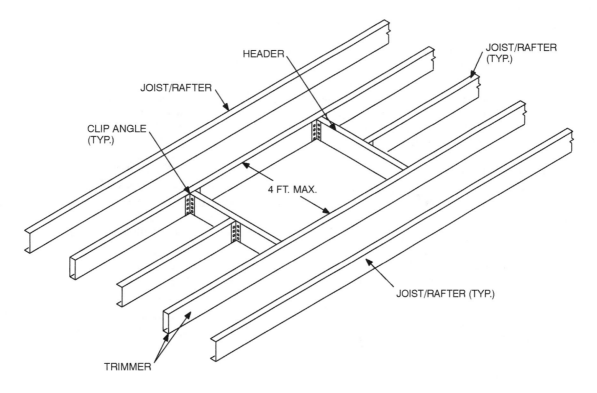

For SI: 1 foot = 304.8 mm.

FIGURE R804.3.10(1)
ROOF OPENING

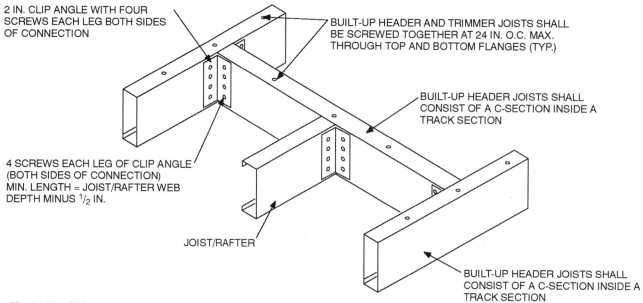

2 IN. CLIP ANGLE WITH FOUR
SCREWS EACH LEG BOTH SIDES
OF CONNECTION

BUILT-UP HEADER AND TRIMMER JOISTS SHALL
BE SCREWED TOGETHER AT 24 IN. O.C. MAX.
THROUGH TOP AND BOTTOM FLANGES (TYP.)

BUILT-UP HEADER JOISTS SHALL
CONSIST OF A C-SECTION INSIDE A
TRACK SECTION

4 SCREWS EACH LEG OF CLIP ANGLE
(BOTH SIDES OF CONNECTION)
MIN. LENGTH = JOIST/RAFTER WEB
DEPTH MINUS ¹/₂ IN.

JOIST/RAFTER

BUILT-UP HEADER JOISTS SHALL
CONSIST OF A C-SECTION INSIDE A
TRACK SECTION

For SI: 1 inch = 25.4 mm.

**FIGURE R804.3.10(2)
HEADER TO TRIMMER CONNECTION**

SECTION R805
CEILING FINISHES

R805.1 Ceiling installation. Ceilings shall be installed in accordance with the requirements for interior wall finishes as provided in Section R702.

SECTION R806
ROOF VENTILATION

R806.1 Ventilation required. Enclosed attics and enclosed rafter spaces formed where ceilings are applied directly to the underside of roof rafters shall have cross ventilation for each separate space by ventilating openings protected against the entrance of rain or snow. Ventilating openings shall be provided with corrosion-resistant wire mesh, with $^1/_8$ inch (3.2 mm) minimum to $^1/_4$ inch (6 mm) maximum openings.

R806.2 Minimum area. The total net free ventilating area shall not be less than $^1/_{150}$ of the area of the space ventilated except that reduction of the total area to $^1/_{300}$ is permitted, provided that at least 50 percent and not more than 80 percent of the required ventilating area is provided by ventilators located in the upper portion of the space to be ventilated at least 3 feet (914 mm) above the eave or cornice vents with the balance of the required ventilation provided by eave or cornice vents. As an alternative, the net free cross-ventilation area may be reduced to $^1/_{300}$ when a vapor barrier having a transmission rate not exceeding 1 perm (5.7×10^{-11} kg/s · m² · Pa) is installed on the warm-in-winter side of the ceiling.

R806.3 Vent and insulation clearance. Where eave or cornice vents are installed, insulation shall not block the free flow of air. A minimum of a 1-inch (25 mm) space shall be provided between the insulation and the roof sheathing and at the location of the vent.

SECTION R807
ATTIC ACCESS

R807.1 Attic access. Buildings with combustible ceiling or roof construction shall have an attic access opening to attic areas that exceed 30 square feet (2.8 m²) and have a vertical height of 30 inches (762 mm) or more.

The rough-framed opening shall not be less than 22 inches by 30 inches (559 mm by 762 mm) and shall be located in a hallway or other readily accessible location. A 30-inch (762 mm) minimum unobstructed headroom in the attic space shall be provided at some point above the access opening. See Section M1305.1.3 for access requirements where mechanical equipment is located in attics.

SECTION R808
INSULATION CLEARANCE

R808.1 Combustible insulation. Combustible insulation shall be separated a minimum of 3 inches (76 mm) from recessed luminaires, fan motors and other heat-producing devices.

Exception: Where heat-producing devices are listed for lesser clearances, combustible insulation complying with the listing requirements shall be separated in accordance with the conditions stipulated in the listing.

Recessed luminaires installed in the building thermal envelope shall meet the requirements of Section N1102.4.3.

CHAPTER 9
ROOF ASSEMBLIES

SECTION R901
GENERAL

R901.1 Scope. The provisions of this chapter shall govern the design, materials, construction and quality of roof assemblies.

SECTION R902
ROOF CLASSIFICATION

R902.1 Roofing covering materials. Roofs shall be covered with materials as set forth in Sections R904 and R905. Class A, B or C roofing shall be installed in areas designated by law as requiring their use or when the edge of the roof is less than 3 feet (914 mm) from a property line. Classes A, B and C roofing required to be listed by this section shall be tested in accordance with UL 790 or ASTM E 108. Roof assemblies with coverings of brick, masonry, slate, clay or concrete roof tile, exposed concrete roof deck, ferrous or copper shingles or sheets, and metal sheets and shingles, shall be considered Class A roof coverings.

R902.2 Fire-retardant-treated shingles and shakes. Fire-retardant-treated wood shakes and shingles shall be treated by impregnation with chemicals by the full-cell vacuum-pressure process, in accordance with AWPA C1. Each bundle shall be marked to identify the manufactured unit and the manufacturer, and shall also be labeled to identify the classification of the material in accordance with the testing required in Section R902.1, the treating company and the quality control agency.

SECTION R903
WEATHER PROTECTION

R903.1 General. Roof decks shall be covered with approved roof coverings secured to the building or structure in accordance with the provisions of this chapter. Roof assemblies shall be designed and installed in accordance with this code and the approved manufacturer's installation instructions such that the roof assembly shall serve to protect the building or structure.

R903.2 Flashing. Flashings shall be installed in a manner that prevents moisture from entering the wall and roof through joints in copings, through moisture permeable materials and at intersections with parapet walls and other penetrations through the roof plane.

R903.2.1 Locations. Flashings shall be installed at wall and roof intersections, wherever there is a change in roof slope or direction and around roof openings. Where flashing is of metal, the metal shall be corrosion resistant with a thickness of not less than 0.019 inch (0.5 mm) (No. 26 galvanized sheet).

R903.2.2 Kick-out flashing/diverter. A kick-out flashing shall be installed where the lower portion of a sloped roof stops within the plane of an intersecting wall cladding, in such a manner as to divert or kick out water away from the assembly.

R903.3 Coping. Parapet walls shall be properly coped with noncombustible, weatherproof materials of a width no less than the thickness of the parapet wall.

R903.4 Roof drainage. Unless roofs are sloped to drain over roof edges, roof drains shall be installed at each low point of the roof. Where required for roof drainage, scuppers shall be placed level with the roof surface in a wall or parapet. The scupper shall be located as determined by the roof slope and contributing roof area.

R903.4.1 Overflow drains and scuppers. Where roof drains are required, overflow drains having the same size as the roof drains shall be installed with the inlet flow line located 2 inches (51 mm) above the low point of the roof, or overflow scuppers having three times the size of the roof drains and having a minimum opening height of 4 inches (102 mm) shall be installed in the adjacent parapet walls with the inlet flow located 2 inches (51 mm) above the low point of the roof served. The installation and sizing of overflow drains, leaders and conductors shall comply with the *International Plumbing Code*.

Overflow drains shall discharge to an approved location and shall not be connected to roof drain lines.

R903.5 Hail exposure. Hail exposure, as specified in Sections R903.5.1 and R903.5.2, shall be determined using Figure R903.5.

R903.5.1 Moderate hail exposure. One or more hail days with hail diameters larger than 1.5 inches (38 mm) in a 20-year period.

R903.5.2 Severe hail exposure. One or more hail days with hail diameters larger than or equal to 2.0 inches (51 mm) in a 20-year period.

SECTION R904
MATERIALS

R904.1 Scope. The requirements set forth in this section shall apply to the application of roof covering materials specified herein. Roof assemblies shall be applied in accordance with this chapter and the manufacturer's installation instructions. Installation of roof assemblies shall comply with the applicable provisions of Section R905.

R904.2 Compatibility of materials. Roof assemblies shall be of materials that are compatible with each other and with the building or structure to which the materials are applied.

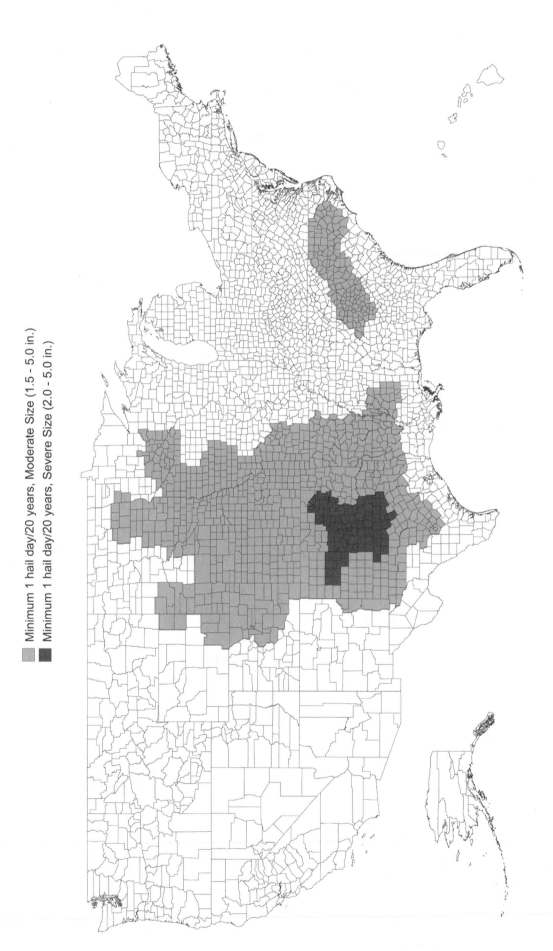

Minimum 1 hail day/20 years, Moderate Size (1.5 - 5.0 in.)

Minimum 1 hail day/20 years, Severe Size (2.0 - 5.0 in.)

FIGURE R903.5
HAIL EXPOSURE MAP

R904.3 Material specifications and physical characteristics. Roof covering materials shall conform to the applicable standards listed in this chapter. In the absence of applicable standards or where materials are of questionable suitability, testing by an approved testing agency shall be required by the building official to determine the character, quality and limitations of application of the materials.

R904.4 Product identification. Roof covering materials shall be delivered in packages bearing the manufacturer's identifying marks and approved testing agency labels when required. Bulk shipments of materials shall be accompanied by the same information issued in the form of a certificate or on a bill of lading by the manufacturer.

SECTION R905
REQUIREMENTS FOR ROOF COVERINGS

R905.1 Roof covering application. Roof coverings shall be applied in accordance with the applicable provisions of this section and the manufacturer's installation instructions. Unless otherwise specified in this section, roof coverings shall be installed to resist the component and cladding loads specified in Table R301.2(2), adjusted for height and exposure in accordance with Table R301.2(3).

R905.2 Asphalt shingles. The installation of asphalt shingles shall comply with the provisions of this section.

R905.2.1 Sheathing requirements. Asphalt shingles shall be fastened to solidly sheathed decks or 1 inch thick nominal wood boards.

R905.2.2 Slope. Asphalt shingles shall be used only on roof slopes of two units vertical in 12 units horizontal (2:12) or greater. For roof slopes from two units vertical in 12 units horizontal (2:12) up to four units vertical in 12 units horizontal (4:12), double underlayment application is required in accordance with Section R905.2.7.

R905.2.3 Underlayment. Unless otherwise noted, required underlayment shall conform to ASTM D 226 Type I, ASTM D 4869 Type I, or ASTM D 6757.

Self-adhering polymer modified bitumen sheet shall comply with ASTM D 1970.

R905.2.4 Asphalt shingles. Asphalt shingles shall have self-seal strips or be interlocking, and comply with ASTM D 225 or D 3462.

R905.2.4.1 Wind resistance of asphalt shingles. Asphalt shingles shall be installed in accordance with Section R905.2.6. Shingles classified using ASTM D 3161 are acceptable for use in wind zones less than 110 mph (49 m/s). Shingles classified using ASTM D 3161, Class F, are acceptable for use in all cases where special fastening is required.

R905.2.5 Fasteners. Fasteners for asphalt shingles shall be galvanized steel, stainless steel, aluminum or copper roofing nails, minimum 12 gage [0.105 inch (3 mm)] shank with a minimum $^3/_8$-inch (10 mm) diameter head, ASTM F 1667, of a length to penetrate through the roofing materials and a minimum of $^3/_4$ inch (19 mm) into the roof sheathing. Where the roof sheathing is less than $^3/_4$ inch (19 mm) thick, the fasteners shall penetrate through the sheathing. Fasteners shall comply with ASTM F 1667.

R905.2.6 Attachment. Asphalt shingles shall have the minimum number of fasteners required by the manufacturer. For normal application, asphalt shingles shall be secured to the roof with not less than four fasteners per strip shingle or two fasteners per individual shingle. Where the roof slope exceeds 20 units vertical in 12 units horizontal (167 percent slope), special methods of fastening are required. For roofs located where the basic wind speed per Figure R301.2(4) is 110 mph (49 m/s) or higher, special methods of fastening are required. Special fastening methods shall be tested in accordance with ASTM D 3161, Class F. Asphalt shingle wrappers shall bear a label indicating compliance with ASTM D 3161, Class F.

R905.2.7 Underlayment application. For roof slopes from two units vertical in 12 units horizontal (17-percent slope), up to four units vertical in 12 units horizontal (33-percent slope), underlayment shall be two layers applied in the following manner. Apply a 19-inch (483 mm) strip of underlayment felt parallel to and starting at the eaves, fastened sufficiently to hold in place. Starting at the eave, apply 36-inch-wide (914 mm) sheets of underlayment, overlapping successive sheets 19 inches (483 mm), and fastened sufficiently to hold in place. Distortions in the underlayment shall not interfere with the ability of the shingles to seal. For roof slopes of four units vertical in 12 units horizontal (33-percent slope) or greater, underlayment shall be one layer applied in the following manner. Underlayment shall be applied shingle fashion, parallel to and starting from the eave and lapped 2 inches (51 mm), fastened sufficiently to hold in place. Distortions in the underlayment shall not interfere with the ability of the shingles to seal. End laps shall be offset by 6 feet (1829 mm).

R905.2.7.1 Ice barrier. In areas where there has been a history of ice forming along the eaves causing a backup of water as designated in Table R301.2(1), an ice barrier that consists of a least two layers of underlayment cemented together or of a self-adhering polymer modified bitumen sheet, shall be used in lieu of normal underlayment and extend from the lowest edges of all roof surfaces to a point at least 24 inches (610 mm) inside the exterior wall line of the building.

Exception: Detached accessory structures that contain no conditioned floor area.

R905.2.7.2 Underlayment and high wind. Underlayment applied in areas subject to high winds [above 110 mph (49 m/s) per Figure R301.2(4)] shall be applied with corrosion-resistant fasteners in accordance with manufacturer's installation instructions. Fasteners are to be applied along the overlap not farther apart than 36 inches (914 mm) on center.

R905.2.8 Flashing. Flashing for asphalt shingles shall comply with this section.

R905.2.8.1 Base and cap flashing. Base and cap flashing shall be installed in accordance with manufacturer's installation instructions. Base flashing shall be of either corrosion-resistant metal of minimum nominal 0.019-inch (0.5 mm) thickness or mineral surface roll roofing weighing a minimum of 77 pounds per 100 square feet (4 kg/m²). Cap flashing shall be corrosion-resistant metal of minimum nominal 0.019-inch (0.5 mm) thickness.

R905.2.8.2 Valleys. Valley linings shall be installed in accordance with the manufacturer's installation instructions before applying shingles. Valley linings of the following types shall be permitted:

1. For open valley (valley lining exposed) lined with metal, the valley lining shall be at least 24 inches (610 mm) wide and of any of the corrosion-resistant metals in Table R905.2.8.2.

2. For open valleys, valley lining of two plies of mineral surfaced roll roofing, complying with ASTM D 3909 or ASTM D 6380 Class M, shall be permitted. The bottom layer shall be 18 inches (457mm) and the top layer a minimum of 36 inches (914 mm) wide.

3. For closed valleys (valley covered with shingles), valley lining of one ply of smooth roll roofing complying with ASTM D 6380 Class S Type III, Class M Type II, or ASTM D 3909 and at least 36 inches wide (914 mm) or valley lining as described in Items 1 and 2 above shall be permitted. Specialty underlayment complying with ASTM D 1970 may be used in lieu of the lining material.

TABLE R905.2.8.2
VALLEY LINING MATERIAL

MATERIAL	MINIMUM THICKNESS (inches)	GAGE	WEIGHT (pounds)
Cold–rolled copper	0.0216 nominal	—	ASTM B 370, 16 oz. per square foot
Lead–coated copper	0.0216 nominal	—	ASTM B 101, 16 oz. per square foot
High–yield copper	0.0162 nominal	—	ASTM B 370, 12 oz. per square foot
Lead–coated high–yield copper	0.0162 nominal	—	ASTM B 101, 12 oz. per square foot
Aluminum	0.024	—	—
Stainless steel	—	28	—
Galvanized steel	0.0179	26 (zinc coated G90)	—
Zinc alloy	0.027	—	—
Lead	—	—	2¹/₂
Painted terne	—	—	20

For SI: 1 inch = 25.4 mm, 1 pound = 0.454 kg.

R905.2.8.3 Crickets and saddles. A cricket or saddle shall be installed on the ridge side of any chimney or penetration more than 30 inches (762 mm) wide as measured perpendicular to the slope. Cricket or saddle coverings shall be sheet metal or of the same material as the roof covering.

R905.2.8.4 Sidewall flashing. Flashing against a vertical sidewall shall be by the step-flashing method.

R905.2.8.5 Other flashing. Flashing against a vertical front wall, as well as soil stack, vent pipe and chimney flashing, shall be applied according to the asphalt shingle manufacturer's printed instructions.

R905.3 Clay and concrete tile. The installation of clay and concrete shall comply with the provisions of this section. Clay roof tile shall comply with ASTM C 1167.

R905.3.1 Deck requirements. Concrete and clay tile shall be installed only over solid sheathing or spaced structural sheathing boards.

R905.3.2 Deck slope. Clay and concrete roof tile shall be installed on roof slopes of two and one-half units vertical in 12 units horizontal (2¹/₂:12) or greater. For roof slopes from two and one-half units vertical in 12 units horizontal (2¹/₂:12) to four units vertical in 12 units horizontal (4:12), double underlayment application is required in accordance with Section R905.3.3.

R905.3.3 Underlayment. Unless otherwise noted, required underlayment shall conform to ASTM D 226 Type II; ASTM D 2626 Type I; or ASTM D 6380 Class M mineral surfaced roll roofing.

R905.3.3.1 Low slope roofs. For roof slopes from two and one-half units vertical in 12 units horizontal (2¹/₂:12), up to four units vertical in 12 units horizontal (4:12), underlayment shall be a minimum of two layers underlayment applied as follows:

1. Starting at the eave, a 19-inch (483 mm) strip of underlayment shall be applied parallel with the eave and fastened sufficiently in place.

2. Starting at the eave, 36-inch-wide (914 mm) strips of underlayment felt shall be applied, overlapping successive sheets 19 inches (483 mm), and fastened sufficiently in place.

R905.3.3.2 High slope roofs. For roof slopes of four units vertical in 12 units horizontal (4:12) or greater, underlayment shall be a minimum of one layer of underlayment felt applied shingle fashion, parallel to and starting from the eaves and lapped 2 inches (51 mm), fastened sufficiently in place.

R905.3.3.3 Underlayment and high wind. Underlayment applied in areas subject to high wind [over 110 miles per hour (49 m/s) per Figure R301.2(4)] shall be applied with corrosion-resistant fasteners in accordance with manufacturer's installation instructions. Fasteners are to be applied along the overlap not farther apart than 36 inches (914 mm) on center.

R905.3.4 Tile. Clay roof tile shall comply with ASTM C 1167.

R905.3.5 Concrete tile. Concrete roof tile shall comply with ASTM C 1492.

R905.3.6 Fasteners. Nails shall be corrosion resistant and not less than 11 gage, $^5/_{16}$-inch (11 mm) head, and of sufficient length to penetrate the deck a minimum of $^3/_4$ inch (19 mm) or through the thickness of the deck, whichever is less. Attaching wire for clay or concrete tile shall not be smaller than 0.083 inch (2 mm). Perimeter fastening areas include three tile courses but not less than 36 inches (914 mm) from either side of hips or ridges and edges of eaves and gable rakes.

R905.3.7 Application. Tile shall be applied in accordance with this chapter and the manufacturer's installation instructions, based on the following:

1. Climatic conditions.

2. Roof slope.

3. Underlayment system.

4. Type of tile being installed.

Clay and concrete roof tiles shall be fastened in accordance with this section and the manufacturer's installation instructions. Perimeter tiles shall be fastened with a minimum of one fastener per tile. Tiles with installed weight less than 9 pounds per square foot (0.4 kg/m^2) require a minimum of one fastener per tile regardless of roof slope. Clay and concrete roof tile attachment shall be in accordance with the manufacturer's installation instructions where applied in areas where the wind speed exceeds 100 miles per hour (45 m/s) and on buildings where the roof is located more than 40 feet (12 192 mm) above grade. In areas subject to snow, a minimum of two fasteners per tile is required. In all other areas, clay and concrete roof tiles shall be attached in accordance with Table R905.3.7.

TABLE R905.3.7
CLAY AND CONCRETE TILE ATTACHMENT

SHEATHING	ROOF SLOPE	NUMBER OF FASTENERS
Solid without battens	All	One per tile
Spaced or solid with battens and slope < 5:12	Fasteners not required	—
Spaced sheathing without battens	5:12 ≤ slope < 12:12	One per tile/every other row
	12:12 ≤ slope < 24:12	One per tile

R905.3.8 Flashing. At the juncture of roof vertical surfaces, flashing and counterflashing shall be provided in accordance with this chapter and the manufacturer's installation instructions and, where of metal, shall not be less than 0.019 inch (0.5 mm) (No. 26 galvanized sheet gage) corrosion-resistant metal. The valley flashing shall extend at least 11 inches (279 mm) from the centerline each way and have a splash diverter rib not less than 1 inch (25 mm) high at the flow line formed as part of the flashing. Sections of flashing shall have an end lap of not less than 4 inches (102 mm). For roof slopes of three units vertical in 12 units horizontal (25-percent slope) and greater, valley flashing shall have a 36-inch-wide (914 mm) underlayment of one layer of Type I underlayment running the full length of the valley, in addition to other required underlayment. In areas where the average daily temperature in January is 25°F (-4°C) or less, metal valley flashing underlayment shall be solid-cemented to the roofing underlayment for slopes less than seven units vertical in 12 units horizontal (58-percent slope) or be of self-adhering polymer modified bitumen sheet.

R905.4 Metal roof shingles. The installation of metal roof shingles shall comply with the provisions of this section.

R905.4.1 Deck requirements. Metal roof shingles shall be applied to a solid or closely fitted deck, except where the roof covering is specifically designed to be applied to spaced sheathing.

R905.4.2 Deck slope. Metal roof shingles shall not be installed on roof slopes below three units vertical in 12 units horizontal (25-percent slope).

R905.4.3 Underlayment. Underlayment shall comply with ASTM D 226, Type I or ASTM D 4869, Type I or II.

R905.4.3.1 Ice barrier. In areas where there has been a history of ice forming along the eaves causing a backup of water as designated in Table R301.2(1), an ice barrier that consists of at least two layers of underlayment cemented together or a self-adhering polymer modified bitumen sheet shall be used in place of normal underlayment and extend from the lowest edges of all roof surfaces to a point at least 24 inches (610 mm) inside the exterior wall line of the building.

Exception: Detached accessory structures that contain no conditioned floor area.

R905.4.4 Material standards. Metal roof shingle roof coverings shall comply with Table R905.10.3(1). The materials used for metal roof shingle roof coverings shall be naturally corrosion resistant or be made corrosion resistant in accordance with the standards and minimum thicknesses listed in Table R905.10.3(2).

R905.4.5 Application. Metal roof shingles shall be secured to the roof in accordance with this chapter and the approved manufacturer's installation instructions.

R905.4.6 Flashing. Roof valley flashing shall be of corrosion-resistant metal of the same material as the roof covering or shall comply with the standards in Table R905.10.3(1). The valley flashing shall extend at least 8 inches (203 mm) from the center line each way and shall have a splash diverter rib not less than $^3/_4$ inch (19 mm) high at the flow line formed as part of the flashing. Sections of flashing shall have an end lap of not less than 4 inches (102 mm). The metal valley flashing shall have a 36-inch-wide (914 mm) underlayment directly under it consisting of one layer of underlayment running the full length of the valley, in addition to underlayment required for metal roof shingles. In areas where the average daily temperature in January is 25°F (-4°C) or less, the metal valley flashing underlayment shall be solid cemented to the roofing underlayment for roof slopes under seven units vertical in 12 units horizontal (58-percent slope) or self-adhering polymer modified bitumen sheet.

R905.5 Mineral-surfaced roll roofing. The installation of mineral-surfaced roll roofing shall comply with this section.

R905.5.1 Deck requirements. Mineral-surfaced roll roofing shall be fastened to solidly sheathed roofs.

R905.5.2 Deck slope. Mineral-surfaced roll roofing shall not be applied on roof slopes below one unit vertical in 12 units horizontal (8-percent slope).

R905.5.3 Underlayment. Underlayment shall comply with ASTM D 226, Type I or ASTM D 4869, Type I or II.

R905.5.3.1 Ice barrier. In areas where there has been a history of ice forming along the eaves causing a backup of water as designated in Table R301.2(1), an ice barrier that consists of at least two layers of underlayment cemented together or a self-adhering polymer modified bitumen sheet shall be used in place of normal underlayment and extend from the lowest edges of all roof surfaces to a point at least 24 inches (610 mm) inside the exterior wall line of the building.

Exception: Detached accessory structures that contain no conditioned floor area.

R905.5.4 Material standards. Mineral-surfaced roll roofing shall conform to ASTM D 3909 or ASTM D 6380, Class M.

R905.5.5 Application. Mineral-surfaced roll roofing shall be installed in accordance with this chapter and the manufacturer's installation instructions.

R905.6 Slate and slate-type shingles. The installation of slate and slate-type shingles shall comply with the provisions of this section.

R905.6.1 Deck requirements. Slate shingles shall be fastened to solidly sheathed roofs.

R905.6.2 Deck slope. Slate shingles shall be used only on slopes of four units vertical in 12 units horizontal (33-percent slope) or greater.

R905.6.3 Underlayment. Underlayment shall comply with ASTM D 226, Type I or ASTM D 4869, Type I or II.

R905.6.3.1 Ice barrier. In areas where there has been a history of ice forming along the eaves causing a backup of water as designated in Table R301.2(1), an ice barrier that consists of at least two layers of underlayment cemented together or a self-adhering polymer modified bitumen sheet shall be used in lieu of normal underlayment and extend from the lowest edges of all roof surfaces to a point at least 24 inches (610 mm) inside the exterior wall line of the building.

Exception: Detached accessory structures that contain no conditioned floor area.

R905.6.4 Material standards. Slate shingles shall comply with ASTM C 406.

R905.6.5 Application. Minimum headlap for slate shingles shall be in accordance with Table R905.6.5. Slate shingles shall be secured to the roof with two fasteners per slate. Slate shingles shall be installed in accordance with this chapter and the manufacturer's installation instructions.

TABLE R905.6.5
SLATE SHINGLE HEADLAP

SLOPE	HEADLAP (inches)
4:12 ≤ slope < 8:12	4
8:12 ≤ slope < 20:12	3
Slope ≤ 20:12	2

For SI: 1 inch = 25.4 mm.

R905.6.6 Flashing. Flashing and counterflashing shall be made with sheet metal. Valley flashing shall be a minimum of 15 inches (381 mm) wide. Valley and flashing metal shall be a minimum uncoated thickness of 0.0179-inch (0.5 mm) zinc coated G90. Chimneys, stucco or brick walls shall have a minimum of two plies of felt for a cap flashing consisting of a 4-inch-wide (102 mm) strip of felt set in plastic cement and extending 1 inch (25 mm) above the first felt and a top coating of plastic cement. The felt shall extend over the base flashing 2 inches (51 mm).

R905.7 Wood shingles. The installation of wood shingles shall comply with the provisions of this section.

R905.7.1 Deck requirements. Wood shingles shall be installed on solid or spaced sheathing. Where spaced sheathing is used, sheathing boards shall not be less than 1-inch by 4-inch (25.4 mm by 102 mm) nominal dimensions and shall be spaced on centers equal to the weather exposure to coincide with the placement of fasteners.

R905.7.1.1 Solid sheathing required. In areas where the average daily temperature in January is 25°F (-4°C) or less, solid sheathing is required on that portion of the roof requiring the application of an ice barrier.

R905.7.2 Deck slope. Wood shingles shall be installed on slopes of three units vertical in 12 units horizontal (25-percent slope) or greater.

R905.7.3 Underlayment. Underlayment shall comply with ASTM D 226, Type I or ASTM D 4869, Type I or II.

R905.7.3.1 Ice barrier. In areas where there has been a history of ice forming along the eaves causing a backup of water as designated in Table R301.2(1), an ice barrier that consists of at least two layers of underlayment cemented together or a self-adhering polymer modified bitumen sheet shall be used in lieu of normal underlayment and extend from the lowest edges of all roof surfaces to a point at least 24 inches (610 mm) inside the exterior wall line of the building.

Exception: Detached accessory structures that contain no conditioned floor area.

R905.7.4 Material standards. Wood shingles shall be of naturally durable wood and comply with the requirements of Table R905.7.4.

TABLE R905.7.4
WOOD SHINGLE MATERIAL REQUIREMENTS

MATERIAL	MINIMUM GRADES	APPLICABLE GRADING RULES
Wood shingles of naturally durable wood	1, 2 or 3	Cedar Shake and Shingle Bureau

R905.7.5 Application. Wood shingles shall be installed according to this chapter and the manufacturer's installation instructions. Wood shingles shall be laid with a side lap not less than $1^{1}/_{2}$ inches (38 mm) between joints in courses, and no two joints in any three adjacent courses shall be in direct alignment. Spacing between shingles shall not be less than $^{1}/_{4}$ inch to $^{3}/_{8}$ inch (6 mm to 10 mm). Weather exposure for wood shingles shall not exceed those set in Table R905.7.5. Fasteners for wood shingles shall be corrosion resistant with a minimum penetration of $^{1}/_{2}$ inch (13 mm) into the sheathing. For sheathing less than $^{1}/_{2}$ inch (13 mm) in thickness, the fasteners shall extend through the sheathing. Wood shingles shall be attached to the roof with two fasteners per shingle, positioned no more than $^{3}/_{4}$ inch (19 mm) from each edge and no more than 1 inch (25 mm) above the exposure line.

TABLE R905.7.5
WOOD SHINGLE WEATHER EXPOSURE AND ROOF SLOPE

ROOFING MATERIAL	LENGTH (inches)	GRADE	EXPOSURE (inches)	
			3:12 pitch to < 4:12	4:12 pitch or steeper
Shingles of naturally durable wood	16	No. 1	$3^{3}/_{4}$	5
		No. 2	$3^{1}/_{2}$	4
		No. 3	3	$3^{1}/_{2}$
	18	No. 1	$4^{1}/_{4}$	$5^{1}/_{2}$
		No. 2	4	$4^{1}/_{2}$
		No. 3	$3^{1}/_{2}$	4
	24	No. 1	$5^{3}/_{4}$	$7^{1}/_{2}$
		No. 2	$5^{1}/_{2}$	$6^{1}/_{2}$
		No. 3	5	$5^{1}/_{2}$

For SI: 1 inch = 25.4 mm.

R905.7.6 Valley flashing. Roof flashing shall be not less than No. 26 gage [0.019 inches (0.5 mm)] corrosion-resistant sheet metal and shall extend 10 inches (254 mm) from the centerline each way for roofs having slopes less than 12 units vertical in 12 units horizontal (100-percent slope), and 7 inches (178 mm) from the centerline each way for slopes of 12 units vertical in 12 units horizontal and greater. Sections of flashing shall have an end lap of not less than 4 inches (102 mm).

R905.7.7 Label required. Each bundle of shingles shall be identified by a label of an approved grading or inspection bureau or agency.

R905.8 Wood shakes. The installation of wood shakes shall comply with the provisions of this section.

R905.8.1 Deck requirements. Wood shakes shall be used only on solid or spaced sheathing. Where spaced sheathing is used, sheathing boards shall not be less than 1-inch by 4-inch (25 mm by 102 mm) nominal dimensions and shall be spaced on centers equal to the weather exposure to coincide with the placement of fasteners. Where 1-inch by 4-inch (25 mm by 102 mm) spaced sheathing is installed at 10 inches (254 mm) on center, additional 1-inch by 4-inch (25 mm by 102 mm) boards shall be installed between the sheathing boards.

R905.8.1.1 Solid sheathing required. In areas where the average daily temperature in January is 25°F (-4°C) or less, solid sheathing is required on that portion of the roof requiring an ice barrier.

R905.8.2 Deck slope. Wood shakes shall only be used on slopes of three units vertical in 12 units horizontal (25-percent slope) or greater.

R905.8.3 Underlayment. Underlayment shall comply with ASTM D 226, Type I or ASTM D 4869, Type I or II.

R905.8.3.1 Ice barrier. In areas where there has been a history of ice forming along the eaves causing a backup of water as designated in Table R301.2(1), an ice barrier that consists of at least two layers of underlayment cemented together or a self-adhering polymer modified bitumen sheet shall be used in place of normal underlayment and extend from the lowest edges of all roof surfaces to a point at least 24 inches (610 mm) inside the exterior wall line of the building.

> **Exception:** Detached accessory structures that contain no conditioned floor area.

R905.8.4 Interlayment. Interlayment shall comply with ASTM D 226, Type I.

R905.8.5 Material standards. Wood shakes shall comply with the requirements of Table R905.8.5.

TABLE R905.8.5
WOOD SHAKE MATERIAL REQUIREMENTS

MATERIAL	MINIMUM GRADES	APPLICABLE GRADING RULES
Wood shakes of naturally durable wood	1	Cedar Shake and Shingle Bureau
Taper sawn shakes of naturally durable wood	1 or 2	Cedar Shake and Shingle Bureau
Preservative-treated shakes and shingles of naturally durable wood	1	Cedar Shake and Shingle Bureau
Fire-retardant-treated shakes and shingles of naturally durable wood	1	Cedar Shake and Shingle Bureau
Preservative-treated taper sawn shakes of Southern pine treated in accordance with AWPA Standard U1 (Commodity Specification A, Use Category 3B and Section 5.6)	1 or 2	Forest Products Laboratory of the Texas Forest Services

R905.8.6 Application. Wood shakes shall be installed according to this chapter and the manufacturer's installation instructions. Wood shakes shall be laid with a side lap not less than $1^{1}/_{2}$ inches (38 mm) between joints in adjacent courses. Spacing between shakes in the same course shall be $^{1}/_{8}$ inch to $^{5}/_{8}$ inch (3 mm to 16 mm) for shakes and tapersawn shakes of naturally durable wood and shall be $^{1}/_{4}$ inch to $^{3}/_{8}$ inch (6 mm to 10 mm) for preservative treated taper sawn shakes. Weather exposure for wood shakes shall not exceed those set forth in Table R905.8.6. Fasteners for wood shakes shall be corrosion-resistant, with a minimum penetration of $^1/_2$ inch (12.7 mm) into the sheathing. For sheathing less than $^1/_2$ inch (12.7 mm) in thickness, the fasteners shall extend through the sheathing. Wood shakes shall be attached to the roof with two fasteners per shake, positioned no more than 1 inch (25 mm) from each edge and no more than 2 inches (51 mm) above the exposure line.

R905.8.7 Shake placement. The starter course at the eaves shall be doubled and the bottom layer shall be either 15-inch (381 mm), 18-inch (457 mm) or 24-inch (610 mm) wood shakes or wood shingles. Fifteen-inch (381 mm) or 18-inch (457 mm) wood shakes may be used for the final course at the ridge. Shakes shall be interlaid with 18-inch-wide (457 mm) strips of not less than No. 30 felt shingled between each course in such a manner that no felt is exposed to the weather by positioning the lower edge of each felt strip above the butt end of the shake it covers a distance equal to twice the weather exposure.

TABLE R905.8.6
WOOD SHAKE WEATHER EXPOSURE AND ROOF SLOPE

ROOFING MATERIAL	LENGTH (inches)	GRADE	EXPOSURE (inches) 4:12 pitch or steeper
Shakes of naturally durable wood	18	No. 1	$7^1/_2$
	24	No. 1	10^a
Preservative-treated taper sawn shakes of Southern Yellow Pine	18	No. 1	$7^1/_2$
	24	No. 1	10
	18	No. 2	$5^1/_2$
	24	No. 2	$7^1/_2$
Taper-sawn shakes of naturally durable wood	18	No. 1	$7^1/_2$
	24	No. 1	10
	18	No. 2	$5^1/_2$
	24	No. 2	$7^1/_2$

For SI: 1 inch = 25.4 mm.

a. For 24-inch by $^3/_8$-inch handsplit shakes, the maximum exposure is $7^1/_2$ inches.

R905.8.8 Valley flashing. Roof valley flashing shall not be less than No. 26 gage [0.019 inch (0.5 mm)] corrosion-resistant sheet metal and shall extend at least 11 inches (279 mm) from the centerline each way. Sections of flashing shall have an end lap of not less than 4 inches (102 mm).

R905.8.9 Label required. Each bundle of shakes shall be identified by a label of an approved grading or inspection bureau or agency.

R905.9 Built-up roofs. The installation of built-up roofs shall comply with the provisions of this section.

R905.9.1 Slope. Built-up roofs shall have a design slope of a minimum of one-fourth unit vertical in 12 units horizontal (2-percent slope) for drainage, except for coal-tar built-up roofs, which shall have a design slope of a minimum one- eighth unit vertical in 12 units horizontal (1-percent slope).

R905.9.2 Material standards. Built-up roof covering materials shall comply with the standards in Table R905.9.2.

R905.9.3 Application. Built-up roofs shall be installed according to this chapter and the manufacturer's installation instructions.

R905.10 Metal roof panels. The installation of metal roof panels shall comply with the provisions of this section.

R905.10.1 Deck requirements. Metal roof panel roof coverings shall be applied to solid or spaced sheathing, except where the roof covering is specifically designed to be applied to spaced supports.

R905.10.2 Slope. Minimum slopes for metal roof panels shall comply with the following:

1. The minimum slope for lapped, nonsoldered-seam metal roofs without applied lap sealant shall be three units vertical in 12 units horizontal (25-percent slope).

2. The minimum slope for lapped, nonsoldered-seam metal roofs with applied lap sealant shall be one-half vertical unit in 12 units horizontal (4-percent slope). Lap sealants shall be applied in accordance with the approved manufacturer's installation instructions.

3. The minimum slope for standing-seam roof systems shall be one-quarter unit vertical in 12 units horizontal (2-percent slope).

R905.10.3 Material standards. Metal-sheet roof covering systems that incorporate supporting structural members shall be designed in accordance with the *International Building Code*. Metal-sheet roof coverings installed over structural decking shall comply with Table R905.10.3(1). The materials used for metal-sheet roof coverings shall be naturally corrosion resistant or provided with corrosion resistance in accordance with the standards and minimum thicknesses shown in Table R905.10.3(2).

R905.10.4 Attachment. Metal roof panels shall be secured to the supports in accordance with this chapter and the manufacturer's installation instructions. In the absence of manufacturer's installation instructions, the following fasteners shall be used:

1. Galvanized fasteners shall be used for steel roofs.

2. Three hundred series stainless steel fasteners shall be used for copper roofs.

3. Stainless steel fasteners are acceptable for metal roofs.

TABLE R905.9.2
BUILT-UP ROOFING MATERIAL STANDARDS

MATERIAL STANDARD	STANDARD
Acrylic coatings used in roofing	ASTM D 6083
Aggregate surfacing	ASTM D 1863
Asphalt adhesive used in roofing	ASTM D 3747
Asphalt cements used in roofing	ASTM D 3019; D 2822; D 4586
Asphalt-coated glass fiber base sheet	ASTM D 4601
Asphalt coatings used in roofing	ASTM D 1227; D 2823; D 2824; D 4479
Asphalt glass felt	ASTM D 2178
Asphalt primer used in roofing	ASTM D 41
Asphalt-saturated and asphalt-coated organic felt base sheet	ASTM D 2626
Asphalt-saturated organic felt (perforated)	ASTM D 226
Asphalt used in roofing	ASTM D 312
Coal tar cements used in roofing	ASTM D 4022; D 5643
Coal-tar primer used in roofing, dampproofing and waterproofing	ASTM D 43
Coal-tar saturated organic felt	ASTM D 227
Coal-tar used in roofing	ASTM D 450, Types I or II
Glass mat, coal tar	ASTM D 4990
Glass mat, venting type	ASTM D 4897
Mineral-surfaced inorganic cap sheet	ASTM D 3909
Thermoplastic fabrics used in roofing	ASTM D 5665; D 5726

TABLE R905.10.3(1)
METAL ROOF COVERINGS STANDARDS

ROOF COVERING TYPE	STANDARD APPLICATION RATE/THICKNESS
Galvanized Steel	ASTM A 653 G90 Zinc Coated
Stainless Steel	ASTM A 240, 300 Series Alloys
Steel	ASTM A 924
Lead-coated Copper	ASTM B 101
Cold Rolled Copper	ASTM B 370 minimum 16 oz/square ft and 12 oz/square ft high yield copper for metal-sheet roof-covering systems; 12 oz/square ft for preformed metal shingle systems.
Hard Lead	2 lb/ sq ft
Soft Lead	3 lb/ sq ft
Aluminum	ASTM B 209, 0.024 minimum thickness for rollformed panels and 0.019 inch minimum thickness for pressformed shingles.
Terne (tin) and terne-coated stainless	Terne coating of 40 lb per double base box, field painted where applicable in accordance with manufacturer's installation instructions.
Zinc	0.027 inch minimum thickness: 99.995% electrolytic high grade zinc with alloy additives of copper (0.08 - 0.20%), titanium (0.07% - 0.12%) and aluminum (0.015%).

For SI: 1 ounce per square foot = 0.305 kg/m^2, 1 pound per square foot = 4.214 kg/m^2, 1 inch = 25.4 mm, 1 pound = 0.454 kg.

R905.11 Modified bitumen roofing. The installation of modified bitumen roofing shall comply with the provisions of this section.

TABLE R905.10.3(2)
MINIMUM CORROSION RESISTANCE

55% Aluminum-zinc alloy coated steel	ASTM A 792 AZ 50
5% aluminum alloy-coated steel	ASTM A 875 GF60
Aluminum-coated steel	ASTM A 463 T2 65
Galvanized steel	ASTM A 653 G-90
Prepainted steel	ASTM A 755[a]

a. Paint systems in accordance with ASTM A 755 shall be applied over steel products with corrosion-resistant coatings complying with ASTM A 792, ASTM A 875, ASTM A 463, or ASTM A 653.

R905.11.1 Slope. Modified bitumen membrane roofs shall have a design slope of a minimum of one-fourth unit vertical in 12 units horizontal (2-percent slope) for drainage.

R905.11.2 Material standards. Modified bitumen roof coverings shall comply with the standards in Table R905.11.2.

TABLE R905.11.2
MODIFIED BITUMEN ROOFING MATERIAL STANDARDS

MATERIAL	STANDARD
Acrylic coating	ASTM D 6083
Asphalt adhesive	ASTM D 3747
Asphalt cement	ASTM D 3019
Asphalt coating	ASTM D 1227; D 2824
Asphalt primer	ASTM D 41
Modified bitumen roof membrane	ASTM D 6162; D 6163; D 6164; D 6222; D 6223; D 6298; CGSB 37–56M

R905.11.3 Application. Modified bitumen roofs shall be installed according to this chapter and the manufacturer's installation instructions.

R905.12 Thermoset single-ply roofing. The installation of thermoset single-ply roofing shall comply with the provisions of this section.

R905.12.1 Slope. Thermoset single-ply membrane roofs shall have a design slope of a minimum of one-fourth unit vertical in 12 units horizontal (2-percent slope) for drainage.

R905.12.2 Material standards. Thermoset single-ply roof coverings shall comply with ASTM D 4637, ASTM D 5019 or CGSB 37-GP-52M.

R905.12.3 Application. Thermoset single-ply roofs shall be installed according to this chapter and the manufacturer's installation instructions.

R905.13 Thermoplastic single-ply roofing. The installation of thermoplastic single-ply roofing shall comply with the provisions of this section.

R905.13.1 Slope. Thermoplastic single-ply membrane roofs shall have a design slope of a minimum of one-fourth unit vertical in 12 units horizontal (2-percent slope).

R905.13.2 Material standards. Thermoplastic single-ply roof coverings shall comply with ASTM D 4434, ASTM D 6754, ASTM D 6878, or CGSB CAN/CGSB 37.54.

R905.13.3 Application. Thermoplastic single-ply roofs shall be installed according to this chapter and the manufacturer's installation instructions.

R905.14 Sprayed polyurethane foam roofing. The installation of sprayed polyurethane foam roofing shall comply with the provisions of this section.

R905.14.1 Slope. Sprayed polyurethane foam roofs shall have a design slope of a minimum of one-fourth unit vertical in 12 units horizontal (2-percent slope) for drainage.

R905.14.2 Material standards. Spray-applied polyurethane foam insulation shall comply with ASTM C 1029.

R905.14.3 Application. Foamed-in-place roof insulation shall be installed in accordance with this chapter and the manufacturer's installation instructions. A liquid-applied protective coating that complies with Section R905.15 shall be applied no less than 2 hours nor more than 72 hours following the application of the foam.

R905.14.4 Foam plastics. Foam plastic materials and installation shall comply with Section R314.

R905.15 Liquid-applied coatings. The installation of liquid-applied coatings shall comply with the provisions of this section.

R905.15.1 Slope. Liquid-applied roofs shall have a design slope of a minimum of one-fourth unit vertical in 12 units horizontal (2-percent slope).

R905.15.2 Material standards. Liquid-applied roof coatings shall comply with ASTM C 836, C 957, D 1227, D 3468, D 6083 or D 6694.

R905.15.3 Application. Liquid-applied roof coatings shall be installed according to this chapter and the manufacturer's installation instructions.

SECTION R906
ROOF INSULATION

R906.1 General. The use of above-deck thermal insulation shall be permitted provided such insulation is covered with an approved roof covering and passes FM 4450 or UL 1256.

R906.2 Material standards. Above-deck thermal insulation board shall comply with the standards in Table R906.2.

TABLE R906.2
MATERIAL STANDARDS FOR ROOF INSULATION

Cellular glass board	ASTM C 552
Composite boards	ASTM C 1289, Type III, IV, V, or VI
Expanded polystyrene	ASTM C 578
Extruded polystyrene board	ASTM C 578
Perlite Board	ASTM C 728
Polyisocyanurate Board	ASTM C 1289, Type I or Type II
Wood fiberboard	ASTM C 208

SECTION R907
REROOFING

R907.1 General. Materials and methods of application used for re-covering or replacing an existing roof covering shall comply with the requirements of Chapter 9.

Exception: Reroofing shall not be required to meet the minimum design slope requirement of one-quarter unit vertical in 12 units horizontal (2-percent slope) in Section R905 for roofs that provide positive roof drainage.

R907.2 Structural and construction loads. The structural roof components shall be capable of supporting the roof covering system and the material and equipment loads that will be encountered during installation of the roof covering system.

R907.3 Re-covering versus replacement. New roof coverings shall not be installed without first removing existing roof coverings where any of the following conditions occur:

1. Where the existing roof or roof covering is water-soaked or has deteriorated to the point that the existing roof or roof covering is not adequate as a base for additional roofing.

2. Where the existing roof covering is wood shake, slate, clay, cement or asbestos-cement tile.

3. Where the existing roof has two or more applications of any type of roof covering.

4. For asphalt shingles, when the building is located in an area subject to moderate or severe hail exposure according to Figure R903.5.

Exceptions:

1. Complete and separate roofing systems, such as standing-seam metal roof systems, that are designed to transmit the roof loads directly to the building's structural system and that do not rely on existing roofs

and roof coverings for support, shall not require the removal of existing roof coverings.

2. Installation of metal panel, metal shingle, and concrete and clay tile roof coverings over existing wood shake roofs shall be permitted when the application is in accordance with Section R907.4.

3. The application of new protective coating over existing spray polyurethane foam roofing systems shall be permitted without tear-off of existing roof coverings.

R907.4 Roof recovering. Where the application of a new roof covering over wood shingle or shake roofs creates a combustible concealed space, the entire existing surface shall be covered with gypsum board, mineral fiber, glass fiber or other approved materials securely fastened in place.

R907.5 Reinstallation of materials. Existing slate, clay or cement tile shall be permitted for reinstallation, except that damaged, cracked or broken slate or tile shall not be reinstalled. Existing vent flashing, metal edgings, drain outlets, collars and metal counterflashings shall not be reinstalled where rusted, damaged or deteriorated. Aggregate surfacing materials shall not be reinstalled.

R907.6 Flashings. Flashings shall be reconstructed in accordance with approved manufacturer's installation instructions. Metal flashing to which bituminous materials are to be adhered shall be primed prior to installation.

CHAPTER 10

CHIMNEYS AND FIREPLACES

SECTION R1001
MASONRY FIREPLACES

R1001.1 General. Masonry fireplaces shall be constructed in accordance with this section and the applicable provisions of Chapters 3 and 4.

R1001.2 Footings and foundations. Footings for masonry fireplaces and their chimneys shall be constructed of concrete or solid masonry at least 12 inches (305 mm) thick and shall extend at least 6 inches (152 mm) beyond the face of the fireplace or foundation wall on all sides. Footings shall be founded on natural, undisturbed earth or engineered fill below frost depth. In areas not subjected to freezing, footings shall be at least 12 inches (305 mm) below finished grade.

R1001.2.1 Ash dump cleanout. Cleanout openings located within foundation walls below fireboxes, when provided, shall be equipped with ferrous metal or masonry doors and frames constructed to remain tightly closed except when in use. Cleanouts shall be accessible and located so that ash removal will not create a hazard to combustible materials.

R1001.3 Seismic reinforcing. Masonry or concrete chimneys in Seismic Design Category D_0, D_1 or D_2 shall be reinforced. Reinforcing shall conform to the requirements set forth in Table R1001.1 and Section R609, Grouted Masonry.

R1001.3.1 Vertical reinforcing. For chimneys up to 40 inches (1016 mm) wide, four No. 4 continuous vertical bars shall be placed between wythes of solid masonry or within the cells of hollow unit masonry and grouted in accordance with Section R609. Grout shall be prevented from bonding with the flue liner so that the flue liner is free to move with thermal expansion. For chimneys more than 40 inches (1016 mm) wide, two additional No. 4 vertical bars shall be provided for each additional flue incorporated into the chimney or for each additional 40 inches (1016 mm) in width or fraction thereof.

R1001.3.2 Horizontal reinforcing. Vertical reinforcement shall be placed within $^1/_4$-inch (6 mm) ties, or other reinforcing of equivalent net cross-sectional area, placed in the bed joints according to Section R607 at a minimum of every 18 inches (457 mm) of vertical height. Two such ties shall be installed at each bend in the vertical bars.

R1001.4 Seismic anchorage. Masonry or concrete chimneys in Seismic Design Categories D_0, D_1 or D_2 shall be anchored at each floor, ceiling or roof line more than 6 feet (1829 mm) above grade, except where constructed completely within the exterior walls. Anchorage shall conform to the requirements of Section R1001.4.1.

R1001.4.1 Anchorage. Two $^3/_{16}$-inch by 1-inch (5 mm by 25 mm) straps shall be embedded a minimum of 12 inches (305 mm) into the chimney. Straps shall be hooked around the outer bars and extend 6 inches (152 mm) beyond the bend. Each strap shall be fastened to a minimum of four floor ceiling or floor joists or rafters with two $^1/_2$-inch (13 mm) bolts.

R1001.5 Firebox walls. Masonry fireboxes shall be constructed of solid masonry units, hollow masonry units grouted solid, stone or concrete. When a lining of firebrick at least 2 inches (51 mm) thick or other approved lining is provided, the minimum thickness of back and side walls shall each be 8 inches (203 mm) of solid masonry, including the lining. The width of joints between firebricks shall not be greater than $^1/_4$ inch (6 mm). When no lining is provided, the total minimum thickness of back and side walls shall be 10 inches (254 mm) of solid masonry. Firebrick shall conform to ASTM C 27 or C 1261 and shall be laid with medium duty refractory mortar conforming to ASTM C 199.

R1001.5.1 Steel fireplace units. Installation of steel fireplace units with solid masonry to form a masonry fireplace is permitted when installed either according to the requirements of their listing or according to the requirements of this section. Steel fireplace units incorporating a steel firebox lining, shall be constructed with steel not less than $^1/_4$ inch (6 mm) thick, and an air circulating chamber which is ducted to the interior of the building. The firebox lining shall be encased with solid masonry to provide a total thickness at the back and sides of not less than 8 inches (203 mm), of which not less than 4 inches (102 mm) shall be of solid masonry or concrete. Circulating air ducts used with steel fireplace units shall be constructed of metal or masonry.

R1001.6 Firebox dimensions. The firebox of a concrete or masonry fireplace shall have a minimum depth of 20 inches (508 mm). The throat shall not be less than 8 inches (203 mm) above the fireplace opening. The throat opening shall not be less than 4 inches (102 mm) deep. The cross-sectional area of the passageway above the firebox, including the throat, damper and smoke chamber, shall not be less than the cross-sectional area of the flue.

Exception: Rumford fireplaces shall be permitted provided that the depth of the fireplace is at least 12 inches (305 mm) and at least one-third of the width of the fireplace opening, that the throat is at least 12 inches (305 mm) above the lintel and is at least $^1/_{20}$ the cross-sectional area of the fireplace opening.

R1001.7 Lintel and throat. Masonry over a fireplace opening shall be supported by a lintel of noncombustible material. The minimum required bearing length on each end of the fireplace opening shall be 4 inches (102 mm). The fireplace throat or damper shall be located a minimum of 8 inches (203 mm) above the lintel.

R1001.7.1 Damper. Masonry fireplaces shall be equipped with a ferrous metal damper located at least 8 inches (203 mm) above the top of the fireplace opening. Dampers shall be installed in the fireplace or the chimney venting the fireplace, and shall be operable from the room containing the fireplace.

TABLE R1001.1
SUMMARY OF REQUIREMENTS FOR MASONRY FIREPLACES AND CHIMNEYS

ITEM	LETTER[a]	REQUIREMENTS
Hearth slab thickness	A	4″
Hearth extension (each side of opening)	B	8″ fireplace opening < 6 square foot. 12″ fireplace opening ≥ 6 square foot.
Hearth extension (front of opening)	C	16″ fireplace opening < 6 square foot. 20″ fireplace opening ≥ 6 square foot.
Hearth slab reinforcing	D	Reinforced to carry its own weight and all imposed loads.
Thickness of wall of firebox	E	10″ solid brick or 8″ where a firebrick lining is used. Joints in firebrick $^1/_4$″ maximum.
Distance from top of opening to throat	F	8″
Smoke chamber wall thickness Unlined walls	G	6″ 8″
Chimney Vertical reinforcing[b]	H	Four No. 4 full-length bars for chimney up to 40″ wide. Add two No. 4 bars for each additional 40″ or fraction of width or each additional flue.
Horizontal reinforcing	J	$^1/_4$″ ties at 18″ and two ties at each bend in vertical steel.
Bond beams	K	No specified requirements.
Fireplace lintel	L	Noncombustible material.
Chimney walls with flue lining	M	Solid masonry units or hollow masonry units grouted solid with at least 4 inch nominal thickness.
Distances between adjacent flues	—	See Section R1003.13.
Effective flue area (based on area of fireplace opening)	P	See Section R1003.15.
Clearances: Combustible material Mantel and trim Above roof	R	See Sections R1001.11 and R1003.18. See Section R1001.11, Exception 4. 3′ at roofline and 2′ at 10′.
Anchorage[b] Strap Number Embedment into chimney Fasten to Bolts	S	$^3/_{16}$″ × 1″ Two 12″ hooked around outer bar with 6″ extension. 4 joists Two $^1/_2$″ diameter.
Footing Thickness Width	T	12″ min. 6″ each side of fireplace wall.

For SI: 1 inch = 25.4 mm, 1 foot = 304.8 mm, 1 square foot = 0.0929 m².

NOTE: This table provides a summary of major requirements for the construction of masonry chimneys and fireplaces. Letter references are to Figure R1001.1, which shows examples of typical construction. This table does not cover all requirements, nor does it cover all aspects of the indicated requirements. For the actual mandatory requirements of the code, see the indicated section of text.

a. The letters refer to Figure R1001.1.

b. Not required in Seismic Design Category A, B or C.

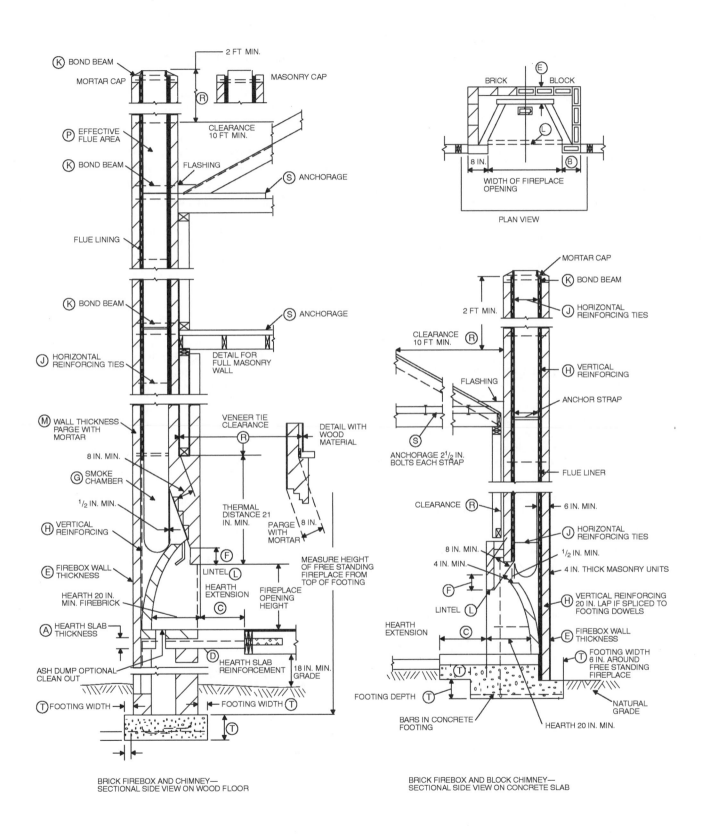

For SI: 1 inch = 25.4 mm, 1 foot = 304.8 mm.

FIGURE R1001.1
FIREPLACE AND CHIMNEY DETAILS

R1001.8 Smoke chamber. Smoke chamber walls shall be constructed of solid masonry units, hollow masonry units grouted solid, stone or concrete. Corbelling of masonry units shall not leave unit cores exposed to the inside of the smoke chamber. When a lining of firebrick at least 2 inches (51 mm) thick, or a lining of vitrified clay at least $^5/_8$ inch (16 mm) thick, is provided, the total minimum thickness of front, back and side walls shall be 6 inches (152 mm) of solid masonry, including the lining. Firebrick shall conform to ASTM C 27 or C 1261 and shall be laid with medium duty refractory mortar conforming to ASTM C 199. Where no lining is provided, the total minimum thickness of front, back and side walls shall be 8 inches (203 mm) of solid masonry. When the inside surface of the smoke chamber is formed by corbeled masonry, the inside surface shall be parged smooth.

R1001.8.1 Smoke chamber dimensions. The inside height of the smoke chamber from the fireplace throat to the beginning of the flue shall not be greater than the inside width of the fireplace opening. The inside surface of the smoke chamber shall not be inclined more than 45 degrees (0.79 rad) from vertical when prefabricated smoke chamber linings are used or when the smoke chamber walls are rolled or sloped rather than corbeled. When the inside surface of the smoke chamber is formed by corbeled masonry, the walls shall not be corbeled more than 30 degrees (0.52 rad) from vertical.

R1001.9 Hearth and hearth extension. Masonry fireplace hearths and hearth extensions shall be constructed of concrete or masonry, supported by noncombustible materials, and reinforced to carry their own weight and all imposed loads. No combustible material shall remain against the underside of hearths and hearth extensions after construction.

R1001.9.1 Hearth thickness. The minimum thickness of fireplace hearths shall be 4 inches (102 mm).

R1001.9.2 Hearth extension thickness. The minimum thickness of hearth extensions shall be 2 inches (51 mm).

Exception: When the bottom of the firebox opening is raised at least 8 inches (203 mm) above the top of the hearth extension, a hearth extension of not less than $^3/_8$-inch-thick (10 mm) brick, concrete, stone, tile or other approved noncombustible material is permitted.

R1001.10 Hearth extension dimensions. Hearth extensions shall extend at least 16 inches (406 mm) in front of and at least 8 inches (203 mm) beyond each side of the fireplace opening. Where the fireplace opening is 6 square feet (0.6 m²) or larger, the hearth extension shall extend at least 20 inches (508 mm) in front of and at least 12 inches (305 mm) beyond each side of the fireplace opening.

R1001.11 Fireplace clearance. All wood beams, joists, studs and other combustible material shall have a clearance of not less than 2 inches (51 mm) from the front faces and sides of masonry fireplaces and not less than 4 inches (102 mm) from the back faces of masonry fireplaces. The air space shall not be filled, except to provide fire blocking in accordance with Section R1001.12.

Exceptions:

1. Masonry fireplaces listed and labeled for use in contact with combustibles in accordance with UL 127 and installed in accordance with the manufacturer's installation instructions are permitted to have combustible material in contact with their exterior surfaces.

2. When masonry fireplaces are part of masonry or concrete walls, combustible materials shall not be in contact with the masonry or concrete walls less than 12 inches (306 mm) from the inside surface of the nearest firebox lining.

3. Exposed combustible trim and the edges of sheathing materials such as wood siding, flooring and drywall shall be permitted to abut the masonry fireplace side walls and hearth extension in accordance with Figure R1001.11, provided such combustible trim or sheath-

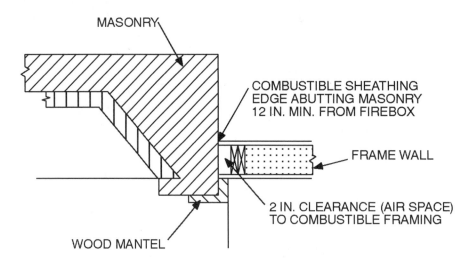

MASONRY

COMBUSTIBLE SHEATHING
EDGE ABUTTING MASONRY
12 IN. MIN. FROM FIREBOX

FRAME WALL

2 IN. CLEARANCE (AIR SPACE)
TO COMBUSTIBLE FRAMING

WOOD MANTEL

For SI: 1 inch = 25.4 mm.

FIGURE R1001.11
CLEARANCE FROM COMBUSTIBLES

ing is a minimum of 12 inches (305 mm) from the inside surface of the nearest firebox lining.

4. Exposed combustible mantels or trim may be placed directly on the masonry fireplace front surrounding the fireplace opening providing such combustible materials are not placed within 6 inches (152 mm) of a fireplace opening. Combustible material within 12 inches (306 mm) of the fireplace opening shall not project more than $^1/_8$ inch (3 mm) for each 1-inch (25 mm) distance from such an opening.

R1001.12 Fireplace fireblocking. Fireplace fireblocking shall comply with the provisions of Section R602.8.

SECTION R1002
MASONRY HEATERS

R1002.1 Definition. A masonry heater is a heating appliance constructed of concrete or solid masonry, hereinafter referred to as masonry, which is designed to absorb and store heat from a solid-fuel fire built in the firebox by routing the exhaust gases through internal heat exchange channels in which the flow path downstream of the firebox may include flow in a horizontal or downward direction before entering the chimney and which delivers heat by radiation from the masonry surface of the heater.

R1002.2 Installation. Masonry heaters shall be installed in accordance with this section and comply with one of the following:

1. Masonry heaters shall comply with the requirements of ASTM E 1602; or

2. Masonry heaters shall be listed and labeled in accordance with UL 1482 and installed in accordance with the manufacturer's installation instructions.

R1002.3 Footings and foundation. The firebox floor of a masonry heater shall be a minimum thickness of 4 inches (102 mm) of noncombustible material and be supported on a noncombustible footing and foundation in accordance with Section R1003.2.

R1002.4 Seismic reinforcing. In Seismic Design Categories D_0, D_1 and D_2, masonry heaters shall be anchored to the masonry foundation in accordance with Section R1003.3. Seismic reinforcing shall not be required within the body of a masonry heater whose height is equal to or less than 3.5 times it's body width and where the masonry chimney serving the heater is not supported by the body of the heater. Where the masonry chimney shares a common wall with the facing of the masonry heater, the chimney portion of the structure shall be reinforced in accordance with Section R1003.

R1002.5 Masonry heater clearance. Combustible materials shall not be placed within 36 inches (914 mm) of the outside surface of a masonry heater in accordance with NFPA 211 Section 8-7 (clearances for solid-fuel-burning appliances), and the required space between the heater and combustible material shall be fully vented to permit the free flow of air around all heater surfaces.

Exceptions:

1. When the masonry heater wall is at least 8 inches (203 mm) thick of solid masonry and the wall of the heat exchange channels is at least 5 inches (127 mm) thick of solid masonry, combustible materials shall not be placed within 4 inches (102 mm) of the outside surface of a masonry heater. A clearance of at least 8 inches (203 mm) shall be provided between the gas-tight capping slab of the heater and a combustible ceiling.

2. Masonry heaters tested and listed by an American National Standards Association (ANSI)-accredited laboratory to the requirements of UL1482 may be installed in accordance with the listing specifications and the manufacturer's written instructions.

SECTION R1003
MASONRY CHIMNEYS

R1003.1 Definition. A masonry chimney is a chimney constructed of concrete or masonry, hereinafter referred to as masonry. Masonry chimneys shall be constructed, anchored, supported and reinforced as required in this chapter.

R1003.2 Footings and foundations. Footings for masonry chimneys shall be constructed of concrete or solid masonry at least 12 inches (305 mm) thick and shall extend at least 6 inches (152 mm) beyond the face of the foundation or support wall on all sides. Footings shall be founded on natural undisturbed earth or engineered fill below frost depth. In areas not subjected to freezing, footings shall be at least 12 inches (305 mm) below finished grade.

R1003.3 Seismic reinforcing. Masonry or concrete chimneys shall be constructed, anchored, supported and reinforced as required in this chapter. In Seismic Design Category D_0, D_1 or D_2 masonry and concrete chimneys shall be reinforced and anchored as detailed in Section R1003.3.1, R1003.3.2 and R1003.4. In Seismic Design Category A, B or C, reinforcement and seismic anchorage is not required.

R1003.3.1 Vertical reinforcing. For chimneys up to 40 inches (1016 mm) wide, four No. 4 continuous vertical bars, anchored in the foundation, shall be placed in the concrete, or between wythes of solid masonry, or within the cells of hollow unit masonry, and grouted in accordance with Section R609.1.1. Grout shall be prevented from bonding with the flue liner so that the flue liner is free to move with thermal expansion. For chimneys more than 40 inches (1016 mm) wide, two additional No. 4 vertical bars shall be installed for each additional 40 inches (1016 mm) in width or fraction thereof.

R1003.3.2 Horizontal reinforcing. Vertical reinforcement shall be placed enclosed within $^1/_4$-inch (6 mm) ties, or other reinforcing of equivalent net cross-sectional area, spaced not to exceed 18 inches (457 mm) on center in concrete, or placed in the bed joints of unit masonry, at a minimum of every 18 inches (457 mm) of vertical height. Two such ties shall be installed at each bend in the vertical bars.

R1003.4 Seismic anchorage. Masonry and concrete chimneys and foundations in Seismic Design Category D_0, D_1 or D_2 shall be anchored at each floor, ceiling or roof line more than 6 feet (1829 mm) above grade, except where constructed completely within the exterior walls. Anchorage shall conform to the requirements in Section R1003.4.1.

R1003.4.1 Anchorage. Two $^3/_{16}$-inch by 1-inch (5 mm by 25 mm) straps shall be embedded a minimum of 12 inches (305 mm) into the chimney. Straps shall be hooked around the outer bars and extend 6 inches (152 mm) beyond the bend. Each strap shall be fastened to a minimum of four floor joists with two $^1/_2$-inch (13 mm) bolts.

R1003.5 Corbeling. Masonry chimneys shall not be corbeled more than one-half of the chimney's wall thickness from a wall or foundation, nor shall a chimney be corbeled from a wall or foundation that is less than 12 inches (305 mm) thick unless it projects equally on each side of the wall, except that on the second story of a two-story dwelling, corbeling of chimneys on the exterior of the enclosing walls may equal the wall thickness. The projection of a single course shall not exceed one-half the unit height or one-third of the unit bed depth, whichever is less.

R1003.6 Changes in dimension. The chimney wall or chimney flue lining shall not change in size or shape within 6 inches (152 mm) above or below where the chimney passes through floor components, ceiling components or roof components.

R1003.7 Offsets. Where a masonry chimney is constructed with a fireclay flue liner surrounded by one wythe of masonry, the maximum offset shall be such that the centerline of the flue above the offset does not extend beyond the center of the chimney wall below the offset. Where the chimney offset is supported by masonry below the offset in an approved manner, the maximum offset limitations shall not apply. Each individual corbeled masonry course of the offset shall not exceed the projection limitations specified in Section R1003.5.

R1003.8 Additional load. Chimneys shall not support loads other than their own weight unless they are designed and constructed to support the additional load. Construction of masonry chimneys as part of the masonry walls or reinforced concrete walls of the building shall be permitted.

R1003.9 Termination. Chimneys shall extend at least 2 feet (610 mm) higher than any portion of a building within 10 feet (3048 mm), but shall not be less than 3 feet (914 mm) above the highest point where the chimney passes through the roof.

R1003.9.1 Spark arrestors. Where a spark arrestor is installed on a masonry chimney, the spark arrestor shall meet all of the following requirements:

1. The net free area of the arrestor shall not be less than four times the net free area of the outlet of the chimney flue it serves.

2. The arrestor screen shall have heat and corrosion resistance equivalent to 19-gage galvanized steel or 24-gage stainless steel.

3. Openings shall not permit the passage of spheres having a diameter greater than $^1/_2$ inch (13 mm) nor block the passage of spheres having a diameter less than $^3/_8$ inch (10 mm).

4. The spark arrestor shall be accessible for cleaning and the screen or chimney cap shall be removable to allow for cleaning of the chimney flue.

R1003.10 Wall thickness. Masonry chimney walls shall be constructed of solid masonry units or hollow masonry units grouted solid with not less than a 4-inch (102 mm) nominal thickness.

R1003.10.1 Masonry veneer chimneys. Where masonry is used to veneer a frame chimney, through-flashing and weep holes shall be installed as required by Section R703.

R1003.11 Flue lining (material). Masonry chimneys shall be lined. The lining material shall be appropriate for the type of appliance connected, according to the terms of the appliance listing and manufacturer's instructions.

R1003.11.1 Residential-type appliances (general). Flue lining systems shall comply with one of the following:

1. Clay flue lining complying with the requirements of ASTM C 315 or equivalent.

2. Listed chimney lining systems complying with UL 1777.

3. Factory-built chimneys or chimney units listed for installation within masonry chimneys.

4. Other approved materials that will resist corrosion, erosion, softening or cracking from flue gases and condensate at temperatures up to 1,800°F (982°C).

R1003.11.2 Flue linings for specific appliances. Flue linings other than these covered in Section R1003.11.1, intended for use with specific types of appliances, shall comply with Sections R1003.11.3 through R1003.11.6.

R1003.11.3 Gas appliances. Flue lining systems for gas appliances shall be in accordance with Chapter 24.

R1003.11.4 Pellet fuel-burning appliances. Flue lining and vent systems for use in masonry chimneys with pellet fuel-burning appliances shall be limited to the following:

1. Flue lining systems complying with Section R1003.11.1.

2. Pellet vents listed for installation within masonry chimneys. (See Section R1003.11.6 for marking.)

R1003.11.5 Oil-fired appliances approved for use with Type L vent. Flue lining and vent systems for use in masonry chimneys with oil-fired appliances approved for use with Type L vent shall be limited to the following:

1. Flue lining systems complying with Section R1003.11.1.

2. Listed chimney liners complying with UL 641. (See Section R1003.11.6 for marking.)

R1003.11.6 Notice of usage. When a flue is relined with a material not complying with Section R1003.11.1, the chimney shall be plainly and permanently identified by a label attached to a wall, ceiling or other conspicuous location adjacent to where the connector enters the chimney. The label shall include the following message or equivalent language:

THIS CHIMNEY FLUE IS FOR USE ONLY WITH [TYPE OR CATEGORY OF APPLIANCE] APPLIANCES THAT BURN [TYPE OF FUEL]. DO NOT CONNECT OTHER TYPES OF APPLIANCES.

R1003.12 Clay flue lining (installation). Clay flue liners shall be installed in accordance with ASTM C 1283 and extend from a point not less than 8 inches (203 mm) below the lowest inlet or, in the case of fireplaces, from the top of the smoke chamber to a point above the enclosing walls. The lining shall be carried up vertically, with a maximum slope no greater than 30 degrees (0.52 rad) from the vertical.

Clay flue liners shall be laid in medium-duty refractory mortar conforming to ASTM C 199 with tight mortar joints left smooth on the inside and installed to maintain an air space or insulation not to exceed the thickness of the flue liner separating the flue liners from the interior face of the chimney masonry walls. Flue liners shall be supported on all sides. Only enough mortar shall be placed to make the joint and hold the liners in position.

R1003.12.1 Listed materials. Listed materials used as flue linings shall be installed in accordance with the terms of their listings and manufacturer's instructions.

R1003.12.2 Space around lining. The space surrounding a chimney lining system or vent installed within a masonry chimney shall not be used to vent any other appliance.

Exception: This shall not prevent the installation of a separate flue lining in accordance with the manufacturer's installation instructions.

R1003.13 Multiple flues. When two or more flues are located in the same chimney, masonry wythes shall be built between adjacent flue linings. The masonry wythes shall be at least 4 inches (102 mm) thick and bonded into the walls of the chimney.

Exception: When venting only one appliance, two flues may adjoin each other in the same chimney with only the flue lining separation between them. The joints of the adjacent flue linings shall be staggered at least 4 inches (102 mm).

R1003.14 Flue area (appliance). Chimney flues shall not be smaller in area than that of the area of the connector from the appliance [see Tables R1003.14(1) and R1003.14(2)]. The sizing of a chimney flue to which multiple appliance venting systems are connected shall be in accordance with Section M1805.3.

R1003.15 Flue area (masonry fireplace). Flue sizing for chimneys serving fireplaces shall be in accordance with Section R1003.15.1 or Section R1003.15.2.

R1003.15.1 Option 1. Round chimney flues shall have a minimum net cross-sectional area of at least $^1/_{12}$ of the fireplace opening. Square chimney flues shall have a minimum net cross-sectional area of $^1/_{10}$ of the fireplace opening. Rectangular chimney flues with an aspect ratio less than 2 to 1 shall have a minimum net cross-sectional area of $^1/_{10}$ of the fireplace opening. Rectangular chimney flues with an aspect ratio of 2 to 1 or more shall have a minimum net cross-sec-

tional area of $^1/_8$ of the fireplace opening. Cross-sectional areas of clay flue linings are shown in Tables R1001.14(1) and R1001.14(2) or as provided by the manufacturer or as measured in the field.

R1003.15.2 Option 2. The minimum net cross-sectional area of the chimney flue shall be determined in accordance with Figure R1003.15.2. A flue size providing at least the equivalent net cross-sectional area shall be used. Cross-sectional areas of clay flue linings are shown in Tables R1003.14(1) and R1003.14(2) or as provided by the manufacturer or as measured in the field. The height of the chimney shall be measured from the firebox floor to the top of the chimney flue.

TABLE R1003.14(1)
NET CROSS–SECTIONAL AREA OF ROUND FLUE SIZES[a]

FLUE SIZE, INSIDE DIAMETER (inches)	CROSS–SECTIONAL AREA (square inches)
6	28
7	38
8	50
10	78
10$^3/_4$	90
12	113
15	176
18	254

For SI: 1 inch = 25.4 mm, 1 square inch = 645.16 mm².
a. Flue sizes are based on ASTM C 315.

TABLE R1003.14(2)
NET CROSS–SECTIONAL AREA OF SQUARE AND RECTANGULAR FLUE SIZES

FLUE SIZE, OUTSIDE NOMINAL DIMENSIONS (inches)	CROSS–SECTIONAL AREA (square inches)
4.5 × 8.5	23
4.5 × 13	34
8 × 8	42
8.5 × 8.5	49
8 × 12	67
8.5 × 13	76
12 × 12	102
8.5 × 18	101
13 × 13	127
12 × 16	131
13 × 18	173
16 × 16	181
16 × 20	222
18 × 18	233
20 × 20	298
20 × 24	335
24 × 24	431

For SI: 1 inch = 25.4 mm, 1 square inch = 645.16 mm².

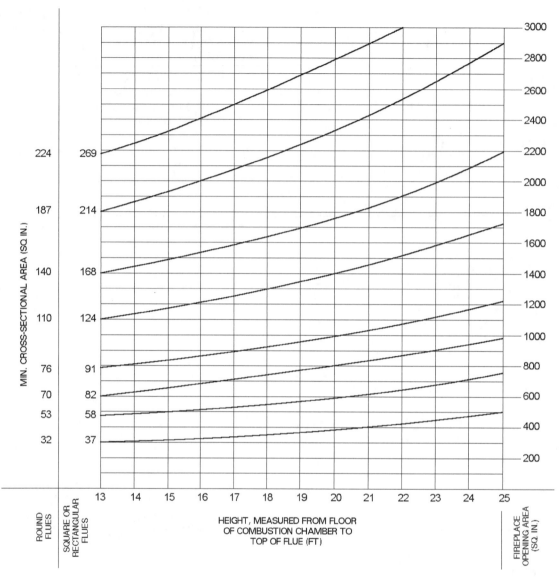

For SI: 1 foot = 304.8 mm, 1 square inch = 645.16 mm².

FIGURE R1003.15.2
FLUE SIZES FOR MASONRY CHIMNEYS

R1003.16 Inlet. Inlets to masonry chimneys shall enter from the side. Inlets shall have a thimble of fireclay, rigid refractory material or metal that will prevent the connector from pulling out of the inlet or from extending beyond the wall of the liner.

R1003.17 Masonry chimney cleanout openings. Cleanout openings shall be provided within 6 inches (152 mm) of the base of each flue within every masonry chimney. The upper edge of the cleanout shall be located at least 6 inches (152 mm) below the lowest chimney inlet opening. The height of the opening shall be at least 6 inches (152 mm). The cleanout shall be provided with a noncombustible cover.

Exception: Chimney flues serving masonry fireplaces where cleaning is possible through the fireplace opening.

R1003.18 Chimney clearances. Any portion of a masonry chimney located in the interior of the building or within the exterior wall of the building shall have a minimum air space clearance to combustibles of 2 inches (51 mm). Chimneys located entirely outside the exterior walls of the building, including chimneys that pass through the soffit or cornice, shall have a minimum air space clearance of 1 inch (25 mm). The air space shall not be filled, except to provide fire blocking in accordance with Section R1003.19.

Exceptions:

1. Masonry chimneys equipped with a chimney lining system listed and labeled for use in chimneys in contact with combustibles in accordance with UL 1777 and installed in accordance with the manufacturer's installation instructions are permitted to have combustible material in contact with their exterior surfaces.

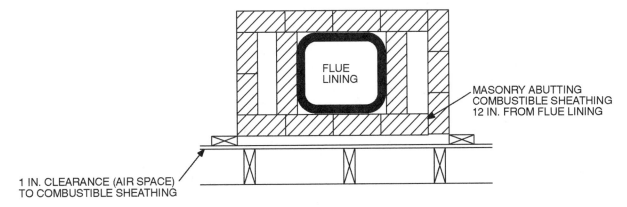

1 IN. CLEARANCE (AIR SPACE)
TO COMBUSTIBLE SHEATHING

For SI: 1 inch = 25.4 mm.

FIGURE R1003.18
CLEARANCE FROM COMBUSTIBLES

2. When masonry chimneys are constructed as part of masonry or concrete walls, combustible materials shall not be in contact with the masonry or concrete wall less than 12 inches (305 mm) from the inside surface of the nearest flue lining.

3. Exposed combustible trim and the edges of sheathing materials, such as wood siding and flooring, shall be permitted to abut the masonry chimney side walls, in accordance with Figure R1003.18, provided such combustible trim or sheathing is a minimum of 12 inches (305 mm) from the inside surface of the nearest flue lining. Combustible material and trim shall not overlap the corners of the chimney by more than 1 inch (25 mm).

R1003.19 Chimney fireblocking. All spaces between chimneys and floors and ceilings through which chimneys pass shall be fireblocked with noncombustible material securely fastened in place. The fireblocking of spaces between chimneys and wood joists, beams or headers shall be self-supporting or be placed on strips of metal or metal lath laid across the spaces between combustible material and the chimney.

R1003.20 Chimney crickets. Chimneys shall be provided with crickets when the dimension parallel to the ridgeline is greater than 30 inches (762 mm) and does not intersect the ridgeline. The intersection of the cricket and the chimney shall be flashed and counterflashed in the same manner as normal roof-chimney intersections. Crickets shall be constructed in compliance with Figure R1003.20 and Table R1003.20.

TABLE R1003.20
CRICKET DIMENSIONS

ROOF SLOPE	H
12 - 12	$^1/_2$ of W
8 - 12	$^1/_3$ of W
6 - 12	$^1/_4$ of W
4 - 12	$^1/_6$ of W
3 - 12	$^1/_8$ of W

SECTION R1004
FACTORY-BUILT FIREPLACES

R1004.1 General. Factory-built fireplaces shall be listed and labeled and shall be installed in accordance with the conditions of the listing. Factory-built fireplaces shall be tested in accordance with UL 127.

R1004.2 Hearth extensions. Hearth extensions of approved factory-built fireplaces shall be installed in accordance with the listing of the fireplace. The hearth extension shall be readily distinguishable from the surrounding floor area.

R1004.3 Decorative shrouds. Decorative shrouds shall not be installed at the termination of chimneys for factory-built fireplaces except where the shrouds are listed and labeled for use with the specific factory-built fireplace system and installed in accordance with the manufacturer's installation instructions.

R1004.4 Unvented gas log heaters. An unvented gas log heater shall not be installed in a factory-built fireplace unless the fireplace system has been specifically tested, listed and labeled for such use in accordance with UL 127.

SECTION R1005
FACTORY-BUILT CHIMNEYS

R1005.1 Listing. Factory-built chimneys shall be listed and labeled and shall be installed and terminated in accordance with the manufacturer's installation instructions.

R1005.2 Decorative shrouds. Decorative shrouds shall not be installed at the termination of factory-built chimneys except where the shrouds are listed and labeled for use with the specific factory-built chimney system and installed in accordance with the manufacturer's installation instructions.

R1005.3 Solid-fuel appliances. Factory-built chimneys installed in dwelling units with solid-fuel-burning appliances shall comply with the Type HT requirements of UL 103 and shall be marked "Type HT and "Residential Type and Building Heating Appliance Chimney."

Exception: Chimneys for use with open combustion chamber fireplaces shall comply with the requirements of UL 103

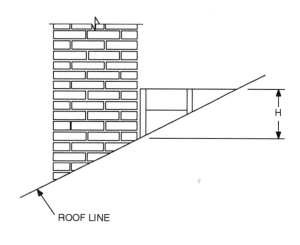

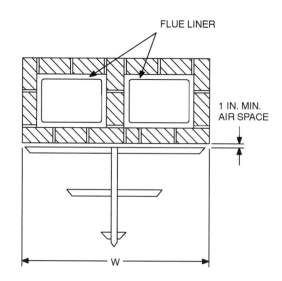

For SI: 1 inch = 25.4 mm.

FIGURE R1003.20
CHIMNEY CRICKET

and shall be marked "Residential Type and Building Heating Appliance Chimney."

Chimneys for use with open combustion chamber appliances installed in buildings other than dwelling units shall comply with the requirements of UL 103 and shall be marked "Building Heating Appliance Chimney" or "Residential Type and Building Heating Appliance Chimney."

R1005.4 Factory-built fireplaces. Chimneys for use with factory-built fireplaces shall comply with the requirements of UL 127.

R1005.5 Support. Where factory-built chimneys are supported by structural members, such as joists and rafters, those members shall be designed to support the additional load.

R1005.6 Medium-heat appliances. Factory-built chimneys for medium-heat appliances producing flue gases having a temperature above 1,000°F (538°C), measured at the entrance to the chimney shall comply with UL 959.

SECTION R1006
EXTERIOR AIR SUPPLY

R1006.1 Exterior air. Factory-built or masonry fireplaces covered in this chapter shall be equipped with an exterior air supply to assure proper fuel combustion unless the room is mechanically ventilated and controlled so that the indoor pressure is neutral or positive.

R1006.1.1 Factory-built fireplaces. Exterior combustion air ducts for factory-built fireplaces shall be a listed component of the fireplace and shall be installed according to the fireplace manufacturer's instructions.

R1006.1.2 Masonry fireplaces. Listed combustion air ducts for masonry fireplaces shall be installed according to the terms of their listing and the manufacturer's instructions.

R1006.2 Exterior air intake. The exterior air intake shall be capable of supplying all combustion air from the exterior of the dwelling or from spaces within the dwelling ventilated with outside air such as non-mechanically ventilated crawl or attic spaces. The exterior air intake shall not be located within the garage or basement of the dwelling nor shall the air intake be located at an elevation higher than the firebox. The exterior air intake shall be covered with a corrosion-resistant screen of $^1/_4$-inch (6 mm) mesh.

R1006.3 Clearance. Unlisted combustion air ducts shall be installed with a minimum 1-inch (25 mm) clearance to combustibles for all parts of the duct within 5 feet (1524 mm) of the duct outlet.

R1006.4 Passageway. The combustion air passageway shall be a minimum of 6 square inches (3870 mm²) and not more than 55 square inches (0.035 m²), except that combustion air systems for listed fireplaces shall be constructed according to the fireplace manufacturer's instructions.

R1006.5 Outlet. Locating the exterior air outlet in the back or sides of the firebox chamber or within 24 inches (610 mm) of the firebox opening on or near the floor is permitted. The outlet shall be closable and designed to prevent burning material from dropping into concealed combustible spaces.

PART IV — Energy Conservation

CHAPTER 11

ENERGY

Provisions for energy, energy conservation, or references to the *International Energy Conservation Code* are deleted and replaced with Minnesota Statutes, Section 16B.617.

PART V — Mechanical

CHAPTER 12

MECHANICAL

$<$

Provisions for mechanical or references to the *International Mechanical Code*, which include Chapter 12 through 24 of the IRC, are deleted and replaced with Minnesota Rules, Chapter 1346, the Minnesota Mechanical Code.

M
N
M
N
M

$<$

PART VII — Plumbing

CHAPTER 25

PLUMBING

Provisions for plumbing or references to the ICC *Plumbing Code*, which include Chapters 25 through 32 of the IRC, shall be deleted and replaced with Minnesota Rules, Chapter 4715, the Minnesota Plumbing Code.

M
N
M
<

PART VIII — Electrical

CHAPTER 34

ELECTRICAL <

Provisions for electrical or references to the ICC *Electrical Code*, which include Chapters 34 through 42 of the IRC, shall be deleted and replaced with Minnesota Rules, Chapter 1315, the Minnesota Electrical Code.

M
N
M

<

Part IX—Referenced Standards

CHAPTER 43

REFERENCED STANDARDS

This chapter lists the standards that are referenced in various sections of this document. The standards are listed herein by the promulgating agency of the standard, the standard identification, the effective date and title, and the section or sections of this document that reference the standard. The application of the referenced standard shall be as specified in Section R102.4.

AAMA

American Architectural Manufacturers Association
1827 Walden Office Square, Suite 550
Schaumburg, IL 60173

Standard reference number	Title	Referenced in code section number
101/I.S.2/A440—05	Specifications for Windows, Doors and Unit Skylights	R308.6.9, R613.4, N1102.4.2
450—00	Voluntary Performance Rating Method for Mulled Fenestration Assemblies	R613.9.1
506—00	Voluntary Specifications for Hurricane Impact and Cycle Testing of Fenestration Products	R613.7.1

ACI

American Concrete Institute
38800 Country Club Drive
Farmington Hills, MI 48333

Standard reference number	Title	Referenced in code section number
318—05	Building Code Requirements for Structural Concrete.	R402.2, R404.1, Table R404.1.1(5), R404.4, R404.4.6.1, Table R404.4(1), Table R404.4(2), Table R404.4(3), Table R404.4(4), Table R404.4(5), R611.1, Table R611.3(1), Table R611.7(1), Table R611.7(2), Table R611.7(3), Table R611.7(4), Table R611.7(5), Table R611.7(6), Table R611.7(7), Table R611.7(9), Table R611.7(10), R611.7.1.1, Table R611.7.4, R612.1
332—05	Requirements for Residential Concrete Construction	R404.1, Table R404.1.1(5)
530—05	Building Code Requirements for Masonry Structures	R404.1, R606.1, R606.1.1, R606.12.1, R606.12.2.2.1, R606.12.2.2.2, R606.12.3.1
530.1—05	Specifications for Masonry Structures	R404.1, R606.1, R606.1.1, R606.12.1, R606.12.2.2.1, R606.12.2.2.2, R606.12.3.1

ACCA

Air Conditioning Contractors of America
2800 Shirlington Road, Suite 300
Arlington, VA 22206

Standard reference number	Title	Referenced in code section number
Manual D—95	Residential Duct Systems	M1601.1, M1602.2
Manual J—02	Residential Load Calculation—Eighth Edition	M1401.3

AFPA

American Forest and Paper Association
111 19th Street, NW, Suite 800
Washington, DC 20036

Standard reference number	Title	Referenced in code section number
NDS—05	National Design Specification (NDS) for Wood Construction—with 2005 Supplement	R404.2.2, R502.2, Table R503.1, R602.3, R802.2
WFCM—2001	Wood Frame Construction Manual for One- and Two-family Dwellings	R301.2.1.1

AHA

American Hardboard Association
1210 West Northwest Highway
Palatine, IL 60067

Standard reference number	Title	Referenced in code section number
A135.4—04	Basic Hardboard	Table R602.3(1)
A135.5—04	Prefinished Hardboard Paneling	R702.5
A135.6—98	Hardboard Siding	Table R703.4

AISI

American Iron and Steel Institute
1140 Connecticut Ave, Suite 705
Washington, DC 20036

Standard reference number	Title	Referenced in code section number
Header—04	Standard for Cold-formed Steel Framing-Header Design	R603.6
PM—2001	Standard for Cold-formed Steel Framing-Prescriptive Method for One- and Two-family Dwellings (including 2004 Supplement)	R301.1.1, R301.2.1.1(4), R301.2.2.4.1, R301.2.2.4.5
Truss—04	Standard for Cold-formed Steel Framing-Truss Design	R804.1.3

AITC

American Institute of Timber Construction
7012 S. Revere Parkway, Suite 140
Englewood, CO 80112

Standard reference number	Title	Referenced in code section number
AITC A 190.1—02	Structural Glued Laminated Timber	R502.1.5, R602.1.2, R802.1.4

ANSI

American National Standards Institute
25 West 43rd Street, Fourth Floor
New York, NY 10036

Standard reference number	Title	Referenced in code section number
A108.1A—99	Installation of Ceramic Tile in the Wet-set Method, with Portland Cement Mortar	R702.4.1
A108.1B—99	Installation of Ceramic Tile, Quarry Tile on a Cured Portland Cement Mortar Setting Bed with Dry-set or Latex-Portland Mortar	R702.4.1
A108.4—99	Installation of Ceramic Tile with Organic Adhesives or Water Cleanable Tile-setting Epoxy Adhesive	R702.4.1
A108.5—99	Installation of Ceramic Tile with Dry-set Portland Cement Mortar or Latex-Portland Cement Mortar	R702.4.1
A108.6—99	Installation of Ceramic Tile with Chemical Resistant, Water Cleanable Tile-setting and -grouting Epoxy	R702.4.1
A108.11—99	Interior Installation of Cementitious Backer Units	R702.4.1
A118.1—99	American National Standard Specifications for Dry-set Portland Cement Mortar	R702.4.1
A118.3—99	American National Standard Specifications for Chemical Resistant, Water Cleanable Tile-setting and Grouting Epoxy and Water Cleanable Tile-setting Epoxy Adhesive	R702.4.1
A136.1—99	American National Standard Specifications for Organic Adhesives for Installation of Ceramic Tile	R702.4.1
A137.1—88	American National Standard Specifications for Ceramic Tile	R702.4.1
A208.1—99	Particleboard	R503.3.1, R605.1
LC1—97	Interior Fuel Gas Piping Systems Using Corrugated Stainless Steel Tubing —with Addenda LC 1a-1999 and LC 1b-2001	G2414.5.3
Z21.1—03	Household Cooking Gas Appliances—with Addenda Z21.1a-2003 and Z21.1b-2003	G2447.1

ANSI—continued

Z21.5.1—02	Gas Clothes Dryers—Volume I—Type I Clothes Dryers—with Addenda Z21.5.1a-2003	G2438.1
Z21.8—94(R2002)	Installation of Domestic Gas Conversion Burners	G2443.1
Z21.10.1—04	Gas Water Heaters—Volume I—Storage, Water Heaters with Input Ratings of 75,000 Btu per hour or Less	G2448.1
Z21.10.3—01	Gas Water Heaters—Volume III—Storage, Water Heaters with Input Ratings above 75,000 Btu per hour, Circulating and Instantaneous Water Heaters—with Addenda Z21.10.3a-2003 and Z21.10.3b-2004	G2448.1
Z21.11.2—02	Gas-fired Room Heaters—Volume II—Unvented Room Heaters—with Addenda Z21.11.2a-2003	G2445.1
Z21.13—04	Gas-fired Low-Pressure Steam and Hot Water Boilers	G2452.1
Z21.15—97(R2003)	Manually Operated Gas Valves for Appliances, Appliance Connector Valves and Hose End Valves —with Addenda Z21.15a-2001 (R2003)	G2420.1.1
Z21.22—99(R2003)	Relief Valves for Hot Water Supply Systems—with Addenda Z21.22a-2000 (R2003) and 21.22b-2001 (R2003)	P2803.2
Z21.24-97	Connectors for Gas Appliances	G2422.1
Z21.40.1—96(R2002)	Gas-fired Heat Activated Air Conditioning and Heat Pump Appliances—with Z21.40.1a-97 (R2002)	G2449.1
Z21.40.2—96(R2002)	Gas-fired Work Activated Air Conditioning and Heat Pump Appliances (Internal Combustion) —with Addenda Z21.40.2a-1997 (R2002)	G2449.1
Z21.42—93(R2002)	Gas-fired Illuminating Appliances	G2450.1
Z21.47—03	Gas-fired Central Furnaces	R617.1, G2442.1
Z21.50—03	Vented Gas Fireplaces—with Addenda Z21.50a-2003	G2434.1
Z21.56—01	Gas-fired Pool Heaters—with Addenda Z21.56a-2004 and Z21.56b—2004	R616.1, G2441.1
Z21.58—95(R2002)	Outdoor Cooking Gas Appliances—with Addenda Z21.58a-1998 (R2002) and Z21.58b-2002	R622.1, G2447.1
Z21.60—03	Decorative Gas Appliances for Installation in Solid Fuel Burning Fireplaces—with Addenda Z21.60a-2003	G2432.1
Z21.69—02	Connectors for Movable Gas Appliances with Addenda Z21.69a—2003	G2422.1
Z21.75/CSA 6.27—01	Connectors for Outdoor Gas Appliances	G2422.1
Z21.80—03	Line Pressure Regulators	G2421.1
Z21.84—02	Manually-listed, Natural Gas Decorative Gas Appliances for Installation in Solid Fuel Burning Fireplaces —with Addenda Z21.84a -2003	G2432.1, G2432.2
Z21.86—04	Gas-fired Vented Space Heating Appliances	G2436.1, G2437.1, G2446.1
Z21.88—02	Vented Gas Fireplace Heaters—with Addenda A21.88a-2003 and Z21.88b—2004	G2435.1
Z21.91—01	Ventless Firebox Enclosures for Gas-fired Unvented Decorative Room Heaters	G2445.7.1
Z83.6—90(R1998)	Gas-fired Infrared Heaters	G2442.1, G2449.1, G2451.1
Z83.8—02	Gas-fired Unit Heaters and Gas-fired Duct Furnaces—with Addenda Z83.8a-2003	G2444.1
Z124.1—95	Plastic Bathtub Units	Table P2701.1
Z124.2—95	Plastic Shower Receptors and Shower Stalls	Table P2701.1
Z124.3—95	Plastic Lavatories	Table P2701.1, P2711.1, P2711.2
Z124.4—96	Plastic Water Closet Bowls and Tanks	Table P2701.1, P2712.1
Z124.6—97	Plastic Sinks	Table P2701.1

APA

APA–The Engineered Wood Association
P. O. Box 11700
Tacoma, WA 98411-0700

Standard reference number	Title	Referenced in code section number
APA E30—03	Engineered Wood Construction Guide	R503.2.2, R803.2.2, R803.2.3

ASCE

American Society of Civil Engineers
1801 Alexander Bell Drive
Reston, VA 20191

Standard reference number	Title	Referenced in code section number
5—05	Building Code Requirements for Masonry Structures	R404.1, R606.1, R606.1.1, R606.12.1, R606.12.2.2.1, R606.12.2.2.2, R606.12.3.1
6—05	Specifications for Masonry Structures	R404.1, R606.1, R606.1.1, R606.12.1, R606.12.2.2.1, R606.12.2.2.2, R606.12.3.1
7—05	Minimum Design Loads for Buildings and Other Structures	R301.2.1.1
32—01	Design and Construction of Frost Protected Shallow Foundations	R403.1.4.1

ASHRAE

American Society of Heating, Refrigerating
and Air-Conditioning Engineers, Inc.
1791 Tullie Circle, NE
Atlanta, GA 30329

Standard reference number	Title	Referenced in code section number
34—2004	Designation and Safety Classification of Refrigerants M1411.1	
ASHRAE—2004	ASHRAE Fundamentals Handbook—2001 . . . . .N1102.1.3, M1502.6, P3001.2, P3002.3, P3101.4, P3103.2	

ASME

American Society of Mechanical Engineers
Three Park Avenue
New York, NY 10016-5990

Standard reference number	Title	Referenced in code section number
A17.1—2004	Safety Code for Elevators. R323.1	
A18.1—2003	Safety Standard for Platforms and Stairway Chair Lifts R323.2	
A112.1.2—1991(R2002)	Air Gaps in Plumbing Systems . . . . .P2902.3.1, Table P2902.3	
A112.1.3—2000	Air Gap Fittings for Use with Plumbing Fixtures, Appliances, and Appurtenances. . . . . Table P2701.1, P2902.3.1	
A112.3.1—93	Performance Standard and Installation Procedures for Stainless Steel Drainage Systems for Sanitary, Storm and Chemical Applications Above and Below Ground . . . . Table P3002.1(1), Table P3002.1(2), P3002.2, P3002.3	
A112.3.4—2000	Macerating Toilet Systems and Related Components . . . . Table P2701.1, P3007.2.1	
A112.4.1—1993(R2002)	Water Heater Relief Valve Drain Tubes. P2803.6.2	
A112.4.3—1999	Plastic Fittings for Connecting Water Closets to the Sanitary Drainage System. P3003.19, P3003.4.5	
A112.6.1M—1997(R2002)	Floor Affixed Supports for Off-the-floor Plumbing Fixtures for Public Use . . . . .P2702.4, Table P2704.1	
A112.6.2—2000	Framing-Affixed Supports for Off-the-floor Water Closets with Concealed Tanks . . . . Table P2701.1, P2702.4	
A112.6.3—2001	Floor and Trench Drains . . . . .Table P2701.1	
A112.18.1—2003	Plumbing Fixture Fittings. . . . . .Table P2701.1, P2708.4, P2722.1, P2902.2	
A112.18.2—2002	Plumbing Fixture Waste Fittings . . . . .Table P2701.1, P2702.2	
A112.18.3M—2002	Performance Requirements for Backflow Protection Devices and Systems in Plumbing Fixture Fittings P2708.4, P2722.3	
A112.18.6—2003	Flexible Water Connectors P2904.7	
A112.19.1M—1994(R1999)	Enameled Cast Iron Plumbing Fixtures—with 1998 and 2000 Supplements. .Table P2701.1, P2711.1	
A112.19.2—2003	Vitreous China Plumbing Fixtures—and Hydraulic Requirements for Water Closets and Urinals . . . . .Table P2701.1, P2705.1, P2711.1, P2712.1, P2712.2	
A112.19.3M—2000	Stainless Steel Plumbing Fixtures (Designed for Residential Use)—with 2002 Supplement. . Table P2701.1, P2705.1, P2711.1	
A112.19.4M—1994(R1999)	Porcelain Enameled Formed Steel Plumbing Fixtures—with 1998 and 2000 Supplements . . . . Table P2701.1, P2711.1	
A112.19.5—1999	Trim for Water-closet Bowls, Tanks, and Urinals. . . . . .Table P2701.1	
A112.19.6—1995	Hydraulic Performance Requirements for Water Closets and Urinals. . . . . .Table P2701.1, P2712.1, P2712.2	
A112.19.7M—1995	Whirlpool Bathtub Appliances . . . . .Table P2701.1	
A112.19.8M—1987(R1996)	Suction Fittings for Use in Swimming Pools, Wading Pools, Spas, Hot Tubs, and Whirlpool Bathtub Appliances . . Table P2701.1	
A112.19.9M—1991(R2002)	Non-vitreous Ceramic Plumbing Fixtures—with 2002 Supplement. . . . . .Table P2701.1, P27.11.1, P2712.1	
A112.19.12—2000	Wall Mounted and Pedestal Mounted, Adjustable and Pivoting Lavatory and Sink Carrier Systems . . . . .Table P2701.1, P2711.4, P2714.2	
A112.19.13—2001	Electrohydraulic Water Closets. P2712.9	
A112.19.15—2001	Bathtub/Whirlpool Bathtubs with Pressure Sealed Doors. . . . . .Table P2701.1, P2713.2	
B1.20.1—1983(R2001)	Pipe Threads, General Purpose (Inch). G2414.9, P3003.3.3, P3003.5.3, P3003.10.4, P3003.12.1, P3003.14.3	
B16.3—1998	Malleable Iron Threaded Fittings Classes 150 and 300 . . . . .Table P2904.6	
B16.4—1998	Gray-iron Threaded Fittings Classes 125 and 250 . . . . .Table P2904.6	
B16.9—2003	Factory-made Wrought Steel Buttwelding Fittings . . . . .Table P2904.6	
B16.11—2001	Forged Fittings, Socket-welding and Threaded . . . . .Table P2904.6	
B16.12—1998	Cast Iron Threaded Drainage Fittings . . . . .Table P2904.6	
B16.15—1985(R1994)	Cast Bronze Threaded Fittings . . . . .Table P2904.6	
B16.18—2001	Cast Copper Alloy Solder Joint Pressure Fittings. . . . . .Table P2904.6	
B16.22—2001	Wrought Copper and Copper Alloy Solder Joint Pressure Fittings . . . . .Table P2904.6	
B16.23—2002	Cast Copper Alloy Solder Joint Drainage Fittings (DWV). . . . . .Table P2904.6, Table P3002.3	
B16.26—1988	Cast Copper Alloy Fittings for Flared Copper Tubes. . . . . .Table P2904.6	
B16.28—1994	Wrought Steel Buttwelding Short Radius Elbows and Returns . . . . .Table P2904.6	
B16.29—2001	Wrought Copper and Wrought Copper Alloy Solder Joint Drainage Fittings-DWV. . . . . Table P2904.6 Table P3002.3	
B16.33—2002	Manually Operated Metallic Gas Valves for Use in Gas Piping Systems up to 125 psig (Sizes $^1\!/_2$ through 2) G2420.1.1	
B16.44-01	Manually Operated Metallic Gas Valves For Use in House Piping Systems . . . . .Table G2420.1.1	
B36.10M—2000	Welded and Seamless Wrought-steel Pipe G2414.4.2	

BPVC—2001	ASME Boiler and Pressure Vessel Code (2001 Edition) (Sections I, II, IV, V, VI & IX) M2001.1.1, G2452.1	
CSD-1—2002	Controls and Safety Devices for Automatically Fired Boilers. M2001.1.1, G2452.1	

ASSE

American Society of Sanitary Engineering
28901 Clemens Road, Suite A
Westlake, OH 44145

Standard reference number	Title	Referenced in code section number
1001—02	Performance Requirements for Atmospheric Type Vacuum Breakers . . . . Table P2902.3, P2902.3.2	
1002—99	Performance Requirements for Antisiphen Fill Valves (Ballcocks) for Gravity Water Closet Flush Tank . . . . Table P2701.1, Table P2902.3, P2902.4.1	
1003—01	Performance Requirements for Water Pressure Reducing Valves. P2903.3.1	
1006—89	Performance Requirements for Residential Use Dishwashers . . . . Table P2701.1	
1007—92	Performance Requirements for Home Laundry Equipment. . . . . Table P2701.1	
1008—89	Performance Requirements for Household Food Waste Disposer Units . . . . Table P2701.1	
1010—96	Performance Requirements for Water Hammer Arresters P2903.5	
1011—93	Performance Requirements for Hose Connection Vacuum Breakers . . . . Table P2902.3, P2902.3.2	
1012—02	Performance Requirements for Backflow Preventers with Intermediate Atmospheric Vent . . . . Table P2902.3 P2902.3.3, P2902.5.1, P2902.5.5	
1013—99	Performance Requirements for Reduced Pressure Principle Backflow Preventers and Reduced Pressure Fire Protection Principle Backflow Preventers. . . . . Table P2902.3, P2902.5.5, P2902.5.1, P2902.5.5	
1014—90	Performance Requirements for Hand-held Shower . . . . Table P2701.1	
1015—99	Performance Requirements For Double Check Backflow Prevention Assemblies and Double Check Fire Protection Backflow Prevention Assemblies . . . . Table P2902.3, P2902.3.6	
1016—96	Performance Requirements for Individual Thermostatic, Pressure Balancing and Combination Control Valves for Bathing Facilities . . . . Table P2701.1, P2708.3, P2722.2	
1017—99	Performance Requirements for Temperature Actuated Mixing Valves for Hot Water Distribution Systems P2802.2	
1019—97	Performance Requirements for Wall Hydrants, Freezeless, Automatic Automatic Draining, Anti-backflow Types . . . . Table P2701.1, Table P2902.3	
1020—98	Performance Requirements for Pressure Vacuum Breaker Assembly . . . . Table P2902.3, P2902.3.4	
1023—79	Performance Requirements for Hot Water Dispensers Household Storage Type Electrical . . . . Table P2701.1	
1024—04	Performance Requirements for Dual Check Valve Type Backflow Preventers . . . . Table P2902.3	
1025—78	Performance Requirements for Diverters for Plumbing Faucets with Hose Spray, Anti-siphon Type, Residential Applications. . . . . Table P2701.1	
1035—02	Performance Requirements for Laboratory Faucet Backflow Preventers . . . . Table P2902.3, P2902.3.2	
1037—90	Performance Requirements for Pressurized Flushing Devices for Plumbing Fixtures. . . . . Table P2701.1	
1047—99	Performance Requirements for Reduced Pressure Detector Fire Protection Backflow Prevention Assemblies . . . . P2902.3.5, Table P2902.3	
1048—99	Performance Requirements for Double Check Detector Fire Protection Backflow Prevention Assemblies . . . . P2902.3.6, Table P2902.3	
1050—02	Performance Requirements for Stack Air Admittance Valves for Sanitary Drainage Systems. P3114.1	
1051—02	Performance Requirements for Individual and Branch Type Air Admittance Valves for Plumbing Drainage Systems P3114.1	
1052—93	Performance Requirements for Hose Connection Backflow Preventers. . . . . Table P2701.1, Table P2902.3, P2902.3.2	
1056—01	Performance Requirements for Spill Resistant Vacuum. . . . . Table P2902.3, P2902.3.4	
1062—97	Performance Requirements for Temperature Actuated, Flow Reduction Valves to Individual Fixture Fittings . . . . Table P2701.1, P2724.1	
1066—97	Performance Requirements for Individual Pressure Balancing Valves for Individual Fixture Fittings . . Table P2701.1, P2722.4	
1070—04	Performance Requirements for Water Temperature Limiting Devices P2713.3, P2721.2	

ASTM

ASTM International
100 Barr Harbor Drive
West Conshohocken, PA 19428

Standard reference number	Title	Referenced in code section number
A 36/A 36M—04	Specification for Carbon Structural Steel. R606.15	
A 53/A 53M—02	Specification for Pipe, Steel, Black and Hot-dipped, Zinc-coated Welded and Seamless . . . . Table M2101.1, G2414.4.2, Table P2904.4.1, Table P2904.5, Table P3002.1(1)	
A 74—04	Specification for Cast Iron Soil Pipe and Fittings. . . . . Table P3002.1(1), Table P3002.1(2), Table P3002.2 Table P3002.3, P3005.2.9	

ASTM—continued

A 106—04	Specification for Seamless Carbon Steel Pipe for High Temperature Service................Table M2101.1, G2414.4.2	
A 126—04	Specification for Gray Iron Castings for Valves, Flanges and Pipe Fittings..........................Table P3002.1(1)	
A 153—03	Specification for Zinc Coating (Hot Dip) on Iron and Steel Hardware.......................R319.3, Table R606.15.1	
A 167—99	Specification for Stainless and Heat-resisting Chromium-nickel Steel Plate, Sheet, and Strip......R606.15, Table R606.15.1	
A 197/A197M—00	Specification for Cupola Malleable Iron...Table P3002.1	
A 240—04	Standard Specification for Chromium and Chromium-nickel Stainless Steel Plate, Sheet and Strip for Pressure Vessels and for General Applications.....................Table R905.10.3(1)	
A 254—97(2002)	Specification for Copper Brazed Steel Tubing................................Table M2101.1, G2414.5.1	
A 312/A 312M—04a	Specification for Seamless and Welded Austenitic Stainless Steel Pipes.................Table P2904.4.1, Table P2904.5, Table P2904.6, P2904.11.2	
A 377—03	Index of Specification for Ductile Iron Pressure Pipe..Table P2904.4	
A463/A 463M—02a	Standard Specification for Steel Sheet, Aluminum-coated by the Hot-Dip Process.................Table R905.10.3(2)	
A 510M—03	Specification for General Requirements for Wire Rods and Coarse Round Wire, Carbon Steel.................R606.15	
A 539—99	Specification for Electronic-resistance-welded Coiled Steel Tubing for Gas and Fuel Oil Lines........M2202.1, G2414.5.1	
A 615/A 0615M—04a	Specification for Deformed and Plain Billet-steel Bars for Concrete Reinforcement...............R404.4.6.1, R611.6.2	
A 641/A 0641M—03	Specification for Zinc-coated (Galvanized) Carbon Steel Wire...............................Table R606.15.1	
A 653/A 0653M—04a	Specification for Steel Sheet, Zinc-coated (Galvanized) or Zinc-iron Alloy-coated (Galvanized) by the Hot-dip Process......................R505.2.1, R505.2.3, R603.2.1, R603.2.3, Table R606.15.1, R804.2.1, R804.2.3, Table R905.10.3(1) M1601.1.1	
A 706/A 706/M—04a	Specification for Low-alloy Steel Deformed and Plain Bars for Concrete Reinforcement............R404.4.6.1, R611.6.2	
A 755/A 755M—01 (2003)	Specification for Steel Sheet, Metallic Coated by the Hot-dip Process and Prepainted by the Coil-coating Process for Exterior Exposed Building Products..................Table R905.10.3(2)	
A 778—01	Specification for Welded Unannealed Austenitic Stainless Steel Tubular Products............Table P2904.4, Table P2904.5, Table P2904.6	
A 792/A 792M—03	Specification for Steel Sheet, 55% Aluminum-zinc Alloy-coated by the Hot-dip Process..................R505.2.1, R603.2.1, R603.2.3, R804.2.1, R804.2.3	
A 875/A 875M—02a	Specification for Steel Sheet, Zinc-5%, Aluminum Alloy-coated by the Hot-dip Process..............R505.2.1, R505.2.3, R603.2.1, R603.2.1, R603.2.3, R804.2.1, R804.2.3, Table R905.10.3	
A 888—04	Specification for Hubless Cast Iron Soil Pipe and Fittings for Sanitary and Storm Drain, Waste, and Vent Piping Application.....................Table P3002.1(1), Table P3002.1(2), Table P3002.2, Table P3002.3, P3005.2.9	
A 924-04	Standard Specification for General Requirements for Steel Sheet, Metallic-Coated by the Hot-Dip Process Table...............................R905.10.3(1)	
A 951—02	Specification for Masonry Joint Reinforcement..R606.15	
A 996/A 996M—04	Specifications for Rail-Steel and Axel-Steel Deformed Bars for Concrete Reinforcement............R404.4.6.1, R611.6.2	
A 1003/A 1003M—00	Standard Specification for Steel Sheet, Carbon, Metallic- and Nonmetallic-Coated for Cold-formed Framing Members....................R505.2.1, R603.2.1, R804.2.1	
B 32—03	Specification for Solder Metal...P3003.10.3, P3003.11.3	
B 42—02e01	Specification for Seamless Copper Pipe, Standard Sizes.......Table M2101.1, G2413.5.2, Table P2904.5, Table P3002.1(1)	
B 43—98(2004)	Specification for Seamless Red Brass Pipe, Standard Sizes.................Table M2101.1, G2413.5.2, Table P2904.4, Table P2904.5, Table P3002.1(1)	
B 75—02	Specification for Seamless Copper Tube...........................Table M2101.1, Table P2904.4, Table P2904.5, Table P3002.1(1), Table P3002.1(2), Table P3002.2	
B 88—03	Specification for Seamless Copper Water Tube.............Table M2101.1, G2414.5.2, Table P2904.4, Table P2904.5, Table P3002.1(1), Table P3002.1(2), Table P3002.2	
B 101—02	Specification for Lead-Coated Copper Sheet and Strip for Building Construction.....................Table R905.10.3(1)	
B 135—02	Specification for Seamless Brass Tube...Table M2101.1	
B 209—04	Specification for Aluminum and Aluminum-alloy Sheet and Plate..........................Table 905.10.3(1)	
B 227—04	Specification for Hard-drawn Copper-clad Steel Wire...R606.15	
B 251—02e01	Specification for General Requirements for Wrought Seamless Copper and Copper-alloy Tube...........................Table M2101.1, Table P2904.4, Table P2904.5 Table P3002.1(1), Table P3002.1(2), Table P3002.2	
B 280—02	Specification for Seamless Copper Tube for Air Conditioning and Refrigeration Field Service.................G2414.5.2	
B 302—02	Specification for Threadless Copper Pipe, Standard Sizes...............Table M2101.1, Table P2904.5, Table P3002.1(1)	
B 306—02	Specification for Copper Drainage Tube (DWV).......Table M2101.1, Table P3002.1(1), Table P3002.1(2), Table P3002.2	
B 370—03	Specification for Copper Sheet and Strip for Building Construction.................Table R905.10.3(1), Table P2701.1	
B 447—02	Specification for Welded Copper Tube...Table P2904.4, Table P2904.5	
B 633—98e01	Specification for Electrodeposited Coatings of Zinc on Iron and Steel.................R505.2.4, R603.2.4, R804.2.4	
B695—00	Standard Specification for Coatings of Zinc Mechanically Deposited on Iron and Steel........................R319.3	
B 813—00e01	Specification for Liquid and Paste Fluxes for Soldering Applications of Copper and Copper Alloy Tube.................Table M2101.1, P2904.13, P3003.3.4 P3003.10.3, P3003.11.3	

ASTM—continued

B 828—02	Practice for Making Capillary Joints by Soldering of Copper and Copper Alloy Tube and Fittings P2904.13,	P3003.10.3, P3003.11.3
C 5—03	Specification for Quicklime for Structural Purposes R702.2	
C 14—03	Specification for Concrete Sewer, Storm Drain and Culvert Pipe . . . . .Table P3002.2	
C 27—98(2002)	Specification for Standard Classification of Fireclay and High-alumina Refractory Brick. R1001.5, R1001.8	
C 28/C28M—00e01	Specification for Gypsum Plasters R702.2	
C 34—03	Specification for Structural Clay Load-Bearing Wall Tile . . . . .Table R301.2(1)	
C 35—95(2001)	Specification for Inorganic Aggregates for Use in Gypsum Plaster R702.2	
C 36/C 0036M—03	Specification for Gypsum Wallboard R702.3.1	
C 37/C 0037M—01	Specification for Gypsum Lath. R702.2	
C 55—03	Specification for Concrete Brick. . . . . .R202, Table R301.2(1)	
C 59/C 0059M—00	Specification for Gypsum Casting and Molding Plaster. R702.2	
C 61/C 0061M—00	Specification for Gypsum Keene's Cement R702.2	
C 62—04	Specification for Building Brick (Solid Masonry Units Made from Clay or Shale) . . . . .R202, Table R301.2(1)	
C 67-03ae01	Test Methods of Sampling and Testing Brick and Structural Clay Tile R905.3.5	
C 73-99a	Specification for Calcium Silicate Face Brick (Sand Lime Brick). . . . . .R202, Table R301.2(1)	
C 76—04a	Specification for Reinforced Concrete Culvert, storm Drain, and Sewer Pipe. . . . . .Table P3002.2	
C79/C 79—04a	Specification for Treated Core and Nontreated Core Gypsum Sheathing Board . . . . .Table R602.3(1), R702.3.1	
C 90—03	Specification for Load-bearing Concrete Masonry Units . . . . .Table R301.2(1)	
C 129—03	Specification for Nonload-bearing Concrete Masonry Units . . . . .Table R301.2(1)	
C140—03	Test Methods of Sampling and Testing Concrete Masonry Units and Related Units. R905.3.5	
C 143/C 0143M—03	Test Method for Slump or Hydraulic Cement Concrete. R404.4.5, R611.6.1	
C 145—85	Specification for Solid Load-bearing Concrete Masonry Units . . . . .R202, Table R301.2(1)	
C 199—84(2000)	Test Method for Pier Test for Refractory Mortar R1001.9, R1003.5, R1003.8	
C 207—04	Specification for Hydrated Lime for Masonry Purposes . . . . .Table R607.1	
C 208—95(2001)	Specification for Cellulosic Fiber Insulating Board . . . . .Table R602.3(1)	
C 216—04a	Specification for Facing Brick (Solid Masonry Units Made from Clay or Shale). . . . . .R202, Table R301.2(1)	
C 270—04	Specification for Mortar for Unit Masonry R607.1	
C 296—00	Specification for Asbestos Cement Pressure Pipe . . . . .Table P2904.4	
C 315—02	Specification for Clay Flue Linings . . . . .Table R1001.11(1), Table R1001.11(2), R1001.8.1, G2425.12	
C 406—00	Specifications for Roofing Slate R905.6.4	
C 411—97	Test Method for Hot-surface Performance of High-temperature Thermal Insulation M1601.2.1	
C 425—04	Specification for Compression Joints for Vitrified Clay Pipe and Fittings . . . . .Table P3002.2,	P3003.15, P3003.18
C428—97(2002)	Specification for Asbestos-Cement Nonpressure Sewer Pipe . . . . .Table P3002.2	
C 443—03	Specification for Joints for Concrete Pipe and Manholes, Using Rubber Gaskets P3003.7, P3003.18	
C 475/C 475M—02	Specification for Joint Compound and Joint Tape for Finishing Gypsum Wallboard. R702.3.1	
C 476—02	Specification for Grout for Masonry. R609.1.1	
C 514—01	Specification for Nails for the Application of Gypsum Wallboard. R702.3.1	
C552—03	Standard Specification for Cellular Glass Thermal Insulation. . . . . .Table R906.2	
C 557—03	Specification for Adhesives for Fastening Gypsum Wallboard to Wood Framing R702.3.1	
C564—04a	Specification for Rubber Gaskets for Cast Iron Soil Pipe and Fittings P3003.6.2, P3003.6.3, P3003.18	
C 578—04	Specification for Rigid, Cellular Polystyrene Thermal Insulation . . . . .R403.3, Table R906.2	
C 587—02	Specification for Gypsum Veneer Plaster. R702.2	
C 588/C 588M—01	Specification for Gypsum Base for Veneer Plasters. R702.2	
C 630/0630M—03	Specification for Water-resistant Gypsum Backing Board. R702.3.1, R702.4.2	
C 631—95a (2000)	Specification for Bonding Compounds for Interior Gypsum Plastering R702.2	
C 645—04	Specification for Nonstructural Steel Framing Members R702.3.3	
C 652—04a	Specification for Hollow Brick (Hollow Masonry Units Made from Clay or Shale). . . . . .R202, Table R301.2(1)	
C 700—02	Specification for Vitrified Clay Pipe, Extra Strength, Standard Strength, and Perforated. . . . . .Table P3002.2	
C 728—97[EI]	Standard Specification for Perlite Thermal Insulation Board . . . . .Table R906.2	
C 836—03	Specification for High Solids Content, Cold Liquid-Applied Elastomeric Waterproofing Membrane for Use with Separate Wearing Course R905.15.2	
C 843—99e01	Specification for Application of Gypsum Veneer Plaster. R702.2	
C 844—99	Specification for Application of Gypsum Base to Receive Gypsum Veneer Plaster. R702.2	
C 847—(2000)	Specification for Metal Lath. R702.2	
C 887—79(2001)	Specification for Packaged, Dry, Combined Materials for Surface Bonding Mortar R406.1	
C 897—00	Specification for Aggregate for Job-mixed Portland Cement-based Plasters R702.2	
C926—98a	Specification for Application of Portland Cement Based-Plaster R703.6	
C 931/C 931M—04	Specification for Exterior Gypsum Soffit Board. R702.3.1	

ASTM—continued

C 933—04	Specification for Welded Wire Lath	R702.2
C 954—00	Specification for Steel Drill Screws for the Application of Gypsum Panel Products or Metal Plaster Bases to Steel Studs from 0.033 in. (0.84 mm) to 0.112 in. (2.84 mm) in Thickness	R505.2.4, R603.2.4, R702.3.6, R804.2.4
C955—03	Specification for Load-Bearing (Transverse and Axial) Steel Studs, Runners (Tracks), and Bracing or Bridging for Screw Application of Gypsum Panel Products and Metal Plaster Bases	R702.3.3
C 957—04	Specification for High-solids Content, Cold Liquid-Applied Elastomeric Waterproofing Membrane for Use with Integral Wearing Surface	R905.15.2
C 960/C960M—04	Specification for Predecorated Gypsum Board	R702.3.1
C 1002—01	Specification for Steel Drill Screws for the Application of Gypsum Panel Products or Metal Plaster Bases	R702.3.1, R702.3.6, Table R702.3.4
C 1029—02	Specification for Spray-Applied Rigid Cellular Polyurethane Thermal Insulation	R905.14.2
C 1032—04	Specification for Woven Wire Plaster Base	R702.2
C 1047—99	Specification for Accessories for Gypsum Wallboard and Gypsum Veneer Base	R702.2, R702.3.1
C 1063—03	Specification for Installation of Lathing and Furring to Receive Interior and Exterior Portland Cement-Based Plaster	R702.2
C 1157—03	Performance Specification for Hydraulic Cements	R402.2
C 1167—03	Specification for Clay Roof Tiles	R905.3, R905.3.4, R905.3.5
C 1173—02	Specification for Flexible Transition Couplings for Underground Piping Systems	P3003.3, P3003.3.5, P3003.7, P3003.8.1, P3003.14.1, P3003.15, P3003.17.2, P3003.18
C 1177/C 1177M—04	Specification for Glass Mat Gypsum Substrate for Use as Sheathing	R702.3.1
C 1178/C 1178M—04	Specification for Glass Mat Water-Resistant Gypsum Backing Panel	R702.3.1, R702.3.8, R702.4.2
C 1186—02	Specification for Flat Nonasbestos Fiber Cement Sheets	R703.4
C 1261—04	Specification for Firebox Brick for Residential Fireplaces	R1001.5, R1001.8
C 1277—04	Specification for Shielded Couplings Joining Hubless Cast Iron Soil Pipe and Fittings	Table P3002.1, Table P3002.2, P3003.6.3
C 1278/C 1278M—03	Specification for Fiber-Reinforced Gypsum Panels	R702.3.1
C 1283—03e01	Practice for Installing Clay Flue Lining	R1003.12
C1288—01	Standard Specification for Discrete Non-asbestos Fiber-Cement Interior Substrate Sheets	R702.4.2
C1289—03	Standard Specification for Faced Rigid Cellular Polyisocyanurate Thermal Insulation Board	Table R906.2
C 1325—04	Standard Specification for Non-abestos Fiber-Mat Reinforced Cement Interior Substrate Sheets	R702.4.2
C 1395/C 1395M—04	Specification for Gypsum Ceiling Board	R702.3.1
C 1396M—04	Specification for Gypsum Board	R702.3.1
C 1440-99e01	Specification for Thermoplastic Elastomeric (TPE) Gasket Materials for Drain, Waste and Vent (DWV), Sewer, Sanitary and Storm Plumbing Systems	P3003.18
C 1460—04	Specification for Shielded Transition Couplings for Use with Dissimilar DWV Pipe and Fittings Above Ground	Table P3002.1, Table P3002.2, P3003.18
C 1461—02	Specification for Mechanical Couplings Using Thermoplastic Elastomeric (TPE) Gaskets for Joining Drain, Waste, and Vent (DWV) Sewer, Sanitary and Storm Plumbing Systems for Above and Below Ground Use	Table P3002.1, Table P3002.2, P3003.18
C 1492—03	Specification for Concrete Roof Tile	R905.3.5
D 41—e01	Specification for Asphalt Primer Used in Roofing, Dampproofing, and Waterproofing	Table R905.9.2, Table R905.11.2
D 43—00	Specification for Coal Tar Primer Used in Roofing, Dampproofing and Waterproofing	Table R905.9.2
D 225—04	Specification for Asphalt Shingles (Organic Felt) Surfaced with Mineral Granules	R905.2.4
D 226—97a	Specification for Asphalt-Saturated (Organic Felt) Used in Roofing and Waterproofing	R703.2, R703.9.1, Table R905.2.3, R905.4.3, R905.5.3, R905.5.4, R905.6.3, R905.7.3, R905.8.3, R905.8.4, Table 905.9.2
D 227—03	Specification for Coal Tar Saturated (Organic Felt) Used in Roofing and Waterproofing	Table R905.9.2
D 312—00	Specification for Asphalt Used in Roofing	Table R905.9.2
D 422—63(2002)	Test Method for Particle-size Analysis of Soils	R403.1.7.5.1
D 449—03	Specification for Asphalt Used in Dampproofing and Waterproofing	R406.2
D 450—96(00)e01	Specification for Coal-Tar Pitch Used in Roofing , Dampproofing and Waterproofing	Table R905.9.2
D 1227—00	Specification for Emulsified Asphalt Used as a Protective Coating for Roofing	Table R905.9.2, Table R905.11.2, R905.15.2
D 1248—02	Specification for Polyethylene Plastics Extrusion Materials for Wire and Cable	M1601.1.2
D 1527—99e01	Specification for Acrylonite-Butadiene-Styrene (ABS) Plastic Pipe, Schedules 40 and 80	Table P2904.4
D 1693—01	Test Method for Environmental Stress-cracking of Ethylene Plastics	Table M2101.1
D 1784—04	Standard Specification for Rigid Poly (Vinyl Chloride) (PVC) Compounds and Chlorinated Poly (Vinyl Chloride) (CPVC) Compounds	M1601.1.2
D 1785—04	Specification for Poly (Vinyl Chloride) (PVC) Plastic Pipe, Schedules 40, 80 and 120	Table P2904.4
D 1863—03	Specification for Mineral Aggregate Used in Built-up Roofs	Table R905.9.2, Table R906.3.2
D 1869—95(2000)	Specification for Rubber Rings for Asbestos-cement Pipe	P2904.17, P3003.4, P3003.18
D 1970—01	Specification for Self-adhering Polymer Modified Bitumen Sheet Materials Used as Steep Roofing Underlayment for Ice Dam Protection	R905.2.3, R905.2.8.3

ASTM—continued

D 2104—03	Specification for Polyethylene (PE) Plastic Pipe, Schedule 40	Table P2904.4
D 2178—97a	Specification for Asphalt Glass Felt Used in Roofing and Waterproofing	Table R905.9.2
D 2235—01	Specification for Solvent Cement for Acrylonitrile-Butadiene-Styrene (ABS) Plastic Pipe and Fittings	P2904.9.1.1, Table P3002.1, Table P3002.2, P3003.3.2, P3003.8.2
D 2239—03	Specification for Polyethylene (PE) Plastic Pipe (SIDR-PR) Based on Controlled Inside Diameter	Table P2904.4
D 2241—04a	Specification for Poly (Vinyl Chloride) (PVC) Pressure-rated Pipe (SDR-Series)	Table P2904.4
D 2282—99e01	Specification for Acrylonitrile-Butadiene-Styrene (ABS) Plastic Pipe (SDR-PR)	Table P2904.4
D 2412—02	Test Method for Determination of External Loading Characteristics of Plastic Pipe by Parallel-plate Loading	M1601.1.2
D 2447—03	Specification for Polyethylene (PE) Plastic Pipe Schedules 40 and 80, Based on Outside Diameter	Table M2101.1
D 2464—99	Specification for Threaded Poly (Vinyl Chloride) (PVC) Plastic Pipe Fittings, Schedule 80	Table P2904.6
D 2466—02	Specification for Poly(Vinyl Chloride) (PVC) Plastic Pipe Fittings, Schedule 40	Table P2904.6
D 2467—04	Specification for Poly (Vinyl Chloride) (PVC) Plastic Pipe Fittings, Schedule 80	Table P2904.6
D 2468—96a	Specification for Acrylonitrile-Butadiene-Styrene (ABS) Plastic Pipe Fittings, Schedule 40	Table P2904.6
D 2513—04a	Specification for Thermoplastic Gas Pressure Pipe, Tubing, and Fittings	Table M2101.1, M2104.2.1.3, G2414.6, G2414.6.1, G2414.11, G2415.14.3
D 2564—02	Specification for Solvent Cements for Poly (Vinyl Chloride) (PVC) Plastic Piping Systems	P2904.9.1.3, Table P3002.1, Table P3002.2, P3003.9.2, P3003.14.2
D 2609—02	Specification for Plastic Insert Fittings for Polyethylene (PE) Plastic Pipe	Table P2904.6
D 2626—04	Specification for Asphalt-Saturated and Coated Organic Felt Base Sheet Used in Roofing	R905.3.3, Table R905.9.2
D 2657—97	Standard Practice for Heat Fusion-joining of Polyolefin Pipe Fittings	P2904.3.1, P3003.17.1
D 2661—02	Specification for Acrylonitrile-Butadiene-Styrene (ABS) Schedule 40 Plastic Drain, Waste, and Vent Pipe and Fittings	Table P3002.1(1), Table P3002.1(2), Table P3002.2, Table P3002.3, Table P3002.4, P3003.3.2, P3003.8.2
D 2662—96a	Specification for Polybutylene (PB) Plastic Pipe (SDR-PR) Based on Controlled Inside Diameter	Table P2904.4
D 2665—04ae01	Specification for Poly (Vinyl Chloride) (PVC) Plastic Drain, Waste, and Vent Pipe and Fittings	Table P3002.1(1), Table P3002.1(2), Table P3002.2, P3002.3, Table P3002.4
D 2666—96a(2003)	Specification for Polybutylene (PB) Plastic Tubing	Table P2904.4
D 2672—03	Specification for Joints for IPS PVC Pipe Using Solvent Cement	Table P3002.1, Table, P3002.2, Table P2904.4
D 2683—98	Specification for Socket-Type Polyethylene Fittings for Outside Diameter-controlled Polyethylene Pipe and Tubing	Table M2101.1, M2104.2.1.1
D 2737—03	Specification for Polyethylene (PE) Plastic Tubing	Table P2904.4
D 2751—96a	Specification for Acrylonitrile-Butadiene-Styrene (ABS) Sewer Pipe and Fittings	Table P3002.2, Table P3002.3
D 2822—91(1997)e01	Specification for Asphalt Roof Cement	Table R905.9.2, Table R905.11.2
D 2823—90(1997)e1	Specification for Asphalt Roof Coatings	Table R905.9.2, Table R905.11.2
D 2824—04	Specification for Aluminum-Pigmented Asphalt Roof Coatings, Non-fibered, Asbestos Fibered, and Fibered without Asbestos	Table R905.9.2, Table R905.11.2
D 2837—04	Test Method for Obtaining Hydrostatic Design Basis for Thermoplastic Pipe Materials	Table M2101.1
D 2846/D 2846M—99	Specification for Chlorinated Poly (Vinyl Chloride) (CPVC) Plastic Hot- and Cold-water Distribution Systems	Table M2101.1, Table P2904.4, Table P2904.5, P2904.9.1.2
D 2855-96(2002)	Standard Practice for Making Solvent-Cemented Joints with Poly (Vinyl Chloride) (PVC) Pipe and Fittings	P3003.9.2, P3003.14.2
D 2898—94(1999)	Test Methods for Accelerated Weathering of Fire-retardant-treated Wood for Fire Testing	R802.1.3.3, R902.2
D 2949—01a	Specification for 3.25-in. Outside Diameter Poly (Vinyl Chloride) (PVC) Plastic Drain, Waste, and Vent Pipe and Fittings	Table P3002.1(1), Table P3002.1(2), Table P3002.2, Table P3002.3
D 3019—e01	Specification for Lap Cement Used with Asphalt Roll Roofing, Non-fibered, Asbestos Fibered, and Non-asbestos Fibered	Table R905.9.2, Table R905.11.2
D 3034—04	Specification for Type PSM Poly (Vinyl Chloride) (PVC) Sewer Pipe and Fittings	Table P3002.2, P3002.3, Table P3002.4
D 3035—03a	Specification for Polyethylene (PE) Plastic Pipe (DR-PR) Based On Controlled Outside Diameter	Table M2101.1
D 3161—03b	Test Method for Wind Resistance of Asphalt Shingles (Fan Induced Method)	R905.2.4.1, R905.2.6
D 3201—94(2003)	Test Method for Hygroscopic Properties of Fire-retardant Wood and Wood-base Products	R802.1.3.4
D 3212—96a(2003)	Specification for Joints for Drain and Sewer Plastic Pipes Using Flexible Elastomeric Seals	Table P3002.2, P3003.3.1, P3003.8.1, P3003.9.1, P3003.14.1, P3003.17.2
D 3309—96a(2002)	Specification for Polybutylene (PB) Plastic Hot- and Cold-water Distribution Systems	Table M2101.1, Table P2904.4, Table P2904.5
D 3311—02	Specification for Drain, Waste, and Vent (DWV) Plastic Fittings Patters	P3002.3
D 3350—02a	Specification for Polyethylene Plastic Pipe and Fitting Materials	Table M2101.1
D 3462—04	Specification for Asphalt Shingles Made From Glass Felt and Surfaced with Mineral Granules	R905.2.4
D 3468—99	Specification for Liquid-applied Neoprene and Chlorosulfanated Polyethylene Used in Roofing and Waterproofing	Table R905.15.2
D 3679—04	Specification for Rigid Poly (Vinyl Chloride) (PVC) Siding	Table R703.4

ASTM—continued

D 3737—03	Practice for Establishing Allowable Properties for Structural Glued Laminated Timber (Glulam)	R502.1.5, R602.1.2, R802.1.4
D 3747—79(2000)e01	Specification for Emulsified Asphalt Adhesive for Adhering Roof Insulation	Table R905.9.2, Table R905.11.2
D 3909—97b	Specification for Asphalt Roll Roofing (Glass Felt) Surfaced with Mineral Granules	R905.2.8.2, R905.3.3, R905.5.4, Table R905.9.2, Table R906.3.2,
D 3957—03	Standard Practices for Establishing Stress Grades for Structural Members Used in Log Buildings	R502.1.6, R602.1.3, R802.1.5
D 4022—94(2000)e01	Specification for Coal Tar Roof Cement, Asbestos Containing	Table R905.9.2
D 4068—01	Specification for Chlorinated Polyethylene (CPE) Sheeting for Concealed Water Containment Membrane	P2709.2.2
D 4318—00	Test Methods for Liquid Limit, Plastic Limit and Plasticity Index of Soils	R403.1.7.5.1
D 4434—04	Specification for Poly (Vinyl Chloride) Sheet Roofing	R905.13.2
D 4479—00	Specification for Asphalt Roof Coatings-Asbestos-free	Table R905.9.2
D 4551—96(2001)	Specification for Poly (Vinyl Chloride) (PVC) Plastic Flexible Concealed Water-containment Membrane	P2709.2.1
D 4586—00	Specification for Asphalt Roof Cement-Asbestos-free	Table R905.9.2
D 4601—98	Specification for Asphalt-coated Glass Fiber Base Sheet Used in Roofing	Table R905.9.2
D 4637—04	Specification for EPDM Sheet Used in Single-ply Roof Membrane	R905.12.2
D 4829—03	Test Method for Expansion Index of Soils	R403.1.8.1
D 4869—04	Specification for Asphalt-Saturated (Organic Felt) Underlayment Used in Steep Slope Roofing	R905.2.3, R905.4.3, R905.5.3, R905.6.3, R905.7.3, R905.8.3
D 4897—01	Specification for Asphalt Coated Glass-fiber Venting Base Sheet Used in Roofing	Table R905.9.2
D 4990—97a	Specification for Coal Tar Glass Felt Used in Roofing and Waterproofing	Table R905.9.2
D 5019-96 e01	Specification for Reinforced Non-Vulcanized Polymeric Sheet Used in Roofing Membrane	R905.12.2
D 5055—04	Specification for Establishing and Monitoring Structural Capacities of Prefabricated Wood I-Joists	R502.1.4
D 5516—03	Test Method for Evaluating the Flexural Properties of Fire-Retardant-treated Softwood Plywood Exposed to the Elevated Temperatures	R802.1.3.2.1
D 5643—94(2000)e01	Specification for Coal Tar Roof Cement Asbestos-free	Table R905.9.2
D 5664—02	Test Methods For Evaluating the Effects of Fire-Retardant Treatments and Elevated Temperatures on Strength Properties of Fire-retardant-treated Lumber	R802.1.3.2.2
D 5665—99a	Specification for Thermoplastic Fabrics Used in Cold-applied Roofing and Waterproofing	Table R905.9.2
D 5726—98	Specification for Thermoplastic Fabrics Used in Hot-applied Roofing and Waterproofing	Table R905.9.2
D 6083—97a	Specification for Liquid Applied Acrylic Coating Used in Roofing	Table R905.9.2, Table R905.11.2, Table R905.15.2
D 6162—00a	Specification for Styrene Butadiene Styrene (SBS) Modified Bituminous Sheet Materials Using a Combination of Polyester and Glass Fiber Reinforcements	Table R905.11.2
D 6163—00e01	Specification for Styrene Butadiene Styrene (SBS) Modified Bituminous Sheet Materials Using Glass Fiber Reinforcements	Table R905.11.2
D 6164—00	Specification for Styrene Butadiene Styrene (SBS) Modified Bituminous Sheet Materials Using Polyester Reinforcements	Table R905.11.2
D 6221—00	Specification for Reinforced Bituminous Flashing Sheets for Roofing and Waterproofing	Table R905.11.2
D 6222—02	Specification for Atactic Polypropelene (APP) Modified Bituminous Sheet Materials Using Polyester Reinforcement	Table R905.11.2
D 6223—02	Specification for Atactic Polypropelene (APP) Modified Bituminous Sheet Materials Using a Combination of Polyester and Glass Fiber Reinforcement	Table R905.11.2
D 6298—00	Specification for Fiberglass Reinforced Styrene-Butadiene-Styrene (SBS) Modified Bituminous Sheets with a Factory Applied Metal Surface	Table R905.11.2
D 6305—02e01	Practice for Calculating Bending Strength Design Adjustment Factors for Fire-Retardant-Treated Plywood Roof Sheathing	R802.1.3.2.1
D 6380—01[E1]	Standard Specification for Asphalt Roll Roofing (Organic Felt)	R905.2.8.2
D 6694—01	Standard Specification Liquid-Applied Silicone Coating Used in spray Polurethane Foam roofing[1]	R905.15.2
D 6754—02	Standard Specification for Ketone Ethylene ester Based Sheet Roofing[1]	R905.13.2
D 6757—02	Standard Specification for Inorganic Underlayment for Use with Steep Slope Roofing Products[1]	R905.2.3
D 6841—03	Standard Practice for Calculating Design Value Treatment Adjustment Factors for Fire-retardant-treated Lumber	R802.1.3.2.2
D 6878—03	Standard Specification for Thermoplastic Polyolefin Based Sheet Roofing[1]	R905.13.2
E 84—04	Test Method for Surface Burning Characteristics of Building Materials	R202, R314.1.1, R314.2.6, R314.3, R315.3, R316.1, R316.2, R802.1.3, M1601.2.1, M1601.4.2
E 96—00e01	Test Method for Water Vapor Transmission of Materials	R202, R806.4, M1411.4, M1601.3.4
E 108—04	Test Methods for Fire Tests of Roof Coverings	R902.1, R902.2
E 119—00	Test Methods for Fire Tests of Building Construction and Materials	R314.1.2, R317.1, R317.3.1
E 136—99e01	Test Method for Behavior of Materials in a Vertical Tube Furnace at 750°C	R202
E 283—04	Test Method for determining the Rate of Air Leakage Through Exterior Windows, Curtain Walls, and Doors Under specified Pressure Differences Across the Specimen	R806.4

ASTM—continued

E 330—02	Test Method for Structural Performance of Exterior Windows, Curtain Walls, and Doors by Uniform Static Air Pressure Difference	R613.3
E 331-00	Test Method for Water Penetration of Exterior Windows, Skylights, Doors and Curtain Walls by uniform Static Air Pressure Difference	R703.1
E 814—02	Test Method for Fire Tests of Through-Penetration Firestops	R317.3.1.2
E 970—00	Test Method for Critical Radiant Flux of Exposed Attic Floor Insulation Using a Radiant Heat Energy Source	R316.5
E 1509—04	Standard Specification for Room Heaters, Pellet Fuel-burning Type	M1410.1
E 1602—03	Guide for Construction of Solid Fuel Burning Masonry Heaters	R1002.2
E 1886—04	Test Method for Performance of Exterior Windows, Curtain Walls, Doors and Storm Shutters Impacted by Missles and Exposed to Cyclic Pressure Differentials	R301.2.1.2, R613.7.1
E 1996—04	Specification for Performance of Exterior Windows, Curtain Walls, Doors and Storm Shutters Impacted by Windborne Debris in Hurricanes	R301.2.1.2, R613.7.1
E 2231—04	Standard Practice for Specimen Preparation and Mounting of Pipe and Duct Insulation Materials to Assess Surface Burning Characteristics	M1601.2.1
F 409—02	Specification for Thermoplastic Accessible and Replaceable Plastic Tube and Tubular Fittings	Table P2701.1, P2702.2, P2702.3
F 437—99	Specification for Threaded Chlorinated Poly (Vinyl Chloride) (CPVC) Plastic Pipe Fittings, Schedule 80	Table P2904.6
F 438—04	Specification for Socket-type Chlorinated Poly (Vinyl Chloride) (CPVC) Plastic Pipe Fittings, Schedule 40	Table P2904.6
F 439—02e01	Specification for Socket-type Chlorinated Poly (Vinyl Chloride) (CPVC) Plastic Pipe Fittings, Schedule 80	Table P2904.6
F 441/F 441M—02	Specification for Chlorinated Poly (Vinyl Chloride) (CPVC) Plastic Pipe, Schedules 40 and 80	Table P2904.4, Table P2904.5
F 442/F 442M—99	Specification for Chlorinated Poly (Vinyl Chloride) (CPVC) Plastic Pipe (SDR-PR)	Table P2904.4, Table P2904.5
F 477—02e01	Specification for Elastomeric Seals (Gaskets) for joining Plastic Pipe	P2904.17, P3003.18
F 493—04	Specification for Solvent Cements for Chlorinated Poly (Vinyl Chloride) (CPVC) Plastic Pipe and Fittings	P2904.9.1.2
F 628—01	Specification for Acrylonitrile-Butadiene-Styrene (ABS) Schedule 40 Plastic Drain, Waste, and Vent Pipe with a Cellular Core	Table 3002.1(1), Table P3002.1(2), Table P3002.2, Table P3002.3, P3003.3.2, P3003.8.2
F 656—02	Specification for Primers for Use in Solvent Cement Joints of Poly (Vinyl Chloride) (PVC) Plastic Pipe and Fittings	P2904.9.1.3, Table P3002.1, Table P3002.2, P3003.9.2, P3003.14.2
F 714—03	Specification for Polyethylene (PE) Plastic Pipe (SDR-PR) Based on Outside Diameter	Table P3002.2
F 789—95a	Specification for Type PS-46 and Type PS-115 Poly (Vinyl Chloride) (PVC) Plastic Gravity Flow Sewer Pipe and Fittings	Table P3002.2
F 876—04	Specification for Cross-linked Polyethylene (PEX) Tubing	Table M2101.1, Table P2904.4
F 877—02e01	Specification for Cross-linked Polyethylene (PEX) Plastic Hot- and Cold-water Distribution Systems	Table M2101.1, Table P2904.4, P2904.9.1.4.2, Table P2904.5, Table 2904.6
F 891—00e01	Specification for Coextruded Poly (Vinyl Chloride) (PVC) Plastic Pipe with a Cellular Core	Table P3002.1(1), Table P3002.1(2), Table P3002.2, Table 3002.3, Table P3002.4
F 1055—98e01	Specification for Electrofusion Type Polyethylene Fittings for Outside Diameter Controlled Polyethylene Pipe and Fittings	Table M2101.1, M2104.2.1.2
F 1281—03	Specification for Crosslinked Polyethylene/Aluminum/Crosslinked Polyethylene (PEX-AL-PEX) Pressure Pipe	Table M2101.1, Table P2904.4, Table P2904.5
F 1282—03	Specification for Polyethylene/Aluminum/Polyethylene (PE-AL-PE) Composite Pressure Pipe	Table P2904.4, Table P2904.5
F 1412—01	Specification for Polyolefin Pipe and Fittings for Corrosive Waste Drainage	Table P3002.2, Table P3002.3, P3003.16.1
F 1488—03	Specification for Coextruded Composite Pipe	Table P3002.1(1), Table P3002.1(2), Table P3002.2
F 1667—03	Specification for Driven Fasteners, Nails, Spikes, and Staples	R905.2.5
F 1807—04	Specification for Metal Insert Fittings Utilizing a Copper Crimp Ring for SDR9 Cross-linked Polyethylene (PEX) Tubing	Table M2101.1, Table P2904.6, P2904.9.1.4.2
F 1866—98	Specification for Poly (Vinyl Chloride) (PVC) Plastic Schedule 40 Drainage and DWV Fabricated Fittings	Table P3002.4
F 1960—04	Specification for Cold Expansion Fittings with PEX Reinforcing Rings for Use with Cross-linked Polyethylene (PEX) Tubing	Table M2101.1, Table P2904.6, P2904.9.1.4.2
F 1974—04	Specification for Metal Insert Fittings for Polyethylene/Aluminum/Polyethylene and Crosslinked Polyethylene/Aluminum/Crosslinked Polyethylene Composite Pressure Pipe	Table P2904.6
F 1986—00a	Multilayer Pipe Type 2, Compression Joints for Hot and Cold Drinking Water Systems	Table P2904.4, Table P2904.5, Table P2904.6
F 2006—00	Standard/Safety Specification for Window Fall Prevention Devices for Non-Emergency Escape (Egress) and Rescue (Ingress) Windows	R613.2
F 2080—04	Specification for Cold-expansion Fittings with Metal Compression-Sleeves for Crosslinked Polyethylene (PEX) Pipe	P2904.6, P2904.9.1.4.2

ASTM—continued

F 2090—01A	Specification for Window Fall Prevention Devices —with Emergency Escape (Egress) Release Mechanisms 613.2	
F 2098—01	Standard Specification for Stainless Steel Clamps for SDR9 PEX Tubing to Metal Insert Fittings . . . . .Table M2101.1	
F 2389—04	Standard for Pressure-rated Polypropylene (PP) Piping Systems . . . . .Table M2101.1, Table P2904.4, Table P2904.5, Table P2904.6, P2904.10.1	

AWS

American Welding Society
550 N. W. LeJeune Road
Miami, FL 33126

Standard reference number	Title	Referenced in code section number
A5.8—04	Specifications for Filler Metals for Brazing and Braze Welding P3003.5.1, P3003.10.1, P3003.11.1	

AWPA

American Wood-Preservers' Association
P.O. Box 5690
Granbury, Texas 76049

Standard reference number	Title	Referenced in code section number
C1—100	All Timber Products—Preservative Treatment by Pressure Processes R902.2	
C33—00	Standard for Preservative Treatment of Structural Composite Lumber by Pressure Processes R324.1	
M4—02	Standard for the Care of Preservative-treated Wood Products. R319.1.1, R320.1.2, R320.3.1	
U1—04	USE CATEGORY SYSTEM: User Specification for Treated Wood Except Section 6 Commodity Specification H .R319.1, R324.1.7, R402.1.2, R504.3, Table R905.8.5	

AWWA

American Water Works Association
6666 West Quincy Avenue
Denver, CO 80235

Standard reference number	Title	Referenced in code section number
C104—98	Standard for Cement-Mortar Lining for Ductile-iron Pipe and Fittings for Water P2904.4	
C110—98	Standard for Ductile-iron and Gray-iron Fittings, 3 Inches through 48 Inches, for Water . . . . . . .Table P2904.6, Table P3002.3	
C115—99	Standard for Flanged Ductile-iron Pipe with Ductile-iron or Gray-iron Threaded Flanges . . . . .Table P2904.4	
C151/A21.51—02	Standard for Ductile-iron Pipe, Centrifugally Cast, for Water . . . . .Table P2904.4	
C153—00	Standard for Ductile-iron Compact Fittings for Water Service . . . . .Table P2904.6.1	
C510—00	Double Check Valve Backflow Prevention Assembly. . . . . Table P2902.3	
C511—00	Reduced-Pressure Principle Backflow Prevention Assembly . . . . .Table P2902.3, P2902.3.5, P2902.5.1	

CGSB

Canadian General Standards Board
Place du Portage 111, 6B1
11 Laurier Street
Gatineau, Quebec, Canada KIA 1G6

Standard reference number	Title	Referenced in code section number
37-GP—52M—(1984)	Roofing and Waterproofing Membrane, Sheet Applied, Elastomeric R905.12.2	
37-GP—56M—(1980)	Membrane, Modified Bituminous, Prefabricated and Reinforced for Roofing— with December 1985 Amendment. . . . . .Table R905.11.2	
CAN/CGSB-37.54—95	Polyvinyl Chloride Roofing and Waterproofing Membrane R905.13.2	

CISPI

Cast Iron Soil Pipe Institute
5959 Shallowford Road, Suite 419
Chattanooga, TN 37421

Standard reference number	Title	Referenced in code section number
301—04	Standard Specification for Hubless Cast Iron Soil Pipe and Fittings for Sanitary and Storm Drain, Waste and Vent Piping Applications..............	Table P3002.1(1), Table P3002.1(2), Table P3002.2, Table P3002.3, Table 3002.4, P3005.2.9
310—04	Standard Specification for Coupling for Use in Connection with Hubless Cast Iron Soil Pipe and Fittings for Sanitary and Storm Drain, Waste, and Vent Piping Applications....	Table P3002.1, Table P3002.2, P3003.6.3

CPSC

Consumer Product Safety Commission
4330 East West Highway
Bethesda, MD 20814-4408

Standard reference number	Title	Referenced in code section number
16 CFR Part 1201— (1977)	Safety Standard for Architectural Glazing	R308.1.1, R308.3
16 CFR Part 1209— (1979)	Interim Safety Standard for Cellulose Insulation	R316.3
16 CFR Part 1404— (1979)	Cellulose Insulation	R316.3

CSA

Canadian Standards Association
5060 Spectrum Way, Suite 100
Mississauga, Ontario, Canada L4W 5N6

Standard reference number	Title	Referenced in code section number
CSA Requirement 3—88	Manually Operated Gas Valves for Use in House Piping Systems........................	Table G2420.1.1
8-93 (Revision 1, 1999)	Requirements for Gas Fired Log Lighters for Wood Burning Fireplaces —with Revisions through January 1999	G2433.1
0325.0—92	Construction Sheathing (Reaffirmed 1998)..	R503.2.1
0437-Series—93	Standards on OSB and Waferboard (Reaffirmed 2001).............................	R503.2.1, R803.2.1
A 257.1M—92	Circular Concrete Culvert, Storm Drain, Sewer Pipe and Fittings......................	Table P3002.2
A 257.2M—92	Reinforced Circular Concrete Culvert, Storm Drain, Sewer Pipe and Fittings	Table P3002.2
A 257.3M—92	Joints for Circular Concrete Sewer and Culvert Pipe, Manhole Sections, and Fittings Using Rubber Gaskets..	P3003.7
101/I.S.2/A440—05	Specifications for Windows, Doors and Unit Skylights.............................	R308.6.9, R613.4, N1102.4.2
B45.1—02	Ceramic Plumbing Fixtures	Table P2701.1, P2711.1, P2712.1
B45.2—02	Enameled Cast Iron Plumbing Fixtures	Table 2701.1, P2711.1
B45.3—02	Porcelain Enameled Steel Plumbing Fixtures	Table P2701.1, Table P2702.2, P2711.1
B45.4—02	Stainless Steel Plumbing Fixtures	Table P2701.1, P2711.1, P2712.1
B45.5—02	Plastic Plumbing Fixtures...	Table P2701.1, P2711.2, P2712.1
B45.9—02	Macerating Systems and Related Components	P3007.1, P3007.2.1
B64.1.1—01	Vacuum Breakers, Atmospheric Type (PVB)	Table P2902.2, P2902.2
B64.1.2—01	Vacuum Breakers, Pressure Type (PVB).................................	Table P2902.2, P2902.2
B64.2—01	Vacuum Breakers, Hose Connection Type (HCVB)........................	Table P2902.2, P2902.2.2
B64.2.1—01	Vacuum Breakers, Hose Connection Type (HCVB) with Manual Draining Feature.............	Table P2902.2, P2902.2.2
B64.2.1.1—01	Vacuum Breakers, Hose Connection Dual Check Type (HCDVB)	Table P2902.2, P2902.2.2
B64.2.2—01	Vacuum Breakers, Hose Connection Type (HCVB) with Automatic Draining Feature.............	Table P2902.2, P2902.2
B64.3—01	Backflow Preventers, Dual Check Valve type with Atmospheric Port (DCAP)............................	Table P2902.2, P2902.2.2, P2902.2.3, P2902.4.1
B64.4—01	Blackflow Preventers, Reduced Pressure Principle Type (RP)	Table P2902.2, P2902.2.3, P2902.2.5, P2902.4.1
B64.4.1—01	Backflow Preventers, Reduced Pressure Principle Type for Fire Systems (RPF)	Table P2902.2, P2902.2.5
B64.5—01	Backflow Preventers, Double Check Valve Type (DCVA)........................	Table P2902.2, P2902.2.6
B64.5.1—01	Backflow Preventers, Double Check Valve Type for Fire Systems (DCVAF)...................	Table P2902.2, P2902.2.6
B64.7—01	Vacuum Breakers, Laboratory Faucet Type (LFVB)	Table P2902.2, P2902.2.2
B125—01	Plumbing Fittings	Table P2701.1, P2702.2, P2708.3, P2722.1, P2722.2, P2722.3
B 125.1—05	Plumbing Supply Fittings	P2708.4

CSA—continued

B137.1—02	Polyethylene Pipe, Tubing and Fittings for Cold Water Pressure Services	Table P2904.4, Table P2904.6
B137.2—02	PVC Injection-moulded Gasketed Fittings for Pressure Applications	Table P2904.6
B137.3—02	Rigid Poly (Vinyl Chloride) (PVC) Pipe for Pressure Applications	Table P2904.4, P3003.9.2, P3003.14.2
B137.5—02	Cross-linked Polyethylene (PEX) Tubing Systems for Pressure Applications	Table P2904.4, Table P2904.5, Table P2904.6
B137.6—02	CPVC Pipe, Tubing and Fittings For Hot and Cold Water Distribution Systems	Table P2904.4, Table P2904.5, Table 2904.6
B137.8—02	Polybutylene (PB) Piping for Pressure Applications	Table 2904.4, Table P2904.5, Table 2904.6
B137.9—02	Polyethylene/Aluminum/Polyethylene Composite Pressure-Pipe Systems	Table 2904.4.1
B137.10—02	Crosslinked Polyethylene/Aluminum/Crosslinked Polyethylene Composite Pressure-Pipe Systems	Table P2904.4.1, Table P2904.5, Table M2101.1
B137.11—02	Polypropylene (PP-R) Pipe and Fittings for Pressure Applications	Table P2904.4.1, Table 2904.5, Table P2904.6
B181.1—02	ABS Drain, Waste and Vent Pipe and Pipe Fittings	Table P3002.1(1), Table P3002.1(2), Table P3002.2, Table P3002.4, P3003.3.2, P3003.8.2
B181.2—02	PVC Drain, Waste and Vent Pipe and Pipe Fittings	Table P3002.1(1), Table P3002.1(2), Table P3002.2, Table P3002.3, P3003.9.2, P3003.14.2
B181.3—02	Polyolefin Laboratory Drainage Systems	Table P3002.2, P3003.16.1
B182.2—02	PVC Sewer Pipe and Fittings (PSM Type)	Table P3002.1(1), Table P3002.1(2), Table P3002.2, Table P3002.3
B182.4—02	Profile PVC Sewer Pipe & Fittings	Table P3002.2, Table P3002.3
B602—02	Mechanical Couplings for Drain, Waste and Vent Pipe and Sewer Pipe	P3003.3.1, P3003.6.3, P3003.7, P3003.8.1, P3003.14.1, P3003.15, P3003.17
LC3—00	Appliance Stands and Drain Pans	P2801.5
CAN/CSA A257.3M—92	Joints for Circular Concrete Sewer and Culvert Pipe, Manhole Sections, and Fittings Using Rubber Gaskets	P3003.3.5
CAN/CSA B64.1.1—01	Vacuum Breakers, Atmospheric Type (AVB)	Table P2902.2, P2902.2.2
CAN/CSA B64.2—01	Vacuum Breakers, Hose Connection Type (HCVP)	Table P2902.2, P2902.2.2
CAN/CSA B64.2.2—01	Vacuum Breakers, Hose Connection Type (HCVP) with Automatic Draining Feature	Table P2902.2, P2902.2.2
CAN/CSA B64.3—01	Backflow Preventers, Dual Check Valve Type with Atmospheric Port (DCAP)	Table P2902.2, P2902.2.3, P2902.4.1
CAN/CSA B64.4—01	Backflow Preventers, Reduced Pressure Principle Type (RP)	Table P2902.2, P2902.2.5
CAN/CSA B137.9—99	Polyethylene/Aluminum/Polyethylene Composite Pressure Pipe Systems	Table P2904.4.1
CAN/CSA B137.10M—02	Crosslinked Polyethylene/Aluminum/Polyethylene Composite Pressure Pipe Systems	Table P2904.4.1, Table P2904.5, Table M2101.1

CSSB

Cedar Shake & Shingle Bureau
515 116th Avenue, NE, Suite 275
Bellevue, WA 98004-5294

Standard reference number	Title	Referenced in code section number
CSSB—97	Grading and Packing Rules for Western Red Cedar Shakes and Western Red Shingles of the Cedar Shake and Shingle Bureau	R702.6, R703.5, Table R905.7.4, Table R905.8.5

DASMA

Door and Access Systems Manufacturers
Association International
1300 Summer Avenue
Cleveland, OH 44115-2851

Standard reference number	Title	Referenced in code section number
108—2002	Standard Method for Testing Garage Doors: Determination of Structural Performance Under Uniform Static Air Pressure Difference	R902.2

DOC

United States Department of Commerce
100 Bureau Drive Stop 3460
Gaithersburg, MD 20899

Standard reference number	Title	Referenced in code section number
PS 1—95	Construction and Industrial Plywood	R404.2.1, Table R404.2.3, R503.2.1, R604.1, R803.2.1
PS 2—92	Performance Standard for Wood-based Structural-use Panels	R404.2.1, Table R404.2.3, R503.2.1, R604.1, R803.2.1
PS 20—99	American Softwood Lumber Standard	R404.2.1, R502.1, R602.1, R802.1

DOTn

Department of Transportation
400 Seventh St. S.W.
Washington, DC 20590

Standard reference number	Title	Referenced in code section number
49 CFR, Parts 192.281(e) & 192.283 (b)	Transportation of Natural and Other Gas by Pipeline: Minimum Federal Safety Standards G2414.6.1	

FEMA

Federal Emergency Management Agency
500 C Street, SW
Washington, DC 20472

Standard reference number	Title	Referenced in code section number
TB-2—93	Flood-resistant Materials Requirements. R324.1.7	
FIA-TB-11—01	Crawlspace Construction for Buildings Located in Special Flood Hazard Area. R408.7	

FM

Factory Mutual Global Research
Standards Laboratories Department
1151 Boston Providence Turnpike
Norwood, MA 02062

Standard reference number	Title	Referenced in code section number
4450—(1989)	Approval Standard for Class 1 Insulated Steel Deck Roofs—with Supplements through July 1992 . . . . R906.1	
4880—(2001)	American National Standard for Evaluating Insulated Wall or Wall and Roof/Ceiling Assemblies, Plastic Interior Finish Materials, Plastic Exterior Building Panels, Wall/Ceiling Coating Systems, Interior or Exterior Finish Systems R314.3	

GA

Gypsum Association
810 First Street, Northeast, Suite 510
Washington, DC 20002-4268

Standard reference number	Title	Referenced in code section number
GA-253—99	Recommended Standard Specification for the Application of Gypsum Sheathing. . . . . Table R602.3(1)	

HPVA

Hardwood Plywood & Veneer Association
1825 Michael Faraday Drive
Reston, Virginia 20190-5350

Standard reference number	Title	Referenced in code section number
HP-1—2000	The American National Standard for Hardwood and Decorative Plywood. R702.5	

ICC

International Code Council, Inc.
500 New Jersey Ave, NW
6th Floor
Washington, D.C. 20001

Standard reference number	Title	Referenced in code section number
IBC—06	International Building Code® R110.2, R322.1, R324.1, R324.1.5, R403.1.8, R1001.8.2, G2402.3	
ICC EC—06	ICC Electrical Code®—Administrative Provisions R107.3, G2402.3	
IEBC—06	International Existing Building Code® R101.2, G2401.1	
IECC—06	International Energy Conservation Code® R104.11	
IFC—06	International Fire Code® R102.7, G2402.3, G2412.2, G2423.1	
IFGC—06	International Fuel Gas Code® R104.11, G2401.1	

ICC—continued

IMC—06	International Mechanical Code®	R104.11, M2106.1, G2402.3
IPC—06	International Plumbing Code®	R104.11, G2402.3
IPSDC—06	International Private Sewage Disposal Code®	R324.1.6
IPMC—06	International Property Maintenance Code®	R102.7
SBCCI SSTD 10—99	Standard for Hurricane Resistant Construction	R301.2.1.1

ISO

International Organization for Standardization
1, rue de Varembé, Case postale 56
CH-1211 Geneva 20, Switzerland

Standard reference number	Title	Referenced in code section number
15874—2002	Polypropylene Plastic Piping Systems for Hot and Cold Water Installations	Table M2101.1

MSS

Manufacturers Standardization Society of the Valve and Fittings Industry
127 Park Street, Northeast
Vienna, VA 22180

Standard reference number	Title	Referenced in code section number
SP-58—93	Pipe Hangers and Supports—Materials, Design and Manufacture	G2418.2

NAIMA

North American Insulation Manufacturers Association
44 Canal Center Plaza, Suite 310
Alexandria, VA 22314

Standard reference number	Title	Referenced in code section number
AH 116 06—02	Fibrous Glass Duct Construction Standards, Fifth Edition	M1601.1.1

NCMA

National Concrete Masonry Association
2302 Horse Pen Road
Herndon, VA 20171-3499

Standard reference number	Title	Referenced in code section number
TR 68-A—75	Design and Construction of Plain and Reinforced Concrete Masonry and Basement and Foundation Walls	R404.1
TR 68B(2001)	Basement Manual Design and Construction Using Concrete Masonry	R404.1

NFPA

National Fire Protection Association
Batterymarch Park
Quincy, MA 02269

Standard reference number	Title	Referenced in code section number
13—02	Installation of Sprinkler Systems	R317.1
31—01	Installation of Oil-burning Equipment	M1801.3.1, M1805.3
58—04	Liquefied Petroleum Gas Code	G2412.2, G2414.6.2
70—05	National Electrical Code	E3301.1, E3301.2, E4201.1, Table E4203.2, E4204.3, E4204.4
72—02	National Fire Alarm Code	R313.1
85—04	Boiler and Construction Systems Hazards Code	G2452.1
211—03	Chimneys, Fireplaces, Vents and Solid Fuel Burning Appliances	R1002.5
259—04	Test Method for Potential Heat of Building Materials	R314.2.5
286—00	Standard Methods of Fire Tests for Evaluating Contribution of Wall and Ceiling Interior Finish to Room Fire Growth	R314.3, R315.4
501—03	Standard on Manufactured Housing	R202
853—03	Standard for the Installation of Stationary Fuel Cell Power Systems	M1903.1

NFRC

National Fenestration Rating Council, Inc.
8484 Georgia Avenue, Suite 320
Silver Spring, MD 20910

Standard reference number	Title	Referenced in code section number
100—2001	Procedure for Determining Fenestration Product U-factors–Second Edition	N1101.5
200—2001	Procedure for Determining Fenestration product Solar Heat Gain Coefficients and Visible Transmittance at Normal Incidence—Second Edition	N1101.5
400—2001	Procedure for Determining Fenestration Product Air Leakage	N1102.4.2

NSF

NSF International
789 N. Dixboro Road
Ann Arbor, MI 48105

Standard reference number	Title	Referenced in code section number
14—2003	Plastic Piping System Components and Related Materials	P2608.3, P2907.3
42—2002e	Drinking Water Treatment Units—Anesthetic Effects	P2907.1, P2907.3
44—2004	Residential Cation Exchange Water Softeners	P2907.1, P2907.3
53—2002e	Drinking Water Treatment Units—Health Effects	P2907.1, P2907.3
58—2004	Reverse Osmosis Drinking Water Treatment Systems	P2907.2, P2907.3
61—2003e	Drinking Water System Components—Health Effects	P2608.5, P2722.1, P2903.9.4, P2904.4, P2904.5, P2904.6, P2907.3

SAE

Society of Automotive Engineers
400 Commonwealth Drive
Warrendale, PA 15096

Standard reference number	Title	Referenced in code section number
J 78—(1998)	Steel Self-drilling Tapping Screws	R505.2.4, R603.2.4, R804.2.4

SMACNA

Sheet Metal & Air Conditioning Contractors National Assoc., Inc.
4021 Lafayette Center Road
Chantilly, VA 22021

Standard reference number	Title	Referenced in code section number
SMACNA—03	Fibrous Glass Duct Construction Standards (2003)	M1601.1.1

TMS

The Masonry Society
3970 Broadway, Suite 201-D
Boulder, CO 80304

Standard reference number	Title	Referenced in code section number
402—05	Building Code Requirements for Masonry Structures	R404.1, R606.1, R606.1.1, R606.12.1, R606.12.2.2.1, R606.11.2.2.2, R606.12.3.1
602—05	Specification for Masonry Structures	R404.1, R606.1, R606.1.1, R606.12.1, R606.12.2.2.1, R606.12.2.2.2, R606.12.3.1

TPI

Truss Plate Institute
583 D'Onofrio Drive, Suite 200
Madison, WI 53719

Standard reference number	Title	Referenced in code section number
TPI 1—2002	National Design Standard for Metal-plate-connected Wood Truss Construction	R502.11.1, R802.10.2,

UL

Underwriters Laboratories, Inc.
333 Pfingsten Road
Northbrook, IL 60062

Standard reference number	Title	Referenced in code section number
17—94	Vent or Chimney Connector Dampers for Oil-fired Appliances—with Revisions through September 1999	M1802.2.2
58—96	Steel Underground Tanks for Flammable and Combustible Liquids—with Revisions through July 1998	M2201.1
80—96	Steel Tanks for Oil-burner Fuel—with Revisions Through June 2003	M2201.1
103—2001	Factory-built Chimneys for Residential Type and Building Heating Appliances—with Revisions through December 2003	R202, R1005.3, G2430.1
127—99	Factory-built Fireplaces—with Revisions through November 1999	R1001.11, R1004.1, R1004.4, R1005.4, G2445.7
174—04	Household Electric Storage Tank Water Heaters—with Revisions through October 1999	M2005.1
181—96	Factory-made Air Ducts and Air Connectors—with Revisions through May 2003	M1601.2, M1601.3.1
181A—98	Closure Systems for Use with Rigid Air Ducts and Air Connectors—with Revisions through December 1998	M1601.2, M1601.3.1
181B—95	Closure Systems for Use with Flexible Air Ducts and Air Connectors—with Revisions through August 2003	M1601.2, M1601.3.1
217—1997	Single and Multiple Station Smoke Alarms—with Revisions Through January 2004	R313.1
325—02	Standard for Door, Drapery, Gate, Louver and Window Operations and Systems—with Revisions through March 2003	R309.6
343—97	Pumps for Oil-Burning Appliances—with Revisions through May 2002	M2204.1
441—96	Gas Vents—with Revisions through December 1999	G2426.1
508—99	Industrial Control Equipment	M1411.3.1
536—97	Flexible Metallic Hose—with Revisions through June 2003	M2202.3
641—95	Type L, Low-temperature Venting Systems—with Revisions through April 1999	R202, R1001.11.5, M1804.2.4, G2426.1
651—05	Schedule 40 and Schedule 80 Rigid PVC Conduit and Fittings	G2414.6.3
726—98	Oil-fired Boiler Assemblies—with Revisions through January 2001	M2001.1.1, M2006.1, G2425.1
727—98	Oil-fired Central Furnaces—with Revisions through January 1999	M1402.1
729—03	Oil-fired Floor Furnaces	M1408.1
730—03	Oil-fired Wall Furnaces	M1409.1
732—95	Oil-fired Storage Tank Water Heaters—with Revisions through January 1999	M2005.1
737—96	Fireplaces Stoves—with Revisions through January 2000	M1414.1
790—04	Standard Test Methods for Fire Tests of Roof Coverings	R902.1
795—99	Commercial-Industrial Gas Heating Equipment	G2442.1, G2452.1
834—04	Heating, Water Supply, and Power Boilers-Electric	M2001.1.1
896—93	Oil-burning Stoves—with Revisions through May 2004	M1410.1
959—01	Medium Heat Appliance Factory-built Chimneys	R1005.6
923—02	Microwave Cooking Appliances—with Revisions through January 2003	M1504.1
1040—96	Fire Test of Insulated Wall Construction—with Revisions through June 2001	R314.3
1256—02	Fire Test of Roof Deck Construction	R906.1
1261—01	Electric Water Heaters for Pools and Tubs—with Revisions through June 2004	M2006.1
1453—04	Electronic Booster and Commercial Storage Tank Water Heaters	M2005.1
1479—03	Fire Tests of Through-Penetration Firestops	R317.3.1.2
1482—98	Solid-fuel Type Room Heaters—with Revisions through January 2000	R1002.2, R1002.5, M1410.1
1715—97	Fire Test of Interior Finish Material—with Revisions through March 2004	R314.4
1738—93	Venting Systems for Gas-burning Appliances, Categories II, III and IV—with Revisions through December 2000	G2426.1
1777—04	Standard for Chimney Liners	R1003.1.8, R1003.11.1, M1801.3.4, G2425.12, G2425.15.4
1995—98	Heating and Cooling Equipment—with Revisions through August 1999	M1402.1, M1403.1, M1407.1
2158A—96	Outline of Investigation for Clothes Dryer Transition Duct	M1502.4

ULC

Underwriters' Laboratories of Canada
7 Crouse Road
Scarborough, Ontario, Canada M1R 3A9

Standard reference number	Title	Referenced in code section number
S 102—1988	Standard Methods for Test for Surface Burning Characteristics of Building Materials and Assemblies—with 2000 Revisions	R316.2

Window & Door Manufacturers Association
1400 East Touhy Avenue, Suite 470
Des Plaines, IL 60018

Standard reference number	Title	Referenced in code section number
101/I.S2/A440—05	Specifications for Windows, Doors and Unit Skylights...................................	R308.6.9, R613.4, N1102.4.2

APPENDIX A

SAMPLE ADOPTION ORDINANCES

REGULAR SAMPLE ORDINANCE - EXAMPLE

Ordinance No. _____ Adopting the Minnesota State Building Code

AN ORDINANCE ADOPTING THE MINNESOTA STATE BUILDING CODE. THIS ORDINANCE: PROVIDES FOR THE APPLICATION, ADMINISTRATION, AND ENFORCEMENT OF THE MINNESOTA STATE BUILDING CODE BY REGULATING THE ERECTION, CONSTRUCTION, ENLARGEMENT, ALTERATION, REPAIR, MOVING, REMOVAL, DEMOLITION, CONVERSION, OCCUPANCY, EQUIPMENT, USE, HEIGHT, AREA, AND MAINTE-NANCE OF ALL BUILDINGS AND/OR STRUCTURES IN THIS MUNICIPALITY; PROVIDES FOR THE ISSUANCE OF PERMITS AND COLLECTION OF FEES THEREOF; PROVIDES PENALTIES FOR VIOLATION THEREOF; REPEALS ALL ORDINANCES AND PARTS OF ORDINANCES THAT CONFLICT THEREWITH.

This municipality does ordain as follows:

Section 1. Application, Administration and Enforcement. The application, administration, and enforcement of the code shall be in accordance with Minnesota Rule Chapter 1300. The code shall be enforced within the extraterritorial limits permitted by Minnesota Statutes, 16B.62, subdivision 1, when so established by this ordinance. The code enforcement agency of this municipality is called the _____. This code shall be enforced by the Minnesota Certified Building Official designated by this Municipality to administer the code (Minnesota statute 16B.65) subdivision 1.

Section 2. Permits and Fees. The issuance of permits and the collection of fees shall be as authorized in Minnesota Statutes, 16B.62, subdivision 1 Permit fees shall be assessed for work governed by this code in accordance with the fee schedule adopted by the municipality in (i.e. City Code #, Ordinance # etc. In addition, a surcharge fee shall be collected on all permits issued for work governed by this code in accordance with Minnesota statute 16B.70.

Section 3. Violations and Penalties. A violation of the code is a misdemeanor (Minnesota statute 16B.69) and Minnesota Rules, Chapter 1300.

Section 4. Building Code. The Minnesota State Building Code, established pursuant to Minnesota Statutes 16B.59 to 16B.75 is hereby adopted as the building code for this Municipality. The code is hereby incorporated in this ordinance as if fully set out herein.

A. The Minnesota State Building Code includes the following chapters of Minnesota Rules:

1. 1300, Administration of the Minnesota State Building Code;

2. 1301, Building Official Certification;

3. 1302, State Building Code Construction Approvals;

4. 1303, Minnesota Provisions;

5. 1305, Adoption of the 2006 International Building Code;

6. 1307, Elevators and Related Devices.

7. 1309, Adoption of the 2006 International Residential Code;

8. 1311, Adoption of the 2000 Guidelines for the Rehabilitation of Existing Buildings;

9. 1315, Adoption of the 2005 National Electrical Code;

10. 1325, Solar Energy Systems;

11. 1330, Fallout Shelters;

12. 1335, Floodproofing Regulations;

13. 1341, Minnesota Accessibility Code;

14. 1346, Adoption of the Minnesota State Mechanical Code;

15. 1350, Manufactured Homes;

16. 1360, Prefabricated Structures;

17. 1361, Industrialized/Modular Buildings;

18. 1370, Storm Shelters (Manufactured Home Parks);

19. 4715, Minnesota Plumbing Code

20. 7670, 7672, 7674, 7676, and 7678, Minnesota Energy Code

B. This municipality may adopt by reference any or all of the following optional chapters of Minnesota Rules: Chapter 1306, Special Fire Protection Systems (with locally designated options); and Chapter 1335, Floodproofing Regulations, parts 1335.0600 to 1335.1200.

C. This municipality may adopt by reference Appendix Chapter J (Grading), of the 2006 International Building Code. The following optional provisions identified in Section 4, Subp. B and C are hereby adopted and incorporated as part of the building code for this municipality.

1.

2. **(Municipality must specifically identify optional provisions elected for code adoption here)**

3.

Section 5. Effective Date of Ordinance. The effective date of this Ordinance is _____.

Signed: _____

Title: _____

Attest: _____

Title: _____

Reviewed By: _____

Title: _____

SELF-PERPETUATING SAMPLE ORDINANCE - EXAMPLE

Ordinance No. _____Adopting the Minnesota State Building Code

AN ORDINANCE ADOPTING THE MINNESOTA STATE BUILDING CODE. THIS ORDINANCE: PROVIDES FOR THE APPLICATION, ADMINISTRATION, AND ENFORCEMENT OF THE MINNESOTA STATE BUILDING CODE BY REGULATING THE ERECTION, CONSTRUCTION, ENLARGEMENT, ALTERATION, REPAIR, MOVING, REMOVAL, DEMOLITION, CONVERSION, OCCUPANCY, EQUIPMENT, USE, HEIGHT, AREA, AND MAINTE-NANCE OF ALL BUILDINGS AND/OR STRUCTURES IN THIS MUNICIPALITY; PROVIDES FOR THE ISSUANCE OF PERMITS AND COLLECTION OF FEES THEREOF; PROVIDES PENALTIES FOR VIOLATION THEREOF; REPEALS ALL ORDINANCES AND PARTS OF ORDINANCES THAT CONFLICT THEREWITH. THIS ORDI-NANCE SHALL PERPETUALLY INCLUDE THE MOST CURRENT EDITION OF THE MINNESOTA STATE BUILD-ING CODE WITH THE EXCEPTION OF THE OPTIONAL APPENDIX CHAPTERS. OPTIONAL APPENDIX CHAPTERS SHALL NOT APPLY UNLESS SPECIFICALLY ADOPTED.

This municipality does ordain as follows:

Section 1 Codes adopted by reference. The Minnesota State Building Code, as adopted by the Commissioner of Labor and Indus-try pursuant to Minnesota Statutes chapter 16B.59 to 16B.75, including all of the amendments, rules and regulations established, adopted and published from time to time by the Minnesota Commissioner of Labor and Industry, through the Building Codes and Standards Unit, is hereby adopted by reference with the exception of the optional chapters, unless specifically adopted in this ordi-nance. The Minnesota State Building Code is hereby incorporated in this ordinance as if fully set out herein.

Section 2. Application, Administration and Enforcement. The application, administration, and enforcement of the code shall be in accordance with Minnesota State Building Code. The code shall be enforced within the extraterritorial limits permitted by Min-nesota Statutes, 16B.62, subdivision 1, when so established by this ordinance. The code enforcement agency of this municipality is called the _____. This code shall be enforced by the Minnesota Certified Building Official designated by this Municipality to administer the code (Minnesota statute 16B.65) subdivision 1.

Section 3. Permits and Fees. The issuance of permits and the collection of fees shall be as authorized in Minnesota Statutes, 16B.62, subdivision 1. Permit fees shall be assessed for work governed by this code in accordance with the fee schedule adopted by the municipality in i.e.: City Code #, Ordinance # etc. In addition, a surcharge fee shall be collected on all permits issued for work governed by this code in accordance with Minnesota statute 16B.70.

Section 4. Violations and Penalties. A violation of the code is a misdemeanor (Minnesota statutes 16B.69).

Section 5. Building Code Optional Chapters. The Minnesota State Building Code, established pursuant to Minnesota Statutes 16B.59 to 16B.75 allows the Municipality to adopt by reference and enforce certain optional chapters of the most current edition of the Minnesota State Building Code. The following optional provisions identified in the most current edition of the State Building Code are hereby adopted and incorporated as part of the building code for this municipality.

1.

2. **(Municipality must specifically identify optional provisions elected for code adoption here)**

3.

Section 6. Effective Date of Ordinance. The effective date of this Ordinance is _____.

Signed: _____

Title: _____

Attest: _____

Title: _____

Reviewed By: _____

Title: _____

ACCESSIBILITY ORDINANCE - EXAMPLE

Ordinance No. _____Adopting the Minnesota State Building Code for Accessibility

AN ORDINANCE ADOPTING THE MINNESOTA STATE BUILDING CODE FOR ACCESSIBILITY. THIS ORDI-NANCE: PROVIDES FOR THE APPLICATION, ADMINISTRATION, AND ENFORCEMENT OF THE MINNESOTA STATE BUILDING CODE FOR ACCESSIBILITY BY REGULATING THE ERECTION, CONSTRUCTION, ENLARGEMENT, ALTERATION, REPAIR, CONVERSION, OCCUPANCY, EQUIPMENT, USE, AND MAINTE-NANCE OF ALL BUILDINGS AND STRUCTURES IN THIS MUNICIPALITY; PROVIDES FOR THE ISSUANCE OF PERMITS AND COLLECTION OF FEES THEREOF; PROVIDES PENALTIES FOR VIOLATION THEREOF; REPEALS ALL ORDINANCES AND PARTS OF ORDINANCES THAT CONFLICT THEREWITH.

This municipality does ordain as follows:

Section 1 Application, Administration and Enforcement. The application, administration, and enforcement of the code shall be in accordance with Minnesota rule chapter 1300. The code enforcement agency of this municipality is called the _____. This code shall be enforced by the Minnesota Certified Building Official designated by this Municipality to administer the code (Minnesota statute 16B.65) subdivision 1.

Section 2. Permits and Fees. Permit fees shall be assessed for work governed by this code in accordance with the fee schedule adopted by the municipality in i.e.: City Code #, Ordinance # etc. In addition, a surcharge fee shall be collected on all permits issued for work governed by this code in accordance with Minnesota statute 16B.70.

Section 3. Violations and Penalties. A violation of the code is a misdemeanor (Minnesota statutes 16B.69).

Section 4. Effective Date of Ordinance. The effective date of this Ordinance is _____.

Signed: _____

Title: _____

Attest: _____

Title: _____

Reviewed By: _____

Title: _____

APPENDIX B

SAMPLE FEE SCHEDULES

EXTRACTED FROM 1997 UNIFORM BUILDING CODE

TABLE NO. 1-A – BUILDING PERMIT FEES

TOTAL VALUATION FEE

$1.00 to $500 . . . . $23.00

$501.00 to $2,000.00 . . . . $23.50 for the first $500.00 plus $3.05 for each additional $100.00, or fraction thereof, to and including $2,000.00

$2,001.00 to $25,000.00 . . . . $69.25 for the first $2,000.00 plus $14.00 for each additional $1,000.00, or fraction thereof, to and including $25,000.00

$25,001.00 to $50,000.00 . . . . $391.25 for the first $25,000.00 plus $10.10 for each additional $1,000.00, or fraction thereof, to and including $50,000.00

$50,001.00 to $100,000.00 . . . . . . $643.75 for the first $50,000.00 plus $7.00 for each additional $1,000.00, or fraction thereof, to and including $100,000.00

$100,001.00 to $500,000.00 . . . . . . $993.75 for the first $100,000.00 plus $5.60 for each additional $1,000.00, or fraction thereof, to and including $500,000.00

$500,001.00 to $1,000,000.00 . . . . $3,233.75 for the first $500,000.00 plus $4.75 for each additional $1,000.00, or fraction thereof, to and including $1,000,000.00

$1,000,001.00 and up $5,608.75 for the first $1,000,000.00 plus $3.15 for each additional $1,000.00, or fraction thereof

Other Inspections and Fees:

1. Inspections outside of normal business hours · $47.00 per hour*

2. Reinspection fees assessed under provisions of Section 305.8 · $47.00 per hour*

3. Inspections for which no fee is specifically indicated · $47.00 per hour* (minimum charge – one-half hour)

4. Additional plan review required by changes, additions or revisions to plans · $47.00 per hour*

5. For use of outside consultants for plan checking and inspections, or both · Actual costs **

* Or the total hourly cost to the jurisdiction, whichever is the greatest. This cost shall include supervision, overhead, equipment, hourly wages and fringe benefits of the employees involved.

** Actual costs include administrative and overhead costs.

EXTRACTED FROM 1994 UNIFORM BUILDING CODE

TOTAL VALUATION FEE

$1.00 to $500 . . . . $21.00

$501.00 to $2,000.00 . . . . $21.00 for the first $500.00 plus $2.75 for each additional $100.00, or fraction thereof, to and including $2,000.00

$2,001.00 to $25,000.00 . . . . $62.25 for the first $2,000.00 plus $12.50 for each additional $1,000.00, or fraction thereof, to and including $25,000.00

$25,001.00 to $50,000.00 . . . . $349.75 for the first $25,000.00 plus $9.00 for each additional $1,000.00, or fraction thereof, to and including $50,000.00

$50,001.00 to $100,000.00 . . . . . . $574.75 for the first $50,000.00 plus $6.25 for each additional $1,000.00, or fraction thereof, to and including $100,000.00

$100,001.00 to $500,000.00 . . . . . $887.25 for the first $100,000.00 plus $5.00 for each additional $1,000.00, or fraction thereof, to and including $500,000.00

$500,001.00 to $1,000,000.00 . . . . $2,887.25 for the first $500,000.00 plus $4.25 for each additional $1,000.00, or fraction thereof, to and including $1,000,000.00

$1,000,001.00 and up $5,012.25 for the first $1,000,000.00 plus $2.75 for each additional $1,000.00, or fraction thereof

Other Inspections and Fees:

1. Inspections outside of normal business hours · $42.00 per hour*

2. Reinspection fees assessed under provisions of Section 305.8 · $42.00 per hour*

3. Inspections for which no fee is specifically indicated · $42.00 per hour*
   (minimum charge – one-half hour)

4. Additional plan review required by changes, additions or revisions to plans · $42.00 per hour*

5. For use of outside consultants for plan checking and inspections, or both · Actual costs **

* Or the total hourly cost to the jurisdiction, whichever is the greatest. This cost shall include supervision, overhead, equipment, hourly wages and fringe benefits of the employees involved.

** Actual costs include administrative and overhead costs.

EXTRACTED FROM THE 1985, 1988 AND 1991 UNIFORM BUILDING CODE

TABLE NO. 3-A – BUILDING PERMIT FEES

TOTAL VALUATION FEE

$1.00 to $500 . . . . $15.00

$501.00 to $2,000.00 . . . . $15.00 for the first $500.00 plus $2.00 for each additional $100.00, or fraction thereof, to and including $2,000.00

$2,001.00 to $25,000.00 . . . . $45.00 for the first $2,000.00 plus $9.00 for each additional $1,000.00, or fraction thereof, to and including $25,000.00

$25,001.00 to $50,000.00 . . . . $252.00 for the first $25,000.00 plus $6.50 for each additional $1,000.00, or fraction thereof, to and including $50,000.00

$50,001.00 to $100,000.00 . . . . . . $414.50 for the first $50,000.00 plus $4.50 for each additional $1,000.00, or fraction thereof, to and including $100,000.00

$100,001.00 to $500,000.00 . . . . . $639.50 for the first $100,000.00 plus $3.50 for each additional $1,000.00, or fraction thereof, to and including $500,000.00

$500,001.00 to $1,000,000.00 . . . . $2,039.50 for the first $500,000.00 plus $3.00 for each additional $1,000.00, or fraction thereof, to and including $1,000,000.00

$1,000,001.00 and up $3,539.50 for the first $1,000,000.00 plus $2.00 for each additional $1,000.00, or fraction thereof

Other Inspections and Fees:

1. Inspections outside of normal business hours · $30.00 per hour*
   (minimum charge – two hours)

2. Reinspection fees assessed under provisions of Section 305 (g) · $30.00 per hour*

3. Inspections for which no fee is specifically indicated · $30.00 per hour*
   (minimum charge – one-half hour)

4. Additional plan review required by changes, additions or revisions to plans · $30.00 per hour*
   (minimum charge – one-half hour)

* Or the total hourly cost to the jurisdiction, whichever is the greatest. This cost shall include supervision, overhead, equipment, hourly wages and fringe benefits of the employees involved.

APPENDIX C

GUIDELINES FOR SPECIAL INSPECTIONS AND TESTING

PURPOSE: To provide a method for complying with requirements of the International Building Code (IBC) 2006 Section 1704 – Special Inspections.

BEFORE PERMIT ISSUANCE: The architect or engineer of record shall prepare and submit a Special Structural Testing and Inspection Program to the building official. The Program may be included in the contract documents or as a separate submittal document. The completed Program Summary Schedule should include the following:

1. A specific listing of the items requiring special inspection (observation and testing).

2. The associated technical scope sections, which define the applicable standard to judge conformance of construction work and describe the duties of special inspectors.

3. The type of special inspector required for each item.

4. The frequency of reporting, i.e., weekly, monthly, per test/inspection, per floor, etc.

5. The parties responsible for performing the special inspections.

6. Acknowledgments by each designated party.

REQUIREMENTS: "Special Inspection" includes inspection (work requiring observation and engineering judgment) and testing (work analyzing materials in accordance with approved standards). Special Inspection shall meet the minimum requirements of the Minnesota State Building Code, which includes IBC Section 1704, and the approved drawings and specifications.

Special Inspectors shall be employed by the owner or engineer/architect of record, but not the contractor. Special Inspection shall not relieve the contractor of responsibility to complete the work in accordance with the approved drawings and specifications

APPENDIX D

MISCELLANEOUS STATUTES RELATED TO
STATE BUILDING CODE ADMINISTRATION

16B.59 State Building Code; policy and purpose.

The State Building Code governs the construction, reconstruction, alteration, and repair of buildings and other structures to which the code is applicable. The commissioner shall administer and amend a state code of building construction which will provide basic and uniform performance standards, establish reasonable safeguards for health, safety, welfare, comfort, and security of the residents of this state and provide for the use of modern methods, devices, materials, and techniques which will in part tend to lower construction costs. The construction of buildings should be permitted at the least possible cost consistent with recognized standards of health and safety.

16B.60 Definitions, State Building Code.

Subdivision 1. **Scope.** For the purposes of Sections 16B.59 to 16B.75, the terms defined in this section have the meanings given them.

Subd. 2. **City.** "City" means a home rule charter or statutory city.

Subd. 3. **Municipality.** "Municipality" means a city, county, or town, the University of Minnesota, or the state for public buildings and state licensed facilities.

Subd. 4. **Code.** "Code" means the State Building Code adopted by the commissioner in accordance with Sections 16B.59 to 16B.75.

Subd. 5. **Agricultural building.** "Agricultural building" means a structure on agricultural land as defined in Section 273.13, subdivision 23, designed, constructed, and used to house farm implements, livestock, or agricultural produce or products used by the owner, lessee, and sublessee of the building and members of their immediate families, their employees, and persons engaged in the pickup or delivery of agricultural produce or products.

Subd. 6. **Public building.** "Public building" means a building and its grounds the cost of which is paid for by the state or a state agency regardless of its cost, and a school district building project the cost of which is $100,000 or more.

Subd. 7. **Physically handicapped.** "Physically handicapped" means having sight disabilities, hearing disabilities, disabilities of incoordination, disabilities of aging, or other disabilities that significantly reduce mobility, flexibility, coordination, or perceptiveness.

Subd. 8. **Remodeling.** "Remodeling" means deliberate reconstruction of an existing public building in whole or in part in order to bring it up to date in conformity with present uses of the structure and to which other rules on the upgrading of health and safety provisions are applicable.

Subd. 9. **Historic building.** "Historic building" means a state-owned building that is on the National Register of Historic Places.

Subd. 10. **Equivalent protection.** "Equivalent protection" means a measure other than a code requirement that provides essentially the same protection that would be provided by a code requirement.

Subd. 11. **State licensed facilities.** "State licensed facilities" means a building and its grounds that are licensed by the state as a hospital, nursing home, supervised living facility, freestanding outpatient surgical center, or correctional facility.

Subd. 12. **Designate.** "Designate" means the formal designation by a municipality's administrative authority of a certified building official accepting responsibility for code administration.

Subd. 13. **Administrative authority.** "Administrative authority" means a municipality's governing body or their assigned administrative authority.

16B.61 General powers of commissioner; State Building Code.

Subdivision 1. Adoption of code. Subject to Sections 16B.59 to 16B.75, the commissioner shall by rule establish a code of standards for the construction, reconstruction, alteration, and repair of buildings, governing matters of structural materials, design and construction, fire protection, health, sanitation, and safety, including design and construction standards regarding heat loss control, illumination, and climate control. The code must also include duties and responsibilities for code administration, including procedures for administrative action, penalties, and suspension and revocation of certification. The code must conform insofar as practicable to model building codes generally accepted and in use throughout the United States, including a code for building conservation. In the preparation of the code, consideration must be given to the existing statewide specialty codes presently in use in the state. Model codes with necessary modifications and statewide specialty codes may be adopted by reference. The code must be based on the application of scientific principles, approved tests, and professional judgment. To the extent possible, the code must be adopted in terms of desired results instead of the means of achieving those results, avoiding wherever possible the incorporation of specifications of particular methods or materials. To that end the code must encourage the use of new methods and new materials. Except as otherwise provided in Sections 16B.59 to 16B.75, the commissioner shall administer and enforce the provisions of those sections. The commissioner shall develop rules addressing the plan review fee assessed to similar buildings without significant modifications including provisions for use of building systems as specified in the indus-

MISCELLANEOUS STATUTES RELATED TO STATE BUILDING CODE ADMINISTRATION

trial/modular program specified in Section 16B.75. Additional plan review fees associated with similar plans must be based on costs commensurate with the direct and indirect costs of the service.

Subd. 1a. **Administration by commissioner.** The commissioner shall administer and enforce the State Building Code as a municipality with respect to public buildings and state licensed facilities in the state. The commissioner shall establish appropriate permit, plan review, and inspection fees for public buildings and state licensed facilities. Fees and surcharges for public buildings and state licensed facilities must be remitted to the commissioner, who shall deposit them in the state treasury for credit to the special revenue fund. Municipalities other than the state having a contractual agreement with the commissioner for code administration and enforcement service for public buildings and state licensed facilities shall charge their customary fees, including surcharge, to be paid directly to the contractual jurisdiction by the applicant seeking authorization to construct a public building or a state licensed facility. The commissioner shall contract with a municipality other than the state for plan review, code administration, and code enforcement service for public buildings and state licensed facilities in the contractual jurisdiction if the building officials of the municipality meet the requirements of Section 16B.65 and wish to provide those services and if the commissioner determines that the municipality has enough adequately trained and qualified building inspectors to provide those services for the construction project. Administration and enforcement in a municipality under this section must apply any optional provisions of the State Building Code adopted by the municipality. A municipality adopting any optional code provision shall notify the state building official within 30 days of its adoption. The commissioner shall administer and enforce the provisions of the code relating to elevators statewide, except as provided for under Section 16B.747, subdivision 3.

Subd. 2. **Enforcement by certain bodies.** Under the direction and supervision of the commissioner, the provisions of the code relating to electrical installations shall be enforced by the state board of electricity, pursuant to the Minnesota Electrical Act, the provisions relating to plumbing shall be enforced by the commissioner of health, the provisions relating to high pressure steam piping and appurtenances shall be enforced by the department of labor and industry. Fees for inspections conducted by the state board of electricity shall be paid in accordance with the rules of the state board of electricity. Under direction of the commissioner of public safety, the state fire marshal shall enforce the Minnesota Uniform Fire Code as provided in chapter 299F. The commissioner, in consultation with the commissioner of labor and industry, shall adopt amendments to the mechanical code portion of the State Building Code to implement standards for process piping.

Subd. 3. **Special requirements.**

(a) Space for commuter vans. The code must require that any parking ramp or other parking facility constructed in accordance with the code include an appropriate number of spaces suitable for the parking of motor vehicles having a capacity of seven to 16 persons and which are principally used to provide prearranged commuter transportation of employees to or from their place of employment or to or from a transit stop authorized by a local transit authority.

(b) Smoke detection devices. The code must require that all dwellings, lodging houses, apartment houses, and hotels as defined in Section 299F.362 comply with the provisions of Section 299F.362.

(c) Doors in nursing homes and hospitals. The State Building Code may not require that each door entering a sleeping or patient's room from a corridor in a nursing home or hospital with an approved complete standard automatic fire extinguishing system be constructed or maintained as self-closing or automatically closing.

(d) Child care facilities in churches; ground level exit. A licensed day care center serving fewer than 30 preschool age persons and which is located in a belowground space in a church building is exempt from the State Building Code requirement for a ground level exit when the center has more than two stairways to the ground level and its exit.

(e) Child care facilities in churches; vertical access. Until August 1, 1996, an organization providing child care in an existing church building which is exempt from taxation under Section 272.02, subdivision 6, shall have five years from the date of initial licensure under chapter 245A to provide interior vertical access, such as an elevator, to persons with disabilities as required by the State Building Code. To obtain the extension, the organization providing child care must secure a $2,500 performance bond with the commissioner of human services to ensure that interior vertical access is achieved by the agreed upon date.

(f) Family and group family day care. Until the legislature enacts legislation specifying appropriate standards, the definition of Group R-3 occupancies in the State Building Code applies to family and group family day care homes licensed by the department of human services under Minnesota Rules, chapter 9502.

(g) Enclosed stairways. No provision of the code or any appendix chapter of the code may require stairways of existing multiple dwelling buildings of two stories or less to be enclosed.

(h) Double cylinder dead bolt locks. No provision of the code or appendix chapter of the code may prohibit double cylinder dead bolt locks in existing single-family homes, townhouses, and first floor duplexes used exclusively as a residential dwelling. Any recommendation or promotion of double cylinder dead bolt locks must include a warning about their potential fire danger and procedures to minimize the danger.

(i) Relocated residential buildings. A residential building relocated within or into a political subdivision of the state need not comply with the State Energy Code or Section 326.371 provided that, where available, an energy audit is conducted on the relocated building.

(j) Automatic garage door opening systems. The code must require all residential buildings as defined in sec-

358

2007 MINNESOTA STATE RESIDENTIAL CODE

tion 325F.82 to comply with the provisions of Sections 325F.82 and 325F.83.

(k) Exit sign illumination. For a new building on which construction is begun on or after October 1, 1993, or an existing building on which remodeling affecting 50 percent or more of the enclosed space is begun on or after October 1, 1993, the code must prohibit the use of internally illuminated exit signs whose electrical consumption during nonemergency operation exceeds 20 watts of resistive power. All other requirements in the code for exit signs must be complied with.

(l) Exterior wood decks, patios, and balconies. The code must permit the decking surface and upper portions of exterior wood decks, patios, and balconies to be constructed of (1) heartwood from species of wood having natural resistance to decay or termites, including redwood and cedars, (2) grades of lumber which contain sapwood from species of wood having natural resistance to decay or termites, including redwood and cedars, or (3) treated wood. The species and grades of wood products used to construct the decking surface and upper portions of exterior decks, patios, and balconies must be made available to the building official on request before final construction approval.

Subd. 3a. **Recycling space.** The code must require suitable space for the separation, collection, and temporary storage of recyclable materials within or adjacent to new or significantly remodeled structures that contain 1,000 square feet or more. Residential structures with fewer than four dwelling units are exempt from this subdivision.

Subd. 4. **Review of plans for public buildings and state licensed facilities.** Construction or remodeling may not begin on any public building or state licensed facility until the plans and specifications have been approved by the commissioner or municipality under contractual agreement pursuant to subdivision 1a. The plans and specifications must be submitted for review, and within 30 days after receipt of the plans and specifications, the commissioner or municipality under contractual agreement shall notify the submitting authority of any corrections.

Subd. 5. **Accessibility.**

(a) Public buildings. The code must provide for making public buildings constructed or remodeled after July 1, 1963, accessible to and usable by physically handicapped persons, although this does not require the remodeling of public buildings solely to provide accessibility and usability to the physically handicapped when remodeling would not otherwise be undertaken.

(b) Leased space. No agency of the state may lease space for agency operations in a nonstate-owned building unless the building satisfies the requirements of the State Building Code for accessibility by the physically handicapped, or is eligible to display the state symbol of accessibility. This limitation applies to leases of 30 days or more for space of at least 1,000 square feet.

(c) Meetings or conferences. Meetings or conferences for the public or for state employees which are sponsored in whole or in part by a state agency must be held in buildings that meet the State Building Code requirements relating to accessibility for physically handicapped persons. This subdivision does not apply to any classes, seminars, or training programs offered by the Minnesota state colleges and universities or the University of Minnesota. Meetings or conferences intended for specific individuals none of whom need the accessibility features for handicapped persons specified in the State Building Code need not comply with this subdivision unless a handicapped person gives reasonable advance notice of an intent to attend the meeting or conference. When sign language interpreters will be provided, meetings or conference sites must be chosen which allow hearing impaired participants to see their signing clearly.

(d) Exemptions. The commissioner may grant an exemption from the requirements of paragraphs (b) and (c) in advance if an agency has demonstrated that reasonable efforts were made to secure facilities which complied with those requirements and if the selected facilities are the best available for access for handicapped persons. Exemptions shall be granted using criteria developed by the commissioner in consultation with the council on disability.

(e) Symbol indicating access. The wheelchair symbol adopted by Rehabilitation International's Eleventh World Congress is the state symbol indicating buildings, facilities, and grounds which are accessible to and usable by handicapped persons. In the interests of uniformity, this symbol is the sole symbol for display in or on all public or private buildings, facilities, and grounds which qualify for its use. The secretary of state shall obtain the symbol and keep it on file. No building, facility, or grounds may display the symbol unless it is in compliance with the rules adopted by the commissioner under subdivision 1. Before any rules are proposed for adoption under this paragraph, the commissioner shall consult with the council on disability. Rules adopted under this paragraph must be enforced in the same way as other accessibility rules of the State Building Code.

(f) Municipal enforcement. Municipalities which have not adopted the State Building Code may enforce the building code requirements for handicapped persons by either entering into a joint powers agreement for enforcement with another municipality which has adopted the State Building Code; or contracting for enforcement with an individual certified under Section 16B.65, subdivision 3, to enforce the State Building Code.

(g) Equipment allowed. The code must allow the use of vertical wheelchair lifts and inclined stairway wheelchair lifts in public buildings. An inclined stairway wheelchair lift must be equipped with light or sound signaling device for use during operation of the lift. The stairway or ramp shall be marked in a bright color that clearly indicates the outside edge of the lift when in operation. The code shall not require a guardrail between the lift and the stairway or ramp. Compliance with this provision by itself does not mean other handicap accessibility requirements have been met.

Subd. 6. **Energy efficiency.** The code must provide for building new low-income housing in accordance with energy efficiency standards adopted under subdivision 1. For purposes of this subdivision, low-income housing means residential housing built for low-income persons and families under a program of a housing and redevelopment authority, the Minnesota housing finance agency, or another entity receiving money from the state to construct such housing.

Subd. 7. **Access for the hearing-impaired.** All rooms in the state office building and in the capitol that are used by the house of representatives or the senate for legislative hearings, and the public galleries overlooking the house and senate chambers, must be fitted with assistive listening devices for the hearing-impaired. Each hearing room and the public galleries must have a sufficient number of receivers available so that hearing-impaired members of the public may participate in the committee hearings and public sessions of the house and senate.

16B.617 Energy code rules remain in effect.

(a) Notwithstanding Laws 1999, chapter 135, Section 9, Minnesota Rules, chapter 7670, does not expire on April 15, 2000, but remains in effect for residential buildings not covered by Minnesota Rules, chapter 7676. The provisions of Minnesota Rules, chapter 7670, that apply to category 1 buildings govern new, detached single one- and two-family R-3 occupancy residential buildings. All new, detached single one- and two-family R-3 occupancy buildings subject to Minnesota Rules, chapter 7670, submitting an application for a building permit after April 14, 2000, must meet the requirements for category 1 buildings, as set out in Minnesota Rules, chapter 7670.

(b) As an alternative to compliance with paragraph (a), compliance with Minnesota Rules, chapters 7672 and 7674, is optional for a contractor or owner.

(c) The department of administration, building codes and standards division (BCSD), shall issue a report to the legislature by December 1, 2001, addressing the cost benefit, as well as air quality, building durability, moisture, enforcement, enforceability, and liability regarding implementation of Minnesota Rules, chapters 7670, 7672, and 7674. The report must include a feasibility study of establishing new criteria for category 2 detached single one- and two-family R-3 occupancy buildings that are energy efficient, enforceable, and provide sufficient non-mechanical ventilation or permeability for a home to maintain good air quality, building durability, and adequate release of moisture

(d) This section expires when the commissioner of administration adopts a new energy code in accordance with Laws 2002, chapter 317, Section 4.

* NOTE: The amendment to this section by Laws 2002, chapter 317, Section 1, is effective when rules are adopted by the commissioner of administration containing appropriate provisions addressing combustion air and make-up air in residential construction as part of the mechanical code. Laws 2002, chapter *317, Section 4.

16B.6175 Energy code.

Notwithstanding Section 16B.617, the commissioner of administration, in consultation with the construction codes advisory council, shall explore and review the availability and appropriateness of any model energy codes related to the construction of single one- and two family residential buildings. In consultation with the council, the commissioner shall take steps to adopt the chosen code with all necessary and appropriate amendments. The commissioner may not adopt all or part of a model energy code relating to the construction of residential buildings without research and analysis that addresses, at a minimum, air quality, building durability, moisture, enforcement, enforceability cost benefit, and liability. The research and analysis must be completed in cooperation with practitioners in residential construction and building science and an affirmative recommendation by the construction codes advisory council.

16B.62 State Building Code; application.

Subdivision 1. **Municipal enforcement.** The State Building Code applies statewide and supersedes the building code of any municipality. A municipality must not by ordinance or through development agreement require building code provisions regulating components or systems of any residential structure that are different from any provision of the State Building Code. A municipality may, with the approval of the state building official, adopt an ordinance that is more restrictive than the State Building Code where geological conditions warrant a more restrictive ordinance. A municipality may appeal the disapproval of a more restrictive ordinance to the commissioner. An appeal under this subdivision is subject to the schedule, fee, procedures, cost provisions, and appeal rights set out in Section 16B.67. The State Building Code does not apply to agricultural buildings except with respect to state inspections required or rulemaking authorized by Sections 103F.141, 216C.19, subdivision 8, and 326.244. All municipalities shall adopt and enforce the State Building Code with respect to new construction within their respective jurisdictions. If a city has adopted or is enforcing the State Building Code on June 3, 1977, or determines by ordinance after that date to undertake enforcement, it shall enforce the code within the city. A city may by ordinance extend the enforcement of the code to contiguous unincorporated territory not more than two miles distant from its corporate limits in any direction. Where two or more noncontiguous cities which have elected to enforce the code have boundaries less than four miles apart, each is authorized to enforce the code on its side of a line equidistant between them. Once enforcement authority is extended extraterritorially by ordinance, the authority may continue to be exercised in the designated territory even though another city less than four miles distant later elects to enforce the code. After the extension, the city may enforce the code in the designated area to the same extent as if the property were situated within its corporate limits. A city which, on June 3, 1977, had not adopted the code may not commence enforcement of the code within or outside of its jurisdiction until it has provided written notice to the commissioner, the county auditor, and the town clerk of each town in which it intends to enforce the code. A public hearing on the proposed enforcement must be held not less than 30 days after the notice has been provided. Enforcement of the code by the city outside of its jurisdiction commences on the first day of January in the year following the notice and hearing. Municipalities may provide for the issuance of permits, inspection, and enforcement within their jurisdictions by means which are convenient, and lawful, including by means of contracts with other municipalities pursuant to section 471.59, and with qualified individuals. The other municipalities or qualified individuals may be reimbursed by retention or remission of some or all of the building permit fee collected or by other means. In areas of the state where inspection and enforcement is unavailable from qualified employees of municipalities, the commissioner shall train and designate individuals available to carry out inspection and enforcement on a fee basis. Nothing in this section prohibits a municipality from adopting ordinances relating to zoning, subdivision, or planning unless the ordinance conflicts with a provision of the State Building Code that regulates components or systems of any residential structure.

Subd. 2. **Enforcement by state building official.** If the commissioner determines that a municipality is not properly administering and enforcing the State Building Code as provided in Section 16B.71, the commissioner may have the administration and enforcement in the involved municipality undertaken by the state building official. The commissioner shall notify the affected municipality in writing immediately upon making the determination, and the municipality may challenge the determination as a contested case before the commissioner pursuant to the Administrative Procedure Act. In municipalities not properly administering and enforcing the State Building Code, and in municipalities who determine not to administer and enforce the State Building Code, the commissioner shall have administration and enforcement undertaken by the state building official or by another inspector certified by the state. In carrying out administration and enforcement under this subdivision, the commissioner shall apply any optional provision of the State Building Code adopted by the municipality. A municipality adopting any optional code provision shall notify the state building official within 30 days of its adoption. The commissioner shall determine appropriate fees to be charged for the administration and enforcement service rendered. Any cost to the state arising from the state administration and enforcement of the State Building Code shall be borne by the subject municipality.

16B.625 Exemptions.

The commissioner may exempt a part of a historic building occupied by the state from the state or another building, fire, safety, or other code if the exemption is necessary to preserve the historic or esthetic character of the building or to prevent theft, vandalism, terrorism, or another crime. When the commissioner grants an exemption, the commissioner shall consider providing equivalent protection. A certificate of occupancy may not be denied because of an exemption under this section.

16B.63 State building official.

Subdivision 1. **Appointment.** The commissioner shall appoint a state building official who under the direction and supervision of the commissioner shall administer the code.

Subd. 2. **Qualifications.** To be eligible for appointment as state building official an individual must be competent in the field of administration and shall have the experience in building design, construction, and supervision which the commissioner considers necessary.

Subd. 3. **Powers and duties.** The state building official may, with the approval of the commissioner, employ personnel necessary to carry out the inspector's function under Sections 16B.59 to 16B.75. The state building official shall distribute without charge one copy of the code to each municipality within the state. Additional copies shall be made available to municipalities and interested parties for a fee prescribed by the commissioner. The state building official shall perform other duties in administering the code assigned by the commissioner.

Subd. 4. **Accessibility specialists.** The state building official shall, with the approval of the commissioner, assign three department employees to assist municipalities in complying with Section 16B.61, subdivision 5.

Subd. 5. **Interpretative authority.** To achieve uniform and consistent application of the State Building Code, the state building official has final interpretative authority applicable to all codes adopted as part of the State Building Code except for the plumbing code and the electrical code when enforced by the state board of electricity. A final interpretative committee composed of seven members, consisting of three building officials, two inspectors from the affected field, and two construction industry representatives, shall review requests for final interpretations relating to that field. A request for final interpretation must come from a local or state level building code board of appeals. The state building official must establish procedures for membership of the interpretative committees. The appropriate committee shall review the request and make a recommendation to the state building official for the final interpretation within 30 days of the request. The state building official must issue an interpretation within ten business days from the recommendation from the review committee. A final interpretation may be appealed within 30 days of its issuance to the commissioner under Section 16B.67. The final interpretation must be published within ten business days of its issuance and made available to the public. Municipal building officials shall administer all final interpretations issued by the state building official until the final interpretations are considered for adoption as part of the State Building Code.

16B.64 Application of Administrative Procedure Act.

Subdivision 1. Applicability. Subject to this section, the adoption of the code and amendment is subject to the Administrative Procedure Act.

Subd. 2. **Distribution of incorporations by reference.** The commissioner need not publish or distribute those parts of the code which are adopted by reference pursuant to Section 14.07, subdivision 4.

Subd. 3. **Filing.** The commissioner shall file one copy of the complete code with the secretary of state, except that all standards referred to in any model or statewide specialty code or any of the modifications of a code need not be filed. All standards referred to in the code must be kept on file and available for inspection in the office of the commissioner.

Subd. 4. Hearings. The commissioner shall hold all state hearings and make all determinations regarding any subject matter dealt with in the code including those in which another state agency proposes to adopt or amend rules which are incorporated by reference into the code or whenever the commissioner proposes to incorporate those rules into the State Building Code. In no event may a state agency subsequently authorized to adopt rules involving State Building Code subject matter proceed to adopt the rules without prior consultation with the commissioner.

Subd. 5. Proposed amendments; hearings. Any interested person may propose amendments to the code which may be either applicable to all municipalities or, where it is alleged and established that conditions exist within a municipality which are not generally found within other municipalities, amendments may be restricted in application to that municipality. Notice of public hearings on proposed amendments shall be given to the governing bodies of all municipalities in addition to those persons entitled to notice under the Administrative Procedure Act.

Subd. 6. Adoption. The commissioner shall approve any proposed amendments deemed by the commissioner to be reasonable in conformity with the policy and purpose of the code and justified under the particular circumstances involved. Upon adoption, a copy of each amendment must be distributed to the governing bodies of all affected municipalities.

Subd. 7. Investigation and research. With the approval of the commissioner the state building official shall investigate or provide for investigations, or may accept authenticated reports from authoritative sources, concerning new materials or modes of construction intended for use in the construction of buildings or structures, and shall propose amendments to the code setting forth the conditions under which the new materials or modes may be used.

16B.65 Building officials.

Subdivision 1. Designation. By January 1, 2002, each municipality shall designate a building official to administer the code. A municipality may designate no more than one building official responsible for code administration defined by each certification category established in rule. Two or more municipalities may combine in the designation of a building official for the purpose of administering the provisions of the code within their communities. In those municipalities for which no building officials have been designated, the state building official may use whichever state employees are necessary to perform the duties of the building official until the municipality makes a temporary or permanent designation. All costs incurred by virtue of these services rendered by state employees must be borne by the involved municipality and receipts arising from these services must be paid into the state treasury and credited to the special revenue fund.

Subd. 2. Qualifications. A building official, to be eligible for designation, must be certified and have the experience in design, construction, and supervision which the commissioner deems necessary and must be generally informed on the quality and strength of building materials, accepted building construction requirements, and the nature of equipment and needs conducive to the safety, comfort, and convenience of building occupants. No person may be designated as a building official for a municipality unless the commissioner determines that the official is qualified as provided in subdivision 3.

Subd. 3. Certification. The commissioner shall:

(1) Prepare and conduct written and practical examinations to determine if a person is qualified pursuant to subdivision 2 to be a building official;

(2) Accept documentation of successful completion of testing programs developed by nationally recognized testing agencies, as proof of qualification pursuant to subdivision 2; or

(3) Determine qualifications by both clauses (1) and (2).

Upon a determination of qualification under clause (1), (2), or both of them, the commissioner shall issue a certificate to the building official stating that the official is certified. Each person applying for examination and certification pursuant to this section shall pay a nonrefundable fee of $70. The commissioner or a designee may establish categories of certification that will recognize the varying complexities of code enforcement in the municipalities within the state. The commissioner shall provide educational programs designed to train and assist building officials in carrying out their responsibilities. The department of employee relations may, at the request of the commissioner, provide statewide testing services.

Subd. 4. Duties. Building officials shall, in the municipality for which they are designated, be responsible for all aspects of code administration for which they are certified, including the issuance of all building permits and the inspection of all manufactured home installations. The commissioner may direct a municipality with a building official to perform services for another municipality, and in that event the municipality being served shall pay the municipality rendering the services the reasonable costs of the services. The costs may be subject to approval by the commissioner.

Subd. 5. Oversight committee.

(a) The commissioner shall establish a code administration oversight committee to evaluate, mediate, and recommend to the commissioner any administrative action, penalty, suspension, or revocation with respect to complaints filed with or information received by the commissioner alleging or indicating the unauthorized performance of official duties or unauthorized use of the title certified building official, or a violation of statute, rule, or order that the commissioner has issued or is empowered to enforce. The committee consists of five certified building officials, at least two of whom must be from non-metropolitan counties. Committee members must be compensated according to Section 15.059, subdivision 3. The commissioner's designee shall act as an ex-officio member of the oversight committee.

(b) If the commissioner has a reasonable basis to believe that a person has engaged in an act or practice constituting the unauthorized performance of official duties, the unauthorized use of the title certified building official, or a violation of a statute, rule, or order that the commissioner has issued or is empowered to enforce, the commissioner may proceed with administrative actions or penalties as described in subdivision 5a or suspension or revocation as described in subdivision 5b.

Subd. 5a. Administrative action and penalties. The commissioner shall, by rule, establish a graduated schedule of administrative actions for violations of Sections 16B.59 to 16B.75 and rules adopted under those sections. The schedule must be based on and reflect the culpability, frequency, and severity of the violator's actions. The commissioner may impose a penalty from the schedule on a certification holder for a violation of Sections 16B.59 to 16B.75 and rules adopted under those sections. The penalty is in addition to any criminal penalty imposed for the same violation. Administrative monetary penalties imposed by the commissioner must be paid to the special revenue fund.

Subd. 5b. Suspension; revocation. Except as otherwise provided for by law, the commissioner may, upon notice and hearing, revoke or suspend or refuse to issue or reissue a building official certification if the applicant, building official, or certification holder:

(1) Violates a provision of Sections 16B.59 to 16B.75 or a rule adopted under those sections;

(2) Engages in fraud, deceit, or misrepresentation while performing the duties of a certified building official;

(3) Makes a false statement in an application submitted to the commissioner or in a document required to be submitted to the commissioner; or (4) violates an order of the commissioner. Notice must be provided and the hearing conducted in accordance with the provisions of chapter 14 governing contested case proceedings. Nothing in this subdivision limits or otherwise affects the authority of a municipality to dismiss or suspend a building official at its discretion, except as otherwise provided for by law.

Subd. 6. Vacancies. In the event that a designated building official position is vacant within a municipality, that municipality shall designate a certified building official to fill the vacancy as soon as possible. The commissioner must be notified of any vacancy or designation in writing within 15 days. If the municipality fails to designate a certified building official within 15 days of the occurrence of the vacancy, the state building official may provide state employees to serve that function as provided in subdivision 1 until the municipality makes a temporary or permanent designation. Municipalities must not issue permits without a designated certified building official.

Subd. 7. Continuing education. Subject to Sections 16B.59 to 16B.75, the commissioner may by rule establish or approve continuing education programs for municipal building officials dealing with matters of building code administration, inspection, and enforcement. Each person certified as a building official for the state must satisfactorily complete applicable educational programs established or approved by the commissioner every three calendar years to retain certification. Each person certified as a building official must submit in writing to the commissioner an application for renewal of certification within 60 days of the last day of the third calendar year following the last certificate issued. Each application for renewal must be accompanied by proof of satisfactory completion of minimum continuing education requirements and the certification renewal fee established by the commissioner.

16B.66 Certain inspections.
The state building official may, upon an application setting forth a set of plans and specifications that will be used in more than one municipality to acquire building permits, review and approve the application for the construction or erection of any building or structure designed to provide dwelling space for no more than two families if the set of plans meets the requirements of the State Building Code. All costs incurred by the state building official by virtue of the examination of the set of plans and specifications must be paid by the applicant. A building official shall issue a building permit upon application and presentation to the official of a set of plans and specifications bearing the approval of the state building official if the requirements of all other local ordinances are satisfied.

16B.665 Permit fee limitation on minor residential improvements.
A municipality as defined in Section 16B.60, subdivision 3, or a town may not charge a permit fee that exceeds $15 or 5 percent of the cost of the improvement, installation, or replacement, whichever is greater, for the improvement, installation, or replacement of a residential fixture or appliance that:

(1) Does not require modification to electric or gas service;

(2) Has a total cost of $500 or less, excluding the cost of the fixture or appliance; and

(3) Is improved, installed, or replaced by the home owner or a licensed contractor.

16B.67 Appeals.
A person aggrieved by the final decision of any municipality as to the application of the code, including any rules adopted under Sections 471.465 to 471.469, may, within 180 days of the decision, appeal to the commissioner. Appellant shall submit a nonrefundable fee of $70, payable to the commissioner, with the request for appeal. An appeal must be heard as a contested case under chapter 14. The commissioner shall submit written findings to the parties. The party not prevailing shall pay the costs of the contested case hearing, including fees charged by the office of administrative hearings and the expense of transcript preparation. Costs under this section do not include attorney fees. Any person aggrieved by a ruling of the commissioner may appeal in accordance with chapter 14. For the purpose of this section "any person aggrieved" includes the council on disability. No fee or costs shall be required when the council on disability is the appellant.

16B.68 Certain permits.
Building permits or certificates of occupancy validly issued before July 1, 1972, regarding buildings or structures being constructed or altered according to the permits or certificates, are valid after that date. The construction may be completed according to the building permit, unless the building official determines that life or property is in jeopardy.

16B.685 Annual report.
Beginning with the first report filed by April 1, 2003, each municipality shall annually report by April 1 to the department, in a format prescribed by the department, all construction and development-related fees collected by the municipality from

developers, builders, and subcontractors. The report must include:

(1) The number and valuation of units for which fees were paid;

(2) The amount of building permit fees, plan review fees, administrative fees, engineering fees, infrastructure fees, and other construction and development-related fees; and

(3) The expenses associated with the municipal activities for which fees were collected.

16B.69 Violation, penalty.

A violation of the code is a misdemeanor.

16B.70 Surcharge.

Subdivision 1. Computation. To defray the costs of administering Sections 16B.59 to 16B.76, a surcharge is imposed on all permits issued by municipalities in connection with the construction of or addition or alteration to buildings and equipment or appurtenances after June 30, 1971. The commissioner may use any surplus in surcharge receipts to award grants for code research and development and education.

If the fee for the permit issued is fixed in amount the surcharge is equivalent to one-half mill (.0005) of the fee or 50 cents, whichever amount is greater. For all other permits, the surcharge is as follows:

(1) If the valuation of the structure, addition, or alteration is $1,000,000 or less, the surcharge is equivalent to one-half mill (.0005) of the valuation of the structure, addition, or alteration;

(2) If the valuation is greater than $1,000,000, the surcharge is $500 plus two-fifths mill (.0004) of the value between $1,000,000 and $2,000,000;

(3) If the valuation is greater than $2,000,000, the surcharge is $900 plus three-tenths mill (.0003) of the value between $2,000,000 and $3,000,000;

(4) If the valuation is greater than $3,000,000, the surcharge is $1,200 plus one-fifth mill (.0002) of the value between $3,000,000 and $4,000,000;

(5) If the valuation is greater than $4,000,000, the surcharge is $1,400 plus one-tenth mill (.0001) of the value between $4,000,000 and $5,000,000; and

(6) If the valuation exceeds $5,000,000, the surcharge is $1,500 plus one-twentieth mill (.00005) of the value that exceeds $5,000,000.

Subd. 2. **Collection and reports.** All permit surcharges must be collected by each municipality and a portion of them remitted to the state. Each municipality having a population greater than 20,000 people shall prepare and submit to the commissioner once a month a report of fees and surcharges on fees collected during the previous month but shall retain the greater of two percent or that amount collected up to $25 to apply against the administrative expenses the municipality incurs in collecting the surcharges. All other municipalities shall submit the report and surcharges on fees once a quarter but shall retain the greater of four percent or that amount collected up to $25 to apply against the administrative expenses the municipalities

incur in collecting the surcharges. The report, which must be in a form prescribed by the commissioner, must be submitted together with a remittance covering the surcharges collected by the 15th day following the month or quarter in which the surcharges are collected. All money collected by the commissioner through surcharges and other fees prescribed by Sections 16B.59 to 16B.75 shall be deposited in the state government special revenue fund and is appropriated to the commissioner for the purpose of administering and enforcing the State Building Code under Sections 16B.59 to 16B.75.

Subd. 3. **Revenue to equal costs.** Revenue received from the surcharge imposed in subdivision 1 should approximately equal the cost, including the overhead cost, of administering Sections 16B.59 to 16B.75. By November 30 each year, the commissioner must report to the commissioner of finance and to the legislature on changes in the surcharge imposed in subdivision 1 needed to comply with this policy. In making this report, the commissioner must assume that the services associated with administering Sections 16B.59 to 16B.75 will continue to be provided at the same level provided during the fiscal year in which the report is made.

16B.71 Permit fees, to whom applicable.

Municipal building officials shall administer and enforce the State Building Code with respect to all subject structures constructed within their jurisdiction, including all buildings constructed by municipalities other than the state, as defined in Section 16B.60, and the University of Minnesota. These governmental bodies shall pay the building permit fees and surcharges that the inspecting municipality customarily imposes for its administration and enforcement of the code.

16B.72 Referenda on State Building Code in non-metropolitan counties.

Notwithstanding any other provision of law to the contrary, a county that is not a metropolitan county as defined by section 473.121, subdivision 4, may provide, by a vote of the majority of its electors residing outside of municipalities that have adopted the State Building Code before January 1, 1977, that no part of the State Building Code except the building requirements for handicapped persons, the requirements for bleacher safety, and the requirements for elevator safety applies within its jurisdiction. The county board may submit to the voters at a regular or special election the question of adopting the building code. The county board shall submit the question to the voters if it receives a petition for the question signed by a number of voters equal to at least five percent of those voting in the last general election. The question on the ballot must be stated substantially as follows:

"Shall the State Building Code be adopted in .... County?"

If the majority of the votes cast on the proposition is in the negative, the State Building Code does not apply in the subject county, outside home rule charter or statutory cities or towns that adopted the building code before January 1, 1977, except the building requirements for handicapped persons, the requirements for bleacher safety, and the requirements for elevator safety do apply. Nothing in this section precludes a municipality or town that has not adopted the State Building Code from adopting and enforcing by ordinance or other legal means the State Building Code within its jurisdiction.

16B.73 State Building Code in municipalities under 2,500; local option.

The governing body of a municipality whose population is less than 2,500 may provide that the State Building Code, except the requirements for handicapped persons, the requirements for bleacher safety, and the requirements for elevator safety, will not apply within the jurisdiction of the municipality, if the municipality is located in whole or in part within a county exempted from its application under Section 16B.72. If more than one municipality has jurisdiction over an area, the State Building Code continues to apply unless all municipalities having jurisdiction over the area have provided that the State Building Code, except the requirements for handicapped persons, the requirements for bleacher safety, and the requirements for elevator safety, does not apply within their respective jurisdictions. Nothing in this section precludes a municipality or town from adopting and enforcing by ordinance or other legal means the State Building Code within its jurisdiction.

Annual Report filing (16B.685)

16B.685 Annual report. Beginning with the first report filed by June 30, 2003, each municipality shall annually report by June 30 to the department, in a format prescribed by the department, all construction and development-related fees collected by the municipality from developers, builders, and subcontractors if the cumulative fees collected exceeded $5,000 in the reporting year. The report must include:

(1) The number and valuation of units for which fees were paid;

(2) The amount of building permit fees, plan review fees, administrative fees, engineering fees, infrastructure fees, and other construction and development-related fees; and

(3) The expenses associated with the municipal activities for which fees were collected.

Automatic garage door opening systems 325F.82 – 325F.83

325F.82 Definitions.

Subdivision 1. Scope. For the purposes of Section 325F.83, the terms defined in this section have the meanings given them.

Subd. 2. **Automatic garage door opening system.** "Automatic garage door opening system" means a system of devices and equipment that, when connected to a garage door, automatically opens and closes a garage door.

Subd. 3. **Garage.** "Garage" means a building, or a portion of a building, designed or used for the storage, repair, or keeping of a motor vehicle.

Subd. 4. **Residential building.** "Residential building" means a building such as a home or apartment for one or more families or persons that includes an attached or unattached garage.

Subd. 5. **Automatic reversing requirement.** "Automatic reversing requirement" means the requirements specified in paragraphs 30.1 and 30.2 of Underwriters Laboratories, Inc., Standards for Safety-UL 325, third edition, as revised May 4, 1988, for a residential automatic garage door opening system or the requirements specified in paragraph 29.1 of Underwriters Laboratories, Inc., Standards for Safety-UL 325, third edition, as revised May 4, 1988, for a commercial vehicular door operator.

Hazardous and substandard buildings

463.15 Definitions.

Subdivision 1. **Coverage.** For purposes of Sections 463.15 to 463.26 the terms defined in this section have the meanings given them.

Subd. 2. **Building.** "Building" includes any structure or part of a structure.

Subd. 3. **Hazardous building or hazardous property.** "Hazardous building or hazardous property" means any building or property, which because of inadequate maintenance, dilapidation, physical damage, unsanitary condition, or abandonment, constitutes a fire hazard or a hazard to public safety or health.

Subd. 4. **Owner, owner of record, and lien holder of record.** "Owner," "owner of record," and "lien holder of record" means a person having a right or interest in property described in subdivision 3 and evidence of which is filed and recorded in the office of the county recorder or registrar of titles in the county in which the property is situated.

463.151 Removal by municipality; consent; cost.

The governing body of any city or town may remove or raze any hazardous building or remove or correct any hazardous condition of real estate upon obtaining the consent in writing of all owners of record, occupying tenants, and all lien holders of record; the cost shall be charged against the real estate as provided in Section 463.21, except the governing body may provide that the cost so assessed may be paid in not to exceed five equal annual installments with interest thereon, at eight percent per annum.

463.152 Exercise of eminent domain.

Subdivision 1. **Purpose, public interest.** In order to maintain a sufficient supply of adequate, safe, and sanitary housing and buildings used for living, commercial, industrial, or other purposes or any combination of purposes, it is found that the public interest requires that municipalities be authorized to acquire buildings, real estate on which buildings are located, or vacant or undeveloped real estate which are found to be hazardous within the meaning of Section 463.15, subdivision 3, and the acquisition of such buildings and real estate is hereby declared to be a public purpose.

Subd. 2. **Acquisition; procedure.** In furtherance of the public policy declared in subdivision 1, the governing body of any city or town may acquire any hazardous building, real estate on which any such building is located, or vacant or undeveloped real estate by eminent domain in the manner provided by chapter 117.

463.16 Repair or remove hazardous property condition.

The governing body of any city or town may order the owner of any hazardous building or property within the municipality to correct or remove the hazardous condition of the building or property or to raze or remove the building.

463.161 Abatement.

In the manner prescribed in Section 463.21 the governing body of any city or town may correct or remove the hazardous condition of any hazardous building or property; the cost of which shall be charged against the real estate as provided in Section 463.21 except the governing body may provide that the cost so assessed may be paid in not to exceed five equal annual installments with interest therein, at eight percent per annum.

463.17 The order.

Subdivision 1. **Contents.** The order shall be in writing; recite the grounds therefore; specify the necessary repairs, if any, and provide a reasonable time for compliance; and shall state that a motion for summary enforcement of the order will be made to the district court of the county in which the hazardous building or property is situated unless corrective action is taken, or unless an answer is filed within the time specified in Section 463.18.

Subd. 2. **Service.** The order shall be served upon the owner of record, or the owner's agent if an agent is in charge of the building or property, and upon the occupying tenant, if there is one, and upon all lien holders of record, in the manner provided for service of a summons in a civil action. If the owner cannot be found, the order shall be served upon the owner by posting it at the main entrance to the building or, if there is no building, in a conspicuous place on the property, and by four weeks' publication in the official newspaper of the municipality if it has one, otherwise in a legal newspaper in the county.

Subd. 3. **Filing.** A copy of the order with proof of service shall be filed with the court administrator of district court of the county in which the hazardous building or property is located not less than five days prior to the filing of a motion pursuant to Section 463.19 to enforce the order. At the time of filing such order the municipality shall file for record with the county recorder or registrar of titles a notice of the pendency of the proceeding, describing with reasonable certainty the lands affected and the nature of the order. If the proceeding be abandoned the municipality shall within ten days thereafter file with the county recorder a notice to that effect. Within 20 days from the date of service, any person upon whom the order is served may serve an answer in the manner provided for the service of an answer in a civil action, specifically denying such facts in the order as are in dispute.

463.19 Default cases.

If no answer is served, the governing body may move the court for the enforcement of the order. If such a motion is made the court may, upon the presentation of such evidence as it may require, affirm or modify the order and enter judgment accordingly, fixing a time after which the governing body may proceed with the enforcement of the order. The court administrator shall cause a copy of the judgment to be mailed forthwith to persons upon whom the original order was served.

463.20 Contested cases.

If an answer is filed and served as provided in Section 463.18, further proceedings in the action shall be governed by the Rules of Civil Procedure for the District Courts, except that the action has priority over all pending civil actions and shall be tried forthwith. If the order is sustained following the trial, the court shall enter judgment and shall fix a time after which the building must be destroyed or repaired or the hazardous condition removed or corrected, as the case may be, in compliance with the order as originally filed or modified by the court. If the order is not sustained, it shall be annulled and set aside. The court administrator of the court shall cause a copy of the judgment to be mailed forthwith to the persons upon whom the original order was served.

463.21 Enforcement of judgment.

If a judgment is not complied with in the time prescribed, the governing body may cause the building to be repaired, razed, or removed or the hazardous condition to be removed or corrected as set forth in the judgment, or acquire the building, if any, and real estate on which the building or hazardous condition is located by eminent domain as provided in Section 463.152. The cost of the repairs, razing, correction, or removal may be: a lien against the real estate on which the building is located or the hazardous condition exists, or recovered by obtaining a judgment against the owner of the real estate on which the building is located or the hazardous condition exists. A lien may be levied and collected only as a special assessment in the manner provided by Minnesota Statutes 1961, Sections 429.061 to 429.081, but the assessment is payable in a single installment. When the building is razed or removed by the municipality, the governing body may sell the salvage and valuable materials at public auction upon three days' posted notice.

463.22 Statement of moneys received.

The municipality shall keep an accurate account of the expenses incurred in carrying out the order and of all other expenses theretofore incurred in connection with its enforcement, including specifically, but not exclusively, filing fees, service fees, publication fees, attorney's fees, appraisers' fees, witness fees, including expert witness fees, and traveling expenses incurred by the municipality from the time the order was originally made, and shall credit thereon the amount, if any, received from the sale of the salvage, or building or structure, and shall report its action under the order, with a statement of moneys received and expenses incurred to the court for approval and allowance. Thereupon the court shall examine, correct, if necessary, and allow the expense account, and, if the amount received from the sale of the salvage, or of the building or structure, does not equal or exceed the amount of expenses as allowed, the court shall by its judgment certify the deficiency in the amount so allowed to the municipal clerk for collection. The owner or other party in interest shall pay the same, without penalty added thereon, and in default of payment by October 1, the clerk shall certify the amount of the expense to the county auditor for entry on the tax lists of the county as a special charge against the real estate on which the building or hazardous condition is or was situated and the same shall be collected in the same manner as other taxes and the amount so collected shall be paid into the municipal treasury. If the amount received for the sale of the salvage or of the building or structure exceeds the expense incurred by the municipality as allowed by the court, and if there are no delinquent taxes, the court shall direct the payment of the surplus to the owner or the payment of the same into court, as provided in Sections 463.15 to 463.26. If there are delinquent taxes against the property, the court shall direct the payment of the surplus to the county treasurer to be applied on such taxes.

463.23 Payment, tender, deposit in court.

The net proceeds of a sale under Section 463.21 or Section 463.24 shall be paid to persons designated in the judgment in the proportions as their interests shall appear therein. Acceptance of such payment shall be taken as a waiver of all objections to the payment and to the proceedings leading thereto on the part of the payee and of all persons for whom the payee is lawfully empowered to act. In case any party to whom a payment of damages is made be not a resident of the state, or the place of residence be unknown, or the party be an infant or other person under legal disability, or, being legally capable, refuses to accept payment, or if for any reason it be doubtful to whom any payment should be paid, the municipality may pay the same to the clerk, to be paid out under the direction of the court; and, unless an appeal be taken such deposit with the clerk shall be deemed a payment of the award.

463.24 Personal property or fixtures.

If any building ordered razed, removed, or made safe and sanitary by repairs contains personal property or fixtures which will unreasonably interfere with the razing, removal, or repair of such building, or if the razing or removal of the building makes necessary the removal of such personal property or fixtures, the original order of the governing body may direct the removal of such personal property or fixtures within a reasonable time. If the property or fixtures are not removed by the time specified, and the governing body subsequently desires to enforce a judgment under Sections 463.15 to 463.26, it may sell the same at public auction as provided in Section 463.21, or if without appreciable value, the governing body may destroy the same.

463.25 Hazardous excavations.

If in any city, an excavation for building purposes is left open for more than six months without proceeding with the erection of a building thereon, whether or not completed, or if any excavation or basement is not filled to grade or otherwise protected after a building is destroyed, demolished or removed, the governing body may order such excavation to be filled or protected or in the alternative that erection of a building begin forthwith if the excavation is for building purposes. The order shall be served upon the owner or the owner's agent in the manner provided by Section 463.17. If the owner of the land fails to comply with the order within 15 days after the order is served, the governing body shall cause the excavation to be filled to grade or protected and the cost shall be charged against the real estate as provided in Section 463.21.

463.251 Securing vacant buildings.

Subdivision 1. **Definitions.** The following terms have the meanings given them for the purposes of this section.

(a) "City" means a statutory or home rule charter city.

(b) "Neighborhood association" means an organization recognized by the city as representing a neighborhood within the city.

(c) "Secure" may include, but is not limited to, installing locks, repairing windows and doors, boarding windows and doors, posting "no-trespassing" signs, installing exterior lighting or motion-detecting lights, fencing the property, and installing a monitored alarm or other security system.

Subd. 2. **Order; notice.** If in any city a building becomes vacant or unoccupied and is deemed hazardous due to the fact that the building is open to trespass and has not been secured and the building could be made safe by securing the building, the governing body may order the building secured and shall cause notice of the order to be served upon the owner of record of the premises or the owner's agent, the taxpayer identified in the property tax records for that parcel, the holder of the mortgage or sheriff's certificate, and any neighborhood association for the neighborhood in which the building is located that has requested notice, by delivering or mailing a copy to the owner or agent, the identified taxpayer, the holder of the mortgage or sheriff's certificate, and the neighborhood association, at the last known address. Service by mail is complete upon mailing.

Subd. 3. **Securing building by city; lien.** If the owner of the building fails to either comply or provide to the governing body a reasonable plan and schedule to comply with an order issued under subdivision 2 within six days after the order is served, the governing body shall cause the building to be properly secured and the cost of securing the building may be charged against the real estate as provided in Section 463.21. In the metropolitan area, as defined in Section 473.121, subdivision 2, the governing body may work with neighborhood associations to develop and implement plans to secure vacant buildings in a timely and cost-effective fashion. The city may use rehabilitation and revitalization funds in implementing this section. Subd. 4. Emergency securing. A city may provide by ordinance for emergency securing of a building that presents an immediate danger to the health and safety of persons in the community.

463.26 Local acts and charter provisions.

Sections 463.15 to 463.26 are supplementary to other statutory and charter provisions and do not limit the authority of any city to enact and enforce ordinances on the same subject.

463.261 Relocation benefits.

Notwithstanding the provisions of Section 117.56, or any other law to the contrary, all acquisitions of buildings and real estate upon which buildings are located by governmental subdivisions pursuant to the exercise of the power of eminent domain as provided in Section 463.152 shall be acquisitions for the purposes of Sections 117.50 to 117.56.

471.59 Joint exercise of powers.

Subdivision 1. Agreement. Two or more governmental units, by agreement entered into through action of their governing bodies, may jointly or cooperatively exercise any power common to the contracting parties or any similar powers, including those which are the same except for the territorial limits within which they may be exercised. The agreement may provide for the exercise of such powers by one or more of the participating governmental units on behalf of the other participating units. The term "governmental unit" as used in this section includes every city, county, town, school district, other political subdivision of this or another state, another state, the University of Minnesota, and any agency of the state of Minnesota or the United States, and includes any instrumentality of a governmental unit. For the purpose of this section, an instrumentality of a governmental unit means an instrumentality having independent policy making and appropriating authority.

Subd. 2. **Agreement to state purpose.** Such agreement shall state the purpose of the agreement or the power to be exercised and it shall provide for the method by which the purpose sought shall be accomplished or the manner in which the power shall be exercised. When the agreement provides for use of a joint board, the board shall be representative of the parties to the agreement. A joint board that is formed for educational purposes may conduct public meetings via interactive television if the board complies with chapter 13D in each location where board members are present. Irrespective of the number, composition, terms, or qualifications of its members, such board is deemed to comply with statutory or charter provisions for a board for the exercise by any one of the parties of the power which is the subject of the agreement.

Subd. 3. **Disbursement of funds.** The parties to such agreement may provide for disbursements from public funds to carry out the purposes of the agreement. Funds may be paid to and disbursed by such agency as may be agreed upon, but the method of disbursement shall agree as far as practicable with the method provided by law for the disbursement of funds by the parties to the agreement. Contracts let and purchases made under the agreement shall conform to the requirements applicable to contracts and purchases of any one of the parties, as specified in the agreement. Strict accountability of all funds and report of all receipts and disbursements shall be provided for.

Subd. 4. **Termination of agreement.** Such agreement may be continued for a definite term or until rescinded or terminated in accordance with its terms.

Subd. 5. **Shall provide for distribution of property.** Such agreement shall provide for the disposition of any property acquired as the result of such joint or cooperative exercise of powers, and the return of any surplus moneys in proportion to contributions of the several contracting parties after the purpose of the agreement has been completed.

Subd. 6. **Residence requirement.** Residence requirements for holding office in any governmental unit shall not apply to any officer appointed to carry out any such agreement.

Subd. 7. **Not to affect other acts.** This section does not dispense with procedural requirements of any other act providing for the joint or cooperative exercise of any governmental power.

Subd. 8. **Services performed by county, commonality of powers.** Notwithstanding the provisions of subdivision 1 requiring commonality of powers between parties to any agreement the board of county commissioners of any county may by resolution enter into agreements with any other governmental unit as defined in subdivision 1 to perform on behalf of that unit any service or function which that unit would be authorized to provide for itself.

Subd. 9. **Exercise of power.** For the purposes of the development, coordination, presentation and evaluation of training programs for local government officials, governmental units may exercise their powers under this section in conjunction with organizations representing governmental units and local government officials.

Subd. 10. **Services performed by governmental units; commonality of powers.** Notwithstanding the provisions of subdivision 1 requiring commonality of powers between parties to any agreement, the governing body of any governmental unit as defined in subdivision 1 may enter into agreements with any

other governmental unit to perform on behalf of that unit any service or function which the governmental unit providing the service or function is authorized to provide for itself.

Subd. 11. **Joint powers board.**

(a) Two or more governmental units, through action of their governing bodies, by adoption of a joint powers agreement that complies with the provisions of subdivisions 1 to 5, may establish a joint board to issue bonds or obligations under any law by which any of the governmental units establishing the joint board may independently issue bonds or obligations and may use the proceeds of the bonds or obligations to carry out the purposes of the law under which the bonds or obligations are issued. A joint board established under this section may issue obligations and other forms of indebtedness only in accordance with express authority granted by the action of the governing bodies of the governmental units that established the joint board. Except as provided in paragraphs (b) and (c), the joint board established under this subdivision must be composed solely of members of the governing bodies of the governmental unit that established the joint board. A joint board established under this subdivision may not pledge the full faith and credit or taxing power of any of the governmental units that established the joint board. The obligations or other forms of indebtedness must be obligations of the joint board issued on behalf of the governmental units creating the joint board. The obligations or other forms of indebtedness must be issued in the same manner and subject to the same conditions and limitations that would apply if the obligations were issued or indebtedness incurred by one of the governmental units that established the joint board, provided that any reference to a governmental unit in the statute, law, or charter provision authorizing the issuance of the bonds or the incurring of the indebtedness is considered a reference to the joint board.

(b) Notwithstanding paragraph (a), one school district, one county, and one public health entity, through action of their governing bodies, may establish a joint board to establish and govern a family services collaborative under Section 124D.23. The school district, county, and public health entity may include other governmental entities at their discretion. The membership of a board established under this paragraph, in addition to members of the governing bodies of the participating governmental units, must include the representation required by Section 124D.23, subdivision 1, paragraph (a), selected in accordance with Section 124D.23, subdivision 1, paragraph (c).

(c) Notwithstanding paragraph (a), counties, school districts, and mental health entities, through action of their governing bodies, may establish a joint board to establish and govern a children's mental health collaborative under Sections 245.491 to 245.496, or a collaborative established by the merger of a children's mental health collaborative and a family services collaborative under section 124D.23. The county, school district, and mental health entities may include other entities at their discretion. The membership of a board established under this paragraph, in addition to members of the governing bodies of the participating governmental units, must include the representation provided by section 245.493, subdivision 1.

Subd. 12. **Joint exercise of police power.** In the event that an agreement authorizes the exercise of peace officer or police powers by an officer appointed by one of the governmental units within the jurisdiction of the other governmental unit, an officer acting pursuant to that agreement has the full and complete authority of a peace officer as though appointed by both governmental units and licensed by the state of Minnesota, provided that:

(1) The peace officer has successfully completed professionally recognized peace officer

Pre-employment education which the Minnesota board of peace officer standards and training has found comparable to Minnesota peace officer pre-employment education; and

(2) The officer is duly licensed or certified by the peace officer licensing or certification authority of the state in which the officer's appointing authority is located.

Subd. 13. **Joint powers board for housing.**

(a) For purposes of implementing a federal court order or decree, two or more housing and redevelopment authorities, or public entities exercising the public housing powers of housing and redevelopment authorities, may by adoption of a joint powers agreement that complies with the provisions of subdivisions 1 to 5, establish a joint board for the purpose of acquiring an interest in, rehabilitating, constructing, owning, or managing low-rent public housing located in the metropolitan area, as defined in Section 473.121, subdivision 2, and financed, in whole or in part, with federal financial assistance under Section 5 of the United States Housing Act of 1937. The joint board established pursuant to this subdivision shall:

(1) Be composed of members designated by the governing bodies of the governmental units which established such joint board and possess such representative and voting power provided by the joint powers agreement;

(2) Constitute a public body, corporate, and politic; and

(3) Notwithstanding the provisions of subdivision 1, requiring commonality of powers between parties to a joint powers agreement, and solely for the purpose of acquiring an interest in, rehabilitating, constructing, owning, or managing federally financed low-rent public housing, shall possess all of the powers and duties contained in Sections 469.001 to 469.047 and, if at least one participant is an economic development authority, Sections 469.090 to 469.1081, except (i) as may be otherwise limited by the terms of the joint powers agreement; and (ii) a joint board shall not have the power to tax pursuant to Section 469.033, subdivision 6, or 469.107, nor shall it

exercise the power of eminent domain. Every joint powers agreement establishing a joint board shall specifically provide which and under what circumstances the powers granted herein may be exercised by that joint board.

(b) If a housing and redevelopment authority exists in a city which intends to participate in the creation of a joint board pursuant to paragraph (a), such housing and redevelopment authority shall be the governmental unit which enters into the joint powers agreement unless it determines not to do so, in which event the governmental entity which enters into the joint powers agreement may be any public entity of that city which exercises the low-rent public housing powers of a housing and redevelopment authority.

(c) A joint board shall not make any contract with the federal government for low-rent public housing, unless the governing body or bodies creating the participating authority in whose jurisdiction the housing is located has, by resolution, approved the provision of that low-rent public housing.

(d) This subdivision does not apply to any housing and redevelopment authority, or public entity exercising the powers of a housing and redevelopment authority, within the jurisdiction of a county housing and redevelopment authority which is actively carrying out a public housing program under Section 5 of the United States Housing Act of 1937. For purposes of this paragraph, a county housing and redevelopment authority is considered to be actively carrying out a public housing program under Section 5 of the United States Housing Act of 1937, if it

(1) Owns 200 or more public housing units constructed under Section 5 of the United States Housing Act of 1937, and

(2) Has applied for public housing development funds under Section 5 of the United States Housing Act of 1937, during the three years immediately preceding January 1, 1996.

(e) For purposes of Sections 469.001 to 469.047, "city" means the city in which the housing units with respect to which the joint board was created are located and "governing body" or "governing body creating the authority" means the council of such city. 13.44 Property data.

Subdivision 1. **Real property; complaint data.** The identities of individuals who register complaints with state agencies or political subdivisions concerning violations of state laws or local ordinances concerning the use of real property are classified as confidential data, pursuant to Section 13.02, subdivision 3.

Subd. 2. **Real property; building code violations.** Code violation records pertaining to a particular parcel of real property and the buildings, improvements, and dwelling units located on it that are kept by any state, county, or city agency charged by the governing body of the appropriate political subdivision with the responsibility for enforcing a state, county, or city health, housing, building, fire prevention, or housing maintenance code are public data; except as otherwise provided by Section 13.39, subdivision 2; 13.44; or 13.82, subdivision 7.

Subd. 3. **Real property; appraisal data.**

(a) **Confidential or protected nonpublic data.** Estimated or appraised values of individual parcels of real property which are made by personnel of the state, its agencies and departments, or a political subdivision or by independent appraisers acting for the state, its agencies and departments, or a political subdivision for the purpose of selling or acquiring land through purchase or condemnation are classified as confidential data on individuals or protected nonpublic data.

(b) **Public data.** The data made confidential or protected nonpublic by the provisions of paragraph (a) shall become public upon the occurrence of any of the following:

(1) the negotiating parties exchange appraisals;

(2) the data are submitted to a court appointed condemnation commissioner;

(3) the data are presented in court in condemnation proceedings; or

(4) the negotiating parties enter into an agreement for the purchase and sale of the property.

299G.11 Door or sidelight of public buildings.

If doors or side lights of a public building, whether privately or publicly owned, are constructed with clear glass, markings shall be placed on such clear glass or the clear glass shall be manufactured with markings. Sidelights are defined as the clear glass panels not less than 15 inches wide immediately adjacent to the door.

299G.13 Safety glazing; definitions.

Subdivision 1. Scope. As used in Sections 299G.13 to 299G.18, the following words and phrases have the meaning here given them.

Subd. 2. **Safety glazing material.** "Safety glazing material" means any glazing material, such as tempered glass, laminated glass, wire glass or rigid plastic, which meets the test requirements of the American National Standards Institute Standard Z-97.1-1972, and which is so constructed, treated, or combined with other materials as to minimize the likelihood of cutting and piercing injuries resulting from human contact with the glazing material.

Subd. 3. **Hazardous locations.** "Hazardous locations" means those structural elements, glazed or to be glazed, in residential buildings and other structures used as dwellings, commercial buildings, industrial buildings, and public buildings, known as interior and exterior commercial entrance and exit doors, and the immediately adjacent operable and inoperable glazed panels, sliding glass door units including the fixed glazed panels which are part of such units, storm or combination doors, shower and bathtub enclosures, primary residential entrance and exit doors and the operable and inoperable adjacent sidelights, whether or not the glazing in such doors, panels and enclosures is transparent.

Subd. 4. **Residential buildings.** "Residential buildings" means buildings such as homes and apartments used as dwellings for one or more families or persons.

Subd. 5. **Other structures used as dwellings.** "Other structures used as dwellings" means buildings such as manufactured homes, manufactured or industrialized housing and lodging homes.

Subd. 6. **Commercial buildings.** "Commercial buildings" means buildings such as wholesale and retail stores and storerooms, and office buildings.

Subd. 7. **Industrial buildings.** "Industrial buildings" means buildings such as factories.

Subd. 8. **Public buildings.** "Public buildings" means buildings such as hotels, hospitals, motels, dormitories, sanitariums, nursing homes, theaters, stadiums, gymnasiums, amusement park buildings, schools and other buildings used for educational purposes, museums, restaurants, bars, correctional institutions, places of worship and other buildings of public assembly.

Subd. 9. **Commercial entrance and exit door.** "Commercial entrance and exit door" means a hinged, pivoting, revolving or sliding door which is glazed or to be glazed and used alone or in combination with doors, other than those described in subdivision 11, on interior or exterior walls of a commercial, public or industrial building as a means of passage, ingress or egress.

Subd. 10. **Operable and inoperable glazed panels immediately adjacent to entrance or exit doors.** "Operable and inoperable glazed panels immediately adjacent to entrance or exit doors" means the flat glazed panels on either or both sides of interior or exterior doors, and within the same wall-plane as the door, whose nearest vertical edge is within 12 inches of the door in a closed position and whose bottom edge is less than 60 inches above the floor or walking surface.

Subd. 11. **Sliding glass door units.** "Sliding glass door units" means an assembly of glazed or to be glazed panels contained in an overall frame, installed in residential buildings and other structures used as dwellings, commercial, industrial or public buildings, and so designed that one or more of the panels is movable in a horizontal direction to produce or close off an opening for use as a means of passage, ingress or egress.

Subd. 12. **Storm or combination door.** "Storm or combination door" means a door which is glazed or to be glazed, and used in tandem with a primary residential or commercial entrance and exit door to protect the primary residential or commercial entrance or exit door against weather elements and to improve indoor climate control.

Subd. 13. **Shower enclosure.** "Shower enclosure" or "bathtub enclosure" means a hinged, pivoting, or sliding door and fixed panels which are glazed or to be glazed and used to form a barrier between the shower stall or bathtub and the rest of the room area.

Subd. 14. **Primary residential entrance and exit door.** "Primary residential entrance and exit door" means a door, other than that described in subdivision 11, which is glazed or to be glazed and used in an exterior wall of a residential building and other structures used as dwellings, as a means of ingress or egress.

Subd. 15. **Glazing.** "Glazing" means the act of installing and securing glass or other glazing material into prepared openings in structural elements such as doors, enclosures, and panels.

Subd. 16. **Glazed.** "Glazed" means the accomplished act of glazing.

299G.14 Glazing material; labeling required.

Subdivision 1. **Permanent labeling; identification; standard.** Each lite of safety glazing material manufactured, distributed, imported, or sold for use in hazardous locations, or installed in such a location within this state shall be permanently labeled by such means as etching, sandblasting, firing of ceramic material, hot-die stamping, transparent pressure sensitive labels, or by other suitable means. The label shall identify the seller, manufacturer, fabricator, or installer, the nominal thickness and the type of safety glazing material, and the fact that said material meets the test requirements of the American National Standards Institute Standard Z-97.1-1972. The label must be legible and visible after installation.

Subd. 2. **Limited use.** Such safety glazing labeling shall not be used on other than safety glazing materials.

299G.15 Safety glazing material required.

It shall be unlawful to knowingly install, cause to be installed or consent to the installation of glazing materials other than safety glazing materials in any hazardous location in this state.

299G.16 Employees not covered.

No liability shall be created under Sections 299G.13 to 299G.15 as to workers who are employees of a material supplier, contractor, subcontractor, or other employer responsible for compliance with the provisions herein.

299G.17 Misdemeanor.

Whoever violates the provisions of Sections 299G.13 to 299G.15 is guilty of a misdemeanor.

299G.18 Local ordinance superseded.

The provisions of Sections 299G.13 to 299G.18 shall supersede any local, municipal or county ordinance or parts thereof relating to the subject matter hereof.

299F.362 Smoke detector; installation; rules; penalty.

Subdivision 1. **Definitions.** For the purposes of this section, the following definitions shall apply:

(a) "Apartment house" is any building, or portion thereof, which is designed, built, rented, leased, let, or hired out to be occupied, or which is occupied as the home or residence of three or more families living independently of each other and doing their own cooking in the building, and shall include buildings containing three or more flats or apartments.

(b) "Dwelling" is any building, or any portion thereof, which is not an apartment house, lodging house, or a hotel and which contains one or two "dwelling units" which are, or are intended or designed to be, occupied for living purposes.

(c) "Dwelling unit" is a single unit providing complete, independent living facilities for one or more persons including permanent provisions for living, sleeping, eating, cooking, and sanitation, or a single unit used by one or more persons for sleeping and sanitation pursuant to a work practice or labor agreement.

(d) "Hotel" is any building, or portion thereof, containing six or more guest rooms intended or designed to be used, or which are used, rented, or hired out to be occupied, or which are occupied for sleeping purposes by guests.

(e) "Lodging house" is any building, or portion thereof, containing not more than five guest rooms which are used or are intended to be used for sleeping purposes by guests and where rent is paid in money, goods, labor, or otherwise.

Subd. 2. **Rules, smoke detector location.** The commissioner of public safety shall promulgate rules concerning the placement of smoke detectors in dwellings, apartment houses, hotels, and lodging houses. The rules shall take into account designs of the guest rooms or dwelling units.

Subd. 3. **Smoke detector for any dwelling.** Every dwelling unit within a dwelling shall be provided with a smoke detector meeting the requirements of Underwriters Laboratories, Inc., or approved by the International Conference of Building Officials. The detector shall be mounted in accordance with the rules regarding smoke detector location promulgated under the provisions of subdivision 2. When actuated, the detector shall provide an alarm in the dwelling unit.

Subd. 3a. **Smoke detector for new dwelling.** In construction of a new dwelling, each smoke detector must be attached to a centralized power source.

Subd. 4. **Smoke detector for apartment, lodging house, or hotel.** Every dwelling unit within an apartment house and every guest room in a lodging house or hotel used for sleeping purposes shall be provided with a smoke detector conforming to the requirements of Underwriters Laboratories, Inc., or approved by the International Conference of Building Officials. In dwelling units, detectors shall be mounted in accordance with the rules regarding smoke detector location promulgated under the provisions of subdivision 2. When actuated, the detector shall provide an alarm in the dwelling unit or guest room.

Subd. 5. **Maintenance responsibilities.** For all occupancies covered by this section where the occupant is not the owner of the dwelling unit or the guest room, the owner is responsible for maintenance of the smoke detectors. An owner may file inspection and maintenance reports with the local fire marshal for establishing evidence of inspection and maintenance of smoke detectors.

Subd. 5a. **Inform owner; no added liability.** The occupant of a dwelling unit must inform the owner of the dwelling unit of a nonfunctioning smoke detector within 24 hours of discovering that the smoke detector in the dwelling unit is not functioning. If the occupant fails to inform the owner under this subdivision, the occupant's liability for damages is not greater than it otherwise would be.

Subd. 6. **Penalties.**

(a) Any person who violates any provision of this section shall be subject to the same penalty and the enforcement mechanism that is provided for violation of the Uniform Fire Code, as specified in Section 299F.011, subdivision 6.

(b) An occupant who willfully disables a smoke detector or causes it to be nonfunctioning, resulting in damage or injury to persons or property, is guilty of a misdemeanor.

Subd. 7. **Local government preempted.** This section prohibits a local unit of government from adopting standards different from those provided in this section.

Subd. 8. Repealed, 1991 c 199 art 1 s 67

Subd. 9. **Local government ordinance; installation in single-family residence.** Notwithstanding subdivision 7, or other law, a local governing body may adopt, by ordinance, rules for the installation of a smoke detector in single-family homes in the city that are more restrictive than the standards provided by this section. Rules adopted pursuant to this subdivision may be enforced through a truth-in-housing inspection.

Subd. 10. **Public fire safety educator.** The position of Minnesota public fire safety educator is established in the department of public safety.

Subd. 11. **Insurance claim.** No insurer shall deny a claim for loss or damage by fire for failure of a person to comply with this section.

471.62 Statutes or rules may be adopted by reference.
Any city or town, however organized, may incorporate in an ordinance by reference any statute of Minnesota, any administrative rule of any department of the state of Minnesota affecting the municipality, or any code. Any such municipality situated wholly or partly within 20 miles of the limits of a city of the first class may similarly adopt by reference any ordinance of such first class city or of any contiguous first class city regulating the construction, alteration, improvement, repair, or maintenance of buildings or the installation of equipment therein. All requirements of statutes and charters for the publication or posting of ordinances shall be satisfied in such case if the ordinance incorporating the statute, rule, ordinance or code is published or posted in the required manner and if, prior to such posting or publication, at least one copy of the ordinance or code is marked as the official copy and filed for use and examination by the public in the office of the municipal clerk or recorder. Provisions of the statute, rule, ordinance or code thus incorporated in such ordinance by reference shall be as much a part of the ordinance as if they had been set out in full therein. The clerk or recorder of the municipality shall furnish a copy of any such ordinance thus incorporated by reference at cost to any person upon request. This section does not authorize any municipality to adopt ordinances on any subject on which it does not have power by statute or charter to legislate. The term "code" as used herein means any compilation of regulations or standards or part thereof prepared by any governmental agency, including regional and county planning agencies or any trade or professional association for general distribution in printed form as a standard or model on the subject of building construction, plumbing, electric wiring, inflammable liquids, sanitary provisions, planning, zoning, subdivision, housing, public health, safety, or welfare.

394.25 Forms of control.
Subdivision 1. **Adopted by ordinance.** Official controls shall be adopted by ordinance and may include but are not limited to the features set forth in this section.

Subd. 2. **Districts set by zoning ordinances.** Zoning ordinances establishing districts within which the use of land or the use of water or the surface of water pursuant to Section 86B.205 for agriculture, forestry, recreation, residence, industry, trade, soil conservation, water supply conservation, surface water drainage and removal, conservation of shore-lands, as defined in Sections 103F.201 to 103F.221, and additional uses of land and of the surface of water pursuant to Section 86B.205, may be by official controls encouraged, regulated, or prohibited and for such purpose the board may divide the county into districts of such number, shape, and area as may be deemed best suited to carry out the comprehensive plan. Official controls may also be applied to wetlands preservation, open space, parks, sewage disposal, protection of groundwater, protection of floodplains as defined in Section 103F.111, protection of wild, scenic, or recreational rivers as defined in Sections 103F.311 and 103F.315, protection of slope, soils, unconsolidated materials or bedrock from potentially damaging development, preservation of forests, woodlands and essential wildlife habitat, reclamation of nonmetallic mining lands; protection and encouragement of access to direct sunlight for solar energy systems as defined in Section 216C.06, subdivision 17; and the preservation of agricultural lands. Official controls may include provisions for purchase of development rights by the board in the form of conservation easements under chapter 84C in areas where preservation is considered by the board to be desirable, and the transfer of development rights from those areas to areas the board considers more desirable for development.

Subd. 3. **In district zoning, maps.** Within each such district zoning ordinances or maps may also be adopted designating or limiting the location, height, width, bulk, type of foundation, number of stories, size of, and the specific uses for which dwellings, buildings, and structures may be erected or altered; the minimum and maximum size of yards, courts, or other open spaces; setback from existing roads and highways and roads and highways designated on an official map; protective measures necessary to protect the public interest including but not limited to controls relating to appearance, signs, lighting, hours of operation and other aesthetic performance characteristics including but not limited to noise, heat, glare, vibrations and smoke; the area required to provide for off street loading and parking facilities; heights of trees and structures near airports; and to avoid too great concentration or scattering of the population. All such provisions shall be uniform for each class of land or building throughout each district, but the provisions in one district may differ from those in other districts. No provision may prohibit earth sheltered construction as defined in Section 216C.06, subdivision 14, or manufactured homes built in conformance with Sections 327.31 to 327.35 that comply with all other zoning ordinances promulgated pursuant to this section.

Subd. 3a. **Pre-1995 manufactured home park.** A county must not enact, amend, or enforce a zoning ordinance that has the effect of altering the existing density, lot-size requirements, or manufactured home setback requirements in any manufactured home park constructed before January 1, 1995, if the manufactured home park, when constructed, complied with the then existing density, lot-size and setback requirements.

Subd. 3b. **Conditional uses.** A manufactured home park, as defined in Section 327.14, subdivision 3, is a conditional use in a zoning district that allows the construction or placement of a building used or intended to be used by two or more families.

Subd. 3c. Feedlot zoning ordinances.

(a) A county proposing to adopt a new feedlot ordinance or amend an existing feedlot ordinance must notify the pollution control agency and commissioner of agriculture at the beginning of the process.

(b) Prior to final approval of a feedlot ordinance, a county board may submit a copy of the proposed ordinance to the pollution control agency and to the commissioner of agriculture and request review, comment, and preparation of a report on the environmental and agricultural effects from specific provisions in the ordinance.

(c) The report may include:

(1) Any recommendations for improvements in the ordinance; and

(2) The legal, social, economic, or scientific justification for each recommendation under clause (1).

(d) A local ordinance that contains a setback for new feedlots from existing residences must also provide for a new residence setback from existing feedlots located in areas zoned agricultural at the same distances and conditions specified in the setback for new feedlots, unless the new residence is built to replace an existing residence. A county may grant a variance from this requirement under Section 394.27, subdivision 7.

Subd. 4. **Official maps.** Official maps as defined in Section 394.22, subdivision 12.

Subd. 5. Repealed, 1974 c 571 s 51

Subd. 5a. **Metro counties; special areas.** In counties in the metropolitan area as defined in Section 473.121, official maps may for a period of up to five years designate the boundaries of areas reserved for purposes of soil conservation, water supply conservation, flood control and surface water drainage and removal.

Subd. 6. Repealed, 1974 c 571 s 51

Subd. 7. **Specific controls; other subjects.** Specific controls pertaining to other subjects incorporated in the comprehensive plan or establishing standards and procedures to be employed in land development including, but not limited to, subdividing of land and the approval of land plats and the preservation and dedication of streets and land for other public purposes and the general design of physical improvement.

Subd. 8. **Law adopted by reference.** Any statute of Minnesota, any administrative rule of any department of the state of Minnesota affecting the county, or any code, adopted by reference as part of the official control. The term "code" as used herein means any compilation of rules or standards or part thereof prepared by any governmental agency or any trade or professional association for general distribution in printed form as a standard or model on the subject of building construction, plumbing, electric wiring, inflammable liquids, sanitary provisions, public health, safety, or welfare. Prior to adoption at least one copy of the statute, rule, ordinance or code shall be marked as official copies and filed for use and examination by the public in the office of the county auditor. Provisions of the statute, rule, ordinance or code thus incorporated in such ordinance by reference shall be as much a part of the ordinance as I they had been set out in full therein.

Subd. 9. **Erosion and sediment controls.** Erosion and sediment controls with regard to clearing, grading, excavation, transporting and filling of lands. Erosion and sediment controls may include, but need not be limited to requiring the development of plans before any land is disturbed. Plans for disturbing land may be submitted to the appropriate soil and water conservation district for comment and review.

Subd. 10. **Amendments.** An amendment to official controls may be initiated by the board, the planning commission, or by petition of affected property owners as defined in the official controls. An amendment not initiated by the planning commission shall be referred to the planning commission, if there is one, for study and report and may not be acted upon by the board until it has received the recommendation of the planning commission.

462.357 Procedure to effect plan: zoning.

Subdivision 1. **Authority for zoning.** For the purpose of promoting the public health, safety, morals, and general welfare, a municipality may by ordinance regulate on the earth's surface, in the air space above the surface, and in subsurface areas, the location, height, width, bulk, type of foundation, number of stories, size of buildings and other structures, the percentage of lot which may be occupied, the size of yards and other open spaces, the density and distribution of population, the uses of buildings and structures for trade, industry, residence, recreation, public activities, or other purposes, and the uses of land for trade, industry, residence, recreation, agriculture, forestry, soil conservation, water supply conservation, conservation of shore-lands, as defined in Sections 103F.201 to 103F.221, access to direct sunlight for solar energy systems as defined in section 216C.06, flood control or other purposes, and may establish standards and procedures regulating such uses. To accomplish these purposes, official controls may include provision for purchase of development rights by the governing body in the form of conservation easements under chapter 84C in areas where the governing body considers preservation desirable and the transfer of development rights from those areas to areas the governing body considers more appropriate for development. No regulation may prohibit earth sheltered construction as defined in section 216C.06, subdivision 14, relocated residential buildings, or manufactured homes built in conformance with Sections 327.31 to 327.35 that comply with all other zoning ordinances promulgated pursuant to this section. The regulations may divide the surface, above surface, and subsurface areas of the municipality into districts or zones of suitable numbers, shape, and area. The regulations shall be uniform for each class or kind of buildings, structures, or land and for each class or kind of use throughout such district, but the regulations in one district may differ from those in other districts. The ordinance embodying these regulations shall be known as the zoning ordinance and shall consist of text and maps. A city may by ordinance extend the application of its zoning regulations to unincorporated territory located within two miles of its limits in any direction, but not in a county or town which has adopted zoning regulations; provided that where two or more noncontiguous municipalities have boundaries less than four miles apart, each is authorized to control the zoning of land on its side of a line equidistant between the two noncontiguous municipalities unless a town or county in the affected area has adopted zoning regulations. Any city may thereafter enforce such regulations in the area to the same extent as if such property were situated within its corporate limits, until the county or town board adopts a comprehensive zoning regulation which includes the area.

Subd. 1a. **Certain zoning ordinances.** A municipality must not enact, amend, or enforce a zoning ordinance that has the effect of altering the existing density, lot-size requirements, or manufactured home setback requirements in any manufactured home park constructed before January 1, 1995, if the manufactured home park, when constructed, complied with the then existing density, lot-size and setback requirements.

Subd. 1b. **Conditional uses.** A manufactured home park, as defined in Section 327.14, subdivision 3, is a conditional use in a zoning district that allows the construction or placement of a building used or intended to be used by two or more families.

Subd. 1c. **Amortization prohibited.** Except as otherwise provided in this subdivision, a municipality must not enact, amend, or enforce an ordinance providing for the elimination or termination of a use by amortization which use was lawful at the time of its inception. This subdivision does not apply to adults-only bookstores, adults-only theaters, or similar adults-only businesses, as defined by ordinance.

Subd. 1d. **Nuisance.** Subdivision 1c does not prohibit a municipality from enforcing an ordinance providing for the prevention or abatement of nuisances, as defined in Section 561.01, or eliminating a use determined to be a public nuisance, as defined in Section 617.81, subdivision 2, paragraph (a), clauses (1) to (9), without payment of compensation.

Subd. 1e. **Nonconformities.** Any nonconformity, including the lawful use or occupation of land or premises existing at the time of the adoption of an additional control under this chapter, may be continued, including through repair or maintenance, but if the nonconformity or occupancy is discontinued for a period of more than one year, or any nonconforming use is destroyed by fire or other peril to the extent of greater than 50 percent of its market value, any subsequent use or occupancy of the land or premises shall be a conforming use or occupancy. A municipality may by ordinance impose upon nonconformities reasonable regulations to prevent and abate nuisances and to protect the public health, welfare, or safety. This subdivision does not prohibit a municipality from enforcing an ordinance

that applies to adults-only bookstores, adults-only theaters, or similar adults-only businesses, as defined by ordinance.

Subd. 1f. **Substandard structures.** Notwithstanding subdivision 1e, Minnesota Rules, parts 6105.0351 to 6105.0550, may allow for the continuation and improvement of substandard structures, as defined in Minnesota Rules, part 6105.0354, subpart 30, in the Lower Saint Croix National Scenic Riverway.

Subd. 2. **General requirements.**

(a) At any time after the adoption of a land use plan for the municipality, the planning agency, for the purpose of carrying out the policies and goals of the land use plan, may prepare a proposed zoning ordinance and submit it to the governing body with its recommendations for adoption.

(b) Subject to the requirements of subdivisions 3, 4, and 5, the governing body may adopt and amend a zoning ordinance by a majority vote of all its members. The adoption or amendment of any portion of a zoning ordinance which changes all or part of the existing classification of a zoning district from residential to either commercial or industrial requires a two-thirds majority vote of all members of the governing body.

(c) The land use plan must provide guidelines for the timing and sequence of the adoption of official controls to ensure planned, orderly, and staged development and redevelopment consistent with the land use plan.

Subd. 3. **Public hearings.** No zoning ordinance or amendment thereto shall be adopted until a public hearing has been held thereon by the planning agency or by the governing body. A notice of the time, place and purpose of the hearing shall be published in the official newspaper of the municipality at least ten days prior to the day of the hearing. When an amendment involves changes in district boundaries affecting an area of five acres or less, a similar notice shall be mailed at least ten days before the day of the hearing to each owner of affected property and property situated wholly or partly within 350 feet of the property to which the amendment relates. For the purpose of giving mailed notice, the person responsible for mailing the notice may use any appropriate records to determine the names and addresses of owners. A copy of the notice and a list of the owners and addresses to which the notice was sent shall be attested to by the responsible person and shall be made a part of the records of the proceedings. The failure to give mailed notice to individual property owners, or defects in the notice shall not invalidate the proceedings, provided a bona fide attempt to comply with this subdivision has been made.

Subd. 4. **Amendments.** An amendment to a zoning ordinance may be initiated by the governing body, the planning agency, or by petition of affected property owners as defined in the zoning ordinance. An amendment not initiated by the planning agency shall be referred to the planning agency, if there is one, for study and report and may not be acted upon by the governing body until it has received the recommendation of the planning agency on the proposed amendment or until 60 days have elapsed from the date of reference of the amendment without a report by the planning agency.

Subd. 5. Amendment; certain cities of the first class. The provisions of this subdivision apply to the adoption or amendment of any portion of a zoning ordinance which changes all or part of the existing classification of a zoning district from residential to either commercial or industrial of a property located in a city of the first class, except a city of the first class in which a different process is provided through the operation of the city's home rule charter. In a city to which this subdivision applies, amendments to a zoning ordinance shall be made in conformance with this section but only after there shall have been filed in the office of the city clerk a written consent of the owners of two-thirds of the several descriptions of real estate situate within 100 feet of the total contiguous descriptions of real estate held by the same owner or any party purchasing any such contiguous property within one year preceding the request, and after the affirmative vote in favor thereof by a majority of the members of the governing body of any such city. The governing body of such city may, by a two-thirds vote of its members, after hearing, adopt a new zoning ordinance without such written consent whenever the planning commission or planning board of such city shall have made a survey of the whole area of the city or of an area of not less than 40 acres, within which the new ordinance or the amendments or alterations of the existing ordinance would take effect when adopted, and shall have considered whether the number of descriptions of real estate affected by such changes and alterations renders the obtaining of such written consent impractical, and such planning commission or planning board shall report in writing as to whether in its opinion the proposals of the governing body in any case are reasonably related to the overall needs of the community, to existing land use, or to a plan for future land use, and shall have conducted a public hearing on such proposed ordinance, changes or alterations, of which hearing published notice shall have been given in a daily newspaper of general circulation at least once each week for three successive weeks prior to such hearing, which notice shall state the time, place and purpose of such hearing, and shall have reported to the governing body of the city its findings and recommendations in writing.

Subd. 6. Appeals and adjustments. Appeals to the board of appeals and adjustments may be taken by any affected person upon compliance with any reasonable conditions imposed by the zoning ordinance. The board of appeals and adjustments has the following powers with respect to the zoning ordinance:

(1) To hear and decide appeals where it is alleged that there is an error in any order, requirement, decision, or determination made by an administrative officer in the enforcement of the zoning ordinance.

(2) To hear requests for variances from the literal provisions of the ordinance in instances where their strict enforcement would cause undue hardship because of circumstances unique to the individual property under consideration, and to grant such variances only when it is demonstrated that such actions will be in keeping with the spirit and intent of the ordinance. "Undue hardship" as used in connection with the granting of a variance means the property in question cannot be put to a reasonable use if used under conditions allowed by the official controls, the plight of the landowner is due

to circumstances unique to the property not created by the landowner, and the variance, if granted, will not alter the essential character of the locality. Economic considerations alone shall not constitute an undue hardship if reasonable use for the property exists under the terms of the ordinance. Undue hardship also includes, but is not limited to, inadequate access to direct sunlight for solar energy systems. Variances shall be granted for earth sheltered construction as defined in Section 216C.06, subdivision 14, when in harmony with the ordinance. The board of appeals and adjustments or the governing body as the case may be, may not permit as a variance any use that is not permitted under the ordinance for property in the zone where the affected person's land is located. The board or governing body as the case may be, may permit as a variance the temporary use of a one family dwelling as a two family dwelling. The board or governing body as the case may be may impose conditions in the granting of variances to insure compliance and to protect adjacent properties.

Subd. 6a. Normal residential surroundings for handicapped. It is the policy of this state that handicapped persons and children should not be excluded by municipal zoning ordinances or other land use regulations from the benefits of normal residential surroundings. For purposes of subdivisions 6a through 9, "person" has the meaning given in Section 245A.02, subdivision 11.

Subd. 7. Permitted single family use. A state licensed residential facility or a housing with services establishment registered under chapter 144D serving six or fewer persons, a licensed day care facility serving 12 or fewer persons, and a group family day care facility licensed under Minnesota Rules, parts 9502.0315 to 9502.0445 to serve 14 or fewer children shall be considered a permitted single family residential use of property for the purposes of zoning, except that a residential facility whose primary purpose is to treat juveniles who have violated criminal statutes relating to sex offenses or have been adjudicated delinquent on the basis of conduct in violation of criminal statutes relating to sex offenses shall not be considered a permitted use.

Subd. 8. Permitted multifamily use. Except as otherwise provided in subdivision 7 or in any town, municipal or county zoning regulation as authorized by this subdivision, a state licensed residential facility serving from 7 through 16 persons or a licensed day care facility serving from 13 through 16 persons shall be considered a permitted multifamily residential use of property for purposes of zoning. A township, municipal or county zoning authority may require a conditional use or special use permit in order to assure proper maintenance and operation of a facility, provided that no conditions shall be imposed on the facility which are more restrictive than those imposed on other conditional uses or special uses of residential property in the same zones, unless the additional conditions are necessary to protect the health and safety of the residents of the residential facility. Nothing herein shall be construed exclude or prohibit residential or day care facilities from single family zones if otherwise permitted by a local zoning regulation.

APPENDIX E

STATUTORY HOUSING WARRANTIES

327A.01 Definitions.

Subdivision 1. **Scope.** As used in sections 327A.01 to 327A.07, the terms in this section shall have the meanings assigned to them.

Subd. 2. **Building standards.** "Building standards" means the State Building Code, adopted by the commissioner of administration pursuant to sections 16B.59 to 16B.75, that is in effect at the time of the construction or remodeling.

Subd. 3. **Dwelling.** "Dwelling" means a new building, not previously occupied, constructed for the purpose of habitation; but does not include appurtenant recreational facilities, detached garages, driveways, walkways, patios, boundary walls, retaining walls not necessary for the structural stability of the dwelling, landscaping, fences, nonpermanent construction materials, off-site improvements, and all other similar items.

Subd. 4. **Initial vendee.** "Initial vendee" means a person who first contracts to purchase a dwelling from a vendor for the purpose of habitation and not for resale in the ordinary course of trade.

Subd. 5. **Major construction defect.** "Major construction defect" means actual damage to the load-bearing portion of the dwelling or the home improvement, including damage due to subsidence, expansion or lateral movement of the soil, which affects the load-bearing function and which vitally affects or is imminently likely to vitally affect use of the dwelling or the home improvement for residential purposes. "Major construction defect" does not include damage due to movement of the soil caused by flood, earthquake or other natural disaster.

Subd. 6. **Vendee.** "Vendee" means any purchaser of a dwelling and includes the initial vendee and any subsequent purchasers.

Subd. 7. **Vendor.** "Vendor" means any person, firm or corporation which constructs dwellings for the purpose of sale, including the construction of dwellings on land owned by vendees.

Subd. 8. **Warranty date.** "Warranty date" means the date from and after which the statutory warranties provided in section 327A.02 shall be effective, and is the earliest of

(a) The date of the initial vendee's first occupancy of the dwelling; or

(b) The date on which the initial vendee takes legal or equitable title in the dwelling.

In the case of a home improvement, the warranty date is the date on which the home improvement work was completed.

Subd. 9. **Home improvement.** "Home improvement" means the repairing, remodeling, altering, converting or modernizing of, or adding to a residential building. For the purpose of this definition, residential building does not include appurtenant recreational facilities, detached garages, driveways, walkways, patios, boundary walls, retaining walls not necessary for the structural stability of the building, landscaping, fences, non-permanent construction materials, off-site improvements, and all other similar items.

Subd. 10. **Home improvement contractor.** "Home improvement contractor" means a person who is engaged in the business of home improvement either full time or part time, and who holds out to the public as having knowledge or skill peculiar to the business of home improvement.

Subd. 11. **Owner.** "Owner" means any person who owns a residential building on which home improvement work is performed, and includes any subsequent owner of the residential building.

327A.02 Statutory warranties.

Subdivision 1. **Warranties by vendors.** In every sale of a completed dwelling, and in every contract for the sale of a dwelling to be completed, the vendor shall warrant to the vendee that:

(a) During the one-year period from and after the warranty date the dwelling shall be free from defects caused by faulty workmanship and defective materials due to non-compliance with building standards;

(b) During the two-year period from and after the warranty date, the dwelling shall be free from defects caused by faulty installation of plumbing, electrical, heating, and cooling systems due to noncompliance with building standards; and

(c) During the ten-year period from and after the warranty date, the dwelling shall be free from major construction defects due to noncompliance with building standards.

Subd. 2. **Warranties to survive passage of title.** The statutory warranties provided in this section shall survive the passing of legal or equitable title in the dwelling to the vendee.

Subd. 3. **Home improvement warranties.**

(a) In a sale or in a contract for the sale of home improvement work involving major structural changes or additions to a residential building, the home improvement contractor shall warrant to the owner that:

(1) During the one-year period from and after the warranty date the home improvement shall be free from defects caused by faulty workmanship and defective materials due to noncompliance with building standards; and

(2) During the ten-year period from and after the warranty date the home improvement shall be free from major construction defects due to noncompliance with building standards.

(b) In a sale or in a contract for the sale of home improvement work involving the installation of plumbing, electrical, heating or cooling systems, the home improvement contractor shall warrant to the owner that, during the two-year period from and after the warranty date, the home improvement shall be free from defects caused by the faulty installation of the system or systems due to non-compliance with building standards.

(c) In a sale or in a contract for the sale of any home improvement work not covered by paragraph (a) or (b), the home improvement contractor shall warrant to the owner that, during the one-year period from and after the warranty date, the home improvement shall be free from defects caused by faulty workmanship or defective materials due to noncompliance with building standards.

327A.03 Exclusions.

The liability of the vendor or the home improvement contractor under sections 327A.01 to 327A.07 is limited to the specific items set forth in sections 327A.01 to 327A.07 and does not extend to the following:

(a) Loss or damage not reported by the vendee or the owner to the vendor or the home improvement contractor in writing within six months after the vendee or the owner discovers or should have discovered the loss or damage;

(b) Loss or damage caused by defects in design, installation, or materials which the vendee or the owner supplied, installed, or directed to be installed;

(c) Secondary loss or damage such as personal injury or property damage;

(d) Loss or damage from normal wear and tear;

(e) Loss or damage from normal shrinkage caused by drying of the dwelling or the home improvement within tolerances of building standards;

(f) Loss or damage from dampness and condensation due to insufficient ventilation after occupancy;

(g) Loss or damage from negligence, improper maintenance or alteration of the dwelling or the home improvement by parties other than the vendor or the home improvement contractor;

(h) Loss or damage from changes in grading of the ground around the dwelling or the home improvement by parties other than the vendor or the home improvement contractor;

(i) Landscaping or insect loss or damage;

(j) Loss or damage from failure to maintain the dwelling or the home improvement in good repair;

(k) Loss or damage which the vendee or the owner, whenever feasible, has not taken timely action to minimize;

(l) Loss or damage which occurs after the dwelling or the home improvement is no longer used primarily as a residence;

(m) Accidental loss or damage usually described as acts of God, including, but not limited to: fire, explosion, smoke, water escape, windstorm, hail or lightning, falling trees, aircraft and vehicles, flood, and earthquake, except when the loss or damage is caused by failure to comply with building standards;

(n) Loss or damage from soil movement which is compensated by legislation or covered by insurance;

(o) Loss or damage due to soil conditions where construction is done upon lands owned by the vendee or the owner and obtained by the vendee or owner from a source independent of the vendor or the home improvement contractor;

(p) In the case of home improvement work, loss or damage due to defects in the existing structure and systems not caused by the home improvement.

327A.04 Waiver and modification limited.

Subdivision 1. Except as provided in subdivisions 2 and 3, the provisions of sections 327A.01 to 327A.07 cannot be waived or modified by contract or otherwise. Any agreement which purports to waive or modify the provisions of sections 327A.01 to 327A.07, except as provided in subdivisions 2 and 3 of this section, shall be void.

Subd. 2. At any time after a contract for the sale of a dwelling is entered into by and between a vendor and a vendee or a contract for home improvement work is entered into by and between a home improvement contractor and an owner, any of the statutory warranties provided for in section 327A.02 may be excluded or modified only by a written instrument, printed in boldface type of a minimum size of ten points, which is signed by the vendee or the owner and which sets forth in detail the warranty involved, the consent of the vendee or the owner, and the terms of the new agreement contained in the writing. No exclusion or modification shall be effective unless the vendor or the home improvement contractor provides substitute express warranties offering substantially the same protections to the vendee or the owner as the statutory warranties set forth in section 327A.02. Any modification or exclusion agreed to by vendee and vendor or the owner and home improvement contractor pursuant to this subdivision shall not require the approval of the commissioner of administration pursuant to section 327A.07.

Subd. 3. If a major construction defect is discovered prior to the sale of a dwelling, the statutory warranty set forth in section 327A.02, subdivision 1, clause (c) may be waived for the defect identified in the waiver instrument, after full oral disclosure of the specific defect, by an instrument which sets forth in detail: the specific defect; the difference between the value of the dwelling without the defect and the value of the dwelling with the defect, as determined attested to by an independent appraiser, contractor, insurance adjuster, engineer or any other similarly knowledgeable person selected by the vendee; the price reduction; the date the construction was completed; the legal description of the dwelling; the consent of the vendee to the waiver; and the signatures of the vendee, the vendor, and two witnesses. A single waiver agreed to pursuant to this subdivision may not apply to more than one major construction defect in a dwelling. The waiver shall not be effective unless filed for recording with the county recorder or registrar of titles who shall file the waiver for record.

327A.05 Remedies.

Subdivision 1. **New home warranties.** Upon breach of any warranty imposed by section 327A.02, subdivision 1, the vendee shall have a cause of action against the vendor for damages arising out of the breach, or for specific performance. Damages shall be limited to:

(a) The amount necessary to remedy the defect or breach; or

(b) The difference between the value of the dwelling without the defect and the value of the dwelling with the defect.

Subd. 2. **Home improvement warranty.** Upon breach of any warranty imposed by section 327A.02, subdivision 3, the owner shall have a cause of action against the home improvement contractor for damages arising out of the breach, or for specific performance. Damages shall be limited to the amount necessary to remedy the defect or breach.

327A.06 Other warranties.

The statutory warranties provided for in section 327A.02 shall be in addition to all other warranties imposed by law or agreement. The remedies provided in section 327A.05 shall not be construed as limiting the remedies in any action not predicated upon breach of the statutory warranties imposed by section 327A.02.

327A.07 Variations.

The commissioner of administration may approve pursuant to sections 14.05 to 14.28, variations from the provisions of sections 327A.02 and 327A.03 if the warranty program of the vendor or the home improvement contractor requesting the variation offers at least substantially the same protections to the vendee or owner as provided by the statutory warranties set forth in section 327A.02.

327A.08 Limitations.

Notwithstanding any other provision of sections 327A.01 to 327A.07:

(a) The terms of the home improvement warranties required by sections 327A.01 to 327A.07 commence upon completion of the home improvement and the term shall not be required to be renewed or extended if the home improvement contractor performs additional improvements required by warranty;

(b) The home improvement warranties required by sections 327A.01 to 327A.07 shall not include products or materials installed that are already covered by implied or written warranty; and

(c) The home improvement warranties required by sections 327A.01 to 327A.07 are intended to be implied warranties imposing an affirmative obligation upon home improvement contractors, and sections 327A.01 to 327A.07 do not require that written warranty instruments be created and conveyed to the owner.

APPENDIX F

DOCUMENT AND AGENCY RESOURCES

The Minnesota State Building Code is comprised of many documents published by various organizations some of which are available from Minnesota's Bookstore or from the sources listed below. Please note that code publications are amended or updated periodically. Contact the organization or the State Building Codes and Standards Division regarding current applicable codes.

Minnesota's Bookstore
(for State Building Code and International Codes)
660 Olive Street, St. Paul, MN 55155
1-651-297-3000 1-800-657-3757
TTY: 1-651-282-5077 1-800-657-3706
http://www.minnesotabookstore.com

ICC - International Code Council
(for International Codes)
500 New Jersey Avenue, NW, 6th Floor,
Washington, DC 20001-2070
[P] 1-888-ICC-SAFE (422-7233); [F] (202) 783-2348;
http://www.iccsafe.org/index.html

NFPA - National Fire Protection Association
1 Batterymarch Park,
P.O. Box 9101, Quincy, MA 02269-9101 USA
617-770-3000 Fax: 617 770-0700
http://www.nfpa.org

ASHRAE - American Society of Heating, Refrigerating and Air-Conditioning Engineers, Inc.
1791 Tullie Circle, N.E.,
Atlanta, GA 30329
(800) 527-4723 (U.S. and Canada only) 404-636-8400
Fax: 404-321-5478
http://ashrae.org

ASME - International (American Society of Mechanical Engineers)
Three Park Avenue,
New York, NY 10016-5990
800-843-2763 (U.S/Canada)
Email: infocentral@asme.org http://www.asme.org

CODES AND REFERENCE MANUALS - 2007 MSBC

* 2006 International Building Code (Latest Printing)

* 2006 International Residential Code (Latest Printing)

* 2006 International Fire Code (Latest Printing)

* 2006 International Mechanical Code (Latest Printing)

* 2006 International Fuel Gas Code (Latest Printing)

* 2005 National Electrical Code (NFPA 70)

* ASHRAE 62 – 2001 Ventilation/Indoor Air Quality

* ASHRAE 62n – 2001 Mechanical Design Ventilation Rates (supplement)

* ASHRAE 15 – 2001 Mechanical Refrigeration Safety Code

* ASHRAE 34 – 2004 Refrigerant Designation and Safety Code

* SMACNA – 1995 HVAC Duct Construction Standard

* NFPA 96 – 2001 Ventilation and Fire Protection for Commercial Cooking Hoods

* NFPA 58 – 2004 Liquefied Petroleum Gases

* NFPA 13 – 2002 Installation of Fire Sprinklers

* NFPA 13R – 2002 Installation of Fire Sprinklers for Multifamily

* NFPA 13D – 2002 Installation of Fire Sprinklers for Dwellings

* NFPA 72 – 2002 Installation of Fire Alarm Systems

* 207 Minnesota Building Conservation Code (MN Rule 1311/GREB)

* ACI 318-2005 Building Code Requirements for Structural Concrete

* ACI 530-05/ASCE 5-05/TMS 402-05 Building Code Requirements for Masonry Structures (in one comprehensive manual from ICC)

* ASCE 7 – 2005 Minimum Design Loads for Buildings and Other Structures

* 2007 Minnesota State Building Code (Will contain MN Rules 1300, 1301, 1302, 1303, 1305, 1306, 1307, 1309, 1311, 1315, 1325, 1335, 1350, 1360, 1361 and 1370.)

* 2007 Minnesota State Fire Code (MN Rule 7510)

* MN Rule 1323 – MN Energy Code for Commercial Buildings

* ANSI/ASHRAE 90.1 – 2004 Commercial Building Energy Code

* MN Rule 1322 – MN Energy Code for Dwelling Construction

* MN Rule 4715 – 2003 Minnesota State Plumbing Code

* MN Rule 1346 – 2007 Minnesota Mechanical Code – MN Amendments to the 2000 IMC and 2000 IFGC

* ICC A117.1 – 2003 Accessibility Code

* NDS – 2005 National Design Specification for Wood Construction

* ICC 300 – 2002 ICC Standard on Bleachers, Folding and Telescoping Seating and Grandstands.

* "Must Have" Codes and Rules for a Building Department in Minnesota

DESIRABLE HANDBOOKS AND/OR STANDARDS FOR CODE ENFORCEMENT

2006 IBC Commentary Manual Volume I & II

Handbook to the 2006 IFC

2006 IRC Commentary Manual Volume I & II

Handbook to the 2006 IRC

Handbook to the 2006 IFGC

2006 IBC/ASTM Reference Standards

2006 IBC Nonstructural Q & A Manual

2006 IBC Structural Provisions

2006 IBC Structural Q & A Guide

2006 Quick Reference Guide to the IBC

ASTM Standards Manual for the 2006 IBC

GA-600 Fire Resistance Design Manual – 17th edition

Fire Protection Handbook

Fire Sprinkler & Standpipe Handbook

Hazardous Materials Guide

NFPA 80 – 1999 Installation of Fire-Resistive Doors and Windows

NFPA Life Safety Code 101 – 2000 Edition

Handbook to the Life Safety Code

2001 ICC Performance Code for Buildings and Facilities

ASME A17.1 Elevator Safety Code – addenda, and supplement (3 documents)

Building Department Administration

Administrative Guidelines for Building Departments

Building Official Management Manual

Building Department Guide to Disaster Mitigation

Legal Aspects of Code Administration

Architectural Graphic Standards (Most current edition)

Webster's Dictionary

2006 IBC UL Standards Manual

U.L's and/or Warnock Hersey's Fire Resistive Directories, Building Materials Directories, Roofing Materials & System's Directories, etc.

Permanent Wood Foundation Design and Construction Guide

MN Rule 1800 & 1805 Board of Architecture and Engineering Rules

MPCA Rule 7080, 7081, 7082, 7083 – On-Site Septic System Rules

RESPONSIBLE STATE AGENCIES AND INDUSTRY RESOURCES

Northstar – State of Minnesota's website
Website address: www.state.mn.us

Access to – information related to Minnesota business, travel and leisure, health and safety, environment, government, learning and education, and living and working. All of the government information listed in this section can be accessed from Northstar.

Construction Codes and Licensing Division
443 Lafayette Road North,
St. Paul, MN 55155
Phone: 651-284-5068 Fax: 651-284-5749
TTY: 651- 297-4198
http://www.doli.state.mn.us

Code responsibilities: Adoption of the Minnesota State Building Code, Boiler Code, High Pressure Piping Code, Boats-for-hire Code and regulations for Residential Building Contractors. Services include: State owned building inspection and plan review, plumbing plan review and inspection, plan review and inspection for industrialized modular buildings, education, elevator inspection, code administration and electrical inspection. Licensing for building officials, manufactured home manufacturers/ dealers and installers, electricians, plumbers, residential building contractors, boiler operators, high pressure piping fitters. Enforcement of licensing laws.

Minnesota Legislature http://www.leg.state.mn.us

Resource for information regarding state laws, statutes, and rules. Includes a Frequently Asked Questions About Laws, Statutes and Rules.

Board of Architecture, Engineering, Land Surveying, Landscape Architecture, Geoscience, and Interior Design (AELSLAGID)
85 East 7th Place, Suite 160,
St. Paul, MN 55101
Phone: 651-296-2388 Fax: 651-297-5310
TTY: 1-800-627-3529
http://www.aelslagid.state.mn.us

Code responsibilities: The AELSLAGID board examines, licenses, and regulates the practice of architecture, professional engineering, land surveying, landscape architecture, geoscience, and interior design.

STATE AGENCY RESOURCES:

Department of Agriculture
Minnesota Department of Agriculture,
90 West Plato Boulevard,
St. Paul, MN 55107
651-297-2200 1-800-967-2474 TTY: 1-800-627-3529
http://www.mda.state.mn.us

Code responsibilities: Pesticide management, feedlots, and useful information.

RESPONSIBLE STATE AGENCIES AND INDUSTRY RESOURCES

Department of Commerce Energy Code Information:

Minnesota Commerce Department
85 - 7th Place East,
St. Paul, MN 55101
http://www.commerce.state.mn.us
Energy Information Center 651-296-5175 1-800-657-3710 (MN only)
energy.info@state.mn.us

Responsibilities: Energy information.

Department of Human Services

DHS Central Office
444 Lafayette Road North,
St. Paul, MN 55155
651-297-3933 TTY Service: 1-800-627-3529

General questions: DHS.Info@state.mn.us
Non-general questions: DHS.Info@state.mn.us
http://www.dhs.state.mn.us

Code responsibilities: Licensing and inspection of care facilities, etc.

Department of Natural Resources

500 Lafayette Road, St. Paul, MN 55155-4040
651-296-6157
http://www.dnr.state.mn.us/index.html

Code responsibilities: Flood-proofing regulations and shore land management.

Pollution Control Agency

520 Lafayette Road North,
St. Paul, MN 55155-4194
800-657-3864

Code responsibilities: Asbestos, storage tanks, feedlots, hazardous spills, solid waste, demolition permits, lead paint, wells, etc.

Department of Public Safety – Minnesota Fire Marshal Division

Suite 145, 444 Cedar Street,
St. Paul, MN 55101-5145
651-215-0500 Fax: 651-215-0525 TTY: 651-282-6555
http://www.dps.state.mn.us/fmarshal/fmarshal.html

Code responsibilities: Minnesota State Fire Code, fire suppression system plan review, contractor and designer licensing, inspections.

Code Administrative Services/Rules/Information Section:

The section works with the Commerce Department investigating consumer complaints and provides review and assistance to building departments.

RELATED USEFUL WEB SITES

LOCAL ORGANIZATIONS

AIA - American Institute of Architects – Minnesota
http://www.aia-mn.org

AMC - Association of Minnesota Counties
http://www.mncounties.org

BAM - Builders Association of Minnesota
http://www.bamn.org

FMAM - Fire Marshal's Association of Minnesota
http://www.fmam.org

LMC - League of Minnesota Cities
http://www.lmnc.org

AMBO - Association of Minnesota Building Officials
http://www.ambo.us

10,000 Lakes Chapter
http://www.10klakes.org

Municipal Telephone Number Contacts
http://www.municipaltelenumbers.html

NATIONAL ORGANIZATIONS

Access Board
http://www.access-board.gov

ADAAG - Americans with Disabilities Act Accessibility Guidelines
http://www.access-board.gov/adaag/html/adaag.htm

ANSI- American National Standards Institute
http://www.ansi.org

ASTM- American Society for Testing and Materials
http://www.astm.org

BOMA - Building Owners and Managers Association
http://www.boma.org/index.htm

DOJ - Department of Justice
http://www.usdoj.gov/crt/ada/adahom1.htm

HUD - Department of Housing and Urban Development
http://www.hud.gov/fhe/fheo.html

ICC - International Code Council
http://www.iccsafe.org/index.html

NAHB - National Association of Home Builders
http://www.nahb.org

NFPA - National Fire Protection Association
http://www.nfpa.org

INDEX

Y

YARD